Innovations in BANK MANAGEMENT

Innovations in

HOLT, RINEHART AND WINSTON, INC.

Bank Management

Selected Readings

PAUL F. JESSUP

UNIVERSITY OF MINNESOTA

New York Chicago San Francisco Atlanta Dallas
Montreal Toronto London Sydney

Library of Congress Catalog Card Number: 72-81178
SBN: 03-078055-1
Printed in the United States of America
1 2 3 4 5 6 7 8 9

Preface

Significant and rapid changes confront contemporary bank management. Decisions about profitability, growth, sources of funds, and resource allocation must consider such new instruments and techniques as: federal funds, equipment leasing, credit cards, negotiable certificates of deposit, and debt capital. Important changes in the regulatory framework have facilitated—and, at times, stimulated—the introduction and growth of these new areas of banking. Also, as American banks increase their international commitments and as they adapt to the advent of a "checkless society," traditional concepts of bank management warrant reexamination.

New and powerful tools are available to assist bankers. Computers are now an important resource of banks—not just for the routine processing of data but also as an aid in structuring and solving complex decision problems. Furthermore, techniques of management science can provide financial decision-makers with carefully specified courses of action, as well as measures of probable outcomes of each alternative. In this way bank management has become a major user of analytical methods.

This book is intended to provide a convenient, comprehensive set of readings for modern bankers. Although there are many recent articles in this area, their diverse locations and varying quality suggest the need for critical selection.

A systematic selection process requires a set of criteria. Emphasized here are articles which treat modern bank management lucidly and analytically. By stressing provocative issues and innovative techniques, this book hopes to stimulate individual reflection and public discussion.

A well-structured book of readings requires an appropriate conceptual framework. Adopted here is the point of view of a bank manager operating in a dynamic environment. Chapters 1 through 3 focus on developments in the principal areas outlined on a bank's balance sheet: liquidity, investments, loans, deposits, and capital. Decisions in these areas are interrelated and furthermore are linked to profit planning and cost analysis, the subject of Chapter 4. The accelerating use of computers and management science techniques receives considerable emphasis in Chapter 5. The articles in Chapter 6 demonstrate that bankers must function in an extensive and rapidly changing regulatory framework. Successful management strategies often anticipate and adapt to major changes in this regulatory environment. As developed in Chapter 7, international operations are broadening the decision issues of American bankers. On the horizon are revolutionary developments in the nation's payments mechanism—developments frequently referred to in such terms as "electronic money" and "the checkless society." The concluding chapter outlines the probable transformation of the payments mechanism and considers the implications for public policy and bank management.

While the articles are organized into chapters, each introduced by editorial comments, the reader should recognize that many of the issues and variables are interrelated. To give but one example, the decision whether, and how, to seek substantial new deposits is associated with: liquidity management, investment and loan opportunities, capital adequacy, probable contribution to profits, regulatory policy concerning deposit instruments and interest-rate ceilings, money market conditions, and even international opportunities (Euro-dollars). To structure and quantify these many interrelationships demonstrates the potential value of computers and management science techniques.

Hopefully this book will assist students and financial practitioners in understanding the dynamic changes in banking, as well as the analytical methods capable of improving financial decisions.

Grateful acknowledgment is given to the copyright holders for granting permission to reprint these selected articles. Also recognized by the editor are the authors' contributions to scholarship. By inclusion in this volume, it is hoped that their contributions will be more broadly appreciated by bankers and students of banking.

Much of the framework for this book was developed while teaching classes in bank management at the University of Minnesota. Two graduate students, Miss Carmencita Hernandez and Mr. John D. Chrisney, provided particularly valuable assistance in the development of this volume. Professor W. Bruce Erickson, an academic colleague, spent long hours discussing and reviewing the selections and editorial comments. During the extensive search procedure for appropriate articles, the library staff of the Federal Reserve Bank of Minneapolis provided courteous assistance. The secretarial tasks were done primarily by Miss Ilona Hanka, whose cheerful cooperation is most appreciated.

Paul F. Jessup

Minneapolis, Minnesota
June 1969

Contents

4 PROFIT PLANNING AND COST ANALYSIS

5 COMPUTERS AND MANAGEMENT SCIENCE

7 INTERNATIONAL BANKING: A NEW FRONTIER

8 FRONTIERS OF BANK MANAGEMENT: "THE CHECKLESS SOCIETY"

1

Asset Management

While a bank's assets can be conceptually subdivided into components such as reserves, investments, and loans, management policies and decisions should serve to identify and measure the interrelationships among these elements. As shown in several of these readings, decisions concerning loan and investment strategies are closely linked to management of a bank's liquidity position. In subsequent sections, other elements such as the structure and variability of deposits, capital structure, and international operations also are seen to be interrelated with effective asset management.

In managing its liquidity position, a bank is confronted by a trade-off between liquidity and profitability. Because liquid assets often provide a zero or low return, bank managers must constantly analyze the opportunity costs involved in not reducing liquid assets and increasing higher yielding assets.

The first reading outlines certain difficulties in defining and measuring liquidity. Recent changes in the structure of bank assets and liabilities place doubt on the significance of traditional liquidity ratios. The article by James L. Pierce also questions the traditional measures in view of new techniques by which banks can affect their liquidity—particularly by means of endogenous deposit determination. He suggests that an appropriate concept of liquidity must consider the time dimension involved in selling an asset and demonstrates that the liquidity decision is closely linked to the loan-supply function of banks.

Questioning the price of liquidity, the third reading analyzes the reasons why bankers have been more closely managing their cash positions. In the following two selections D. R. Cawthorne outlines the techniques and importance of reserve adjustment in city banks, while N. D. Baxter suggests reasons why country banks are becoming more active participants in the federal funds market.

The essay published by the Federal Reserve Bank of Atlanta examines recent trends in bank investments. Although the study is based on sample banks in a limited geographical area, its conclusions seem more generally applicable. The analysis recognizes important interrelationships among such variables as liquidity, investments, loan policy, and deposit structure. Furthermore, the reading indicates the significance of changes in bank holdings of municipal securities.

In another essay published by the Federal Reserve Bank of Chicago, the relative decline in bank holdings of United States government securities is recognized as a possible constraint on public deposits and on the traditional borrowing procedure at the discount window of the Federal Reserve Bank. To assure adequate flexibility for bank managers, this article advocates reexamination of the traditional procedures by which banks post collateral.

The next reading provides insights concerning appropriate strategies for managing a bank's bond portfolio. In testing the "lock-in" hypothesis, Sam B. Chase, Jr., recognizes the importance of opportunity costs and tax treatment of security transactions.

Although based on a regional sample of banks, the essay by Charles T. Taylor provides a useful analysis of significant interrelationships among seasonal loan demands and such variables as liquidity and investment management, deposit structure, borrowing strategies, and Federal Reserve policy.

Bank credit cards have been a major innovation in recent years. In a lucid article, Robert Johnston surveys the principal types of credit cards and estimates the extent of such operations. Also considered are various implications for bank management decisions and bank structure.

An important alternative to direct lending has been the introduction and recent expansion of direct leasing of equipment by banks. The concluding article discusses lessees' motives for such arrangements and relates these motives to the activity and decision problems in this new area of banking.

Bank Liquidity Reexamined

Liquidity is of unusual importance to banks. Compared with nonfinancial businesses', their cash flows, both in and out, are large in relation to their capital base. Also, their cash outflows are to a much larger extent unpredictable. Moreover, bank liabilities constitute the major portion of the nation's money supply and a bank's ability to meet the claims of its depositors is thus a matter critical to the public and to supervisory authorities.

As for any business, "liquidity" may be defined as the ability to meet claims presented for immediate payment. The ultimate source of liquidity for the banking system as a whole, of course, is the Federal Reserve, which stands ready to supply funds adequate to satisfy any demand by depositors to exchange deposits for currency and provides the reserve base for an appropriate growth of the aggregate volume of credit and deposits to serve the economy's needs. It is not bank liquidity in this sense, but rather the ability of individual banks to meet cash demands on them, with which this article is concerned.

Cash demands on individual banks arise mainly from adverse clearings. A cash outflow from one bank, it is important to note, has its counterpart in an inflow to another. Checks presented for collection must be paid in cash and a most important challenge to bank management is to provide for the satisfaction of these claims at the lowest cost. The relevant costs include both the earnings foregone on cash that might have been invested and the sale of assets at a loss in order to acquire cash.

HARD TO MEASURE

There is no single statistic that can adequately measure bank liquidity nor is it possible to develop one. Holdings of cash or assets readily convertible into cash in relation to deposits and the ratio of loans (assumed to be non-liquid assets) to deposits are often used as rough indicators. Any such ratio can indicate only a relative degree of liquidity. Differences in ratios are not adequate to compare liquidity differences between banks since the need for liquid assets varies, depending upon the behavior of a bank's deposits. Moreover, the loan ratio one bank considers "comfort-

Reprinted with the permission of the Federal Reserve Bank of Chicago from *Business Conditions,* July 1966.

able" is in part dependent on the overall composition of its assets—their maturity, marketability and degree of diversification. Variation in loan or liquid asset ratios among banks thus reflects differences in risk factors as well as differences in liquidity needs. Changes in the overall average of these ratios nevertheless may provide broad indications of whether it is easier or harder for most banks to make adjustments necessary to meet potential deposit drains.

The combined effects of strong loan expansion, shrinking portfolios of Government securities and Federal Reserve restraint on deposit expansion over the past year have given rise to expressions of concern about the adequacy of bank liquidity. For all commercial banks, aggregate loan volume now exceeds 65 percent of total deposits while holdings of short-term U.S. Government securities have dropped to less than 6 percent of deposits. These measures suggest that bank liquidity is at a new low in postwar experience. The loan-deposit ratio is well above the level reached in the 1959–1960 period of monetary restraint while the short-term Governments ratio is very near the low reached at that time (Figure 1).

Although higher loan ratios may make banks more cautious about increasing their risk assets—at least at a faster pace than their deposits rise—such ratios do not necessarily indicate impairment of their ability to meet cash demands without suffering capital losses. The adequacy of

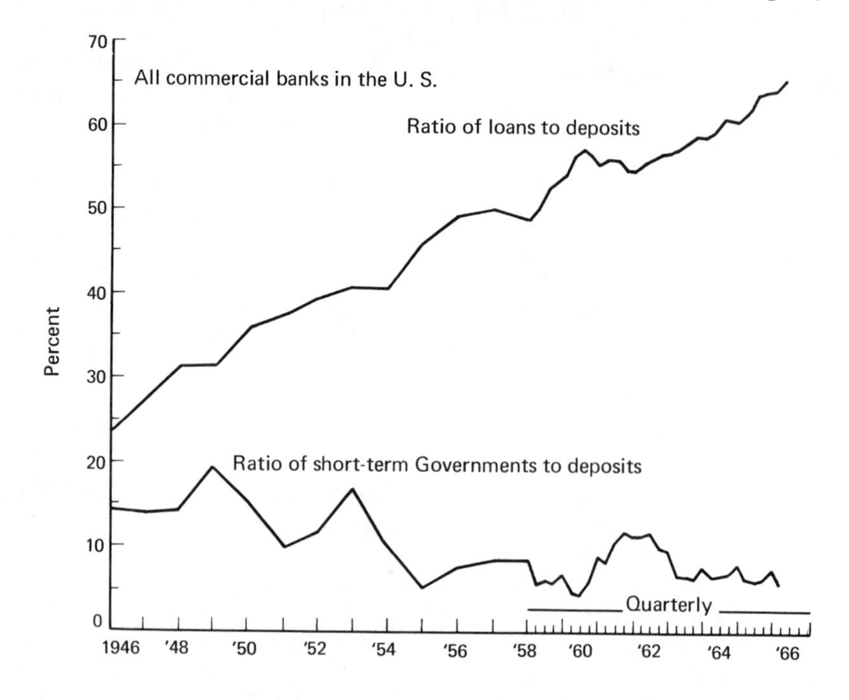

FIG. 1 Bank "liquidity ratios" tighter.

Note: Loans exclude loans to banks; Government securities include issues maturing within one year; deposits are adjusted to exclude cash items in process of collection.

liquidity is a function of both needs, as related to deposit fluctuations, and potential sources of funds. The volume of liquid assets a bank holds is an important but not an exclusive element in its ability to raise cash. Alternatives to the holding of liquid assets, however, are not equally available to all banks or at all times.

Interpretation of the loan-deposit and liquid asset ratios as indicators of the liquidity situation requires consideration of three related questions: 1) Do these ratios accurately reflect the relevant asset-deposit relationships, that is, have changes in the composition of loans, investments and deposits affected liquidity in a direction which either modifies or intensifies the trend shown by these measures? 2) To what extent have other developments modified the importance of holding a stock of short-term Governments for liquidity purposes? and 3) Do banks show differing declines in their liquidity ratios and are those most affected best able to meet their liquidity needs in other ways? Some of the available evidence on these questions is reviewed below.

LIQUIDITY IN LOANS

Although the "liquidity ratios" normally exclude loans from liquid assets, there is a large element of liquidity in the loan portfolio of most banks. This is of two types. First, certain assets classed as loans, including bankers acceptances, CCC certificates of indebtedness and FHA- and VA-guaranteed mortgages, are readily marketable. Second, there is a very large cash inflow from maturing loans, and amortized loans are an increasing proportion of total outstandings. Also important at some banks is the large volume of one-day or demand loans made to other banks and to securities dealers.

Cash inflow from loan repayment is, of course, largely dependent on the average maturity of the loan portfolio. To the extent that the proportion of mortgages, consumer loans and term loans to business has increased, liquidity may have declined. In the past five years, mortgage and consumer loans have risen only slightly in relation to total loans. The average maturity of consumer and mortgage loans at banks is less than 15 months and 5 years, respectively.

Available data on loans of the larger banks in the New York and Cleveland Federal Reserve Districts at the end of March show that business loans with maturities longer than a year amounted to 62 percent and 46 percent, respectively, of all business loans in these banks and that the proportion has tended to rise over the past five years. These data, however, include loans made under revolving credit agreements. Although such agreements normally are for two to three years, the individual loans made under them are often for 90 days or less.

Term loans do not necessarily imply reduced cash inflow since they are usually amortized whereas many short-term business loans are renewed at maturity. Reports by large Seventh District banks on new loans made during a 15 calendar-day period each quarter indicate that at these banks term loans as a proportion of the total dollar volume of extensions in the largest loan size category dropped in December 1965 and March 1966 to about 10 percent after having reached a peak of nearly 17 percent late in 1964. Revolving credits appear to have shrunk somewhat in importance, but this is offset to some extent by a shortening in the average maturity of ordinary term loans to 48 months in December 1965 from 65 months in the same period of 1959.

Investments also provide varying degrees of liquidity. Because of the broad market for both direct U.S. Government securities and for obligations of U.S. Agencies, all of these issues can be easily converted to cash and with little or no loss, especially if they are short term. Markets for state and local obligations, on the other hand, are much more limited. Even short-term Governments, insofar as they are pledged to secure deposits of governmental units, are not available to meet cash needs. Public deposits vary within the year roughly between 6 and 12 percent of the aggregate deposits of all member banks. Although public deposits tend to be the most volatile of the major deposit categories, the pledging of securities against particular types of deposits unquestionably impairs the general liquidity of the banks holding them.

The very substantial change that has occurred in the composition of deposits in recent years also has an important bearing on the need for liquidity. Historically, time deposits have shown much greater stability over short periods (although they have undergone very wide swings secularly) than have demand deposits. Because of the rapid growth in time and savings balances during the past six years, many banks may feel comfortable with relatively small holdings of liquid assets. Whether total deposits are actually more stable, given the large volume of time and savings deposits and the greater importance of fixed maturity certificates as a component of such deposits is not entirely clear.

Average week-to-week percentage changes in total deposits, less uncollected items, computed for 14 weekly reporting banks in seven Midwest cities were not significantly different in 1961 and 1965 although there was some evidence of reduced overall volatility at banks where fluctuations were relatively high in the earlier year. The average percentage decline in those weeks when deposits dropped was slightly larger in 1965 at the majority of these banks. Greater predictability of potential deposit declines associated with the certificates, however, may more than offset the tendency for withdrawals to be somewhat larger when they occur.

MONEY MOBILITY

At any given time some banks find themselves in need of cash while others are seeking profitable outlets for funds. Liquidity for individual banks, then, is to a large extent a matter of the redistribution of funds among banks. Anything that increases a bank's ability to tap the money market for funds contributes to its liquidity. One way banks can do this is through the sale of assets. Another way that has become increasingly important in recent years is by the acquisition of liabilities—borrowed funds or deposits. To the extent a bank possesses the ability to offset cash drains due to withdrawals by some depositors by the acquisition of new deposits or by borrowing, its need to hold a stock of liquid assets is correspondingly less.

There is abundant evidence that many banks have gained increasing control over the amount of their liabilities. While this has been true especially at the large banks which can affect the inflow of their time deposits by varying the rates they offer on negotiable certificates of deposit, many small banks have also found that they are able to attract a larger share of local savings and short-term public funds by issuing time and savings certificates.

The growing practice of overnight interbank loans is a second factor of great importance in facilitating the redistribution of funds to banks with short-term needs. The ability to "buy" Federal funds is an important source of liquidity for the borrower while the "sale" of Federal funds is an extremely liquid investment for the lender. With the Federal funds rate now fully competitive with other money market yields, many banks rely heavily on this market to meet their short-term cash needs. In the past the Federal funds market has been a source of funds mainly for large banks where daily fluctuations in cash needs can be counted in millions of dollars. But more and more relatively small banks are participating in this market by buying and selling funds through their correspondents.

Finally, the discount facilities of the Federal Reserve Banks are available to carry member banks over temporary periods of cash drains. Advances to member banks tend to rise in periods when the overall availability of credit is restricted. The increase in the total volume of borrowing—to a 600–800 million dollar range in recent months—has been accounted for largely by country banks. But this may reflect not so much their inability to obtain accommodation from other banks or in the money market as their reluctance to pay rates substantially above the cost of borrowing at the discount window. There is little doubt that the larger amount of country bank borrowing is due in part to some shrinkage in their stocks of short-term liquid securities. At the same time, the ability of these banks to obtain advances is evidence that they still hold a sufficient volume of securities eligible to collateralize this borrowing.

VARIATION AMONG BANKS

How widespread is the apparent liquidity squeeze? Which banks have been most affected? What kinds of changes in the composition of assets and deposits have accompanied the shrinkage in the liquidity ratios?

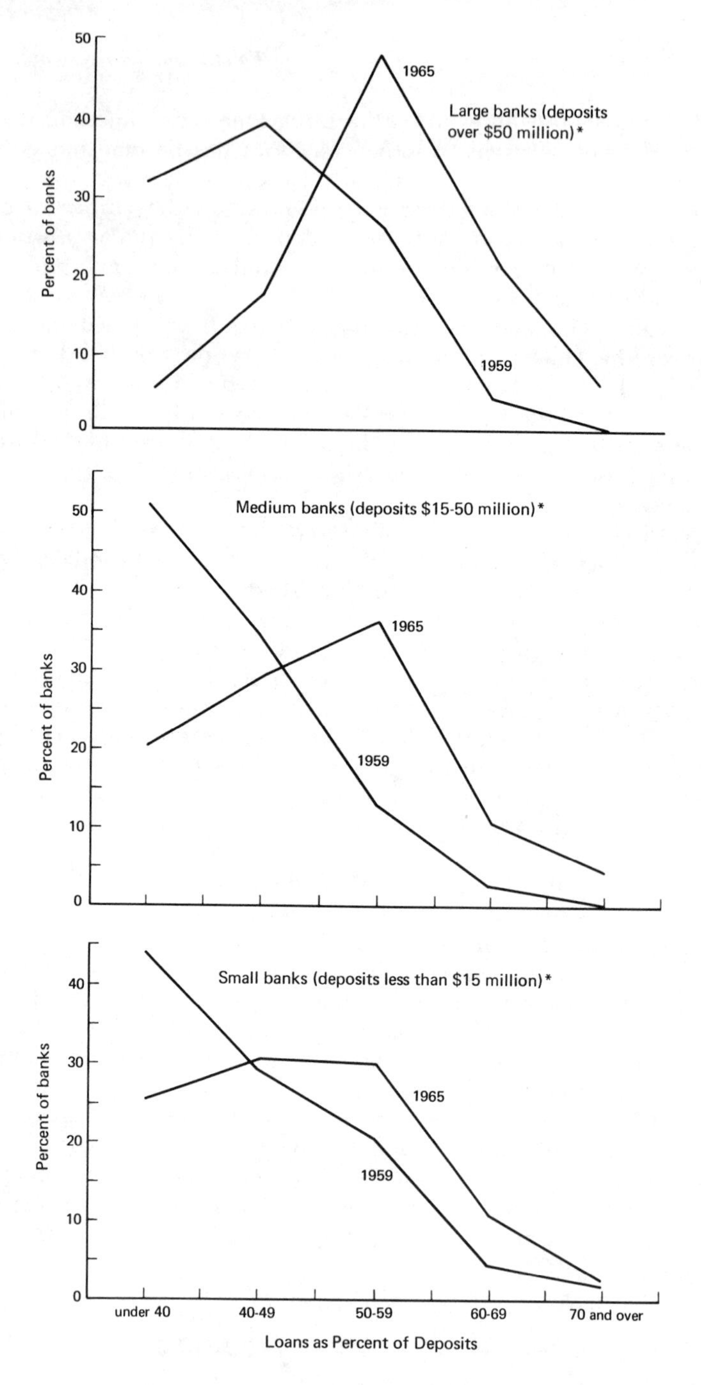

FIG. 2 Proportion of banks with high loan-deposit ratios sharply higher than in 1959.
* *Seventh District member banks by size of gross deposits.*

Note: Loans exclude loans to banks.

Changes in loan-deposit and related ratios of individual Seventh District member banks from December 1959 to December 1965 were examined to provide some additional insight into these questions.[1]

In each of the three size groups analyzed, the percentage of banks with relatively high loan-deposit ratios increased over the six-year period, but the shift was greater at the larger banks (Figure 2). The number of banks in the large size category is, of course, relatively small, accounting for about 12 percent of all District member banks. Only 31 out of almost 950 member banks examined had ratios of 70 percent or more at the end of last year. At more than 200 banks, on the other hand, loans amounted to less than 40 percent of deposits. Many banks have seen these ratios move higher since last December. In mid-June, loan-deposit ratios for the 41 banks that report weekly ranged from 39 to 83 percent but averaged only one percentage point higher than at year-end.

Table 1 shows averages of several liquidity-related ratios for banks in various size and area groupings as of the end of 1965 and the percent change in these ratios compared with six years earlier. In addition to the loan ratio, the table includes average ratios to deposits of selected combinations of asset items—based on their relative liquidity—and of deposit components for the banks in these groups. Within the small, medium and large bank size groups, averages of these ratios are also shown for banks within certain loan-deposit ratio ranges. "Liquid assets" shown in the table are those identifiable from condition statements; besides U.S. Government and Agency securities, they include loans to other commercial banks, loans to brokers and dealers in securities, FHA and VA mortgages, CCC certificates and demand balances with other banks.

Because an average of ratios of individual banks gives equal weight to each bank included regardless of size, this type of measure tends to yield loan-deposit ratios that appear low and liquid asset ratios that appear high compared with the more commonly used ratio of the aggregate asset items of all banks in a group to their aggregate deposits. Furthermore, levels vary seasonally (end of year figures are usually low due to peak deposit volume at that time) and according to the deposit concept chosen (exclusion of uncollected items results in higher ratios). The levels shown as averages of ratios in the table are less significant than the comparison of these averages among various bank groups and over time.

At the end of last year, the average of all individual bank loan-deposit ratios was 49 percent compared with an aggregate ratio of 60 percent. For the 344 medium and large banks—those with total deposits of 15 million dollars or more at the end of 1965—the average loan-deposit ratio was 26 percent above the end of 1959, exactly twice the relative increase in the average ratio of the small banks.

[1] The loan-deposit ratio as used in this article is total loans after deductions of valuation reserves divided by gross deposits. Loan figures do not include sales of Federal funds.

Table 1 Liquidity-related Ratios of Seventh District Member Banks

		AVERAGES OF INDIVIDUAL BANK RATIOS, DECEMBER 31, 1965					
		To Gross Deposits:		To Net Deposits: [2]			
	Number of Banks	*Loans* [1]	*U.S. Govts. and Agencies*	*Real Estate Loans and Municipals* [3]	*Liquid Assets* [4]	*Time Deposits*	*Savings Deposits* [5]
				(percent)			
By Size and Loan-deposit Ratio, December 31, 1965							
Small banks (total deposits under 15 million dollars)							
Total	599	48	36	24	45	48	27
0–39%	153	32	50	19	60	42	23
40–49	183	45	37	24	47	48	28
50–59	180	55	30	28	39	52	29
60–69	67	64	23	25	31	53	29
70–100	16	74	20	23	26	26	34
Medium banks (total deposits 15–50 million dollars)							
Total	223	49	31	30	40	53	39
0–39%	45	34	43	26	53	52	43
40–49	65	45	34	29	43	52	37
50–59	81	55	26	31	36	55	37
60–69	24	63	21	32	29	56	38
70–100	8	73	15	35	24	55	35
Large banks (total deposits over 50 million dollars)							
Total	121	55	24	29	35	53	40
0–39%	6	31	41	26	53	54	49
40–49	21	46	31	30	41	53	43
50–59	59	55	24	30	34	52	38
60–69	28	63	17	29	29	52	36
70–100	7	74	16	19	30	64	47
By Area							
Metropolitan area banks							
Chicago							
Major[6]	19	58	19	23	26	52	41
Other	119	45	36	28	44	56	47
Indianapolis							
Major[6]	3	62	18	24	32	40	21
Other	13	49	35	20	46	45	26
Des Moines	9	51	21	25	39	42	31

[1] Loans, less loans to banks and valuation reserves to gross deposits.
[2] Deposits net of cash items in process of collection.
[3] Excludes VA- and FHA-guaranteed loans.
[4] Includes U.S. Government and agency securities, VA- and FHA-guaranteed loans, CCC certificates, loans to banks, loans to dealers and brokers in securities and balances with domestic banks.
[5] Change from 1961.
[6] Gross deposits over 100 million dollars.

Table 1 (Continued)

		CHANGE IN AVERAGES OF RATIOS FROM DECEMBER 31, 1959 TO DECEMBER 31, 1965					
		To Gross Deposits:		To Net Deposits: [2]			
	Number of Banks	Loans [1]	U.S. Govts. and Agencies	Real Estate Loans and Municipals [3]	Liquid Assets [4]	Time Deposits	Savings Deposits [5]
				(percent)			
Detroit							
Major[6]	8	62	17	28	34	63	52
Other	22	54	31	31	44	69	53
Milwaukee							
Major[6]	3	64	12	26	21	41	24
Other	13	51	34	28	45	54	41
Other metropolitan area banks							
Illinois	72	47	34	22	44	46	30
Indiana	31	43	36	27	49	45	31
Iowa	16	53	28	21	40	42	26
Michigan	52	57	26	36	34	64	45
Wisconsin	10	57	24	36	34	53	31
Rural area banks							
Illinois	150	45	38	21	46	39	23
Indiana	107	45	39	24	49	47	27
Iowa	129	51	32	19	44	41	17
Michigan	79	56	28	37	34	63	39
Wisconsin	88	49	34	31	43	59	31
By Size and Loan-deposit Ratio, December 31, 1965							
Small banks (total deposits under 15 million dollars)							
Total	599	13	−11	16	−10	26	−13
0–39%	153	−2	2	5	1	24	−13
40–49	183	11	−9	14	−7	30	−11
50–59	180	18	−19	22	−18	26	−13
60–69	67	20	−28	22	−24	26	−14
70–100	16	40	−45	5	−44	16	−13
Medium banks (total deposits 15–50 million dollars)							
Total	223	26	−25	31	−22	24	−3
0–39%	45	13	−13	35	−13	22	6
40–49	65	27	−21	31	−20	28	−1
50–59	81	25	−30	29	−26	23	−8
60–69	24	29	−36	30	−33	21	−7
70–100	8	55	−45	29	−39	22	−2
Large banks (total deposits over 50 million dollars)							
Total	121	26	−33		−28	29	4
0–39%	6	16	−16	68	−16	9	3

Table 1 (Continued)

		CHANGE IN AVERAGES OF RATIOS FROM DECEMBER 31, 1959 TO DECEMBER 31, 1965					
		To Gross Deposits:		To Net Deposits: [2]			
	Number of Banks	Loans [1]	U.S. Govts. and Agencies	Real Estate Loans and Municipals [3]	Liquid Assets [4]	Time Deposits	Savings Deposits [5]
Large banks (continued)							
40–49	21	30	−27	47	−24	29	7
50–59	59	25	−31	49	−28	32	5
60–69	28	26	−42	43	−33	33	−1
70–100	7	35	−54	56	−40	19	−3
By Area							
Metropolitan area banks							
Chicago							
Major[6]	19	29	−37	65	−37	52	24
Other	119	36	−24	36	−22	19	4
Indianapolis							
Major[6]	3	38	−41	99	−30	72	−8
Other	13	28	−19	1	−13	46	−9
Des Moines	9	3	−19	42	−20	46	16
Detroit							
Major[6]	8	28	−43	45	−27	23	13
Other	22	24	−19	−3	−9	11	−6
Milwaukee							
Major[6]	3	27	−49	112	−45	51	−4
Other	13	31	−23	40	−23	13	1
Other metropolitan area banks							
Illinois	72	19	−19	30	−17	40	1
Indiana	31	9	−11	24	−9	98	−8
Iowa	16	22	−17	4	−13	23	1
Michigan	52	16	−21	21	−21	17	−6
Wisconsin	10	47	−40	57	−38	15	−24
Rural area banks							
Illinois	150	19	−15	24	−13	45	−5
Indiana	107	15	−12	20	−12	27	−15
Iowa	129	1	4	9	1	39	−12
Michigan	79	15	−19	16	−18	14	−19
Wisconsin	88	26	−23	30	−23	14	−24

In general, the various asset to deposit ratios show a high degree of consistency in their implications with respect to liquidity. For example, banks whose average loan-deposit ratios were highest also tended to have relatively low average liquid asset ratios whether broadly or narrowly defined. The more inclusive ratio dropped somewhat less sharply over the six-year period, however, especially at the large banks. On the other hand, banks with the highest loan-deposit ratios also had the highest share of total time deposits and a relatively high, but shrinking, proportion of savings deposits. The average ratio of real estate loans and municipal securities to deposits increased sharply for almost every bank group with the biggest gains at the largest banks. These are the banks where these assets were relatively small in earlier years.

The average ratios for the area groups show a rather sharp contrast between the largest banks (over 100 million dollars in total deposits) in the major District cities and other banks. Wisconsin banks in both urban and rural areas showed the most severe decline in liquidity by these measures. The average ratio of passbook savings to total deposits showed significant gains from 1961 only for the large banks in Chicago, Detroit and Des Moines and declined in most metropolitan and rural area banks. With higher rates offered on individual certificates in recent months mainly at the major banks, it seems probable that these inter-area divergences in savings trends have now been substantially reduced.

On balance, it appears that the decline in liquid assets relative to deposits has been general but much greater where loan volume was already high. High-ratio banks are to a large extent banks with the ability to compete in the money market for short-term funds offered by other banks, corporations and large individual savers. This source is an effective, although perhaps somewhat uncomfortable, substitute for liquid assets for these banks. The problem may be greater for those few smaller banks with high loan-deposit ratios.

Probably the most important element in assuring liquidity to individual banks is the mobility of funds within the banking system in response to peak needs in different areas at different times. With today's adjustment practices, anything that tends to restrict these flows would cause problems. Rate flexibility is a major factor and, so far, adjustments in ceilings on rates paid on time deposits have permitted large banks to bid for funds as needed. Other measures, such as broadening eligibility rules for collateral against Federal Reserve advances and elimination of the pledge of securities against public deposits, would contribute additional flexibility to the adjustment process.

Commercial Bank Liquidity

James L. Pierce

Bank liquidity is of concern because of its direct connection with two different, but related, problems. Inadequate liquidity of the banking system, on the one hand, raises the possibility that a number of banks more or less simultaneously may discover that they are incapable of meeting deposit withdrawals by selling assets or by other means. On the other hand, the liquidity of the banking system may be regarded as a basic factor shaping the lending policies of banks, and consequently as a principal determinant of the cost and availability of bank credit to borrowers.

This study deals only with the second of these two problems. The first problem is concerned with the adequacy of the powers of a central bank to cope with major crises, and is outside the scope of the study.

Of obvious and justifiable concern however, is the problem of bank liquidity and its relation to lending policies of commercial banks. Because these policies cannot be observed directly, statistics such as ratios of loans to deposits or ratios of liquid assets to total assets are often used to measure variations in the willingness of banks to lend.

In this study, it is argued that, although liquidity is an important element in an individual bank's decisions regarding the composition of its asset portfolio, no liquidity ratio provides an unambiguous picture of either asset characteristics or lending behavior. The study also points out that recent developments in banking have reduced—but not eliminated—the importance of asset liquidity in the determination of bank lending practices. Before considering the role of liquidity in bank portfolio management, it is desirable to develop a precise definition of asset liquidity. This requires careful consideration of the characteristics of assets, and in particular of the ease and speed with which assets can be sold.

Note. An earlier draft of this paper was presented at a meeting of the Federal Reserve System Committee on Financial Analysis, Philadelphia, Pennsylvania, on April 19–21, 1966. The author would like to thank Lyle E. Gramley for the many useful suggestions offered on the earlier draft.

Reprinted with the permission of the Board of Governors of the Federal Reserve System from the *Federal Reserve Bulletin,* August 1966.

A CONCEPT OF ASSET LIQUIDITY[1]

At any given time, t, an asset has a maximum expected market price, which may be designated P_t^*. P_t^* is the highest price the owner of the asset expects to obtain by liquidating one unit of the asset if he is allowed all useful preparation prior to its disposal. If the unit of the asset must be sold more quickly, the owner at time t can expect to receive an actual price designated P_t that is less than P_t^*. "Quick" sales require acceptance of less than the full market value of the asset; this is the essence of illiquidity.

The value of the ratio P_t/P_t^* is thus determined by the length of time available between the decision to sell a unit of the asset and its actual sale. The longer is this interval, the higher is the ratio P_t/P_t^*. Let n be the number of units of time required to obtain P_t^*, and let i be a variable representing the number of units of time available ($i = 0, \ldots, n$). If the decision to sell an asset is made in period t, and if the sale is made in period t_{+i}, the price received may be designated P_{t+i}; $P_{t+i} < P_t^*$ for all $i < n$ and $P_{t+n} = P_t^*$. The ratio P_{t+i}/P_t^* then shows the relation between actual and full realizable sales price at any given time of sale, $_{t+i}$, when a single unit of the asset is sold. That ratio may be plotted graphically to show its relation with the length of time for sale, as in Figure 1.

Figure 1 portrays a hypothetical situation in which the relationship between P_{t+i}/P_t^* and i is continuous. It is assumed that at time t ($i = 0$), the seller can obtain no positive price for the asset. If the holder spends m periods finding a buyer, he realizes 50 per cent of the maximum price, P_t^*. Finally, if he spends n periods prior to the disposal of the asset, he realizes the maximum price.

The shape of the relationship between P_{t+i}/P_t^* and i, for any asset, depends upon the characteristics of the market in which the asset is traded. Cash is a perfectly liquid asset; its ratio of P_{t+i}/P_t^* is always unity. Treasury bills can be sold quickly at low cost; the actual sales price P_{t+i} rises rapidly to P_t^*. Mortgages often can be sold, but the market is sufficiently imperfect to require that the holder shop around to avoid low values of P_{t+i}/P_t^*. Many types of bank loans normally are not traded on secondary markets, and as a limiting case it may be supposed that they can be liquidated only at maturity. For these loans $P_{t+i}/P_t^* = 0$ for all $i < n$ and $P_{t+n}/P_t = 1$, where n is time to maturity.

The liquidity of an asset is defined in terms of the function describing the relationship between the ratio P_{t+i}/P_t^* and the time available for disposal. At any given point in the horizontal time scale of Figure 1, an

[1] The treatment of liquidity provided here is an elaboration and extension of that provided by Professor James Tobin, of Yale University, in his unpublished book on monetary theory, Ch. II, "Properties of Assets."

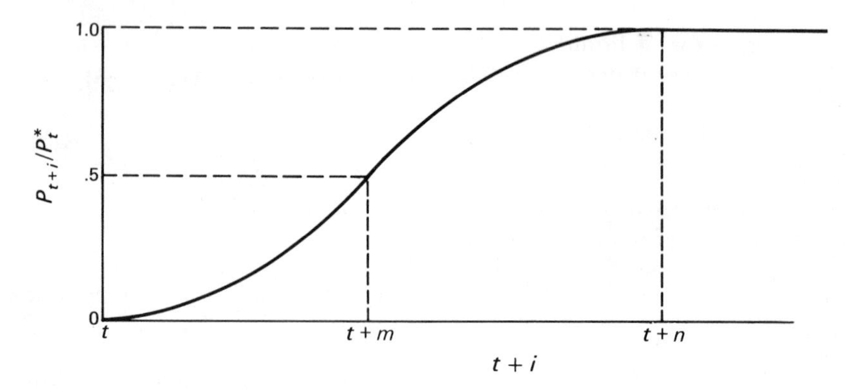

FIG. 1

asset is the more liquid the higher is its ratio of P_{t+i}/P_t^*. But apart from those assets that are perfectly liquid and those for which sale prior to maturity is impossible, assets cannot be uniquely ranked by degrees of liquidity. Liquidity curves of two assets similar to that shown in Figure 1 may cross at some value of $i < n$.

Whether or not a commercial bank's portfolio is liquid thus depends upon the time period being considered. Knowledge of the relationship between the ratio P_{t+i}/P_t^* and i for each asset in the portfolio would permit construction of a liquidity index for a given value of i. For any fixed time horizon (any given value of i), a liquidity index I^i would weight each asset's liquidity by the share of that asset in the total portfolio. Let P^*_{kt} be the maximum price of the kth asset and a_{kt} be the number of units of that asset held at time t ($k = 1, \ldots, N$). The value of the index is given by

$$I^i = \sum_{k=1}^{N} [(W_k)(P_{kt+i}/P^*_{kt})]$$

where

$$W_k = a_{kt}\,(P^*_{kt}) / \sum_{k=1}^{N} a_{kt}\,(P^*_{kt}),$$

$$\sum_{k=1}^{N} W_k = 1, \text{ and } 0 \leq I^i \leq 1.$$

A vector of liquidity indices could be constructed from the I^i for each value of i from 0 to the value of n for the longest term asset. The elements of this vector would obviously bear only a loose relation to conventional liquidity ratios; liquidity measures cannot be compressed into a single number.

Such a vector of liquidity indices would have only limited usefulness, however, because it does not recognize that, for some assets, the price per unit depends on the number of units sold. For example, it might be possible to dispose of a single mortgage loan quickly and at relatively low cost. But the larger the number of mortgages to be sold, the longer the time needed to find buyers and the lower the ratio P_{t+i}/P_t^* for any given value of i. The relationship between P_{t+i}/P_t^* and the time to disposal for different sizes of transactions, s ($s = 1, 2, \ldots, S$), is shown in Figure 2, where $s_1 < s_2 < s_3$.

Thus the price that can be obtained by liquidating an asset depends on both the time available prior to its disposal and the number of units to be sold. For each asset in the portfolio there is a matrix of possible prices with elements defined for given values of i and s. An index of total portfolio liquidity implied by combining the N individual asset matrices could be constructed, but it would be of dubious operational significance.

The concept of liquidity used here provides a clear distinction between liquidity and solvency. Solvency measures the difference between the value of a bank's assets at maximum expected prices and its liabilities. Liquidity refers to realizable value of the asset portfolio for a given time to sale and a given size of the actual sale. A bank can be illiquid and still be solvent.

Brokerage fees, although not an element of liquidity as defined for this study, are important in determining the net return on an asset. Brokerage fees are defined to include all fees charged by middlemen in asset markets, and are assumed to be collected only when assets are sold. If an asset is sold prior to maturity, the brokerage fee must be deducted from P_t^*. Payment of the fee reduces realized rates of return. If an asset is purchased and then sold quickly, brokerage costs could exceed the accumulated interest on the asset, and the rate of return would then be

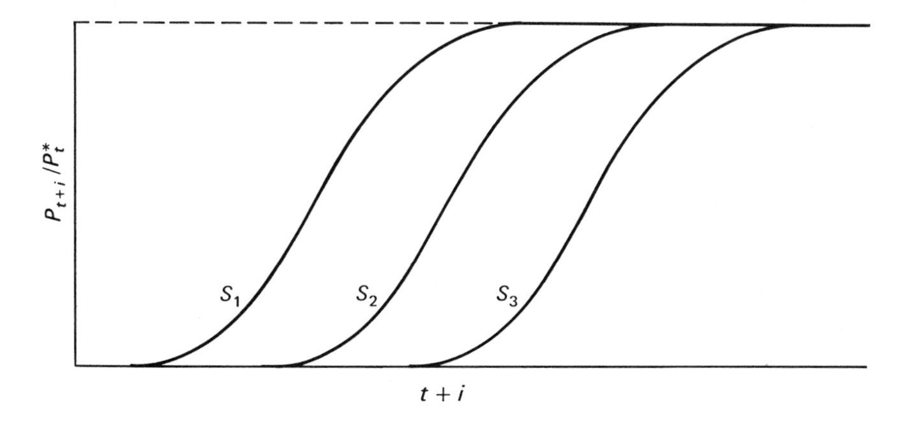

FIG. 2

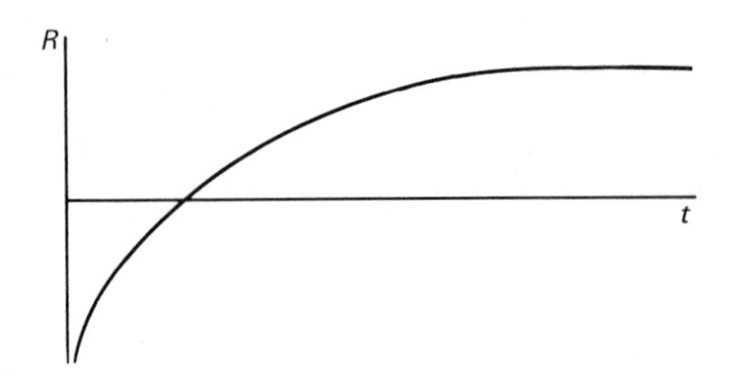

FIG. 3

negative. In general, the greater the fee, the longer an asset must be held to yield any given rate of return. Because it is imposed only once, the brokerage fee becomes less important as a determinant of the realized rate of return the longer an asset is held. A hypothetical relationship between the length of time an asset is held, t, and its rate of return, R—given the brokerage fee, the purchase price, the sale price, and the coupon rate—is shown in Figure 3.

By definition, brokerage fees are independent of the length of time an asset is held and of the number of units sold. They are, therefore, different in concept from liquidity. Nevertheless, both liquidity and brokerage fees represent sources of inertia in the sale of assets.

THE ROLE OF LIQUIDITY IN BANK PORTFOLIO MANAGEMENT

This concept of liquidity permits a more careful consideration of the role of liquidity in a bank's decisions to make loans. To simplify the analysis and to focus sharply on the role of liquidity in decision-making, the analysis that follows ignores brokerage costs, expected rates of return, predictability of return, and similar matters. It also assumes that all deposit liabilities are demand balances and are exogenously determined.[2] Thus, banks are assumed to stand ready to issue demand deposits at a given and constant yield to anyone willing to hold them. The amount of demand deposits issued by any bank at a given point in time is assumed to be a random variable with constant mean and variance. Also for simplicity, it is assumed that the only other type of bank liability available is a loan from the Federal Reserve obtained at an interest rate exceeding the return on any asset.

The analysis is simplified greatly by assuming also that total assets can be separated arbitrarily into two homogeneous groups called "loans" and "liquid assets." Though salable prior to maturity, a unit of loans is as-

[2] This assumption will be relaxed later.

sumed to command a smaller proportion of its full value for a given value of i $(i < n)$ than a unit of liquid assets.

The portfolio of liquid assets serves as a buffer that insulates loans from unexpected variations in deposits. When a bank experiences an unexpected loss of funds, it can meet at least part of the loss from its liquid assets.[3] Ownership of liquid assets reduces the probability that the bank has to sell loans under unfavorable terms.

Similarly, when a bank experiences an unexpected net inflow of deposits, the inflow might be viewed as transitory and the funds held in liquid form. Generally speaking, it is not profitable to invest funds in loans if there is reason to believe that an inflow soon will be reversed.[4]

With this simple division of bank assets into two categories, the determinants of loans and of the buffer stock of liquid assets are one and the same. Before considering these determinants, it may be helpful to digress a bit to discuss the institutional approach to commercial banking.[5]

The institutional approach asserts that banks assign priorities to the use of their funds. Liquidity receives first priority, and each bank has a subjective liquidity standard which it attempts to meet at all times. The standard for each bank depends upon its deposit stability and upon its preferences, and is fixed in the short run. Loans are accorded second priority. Once the fixed liquidity ratio is attained, each bank stands ready to grant loans to all borrowers who qualify as acceptable loan customers and are willing to pay a given and constant loan rate. For a bank with "adequate" capital and "healthy" loans, the conceptual limits to the size of the loan account are the value of the bank's resources (deposits and capital) and its invariate commitment to liquidity. The ratio of loans to total assets is thought to be limited, under most circumstances, by the paucity of acceptable loans. If a paucity exists, banks move on to their third priority, the purchase of securities for income.

If banks did behave this way, simple liquidity ratios would be useful. Each bank would have a maximum loan-to-deposit ratio determined by its liquidity standard, the size of its capital, and the quality of available loans. A bank could be fully "loaned up" before all its resources were devoted to loans, since the bank would refuse to grant new loans to acceptable customers if its liquidity standard were not met. Differences

[3] Assets in the buffer stock need not and typically are not in cash form. Interest-bearing liquid assets provide some current income and they can be sold quickly at low cost should the need arise.

[4] Many of the considerations involved in liquidity and asset sales are also involved in asset purchases. The price a bank pays for an asset is, in part, a function of the time available to find the most eager seller and of the size of the transaction. For an extended discussion of the role of costs of asset acquisition in bank portfolio management, see James L. Pierce, "A Cross Section Analysis of Commercial Bank Portfolio Management," presented before the 1965 winter meetings of the Econometric Society.

[5] One of the most coherent statements of this position is found in Roland Robinson, *The Management of Bank Funds,* 2d ed., McGraw-Hill, 1962.

among banks in liquidity standards, and variations from one bank to another in the strength of loan demands, would alter the significance of an aggregate loan-to-deposit ratio—even during periods of high aggregate loan demand. However, unless subjective preferences for liquidity were highly variable from bank to bank, a higher aggregate ratio of loans to deposits at all banks would generally imply a greater number of banks turning away loan customers.

While the use of an aggregate loan-to-deposit ratio is defensible in this context, the assumption that banks behave in the manner contemplated by the institutional approach is not compelling. Asset returns are not constant over a period of time, and the liquidity standard is unlikely to be independent of alternative rates of return. Decision-making at commercial banks is more complex than the institutional approach assumes.

In the last few years, several efforts have been made to bring a higher level of economic analysis to bear on bank decision-making.[6] A primary feature of the new approach is the treatment of banks as economic units interested in maximizing profits. The theory of the firm and the theory of portfolio management have been combined to analyze the financial firm. The results obtained are quite different from those of the institutional approach.

The new approach argues that banks seek to maximize some function of their discounted future stream of profits over a period of time for which neither future deposit levels nor future rates of return are known with certainty.[7] Since the only absolutely safe liquidity standard is to hold all deposits in cash, the size of the liquid asset portfolio is inseparably related to the size of the bank's total portfolio.[8] The contribution to current and future profits provided by the flexibility of liquid assets is balanced against the relatively high expected return on less liquid assets. A profit-maximizing assumption implies that the balance point depends both upon deposit levels expected in the future and upon expected rates of return on liquid and illiquid assets.

In this approach, an increase in the expected return on loans relative to liquid assets encourages banks to shift funds into loans. Even though

[6] The references most relevant to this paper are as follows: Richard C. Porter, "A Model of Bank Portfolio Selection," *Yale Economic Essays* (Fall 1961), pp. 323–359. Daniel Orr and W. Mellon, "Stochastic Reserve Losses and Expansion of Bank Credit," *American Economic Review* (Sept. 1961), pp. 614–623. David Chambers and Abraham Charnes, "Inter-Temporal Analysis and Optimization of Bank Portfolios," *Management Science* (July 1961), pp. 393–410.

[7] The models that deal explicitly with stochastic deposit losses are restricted to static, single-period, expected-profit maximization problems. Dynamic models that allow for covariances of asset returns are difficult to solve, but some work is being conducted in this area.

[8] A possible rationalization of the fixed liquidity standard of the institutional approach is to assume that banks seek to maximize expected profit subject to a liquidity constraint.

this shift of funds reduces the liquidity of the asset portfolio, a bank is willing to accept an increased probability of either unforeseen asset sales or borrowing from its Reserve Bank if it is sufficiently compensated by an increased rate of return on loans.[9] Liquidity is relevant to the contribution that it makes to profits. Liquid asset purchases are not made independently of profit considerations.

Viewed in this context, the relation between the maintenance of liquidity and the decision to lend is but one part of the more general problem of specifying a function describing a bank's desired allocation of funds to loans, that is, a loan-supply function. The approach clearly does not imply that the willingness to lend is unrelated to the existing ratio of loans to deposits. Rather it suggests that there is no fixed loan limit for a given value of deposits, but there is a limit that is related to the rate of return on loans. With given deposit characteristics, the greater the share of loans in total assets, the greater the probability that a bank will have to dispose of some part of its loan portfolio at unfavorable terms. Consequently, if a bank is to be induced to hold more loans relative to total assets, it must be compensated for the increased probability of loan sales.

To illustrate, assume for the moment that the terms on which loans are supplied (and demanded) can be represented by a single interest rate, r. Let L represent loans, and D deposits. The approach discussed here suggests a supply-of-loans function of the sort depicted in Figure 4, where the quantity of deposits, D, and the rate of return on liquid assets are given.

The actual shape of this functional relation is by no means obvious.[10] It depends upon such factors as the characteristics of the bank's deposits, the liquidity characteristics of its loans, and the cost of borrowing as a means of adjusting to deposit withdrawals. Nevertheless, there are some reasons for believing that the supply of loans function would have the generally nonlinear shape depicted in Figure 4.

This shape is indicated because the higher is a bank's loan-to-deposit ratio, the greater is the probability that a loss of deposits would force the bank to dispose of loans on unfavorable terms. Consequently, the higher is the value of L/D, the greater is the increase in r required to induce the bank to supply an additional unit of loans.[11]

At least one further reason exists for believing that the supply-of-loans function has the shape described. The lack of insurance on the greater part of large deposit accounts may induce these depositors to favor banks with higher degrees of liquidity. The higher the value of L / D for any given bank, the greater the probability that a marginal rise

[9] This "free choice" can, of course, clash with bank examination rules. To the extent that it does, profit maxima are constrained by the rules.

[10] The quantity of loans supplied at various rates is deflated by deposits so as to present the argument in terms of the loan-to-deposit ratio.

[11] This condition appears to hold even for banks that are risk neutral, that is, for banks guided solely by expected profit.

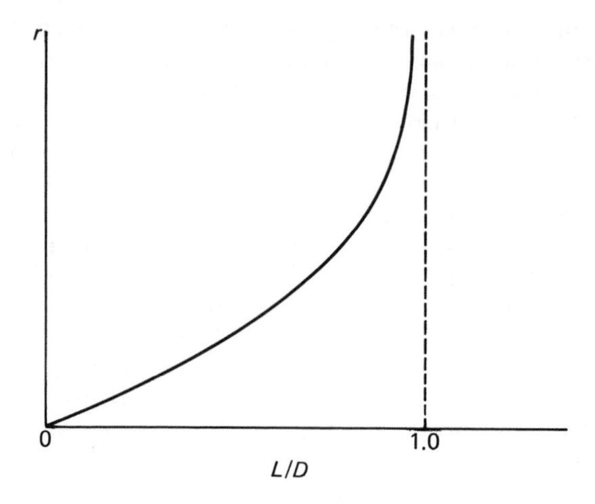

FIG. 4

in the ratio would induce these depositors to move their funds elsewhere. If this is true, a rise in L/D increases the risk of a deposit loss, and banks must be compensated for this added risk.

The position of the loan-supply function in Figure 4 depends upon expected rates of return on liquid assets, the degree of deposit variability, and other factors. The loan-to-deposit ratio expresses its influence on the slope of the loan-supply function, but it is only one element among the several that determine a bank's lending policies. To isolate the role of L/D in the lending decision, it is necessary to specify a loan-supply function that explicitly takes these other elements into account. Before turning to this matter, the discussion must first consider the effects of introducing endogenous liabilities into the argument.

SIGNIFICANCE OF ENDOGENOUS DEPOSIT DETERMINATION

The role of liquidity in a bank's decision to lend is complicated further when the assumption is relaxed that deposits are determined exogenously, but the significance of endogenous deposit determination is well worth pursuing. Markets have developed in recent years that permit banks, within rather wide limits, to obtain funds if they are willing to pay the price.[12] By varying the rates they pay for Federal funds and for certificates of deposit, banks can—within limits—determine the size of

[12] For purposes of the present discussion it is assumed that all banks have equal access to liability markets. It is further assumed that there are no legal maxima on the rates paid for these liabilities. Both assumptions are relaxed in the section on loan-supply function (p. 26).

their total liabilities.[13] To draw out the implications of these markets for liquidity and lending decisions, it may be supposed that the only form of endogenous deposit liability is a certificate of deposit [CD] that has a single maturity, on which banks can pay any interest rate they choose.

Banks are not assumed to be strictly price takers in markets for endogenous deposit liabilities. The rate paid by an individual bank is an increasing function of the average rate prevailing in the market, of the amount of CD's that the bank has outstanding, and of the size of the new issue offered by the bank. Banks, like other borrowers, do not face perfectly elastic demand schedules for their liabilities.

As its most significant feature for the problem at hand, the CD market provides banks with an alternative method of portfolio adjustment. To meet an exogenous loss of funds, banks may sell assets or issue new liabilities, or both. Profit-maximizing banks would make adjustments by the method that costs the least. For any given loss of deposits there is a particular least-cost combination of asset and liability sales. Since the mere existence of a CD market does not remove the option of selling assets, this mix must be at least as inexpensive as relying strictly on asset sales to meet deposit losses. Thus, the development of markets permitting endogenous determination of liabilities tends to reduce the costs of portfolio adjustment. The existence of such markets also reduces the size of the desired buffer of liquid assets.

But endogenous liabilities also allow a bank to determine the total size, as well as composition, of its asset portfolio. A positive differential between the expected return on loans and the existing CD rate—if it is large enough—would induce a bank to issue CD's and purchase new loans.[14] Issuance of new CD's tends to raise the marginal cost of liabilities, and the acquisition of new loans tends to depress the return expected on loans. Equilibrium is achieved when there is no longer any net advantage to issuing CD's to acquire additional loans.

Sales of liabilities to purchase assets, however, are not likely to be carried to the point at which the marginal cost of new CD's equals the marginal expected return on new loans. When a bank issues a CD and purchases a loan, it runs the risk that CD rates will rise prior to the maturity date of the loan. Most banks would require compensation for this risk.[15]

Endogenous liabilities appear to have some clear qualitative implications for lending practices of banks. The ability of banks to market their liabilities induces them to desire a higher loan-to-deposit ratio for every value of the terms on new loans. The loan-supply relation in Figure 4

[13] The stochastic processes which generate exogenous deposit liabilities prevent this control from being complete.

[14] The possibility is ignored that yield relationships might permit banks profitably to issue CD's and purchase liquid assets.

[15] If ceiling rates on CD's are introduced, the bank runs the risk that the rate will rise to the ceiling. If it does, CD's become exogenous and the bank must rely upon liquid assets for short-term portfolio adjustments.

shifts down and to the right. The constraint on the volume of loans is no longer determined by the value of D, the level of exogenous deposits, but by the total size of the bank's portfolio.[16]

More important, the function also becomes less steeply sloped. The probability of costly adjustments through large asset sales rises less rapidly when adjustments are permitted in liability markets. Since the market for CD's is relatively well developed (as is the market for Federal funds), adjustment costs for the individual bank are likely to rise less rapidly with the scale of transactions than in markets for assets other than Treasury bills. It is very unlikely that the interest-rate elasticity of demand for CD's facing an individual bank is low enough to produce the sharply rising costs of adjustments to deposit losses implied in Figure 4. The slope of the function tends to be reduced by the introduction of endogenous liabilities.

It was observed earlier that bank liquidity is a relative term, even in a world of exogenous liabilities. And when endogenous liabilities are introduced, asset liquidity loses much of its crucial importance. Markets for CD's and other endogenous liabilities bear part of the burden of adjustment to exogenous deposit losses. Conventional measures of liquidity that focus on the share of liquid assets in the total portfolio tend to lose their significance. Statistics such as aggregate loan-to-deposit ratios and ratios of liquid assets to total assets provide at best only incomplete information, and this information may often be quite misleading. To analyze decision-making in today's sophisticated financial markets, more sophisticated measuring techniques are needed.

LOAN-SUPPLY FUNCTION

Although the above remarks are admittedly rather negative, they point to the direction in which further research might illuminate the relation between bank liquidity and bank lending practices. The procedure by which this relation expresses itself is properly formulated in terms of a loan-supply function in which considerations of asset liquidity and costs of making adjustments in endogenous deposit markets are treated explicitly.

Knowledge of the aggregate loan-supply function is of great importance, but almost nothing is known about it. Attempts to obtain statistical estimates of the parameters of the loan-supply function have been thwarted by an almost total lack of information on the terms on which these loans are granted.[17]

[16] This implies, of course, that the maximum value of L/D could exceed unity.

[17] Loan size, maturity, guarantee, and interest rate are examples of important loan terms. For a discussion of the role of such terms in bank loan decisions, see Donald Hester, "An Empirical Examination of a Commercial Bank Loan Offer Function," *Yale Economic Essays* (Spring 1962), pp. 3–57, and Jack Guttentag, "Credit Availability, Interest Rates, and Monetary Policy," *The Southern Economic Journal* (Jan. 1960), pp. 219–228.

Availability of information on loan terms would permit the estimation of the loan-supply function. At any given point in time the following variables might be assumed to enter into the function for a bank: the size and composition of its exogenous liabilities, the rates it pays for endogenous liabilities, the expected rates of return and covariance of return on assets other than loans, the "liquidity" of its portfolio, and finally the set of loan terms. Data on loan terms, coupled with estimates of the extent to which lenders and borrowers trade off elements in the vector of terms in their negotiations, would provide a basis for an approximate identification of the supply-of-loans function.

The specification and estimation of a loan-supply function would be difficult and costly.[18] But the impact of liquidity and other variables on bank lending behavior cannot be known until this supply function is estimated.

[18] A second possible approach lies in a technique which statistically imputes marginal net rates of return to bank assets on a cross section basis. See D. Hester and J. Zoellner, "The Relation Between Bank Portfolios and Earnings: An Econometric Study," a paper presented before the 1964 winter meetings of the Econometric Society. Some preliminary attempts to obtain time series of net loan returns have not been very encouraging, but further efforts are justified.

What Price Liquidity?

Did you ever sit down and figure the return on $1,000,000 at 6 per cent interest for one year? It comes to $60,000, and $60,000 pays a lot of wages, salaries, electric bills, and other expenses that bankers and other businessmen incur in the process of earning a profit.

Now suppose you just happen to have $1,000,000 lying around in a bank vault or elsewhere which you may not need in the form of ready cash or its equivalent. If you lend it out or invest it, you get the $60,000. If you don't, you don't. Interested? More and more bankers have been interested in the past decade for they have steadily decreased the volume of cash assets they hold relative to the total assets they manage.[1]

[1] In this article, the term "cash assets" is used to mean cash in vault, deposits with correspondents, required and excess reserves held with Federal Reserve Banks and cash items (checks and the like) in process of collection. The term "managed cash assets" includes vault cash, deposits with correspondents, and excess reserves held with the Fed.

Reprinted with the permission of the Federal Reserve Bank of Philadelphia from *Business Review,* September 1964.

EARNINGS VERSUS LIQUIDITY: THE BANKER'S AGE-OLD DILEMMA

In many respects a bank is much like any other business. It hires workers such as the tellers who stand at the front desk and accept deposits and pay out currency. It must buy or rent its business quarters and pay for heating, cooling, and lighting. It sells a "product" in the form of checking accounts, loans, and the like. Also, like any other business, a bank wants to maximize its revenues so it can meet its expenses and still turn a profit.

Unlike other businesses, however, a bank's primary stock in trade is the deposits of its customers which it uses to lend and invest. And a large proportion of these deposits, unlike the accounts payable of most businesses, must be paid out on demand.

The banker, for example, must stand ready on a moment's notice to pay out cash to his depositors and others. If he can't, he's in trouble. In the jargon of the trade, the banker must be "liquid." And here we have a seeming paradox. The most liquid asset—cash—provides no earnings. Assets which do provide earnings, on the other hand, (loans and investments) are less liquid; they are more difficult to turn into ready cash.

How does the banker cope with this two-sided problem, with simultaneous need to be (a) liquid enough to meet cash demand and (b) invested and loaned enough to derive a good return? Answer: he keeps sufficient cash assets and near-cash assets to meet the cash demand he may reasonably expect, and then he invests and lends the rest. He thereby obtains both liquidity and earnings.

Yet in recent years, as shown in Figure 1, banks have reduced the proportion of their total assets held in the form of cash, this at the same time that holdings of short-term Governments have been falling and loan-deposit ratios have been rising.

In this article we take a look at the reasons why commercial bankers have decided they can do with less cash. We also examine some of the wider implications of a declining cash-asset ratio.

TO MARKET, TO MARKET

One reason why bankers have decided they can do with less in cash is simply that they can "buy" or borrow funds if they run short, often with little loss or delay. With such funds available, bankers have found that they need not keep cash on hand at all times in amounts large enough to meet peak cash drains.

The traditional methods of obtaining funds to meet immediate cash needs include the sale of near-cash assets such as Treasury bills, borrowing from other banks, and borrowing from the Federal Reserve Banks (a privilege which member banks may exercise in accordance with regulations specified by Federal Reserve authorities).

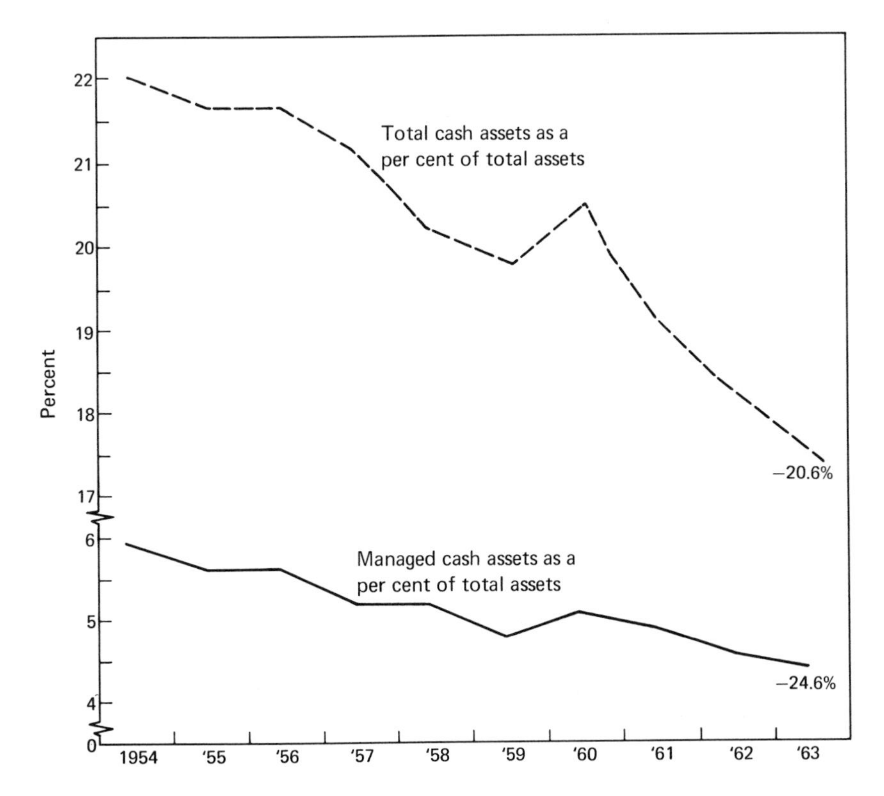

FIG. 1 Cash assets as a percent of total assets.
All member banks, United States.

Sources: Board of Governors, Member Bank Call Reports; data are averages of 4 Call dates.

Another alternative which has become increasingly important in recent years (both in terms of the volume of funds changing hands and in numbers and sizes of participating banks) is the so-called "federal funds market." Through the federal funds market, banks with excess funds may lend to deficit banks who are temporarily deficient. The loan is usually of short duration, say, overnight or for one or two days. A typical transaction might go something like this: Bank A finds that a larger dollar volume of checks have been drawn against it than have been deposited with it, with the result that Bank A experiences a net drain of funds. Bank A contacts a federal funds dealer who puts him in touch with Bank B (Bank B having experienced a net inflow of funds in excess of its immediate needs). Bank A borrows the funds for one or two days then returns them with interest to Bank B.

The federal funds market has made possible the mobilization of excess funds among an ever-widening circle of both large and small banks. In the Third Federal Reserve District, for example, the large Philadelphia reserve city banks stand ready to buy or sell federal funds for the account of their smaller correspondents. They will buy or sell regardless of their own deficit or surplus position, using any excess funds, for example, to cover their own deficiency (if they happen to have a deficiency) or selling these funds to others if they should have a reserve surplus. The majority of transactions are consummated by direct debit or credit to the correspondent account at the prevailing federal funds rate. Typically, the reserve city banks will sell funds to correspondents in amounts of $100,000 or over and will purchase funds in amounts of $200,000 to $250,000 and over. A market for federal funds in such relatively small amounts opens the federal funds mechanism to a very wide range of smaller banks and thus a growing number of institutions feel they may safely decrease the volume of cash they hold.

But this is only one side of the earnings-liquidity coin. Institutional developments such as the federal funds market provide the *opportunity* to reduce cash holdings, but the opportunity might be passed over and indeed a federal funds market might never have developed if there were not some *inducement* to economize on cash holdings. The inducement has come from the earnings side of the coin.

THE PULL OF INTEREST RATES

Interest rates increased significantly in the 1950's from the low levels associated with wartime financing. This rise in interest rates, in effect, has made it more costly for banks to hold cash assets.

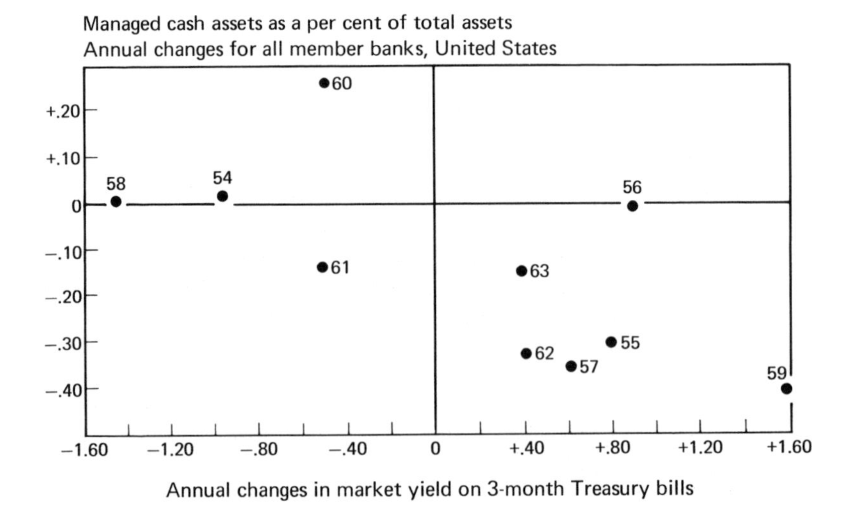

FIG. 2 Changes in cash asset holdings appear to be related to changes in interest rates in the nation.

Sources: Board of Governors, Member Bank Call Reports.

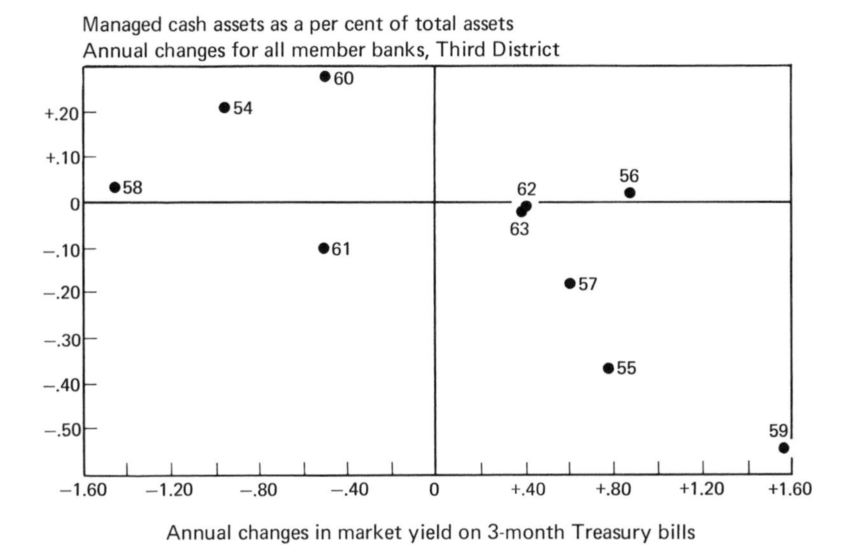

FIG. 3 Changes in cash asset holdings appear to be related to changes in interest rates in the Third Federal Reserve District.

Sources: Federal Reserve Bank of Philadelphia, Member Bank Call Reports.

Whereas it cost banks only about 3⁄8 of 1 per cent to hold cash instead of Treasury bills during the war (by holding cash, banks would give up the 3⁄8 of 1 per cent they could otherwise have made by investing in Treasury bills), it now costs them around 3½ per cent to hold cash instead of bills, and even more to hold cash instead of loans. Since banks are in business to make a profit, one might expect bankers to reduce their cash-asset ratios as interest rates rise (providing, of course, that bankers determine such action to be prudent and in keeping with liquidity needs).

In fact, changes in interest rates do appear to have influenced changes in cash-asset ratios. Figures 2 and 3 show that, more often than not in the 10-year period 1954–1963, bankers economized on the cash assets which they can control or "manage" (vault cash, deposits with correspondents, and excess reserves held with the Fed) [2] in years when interest rates were rising and raised these same cash-asset ratios more often than

[2] The total of these items which can be "managed" or "controlled" (that is, which may more readily be converted from nonearning to earning assets) is actually less than their arithmetic sum at any one point in time. This is because correspondent balances, shifted into loans or investments, would then be subject on the liability side to reserve requirements. Since banks have been allowed to count vault cash as required reserves since 1960, vault cash too, is now less of a "manageable" asset.

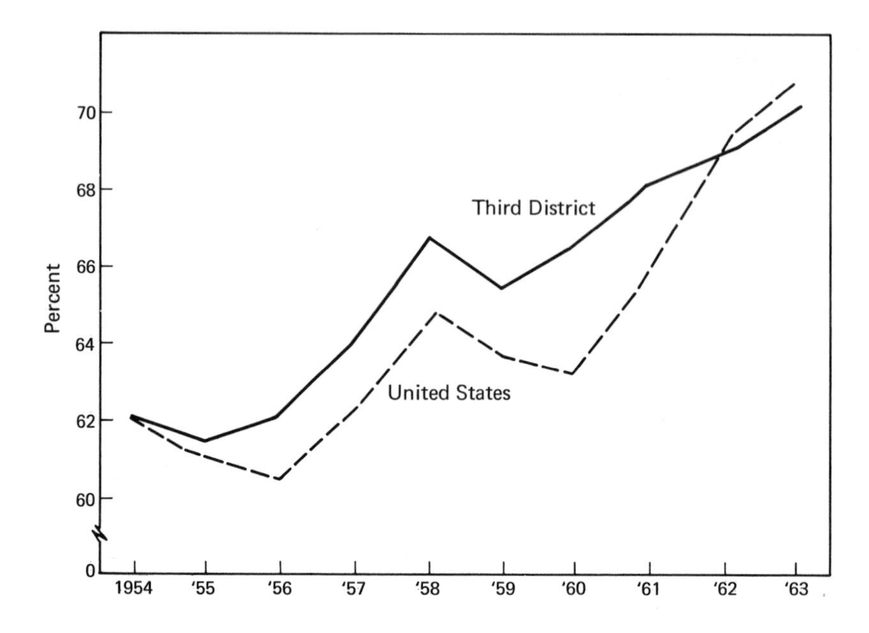

FIG. 4 Total expenses as a percent of total revenue.
All member banks, United States and Third District.

Source: Board of Governors.

not in years when interest rates fell.[3] Thus the pull of earnings reflected in the shifting attractiveness of interest rates does appear to provide an inducement for bankers to adjust their cash assets.

But earnings are a function both of revenues and of costs. We have seen that bankers apparently are influenced by the pull of revenues (interest rates) in managing their cash position; could they also be pushed by rising costs?

THE PUSH OF COSTS

Costs in banking, as for many industries, have risen significantly in the past decade. Wages, salaries, occupancy expenses have increased, and

[3] Despite the limited number of observations, the correlations observed are sufficiently high that they would seldom occur in sampling universes where no correlation existed.

	Number of Observations	*Coefficient of Correlation*	*Correlation Significant at Level*
Member Banks, U.S.	10	−.67	.025
Member Banks, Third District	10	−.72	.01

banks also have experienced rising costs in the form of higher interest rates which they must pay to compete effectively for time and savings deposits.

As can be seen in Figures 4 and 5, bank costs have risen both in terms of revenues and assets. For each dollar of revenues earned in 1954, member banks incurred operating expenses of about 62 cents. In 1963, operating expenses took about 71 cents of each dollar of revenue. Operating expenses per dollar of assets, on the other hand, rose from 1.8 cents in 1954 to over 3.1 cents in 1963. It would not be at all surprising if the reduction in cash-asset ratios were partially related to rising bank costs.

RESERVES HELD WITH THE FED: A SHARPER PENCIL

As already mentioned, one important component of a member bank's cash assets is its cash reserves held with Federal Reserve Banks. Today's banker who wishes to hold his cash assets at a minimum consistent with basic liquidity needs is aided in doing so by a basic improvement with respect to these reserves.

A portion of reserves held with the Fed is, of course, required. Country member banks, for example, must hold 12 per cent of their net demand

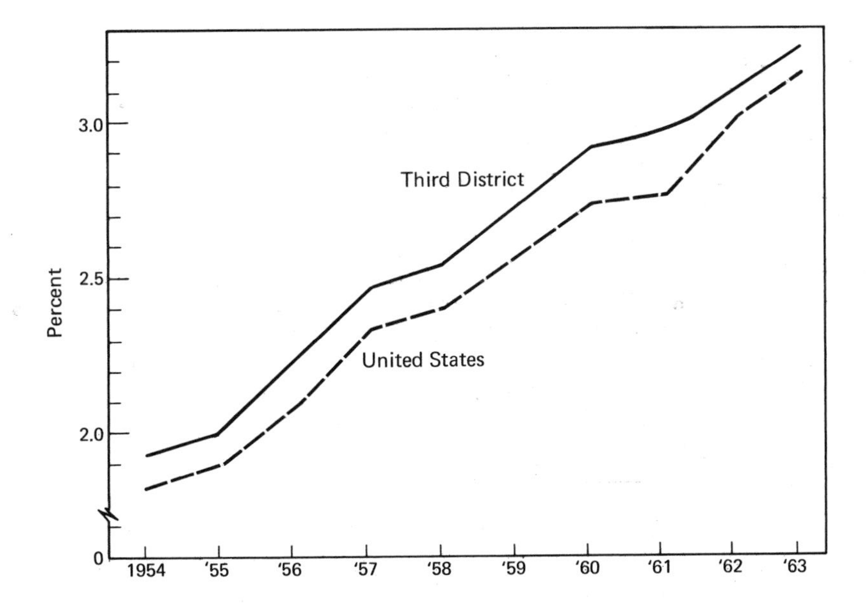

FIG. 5 Total expenses as a percent of total assets.
All member banks, United States and Third District.

Source: Board of Governors.

deposits as required reserves and 4 per cent of their time deposits. The banker need not hold any *more* reserves than are required, however, and to the extent that the banker *does* keep a considerable sum in excess of required reserves, he bypasses loans and investments he might otherwise make and thereby earns less.

Question: how has the banker sharpened his pencil with respect to reserve balances?

Answer: he has become better informed of the day-to-day fluctuations in his reserves—whether he is about on the line with his requirements or whether he is building up a large deficit or surplus. If he is better informed, he is better able to minimize his reserve balances and thereby lend and invest more and improve his earnings.

The Philadelphia Federal Reserve Bank, for example, provides work sheets to member banks which aid them in computing, on a day-to-day basis, the reserves that they are *required* to hold at the Fed. Then, each day, the Philadelphia Fed sends each of its members a statement indicating reserves actually *maintained.* The difference between reserves maintained and reserves required gives the daily excess or deficiency. The member banker is thereby able to see each day if he is building up a con-

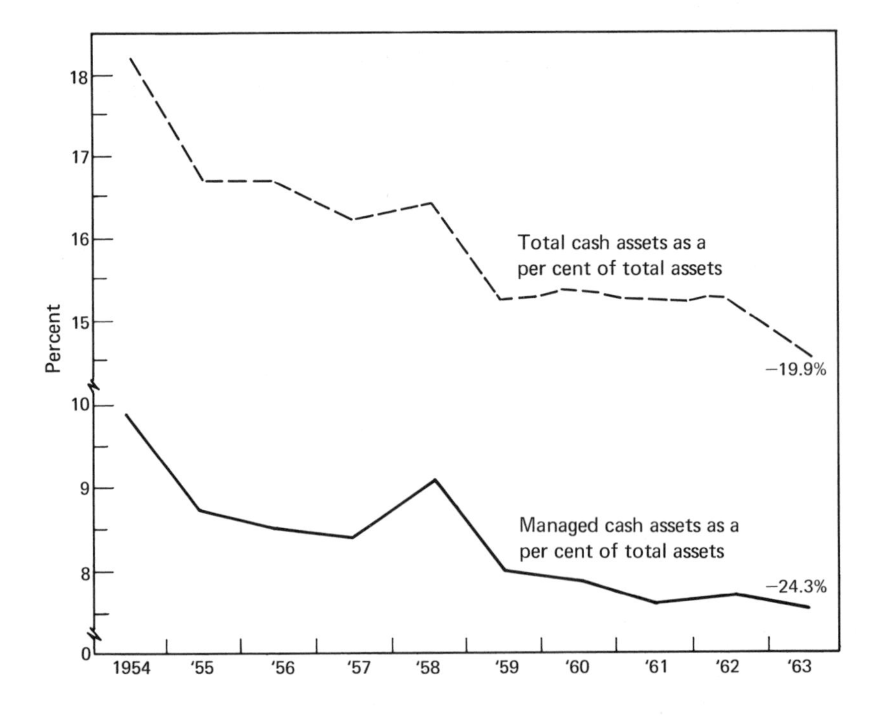

FIG. 6 Cash assets as a percent of total assets.
Third District member banks.

Sources: Federal Reserve Bank of Philadelphia, Member Bank Call Reports, June dates.

siderable excess in his reserve position, and being thus informed, is able to take corrective action if he so desires. In effect, the Fed provides the member banker with a sharper pencil to manage his reserve position.

MANAGING CASH POSITIONS IN THE THIRD FEDERAL RESERVE DISTRICT

In keeping with their counterparts throughout the nation, Third District bankers have sharpened their pencils in the past decade and lowered their holdings of cash assets relative to the total assets they control. Indeed, Figure 6 shows that managed cash assets as a percentage of total assets have declined by a substantial 24 per cent in the past ten years.

What kinds of cash assets have banks reduced the most? What size banks have been most successful in minimizing cash holdings? What are some wider implications of the reduction in cash assets?

Big banks versus their country cousins

Though larger banks have carried a smaller over-all ratio of managed cash assets to total assets, their country cousins have been gaining in the

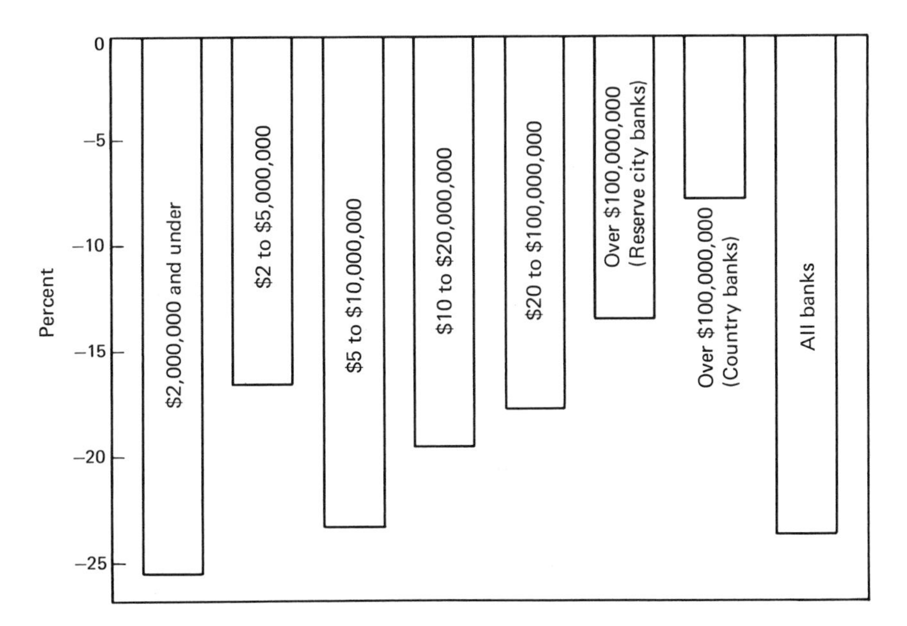

FIG. 7 Managed cash assets as a percent of total assets—percentage decline 1954–1963. *Third District member banks by deposit size.*

Sources: Federal Reserve Bank of Philadelphia, Member Bank Call Reports, June dates.

race to minimize cash holdings. For example, in 1963 banks with under $2 million in deposits held about 8½ per cent of their total assets in the form of managed cash, while the big reserve city banks of Philadelphia held only about 3⅓ per cent. In the decade 1954–1963, however, the $2 million banks reduced their managed-cash-assets ratio by a sizable 25.7 per cent while the city banks pulled down cash by only 13.8 per cent. Figure 7 shows a complete breakdown of the changes in the ratio by bank size. It is notable that all of the smaller-size banks were able to better the reduction achieved by the city banks. Still, it should be remembered that the city banks generally had less room to maneuver as they *started off* with a much lower absolute cash asset ratio.

What kinds of cash assets were cut?

Of the three classes of managed cash assets (vault cash, deposit balances held with correspondents, and excess reserves held with the Fed) only the ratio for excess reserves showed a distinct downward trend during the period 1954–1963 (as shown in Figure 8). For all member banks, the ratio was down by 31.3 per cent while the ratio for balances due from banks

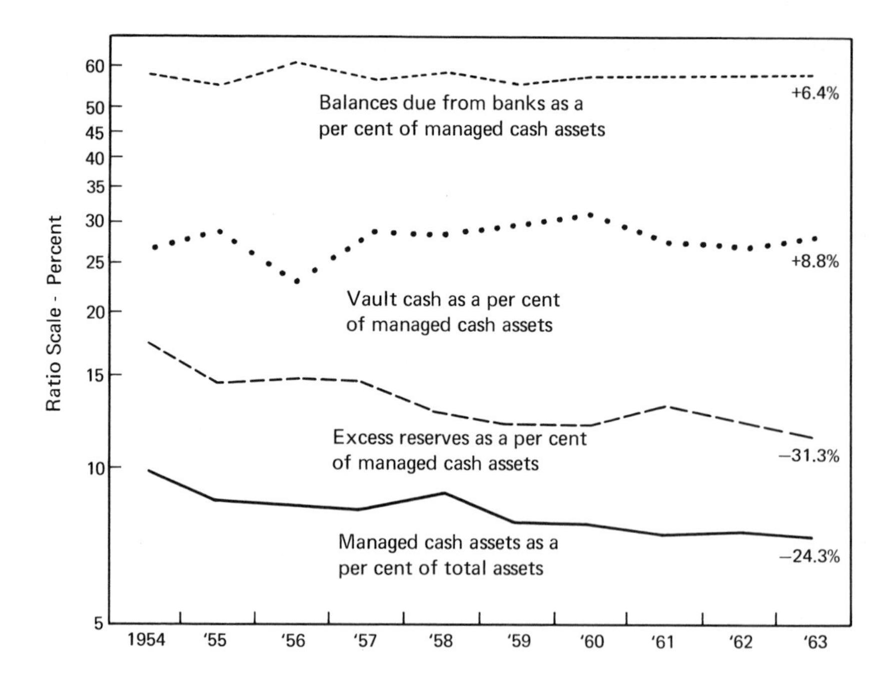

FIG. 8 Cash asset ratios.
All member banks, Third District.

Sources: Federal Reserve Bank of Philadelphia, Member Bank Call Reports, June dates.

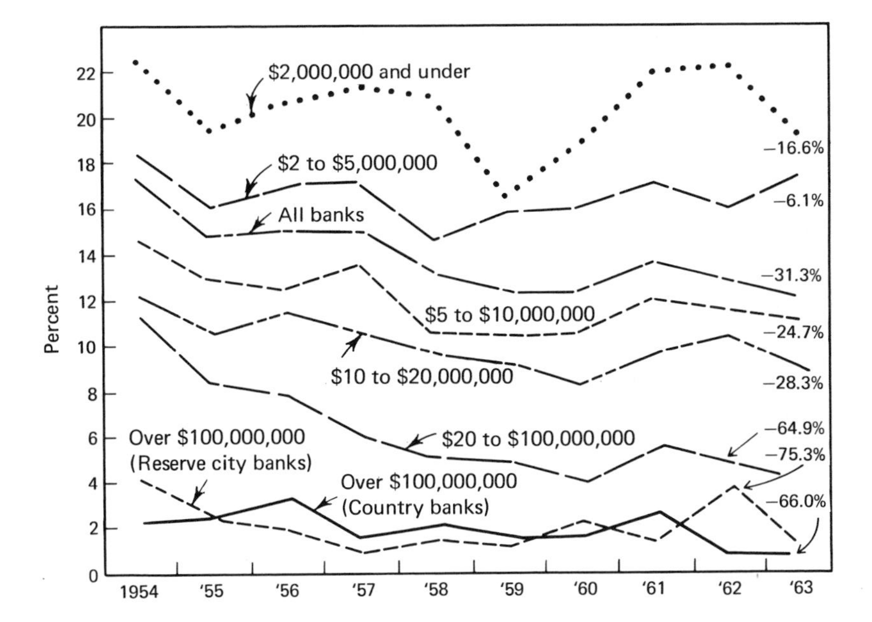

FIG. 9 Excess reserves as a percent of managed cash assets.
Third District member banks by deposit size.

Sources: Federal Reserve Bank of Philadelphia, Member Bank Call Reports, June dates.

actually rose by 6.4 per cent and vault cash as a percentage of managed cash assets increased by 8.8 per cent.

Figure 9 shows that city bankers were most successful in cutting the ratio of excess reserves (even though country banks sliced the total managed-cash-asset ratio most).

For the entire period 1954–1963, city bankers reduced excess reserves by a sizable 75 per cent while country banks in the $2 million and under deposit class clipped excess reserves by 17 per cent and those with $10–20 million in deposits cut the same ratio by 28 per cent.[4]

Table 1 shows a breakdown by size of bank of the classes of managed cash assets. The breakdown reveals the same pattern observed for all member banks—excess reserves fall for all size classifications while vault cash rises for all classes and deposits held with correspondents increase for most.

[4] How can small banks have the largest decline in total managed cash assets while the only managed cash-asset ratio which declined consistently throughout the size classes declined most at larger banks? Explanation: Much of the percentage decline in the excess reserve ratio at larger banks is offset by increases in vault cash. It is also interesting that the rise in vault cash at larger banks—as at smaller ones—occurred largely before and thus is not explained by the recent law allowing member banks to count cash as required reserves.

Table 1 How Third District Member Banks Changed Their Managed-Cash-Assets Ratios

Size Group—Total Deposits (Millions $)	PERCENTAGE CHANGE, 1954–1963, IN THE RATIO OF			
	Managed Cash Assets to Total Assets	*Excess Reserves to Managed Cash Assets*	*Balances Due from Banks to Managed Cash Assets*	*Vault Cash to Managed Cash Assets*
$2 and under	−25.7%	−16.6%	+11.5%	+2.3%
2 to 5	−16.8	−6.1	+2.5	+0.5
5 to 10	−23.5	−24.7	+3.2	+8.5
10 to 20	−19.7	−28.3	−0.1	+17.5
20 to 100	−18.0	−64.9	+1.5	+21.4
Over 100				
Reserve City Banks	−13.8	−75.3	−3.9	+21.9
Country Banks	−8.0	−66.0	−1.8	+9.9
All Banks	−24.3	−31.3	+6.4	+8.8

Source: Federal Reserve Bank of Philadelphia, Member Bank Call Reports.

Do time deposits make a difference?

Earlier it was suggested that costs influence the way a bank manages its cash position. If this suggestion indeed has merit, one would expect the relative importance of time deposits to affect significantly the way the individual bank manages its cash assets. The reason: banks pay interest on their time deposits, thus where time deposits are a relatively large proportion of total deposits, a bank is saddled with a heavier expense burden than would otherwise be the case. To meet this larger burden and still make a reasonable profit, the bank with a large proportion of time deposits might economize on cash and thus maintain a heavier position in earning assets. Moreover, since time deposits are generally considered less volatile than demand, the banker with high time deposits may be able to cut his cash asset ratio with less concern for the decline in his liquidity.

Figure 10 shows that this pattern indeed holds true. During the entire 10-year period 1954–1963, banks with a higher percentage of time deposits maintained lower managed-cash-asset ratios. Conversely, banks with lower time deposits held higher managed cash assets.[5] Moreover, the higher the time-deposit ratio, the greater the percentage cut in managed cash assets.

[5] This behavior is especially significant when one realizes that (a) the over-60 per cent time deposit category contains banks of smaller size on average, and (b) smaller banks tend to have *higher* not *lower* cash-asset ratios, other things remaining the same. In other words, the small bank tendency toward high cash assets is offset when the small banks also have high time deposits.

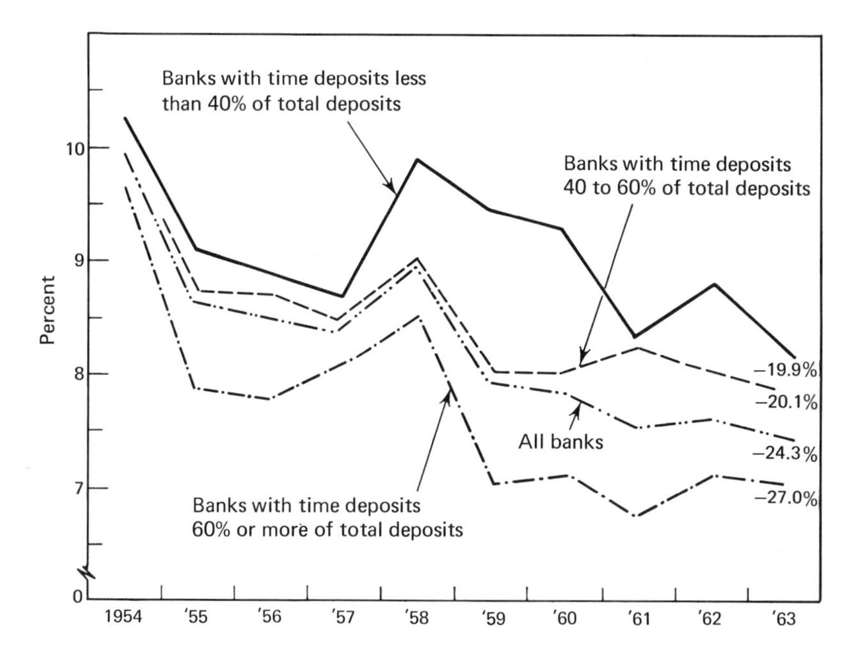

FIG. 10 Managed cash assets as a percent of total assets.
Third District member banks, grouped by the proportion of time deposits to total deposits.

Sources: Federal Reserve Bank of Philadelphia, Member Bank Call Reports, June dates.

The Third District versus the United States

As we have seen, Third District bankers reduced the relative size of their managed cash assets significantly during the past decade. This reduction in managed cash assets was carried out by all sizes of banks—from the small, $2 million country bank to institutions along Chestnut and Broad Streets which count their assets in the hundreds of millions. We have seen also that District bankers looked primarily to their excess reserves as they clipped cash assets in favor of more loans and investments. What are some of the wider implications of these trends?

Excess reserves of Third District banks have fallen not only in relation to District cash assets but, as shown in Figure 11, also relative to excess reserves held by all member banks in the nation, and relative to the District's proportion of total deposits. From a high of almost 6.4 per cent of total excess reserves in 1956, excess reserves of Third District banks fell to a low of around 4.4 per cent in 1961 and in 1963, were around 5 per cent of total excess reserves.

There are several reasons why District bankers have shifted their preference more in the direction of earning assets than have their national counterparts. Probably one of the most important is the increas-

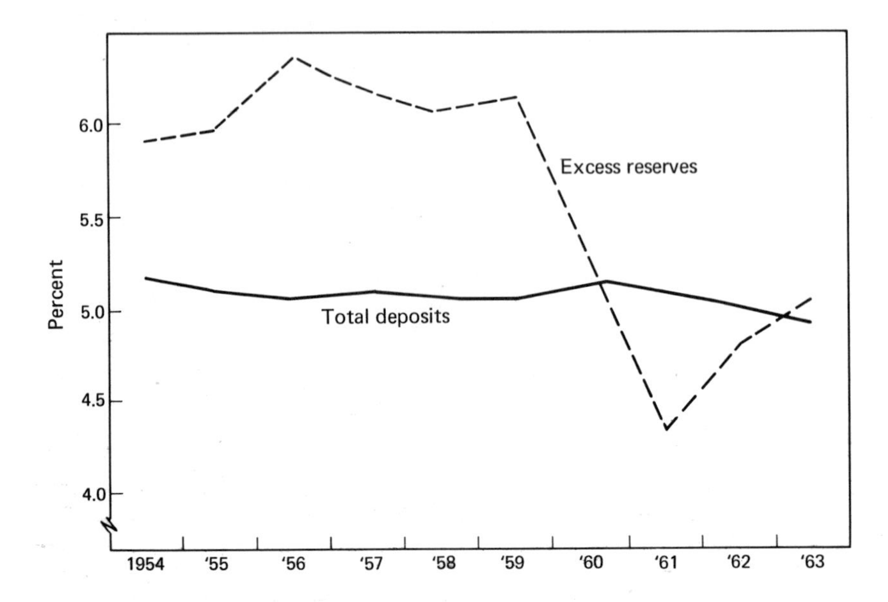

FIG. 11 Total deposits and excess reserves.
Third District member banks as a percent of United States.

Sources: Board of Governors, Federal Reserve Bank of Philadelphia.

ing proportion of time deposits relative to total deposits in the Third District, which increases bank costs and, as we have seen, stimulates bankers to reduce cash holdings. Time deposits, as shown in Figure 12, have increased over the 10-year period 1954–1963 from less than 30 per cent to over 40 per cent of total deposits at Third District banks. Moreover, time-deposit ratios of Third District banks have remained consistently higher than the comparable national figure. The higher time-deposit ratios have probably been a significant influence in inducing banks to bring their excess reserves down.

Another factor which may help to explain the decline in excess reserves of Third District banks relative to the rest of the nation is the improved information and accounting technique with respect to maintained and required reserves. As already noted, the banker using these techniques is better informed of day-to-day fluctuations in his reserve account, and thus is better able to minimize his reserve balance. The reserve-accounting program was begun quite early in the Third District, in the spring of 1960 to be exact, and it is likely that the sharp decline in the District's proportion of total excess reserves after 1959 is partially related to the reserve accounting improvements.

Finally, it is likely that the widening of the federal funds market in the Philadelphia area to include transactions between country correspondents and reserve city banks has contributed to the district's declining excess reserves. Philadelphia banks were among the first to move more

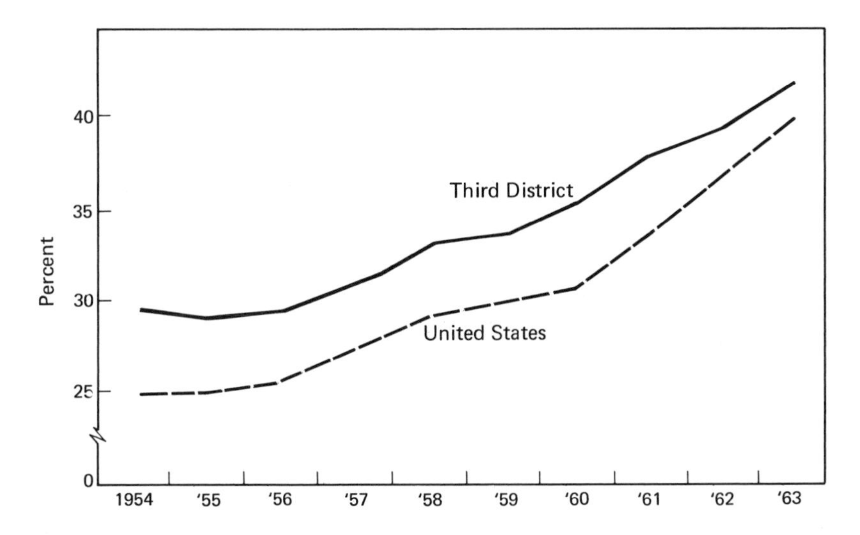

FIG. 12 Time deposits as a percent of total deposits.
All member banks, United States and Third District.

Sources: Board of Governors, Federal Reserve Bank of Philadelphia.

fully into this business and it is likely that their efforts have helped to differentiate the District from the nation.

One further implication of bank cash management in the Third District

In conclusion, the downtrend in excess reserves of Third District banks has some interesting implications for the money and credit policies of the Federal Reserve System. It is quite possible that the declining excess reserve cushion will serve to accentuate any future swings in monetary policy. A move toward greater credit ease by the Fed, for example, would be more quickly and more fully translated into increased earning assets if banks are reluctant to hold excess reserves. A move toward greater credit restraint, on the other hand, would more quickly result in a general tightening, including greater pressure to liquidate Governments as federal funds became less readily available, and perhaps more active utilization of the Fed's discount window.

Reserve Adjustments of City Banks

D. R. Cawthorne

The distribution of bank resources among loans to customers, primary and secondary reserves, and the bond account is one of the major decisions relating to bank asset management. Such decisions often are based on an estimate of the need for liquidity to meet deposit losses or to satisfy loan requests, as well as on expectations about future movements of interest rates. The degree of confidence placed in the reliability of such estimates also is important. Allowance must be made for the fact that deposits fluctuate—sometimes predictably but often without warning—which at times raises the investible reserves of the bank and at other times reduces them.

In this respect, the unique characteristic of large banks compared with smaller institutions is that while the day-to-day fluctuations of reserves are relatively small in percentage terms, the amount is large enough to justify special action to gain earnings on these transitory balances. Larger banks in the Tenth Federal Reserve District encounter widely varying conditions with respect to the short-run volatility of their deposits. In banks where the accounts of oil companies represent a substantial part of the total, intramonth fluctuations are quite wide but have a fairly regular timing and magnitude. Some of the banks in which interbank deposits are important also experience distinct seasonal deposit flows. In still others, state funds produce both predictable and unforeseen changes in deposits. All of these movements, together with the ebb and flow of other depositors' accounts, may either yield short-run gains of reserves or result in short-run losses.

It is common knowledge that, despite this somewhat random movement of deposits and reserves, larger banks are able to hold their excess reserves to low levels, measured in terms of absolute values or percentages. Not so well known is the fact that rather wide disparities exist between the comparative performance of larger banks in minimizing their excess reserves. District reserve city banks, for example, maintain rela-

Reprinted with the permission of the Federal Reserve Bank of Kansas City from *Essays on Commercial Banking*, 1962.

tively high excess reserves in comparison with the national average for all reserve city banks. This fact is often attributed to time differences between New York and District municipalities which make adjustment through the federal funds market more difficult. Another argument is that banks in District cities having no Federal Reserve office are handicapped in adjusting reserves through the use of discounting. It appears, however, that the widely varying holdings of excess reserves by larger District banks cannot be explained by these factors.

It is the purpose of the ensuing discussion to examine the nature of the reserve adjustment problem, the process by which excess reserves are minimized, the instruments employed in making the adjustment, and the comparative behavior of large District banks in their holdings of excess reserves.

THE OPERATION OF THE ADJUSTMENT PROCESS

The task of adjusting the reserve position of a large bank is assigned to a money desk which may be operated by the cashier, the investment vice president, or, less frequently, by another officer of the bank. The principal bank policies which affect the nature of the operation are management's attitude toward borrowing, whether from the Reserve bank or from the federal funds market, and restrictions on the method employed to dispose of excess funds.

One of the requisites of the management of the reserve position is the establishment of a system throughout the bank whereby the money desk is informed of all major actions that affect the money position. Such actions include large transfers into or out of customers' accounts, purchases or sales of securities for customers or the bank's own portfolio, withdrawals from or additions to the U. S. Treasury Tax and Loan accounts, and sizable loan extensions or retirements. These known changes, together with any events whose effects can be foreseen—such as redemptions of securities, loan commitments, and so forth—constitute the principal data used to gauge the forces affecting the current reserve position of the bank.

Federal Reserve regulations governing the determination of legal required reserves form another part of the framework within which the adjustment is made. Reserve requirements are applied to average deposits in a week that begins with the opening of business on Thursday morning and closes the following Wednesday morning. The balances which fulfill these requirements are the deposits of the bank at the Reserve bank in the week which begins with the close of business on Thursday and ends with the close of business on the following Wednesday.[1] Thus, on any Wednesday morning, the bank knows its requirement for the pre-

[1] Since November 24, 1960, all vault cash held by member banks also has counted as reserves in meeting legal requirements.

ceding 7 days and its reserve balance for the preceding 6 days. Therefore, if it becomes evident during the day that a deficiency will occur, steps can be taken to raise the balance by a sufficient amount to meet the minimum requirement. On the other hand, expected surpluses can be placed in assets that will yield earnings for the bank.

Subject to approval in the individual case, current regulations allow a member bank to carry a reserve deficiency of not more than 2 per cent into the succeeding reserve period, provided a deficiency did not occur in the preceding period and provided the reserve balance in the next period is sufficient to counterbalance the deficiency. Banks occasionally employ this privilege, not perhaps as a conscious policy, but rather as a result of minor errors in forecasts. Penalities are assessed against larger reserve deficiencies at a rate 2 per cent above the discount rate, so banks have an incentive to hold somewhat more than the minimum to avoid this charge.

The process of reserve adjustment may be illustrated from the records of two District banks of approximately equal size. One trims its reserve position very closely and the other runs larger-than-average excesses, as shown by Table 1. Bank A had a cumulative excess reserve of $663,000 in the reserve period which on a daily basis was $94,714. Bank B had a cumulative excess of $13,124,000, an average daily excess of almost $1,-875,000. Bank A curtailed its reserves on the last day of the reserve period by sales of federal funds, but the cumulative excess of Bank B expired, as the surpluses of one reserve period cannot be used to meet the require-

Table 1 Comparison of Two District Banks

	Bank A	Bank B
	Excess (+) or deficiency (—) of reserves	
Thursday	$−1,144,000	$+1,650,000
Friday	+996,000	+986,000
2-day total	−148,000	+2,636,000
Saturday	+273,000	+392,000
3-day total	+125,000	+3,028,000
Sunday	+273,000	+392,000
4-day total	+398,000	+3,420,000
Monday	+579,000	+1,594,000
5-day total	+977,000	+5,014,000
Tuesday	+1,160,000	+5,642,000
6-day total	+2,137,000	+10,656,000
Wednesday	−1,474,000	+2,468,000
7-day total	$ +663,000	$+13,124,000

ments of the following period. Assuming an interest rate of 3 per cent, a sale of $13 million for 1 day would have produced earnings of $1,083; at a rate of 3½ per cent, the transaction would have yielded $1,264.

METHODS OF RESERVE ADJUSTMENT

The principal methods employed by the larger District banks in adjusting reserve positions include variations of indebtedness to the Reserve bank, purchases or sales of funds in the federal funds market, and purchases or sales of short-term Treasury issues. These three methods may be compared first as ways of covering a deficiency of reserves and then as methods for disposing of excess funds.

The use of the Reserve bank discount privilege has the advantage that the exact sum needed to cover the deficit of reserves can be borrowed. Also important to some banks is the fact that no borrowing limit is imposed apart from the necessity of having acceptable collateral or rediscountable paper. Banks which experience rather wide fluctuations of deposits may rely heavily on this source of reserves since their ability to borrow from other sources is limited by law. Other advantages of discounting are the ease with which the transaction is consummated and the ready availability of funds. A bank can wait until very late in the business day before covering its deficiency, and while this also may be possible in the securities and federal funds markets, the earlier closing of eastern markets would make these avenues of adjustment less reliable for District banks.

Funds also may be borrowed—usually for 1 day—from other banks, security dealers, or other organizations, in what is known as the federal funds market. Most of these transactions flow through the wire transfer system of the Federal Reserve banks, moving reserve balances from banks having excess funds to banks having deficiencies. Under normal circumstances, the minimum transaction is $1 million. This restriction prevents banks from borrowing from the federal funds market when they require less than $1 million, or from using that market to dispose of excess reserves of less than $1 million. Another important restriction on use of this market is the prohibition against national banks' borrowing a greater amount than their capital stock. Since banks often experience short-term outflows of reserves that exceed their capital, these exigencies cannot be met through the federal funds market.

There are two principal advantages of this market as a source of funds. At times, the rate of interest is less than the discount rate, permitting reserve deficiencies to be covered at reduced cost. A substantial part of the purchases of funds by District banks over the past year has coincided with declines in the federal funds rate. Use of the market also permits a bank to curtail its borrowing from the Reserve bank. Since continuous borrowing is not in accord with the provisions of Federal Reserve Regulation A, a number of banks employ the market for ordinary adjustments and conserve the privilege of borrowing from the Reserve bank for more extreme emergencies.

The chief problem in using the Treasury bill market as a source of funds arises from rate fluctuations and the costs of the transaction. If rates should rise and prices fall after bills are purchased, losses may occur when the security is sold. Moreover, the spread between bid and asked quotations, which is the dealer's margin, may absorb interest earned over a short period. These disadvantages often are surmounted by the use of repurchase agreements in which bills or other securities are sold for immediate delivery and purchased for regular delivery a day later. The rate on the transaction for the one day is usually the same as the rate on federal funds and thus the purchase and sale prices are fixed in advance. Recent rulings have declared these contracts to be loans, rather than purchases and sales of securities, and to be subject to the restrictions placed by law upon loans. In fact, this type of transaction bears a closer resemblance to a reserve adjustment via the federal funds market than to an adjustment through the bill market as such.

Each of these instruments is used as a method of disposing of excess reserves. Banks with indebtedness to the Reserve bank can pay down their discounts. Those without debts either sell funds or acquire Treasury bills. If the excess is large compared with the loan limit of the bank, several transactions in federal funds may be required to reduce the reserve balance to an acceptable level. If the amount is small, the minimum size of a transaction may prevent the use of the funds market. Several banks follow the practice of purchasing the maturing Treasury bill late in the reserve period to be presented for redemption on Thursday—the first day of the new reserve period. This operation carries the excess forward into the next period and a return is earned for the period of investment. Demand for the maturing bill for this purpose frequently makes it difficult to obtain and drives the interest rate below the rate obtainable on federal funds.

The practices of larger District banks in using these methods of reserve adjustment follow no clear-cut pattern. A few banks use all three, both in acquiring and disposing of reserves. Others rely on the Federal Reserve bank when reserves are needed and sell excess funds when their indebtedness has been discharged. Still others employ the federal funds market exclusively, but rarely purchase funds. These are banks which, as a matter of policy, hold comparatively large liquid reserves.

Data are not available through which an evaluation can be made of the comparative importance of the three instruments of adjustment in District bank operations. The information for discounts alone is displayed in Figure 1, tracing the borrowings and repayments of the 23 banks whose performances are compared in a later section. In Figure 1, discounts include the increases of average daily indebtedness to the Reserve bank compared with the preceding week. Repayments reflect the reductions of such indebtedness. The movements of the two lines express

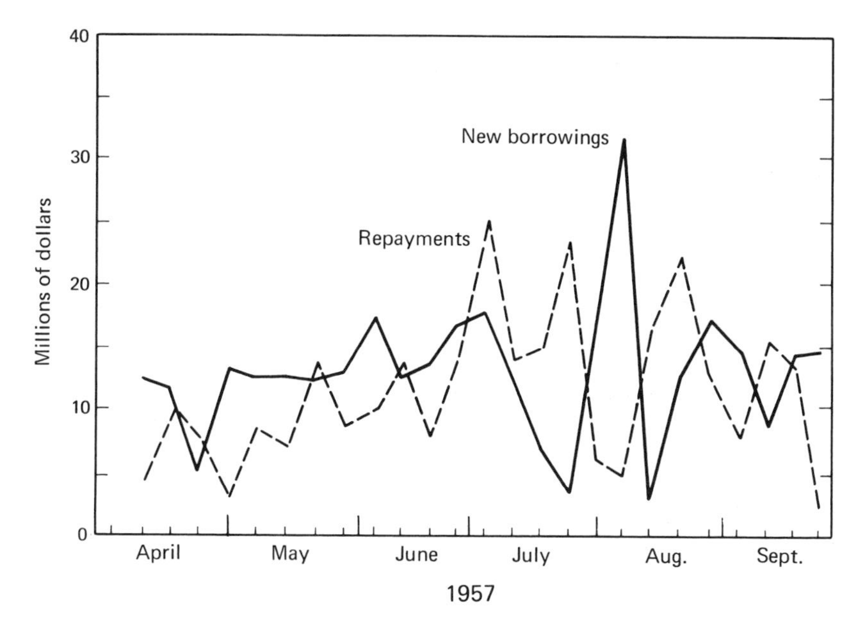

FIG. 1 Borrowings from and repayments to the Reserve Bank.
23 District reserve city member banks.

the volume of reserve adjustments made from week to week through the discount facility. If daily changes had been shown, the variations would have been much greater. Judging on the basis of rough measures, such as week-to-week changes in federal funds borrowed or sold and in bill holdings, a larger volume of reserve adjustments is made through the open market than is made through discounting.

DISTRICT BANK EXPERIENCE

Another aspect of city bank reserve adjustments is the comparative results achieved in minimizing excess reserves. One test of this operation can be made by comparing District results with those of reserve city banks in the United States. Average daily excess reserves in percentages of required reserves for the two groups of banks are shown in Figure 2. There it is evident that District reserve city banks as a group carry excess reserves which are quite high in relation to the national average for reserve city banks. If District banks had achieved the national average in the period shown, their average daily excess reserves would have been lower by $8.9 million, or more than 50 per cent.

The data for individual banks are useful in locating the sources of this difference. The accompanying tables summarize information on 23 of the larger District reserve city member banks having deposits in excess

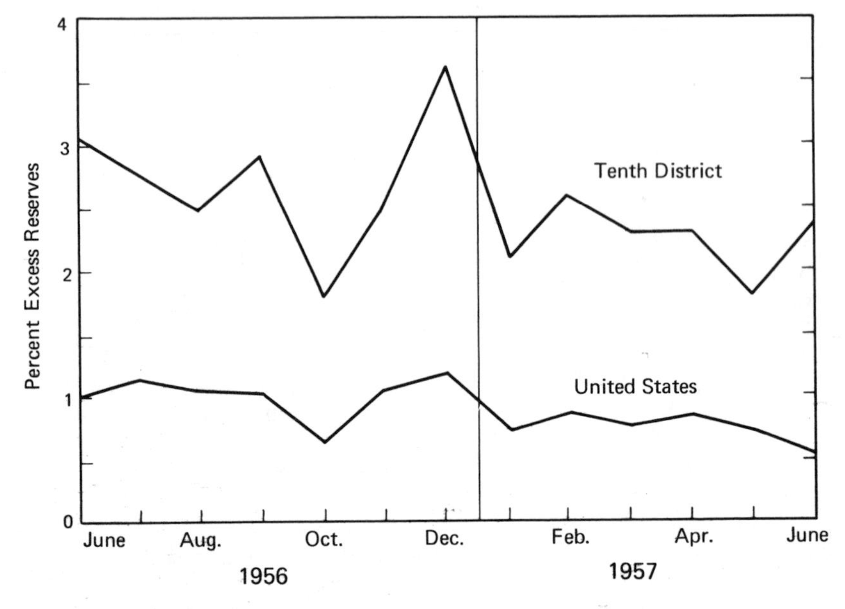

FIG. 2 Excess reserves of reserve city banks.
Tenth District and United States.

of $30 million. Their performance in managing their reserve positions was measured on the basis of 52 reserve periods in 1956 and 34 reserve periods in 1957.

Inspection of Table 2 indicates that among these banks the absolute volume of excess reserves held shows no clear relation to bank size, although in percentage terms the maximum ratio diminishes with increasing size of the bank. Moreover, in each size class, there is a substantial spread between the highest and lowest volume of excess reserves held. However, most of the banks in each class held amounts close to the minimum shown. This is generally indicated in Table 3, showing a frequency distribution of excess reserve holdings in 1956. Most of the

Table 2 Average Daily Excess Reserves by Size of Bank

(23 District Reserve City Member Banks)

Sizes as Indicated by Average Required Reserves (Millions of dollars)	*No. of Banks*	Range of Average Daily Excess Reserves			
		In Thousands of Dollars		*In Percentages of Required Reserves*	
		1956	1957	1956	1957
Less than 10	6	57–1,095	81– 774	1.24–13.61	1.80– 9.39
10 and less than 20	8	28–1,250	37–1,185	0.20– 7.16	0.34–10.34
20 and less than 30	4	208–2,657	160–1,519	0.77– 7.11	0.58– 5.96
30 and over	5	109–1,783	69–1,717	0.30– 3.19	0.32– 2.94

Table 3 Frequency Distribution of Excess Reserves, 1956 Averages
(23 District Reserve City Member Banks)

Amount of Average Daily Excess Reserves (In thousands of dollars)	BANK SIZE EXPRESSED IN TERMS OF AVERAGE REQUIRED RESERVES — No. of Banks	
	$15 million or less	*Over $15 million*
Less than 100	3	1
100–199	4	4
200–299	2	2
300–399	0	0
400–499	0	1
500–999	2	1
1,000 and over	0	3
Total	11	12

smaller banks and more than half of the larger units were able to hold average excess reserves to less than $300,000. It is clear from the two tables that the difference between reserve city banks in the District and the Nation shown in the chart is largely attributable to the performance of a few banks. Approximately half of the 23 banks consistently maintained ratios below the national average, which suggests that regional factors are not the source of the difference.

Other conditions also may be thought to account for the differences in holdings of excess reserves. One is the method of adjustment used by the bank. However, comparisons of banks as to whether preference was given to the open market or to discounting revealed only one interesting difference. Banks whose managements do not employ the discounting privilege or do so only rarely were not among those having comparatively large excess reserves. Since much emphasis is placed upon this privilege as a necessary adjunct to the adjustment process, it is of interest that some banks did not find its use essential to their reserve management.

A second possible explanation is that the accounting systems of some banks cannot supply information with sufficient promptness for action to be taken to dispose of excesses or to cover deficiencies. This may lead some banks to hold a sufficient quantity of excess reserves to assure that the penalties of a reserve deficiency will not be levied. While there may be some differences of accounting, these do not appear likely to explain the larger excesses of reserves. Virtually any system of information would make known the accumulation of an excess through a reserve period—as in the case of Bank B in the illustration given earlier—well in advance of the end of the reserve period. The correction on Wednesdays might not be so close, however, as could be made if the reserve position had been trimmed as the week progressed.

A third possible explanation is that banks holding larger excess reserves frequently encounter extreme changes in their deposits late in the reserve period. Such fluctuations would sharply curtail reserves in some periods and greatly increase them in others and the most adroit reserve management might still leave fairly large excesses.

In order to evaluate this possibility, the records of three banks which held the largest excesses were examined for a period of 62 weeks. Changes in deposits from Tuesday to Wednesday in each week were classified by size of change. In two of the banks, it was found that two thirds of the changes fell between plus and minus $2 million, while in the case of the third, approximately 80 per cent of the changes were within that range. Since an average daily excess of $1.5 million, such as these banks carried, would produce a cumulative excess of $9 million in the first 6 days of the reserve period, it is obvious that these fluctuations were comparatively small. In fact, none of the banks experienced a gain so large as to have created an excess of that size or a loss that would have reduced such an accumulated excess to zero.

Since none of these alternatives seem adequate to explain differences in holdings of excess reserves, it would appear that the reason lies in differences in management objectives at individual banks. In other words, some banks seek to achieve as near zero excess reserves as is possible while others prefer to hold a portion of their liquid assets as excess balances with the Reserve bank.

Why Federal Funds?

Nevins D. Baxter

COUNTRY BANKS AND FEDERAL FUNDS: A CAPSULE

Federal funds are deposits held by banks at the Federal Reserve or with correspondent banks. Banks with temporary excess reserves can lend these funds overnight or for a few days, to banks which are experiencing reserve deficiencies, and can earn interest on the transaction at the federal funds rate.

Until a few years ago, activity in federal funds was limited largely to big banks. At the present time, however, almost half of the country banks in the Third Federal Reserve District buy or sell federal funds, at least on occasion. Even some very small banks participate in the federal funds market. Almost invariably, country banks buy or sell federal funds through their big city correspondents with individual transactions as low as $100,000 not uncommon.

Reprinted with the permission of the Federal Reserve Bank of Philadelphia from *Business Review,* August 1966.

While there is no single explanation which can fully account for the growth in the number of banks using the federal funds market, there are a number of influences which appear to be significant:

Convenience and profitability
Influence of correspondents
Awakening of management
Level of interest rates
The profit squeeze

CONVENIENCE AND PROFITABILITY

In a sense, of course, convenience and profitability are catch-all terms which describe the motivations of so many of the actions of business firms and individuals. It is significant, however, that more than half of the country banks active in federal funds replied on the questionnaire that one reason they participate in this market is that "the federal funds market is the most convenient method to adjust positions for reserve settlement dates." About the same number of banks stressed that federal funds is "generally the most profitable very short-term investment." These factors appear to be about equally important for banks of different deposit sizes, for those in urban and in rural areas and for banks located in different geographic regions of the Third District.[1]

Several banks in the market as buyers suggested that purchasing federal funds is "more convenient" than borrowing from the Reserve Bank. And over one-third of the country banks that deal in federal funds noted that "it is a way to put our balances with correspondent banks to work."

INFLUENCE OF CORRESPONDENTS

Our earlier survey showed that almost all of the country member banks in the Third District which buy or sell federal funds do so through their big city correspondents. But how important an advisory influence does the correspondent have on whether the country bank will make use of federal funds?

Respondents were asked to provide the name of their lead correspondent; most frequently this was was a Philadelphia bank.[2] As Figure 1 shows, there is indeed a relationship between the propensity to use the federal funds market and the choice of lead correspondent. And there

[1] Urban areas were defined as cities with population of at least 25,000. The Third District was divided into six geographic districts for purposes of analysis. This division is illustrated by map in "Country Banks and the Federal Funds Market," *Business Review*, April 1966, p. 4.

[2] The five most frequent Philadelphia correspondents will be referred to as banks A through E; all the remaining banks are classified together as bank group F.

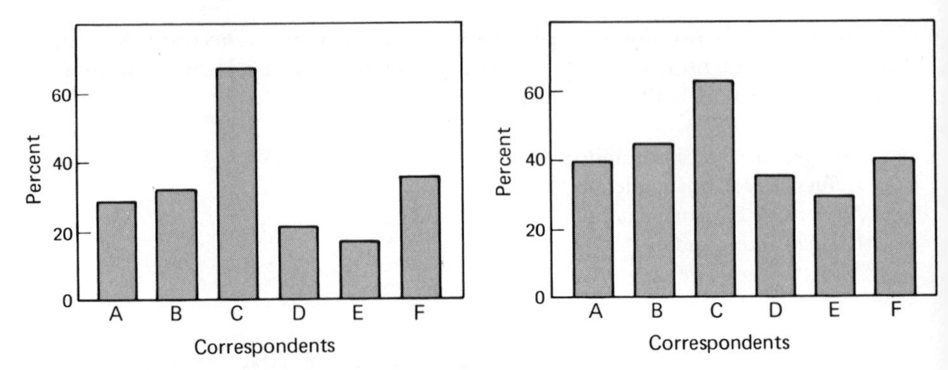

FIG. 1 Federal funds and correspondent relationships.
Country member banks—Third Federal Reserve District.
Country member banks in the Third District with certain correspondents are more active in the federal funds market than are banks with other correspondents, both as buyers* and as sellers**.

* Percentage of country member banks which buy federal funds by lead correspondent.
** Percentage of country member banks which sell federal funds by lead correspondent.

is a definite correlation between the influence of correspondents on banks purchasing federal funds and on banks selling federal funds.[3]

Country banks which deal with correspondent bank C (see Figure 1) are much more likely to buy federal funds or to sell funds than are banks which use other correspondents. And banks using correspondents D and E are least likely to be active in federal funds. This appears to suggest that bank C is most aggressive in acquainting its country cousins with the opportunities of the federal funds market, or in some way renders a better federal funds service.

AWAKENING OF MANAGEMENT

Since certain correspondent banks are especially likely to influence country banks to utilize the federal funds market, it is reasonable that they do so by informing the small-town bankers about the advantages of this market. How important an obstacle is unfamiliarity with federal funds? Can the recent growth in participation in the federal funds market be attributed to increased awareness of the opportunities the market affords?

The answer is an emphatic "yes." Banks were asked to indicate those factors which were important in influencing their decision to enter the federal funds market for the first time. Nearly one-half of the banks answering this question indicated that prior to their first transactions in

[3] Correspondents were also deemed to have an important influence on participation in the fed funds market in a study conducted by the Federal Reserve Bank of New York. See "Second District 'Country' Member Banks and the Federal Funds Market," Federal Reserve Bank of New York, *Monthly Review,* May 1966.

federal funds, they "were unaware of the possibilities of using the federal funds market." This high percentage holds for banks of all sizes, in urban areas and in rural districts, and in all geographic regions of the Third District. A few banks noted that they were prompted to enter the federal funds market because electronic computers enabled them to manage reserve positions more closely.[4]

LEVEL OF INTEREST RATES

Another important reason for the increase in the number of country banks dealing in federal funds is the high level of interest rates in recent years. When interest rates were low, the "penalty" for holding excess reserves was much smaller. For example, $200,000 invested in the federal funds market for one day earns $25 at a rate of 4½ per cent, but only $8.33 at a rate of 1½ per cent. The result is simple: as money gets tighter, funds earn more and banks tend to manage their reserve positions more closely. Federal funds are an ideal vehicle through which to do so, and hence activity in this market has burgeoned.

Forty-five per cent of country member bank respondents indicated that they were influenced to enter the federal funds market because "higher prevailing interest rates on federal funds made them more worthwhile as a short-term investment." The percentage was about the same for country banks in all size groups and in all areas of the Third District.

A PROFIT SQUEEZE?

High interest rates accompanied by the expanding volume of time deposits have resulted in a large growth in interest paid on time deposits in recent years. Interest rates on loans, however, generally have not risen proportionally and hence many banks have been experiencing a real profit squeeze.[5]

Twenty-six per cent of banks active in fed funds indicated that an important impetus to enter the market for the first time was that "a profit squeeze developed" which induced them to seek out any promising opportunity to improve earnings. The federal funds market offered

[4] Since "more sophisticated" management appears to be an influence on the growth of the federal funds market, banks with better examiners' ratings might be expected to be more active in federal funds. However, the composite rating reflects an evaluation of the safety of the bank at least as much as it does an appraisal of managerial ability, and it is not very revealing in explaining whether a bank will participate in the federal funds market.

[5] For a discussion of the influence of the profit squeeze based on a study of the federal funds market conducted last year, see "Federal Funds and the Profit Squeeze—A New Awareness at Country Banks," *Business Reiew,* March 1965.

such an opportunity with virtually no sacrifice of bank liquidity. The influence attributed to the profit squeeze varied little among size groups of banks and geographic areas within the Third District.

What were the main causes of the profit squeeze? Higher interest rates on time deposits headed the list and were especially important for smaller banks in rural areas. Higher operating costs were a close second, and appear to have hit rural and urban banks about equally. Greater dependence on time deposits as a source of bank funds was significant, but mostly for smaller banks in rural areas. The lack of profitable lending opportunities does not seem to have been a major problem; it was noted by only 10 per cent of the banks that reported a profit squeeze. These results are summarized in Table 1.

One would expect that banks with higher ratios of time to total deposits and with higher interest rates paid on time deposits, other things equal, would be more inclined to indicate a profit squeeze. Likewise, an institution with a greater net income-to-asset ratio would be less likely to note a profit squeeze.

Table 2 shows how banks reporting a profit squeeze and active in the federal funds market actually compared with respect to several measures bearing on profitability. Logically enough, banks with low ratios of net income to assets, were especially likely to be motivated by a profit squeeze in entering the federal funds market. This result remains even if we hold size of bank constant.

An examination of the other operating ratios in Table 2, however, does not yield the results that might be expected. Banks with low loan-

Table 1 Profit Squeeze and Activity in Federal Funds

Of all country member banks that said they entered the federal funds market in response to a profit squeeze, the following proportions referred specifically to each of the following explanations:

	All Banks	*Banks in Urban Areas*	*Banks in Rural Areas*
Per cent citing: Higher interest rates paid on time deposits	69	45	76
Per cent citing: Higher operating costs	63	64	62
Per cent citing: Higher ratio of time to total deposits	44	18	51
Per cent citing: Lack of profitable lending opportunities	10	18	8

Table 2 Federal Funds, Profit Squeeze, and Bank Operating Ratios

Country banks active in the federal funds market and reporting a profits squeeze showed significant variation in ratios bearing on their profitability.

	BANKS PARTICIPATING IN FEDERAL FUNDS MARKET AND REPORTING A PROFIT SQUEEZE, CLASSIFIED BY RANGE OF OPERATING RATIO†			
	Per Cent of Banks Active in the Market			
Operating Ratio	*Having Lowest Ratio*	*Having Low Ratio*	*Having Medium Ratio*	*Having High Ratio*
Net Income after Taxes to Total Assets	31	34	19	19
Loans to Assets	33	26	24	27
Time Deposits to Total Deposits	29	26	22	30
Interest Paid on Time Deposits to Time Deposits	*	*	24	25

* Too few banks to be meaningful.
† Each of the four operating ratios was divided into a frequency distribution with four categories as follows:

	Lowest	*Low*	*Medium*	*High*
Net Income to Assets	Under .5%	.5–.75%	.75–1.00%	Over 1%
Loans to Assets	Under 40%	40–48%	48–55%	Over 55%
Time Deposits to Total Deposits	Under 35%	35–45%	45–60%	Over 60%
Interest Paid on Time Deposits to Time Deposits	Under 2%	2–2½%	2½–3%	Over 3%

asset ratios, for example, were hardly more likely to note the profit squeeze than were fully loaned-up institutions. And neither the ratio of time to total deposits, nor the rate paid on time deposits appears to be a good indicator of whether banks entered the federal funds market because of a profit squeeze.[6] This result does not imply that the operating ratios are not associated with the likelihood of entering the federal funds market in response to a profit squeeze. Rather the relationship may be so complex that it is impossible to hold all other factors constant.[7]

[6] For example, 29 per cent of banks with a time deposit ratio of under 35 per cent noted the profit squeeze, as compared with 30 per cent with a time deposit ratio in excess of 60 per cent.

[7] Even if we compare banks in the same size group the importance of the profit squeeze is not strongly influenced by the time deposit ratio or the rate paid on time deposits. For example, if we consider only banks with deposits between $25 million and $100 million, 40 per cent with the lowest time deposit ratio noted the profit squeeze as compared to 32 per cent within the highest time deposit ratio group. Still other factors (such as other operating ratios) may be disguising the relationship or it may very well be that heavy dependence on time deposits, while indicative of higher interest costs may be associated with a relatively profitable loan and investment portfolio, and hence not imply a profit squeeze.

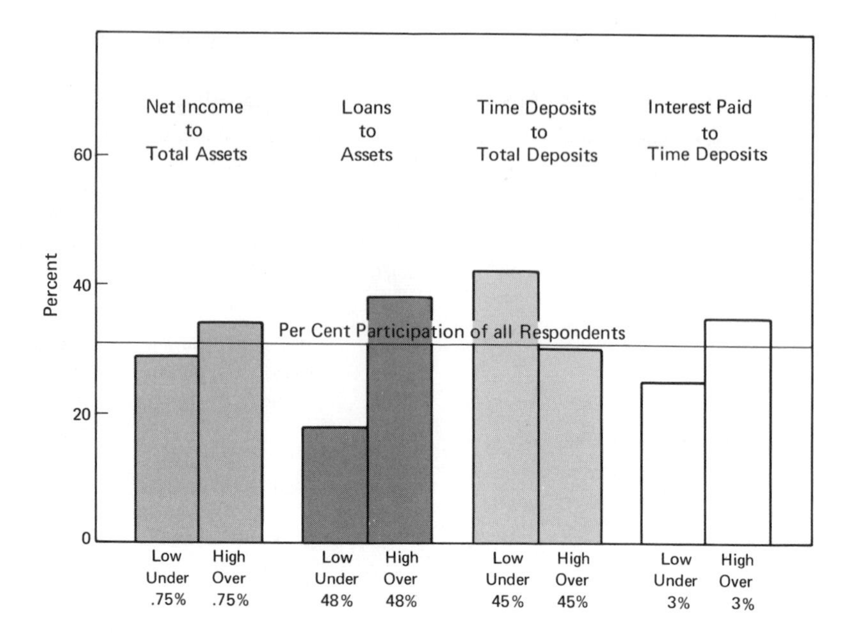

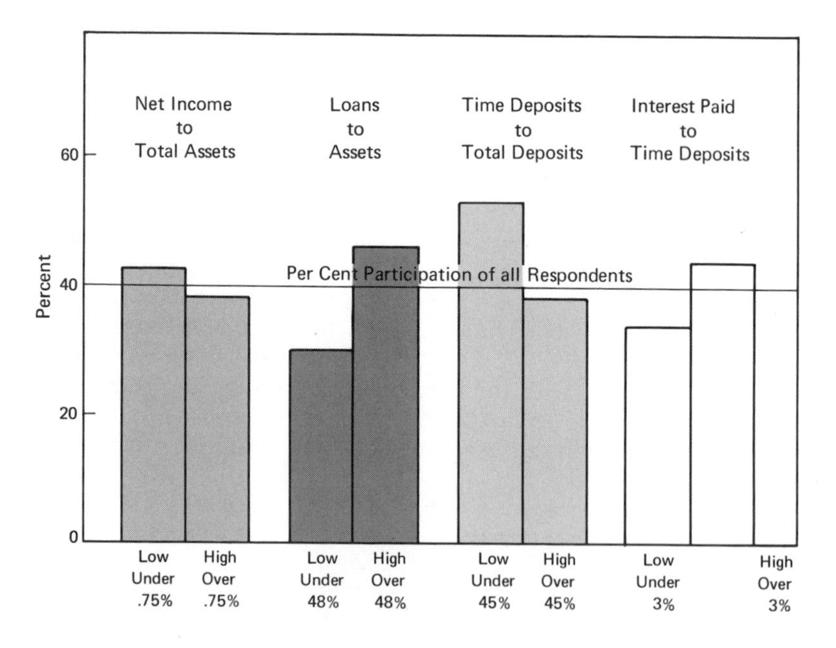

FIG. 2 Federal funds and operating ratios.
Country member banks—Third Federal Reserve District.
Operating ratios are related to whether a country member bank will deal in federal funds as a buyer or as a seller.

* Percentage of respondents in each category who buy federal funds.
** Percentage of respondents in each category who sell federal funds.

To summarize, we can say that there appears to be some causality between earnings and a bank's proclivity to seek opportunities to earn some extra money in the federal funds market. The causal link is "a profit squeeze" and low ratios of income to assets which have pushed banks into the federal funds market. But, although many banks indicated that higher ratios of time deposits and higher interest rates on these deposits were important causes of the profit squeeze, definitive evidence for this view cannot be isolated from the data.

CHARACTERISTICS OF BANKS

Can an analysis of operating ratios help to explain whether a particular bank will be active in federal funds either as a buyer or seller? The answer is a qualified "yes."

In the Third Federal Reserve District about 3 out of 10 country banks are buyers of federal funds and 4 out of 10 are sellers. If we separate all the sellers (for example) into high, medium, low, and lowest ratios of time to total deposits, and if we find that a significantly higher number of those in the bag labeled "high time deposits" are sellers of fed funds (say 7 out of 10 compared to the 4 out of 10 country banks in the District as a whole which sell fed funds) then we might conclude that a high ratio of time to total deposits influences banks to sell fed funds.

On Figure 2 the horizontal lines represent the "3 out of 10" and "4 out of 10" figures for all buyers and all sellers respectively. The bars show how banks with high and low operating ratios compare to this overall participation rate.

On the buy side of the market, banks with higher net income to total assets are more likely to buy fed funds as are banks with higher ratios of loans to assets, with greater interest payments in relation to time deposits and lower ratios of time to total deposits.

Sellers are more likely to have low net income to total assets, low ratios of loans to assets, low interest payments in relation to time deposits, and high ratios of time to total deposits. In short, there are relationships between a bank's operating ratios and the probability that it will be active in federal funds (though, of course, participation of banks in some ratio groupings are more strikingly different from the total participation rate than others).[8]

[8] Smaller banks with high loan-asset ratios are significantly more likely to buy federal funds and to sell federal funds than are institutions not so heavily loaned up. However, there is little correlation between fed funds activity and the loan-asset ratio for banks with deposits over $25 million. Large banks typically have higher loan-asset ratios and are active in the fed funds market. To be sure, high loan-asset ratios and activity in fed funds both characterize the more "aggressive" banks.

High income banks are somewhat less likely to participate in the market as sellers, a result that holds even if size of bank is held constant. An explanation is not hard to find. Banks with the highest rate of return on assets probably keep more fully in-

THE ABSTAINERS

Why are many banks not presently active in the federal funds market? The reasons appear to fall into the following categories:

1. Nonbuyers: The bank almost always has excess reserves and hence is not a buyer of federal funds.
2. Nonsellers: The bank almost never has excess reserves and hence is not a seller.

For banks that neither buy nor sell:

1. The bank is too small to be active in federal funds.
2. The bank is unfamiliar with the opportunities of the federal funds market.
3. The bank prefers other methods of borrowing or lending to federal funds.

Figure 3 summarizes data on the percentage of banks which are not active in the federal funds market as buyers or sellers for each of the above reasons. It is clear that the existence of excess reserves is an important reason why banks do not buy federal funds, but the lack of excess reserves was cited by a smaller proportion of banks which do not sell federal funds. The smallest banks were somewhat less likely to indicate these explanations for their avoidance of the federal funds market, but there is no apparent difference among banks in various geographic areas of the Third District.

Some 30 per cent of nonbuyers and 45 per cent of nonsellers suggested that they feel they are too small to be active in federal funds. As would be expected, these banks are indeed almost exclusively very small, and typically are located in rural areas. It should be emphasized, however, that there are many banks as small or even smaller that *are* active in the federal funds market. The true explanation is, therefore, that management is either unaware of the opportunities afforded by the market or feels that the potential profit from federal funds transactions does not justify the "trouble" of entering the market.

It is perhaps indicative of well-informed bank management that only 15 and 17 per cent of nonbuyers and nonsellers respectively noted that they were unaware of federal funds, and most of these are the smaller banks. Perhaps most interesting, however, is the fact that correspondents of banks D and E were most likely to express unfamiliarity. These banks apparently have not been so active in acquainting their country correspondents with the federal funds market. Forty eight per cent of nonsellers and 38 per cent of nonbuyers that use correspondent bank E indicated they are unfamiliar with the opportunities of federal funds.

---

vested and also manage their reserve positions more closely. Therefore, they are more likely to be short of reserves than to carry excess reserves and are more prone to participate in the federal funds market as buyers than as sellers.

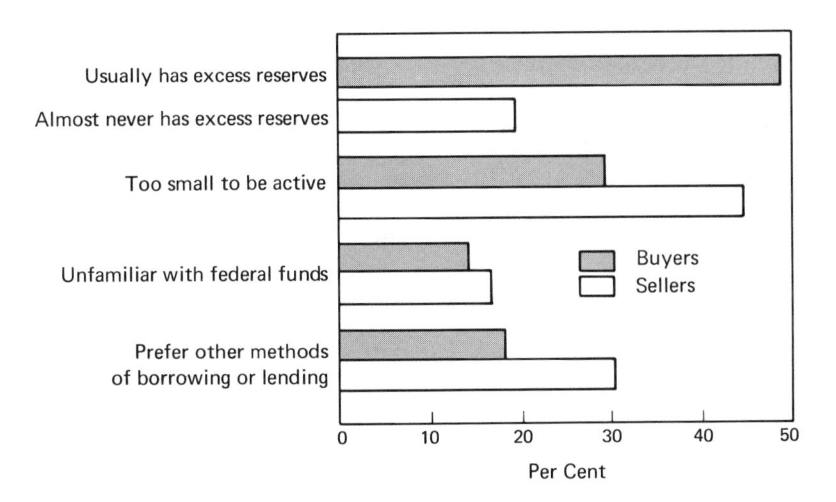

FIG. 3 There are several reasons why some country banks are not active in the federal funds market.
Third Federal Reserve District percentage of banks not active in the federal funds market.

Country member banks which avoided federal funds because they preferred other methods of borrowing and lending were mostly larger institutions, frequently situated in urban areas. Rather than buy federal funds, they borrow directly from correspondents or at the discount window. On the sell side, several banks noted that they prefer to invest surplus funds in Treasury bills, perhaps because of a desire to show a high volume of Government securities on their balance sheets.

CONCLUSIONS

Many country banks find federal funds a convenient and profitable vehicle to adjust their reserve positions. The generally higher level of interest rates of recent years has been one factor which has awakened management to the profitable opportunities of the federal funds market. Big city correspondents have also served in this information-providing role and buy and sell fed funds in small quantities as a service. The choice of correspondents appears to be an important influence on whether a particular country bank is active in the federal funds market. Another influence has been a profit squeeze brought about by higher operating costs (including higher interest rates on time deposits) which has prompted many banks to seek out the opportunities of the federal funds market.

What does this all add up to? Certainly there is no reason to believe that activity in the federal funds market is a temporary phenomenon.

And there is still a substantial number of relatively small banks that may enter the market once they become more familiar with its possibilities.

For the banks, the federal funds market means a more efficient utilization of reserves, and for the monetary authorities it represents an important monetary indicator. With reserves being mobilized and transferred quickly in a national federal funds market, a given volume of net borrowed reserves may imply a different degree of monetary restraint than it would with a less-developed federal funds market. Also, moral suasion at the discount window may become a less effective tool, because the bank in need of reserves can buy federal funds. This is not to say that the federal funds market provides insurmountable difficulties for monetary policy. Rather it is to imply that the authorities must now pay increasing attention to the activities of the federal funds market as a rapidly expanding and important part of the American money market.

A Shift in Banking Philosophy?

An Examination of Bank Investment Practices

Harry Brandt and Robert R. Wyand II

The decline in importance of investments is one of numerous changes characterizing American banking in recent years. At midyear 1966, investments accounted for 32 percent of the earning assets of all U.S. commercial banks, compared with 42 percent in 1961. Fifteen years ago investments averaged 56 percent of assets.

Does this mean bankers have changed their views about investments? Is this merely a passive response to changes in environmental factors? Or is it a combination of changed investment philosophy and adaptation to outside forces?

Reprinted with the permission of the Federal Reserve Bank of Atlanta from *Monthly Review,* August 1966.

Whatever the reasons, this decline in the relative importance of investments is a matter of great concern to some persons. This may have adversely affected bank liquidity, some analysts say. They wonder whether or not the ability of individual banks to meet unusual deposit withdrawals by converting their assets readily into cash with minimum loss has been reduced. Others wonder what this change has done to the ability of banks to meet demands of loan customers by liquidating investments when deposit inflows do not keep up with credit demands. The latter is of some importance in determining the effectiveness of Federal Reserve policy.

Aggregate data on loans and investments, such as those cited above, give inadequate answers. They show only that bankers in recent years have placed more of their funds in loans and less in investments. They do not show the types of securities held, maturity structure, or quality. Yet, these are matters of extreme importance in investment management and in judging the liquidity position of individual banks and the banking system.

A great deal of controversy has arisen about these matters, with inadequate statistical measures complicating a thorough investigation. Such inquiries have had to depend very often on summary statistics for about 14,000 insured banks in the nation or some other large group, such as all-member banks. Therefore, it has been difficult to get more than a bird's-eye view of the problem. Indeed, experience has shown that conclusions about commercial bank behavior, based on aggregate data, may be misleading. Often, they hide important variations among banks of different size and location and fail to stand up in individual instances. Furthermore, some information needed to answer the aforementioned questions has been collected only in isolated studies, and some not at all.

In trying to determine whether bank investment policies did significantly change in the Southeast, we asked 99 banks in Alabama, Florida, Georgia, Louisiana, Mississippi, and Tennessee about some of their investment practices of the last few years. We supplemented this information with data from statistical reports and individual reports of bank examination, distinguishing between institutions by both size and geographical area. Although the study is obviously limited, it seems probable that changes in investment operations of a typical bank in this part of the South have not been too different from those of representative banks elsewhere.

CHANGING INVESTMENT COMPOSITION

Investments held by insured banks in this six-state area shrank in importance over the last few years, as they did in other areas. From the end of 1961 to the end of 1965, investments, measured in relation to total earning assets, declined from over 46 percent to less than 40 percent. This reduction was most rapid in the second half of 1963 and first half

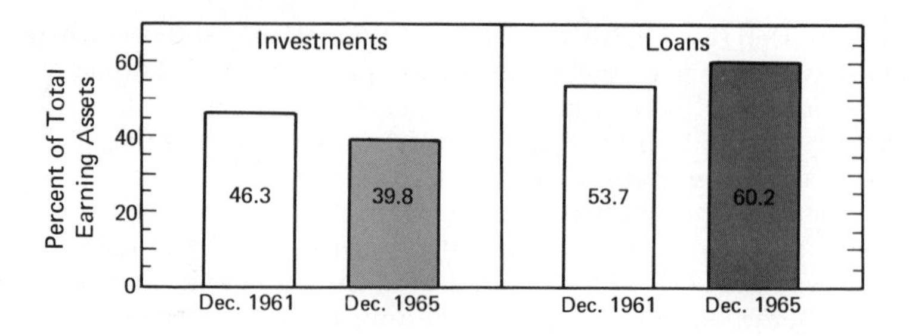

FIG. 1 Earning assets.
Investments at Sixth District insured banks, relative to total earning assets, increased only $2 billion in the December 1961-December 1965 period, while loans advanced $5 billion.

of 1964. However, total investment volume increased, although much less than loans. At the end of 1965, Sixth District insured banks reported a $2.1-billion, or nearly 35-percent, gain from four years earlier (Figure 1).

Aggregate data on securities portfolios alone do not tell the full story. More significantly, most banks bought state and local government issues in heavy volume, so that holdings of state and local government issues doubled in four years. By the end of 1965, over 31 percent of total securities were of this type. In 1961, these investments accounted for only 22 percent. On the other hand, direct and guaranteed U.S. Government securities, as a proportion of total investments, fell from 75 to 63 percent over the same period. The sharpness of these changes supports conclusions that they are the direct result of deliberate bank policy decisions. However, one can overemphasize these shifts if the broader trends into which they fit are not given proper consideration.

Banks were heavy buyers of Treasury obligations during World War II and to a somewhat lesser degree during the Korean War. In years since, they have been more often buyers than sellers, though the relative place of U.S. Government securities among total bank investments has

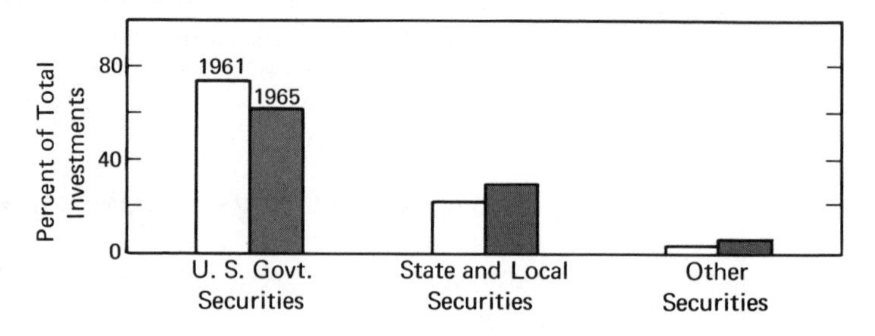

FIG. 1 (cont.)
Among investments held by these banks, U.S. Government securities became relatively less important, and state and local issues more so.

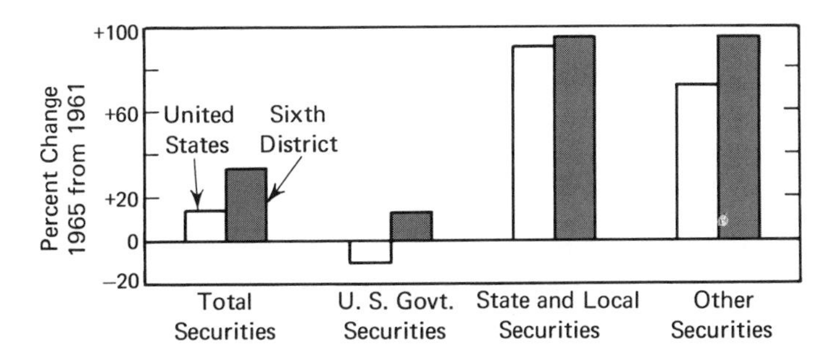

FIG. 1 (cont.)
Except for the expansion of the volume of U.S. Government-held securities, the District pattern resembled that of the nation over the last few years.

shrunk steadily. Thus, owing largely to sizable purchases in 1962, District insured banks held more U.S. Government obligations in December 1965 than four years earlier. In this respect, District banks in the aggregate fared differently in the current business boom than in some other post World War II expansionary periods when heavy liquidations of U.S. Treasury issues were common. Although some U.S. Government issues have been sold this year, they still represent a slightly more important investment to this region's banks than in the late 1920's. District banks' participation in the market for state and local securities, on the other hand, is now greater than it was 35 years ago, although the trend toward greater investment in state and local issues was severely interrupted by World War II (Figure 2).

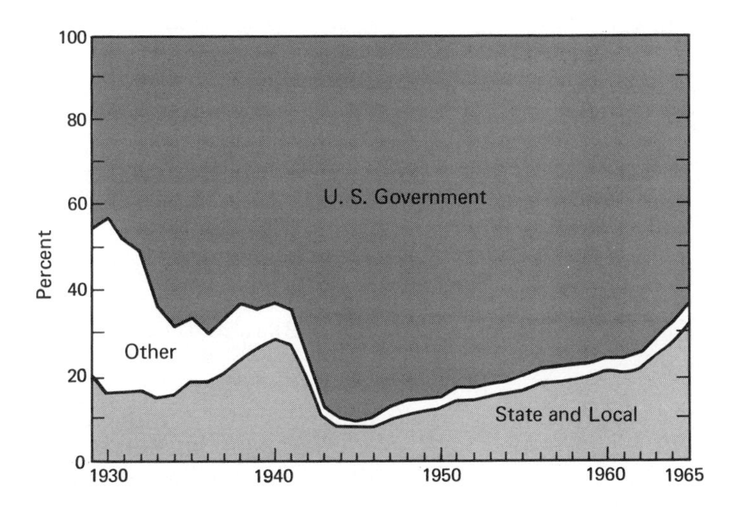

FIG. 2 Composition of investments.
Sixth District Member Banks.

Published statistics fail to separate the exact amounts of corporate, real estate, and foreign bonds that banks hold today, but aggregate figures suggest the amount is insignificant. Similarly, holdings of Federal Agency issues remain fairly small, despite banks' greater than passing interest in these investments recently.

For banks to hold few securities other than U.S. Government and state and local obligations today is in sharp contrast to the 1920's. At that time, many were active buyers of various types of private and foreign bonds. As a result, for all District insured banks, nearly 35 percent of total investments in mid-1929 consisted of obligations of issuers other than the Federal Government and state and local units. In years of depression many of these securities proved difficult to sell even at considerable loss, which partly explains their near absence in portfolios today.

Obviously, not every District bank experienced an absolute increase in total investment volume (or in state and local issues) and a decline in the proportion of investments to total earning assets over the last few years. Nevertheless, every major group—insured nonmember, reserve city member, and country member—did. This differed only in one respect from the national pattern—insured banks sold U.S. Government securities.

Figure 3 gives more insight into what transpired for District banks in various size groupings. There is little doubt that all banks shared the same trends, but smaller banks stayed more heavily invested and retained more U.S. Government obligations than larger ones.

SHIFTS IN PORTFOLIO MANAGEMENT

These portfolio shifts appear to reflect both deliberate changes in banking practices and adjustments to economic and financial conditions. As elsewhere, many District banks have become more aggressive competitors for time and savings deposits and more heavily loaned. The corollary is that they have become less heavily invested.

Why did individual bankers place more funds into loans than investments? In part, the answer lies in a willingness to accept more risks as banks have come to rely on newly developed sources of liquidity. Another explanation is that with the current economic expansion, one of the longest on record, loan demand has been extremely heavy. Total loans rose $5.3 billion between December 1961 and December 1965 at all District insured banks.

Another factor working toward the increased emphasis on loans over this period has been the need to offset the added cost of time and savings deposits, which surged from $4.7 billion to $8.8 billion. Between calendar 1961 and 1965, the interest paid on time deposits climbed from 24 percent of total operating costs to 34 percent.

As rates on time deposits increased, banks needed to move into higher yielding assets. This not only influenced their decision to place greater

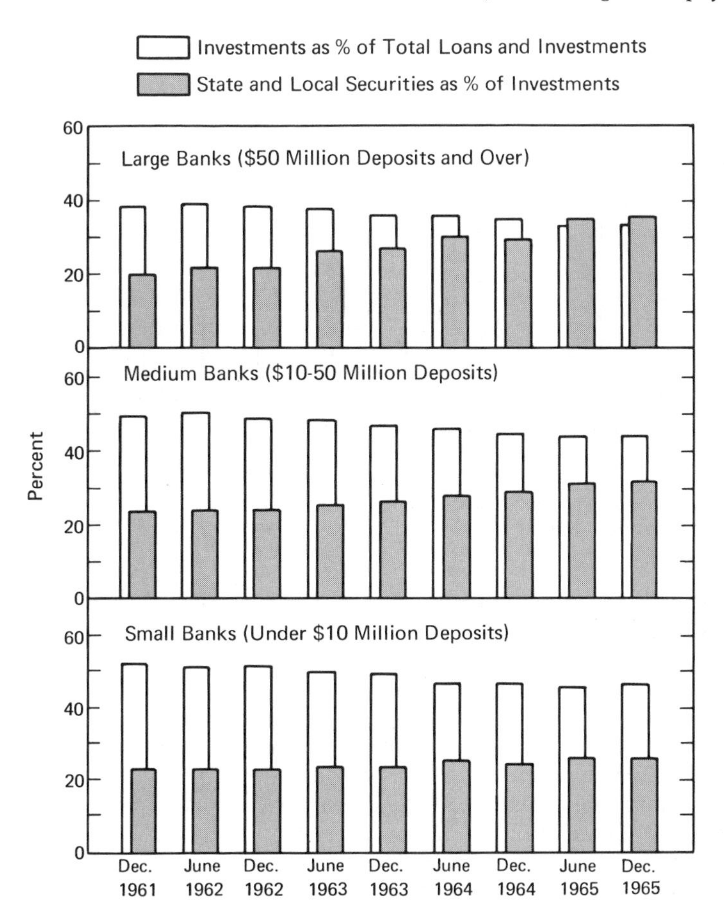

FIG. 3 Composition of earning assets.
Sixth District Insured Banks.

stress on loans (which normally earn more than investments), but also led them to invest more heavily in state and local government issues. Banks with the biggest time-deposit growth showed some of the largest gains in state and local government issues (Figure 4).

This was no accident. State and local securities were favored because of their tax-exempt status. Since 1956, the after-tax yield advantage of high quality long-term tax exempts relative to Treasury bonds has been one percent or better. For short-term issues, this rate advantage has not been quite as high, but still sizable relative to like-maturity Treasury issues. Over the last four years, the comparative after-tax yields in favor of tax-exempt maturities first narrowed and then widened after 1964. However, these fluctuations may have had less to do with banks' favoring these issues than the constant high level of after-tax yields.

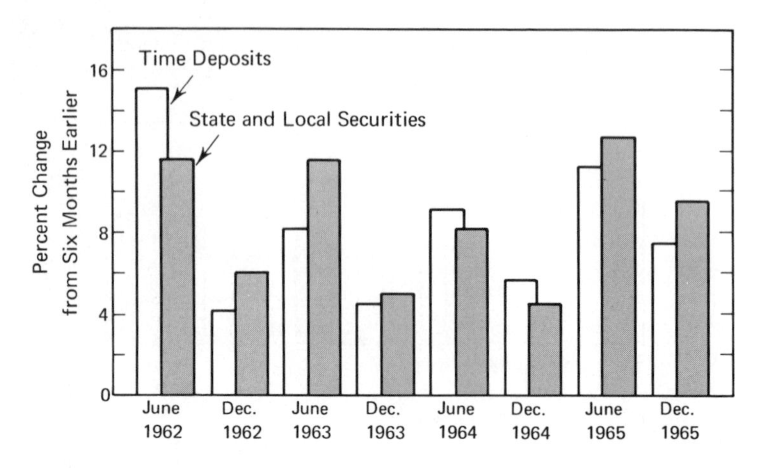

FIG. 4 Growth of time deposits and state and local securities.
Sixth District Insured Banks.

Availability of state and local issues was another factor that encouraged bank buying. The expansion in state and local government debt offered more opportunity to acquire this type of government obligation—especially in comparison to the 1930's and World War II, when these were not too readily available, but U.S. Government securities were. Furthermore, these larger offerings of municipal securities in recent years helped keep yields high enough to attract bank interest.

If monetary policy had been less expansionary during most of this period, bank acquisition of tax-exempts would have been smaller. By providing the banking system with growing reserves, the basis for credit and deposit expansion, the Federal Reserve made it possible for banks to meet the bulk of credit demands from a continued growth of funds and to add to investments at the same time. In recent months, however, with monetary policy aimed at moderating bank credit growth while loan demand continued strong, many banks have felt compelled to supplement deposit growth by selling U.S. Government securities.

LIQUIDITY REDUCED

The appetite for tax-exempt securities over the last few years has been accompanied by some offsetting disadvantages. Generally speaking, these issues are not noted for price stability or for easy marketability relative to U.S. Treasury obligations. Although some widely known state and local issues can be sold readily, even a small block is difficult to liquidate without considerable price concessions in many instances. Therefore, it appears on first glance that, in stressing tax-exempt over U.S. Treasury issues, banks have sacrificed some liquidity to obtain higher yields.

Between 1961 and 1965, District member banks lengthened the average maturity of their total securities. Since the sale of long-term securities usually requires greater price concessions than the sale of short-term ones, this further reduced liquidity. The proportion of securities maturing between five and ten years and those maturing beyond ten years expanded sharply during this period, and issues coming due in the one- to five-year range declined considerably. On the other hand, the under one-year holdings increased slightly. Such maturity lengthening seems to have been most pronounced at reserve city banks.

The overall lengthening in maturity shows up most decisively in the degree to which District member banks acquired long-term state and local government and Federal agency issues. In 1965, for example, about one-fourth of total tax-exempt securities had a maturity of more than ten years, compared with only one-eighth in 1961.

In placing greater emphasis on long-term issues, banks reduced the proportion of one- to five-year maturity U.S. Government obligations, state and local securities, and "other" (mainly Federal agency) issues. Nevertheless, banks did not altogether neglect liquidity considerations. The very short U.S. and state and local maturities increased in importance between 1961 and 1965 (see Figure 5). Still, the greater importance of longer securities has confronted banks with the reality of capital losses where securities were acquired before recent price declines.

Acceptance of greater risk was partly intentional because bankers seemed to feel that less liquidity was necessary than in years past. Many believe time deposits are more stable than demand deposits so that, given the larger volume of time deposits, they can afford to be less liquid. Some feel that additional liquidity has been provided by a broadened market for overnight interbank loans (i.e., Federal funds) and other means available for tapping the money market for short-term cash needs.

Nevertheless, it is not clear how far banks can afford to reduce liquidity. Certain types of time deposits, for instance, are not nearly as stable as total time and savings deposits are often assumed to be. And while larger banks may have found some newly gained ability to offset deposit drains, many smaller banks do not possess this ability to the same degree.

PLEDGING OF BANK ASSETS

Banks have had to accept still another reduction in liquidity because they have had to set aside growing amounts of assets as collateral against public deposits. With more securities tied up for collateral, the amount that banks could conceivably sell in response to demands for loans has diminished. Between 1961–1965, deposits held at District insured banks by governmental units increased by $895 million. Most of this gain was in deposits of state governments and political subdivisions.

Data have not been previously available to permit computation of the amount of securities banks have set aside and the amounts that are still available to meet increased customer borrowings. Such measurements are complicated by the variety of collateral requirements imposed by different governmental units. Some require collateral of value equal to deposits; others demand more than 100 percent of value and others less.

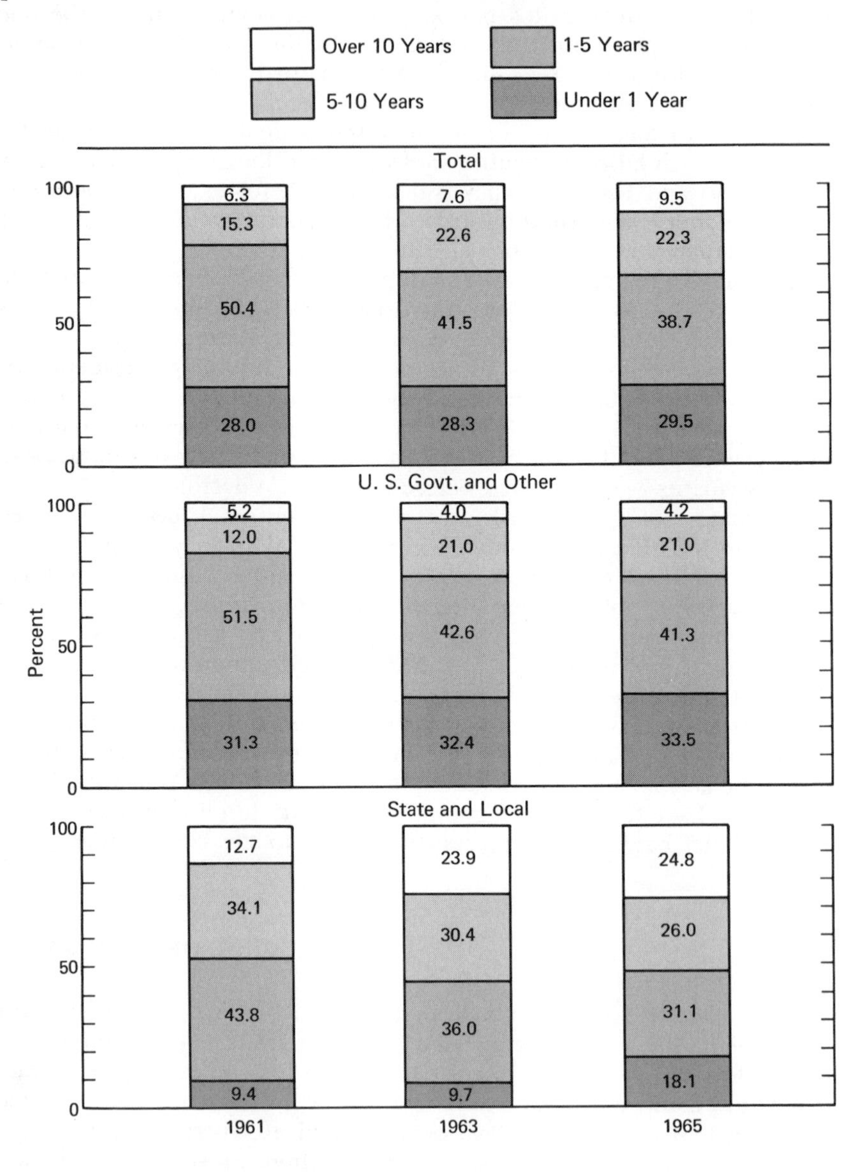

FIG. 5 Maturity distribution of securities.
Sixth District Member Banks.

Moreover, public treasurers are selective in the securities they will accept as collateral. Some insist on Federal Government securities. Others accept bonds of their own city or state; still others take bank guarantees. And for certain public deposits, some types of customer paper are a legitimate form of security.

Measurement of collateral requirements is further complicated by the wide fluctuations common to many public deposits. These gyrations cause sharp changes in assets needed for pledging, although such changes are smaller than they appear because collateral requirements are sometimes based on average deposit levels. Thus, how much in the way of uncommitted funds banks have available for meeting loan demands today is difficult to determine.

Yet there is little doubt that many banks in this District at least still have sizable amounts of securities not pledged against public deposits. Our study of 1965 and early 1966 reports showed about 56 percent of all securities held by these banks were pledged to secure public deposits or were set aside for other purposes. A larger proportion of securities was pledged at reserve city than country banks. About 85 percent of the pledged securities were tied up to secure public deposits; 11 percent, to collateralize trust department funds; and most of the remainder, to serve as collateral for bank borrowings (Figure 6).

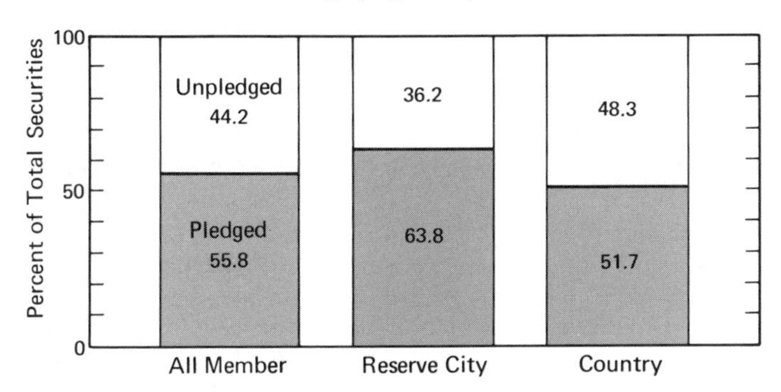

FIG. 6 Pledged and unpledged securities as of 1965 and early 1966.
Sixth District Member Banks.

The dollar value of the pledged securities was considerably in excess of the dollar amount of the deposits and other liabilities that they secured. This was true for both reserve city and country banks, with the excess value amounting to 40 and 49 percent, respectively.

QUALITY REDUCED?

Have bankers reduced the quality of their investments? Because nothing is deemed safer than a U.S. Government security, its shrinking importance and the rising importance of state and local securities are indirect

Table 1 Investment Risk of State and Local Government Securities Portfolio at Selected Sixth District Banks

(Percentage Distribution)

Moody's Rating	*1961*	*1964*	*1965*
Aaa	7.5	7.4	8.3
Aa	26.0	21.7	21.3
A	36.6	38.3	36.7
Baa	15.6	17.8	19.7
Below Baa	0.5	0.6	0.6
Unrated	13.8	14.2	13.4
Total	100.0	100.0	100.0

evidence that bank investments are of lower quality than some years ago. However, the quality of tax-exempt issues—customarily measured by investment ratings—also needs consideration. Since no current information of this kind was available (except for some very large banks in the Cleveland Federal Reserve District) a group of banks holding over one-half of the Sixth District member banks' total state and local securities was asked to classify these. At the end of 1965, three-tenths of these banks' state and local holdings consisted of state and state agency issues; seven-tenths, issues of lower political units, such as counties, cities, and school districts.

Over 13 percent of the bank-held state and local issues lacked investment ratings. Although many unrated issues have excellent investment characteristics, they are usually more difficult to sell. Of the rated ones, about one-twelfth had the highest (Aaa) rating and two-thirds belonged in the three top grades (Aaa, Aa, and A) (Table 1).

Because the proportion of issues in these top grades shrank from four years earlier (and the lower grade issues increased), it is tempting to conclude that credit quality declined. This conclusion is further reinforced by evidence that not only reporting banks with deposits in excess of $100 million but those below shared the same experience. However, not too much significance should be attached to these changes in investment ratings because they were remarkably small. Rather, it would appear that investment quality of state and local issues was maintained quite well.

GEOGRAPHIC DIVERSIFICATION

Geographic diversification is one way in which banks can reduce risk, although some authorities have questioned the need for extensive diversification as long as securities include a few selected issues. On the other hand, the advantage of a bank's buying obligations of political units located in its own area is obvious. Banks are apt to be particularly well informed of fiscal policies and conditions of their own or nearby political units. Some persons, therefore, believe that banks should be heavy buyers of securities issued by their own cities, counties, and states.

Do banks really favor their "own"? The answer—obtained from the same group of District member banks providing data on investment ratings—is a hesitant Yes. For these banks, as a group, the state and local government securities held in late 1965 tended to be weighted in favor of securities issued where the banks were located. A slender majority of their total holdings was of this type.

This should not be interpreted to mean that all reporting banks, or even banks in any one of the six states, followed the same practice. At one extreme, 85 percent of the total state securities owned by the reporting Mississippi banks were Mississippi issues. In contrast, Tennessee banks reported that state of Tennessee obligations accounted for only one-fourth of their total state issues. Tennessee and Florida banks reported that roughly one-half of their total state securities were issued by states outside the District. However, for banks in other District states, the bulk of the issues were either obligations of their own states or other District states.

At banks participating in our survey, securities issued by political subdivisions below the state level were similarly weighted in favor of their own localities. About one-fifth of the municipals held were issued by the same city, county, or district in which the bank was located, and over two-fifths were issued by other governmental units in the same state. Only about one-tenth were issued by political units of District states other than the one in which the reporting banks were located, and one-fourth consisted of out-of-District obligations (Table 2).

Many of these preferences seem to reflect differences in yield, availability, and investment ratings. However, why bank preferences in the various states should be so widely different from each other is not entirely clear.

Table 2 Geographic Characteristics of State and Local Government Securities at Selected Sixth District Banks

(Percentage Distribution)

Securities Issued By	*Mid-1966*
State Government, Agencies, or Authorities of:	100.0
Same State as Bank	52.5
Other Sixth District States	14.4
All Other States	33.1
Local Governments, Agencies, or Authorities Below State Levels of:	100.0
Cities, Counties, etc., in Bank's Metropolitan Area	20.9
Other Cities, Counties, etc., in Same State	43.3
Other Cities, Counties, etc., in Sixth District States	11.5
All Other States	24.3

IN CONCLUSION

Bank investment practices in the Southeast have undergone considerable change in the last four years. Clearly, District bankers have reduced their investment portfolios relative to loans—the result of a change in attitude, as well as a response to environment. Many banks have deliberately chosen to compete aggressively for time deposits and have accepted greater risks by increasing loans relative to deposits, lengthening the maturity of their investments, and taking on less easily marketable securities. These banks were apparently influenced to some degree by a belief that an expanded variety of time and savings deposit instruments, other newly developed sources of funds, and more stable deposits diminished their liquidity requirements. Their eagerness for state and local securities likewise must have been deliberate in part, as these issues seemed to offer special advantages. However, many of the changes in investment policy can be looked upon as being part of longer trends and as responses to monetary policy, loan demands, the availability of different types of securities, and other factors.

To the extent that the District banks' investment policies are typical, what do these conditions imply for future lending and investment policies? Because investment holdings have shrunk relative to deposits and now consist of more longer-term and riskier assets, banks may examine the risk and liquidity position of their portfolios and their lending policies more carefully. Such a development, which may have already occurred, would fit hand in glove with monetary policy actions aimed at curbing bank credit growth. Nevertheless, although the pledging of assets to secure public deposits has reduced the use of securities as a liquidity source, the remaining securities appear to be ample to meet lending needs (assuming District banks are typical) so long as banks are willing to make further reductions in the importance of investments. Meanwhile, greater assumption of risk in investment portfolios has not been accompanied by a significant shift toward lower-rated state and local issues at District banks. Thus, if these findings have wide applications, both adequacy and quality of bank investments may have held up much better in recent years than is sometimes believed.

Banks, Too, Post Collateral

Dorothy M. Nichols

Most people think of collateral as something that a bank requires a borrower to furnish as security for a loan. Such collateral may be in the form of a lien upon a physical asset or it may be a financial asset such as a Government or corporate bond, which itself is an evidence of indebtedness. A bank will accept as collateral, of course, only those assets which it judges to be sufficiently sound and liquid to provide protection against loss in case the borrower should be unable to repay his loan at maturity. Acceptable collateral is typically something easily identified, readily marketable and of fairly stable value. A loan applicant possessing such high-grade assets (and who otherwise meets minimum standards of credit worthiness) normally has little trouble getting credit accommodation.

Not so well understood is that banks themselves must often post collateral against certain of their liabilities. Just as individual or business borrowers pledge houses, stock, bonds, inventory, cattle or equipment as security for bank loans, member banks must pledge specific assets as collateral when they find it necessary to obtain temporary accommodation from their Federal Reserve Banks.

There are two methods by which member banks can obtain credit from their Federal Reserve Banks. One is by endorsing and discounting "eligible" paper at the Reserve Bank. This was the method commonly used in the early days of the Federal Reserve System, and it was this process which gave rise to the term "discount window" and "discount rate." The statute provides that short-term negotiable notes and drafts drawn for specified purposes related to the working capital needs of commercial, agricultural or industrial borrowers are eligible for discount. Such paper constituted a large share of bank assets in the early days of the System, and it was contemplated in the Federal Reserve Act that the provision for discounting this self-liquidating paper would automatically result in the proper amount of money to accommodate the needs of business—in short, an elastic currency.

The second method of extending Federal Reserve credit to a member

Reprinted with the permission of the Federal Reserve Bank of Chicago from *Business Conditions,* February 1965.

bank is through advances on the member's own note, secured either by eligible paper (as described above) or by U.S. Government securities. Such collateral must be delivered and held in custody accounts at the Reserve Bank; in practice, Government securities are often already held there for safekeeping.

In addition, at a premium of 1/2 of 1 percent above the discount rate, member banks can borrow on any other asset judged to be sound by the Reserve Bank even if it does not meet the requirements for eligible paper.[1]

For a good many years member banks have borrowed from Federal Reserve Banks mainly through advances secured by Government securities. This practice reflects the great convenience of such securities for use as collateral because of their unquestioned credit rating, widespread availability and variety of denominations.

WHY BANKS BORROW

When a member bank borrows at the discount window, it receives credit in its deposit balance at the Reserve Bank. These deposits serve as clearing balances and the legal reserves member banks are required to hold against their deposits. While the growth and variation in the aggregate volume of bank reserves are governed mainly by Federal Reserve System open market operations, the distribution of these reserves is determined by the forces of the marketplace. Deposits of individual banks fluctuate widely from day to day and week to week as a result of transactions by the public and the Treasury and even by System open market operations, which have their initial impact on the central money market. Individual banks are subject to frequent, substantial and often totally unexpected deposit drains which, although temporary, force them to take action to maintain their reserves at legally required levels.

A great deal of flexibility in adjusting to these developments is provided by the sale or maturity of liquid assets and, especially for larger banks, the ability to borrow reserves for a day at a time from other banks through the Federal funds market. Nevertheless, it is often appropriate for individual banks to obtain needed funds at the discount window to meet a temporary reserve deficiency.

In many cases the need to borrow results from the bank's efforts to serve unusual credit needs of its customers promptly and adequately. Just as businesses need bank credit to tide them over periods when their

[1] A proposed amendment to the Federal Reserve Act (S.2076, H.R.8505, 88th Congress) is designed to change the provisions with respect to collateral for member bank borrowings in recognition of the changes that have occurred in banking practices and the composition of bank assets. This amendment would remove the present eligibility rules and permit banks to borrow at the regular discount rate on any assets satisfactory to the Federal Reserve Banks, subject to such regulations as the Board of Governors of the Federal Reserve System might prescribe.

resources are out of phase with their outlays, so banks must sometimes borrow when the loan demands of their customers are not perfectly coordinated with the growth in their deposits or with adjustments that could reasonably be expected to be made by disposing of liquid assets. The guiding principles relating to access to the discount facilities are stated in the foreword to Regulation A, which sets forth the rules governing discounts and advances by Federal Reserve Banks, as follows:

> Federal Reserve credit is generally extended on a short-term basis to a member bank in order to enable it to adjust its asset position when necessary because of developments such as a sudden withdrawal of deposits or seasonal requirements for credit beyond those which can reasonably be met by use of the bank's own resources. Federal Reserve credit is also available for longer periods when necessary in order to assist member banks in meeting unusual situations, such as may result from national, regional or local difficulties or from exceptional circumstances involving only particular member banks.

This statement suggests the circumstances under which borrowing by member banks is considered appropriate. Outstanding borrowings at any given time are relatively small—rarely exceeding a billion dollars, or roughly 5 per cent of total member bank reserves—and this is distributed among a constantly changing group of borrowers. But while the aggregates are small, for an individual bank a particular situation may call for a large amount of borrowing in relation to its reserves and, likewise, relatively large amounts of collateral.

SECURITY FOR "PUBLIC DEPOSITS"

Of much greater importance from the standpoint of the total amount of collateral required are the laws providing that certain assets must be pledged as security against deposits of the U.S. Government—mainly Treasury tax and loan accounts—in excess of the amounts insured by the Federal Deposit Insurance Corporation. Acceptable collateral for deposits of public moneys under the Second Liberty Bond Act, as amended, encompasses a wider range of assets than those acceptable as security for borrowing at the discount rate. Included are U.S. Government securities, state and municipal issues, corporate securities, short-term commercial and industrial paper and other designated obligations with specific provisions as to the valuation of these instruments for collateral purposes.[2] The law further provides that such collateral must be held in custody at the Federal Reserve Bank, or in a depository designated by that Bank.

In addition, the laws of most states and political subdivisions require the pledge of specific assets of generally similar types against their funds with custody usually in the hands of a correspondent bank or another

[2] See *Treasury Department Circular No. 92 (Revised)* for detailed description of acceptable collateral and valuation requirements.

legally designated agent. It might be noted that while state and Federal laws require specific collateral against public moneys, banks are generally prohibited from granting prior claims on any segment of their assets to other classes of depositors.

Governmental units are, for many banks, important deposit customers. At mid-1964 total U.S. Treasury and state and local deposits in commercial banks throughout the nation amounted to almost 32 billion dollars, or more than 10 per cent of all commercial bank deposits (Figure 1). Short-

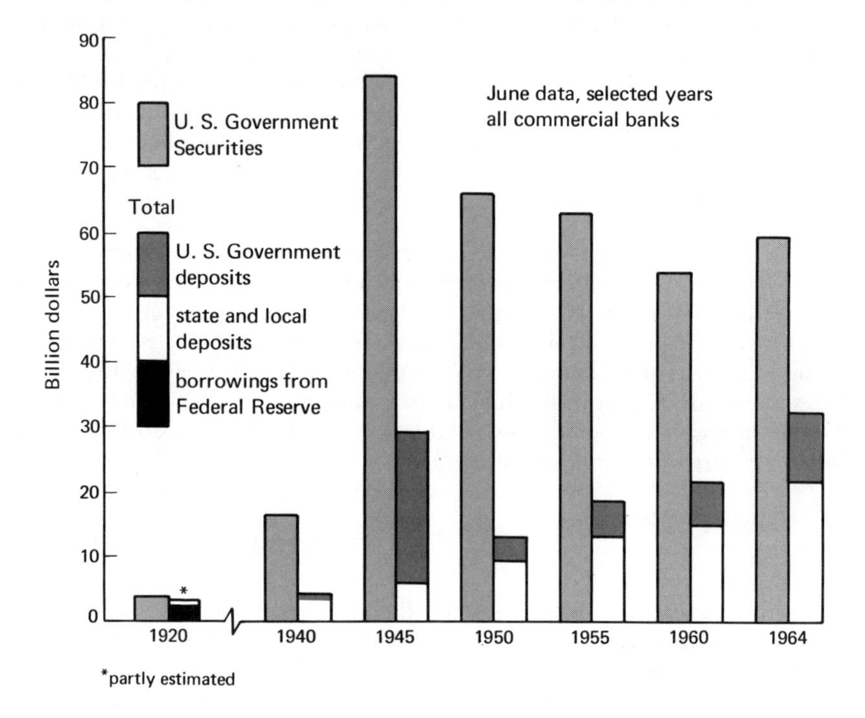

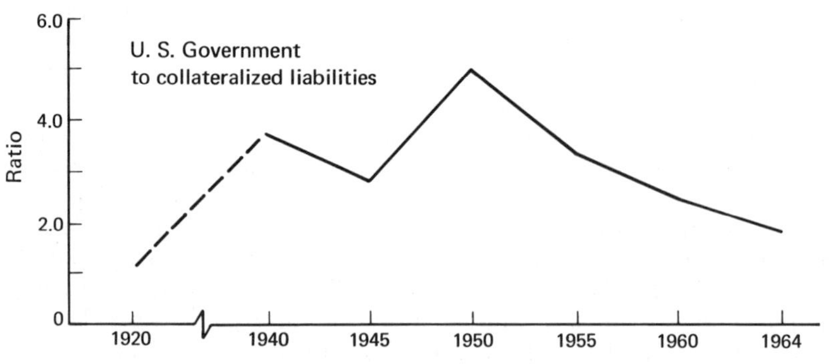

FIG. 1 Banks' U.S. securities have shrunk in relation to collateralized liabilities.

run variations in these totals are wide, due mainly to the uneven impact of Federal tax receipts and expenditure patterns. For individual banks, moreover, fluctuations in state and local balances are also large. With the growing volume of state and local deposits combined with the steady uptrend in the ratio of loans to deposits (and the related decline in holdings of Government securities), the margin of Governments over collateral needs has shrunk and individual banks occasionally find themselves faced with a severe "shortage" of Government securities which may be used as collateral for borrowings. Such shortages occur at times when a high level of public deposits happens to coincide with reserve drains due to adverse clearing on private balances or other temporary needs.

CUSTOMER PAPER AS COLLATERAL

Such occasions have prompted a number of banks to renew their acquaintance with the use of other acceptable collateral in obtaining Reserve Bank credit and in securing their public deposits as well. On the other hand, despite the fact that the discount facilities were set up for this specific purpose, many banks appear to be hesitant either to discount eligible customer paper or to offer it as collateral for Federal Reserve advances, perhaps in part because of uncertain customer reactions. Since, for many years now, the amount of U.S. Government securities held by banks has been more than ample to provide for collateral needs as well as short-run liquidity, bank loan customers have become accustomed to seeing no endorsements on their matured notes.

Endorsement—once fairly common—shows that the notes have been discounted or used as collateral for borrowing by the lender. Bank customers may again see such endorsements on their notes with somewhat greater regularity as banks more closely approach the loan ratios that were more common in the years prior to the depressed period of the Thirties and the acquisition of the huge portfolios of Governments during World War II (Figure 2). This development would simply reflect a continuation of the postwar trend for banks to use their resources less for investment in liquid assets and more for the accommodation of business and industry. Given an appropriate reason for a member bank to borrow, in principle it is of no consequence what type of collateral is used in the implementation of such borrowing. The relative convenience of alternatives is the determining factor.

The banking system as a whole still appears to have ample holdings of Governments to meet its collateral requirements. At the end of 1964 commercial banks held about 60 billion dollars of these securities—nearly twice the total volume of public deposits and borrowings from the Federal Reserve combined. Part of this, however, represents securities in trading positions of large banks that have dealer departments. It has been mainly at the large city institutions which have been aggressive in

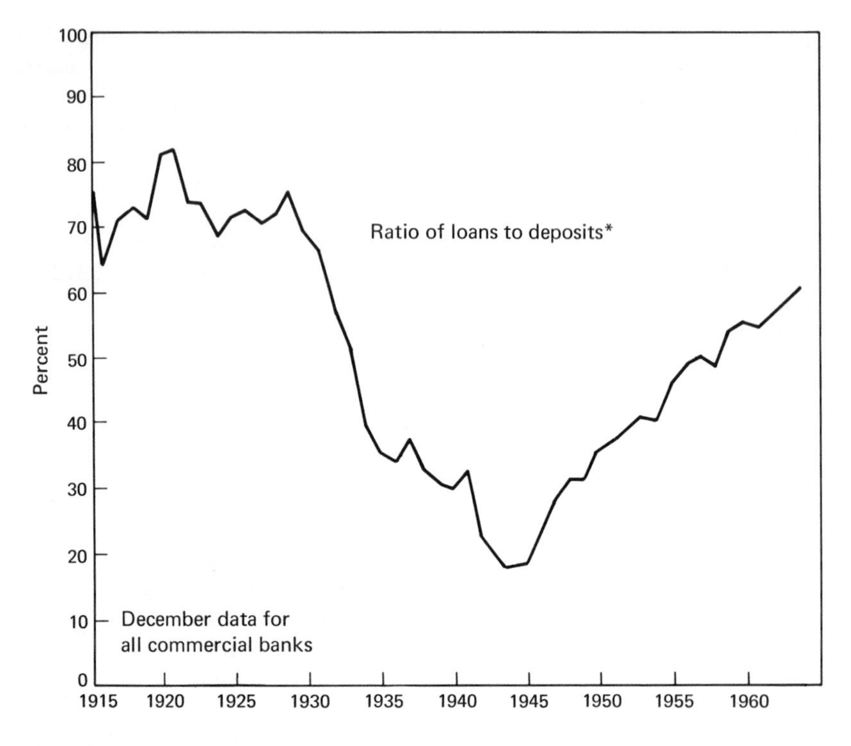

FIG. 2 Loan to deposit ratio of commercial banks reaches level of early Thirties.

* Loans excluding interbank loans; deposits net of cash items in process of collection.

serving their loan customers over the past few years and whose Government deposit and borrowing needs fluctuate widely from day to day that the adequacy of Government security collateral has posed problems. Member banks in New York and Chicago now have only one-third the amount of Governments they held at the end of World War II, while for all other commercial banks Governments are still 75 per cent of the 1945 level.

As indicated earlier, many types of securities, including state and approved municipal obligations, are acceptable at specified valuations as collateral for the deposits of most governmental units, but eligible collateral for borrowing at the discount rate is much more limited. Substitution of other acceptable collateral as security for public deposits would, of course, free Governments not only for use as security against borrowings but also for other purposes—market transactions, liquidity and generally greater flexibility in reserve management. However, a limiting factor in the use of some assets, particularly municipals, is their unit size. Any paper denominated in small units is inconvenient for collateral purposes due to both the physical problems of transport and storage and the necessity to examine each item to determine its acceptability.

For the most part, banks will continue to pledge U.S. Government securities as collateral for both public deposits and borrowings from Federal Reserve Banks. However, some flexibility is required, and it seems likely that the most practical and appropriate alternative would be to resort to the well established precedent but nearly forgotten practice of using prime customer paper to serve banks' collateral needs.

Bank Reactions to Securities Losses

Sam B. Chase, Jr.

During periods of vigorous economic expansion, rising demands for borrowed funds manifest themselves in many ways. One of the clearest indicators of mounting financial tension during such periods is the rising pattern of yields on outstanding U.S. Government securities. As yields rise, prices of outstanding issues other than short-term may decline markedly. This happened in 1959, for example, as it had in 1957 and, to a lesser extent, in 1953.

Since banks hold sizable amounts of intermediate- and long-term Government issues, significant reductions in the market values of bank portfolios occur when interest rates rise abruptly. The reactions of banks to changing prices of the securities they hold are important, both from the viewpoint of bank profits and from the viewpoint of the operation of restrictive monetary policies.

Declining prices of Government securities tend to reduce the willingness of banks to extend additional loan credit, and are therefore an integral part of the operation of restrictive credit policies. The precise implications of a decline in the market values of bank investment portfolios have been a matter of debate, however.

Three reasons have been advanced to explain why banks might be discouraged from expanding their loan credit when Government securities prices fall. Two of these propositions are commonly accepted by nearly all analysts. They are that a declining market value of a bank's investments, which serve partly as liquidity reserves, tends to inhibit sales

Reprinted with the permission of the Federal Reserve Bank of Kansas City from *Essays on Commercial Banking*, 1962.

of Government securities to finance an expansion of loans, and that rising market yields encourage banks to hold Government securities rather than to extend additional loan credit.

However, there is considerably less certainty concerning the validity of a third proposition—that banks are quite reluctant to sell securities when market values have declined because they wish to avoid showing the losses on their books. To the extent that banks refuse to sell securities because market values are below book values, they are sometimes said to be "locked in" to their existing investment portfolios.

It is important to judge the validity of this third proposition. Proponents of the "lock-in" argument contend that it is one of the most powerful of all forces working to reduce the availability of bank loans during periods of credit restraint. Skeptics of the "lock-in" naturally dismiss it as unimportant.

The first part of this article deals with the logic of the "lock-in" argument as it applies to commercial banks. The second section presents certain data that throw light on the actual behavior of banks in the face of the 1959 decline in the market values of their Government securities portfolios. On this basis some conclusions about the strength of the "lock-in" are presented.

REASONING BEHIND THE "LOCK-IN" ARGUMENT

Since Government securities are carried by banks at cost (less amortized premium and valuation reserves in some cases), a decline in their market value is not recorded on the banks' books unless the securities are sold. It is believed that bankers dislike showing securities losses on their books for a number of reasons. These reasons include a desire to refrain from recording losses because they may be mistaken by depositors or others to be evidence of poor management, as well as the more concrete reason that it is advantageous for banks to maximize the current rate of accumulation in capital, surplus, and undivided profits accounts.

The accumulation in these accounts may be important because certain bank regulations are related to bank size. For example, the aggregate amount of real-estate credit extended by a national bank cannot exceed 100 per cent of its unimpaired paid-in capital and surplus, or 60 per cent of its time deposit liabilities, whichever is greater. Similarly, the maximum amount that a national bank can loan to any one borrower is limited, with minor exceptions, to 10 per cent of its capital and surplus accounts. A bank that wishes to increase its loan limits may wish to avoid the recognition of "book" losses from selling securities in depressed markets because such losses would retard the current rate at which undivided profits accumulate and can be transferred to capital and surplus accounts.

However, against the possible advantages of maintaining the book value of its investment portfolio must be weighed two disadvantages, both of which may be significant in certain situations.

LOGICAL ARGUMENTS FOR PORTFOLIO FLEXIBILITY

For the purposes of portfolio management, the prices at which present holdings of Government securities were acquired are irrelevant to the determination of whether present securities portfolios constitute the optimum use of the funds represented by their market values. If a bank can increase its ultimate earnings by selling securities presently held and employing the proceeds of the sale in another use, it makes a distinct sacrifice by refraining from making the switch. Thus, for example, if two Government securities of similar characteristics should have unequal yields to maturity, computed on the basis of their market prices, a bank holding the security with the lower yield could increase the future income on its portfolio by switching its funds to the higher yielding issue. This would be true regardless of the effect of the switch on the book value of its investments.

On the same basis, it can be argued that a bank need not be deterred from expanding its loan portfolio simply because losses are realized when securities are sold to raise funds for loan expansion. Such losses have been suffered whether or not the bank shows them on its books; a decline in the market value of security holdings is a fact that cannot be avoided by refraining from selling the issues.

If a bank is to maximize the earnings on its investible resources, the relevant question in determining whether it should continue to hold any security it now owns is whether, if it held funds equal to the market value of its holdings of the security rather than the security itself, it could find a more attractive alternative use for the funds. If so, the present pattern of investments can be improved upon by selling the security in question and putting the funds into the more attractive alternative use. The only exception to this logical rule of profit-maximizing portfolio management involves the trading cost of switching investments. Switches from one use of funds to another would not be justified if the advantage of the switch, in terms of increased bank earnings, were so marginal as to be completely offset by the cost of making the change.

TAX TREATMENT OF BANK SECURITIES LOSSES

While it is true that an unwillingness to engage in market transactions in Government securities because their prices are depressed may stand in the way of achieving the most profitable use of investible resources, the tax treatment of securities losses realized by banks actually may provide an important stimulus for establishing such losses by market transactions. Although banks are, like other taxpayers, allowed to treat profits on the sale of Treasury securities (other than discount obligations, such as Treasury bills) as capital gains for tax purposes, they are permitted to treat net losses on Government securities in any given year as stock-in-trade losses. This means that they may deduct net losses from ordinary income for that year without limit. Other corporate investors for whom such Government securities are classified as capital assets are allowed only to offset capital losses against capital gains. Noncorporate investors are, in general, allowed to deduct net losses from ordinary income only up to a maximum of $1,000 in any given year, with the privilege of carrying unused losses forward over a 5-year period.

Because of the unlimited deductibility feature of the income tax law as it applies to banks, the principles governing the advisability of bank transactions that establish securities losses differ from those applied to investors subject to restricted deductiblity. The ordinary investor who incurs sizable losses on securities classified as capital assets is well advised to realize them through market transactions during a year in which he realizes capital gains, so as to be able to offset his losses against his gains. A bank has the more attractive alternative of taking securities losses in years other than those in which gains are realized. For a bank with net taxable income exceeding $25,000, after-tax losses are equal to only 48 per cent of the amount of losses recorded when the losses are deducted from ordinary income, but are equal to 75 per cent of the amount of losses recorded when the losses are offset against long-term capital gains.

For example, if at the end of 1959 a bank held 2⅝ per cent Treasury notes maturing in February 1963 that had been acquired at par value when they were issued, the bank could, by selling the securities at the December 31 market price of $92.875 per $100 par value, establish a loss of $7.125 per $100 par value of the notes it held. So long as the bank's securities losses exceeded its gains, it could deduct the loss from ordinary income. The result would be to lower net income subject to tax at the 52 per cent corporate rate (assuming net taxable income exceeds $25,000), reducing the bank's tax liability by 52 per cent of the amount of losses established. The tax saving would then be available for current investment. Supposing that the bank held $1 million par value of these notes, it could, by establishing a $71,250 loss on them, increase the market value of its holdings of securities by $37,050 (52 per cent of $71,250) if it reinvested both the proceeds of the sale and the tax saving. However, should the bank have experienced long-term capital gains sufficient to cover its securities losses during the taxable year in question, the loss on the Treasury notes would have to be offset against the gains. Since long-term gains are taxable at a maximum rate of 25 per cent, the reduction in the bank's current tax liabilities due to the $71,250 loss would be only $17,813.

Thus while it is always possible for a bank to reduce its current tax liabilities by realizing securities losses, the net tax advantage of recording the loss is considerably greater when it can be deducted from ordinary income, which means that securities losses lead to a greater tax saving if they are established during years in which long-term capital gains are not realized.

DEVELOPMENTS DURING 1959

The advantages that may derive from liquidating securities, both in order to transfer funds into more profitable uses and to realize the tax savings made possible by the establishment of losses on Government securities during a year of generally falling securities prices, would seem to constitute an important deterrent to maintaining book values of securities by avoiding market sales.

During 1959, financial developments were such as to put the strength of a "lock in" to a severe test. Mounting loan demands during the year provided a strong inducement for banks, most of which experienced pressures on their reserve positions throughout 1959, to liquidate Government securities in order to expand their loan portfolios.

Offsetting this inducement, and tending to retard a shift from Government securities into loans, were the reduced value of liquid assets held by banks that ensued from the decline in the market prices of Treasury issues, and the more or less steadily increasing return that could be obtained on Government securities.

In addition, any reluctance banks might have to recognizing securities losses on their books may have played an important part in deterring loan expansion during 1959. These losses were particularly important in the case of longer-term Treasury securities such as the 2½ per cent Treasury bonds maturing in September 1972, of which banks across the Nation held well over $1 billion par value at the beginning of the year. The quotation on this bond fell to an all-time low of $79.3125 per $100 par value on December 30, 1959, down from a bid price of $85.5625 on the last day of 1958.

If the "lock-in" effect was an important factor, even banks which did not feel their liquidity positions were being strained would still have been unwilling to liquidate Treasury securities on which prices had fallen sharply because of the book losses that such transactions would entail.

Aggregate figures for all banks in the Nation show that in 1959 they did indeed liquidate substantial amounts of securities on which prices had fallen significantly. But this fact alone cannot be interpreted as an indication that the "lock-in" effect was unimportant. It might be that banks were willing to establish book losses to some extent in order to provide for certain of the most desirable kinds of loan expansion but were more reluctant to extend loans than they would have been if the liquidation of investments could have been effected without recording losses.

However, in addition to the incentive to shift funds from Government securities portfolios to loan expansion, there existed the incentive to establish securities losses in order to reduce current tax liabilities. Banks that did not consider a decline in book values of securities (as distinct from the unavoidable fact of the decline in their market values) to be particularly undesirable might be expected to establish securities losses through market sales of Government issues even if they did not wish to reallocate their resources from Government securities into loans. This is because the advantage of establishing securities losses traces to the immediate tax savings that result, and is the same regardless of how the funds are employed after the securities are sold.

Thus, a bank that considers the advantages of tax savings obtained by realizing losses on its holdings of Government securities to outweigh the disadvantages of showing the losses on its books may simply sell off its existing holdings and reinvest the proceeds in other Government securities.[1] Such "tax switching" is practiced by a number of banks, but no evidence is available bearing directly on the extent of this practice.

LOSSES OF DISTRICT BANKS DURING 1959

Figures submitted by Tenth Federal Reserve District banks in their condition statements and their earnings and dividends reports for 1959 provide information that is helpful in gauging the extent to which they attempted to reduce their tax liabilities by establishing losses on Government securities. This information in turn provides a useful insight into the power of the "lock-in" effect, since banks that establish losses for tax purposes are clearly not "locked in."

An examination of reports for nearly all member banks in the Tenth District indicates that of a total of 752 banks, 473 established net securities losses during the year in excess of .01 per cent of the average value

[1] One technical feature of undertaking tax switches to the nondeductibility of securities losses obtained through wash sales. Whether a specific transaction constitutes a wash sale cannot always be determined in advance of a specific ruling by the Internal Revenue Service. In general, losses are not deductible under the wash sale rule when they are established on "substantially identical" securities in which both sales and purchases were conducted within a 30-day period. However, because of the large number of outstanding Government issues, there are many pairs of issues that may be satisfactory substitutes for one another in terms of bank portfolio management and that are not held to be "substantially identical." For example, the 2½ per cent bonds maturing in September 1972 and callable in September 1967 have been ruled not identical (for purposes of the application of the wash sale rule) with the 2½ per cent issue of December 1972, callable in December 1967. The differences between these two issues, aside from their 3 months' difference in maturity, are largely of a technical nature, and in general would not be such as to make banks unwilling to switch between them.

of their investment portfolios as shown in their condition reports for December 31, 1958, June 6, 1959, and October 6, 1959. Of the remaining 279 banks, 61 reported net gains on securities in excess of .01 per cent of their average investments on the three call dates, while 218 banks showed net gains or losses amounting to less than .01 per cent of the average of their investment portfolios on the three call dates (Table 1).

Among the 473 banks showing net losses of more than .01 per cent, a majority (374 banks) had net losses ranging from .01 to 1 per cent of their investment portfolios. Sixty-eight banks showed net losses on securities amounting to between 1 and 2 per cent of average investment portfolios, while 22 banks recorded net losses of between 2 and 3 per cent. The remaining nine banks showed losses on securities in excess of 3 per cent of their average investment portfolios.

These figures indicate that bank reactions to the decline in the market values of their Treasury securities were subject to extreme variation. A complete examination of a bank's portfolio and a knowledge of its market transactions during the year would be necessary to know the precise extent to which it took advantage of the opportunity to establish securi-

Table 1 Net Gains and Losses on Securities as Per Cent of Average Investment Portfolios

Tenth District Member Banks, 1959

	Net Gains in Excess of .01%		Net Gains or Losses Less Than .01%	
Deposit Size	*No. of Banks*	*Per Cent*	*No. of Banks*	*Per Cent*
Under $2 million	10	5	115	53
$2–$10 million	36	9	90	22
$10–$50 million	10	10	12	11
$50 million and over	5	20	1	4
Total	61	8	218	29

	Net Losses							
	.01-.99%		1.0-1.99%		2.0% and over		Total	
Deposit Size	*No. of Banks*	*Per Cent*	*No. of Banks*	*Per Cent*	*No. of Banks*	*Per Cent*	*No. of Banks*	*Per Cent*
Under $2 million	77	36	10	5	3	1	215	100
$2–$10 million	233	57	35	9	13	3	407	100
$10–$50 million	53	50	20	19	10	10	105	100
$50 million and over	11	44	3	12	5	20	25	100
Total	374	50	68	9	31	4	752	100

ties losses for tax purposes. However, some insight is provided by the figures relating net securities losses to average investment portfolios.

One bank in the District that reported substantial securities losses stated in its annual report to stockholders that it engaged in extensive tax selling during the year, establishing a net after-tax loss on securities of almost $1 million on an investment portfolio that averaged $69 million. Its market transactions in securities maturing in over 1 year amounted to more than $48 million in 1959, a figure clearly in excess of the amount of sales necessary to finance the bank's loan expansion during the year.

Since for this bank the pre-tax losses on Government securities would be equal to slightly more than twice the amount of after-tax losses, the bank's net losses on Government issues amounted to something over 2½ per cent of its total investment portfolio. If the published information of this bank can be used as a benchmark, it would seem safe to conclude that other banks experiencing securities losses in excess of 2 per cent of their average investment portfolios during 1959 also engaged in considerable tax switching for the purpose of establishing losses. Similarly it would seem reasonable to presume that banks that established losses ranging from 1 to 2 per cent of their average holdings of Government securities probably did engage in at least some tax switching. It is clear that banks selling for tax purposes did not consider themselves "locked in" to their holdings of Government securities, so that the decline in the market values of their portfolios below book values could not in itself have been a factor inhibiting them from financing an expansion of loans through securities liquidations.

However, if the interpretation of figures relating to securities losses of District banks set forth above is correct, only 99 of the 752 member banks appear to have taken advantage, to any considerable extent, of the securities loss provisions of the Internal Revenue Code. It might therefore be concluded that most banks either were unaware of the advantages of establishing tax losses or did not consider them desirable, either because they entailed showing book losses, which was repugnant to the bank management, or because the banks did not feel it was worthwhile to devote the time and effort necessary to effect tax switches.

A lack of acquaintance with the provisions of the income tax laws concerning securities losses and a reluctance to devote the necessary time and effort to planning tax switches would presumably be more important factors for small banks than for large ones. Larger banks are likely to have specialized personnel whose time is devoted mainly to managing the securities portfolio.

Thus it might be expected that the management of a large bank would be fully aware of the tax implications of establishing losses, and that the bank would be in a position to exercise the kind of careful planning necessary for the successful execution of tax switches. In addition, many smaller banks have net taxable incomes of less than $25,000, which puts them in the 30 per cent bracket of the corporation income tax, reducing the tax-saving advantages of establishing net securities losses.

From this point of view it is interesting to examine the securities losses of District member banks classified according to bank size. Table 1 shows that while only 6 per cent of District member banks with deposits of less than $2 million established losses in excess of 1 per cent of their average investment portfolios, 32 per cent of the banks with deposits of over $50 million did so. In general the relative amount of net losses on securities increases as the size of the bank increases.

This finding would seem to confirm the notion that the failure of at least some banks to realize the maximum possible securities losses can be traced to such factors as (1) the weaker incentive for smaller banks in the 30 per cent corporation income tax bracket to take advantage of tax provisions regarding securities losses, (2) an inadequate knowledge of these provisions, or (3) a less meticulous management of investment portfolios, perhaps because it does not pay smaller banks to employ specialists in portfolio management.

Nevertheless, the evidence cited here indicates that the attraction of maintaining book values of securities portfolios is strong. This is true even for larger banks which presumably exercise a close supervision over their portfolios and are fully aware of the tax advantages of establishing securities losses. Only a minority of the largest banks in the District showed losses amounting to more than 1 per cent of their investment portfolios.

A FURTHER TEST

The hypothesis that many larger banks in the District carried substantial amounts of unrealized securities losses on their books at the end of 1959 may be further tested by an examination of portfolio figures for reserve city member banks, almost all of which have total deposits of $10 million or more. Figures for all central reserve city and reserve city banks in the Nation are also presented.

The declared book values of U.S. Government securities held by these banks, as they are shown on the December 31, 1959, statements of condition, can be compared with the market values of these holdings on the same date to determine the extent of their unrealized losses at the end of 1959. The market values of securities held by central reserve city and reserve city banks both for the Nation and for the Tenth District were computed by multiplying the par values of their holdings, as reported in the Treasury Survey of Ownership for December 31, by the ratio of market prices to par values of the securities on the same date.

Table 2 shows the declared book values, together with the computed market values, of Treasury notes and bonds for District reserve city banks and for both reserve city and central reserve city banks across the Nation. In the third column of the table are shown aggregate unrealized losses on each type of security, computed by subtracting market values from

Table 2 Estimated Unrealized Losses on Marketable Treasury Notes and Bonds

December 31, 1959

	1		2		3		4	
	Book Values		Market Values		Unrealized Losses		Unrealized Losses as a Per Cent of Book Values	
	Notes	*Bonds*	*Notes*	*Bonds*	*Notes*	*Bonds*	*Notes*	*Bonds*
	(In millions of dollars)							
Tenth District Reserve City Banks	277.0	523.9	270.0	495.1	7.0	28.8	2.54	5.50
All Reserve City Banks	4,108.6	10,936.7	4,019.0	10,336.1	89.6	600.6	2.18	5.49
Central Reserve City Banks	1,744.3	4,183.1	1,718.2	3,985.0	26.1	198.1	1.50	4.74

Sources: U. S. Treasury Department, Board of Governors of the Federal Reserve System, and Federal Reserve Bank of Kansas City.

book values. Column 4 indicates, for each class of security, unrealized losses as a per cent of book values.

One qualification that must be noted is that some banks carry valuation reserves against securities. The effect of building up such a reserve is to reduce book values below original costs, so that the figures shown understate the amount of unrealized losses somewhat. However, the practice of carrying valuation reserves against securities is quite limited; aggregate valuation reserves on securities for District reserve city banks at the end of 1959 amounted to only about $5 million, or less than .6 of 1 per cent of the book values of notes and bonds combined.

In the case of each group of banks the difference between book values and market values is sufficiently large to indicate that they bypassed the opportunity to realize considerable additional losses in 1959. This finding tends to confirm the conclusion that the maintenance of book values may be an important consideration even to larger banks, both in the Tenth District and throughout the Nation. It is notable that unrealized losses are a smaller proportion of book values for central reserve city banks than for reserve city banks, which tends to confirm further the judgment that larger banks are less likely to carry extensive unused securities losses than are smaller banks.

CONCLUDING REMARKS

Judging from the evidence presented concerning the practices of District banks, it appears that there is no hard and fast rule that banks are "locked in" to their holdings of Government securities when market values decline. The fact that many larger banks evidently engaged in tax switching during 1959 may be taken to mean that an aversion to showing book losses on securities was not a factor in limiting their willingness to extend loans.

Nevertheless, a majority of banks appear to have been reluctant to establish sizable net losses on securities, and it would seem correct to conclude that in these cases their willingness to extend additional loan credit was at least to some extent correspondingly tempered. Thus the evidence appears to indicate that the "lock-in" effect, though it is far from being a universal influence, is an important one.

Meeting Seasonal Loan Demands

A Problem of Managing Bank Funds

Charles T. Taylor

Frequently, because of seasonal forces, banks in an area may lose deposits when loan demands are high and gain deposits when loan demands are low. Such alternate periods of "tightness" and "ease" create a problem for an individual bank in managing its funds, regardless of how well Federal Reserve policy reduces the seasonal pressures on the entire banking system. This difficulty occurs because seasonal patterns in local areas frequently differ from those of the entire banking system. This is so because commercial banks make most of their loans to local borrowers and because the economic structures underlying the seasonal loan demands of these borrowers differ from area to area.

At the nation's banks, loans reach their seasonal peak in December; in the Sixth District, however, Florida and Louisiana are the only states

Reprinted with the permission of the Federal Reserve Bank of Atlanta from *Monthly Review,* November 1963.

that have a similar seasonal pattern of loan demand. Seasonal influences cause loans to be highest at the end of July in Alabama, Mississippi, and Tennessee. At Georgia banks, the seasonal peak comes at the end of September. Seasonal lending patterns also differ markedly from area to area within the states (Figure 1).

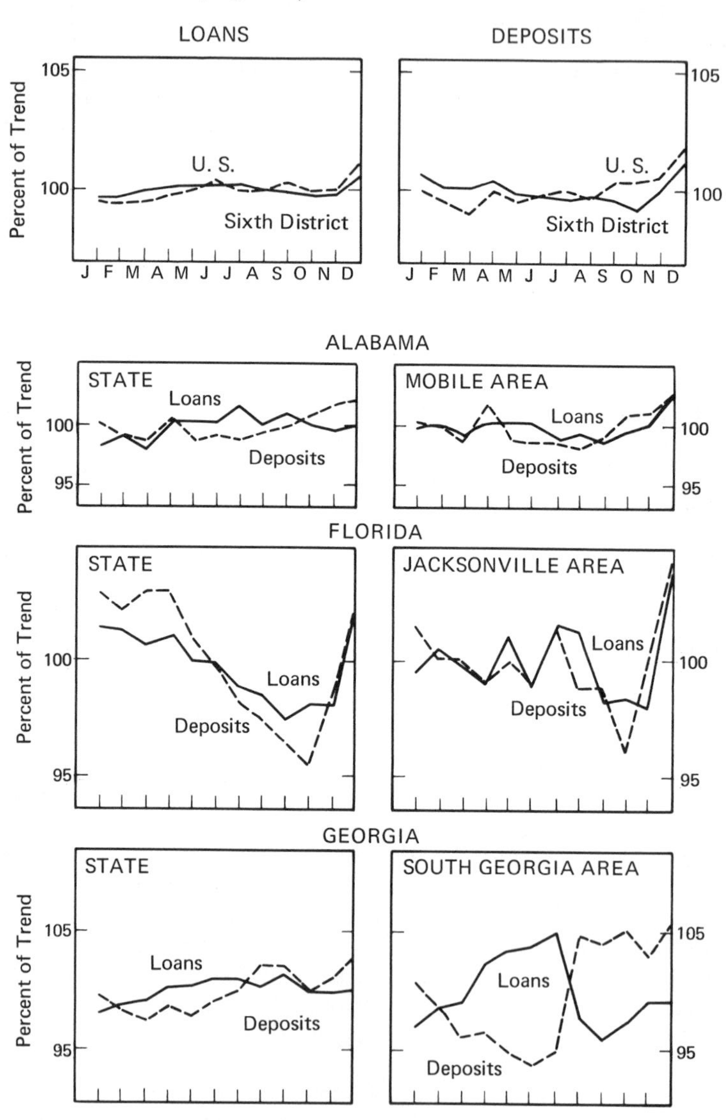

FIG. 1 The seasonal patterns of both the loans and deposits at all member banks in the United States and in the Sixth District are generally similar. Some seasonal patterns differ, however, from state to state and from area to area within each state.

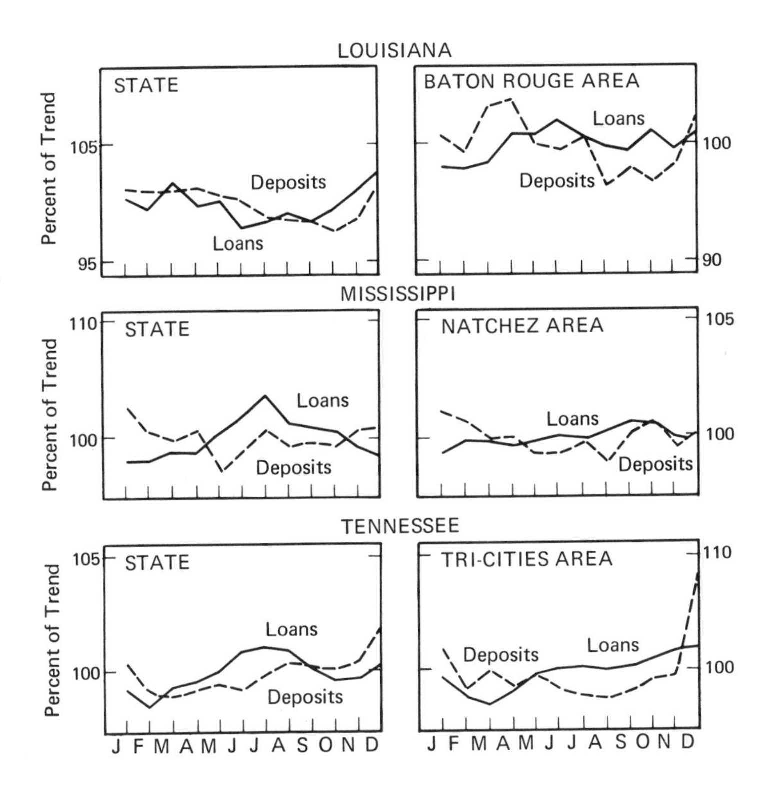

FIG. 1 (cont.)

Every banker knows on the basis of past experience that more of his customers will be requesting loans in certain months than in others and that these months are the same year after year. Thus, the seasonal patterns that are derived from data based on banking reports, used as illustrations in this article, merely formalize what bankers already know. Applying statistical techniques to monthly loan data for recent years, we have developed measures of seasonal movements, technically called seasonal adjustment factors. These factors tell us the typical increase or decrease from month to month, assuming the levels of outstanding loans were influenced solely by seasonal influences and not by general economic conditions, long-term growth or decline, or irregular forces.

THE LOAN MIX

The figure for total loans outstanding is a composite of the loans a bank has made to a wide variety of borrowers with different credit needs. The borrowings of some of these persons have a seasonal pattern; those of others do not. The borrowings that show a seasonal pattern are quite likely to do so because of customers' needs for more short-term working capital during certain months of the year, rather than from their needs for longer-term funds. In this respect, the seasonal loan demands of farmers and businessmen are similar. A farmer needs funds to buy seed and fertilizer, pay hired labor, and cover living expenses until his crops are harvested and sold. The retail merchant needs working capital to accumulate inventories prior to his heaviest selling months and to carry the accounts receivable of his customers after the goods are sold. The home builder needs construction funds to pay for labor and materials used during the good building months before the houses are ready for sale. The mortgage banker may need funds while mortgages acquired during the peak home-buying months are being "seasoned." These and other types of borrowers may differ in their specific seasonal needs, but they all have a greater need for short-term working capital in some months than in others and they receive some of these funds from banks.

With so many different kinds of borrowers, the seasonal lending patterns of total loans outstanding naturally differ from bank to bank and from area to area merely because of the "loan mix." In addition, banks with a high proportion of borrowers whose primary need is for long-term credit are less likely to have a marked seasonal lending pattern than banks with a high proportion of short-term borrowers. For example, although consumers tend to concentrate their car buying in the first half of the year, which causes new automobile instalment loans by banks to be highest then, changes in loans outstanding show less seasonal response than new loans. This may be explained by saying that the new credit granted for comparatively long terms is only a small part of the total outstandings and, in some cases, repayments are heavy in the same months in which new loans are highest.

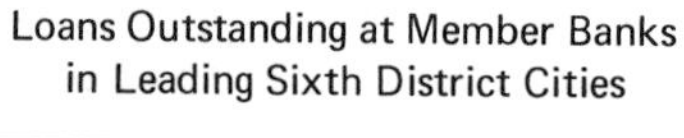

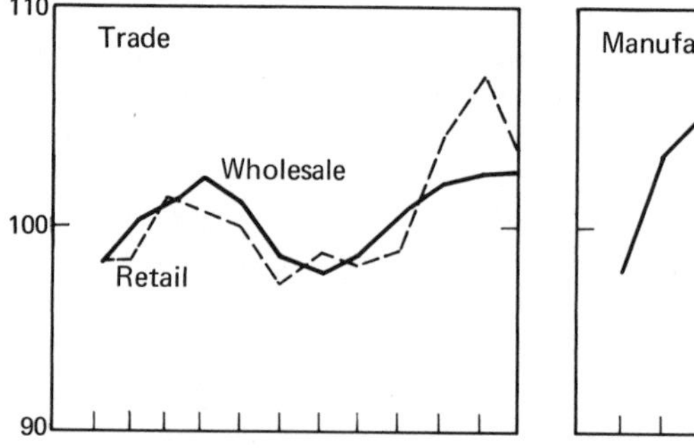

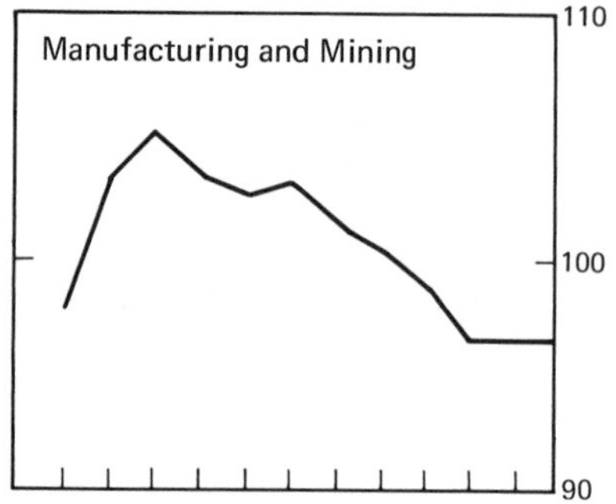

FIG. 2 Loans that provide short-term working capital are most likely to follow a seasonal pattern. Loans made for longer periods show less seasonal variation in outstandings.

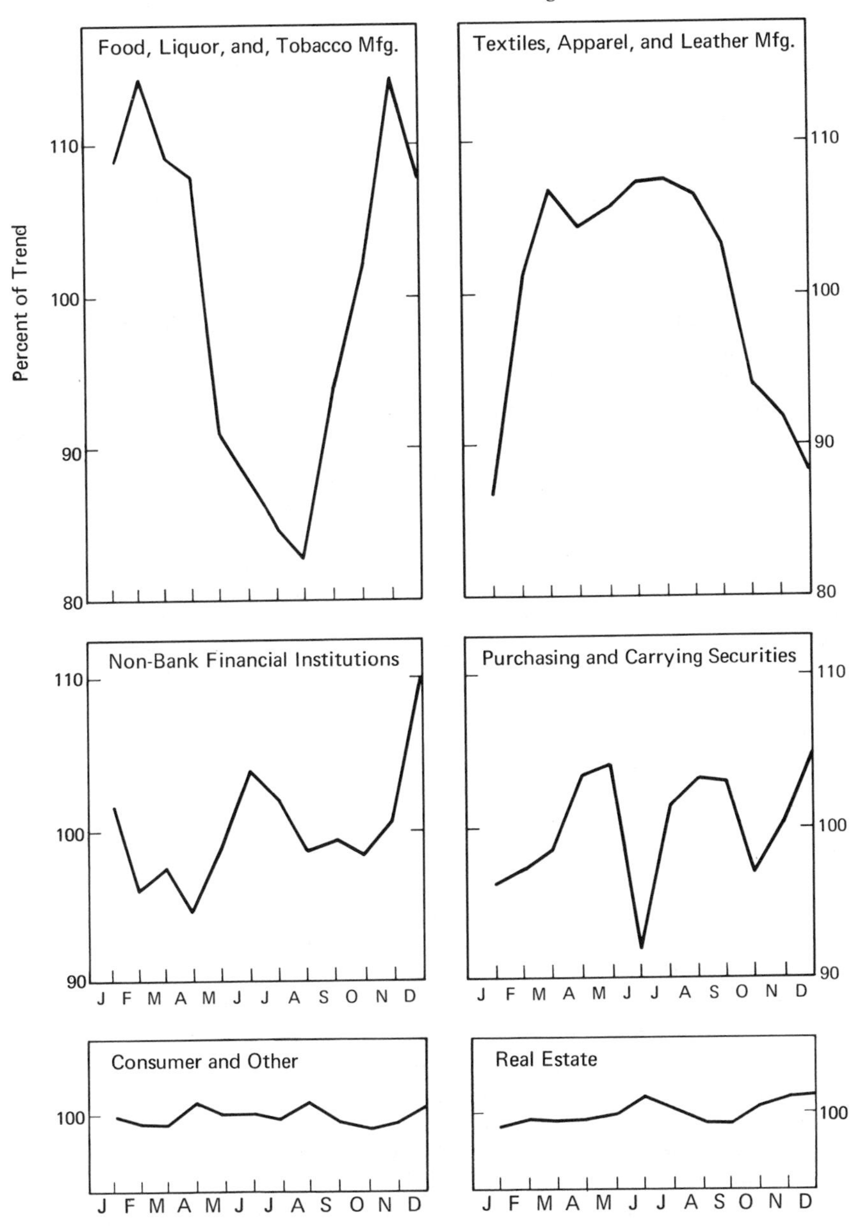

FIG. 2 **(cont.)**

The variety of seasonal loan patterns of some specific types of loans, as well as the contrasting patterns that result in different areas of the District from different "loan mixes" and different local economic characteristics, is illustrated in Figure 2. In general, there is likely to be a stronger seasonal loan pattern in areas where the economic structure is specialized than where it is more diversified. Almost all banks, nevertheless, have a seasonal lending pattern of some sort.

THE BANKER'S PROBLEM

This tendency for loans to rise and fall during the year in a regular recurring pattern is of more than casual interest to the banker. Unless he plans and prepares for these seasonal peaks in lending, he may find himself either unable to meet the usual credit demands of his customers or discover at the same time year after year that he is in an uncomfortably tight "cash position." The very same forces that are determining the seasonal pattern of his loans may also be drawing funds out of his bank when he most needs them and vice versa.

Bankers tend to regard the amount of their deposits as imposing a limit on their loans or investments, even though they may know that the banking system as a whole "creates" deposits when it extends credit on the basis of available reserves. This is so because a bank is likely to gain reserves during a deposit expansion and lose them during a contraction. How much an individual bank can lend or invest, therefore, depends upon its ability to attract or retain deposits. Since both the inflow and withdrawal of deposits are influenced by seasonal forces, the banker must take them into consideration when he formulates his loan and investment policies.

In some farming communities, for example, income is derived principally from the sale of a few specific crops in the late summer and early autumn, and deposits build up during these months. During this period, the banker has ample funds to lend. The demand for loans, however, is then at a seasonal low because farming activity is at a low ebb. After that, deposit declines begin to drain reserves month by month well into the following year until the crops are harvested and sold. Beginning in the spring, money must be spent for seed, fertilizer, and other production expenses; some of this money travels outside the local banking area, thus adding to the bank deposit drains. This is the time, however, when loan demands are high. The banker in such an area finds that when he needs funds most he has a shortage of loanable funds and when loanable funds are abundant he needs them least. Thus, conflicting seasonal deposit and loan patterns may pose serious problems in the management of a bank's funds (Figure 3). Not all banks have identical problems, but most of them have seasonal problems of some sort. Since bankers know with some confidence when there will be "tight" and "easy" periods each year, they plan their operations accordingly to keep available funds fully employed and earning profits and also to meet seasonal drains on their reserves when they occur.

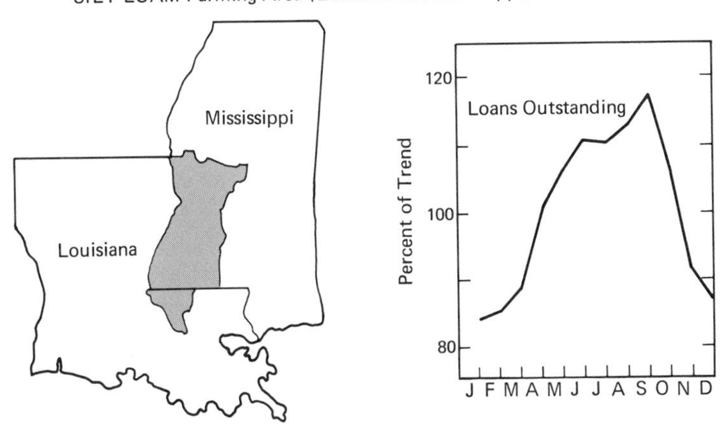

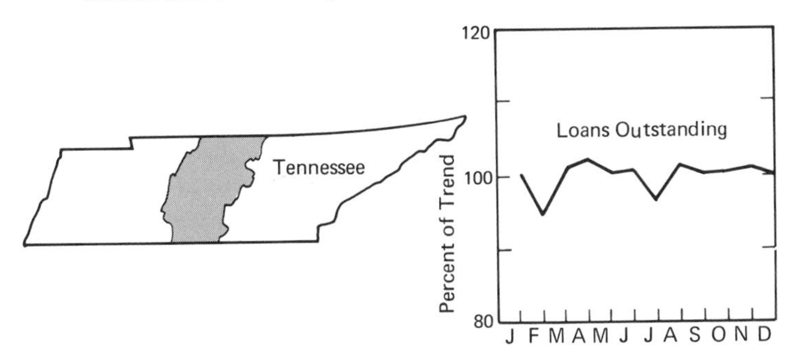

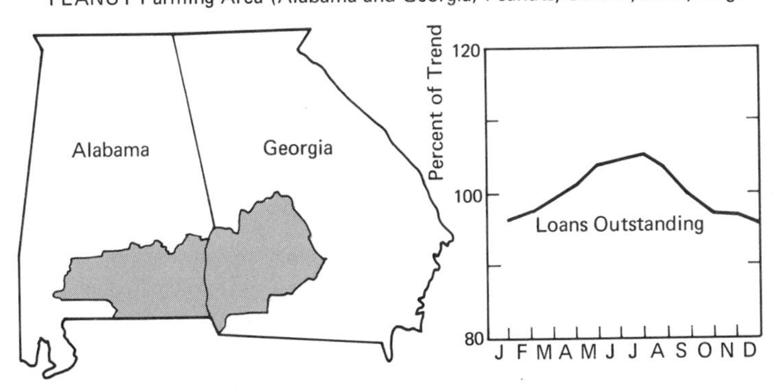

FIG. 3 The kinds of farm enterprise carried on in an area determine the seasonal loan practices of banks serving farmers, as the experience of rural banks in these areas illustrates.

MEETING THE PROBLEM

Bankers meet these seasonal problems by properly managing their secondary reserves, which are, in the words of the money and banking textbooks, those earning assets that may be quickly converted to cash at all times without appreciable loss. Instead of leaving their funds idle during slack periods, they invest them in earning assets that can readily be converted into cash without loss. Since short-term securities of the U.S. Government are subject to fewer price fluctuations than long-term securities, they are the chief components of secondary reserves. Skillful management spaces the maturities of these issues so that securities will mature as funds are needed. Although higher earnings could be obtained from a portfolio consisting entirely of long-term securities, there is the risk that, with a rise in yields and a consequent decline in prices, a loss would be incurred if the securities were sold before maturity.

The management of a bank's cash position is a special art. First of all, some knowledge of seasonal changes in loans and deposits is needed. It also requires a man with a "sharp pencil" who will watch his bank's cash position from day to day or even from hour to hour. He checks by phone with his Federal Reserve Bank to determine his reserve position; he checks within his own bank on any expected large deposit changes; and he knows if large blocks of securities are maturing. He must be able to estimate not only today's position, but also what it will likely be in the future. Only then can he decide whether he should use any existing

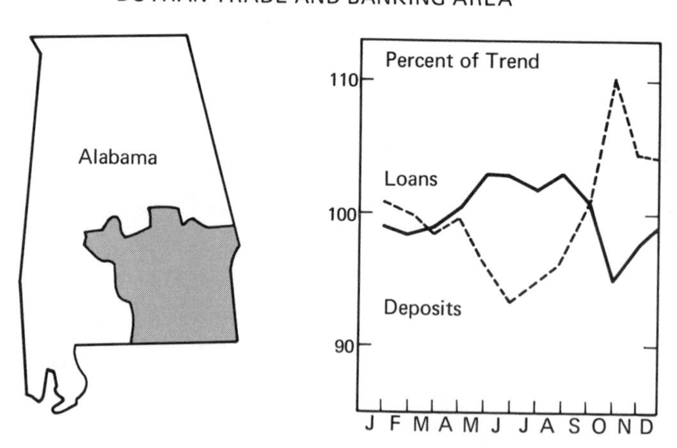

FIG. 4

Proper management of bank funds is especially important in an area where cash crops are an important source of income, as they are in the Dothan, Alabama, trade and banking area. There, deposits decline seasonally and reduce reserves during the months when loans are rising. Deposits rise seasonally when loans decline.

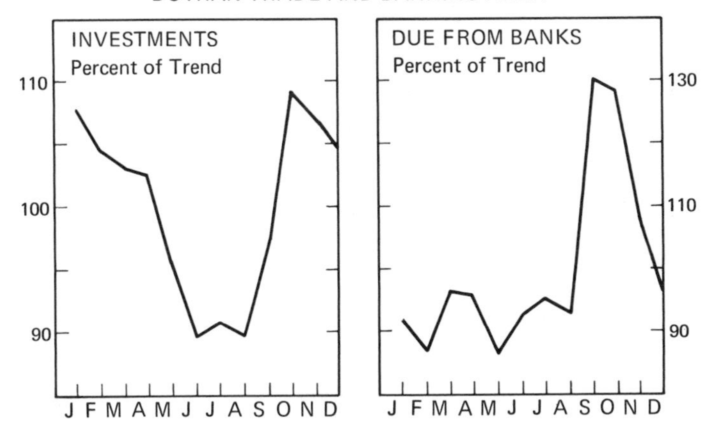

FIG. 4 (cont.)
Member banks in the area meet peak credit demands and absorb excess funds chiefly by adjusting their investment portfolios. They also make adjustments through their excess reserves at the Federal Reserve Bank of Atlanta and their demand deposit balances due from correspondent banks.

excess funds in the Federal funds market, buy short-term securities or commercial paper, or whether the bank could prudently earn higher yields on intermediate- or longer-term Government or municipal securities. When he discovers that the bank is likely to be deficient in reserves, he must decide how to erase the deficiency. Because of the special skills required and the time involved, a money-position specialist is frequently found only at the larger city banks.

For many banks, especially the smaller ones, managing the bank's money position may be only one of the numerous tasks performed by a bank officer. Paying such close attention to the bank's daily cash position, however, may not be compensated by an additional gain in earnings. Some banks, therefore, prefer to keep a cushion of excess reserves and correspondent balances that will meet most emergencies. Sometimes, if not carried to an extreme, such a policy may be the most economical one to follow.

The seasonal patterns derived from statistics reported by the member banks in this District's six county Dothan trade and banking area in southeast Alabama illustrate the asset and liability changes made in response to seasonal forces (Figure 4). This area was chosen as an illustration because it is more dependent upon farming, particularly cotton and peanut production, than many other areas of the District, and, consequently, the seasonal swings in deposits and loans are large. Typically, deposits decline seasonally during the period in which loan demand is expanding and rise when loan demand falls off. Of course, the operations of any one of the banks in the area may not conform specifically to the pattern derived from the experience of all the banks combined. Nevertheless, the asset adjustments that were made are typical of the action many bankers take when faced by such seasonal changes.

The statistics for past years show, for example, that the Dothan area member banks typically reduce their investment holdings month by month during the first half of the year—the period when loans are rising and deposits declining. When deposits increase in the latter part of the year as the crops are marketed, the banks typically add to their investment holdings. They also use their excess reserves with the Federal Reserve Bank of Atlanta, as well as their demand balances with other banks, in making adjustments to seasonal needs.

BORROWING FOR SEASONAL NEEDS

Why, then, if a banker by planning can manage his bank's funds to provide for seasonal needs, do some banks occasionally borrow from the Federal Reserve Bank of Atlanta or from other banks for seasonal needs? There are two general reasons: the imprecision inherent in forecasting and mistakes in bank management.

Changes in the demand for bank loans and in the level of bank deposits are caused, of course, by changes in general economic conditions, the long-term growth of a community, and by other not completely predictable events, as well as by seasonal forces. At times, these forces may push up loan demands or drain off deposits beyond a banker's prudent expectations. Moreover, the seasonal pattern of lending may change as the economic character of the community the bank serves changes. For any such reason, plans for meeting seasonal problems may prove inadequate. Furthermore, the "sharper" the banker's "pencil" and the greater his attempts to remain fully invested at all times, the more likely it is that he will find himself faced with special seasonal problems. Thus, large banks are more frequent borrowers than smaller ones.

A banker may find, for example, that deposit withdrawals are greater than he can meet by liquidating short-term securities. To raise funds by selling his long-term securities on a falling market might incur losses. Sometimes such emergency seasonal needs can be met by borrowing from other banks through the Federal funds market. . . . At other times, member banks exercise their privilege of borrowing from the Federal Reserve Banks (Figure 5).

"Access to the Federal Reserve discount facilities," we are told in *Regulation A* of the Board of Governors, "is granted as a privilege of membership . . . . Federal Reserve credit is generally extended on a short-term basis to a member bank in order to enable it to adjust its asset position when necessary because of a sudden withdrawal of deposits or seasonal requirements beyond those that can be reasonably met from the bank's own resources."

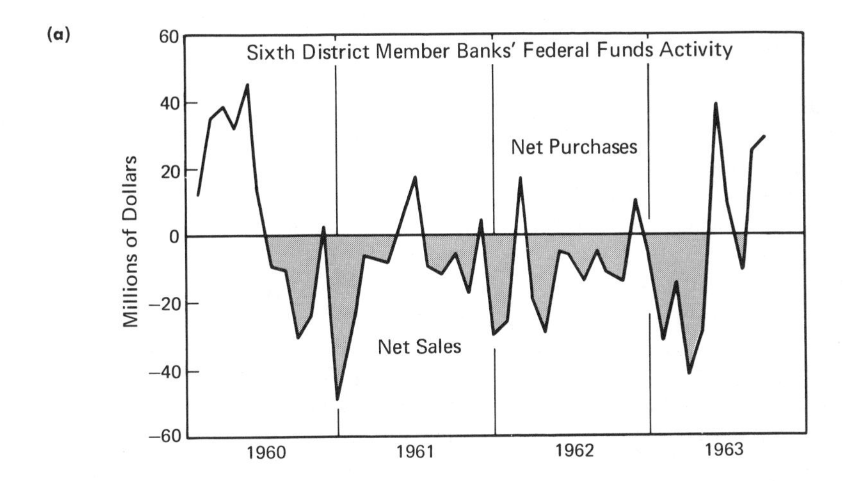

FIG. 5

(a) Some Sixth District banks adjust their reserves through purchase and sale of Federal funds. For all District banks combined, this activity in recent years follows somewhat of a seasonal pattern.

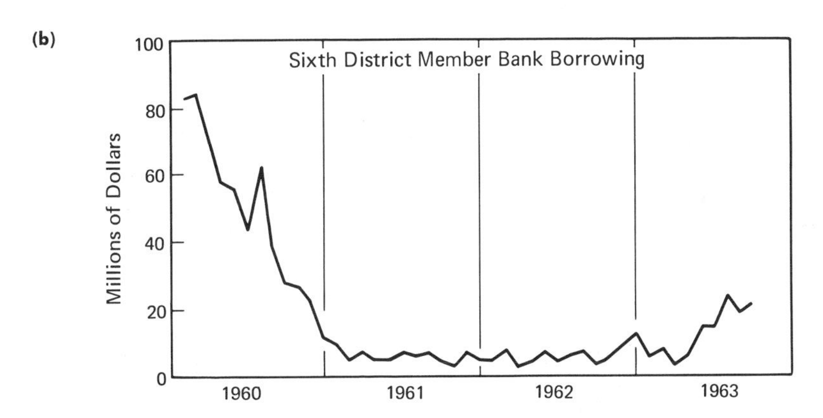

(b) Seasonal requirements beyond those that can be reasonably met from banks' own reserves may be met by short-term borrowing from the Federal Reserve Bank of Atlanta.

Not all seasonal borrowing by member banks can be traced to the fallibility of forecasting and planning for seasonal needs that are to be expected. For example, there is the banker who is surprised year after year to find a seasonal pattern at his bank. He ties up all his funds in long-term securities to take advantage of their yield or income. When confronted by declining deposits, he may find himself in the position of having to replenish his reserves by selling his securities at a loss if money market interest rates have been rising. Or, there is the banker who tries to achieve the seemingly impossible feat of increasing both his loans and investments while his deposits are declining. Circumstances such as these, even though they can be traced to lack of foresight and should have been avoided, can be met temporarily by borrowing at the Federal Reserve Bank's discount window, since assisting banks to maintain a liquid position is one of the primary concerns of the Federal Reserve authorities. However, in such cases, the Federal Reserve Bank authorities take steps to help the member bank avoid such borrowing in the future.

Most banks are able to meet seasonal pressures on their cash positions by properly managing their funds and use the privilege of borrowing from the Federal Reserve Banks only occasionally, if at all. For example, so far this year only 61 of the 458 member banks in this District have used the borrowing privilege. Even in the so-called "tight money" year of 1959, only 115 resorted to borrowing from the Federal Reserve Bank.

Both the American commercial banking system and the Federal Reserve System are unique. In the United States, banking is carried on by over 14,000 unit banks that are privately owned and, for the most part, individually operated; in many parts of the world, commercial banking is highly concentrated among a few large banks.

The burden of serving the needs of the public, therefore, falls upon both the Federal Reserve and the privately owned and operated commercial banks. Neither can do the job alone. Thus, the Federal Reserve System helps this nation's banks meet seasonal needs for money and credit in two ways. By providing the banking system with reserves in accordance with seasonal needs . . . , it helps avoid periods of general seasonal credit stringency; by extending the discount privilege to member banks, it helps the individual bank solve its problem of meeting seasonal credit demands in its own community.

On the other hand, the Federal Reserve System must have the help of local bank management in meeting the seasonal credit needs of individual communities. Together, the Federal Reserve System and individual banks operate to provide that seasonal elasticity in the supply of money and credit envisioned by those who wrote the Federal Reserve Act fifty years ago. If one measure of the success of Federal Reserve policy is the avoidance of periods of general seasonal credit stringency, one measure of commercial bank management is how well it meets the peculiar seasonal needs of its own customers.

Credit—and Credit Cards

Robert A. Johnston

The bank credit card has now spread across the country, bringing both opportunities and problems to the banking system. As late as two years ago, bank credit-card plans were relatively unimportant except in California; almost everywhere else, they were limited to local merchants and operated by small to medium-sized banks. But last year marked a major turning point for these plans.

In early 1966, some of the nation's largest banks, undoubtedly impressed by the profitability of existing credit-card plans, decided to enter this field, and the largest operator (Bank of America) announced the creation of the first nationwide system through a national licensing scheme. In response to these developments, still more banks decided to issue credit cards. By the end of 1966 new plans were either operating or in the planning stage in the Pacific Northwest, the Chicago area, and many areas of the East; the credit card was now the latest in thing.

Although the bank credit card has basked in the spotlight for several years now, relatively few reliable statistics were available on the subject until quite recently. Even now, the available statistics combine bank credit cards with other plans which, though often regarded as substitutes, are not exactly the same as credit cards. The other types are check-credit plans and nonbank credit-card plans—which include the so-called travel and entertainment (T&E) cards such as American Express, Diners Club and Carte Blanche.

TYPE 1: CHECK CREDIT

Check-credit is a method whereby a bank automatically makes consumer loans on a pre-arranged revolving credit. The customer applies for a line of credit and, if the application is accepted, an account is opened on borrowed funds against which the borrower writes checks. In some plans, checks with distinctive designs are provided to identify check-credit accounts, while in other cases, ordinary checks with no special identification beyond the account number are employed.

Reprinted with the permission of the Federal Reserve Bank of San Francisco from *Monthly Review*, September 1967.

Overdraft plans are similar in that the existing account of a customer is assigned an additional line of credit by the bank to cover overdrafts. The overdrafts may be accidental or deliberate; in the latter case the line of credit plays the same role as a check-credit account.

For both the check-credit and the overdraft plan, the check remains the instrument for making purchases, and so the adoption of either variation involves minimum changes in existing banking procedures. Both types of plan compete with credit cards because of their provision of revolving credit, but they avoid the heavy administrative costs and the credit-control problems of a credit-card plan. Furthermore, customer-pleasing features such as check-guarantees can easily be added through the use of identification cards or special checks designed like travellers checks. Nevertheless, in comparison to the bank credit card, these plans do not produce significantly large increases in credit volume. The reason, as will be seen, lies in the special characteristics of the credit card.

TYPE 2: T&E CARD

Intermediate between the check-credit plan and the bank credit-card plan is another revolving-credit plan, the T&E card. Because of some obvious similarities, the bank credit card and the T&E card are frequently lumped together, but they appeal to different markets, and banks play different roles under each plan. With the bank credit card, banks run the entire operation, extending credit from the day a merchant deposits a sales draft to the time the cardholder pays his bill. With the T&E card, a bank becomes involved only if the cardholder, after signing the appropriate bank agreement, decides to let his bill go on a revolving-credit basis or to use his card to borrow from the bank.

The principal advantage of the T&E card is that it allows the bank a credit-card service to its customers with a minimum of direct expense; the bank only has to set up an organization to administer revolving credit. But at the same time, the bank will not obtain as large a volume of operations from this plan as it would from its own plan. First of all, T&E cardholders generally have superior credit ratings and therefore are less likely to resort to revolving-credit to pay their bills—and when they do so, they tend to be in debt for only short periods of time.

T&E cards thus are basically a convenience service for people who want to avoid carrying cash but who do not need credit on a regularly scheduled basis. Furthermore, T&E cardholders need not even sign up with a bank to obtain revolving credit, since they can repay major transportation expenses on a time-payment basis with the card company. This is the only exception to the requirement that accounts are due when billed, but it is an important one, since these big-ticket items are the ones most likely to be deferred and most likely to have otherwise required bank financing.

TYPE 3: BANK CREDIT CARD

The prime advantage of the bank credit card is its simplicity: banks can even use it to attract loan demand without first establishing a regular banking relationship in the traditional sense with the customer. Cardholders do not have to be depositors of the bank which issues the card. Thus, in effect, the card-issuing bank is able to make consumer-type loans to other banks' customers as well as its own.

One alternative, check-credit, is at a disadvantage because most people, when planning on major purchases, will obtain revolving credit through a retail store rather than through a bank. In contrast, the bank credit card fits easily into habits already established by department-store and oil-company cards. In the public's mind, this is just another plastic credit card, but one with a greater acceptance at a number of different businesses. And in further contrast to check-credit and overdraft plans, there is no need to minimize the number of transactions in order to avoid service charges on the checking account.

Another alternative, the T&E card, also has important shortcomings. The excellent credit rating of T&E cardholders means that they are least likely to resort to revolving credit, the stage where the bank finally makes a loan under this plan. In contrast, bank credit cards rely upon a mass market—they are designed for local expenditures on a wide range of items and are issued to people with average incomes.

Of course there is some overlapping of markets, in regard to both the cardholders who use these cards and the purchases they make. Yet the fact remains that the bank relies upon a high volume of revolving credit for its credit-card revenues. There is no membership fee for the cardholder and merchant discounts tend to be low. Therefore, the interest from revolving credit must be the main source of income, and the bank's goal must be to stimulate the regular use of cards by a large number of people for a wide range of purchases. A high volume of card transactions is required to support the credit balances needed to produce sufficient interest income.

A fully-operational credit-card organization has other advantages too. As it is geared to handle a mass of small transactions with a minimum of decision-making, this organization can easily take over from the bank-office level those functions whose processing costs are high relative to their return. A prime example would be small personal loans; in some banks, all personal loans below a certain size are processed as credit-card cash advances, and overdraft facilities for depositors can be treated in a similar fashion. There are also the benefits arising from the usual requirement that merchants accepting cards open an account with the bank operating the plan. In practice this requirement is a further source of new customers; since many merchants dislike having several accounts, non-card banks tend to lose accounts to the card-issuing bank.

The major disadvantages of a full credit-card plan are simply the reverse of its advantages. Mass issuance of cards and high volume of transactions create both heavy start-up costs and high credit risks. The latter can be a particularly difficult problem, since the mass distribution of cards, which is at the heart of the plan's ultimate profitability, prevents application of unduly restrictive credit standards. Lack of a regular banking relationship with all cardholders also increases risk. The pressures to recover initial expenses and to reach a profitable level of operations too quickly may force a bank to be overly generous in its initial issue of cards and may thereby expose it to even higher credit losses.

The first few years are the key ones: this high-cost period determines whether a bank abandons its credit-card plan, as some major banks have done in the past, or whether it finally achieves a profitable position. In a well-run plan, the profits can be substantial—but so too are the costs of reaching that position.

THE STATISTICS

Statistics on the credit-card phenomenon are rather scanty, but some data are available from the April 27 Call Report of the three Federal bank-regulatory agencies. As of that date, $809 million in credit was outstanding at the 627 banks which offered some kind of plan (Table 1).

Unfortunately, no exact breakdown is possible between bank credit-

Table 1 Bank Credit Cards and Check-Credit

Total Credit Outstanding as of April 25, 1967 (Amounts in millions of dollars)

	National banks		State member banks		State non-member banks		All banks	
Federal Reserve District	*No. of banks*	*Total credit*	*No. of banks*	*Total credit*	*No. of banks*	*Total credit*	*No. of banks*	*Total credit*
1. Boston	28	44	11	13	8	2	47	59
2. New York	34	61	25	46	11	9	70	116
3. Philadelphia	23	20	7	40	9	6	39	66
4. Cleveland	27	54	1	*	8	1	36	55
5. Richmond	16	18	5	12	7	2	28	31
6. Atlanta	51	40	7	3	23	5	81	48
7. Chicago	78	95	12	18	48	9	138	122
8. St. Louis	22	10	6	2	17	2	45	13
9. Minneapolis	15	4	1	*	6	*	22	4
10. Kansas City	29	10	6	1	5	*	40	12
11. Dallas	19	3	3	2	11	5	33	10
12. San Francisco	30	248	6	13	12	11	48	272
Total	372	607	90	150	165	52	627	809

* Less than $50,000.

Source: Federal Reserve Board of Governors.

card plans and T&E cards and check-credit plans, although it is estimated that about 60 percent of the total is in bank credit-card systems and the remainder in other plans. Moreover, there are probably more than 627 banks involved with credit cards, since in many areas (Illinois, for example) correspondent banks offer cards and service merchants but do not carry any credit balances. In the Call Report, also, some banks probably over-stated their lending, while others did not report at all, because of some confusion as to what kind of loans should be classified as credit-card and check-credit loans. Despite these qualifications, however, the returns do permit some useful generalizations to be made on the subject.

At the moment, credit cards and check credit appear to be a big bank's game. Of the 40 largest banks—those with deposits of $1 billion or more—all but five offer some kind of credit-card or check-credit plan, and in the $500 million-$1 billion deposit-size category, over two-thirds of the banks have a plan. Thereafter, percentage participation falls off rapidly with size. For banks with less than $5 million in deposits, fewer than .5 percent offer a credit plan. Yet 48 percent of the banks with credit outstanding under these plans had less than $50 million in deposits.

Credit cards and other credit plans are concentrated in a few geographic areas, principally the Pacific Coast, the Midwest and the North East. The Twelfth District leads, having twice the credit outstanding of any other district—or about one-third of the national total—and it is followed by the Chicago and the New York Federal Reserve Districts (Figure 1). On a state basis, the leaders are California, New York, Penn-

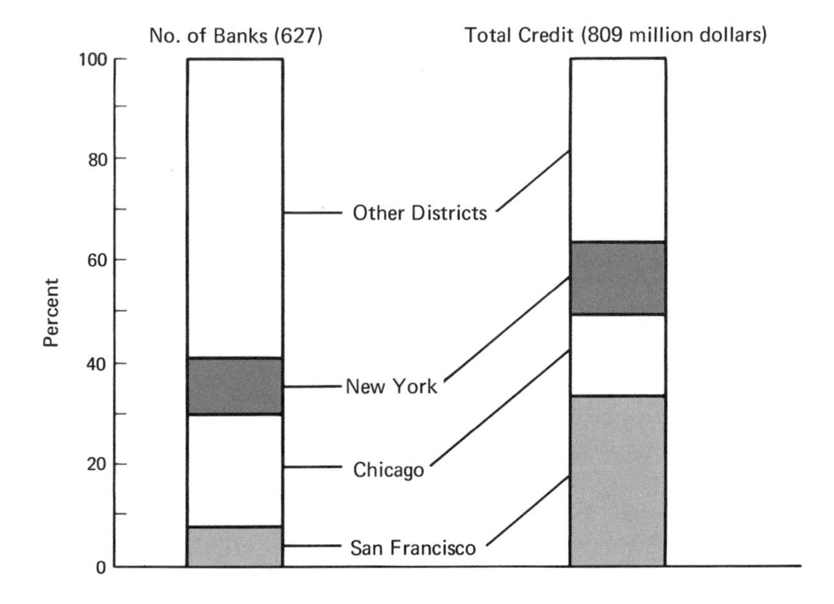

FIG. 1 District holds one-third of credit outstanding in all bank-credit plans.

sylvania, Illinois and Massachusetts, in that order. In terms of numbers, the Chicago District is first because of the local predominance of unit banks.

In the field of bank credit cards alone, the San Francisco District's role is even more striking—bank credit cards account for perhaps 80 percent of the District's credit-plan outstandings, as against roughly 50 percent elsewhere. Indeed, with the single exception of Alaska, the credit card is a regular feature of the District banking scene (Figure 2).

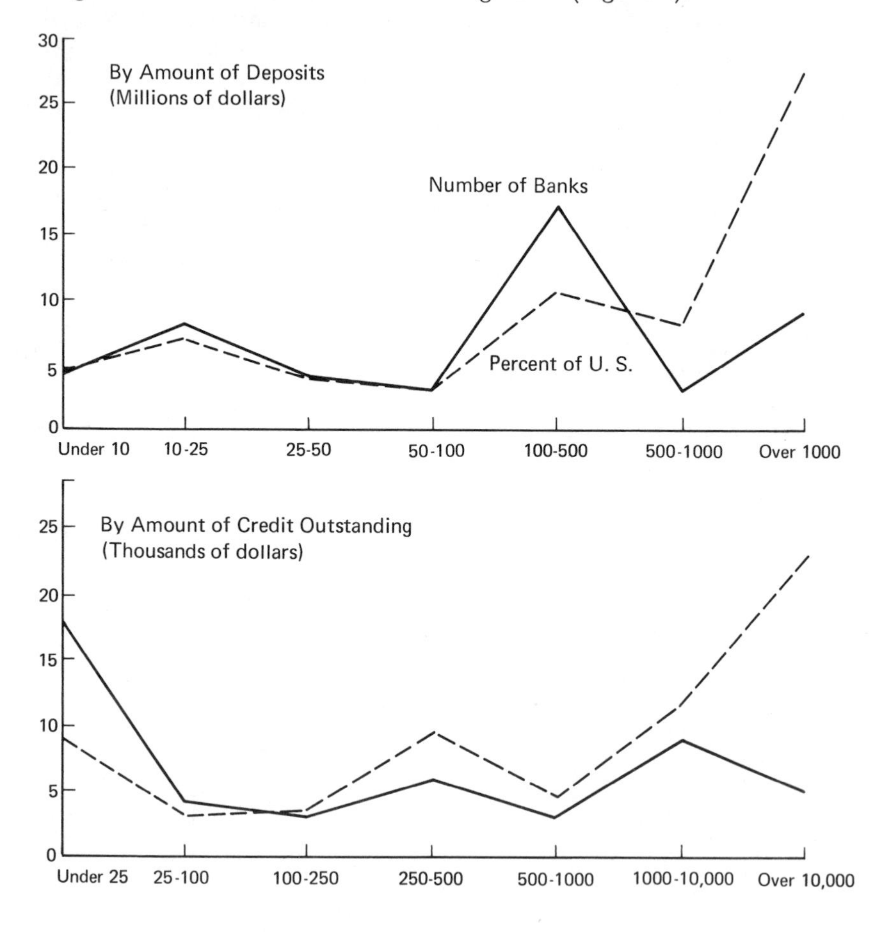

FIG. 2 West dominates large-bank activity in credit-plan accounts.

California leads the way in bank credit cards, followed by Illinois (Chicago), Pennsylvania (Philadelphia and Pittsburgh), and New York. As of the April Call Report, New York City did not have any major bank credit card in operation; that area's large total in outstanding credit was due largely to T&E cards and check-credit. However, one major New York City bank has since started a credit-card operation, and still others might follow.

EFFECTS ON BANKING PRACTICE

The key to a successful credit card program lies in the control of credit —for example, supervising the distribution of cards with their associated lines of credit, and supervising their subsequent use to prevent excessive indebtedness and, most important, fraud. Generally the task of credit control is greatest during the first years, but it then becomes more manageable as the bad cards are gradually eliminated. Credit supervision is ultimately a technical problem but by no means a minor one.

Another aspect of credit control concerns the policy of each bank regarding the amount of credit it commits relative to its total resources. The total commitment can be substantial, since cash advances are a regular feature of most plans. Additionally, since these lines are unsecured and automatic, the bank may expose itself to unpredictable surges in credit demand which it must meet by adjusting its asset portfolio. The bank cannot reduce credit lines that have been widely advertised without destroying much of its earlier selling efforts aimed at creating a credit-card habit. The mass distribution of cards makes it administratively difficult to cut back on credit lines; thus the success of a credit-card plan may require a bank to make fundamental policy changes in its credit priorities.

There is also the administrative problem of handling the mass of paper created by the credit card. It may well be that the credit card reduces the burden of handling checks. Indeed, the credit card is quite likely to reduce the number of checks written, since one check per month can pay for a number of transactions that normally require payment by separate checks. But one problem is now replaced by another; the bank now must process an even larger volume of paper, including both the sales drafts that would normally be paid by check and those that replace former cash purchases.

The immediate effect of the credit card is an increase in internal clearing problems. Ultimately, some have argued, it is a step toward the "checkless society." This is true only in the sense that the system puts pressure on the banks to develop a technology capable of handling transactions more quickly and cheaply. The techniques which can process sales-drafts can also do the same thing for checks. Thus the credit card—although it may be an indirect step toward a more sophisticated payments transfer mechanism—in the meantime tends to increase the banks' burdens.

EFFECTS ON BANKING STRUCTURE

As the statistics indicate, the credit card is typically a service offered by medium- or large-size banks. The high start-up costs put a premium on financial strength, and the recent trend to regional and national coverage points even more to the advantages of size. Consequently, there is concern that the credit card will weaken the competitive position of the smaller banks.

But this pessimism may be unwarranted, since the major banks are now adapting their plans to allow varying degrees of participation by smaller banks. A prime example is the California Bankcard Association, whereby 73 banks of varying sizes have formed a joint program. Under this program, a central organization owned by the banks and set up as a non-profit organization takes care of certain tasks created by the use of a common card. The individual banks can share fully in all plans of the credit-card program, regardless of size. In fact, approximately one-third of the membership consists of banks with deposits of $10 million or less.

In an alternative development, the Bank of America under its licensing program has permitted correspondent banks of its licensees to issue BankAmericards under their own name or some common name, and to extend credit if they wish. This arrangement is being used in Colorado and Ohio. Another variation is the agency-bank arrangement, whereby a bank avoids the risk of a full credit-card operation by participating on a limited basis, accepting sales-drafts deposited by merchants and processing card applications of its customers. The agency arrangement, besides being widespread on the Pacific coast, is dominant in the Chicago area, where unit banking makes it essential to achieve adequate coverage.

These new variants of the normal pattern of "one-bank-one-card" help encourage smaller banks who are trying to enter the credit-card field. As there is no inherent barrier to the entry of smaller banks, it is still too early to tell whether the credit card will ultimately shift the competitive advantage more towards larger banks.

Quite apart from inter-bank competition, the bank credit card may also affect the position of banks relative to other financial institutions. Bank credit cards are already involved in business accounts-receivable financing and in some consumer-credit activities previously financed by non-bank institutions. However, banks are limited in their ability to take over larger-sized contracts by their relatively low credit limits (often only $300) and by credit requirements which are stricter than those of many consumer-finance companies. Nonetheless, the basic administrative machinery of a credit-card plan can, in principle, be adapted to larger credit contracts, and thereby can support the expansion of the banks' competitive position in the lending field.

But this relative improvement should not be exaggerated. Bank credit cards now account for about one-sixth of all credit extended by credit cards, but this still leaves five-sixths in other hands. Moreover, they amount to less than 1 percent of all non-auto consumer credit ($62 billion outstanding in April). Therefore, bank credit cards have far to go before they can become a dominant factor in consumer credit, let alone in bank lending.

FUTURE EFFECTS?

Bank credit cards, to conclude, have attracted well-deserved attention since they are an important innovation in banking services. For the individual bank, the credit card presents a difficult management choice of whether or not to enter this field. If the bank does decide to enter, then there are critical operational problems created by the issuance and control of cards. And while these problems can be costly and difficult to resolve, the trend is toward greater bank participation in this or similar credit programs. After all, cards can be very profitable, and besides they may be necessary as a defensive reaction to a competitor's program.

In the overall banking system, credit cards currently absorb only a small part of total bank resources, and they are not yet an essential banking service. Partly for this reason, the most important policy tasks of the regulatory agencies at this time are likely to be in supervision—to insure that there are proper credit standards—and in market structure—to preserve the ability of small banks to compete in this area—rather than in the area of monetary control. All in all, the bank credit card may create difficulties for individual banks, but its recent growth testifies to its ability to provide a useful and popular banking service.

Equipment Leasing

Harmon H. Haymes

Equipment leasing is a time-honored practice in American industry. For many years, machinery has been leased to users by manufacturers so they could retain control over maintenance and replacement and assure satisfactory service. Sometimes the lease arrangement has been used to avoid local property taxes or to take advantage of other tax considerations.

Reprinted with the permission of the Federal Reserve Bank of Richmond from *Monthly Review,* December 1967.

Frequently, users have leased equipment to avoid tying up scarce capital or going into debt. Lessees have acquired almost every type of equipment in this manner—automobiles, trucks, office equipment, manufacturing machinery, and recently, multi-million dollar jet aircraft. Equipment is available on lease not only from manufacturers and regular suppliers, but also from leasing companies, and in recent years, from commercial banks. In almost every undertaking involving the use of productive goods, leasing is now an alternative to buying and sometimes a more attractive alternative.

TYPES OF LEASES

Equipment leases are often classified as "operating leases," sometimes known as maintenance or service leases, and "financial leases." The operating lease is used when the lessee does not want to buy the equipment, but only wants to use it. He may prefer not to buy either because he needs the equipment only for a limited time or because he would prefer to have the lessor maintain it. This type of lease usually involves payments which add up to less than the price of the equipment over the term of the lease, and the leased property is reclaimed at the expiration of the lease. Usually the lessor agrees to provide maintenance or service over the term of the lease or to replace the equipment if it should become defective. In the case of an automobile or truck lease, for example, the lessor would generally be required to maintain the vehicle in good repair and provide tires, batteries, and other parts, but not gas and oil.

The financial lease resembles more closely the purchase of goods on an instalment basis. Usually such a lease is non-cancellable for its entire term, and payments will total more than the price of the equipment. The agreement frequently provides for the lessee to take possession of the equipment at the termination of the lease after paying an additional nominal fee. The financial lease is used when the lessee actually wants to acquire the property, but when a lease offers some advantage over an instalment purchase, such as a lower down payment or reduced tax liability.

LEASING VERSUS PURCHASING

Leasing in one form or the other frequently provides advantages over outright purchasing. Many smaller businesses find such an arrangement a useful substitute for a loan. The lease may in effect provide 100% financing and on a longer-term basis than any available loan. Sometimes a lease is available to an individual or company who, as a result of a poor credit rating, would be unable to qualify for a loan of equivalent size. Leasing may also provide a hedge against obsolescence. Rapidly advancing technology continually provides new and better machines, but as a result, today's mechanical marvel may be tomorrow's white elephant. To avoid being stuck with outdated equipment, the user may prefer to lease machines for relatively short periods of time, replacing those which have been by-passed by later developments. The lessor must, of course, charge fees which will cover the depreciation of his assets, but the user of the machinery is saved the problem of justifying new purchases, establishing a high rate of depreciation for tax purposes, and marketing the outdated equipment.

For a time, the way in which many government contracts were handled provided an incentive to lease equipment. Under contracts negotiated on a cost-plus basis, the practice in many instances was to allow lease payments in full as costs, but to disallow interest payments on borrowed funds. Depreciation allowances also had to be related to the life of the equipment, rather than to the life of the contract. As a result, many defense contractors found it more profitable to lease equipment than to buy it, especially when its purchase was financed by borrowed funds. Government auditors are aware of this discrepancy, however, and now apparently treat lease payments and similar costs on a comparable basis.

Some firms find leasing preferable to purchasing on credit because it minimizes the amount of debt appearing on the balance sheet. A debt to a supplier or a loan payable is clearly a liability, but in the past large amounts of equipment have been leased with no evidence of indebtedness appearing in the firm's statement of condition. In recent years, however, it has become more common to make some reference to leases, either in a footnote on the balance sheet or as a liability representing the sum of future payments due. The American Institute of Certified Public Accountants, after a study of accounting principles related to leasing, issued a policy statement holding that leases which in effect are instalment purchases should be treated as purchases, and should appear on the books as such. Other leases should be noted on the balance sheet, with sufficient information available to indicate the true financial position of the firm. Strict adherence to these recommended accounting procedures in some instances would dilute or eliminate the advantages of leasing.

Recent developments in Federal tax laws have removed some of the advantages of equipment leasing and in some instances, added others. Accelerated depreciation allowances may make leasing less attractive to the lessee, in that the depreciation deduction may exceed the deduction for rental payments under a lease agreement for several years after the acquisition of an asset. But the 7% investment tax credit now provided under the Internal Revenue Code may offer benefits to both the lessor and lessee. The credit may be claimed by either, but of course not both. If the lessor claims the tax credit, he may give the lessee some of the benefit in the form of lower rental payments. This has the effect of spreading the benefit of the tax credit over a period of years for the lessee.

In some instances, the lessor has claimed the tax credit because the lessee could not take full advantage of it under the law, and then passed on some of the benefit to the lessee. For example, when a major airline placed a multi-million dollar aircraft order, it could not benefit directly from the tax credit because companies can deduct the cost of new equipment from their tax bills only up to $25,000 a year plus 25% of the company's tax liability above $25,000. The airline had heavy expenditures but a small tax liability, and so instead of buying the planes outright, it leased them from a syndicate of banks which could take full advantage of the tax credit and share the benefit with the airline in the form of lower financing costs.

LEASING BY BANKS

Commercial banks have financed equipment leasing for many years. Some of the oldest leasing companies have relied upon banks for operating funds, and banks have frequently looked upon such companies as attractive borrowers with highly acceptable collateral. Bank interest in lease financing was no doubt stimulated somewhat when the amendment of Regulation Q on January 1, 1962, resulted in a substantially larger amount of funds available for intermediate and long-term investment. But bank entry into direct leasing dates from the Comptroller of the Currency's letter of March 13, 1963, to the presidents of all national banks, in which he ruled that direct leasing of equipment constitutes "legal and proper banking activities for National Banks." A number of state banking commissions subsequently granted permission for banks under their jurisdiction to engage in direct leasing. Some of the larger banks immediately moved into the field, and the dollar volume of bank equipment leases quickly reached substantial proportions.

Banks have found many compelling reasons to engage in direct equipment leasing, but the strongest, apparently, is customer demand. Bank customers, noting the advantages of leasing cited above, have asked their banks to purchase equipment on their behalf. Banks have strong incentives to accommodate their customers whenever possible, especially when such accommodation brings respectable earnings, and lessees have been willing to pay rates resulting in attractive yields. Few banks, however, are in a position to offer leases comparable to those of large equipment manufacturers and suppliers. Since banks do not produce the equipment they lease and have no facilities for servicing it, they generally do not provide operating leases. Their activities are confined primarily to financial leases, similar in some respects to instalment or term loans. Financial leases frequently do not yield the tax benefits of an operating lease to the lessee, and the lessor does not claim equipment having a substantial residual value at the termination of the lease, but they still offer advantages for both parties. The lessee may obtain 100% financing, may improve the appearance of his financial statements, and in some instances may derive a tax advantage. The bank may be able to acquire business which otherwise would be lost, and may sometimes earn a higher yield.

Leases do not necessarily bring higher net returns than loans, however. Unless a bank handles enough leases to establish routines for processing them, costs may be considerably higher than loan costs, and may more than offset the difference in rates. The risk factor apparently is about the same as for a comparable loan. The risk of default is essentially the same in each instance. It depends on the ability of the borrower or lessee to pay, not on the type of instrument involved. In the event of default, the lessor, on the one hand, may have some advantage over the lender if the receiver rules that rental payments must be continued during the period of receivership. Such a ruling may be forthcoming if the business continues to operate, using the leased equipment. A lender in similar circumstances might have to wait until a reorganization has been completed or some other statement has been reached. On the other hand, the lender has the advantage over the lessor in that a lender qualifies as a general creditor, and may qualify for the payment of any unsatisfied balance after the disposal of equipment used as collateral, whereas the lessor can only reclaim the equipment in the event of a default on a lease. He has no claim as a general creditor.

For many banks, the departure from traditional banking practices inherent in direct leasing is great enough to discourage them from entering the field. They have found, however, that close affiliation with a nonbank leasing company may offer them the opportunity to meet the demands of their customers through traditional channels. The lessee leases the equipment from the leasing company, and the leasing company discounts the lease with the bank. Then the customer has his equipment, the bank has its loan, and the problems involved in making and servicing direct leases are avoided.

2

Deposits:

Acquisition and Administration

Outside variables and decisions by bank managers have contributed to significant changes in the structure of bank deposits. Furthermore, the acquisition and administration of changing types of deposits have posed new decision problems for bankers.

The first essay introduces this subject area by demonstrating the interactions among liquidity management and demand deposit fluctuations, as well as examining various factors that may explain the volatility of demand deposits. Identification of significant variables associated with deposit fluctuations enables bankers to manage their money positions more effectively.

Although based on banks in the Twelfth Federal Reserve District, the study of public treasurers' money by Ruth Wilson clearly has broader significance. This study, which examines various implications of public deposits for bank management decisions, presents the concept of collateral requirements and their relationship to bank liquidity. The next essay considers Treasury Tax and Loan Accounts as they relate to individual banks and the broader banking system.

Correspondent relationships are an important feature of American banking. Usually in return for deposit balances, large city banks provide services to smaller banks. The article published by the Federal Reserve Bank of Kansas City analyzes various facets of such correspondent relationships and provides some quantitative measures of their importance. Paul S. Nadler's article considers recent changes in correspondent relationships and suggests how such relationships may evolve in the future.

Negotiable certificates of deposit are one of the most significant recent developments in banking. The reasons for this new instrument are well presented in the article about the "creative response" of banks.

Relationships between banks and their depositors are explored in the concluding two articles. In addition to describing the role and implications of compensating balances, the essay by Jack M. Guttentag and Richard G. Davis introduces the concept of link financing. In an interesting brief paper, Neil B. Murphy provides an empirical test of the deposit relationship hypothesis.

Running the Bank's Money Position:

A Study of Demand Deposit Fluctuations

Neil B. Murphy and Paul S. Anderson

All bank assets and liabilities from cash in vault to net worth require careful administration. Loans are made and policed, securities are compared and bought, demand and time deposits are serviced and invested, and the net worth position is increased by retained earnings or stock sales as the bank grows.

At first glance we might assume that a bank's holding of cash in the vault and cash with other banks requires little attention other than bookkeeping. Such may have been the case in the easy money years of the latter 1930's and the 1940's. Cash was allowed to accumulate to high levels since the prevailing low interest rates provided little incentive for investment. But after interest rates began rising during the 1950's, bank attitudes changed. Excess cash meant the bank was losing money, so banks began to invest surplus balances.

The shift to investing surplus cash balances was not made without some cost, however. These excess balances were useful in that they took care of deposit fluctuations. For example, if a bank had $500,000 in excess cash, and suddenly deposits were withdrawn in this amount, the bank had no problem; the excess cash took care of this withdrawal. But when the excess cash was invested and then such a sudden withdrawal occurred, the bank had to scramble to replenish the withdrawn cash and reserves. The bank had to readjust its "money position."

Despite the adjustment problems brought on by a tightly-run money position, banks have found it profitable to invest surplus cash and accept such problems. As a result, a new job has been created at most banks, that of managing the money position.

The function of the manager of the bank's money position is to keep

Reprinted with the permission of the Federal Reserve Bank of Boston from *New England Business Review,* November 1967.

the bank's cash and reserve position down at the minimum, yet not let it run short so that required reserves are deficient or insufficient cash is on hand for withdrawals. The manager keeps a running record of the amount of cash and reserves the bank holds. When this amount becomes excessive, he invests the excess. He may lend reserves to other banks, a process called selling Federal funds. He may buy Treasury bills, commercial paper, bankers' acceptances or other securities. If the bank's cash position is too low, he reverses the above transactions. He may "buy" Federal funds, borrow from the Federal Reserve Banks, sell Treasury bills or commercial paper, and so forth.

DEPOSIT FLUCTUATIONS

What causes money positions of banks to be in excess one period and short the next? The major cause is demand deposit fluctuations. Changes in deposit levels are determined by the desires of depositors and all the bank can do is accommodate the flows.

Demand deposits flow into a bank when customers add to their accounts by depositing the proceeds from sales in the case of businesses, and pay in the case of individuals. These inflows depend on the volume of sales and income of customers. Deposits flow out when customers pay for their various purchases. Thus, inflows and outflows depend on the customers' situations and not on the bank.

Business conditions in a bank's service area naturally affect deposit levels. When business operations rise, demand deposits grow and vice versa. The connection between business activity and deposits is illustrated clearly by the banks located in vacation areas. As shown in Figure 1, demand deposits at Cape Cod banks rise sharply during the summer vacation months, reaching a peak after Labor Day. Then the decline sets in and continues until the next summer. The Cape Cod banks have to make large adjustments to accommodate this large seasonal inflow and outflow of deposits.

FACTORS IN DEMAND DEPOSIT FLUCTUATIONS

Although fluctuations in demand deposits lie largely outside the control of the bank, it is interesting to know what characteristics of a bank and its customers are associated with substantial fluctuations in the level of demand deposits. For example, bankers often claim that extremely large demand deposit accounts are risky because the owner can suddenly withdraw a large sum. From this we can ask the question, do banks with a larger average size of demand deposits have greater fluctuations in their total level of demand deposits?

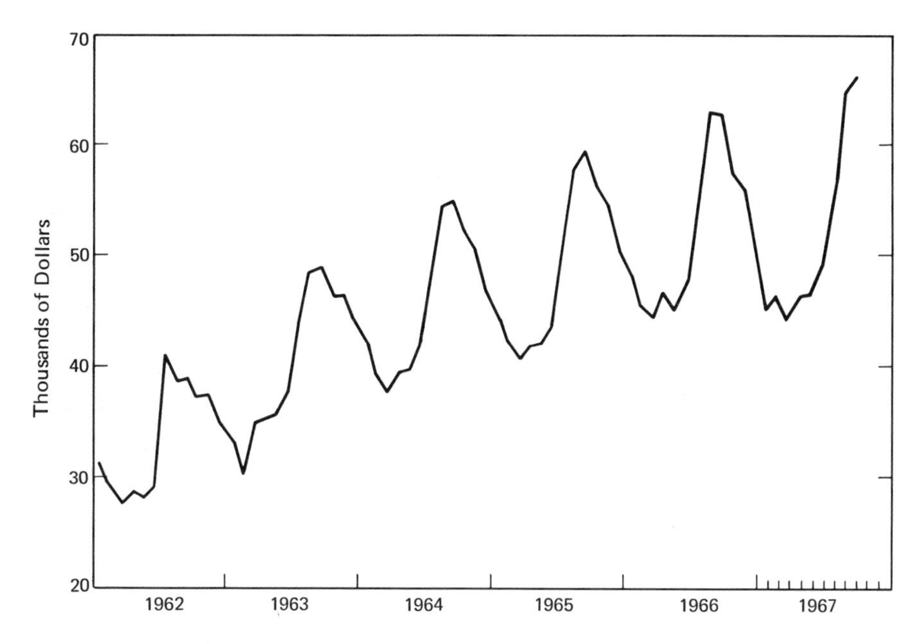

FIG. 1 Demand deposits of Cape Cod banks.
Monthly, 1962–1967

Note: Data are for all 6 member banks which are located in Cape Cod and report monthly averages of daily figures.

To answer this and similar questions, an analysis was made of the 1965 demand deposit fluctuations of 100 banks in New England which cooperate in the Functional Cost Survey conducted by the Federal Reserve Bank of Boston. Fluctuations were measured as the average percentage deviation between the actual level of total demand deposits in each 2-week period and the trend line of demand deposits for the year. For example, if the trend line indicated a level of demand deposits of $20 million for a 2-week period in June, while the actual was $21 million, the measured deviation would be $1 million.

The results of this analysis were rather surprising, both as to what factors seemed to lead to large fluctuations and what factors were associated in a statistically significant way with fluctuations or stability. One factor was the slope of the trend line. The steeper the slope, the greater was the deviation of the actual level of deposits from the trend line. The second important factor was the average size of deposit. The larger the average size, the less fluctuation there was around the trend line. Four other factors—the size of bank, the percentage of U.S. Government and interbank deposits, and the average activity of each account as measured by the number of checks drawn during 1965—were also considered. The more detailed analysis which follows shows that these latter factors appear to have little effect on fluctuations or stability.

SLOPE OF TREND LINE

It is not readily apparent why demand deposit fluctuations around the trend line were generally largest for those banks in the study which had the sharpest rise in the trend line. Perhaps this reflects a more dynamic growth situation and therefore more fluctuations.

Since this study was based on only one year, 1965, the trend line of deposits may not reflect true growth but only seasonal swings in deposits. Most banks have seasonal lows in deposits during the spring and early summer and highs in the fall and at Christmas time. Consequently a trend line for the year rises and the greater the seasonal swing, the steeper its rise. Seasonal swings do not follow a straight line trend, so the larger these swings, the bigger the departures from the straight line trend.

AVERAGE SIZE OF DEMAND DEPOSIT ACCOUNT

Contrary to expectations, the larger the size of the average demand deposit, the more stable the level of total demand deposits appeared among these 100 banks. Most bankers are quite aware of the potential risk of sudden withdrawal inherent in large deposits. Most also can recall instances where such deposits actually were unexpectedly pulled out, leaving the bank in a rather uncomfortable cash position.

But the 1965 experience of our 100 surveyed banks demonstrated rather conclusively that a large average deposit size is associated with stability in the total level of demand deposits. What might be a reasonable explanation? At first blush we might theorize that a large average deposit size reflects total bank size—large bank, large deposits. But bank size by itself was considered separately and was not significantly associated with deposit stability.

Perhaps a better explanation of the larger deposit/stability relation is that larger deposits are managed more carefully by their owners because it pays to do so while small deposits do not have the same profit potential. We can analyze this problem by noting that large fluctuations in the level of a deposit are more likely to reflect the fact that the holder allows the deposit to grow too large at times, rather than that he lets it get too small. For example, a business treasurer might decide that he must not allow the business' demand deposit to fall below $10,000. At times he may slip and allow it to fall to, say $1,000, an "error" of $9,000. But on the excess side, he might well allow the deposit to accumulate to, say, $30,000–$40,000 before taking corrective action. This would be an excess error of $20,000–$30,000, much bigger than the deficiency error.

The larger the average size of account, the more profitable it is for the holder to invest any excesses. Therefore a larger account would tend to be held pretty close to its desired level, while similar exactness—at least in percentage terms—would not pay with a small account. The other side of this problem is seen in time and savings deposits. Large time and savings deposits, like certificates of deposit, tend to be unstable, coming in for, say, 90 days and then being withdrawn. Such large deposits presumably come from the excess of a large demand deposit. Thus the large demand deposit remains quite stable and its possible fluctuations are shifted over to time deposits. The opposite is the case with small depositors—their savings deposits are stable but their demand deposits fluctuate.

SIZE OF BANK

Another unexpected result of the survey was that size of bank, as measured by total demand deposits, had little influence on demand deposit stability. It would have been reasonable to expect larger banks to have more stability, if only because the larger the bank, the more chance that a withdrawal from one account will be deposited in another account of the bank. Also with more industries and a wider area represented among a large bank's depositors, various seasonal influences might tend to offset one another.

Other surveys that have been made of demand deposit fluctuations have shown that larger banks have more stability. It may be that if the New England survey were repeated in another year, bank size would turn out to be a significant factor.

INTERBANK AND U.S. GOVERNMENT DEPOSITS

Neither the share of interbank nor of U.S. Government deposits was significantly associated with total demand deposit fluctuation or stability. This is quite surprising at first glance because both these types of deposits fluctuate a great deal. However, their fluctuations are largely offset by complementary fluctuations in other deposits, mainly of businesses.

U.S. Government deposits, termed Tax and Loan Accounts, rise when tax and loan proceeds are deposited. When a bank customer, especially a business, pays withheld and other Federal taxes, the amounts are simply transferred from the individual or business account to the Tax and Loan Account at the same bank. Thus no change in total demand deposits occurs. The same occurs when a bank customer buys a new U.S. Treasury security through the bank.

The U.S. Treasury withdraws money from these Tax and Loan Accounts as needed for expenditures. But these expenditures go to the public and are deposited back at the banks. So despite the fairly wide fluctuations in Tax and Loan Accounts, the impact on banks is small due to this offsetting.

Interbank deposits behave quite similarly to Tax and Loan Accounts. As an illustration, let us assume that Bank A, a small country bank, holds an interbank deposit in Bank B, a city bank. This deposit is built up when Bank A sends to Bank B checks for clearing drawn on Bank B and perhaps on other banks in B's city. Bank A's deposit is drawn down when customers of Bank B and other banks in B's city present to Bank B checks for clearing drawn on Bank A. Thus, when Bank A's interbank deposit goes up, other demand deposits at Bank B go down for a partial offset, and similarly with declines in Bank A's deposit.

Another factor lessening the impact of Tax and Loan and interbank deposits on the level of total deposits is their relatively small size. Neither makes up as much as 10 percent of total demand deposits at most banks.

DEPOSIT ACTIVITY

The average number of checks drawn per account had no influence on total demand deposit fluctuations of the banks in this study. This really is not surprising because the number of checks drawn simply reflects the nature of the depositor's business. Retail stores, for example, usually write many checks, but they also deposit their receipts daily so the balance may not change much even though the account shows a substantial amount of activity.

CONCLUDING COMMENTS

Demand deposit fluctuations are quite small at most banks, usually averaging for any 2-week period through the year between 3 to 6 percent of the level of deposits. Since the aggregate level of demand deposits in the country remains quite stable around its growth trend, the fluctuations occurring at individual banks reflect deposit shifts that take place due to ebbs and flows of funds arising from seasonal influences and payment patterns.

Regular deposit fluctuations are small and reversible, so they cause little harm except for exacting a little more effort by the bank in managing its money position. Much more serious a problem is the one-way trend that occurs during banking crises, as in 1929–1933. Such liquidation crises require wholesale conversions of relatively illiquid bank assets into cash. When such conversions were not possible, or required too great a capital loss, banks became insolvent or failed. The handling of such crises is beyond the scope of a bank's money manager. Such massive difficulties are better prevented by overall economic policies than cured after they occur. Preventive steps include of course adequate deposit insurance and bank supervision as well as general monetary and fiscal policies that promote financial stability.

TECHNICAL NOTE

This article is based on a statistical study of 100 New England banks for the year 1965. The regression equation which summarizes the findings is as follows:

Dependent variable: the ratio of standard error of estimate for a least-squares trend line fitted to 26 bi-weekly averages of daily demand deposit totals to the mean of the bi-weekly averages × 10,000.

Independent Variable	*Coefficient*	t-*value*
Mean of total demand deposits, in $1,000's	−.00078158	−0.95
Ratio of mean of interbank deposits to total demand deposits × 10,000	−.0968388	−1.29
Ratio of mean of U.S. Government deposits to total demand deposits × 10,000	.138527	1.00
Rate of growth; ratio of slope of trend line to mean × 10,000	5.80319	9.69
Average size of regular account	−.0406257	−1.97
Checks written per account	−.0833659	−0.14

Constant term = 249.536; $R^2 = .6748$; $N = 100$.

Public Treasurers' Money

Ruth V. Wilson

New departures in banking practices have been frequent in recent years as banks have attempted to maintain, or to improve, their competitive position vis-a-vis other financial institutions. On the asset side, banks have increased their penetration into the fields of long-term business lending, mortgages, and municipal financing; on the liability side, they have been more active in soliciting personal savings deposits and in obtaining funds through negotiable time certificates of deposit, capital notes and debentures, and unsecured notes. Not surprisingly, the resultant changes in the composition of banks' assets and liabilities have altered the reading of traditional measures of bank liquidity, so that it

Reprinted with the permission of the Federal Reserve Bank of San Francisco from *Monthly Review,* March 1966.

has become increasingly difficult to assess the margins within which banks can safely and prudently operate.

In this situation the past record of the pacesetting Western banks may provide a useful guide, since many of the recent developments have not represented as basic a change in banking practices for them as for banks elsewhere in the nation. In other words, what for some banks have been innovations have been for Western banks simply extensions of long-established practice—particularly in the time-deposits area. A major case in point is "public" time deposits—that is, time deposits of states, municipalities, and other governmental units (except the Federal Government).

ONE-THIRD OF THE TOTAL

Early in this cyclical expansion (June 1961) Twelfth District commercial banks accounted for one-third of total bank holdings of public time deposits. Their share of this category was even greater than their widely noted one-fifth share of savings deposits, and it was in striking contrast to their one-seventh share of total demand deposits. During the current cyclical upturn, District banks increased their holdings of public time deposits 61 percent, from $1.7 billion in June 1961 to $2.7 billion in June 1965. But banks elsewhere recorded an even faster increase, from $3.5 billion to $7.8 billion, so that the District's share dropped from one-third to about one-fourth of the total over four years' time.

These developments have brought several questions to the fore. Why have Twelfth District banks maintained such a large share of public time deposits over the years? Why have banks elsewhere evidenced such strong interest in such deposits during this cyclical expansion? How stable are such funds? And what effects do they have on banks' problems of liquidity?

DISTRICT DOMINANCE

District banks have built up their public time deposits largely because of deliberate policy decisions. They have been active in the solicitation of such deposits—as they have in the case of savings deposits and corporate time deposits—in order to meet the strong mortgage-financing demands generated by the rapid growth in the West. This development has been made possible, moreover, by the existence in most District states of legislation permitting the investment of state and local funds in interest-bearing deposits. Specific legislative or regulatory authorization is required before the funds of states and political subdivisions may be invested in the form of interest-bearing commercial bank deposits. Each District state, except Idaho, has long authorized such investment, and as a consequence, banks in practically every District state have substantial holdings of public time deposits.

On the surface it might appear that District banks built up these time deposits at the expense of their public demand deposits. In June 1961, for example, public time deposits in District commercial banks were 20 percent greater than public demand deposits, whereas public time deposits amounted to only one-half of public demand deposits at banks elsewhere. But legislation in all District states, except Arizona and Nevada, permits investment of public funds in other forms of interest-bearing assets (generally United States Government securities and municipal issues). Therefore, by accepting time deposits from public treasurers, District banks retained balances which might otherwise have been withdrawn for investment in securities. Thus, at a relatively early date, District banks faced, in connection with public deposits, the type of situation which in 1961 led major banks in the East to introduce negotiable time certificates of deposit in an effort to retain their corporate deposits.

SOLICITATION, LEGISLATION, AND . . .

Active solicitation of funds from states and political subdivisions and legislative authorization permitting investment of public funds in time deposits, therefore, were the basic factors supporting the large holdings of public time deposits at District banks throughout past years. In the 1961–1965 period, however, several other factors as well contributed to the very rapid growth in these deposits. Successive revisions in Federal Reserve Regulation Q allowed banks to pay higher rates on time deposits and thus to remain competitive in a period of rising money rates. These higher rates induced governmental units to invest more of their idle funds in interest-bearing certificates or open time accounts. In fact, state and local treasurers responded with alacrity to these higher rates and became increasingly alert to the earnings possibilities inherent in investing tax receipts between the date of collection and the date of disbursement. At the same time, increasing state and local budgets placed additional pressure on public treasurers to obtain interest income as a means of at least partially stemming steadily rising tax rates. Not surprisingly, then, District banks recorded a 61-percent increase in public time deposits as against an 8-percent rise in public demand deposits between June 1961 and June 1965.

Over the same period, commercial banks and state and local treasurers elsewhere realized the mutual advantages of public time deposits and began to follow the Western lead with enthusiasm. These banks outside the Twelfth District actually increased their public time deposits 121 percent over the four-year period, as against only a 13-percent increase in their public demand deposits.

Throughout the country there existed the same heavy demand for deposit money, the same rate competition among banks, and the same alertness by state-and-local treasurers to the investment possibilities of time deposits. Many banks that had not been interested previously in paying interest on corporate and public deposits finally shifted their policy and actively sought such deposits as a means of augmenting their loanable funds. In the West and elsewhere, banks were increasingly able to attract funds through higher and more competitive rates. Moreover, public treasurers throughout the country became increasingly sophisticated and enthusiastic about the investment of their idle balances. These developments influenced a number of states to enact new legislation (or to broaden existing legislation) regarding the investment of public funds in interest-bearing deposits.

SEASONALITY

In view of this growing dependence of banks on public time deposits, the question arises: How stable are such deposits as a source of loanable funds? How has District-bank experience differed from that of those banks which only recently have begun to move into this field? An analysis of weekly-reporting bank data shows a strong seasonal fluctuation in such funds at District banks, in contrast to a minor seasonal fluctuation and a very strong secular uptrend at banks elsewhere.

Public time deposits at District weekly-reporting banks displayed a distinct seasonal pattern in the 1961–1965 period (Figure 1). These deposits generally peaked in late January, then declined through March, rose again through May, and then dropped steadily until early November. In recent years, the January-March decline has averaged about 6 percent while the May-November decline has averaged almost 18 percent.

The regularity of this seasonal movement has given banks leeway to plan any adjustments in loan and security portfolios needed to meet the withdrawal of these time deposits. (The rising trend in public time deposits of course has eased this task even more.) Moreover, the seasonal peaks in public time deposits have come at very appropriate points of time, since they coincide with the two periods, in April and December, when passbook-savings accounts decline; in fact, as individuals withdraw their savings to pay income and property taxes, the banks recapture these funds in the form of public time deposits.

Public time deposits at banks elsewhere have displayed a smaller seasonal fluctuation, with a 6-percent average decline between April and July being followed each year by a general upward surge from August through March. The strong secular increase in this series has obviously obscured seasonal movements. But whatever the reason may be for the difference in seasonality, it remains true that Western public treasurers are quite accustomed to placing temporarily idle funds in time certificates. They normally deposit funds as collected and schedule the maturities of their certificates to meet expenditure needs. Treasurers elsewhere

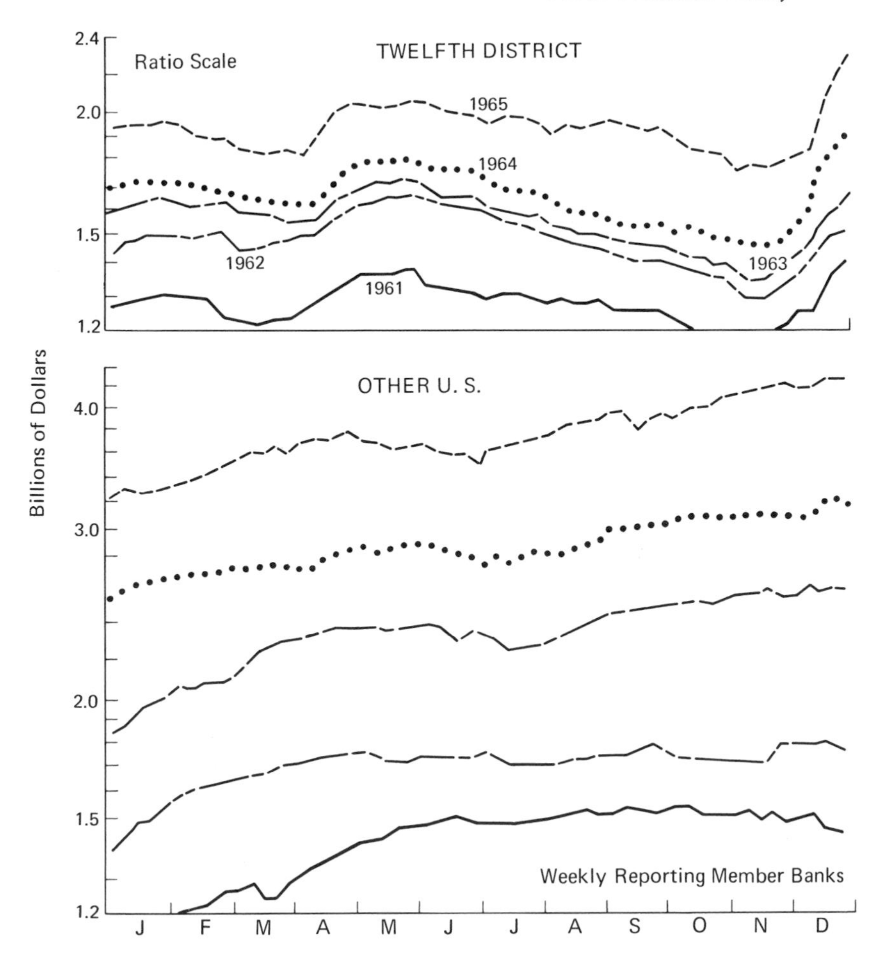

FIG. 1 Public time deposits grow rapidly, but with some seasonal variation.

have been more conservative in this regard, but the increasing seasonality in their deposits in 1965 suggests that they now are beginning to emulate their Western colleagues, depositing funds for shorter time periods than heretofore.

COLLATERAL AND LIQUIDITY

Public time deposits create few worries when allowance is made for the predictability of their seasonal fluctuations. Nonetheless, one aspect of public deposits—collateral requirements—raises important problems of liquidity.

Most state and local governments, along with the U.S. government, require commercial banks to maintain certain specific types of securities as collateral against their deposits. All Western states permitting such deposits (except Utah) require collateral ranging from 100 to 120 percent of the amount of public deposits. The state of California, which accounts for one-fifth of the national total of public time deposits, requires 110-percent collateral against deposited funds. Most District states accept a wide variety of securities for collateral purposes—direct and guaranteed obligations of the U.S. government, Federal agency securities, state, county, municipal and special district bonds, and state and municipal registered warrants. The amount of the collateral demanded sometimes varies with the type of security or with the measure of value (market or par value).

Collateral requirements are no problem when banks are highly liquid, with a high ratio of securities to deposits. But each successive business expansion over the postwar period has entailed a reduction in banks' excess cushion of securities, especially short-term governments. In the Twelfth District the proportion of banks' security holdings immobilized as collateral against Federal and public deposits increased from one-third in June 1961 to one-half in June 1965. (This assumes a 100 percent col-

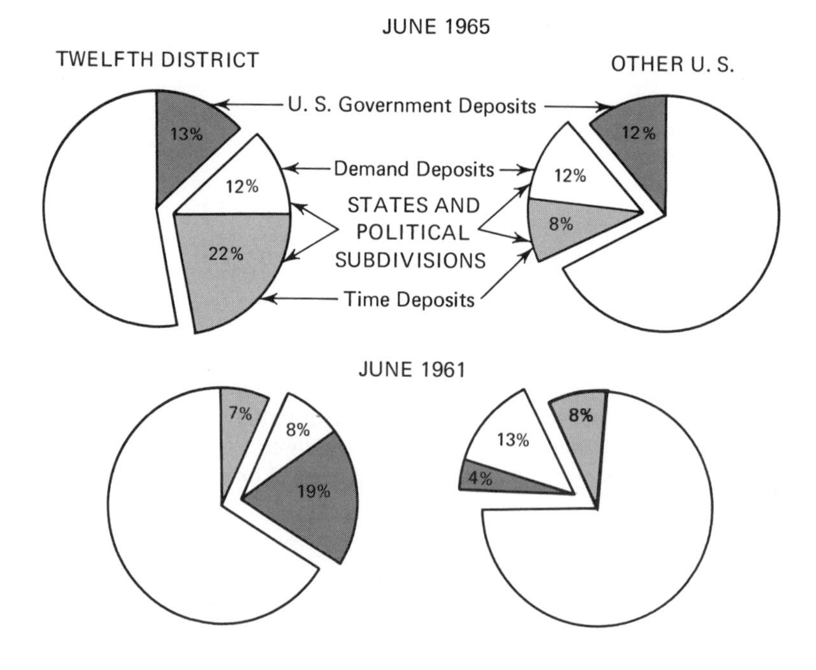

FIG. 2 District collateral requirements immobilize half of security holdings.

Note: Chart shows percentage of banks' security holdings required as collateral for deposits.

lateral requirement, although some states require more.) The increase in this ratio was largely due to the increase, from 15 to 22 percent, in the proportion of banks' security holdings pledged as collateral against public time deposits. Elsewhere in the nation the amount of collateral required against all Federal and public deposits increased from one-fourth to one-third of total security holdings in the 1961–1965 period. Thus, by mid-1965, banks elsewhere approached the one-third involvement that District banks had already reached in 1961 (Figure 2).

At a time like the present—with loan demand strengthening even after a five-year-long expansion, and with the loan-deposit ratio at the highest point since the 1920's—any factor that reduces banks' flexibility in handling their security portfolios also impinges on their liquidity. A security portfolio functions not only as a source of earnings or as a potential source of loanable funds, but also as a liquidity reserve available to meet large and unexpected demands on bank resources. For any individual bank, the margin of liquidity required varies with its asset and liability structure. But any prior demand on a bank's security holdings automatically reduces the flexibility needed for meeting potential liquidity requirements.

Meanwhile, from the standpoint of public treasurers, bank time deposits continue to serve as a worthwhile repository for temporarily idle funds. By placing these funds with banks, treasurers earn an attractive interest return—and, in view of the recent revision in Regulation Q, interest rates offered by banks should remain attractive because banks are presently able to offer rates competitive with other money-market instruments.

Treasury Tax and Loan Accounts

"There is no known mechanism for achieving the balancing effect on the money market now achieved by the Tax and Loan Account System. It is the object of study and, indeed, of envy, by the government of virtually every other large country today." So said Robert Roosa, Undersecretary of the Treasury, in 1962.

Reprinted with the permission of the Federal Reserve Bank of Richmond from *Monthly Review,* January 1966.

The bulk of the U.S. Government's cash operating balance is held in demand deposits, known as Tax and Loan Accounts, in about 12,000 commercial banks. While virtually all Government payments are made by checks drawn on its account with the Federal Reserve Banks, the supplementary depositary system enables the Treasury to maintain a minimum balance with the Federal Reserve, sufficient to cover its daily needs, and simultaneously to minimize the impact of its financial operations on the economic stability of the country.

RELATION TO THE MONEY MARKET

The Tax and Loan Account System is the means used for maintaining a smooth flow of funds from the general public to the Treasury and back again without causing seriously disruptive effects on the banking system and the money market. Government expenditures, tax collections and debt operations involve huge and irregular transfers of funds, many of which fall in certain months, and on certain days in the month. Because receipts and expenditures cannot be synchronized in offsetting amounts, Government financial operations would have an enormous impact on aggregate bank reserves if all funds flowed directly and immediately from the public to the Treasury's Federal Reserve account. This would occur because the Federal Reserve transfers funds by crediting the Treasury's account and debiting the member banks' reserve balances, or vice versa. Thus, Government receipts would drain reserves from the banking system, forcing banks to restrict credit without economic justification or to liquidate securities or short-term paper, thereby depressing security prices and raising yields. Conversely, a large outflow of Government expenditures would provide banks with an excess of reserves, and money market conditions would be suddenly, but temporarily, easy.

In the absence of Tax and Loan Accounts, the Federal Reserve could take action to offset the wide swings in reserves, but this arrangement would be less desirable than the present system for at least two reasons. First, it would be necessary for the System to increase significantly its role as a buyer and seller of Government securities, which it would prefer not to do. The smaller the System's role, the more accurately the market provides useful information about the demand and supply of funds emerging out of the nation's economic processes. In general, the System tries to hold its participation to a minimum consistent with its objectives of economic stabilization and orderly markets. Second, the absence of Tax and Loan Accounts would probably result in more massive shifts in reserves among banks than is presently the case. For example, large purchases of Government securities necessitated by an excess of tax receipts over disbursements would not restore reserves to their original location. Initially they would tend to be concentrated in the banks in the financial centers and would only gradually filter out to banks in other areas.

DEVELOPMENT

The Special Depositary system was devised during World War I to facilitate the sale of bonds necessary to finance the war. Under the terms of the First Liberty Loan Act of 1917, banks which purchased securities issued under the terms of the Act, for their own or their customers' accounts, could deposit the proceeds into special "War Loan Accounts." By leaving the proceeds from the sales on deposit in commercial banks until they were needed, the Treasury was able to insulate the money market, at least partially, from large inflows and outflows of cash, while providing banks with an incentive to sell bonds. While these deposits were not subject to reserve requirements, banks were required to pay 2% interest on them. Interest payments on all demand deposits, including the War Loan Accounts, were abolished by the Banking Act of 1933 and, in 1935, these accounts were made subject to reserve requirements.

Little use was made of War Loan Accounts during the 1930's, but with the advent of World War II they again became very active. To encourage banks to open these accounts reserve requirements against them were suspended between 1943 and 1947. In recognition of the high postwar levels of Government financing, Congress subsequently broadened the use of War Loan Accounts to include deposits of withheld income taxes in addition to proceeds from savings bond sales. In 1950 the Treasury provided for the payment of Social Security taxes through this mechanism, and changed the name to "Tax and Loan Accounts." Since that time other taxes have been made eligible for deposit in these accounts, such as Railroad Retirement taxes, and corporate and personal income taxes under certain circumstances. (The latter taxes are eligible when checks total $10,000 or more and the Treasury grants permission.) Also, to the extent authorized by the Treasury, banks continue to be permitted to pay for their own and their customers' subscriptions to Government marketable securities by crediting their Tax and Loan Accounts.

MECHANICS OF OPERATION

Although all incorporated banks and trust companies have been designated as Special Depositaries by the Secretary of the Treasury, banks must qualify individually to hold Tax and Loan Accounts by filing an application with the District Federal Reserve Bank. In the application, a bank must specify the amount for which it wishes to qualify, within the ceiling established by Treasury regulations. This ceiling is either 30% of the bank's total deposits, exclusive of Treasury Tax and Loan deposits, or 100% of its capital and surplus, whichever is greater. The 30% guideline is used most frequently.

One of the most important requirements for qualification is the pledging of collateral at least equal to that part of the Treasury deposit in excess of the $10,000 limit insured by the Federal Deposit Insurance Corporation. Although U.S. Government securities constitute the principal collateral for these deposits, a wide variety of other types of securities and paper have been pronounced "eligible" by the Treasury, such as obligations of U.S. Government Agencies, State bonds and high-grade corporate and municipal bonds, certain commercial and agricultural paper, bankers' acceptances, and notes representing loans guaranteed by certain U.S. Government departments and bureaus.

Once a bank has qualified to hold a Tax and Loan Account it may deposit proceeds from purchases of new Government securities in the Treasury account, when permitted by the Treasury. In order to receive deposits of Federal taxes, however, a second application must be made to the Federal Reserve.

For administrative purposes Special Depositary banks are classified in three groups, according to the total deposits credited to the individual Tax and Loan Accounts during the period September 1–November 30, 1964. Group A includes all banks which in this period received Tax and Loan deposits in amounts of $600,000 or less, Group B those which received more than $600,000 but less than $32,500,000, and Group C those which received $32,500,000 or more. In the calculation of deposit totals, however, deposits resulting from new Treasury financing or from Treasury adjustments of balances held with C banks are not counted. C banks, which number less than 100, hold about half of all Tax and Loan deposits. The Treasury withdraws funds from these banks by "calling" a certain percentage of the aggregate balance in each group, so that the same per cent is withdrawn from each bank within a group. Calls from A banks are generally made once a month, with partial payment required in a week and the balance in three weeks from the date of call; B calls are usually on Mondays and Thursdays with payment due in four or five days; and C calls are the same as B, except that "special" calls, redeposits, or cancellations of calls may be made at any time. "Special" calls must be paid the day of the call, and usually consist of a certain per cent of the previous day's balance.

In order to minimize fluctuations in total bank reserves, the Treasury endeavors to maintain its balance in the Federal Reserve Banks within a certain range. In fiscal 1965 it averaged about $850 million. Special C bank action is the principal means of adjusting for unexpected changes in this level. Thus, while all Treasury deposits are technically payable on demand, a large number of small banks actually hold relatively predictable balances, balances in larger banks are subject to wider swings on shorter notice, and a small number of very large banks may find their Treasury balances fluctuating sharply on a few minutes notice.

The volume of Tax and Loan Account receipts and disbursements has risen steeply since World War II. Receipts totaled $60.1 billion in fiscal 1965, up from only $8.6 billion in fiscal 1948. During the year balances

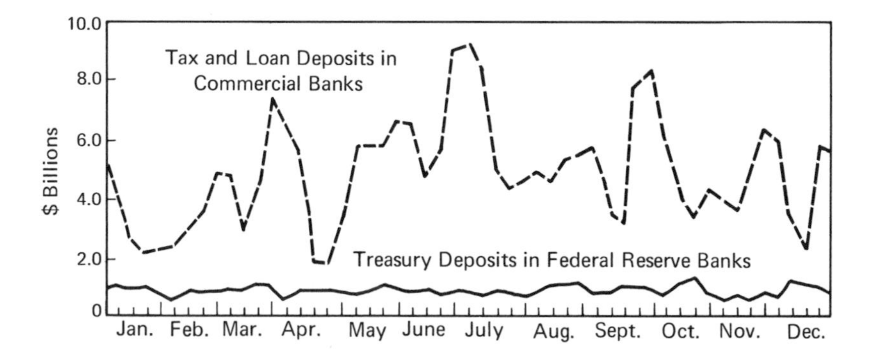

FIG. 1 Treasury operating balances, 1964.

Source: U.S. Treasury Department.

in these accounts fluctuate sharply with a strong seasonal pattern (Figure 1). The low point is usually reached in January and the high in June, when total budget receipts are the greatest. In the past two fiscal years this spread has varied from $2.5 billion to $10 billion. The balances also peak in March and September, due primarily to heavy corporate tax payments. Of the approximately $120 billion total cash budget receipts in fiscal 1965, about 48% were channeled into the Treasury through Tax and Loan Accounts. Most of the other receipts were deposited directly with Federal Reserve Banks.

COMMERCIAL BANKS AS FISCAL AGENTS AND UNDERWRITERS

Most banks perform a wide variety of services for the Treasury, regardless of whether or not they have a Tax and Loan Account. The most commonly performed services are:

1. Issuing and redeeming U.S. savings bonds.
2. Promoting new offerings of and handling subscriptions to U.S. securities.
3. Handling matured Government obligations.
4. Cashing Government checks.
5. Handling "Depositary receipts" relating to withheld income and other Internal Revenue taxes.
6. Reporting large or unusual currency transactions to the Treasury.
7. Submitting information returns to the Internal Revenue Service.
8. Submitting reports relating to certain financial activities of foreigners.
9. Processing letters of credit under programs sponsored by Government agencies.

10. Keeping records and filing reports in connection with the Treasury's Foreign Funds Control Operations.
11. Counseling the general public in regard to savings bonds and marketable Government securities.

All of these services are performed without direct compensation from the Treasury except the redemption of savings bonds, for which banks (per qualified paying agent) are reimbursed 15 cents each for the first 1,000 bonds, and 10 cents each thereafter, during the calendar quarter. While a bank may receive indirect compensation through the increased customer traffic which some of these services might generate, a Tax and Loan Account is profitable only if the bank works hard to build it up. By endeavoring to maintain a flow of funds through its Tax and Loan Account, a bank automatically increases its effectiveness as a fiscal agent for the Treasury while earning profits in connection with certain services which, for the most part, it would be rendering anyway.

In the absence of formal underwriting arrangements, the Treasury depends to a large extent on the commercial banking system for the efficient and successful marketing of Government securities. In the particular instances when the Treasury allows partial or complete payment for a debt offering through credit to Tax and Loan Accounts, however, banks become similar to "underwriters" in that their eagerness to acquire the securities assures the success of the offering. The best example is the sale of tax anticipation bills when Tax and Loan privileges are extended. Banks bid aggressively for these issues, for their own and their customers' accounts, and the resulting rates are much lower than on comparable outstanding issues. Thus, the Treasury incurs a lower interest cost than would otherwise have been possible. This is particularly true when banks are strapped for funds and would not ordinarily be interested in purchasing short-term Government issues.

Tax and Loan Accounts are not maintained to compensate commercial banks for their services to the Treasury, but rather to avoid the reserve fluctuations which would otherwise result from the Treasury's taxing, borrowing, and spending activities. They do, however, provide at least some offset to the cost of performing fiscal agency functions. According to the findings of two recent studies by the Treasury, the cost to the banking system of the services provided for the Government is slightly greater than the potential earning power of the Tax and Loan deposits.

Correspondent Banking

Stuart I. Greenbaum

Commercial banks sell their services to individuals, businesses, and governmental units. Among the business customers of many banks are other commercial banks. As customers, commercial banks purchase the same general types of services—clearing, depository, credit advice and supply, etc.—as nonbank businesses and individuals. Like other customers, banks pay for these services by maintaining balances with the seller as well as by making explicit money payments. However, the relationship between banks as producers of services and other commercial banks as purchasers of bank output is thought to have special importance because of its possible implications for questions of banking structure as well as monetary policy.

Apart from its special importance, correspondent banking is highly complex. Small country banks commonly maintain correspondent relations with 5 or 6 banks, whereas larger banks may maintain balances with 30 or more banks. Flows of services are frequently reciprocal and at times quite circuitous. Nevertheless, the flow of correspondent services through the banking system traces a perceptible hierarchical structure of banks. Small country banks generally maintain balances with a series of larger banks in regional financial centers. Banks in regional financial centers maintain balances with other banks in regional financial centers, as well as with banks in New York and/or Chicago. New York and Chicago banks will, in turn, maintain balances with banks in the national financial centers and also with banks in various regional centers. The intricacy of this network indicates the degree of indirection and complexity that interbank service flows can assume.

PRODUCTION VERSUS PURCHASE OF BANK SERVICES

The basic reason for the flow of services among banks is that in some instances commercial banks find it either impossible or relatively costly to produce certain services required by their customers. When a profit-

Reprinted with the permission of the Federal Reserve Bank of Kansas City from *Monthly Review*, March–April 1965.

conscious bank finds it cheaper to purchase a service from another bank than to produce that service itself, it will resort to a correspondent. In determining which banks are to produce a given type of service and which are to purchase the service, bank size and location appear to be of paramount importance. These two factors, it may be noted, are not entirely independent of each other, since banks rarely grow to great size in sparsely populated or commercially remote areas.

The importance of bank location is, perhaps, best exemplified by clearing services. A bank receiving a check drawn on another bank must arrange for transportation of the check to either the paying bank's premises or to some location where the paying bank maintains an account. If a country bank regularly receives a substantial number of items drawn on a city bank, it may become convenient to maintain an account with the paying bank and use its clearing facilities. Since the volume of clearing flows between banks generally is influenced by the pattern of commerce in an area, the decision to maintain a correspondent relationship derives partly from the geographic location of participants.

Bank size, the second major element rationalizing the production of bank services, appears to have especially pervasive implications for the structure of correspondent relationships. The importance of bank size derives largely from the connection between size and division of labor. Because banks produce such diverse financial services, substantial size is necessary to permit the specialization required to gain expertise in all phases of the business. If the required volume of business is unattainable, it becomes cheaper for a bank to purchase services from other banks with more highly developed facilities. Correspondent banking thus may be viewed as a means for circumventing some of the disadvantages inherent in small size. In effect, the larger bank stands ready to sell or rent factors of production or services flowing from these factors to smaller banks in smaller amounts than are otherwise available.

The following cursory description of selected types of correspondent services is meant to convey an impression of the scope and variety of such services, but is not an exhaustive listing of types of correspondent services. Following the descriptive material are sections devoted to interpretation of the meaning and importance of correspondent banking. Most of the discussion is focused upon the relationship between the small country member bank and larger banks in regional financial centers; however, parts of the discussion are equally relevant to correspondent relationships among other types of banks. Correspondent services will be conveniently, albeit somewhat arbitrarily, grouped under three headings: clearing services, asset management services, and other miscellaneous services.

CLEARING SERVICES

It is significant that a sizable proportion of Federal Reserve member banks prefer to sustain the expense of clearing through correspondents, even though Federal Reserve Banks provide clearing services at no additional cost, once membership has been established. Banks in regional financial centers actively solicit this type of business with notable success. For example, less than one fourth of the member banks in the Tenth Federal Reserve District cleared directly through the Reserve Bank during 1964. It may be assumed that the remainder rely primarily on the facilities of correspondents. On the other hand, city correspondents will submit many of the items originating with their respondents to the Federal Reserve Bank. Thus, the practice of clearing through correspondents will not necessarily result in a material reduction in the volume of clearings handled by the Federal Reserve System, but an element of indirection is introduced into the clearing process.

The ability of city correspondents to sell clearing services to member banks is partly explained by the inclusion of these services as an integral part of a package of highly diverse services that comprise the typical correspondent relationship. However, it is also true that clearing services provided by correspondents are differentiated from those offered by Federal Reserve Banks. For example, the Federal Reserve Bank may require some sorting of items submitted for collection, whereas correspondents commonly accept clearing items unsorted. Federal Reserve Banks will not generally accept nonpar or foreign items, while correspondents do not usually impose such restrictions. In addition, correspondents frequently provide immediate credit for all cash items, whereas the Federal Reserve Bank gives immediate, 1-day, or 2-day credit depending upon the location of the paying bank. The point to be emphasized is that city correspondents augment the clearing services offered member banks by the Federal Reserve System.

ASSET MANAGEMENT SERVICES

With regard to portfolio management, the small bank faces two major problems. First, it does not generate sufficient expert information internally, and second, it is forced to trade in relatively small units. In helping the small bank circumvent these inherent disadvantages, the city correspondent promotes two socially useful ends. Inter-area capital mobility is enhanced and the dissemination of economically valuable information is facilitated.

Expert information, purchased from a correspondent, may relate to problems as broad as the over-all structure of a bank's portfolio, or it may be confined to the merits of a specific municipal security. The intricacies of Treasury advance refundings and the creditworthiness of out-of-area loan applicants also serve as bases for exchanges of information. The city correspondent's highly specialized organization, as well as its numerous contacts with banks large and small, provide it with unique credentials as a purveyor of wide-ranging expertise.

The importance of trading units expresses itself in two ways. First, smaller banks occasionally are confronted by valued customers who wish to negotiate larger loans than these banks can legally or prudently make to any single borrower. These same banks, when in need of funds or outlets for the employment of idle funds, often find that the size of trading units in organized markets preclude their participation. The first type of contingency is often solved with a loan participation, whereby the city correspondent shares in the oversize loans originated by correspondents. The second type of problem may be dealt with by providing loans in which smaller banks may participate. In addition, correspondents may lend or borrow, using federal funds or other instruments, or they may buy or sell various types of earning assets. In effect, the city correspondent "makes a market" in various types of debt instruments designed to serve the needs of smaller banks. Depending on the needs and tastes of participants, the city correspondent may act as dealer, broker, or both. The importance of such a relationship is more fully appreciated by recognizing that assets flowing among banks are at times those for which there are no organized secondary markets.

MISCELLANEOUS SERVICES

In addition to the services already discussed, correspondents provide a group of miscellaneous services, some of which are used infrequently but remain crucial to the efficient operation of smaller banks. Examples of such services include trust and international banking, and consultation on management problems. Personnel problems of smaller, remotely situated banks are often particularly difficult. Correspondents commonly serve as a clearing house for higher level job applicants and openings at such banks. In addition, some smaller banks participate in the group insurance and retirement programs of city correspondents.

City correspondents also facilitate the exchange of equity in smaller banks by bringing together prospective buyers and sellers and by financing the purchase of stock. An indication of the importance of correspondents in financing equity transfers is suggested by a recent study done under the auspices of the House Committee on Banking and Currency. A questionnaire addressed to 6,200 member banks in 1962 revealed that 2,166 loans made by these banks were secured with 10 per cent or more of the equity in other banks. The preponderant majority of these loans was made in areas with large concentrations of relatively small banks. For example, banks within the Tenth District had 470 loans outstanding that were secured by 10 per cent or more of the stock of banks within the Kansas City District. Assuming no duplication, the banks whose stock served as collateral constituted more than one fourth of all commercial banks in the area. The purposes for which these loans were made were not disclosed, but it seems reasonable to expect that the borrowers had a wide variety of purposes. On the other hand, there is no reason to doubt that the acquisition of bank equity was one reason for borrowing.

The general acceptability of bank stock as collateral for bank loans has meaning beyond facilitating the transfer of equity. Since the market for the stock of small banks is not highly developed, owners may find it difficult to dispose of such assets on short notice without accepting sizable losses. So long as loans are readily available to those able to hypothecate bank stock, disposal of the stock on short notice becomes unnecessary. The ready availability of such loans may thus be viewed as enhancing the real rate of return on investments in bank stock.

Still other services commonly provided through correspondent relationships might be discussed in some detail. The provision of coin, electronic data processing services, and advice on building design and equipment are just a few. However, there is little point in trying to make this discussion exhaustive. The field is far too broad and simple enumeration of services conveys little insight.

AN INTERPRETATION OF CORRESPONDENT BANKING

The foregoing discussion suggested that the importance of correspondent banking results largely from economies of scale in the production of banking services. Since large banks can produce some types of bank output at lower cost than their smaller counterparts, the smaller bank can frequently purchase bank services at lower cost than it can produce them. Viewed in this way, interbank service flows become a type of "intermediate product," analogous to the semi-processed goods purchased by a manufacturer.

A measure of the importance of interbank service flows and a possible measure of economies of scale may be obtained by relating bank purchases of correspondent services to sales. Deriving such a measure is, however, complicated by a number of considerations. First, there are difficulties in measuring the volume of interbank service flows because payments for these services are made by explicit money transfers as well as by maintaining balances with the bank supplying services. The balances represent a type of payment "in kind" in which the medium of exchange is a factor of production, an ingredient used by the receiving bank in the further production of output. Surprisingly, "in kind" payments are easily estimated, but explicit interbank money payments are not. This stems from the fact that interbank balances are shown in Reports of Condition, but interbank payments are not generally shown, as such, in Income and Dividend Reports. However, the inability to measure explicit interbank payments may not be a major problem since they are generally far less important than "in kind" payments.

A distinction must be made between Federal Reserve member and nonmember banks in the interpretation of their interbank balances. The correspondent bank receiving balances invests the funds, allowing for reserve requirements, and the earnings on such investments constitute the payment received from its respondent for services rendered. The *member* bank maintaining correspondent balances could alternatively withdraw these funds and purchase earning assets itself, thereby augmenting its income. Thus, interbank balances represent forgone income to the *member* bank maintaining them, as well as a source of income to the depository bank. These balances are maintained in consideration of services received and, provided respondents are profit conscious, the amount of income forgone by the member bank maintaining such balances should not tend to be greater than its estimate of the value of services provided by the depository bank.

In the case of nonmember banks, however, it is important to recognize that their correspondent balances may serve as legal reserves. A nonmember bank that is fully "loaned up"—without excess reserves—will not effectively have the option of withdrawing its correspondent balances for the purchase of earning assets. It is reasonable to assume that these deposits would be maintained even in the absence of services provided by the depository bank. Thus, the nonmember bank holding interbank balances for reserve purposes does not thereby sustain an opportunity cost in the same way as the member bank.[1] Of course, in choosing among possible depositories, the nonmember bank will attempt to select the bank making the most generous offer of correspondent services. However, there is no compelling reason to expect the value of these services to equal the forgone income, as measured by the member bank holding such balances, unless the sellers of bank services are in highly competitive markets.

If strong competition is absent, depository banks need not pay as much —in services—for the correspondent balances of nonmember banks as they would for the balances of member banks. Whether depository banks in fact pay more or less for these deposits is not known. However, it seems reasonable to assume that the earnings a member bank might have obtained by investing its interbank balances, again allowing for reserve requirements, may be used as a measure of the lower limit of the value of services the bank receives from correspondents. On the other hand, such an assumption does not appear warranted when applied to nonmember banks.

A second problem in deriving a measure of the relationship between sales and correspondent services purchased relates to the measurement of bank sales. The major difficulty encountered here relates to problems of asset valuation—the treatment of capital gains and losses. However, detailed discussion of this problem is beyond the scope of this article. Current operating revenue—mainly interest and service charge income—

[1] This argument is predicated on the assumption that the marginal return on vault cash is zero and that banks do not have the option of holding their reserves in the form of earning assets. In cases where these two assumptions are not satisfied, the distinction between member and nonmember banks can be weakened or nullified.

will be used as measure of sales, while recognizing that the measure is not uniquely correct.

Figure 1 shows an estimated relationship between correspondent services purchased, or forgone income on interbank balances, and deposit

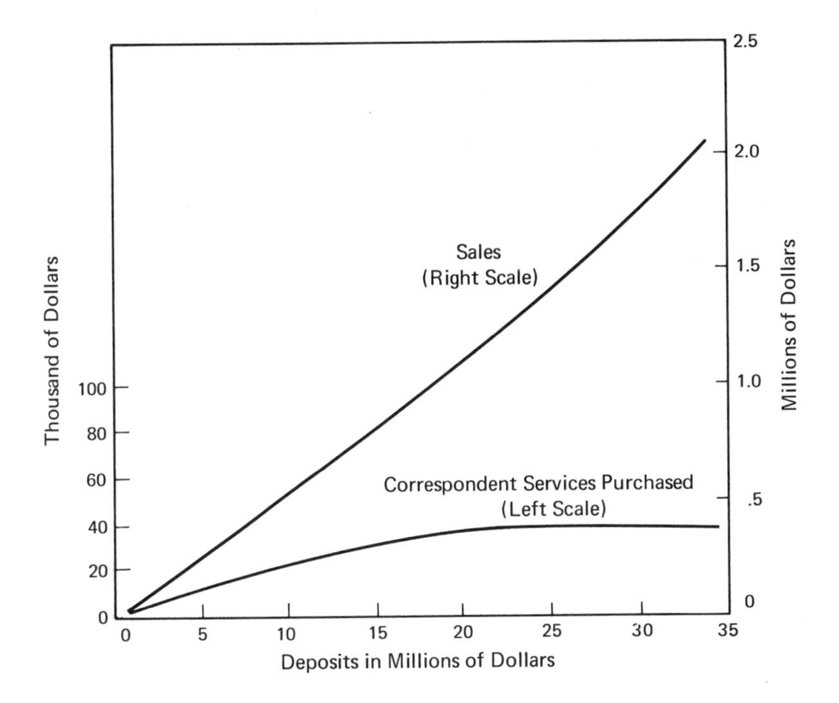

FIG. 1 Sales and correspondent services purchased related to total deposits.

Note: The relationship between correspondent services purchased and total deposits was obtained in three steps. First, a statistical technique—least squares regression—was used to estimate the relationship between demand balances with correspondents and total deposits. The fitted equation—shown in Technical Note 2—was then multiplied by a constant—1 minus the legal reserve requirement against demand deposits for country member banks (1.0 — 0.12 = 0.88)—in order to transform the equation into a relationship between the investible portions of correspondent balances and deposit size. (Correspondent balances are treated as deductions from total demand deposits in the computation of required reserves.) The final step involved multiplying the resulting equation by a second constant—3.5 per cent—which was an assumed value for the rate of return on highly liquid bank investments. This multiplication further transformed the equation into a relationship between forgone income, or correspondent services purchased, and deposit size.

size, for a sample of 602 country member banks in the Tenth Federal Reserve District. Banks in the sample ranged from approximately $0.5 million to $34.2 million in deposit size. The figure indicates that the smallest banks in the sample purchase about $1,400 per year in correspondent services. This value increases at a diminishing rate as deposits grow, and reaches a maximum of $38,500 for banks with deposits of $26.8 million. Thereafter, forgone income falls as deposits rise and at $34.2 million, the maximum deposit size in the sample, banks purchase approximately $35,600 worth of correspondent services per year. The remaining line in Figure 1 depicts the estimated relationship between sales —current operating revenue—and deposit size. (See Technical Note 2.) Sales rise at an increasing rate as bank deposits grow. A bank with $0.5 million in total deposits has estimated sales of $22,900 per year and banks of maximum deposit size—$34.2 million—show sales of $2.07 million.

Figure 2, which is derived from the equations depicted in Figure 1, shows forgone income and sales as a per cent of deposits, and forgone income is also shown as a per cent of sales. The figure indicates that forgone income declines as a per cent of deposits as bank size increases. For the smallest banks in the sample, forgone income on correspondent balances, or correspondent services purchased, amounts to 0.29 per cent of total deposits and for the largest banks the value is 0.10 per cent. In contrast, sales, as a per cent of deposits, rise consistently with bank growth, from a low of 4.6 per cent to a high of 6.1 per cent.

The line marked "correspondent services purchased/sales" is a lower limit estimate of the per cent of sales which are intermediate product— the resold output of other producers—for banks of varying deposit size. The equation underlying the charted relationship was obtained by dividing the correspondent services purchased relationship of Figure 1 by the sales relationship also shown in Figure 1. The resulting equation indicates that correspondent services become less important relative to sales as deposit size of banks increases. However, the ratio of forgone income to sales falls at a declining rate—there is a tendency for the line to flatten out—as deposits grow. For the smallest banks in the sample, 6.2 per cent of sales are intermediate product in the form of correspondent services, but only 1.7 per cent of sales of the largest banks are accounted for by purchased correspondent services. This relationship provides tentative corroboration for the economies of scale explanation for the importance of correspondent banking. As banks become larger, they produce an ever greater percentage of their sales. The derived relationship is also significant in that it provides a measure of the quantitative importance of correspondent banking for small banks in a unit banking environment. On the other hand, it may be worth repeating that the measure of correspondent service flows covers only that portion of correspondent services which are paid for by the maintenance of interbank balances among the sample banks. In addition, the rate of return used in deriving the forgone income measure was selected somewhat arbitrarily, and the measure of sales is not entirely unambiguous. These shortcomings are, how-

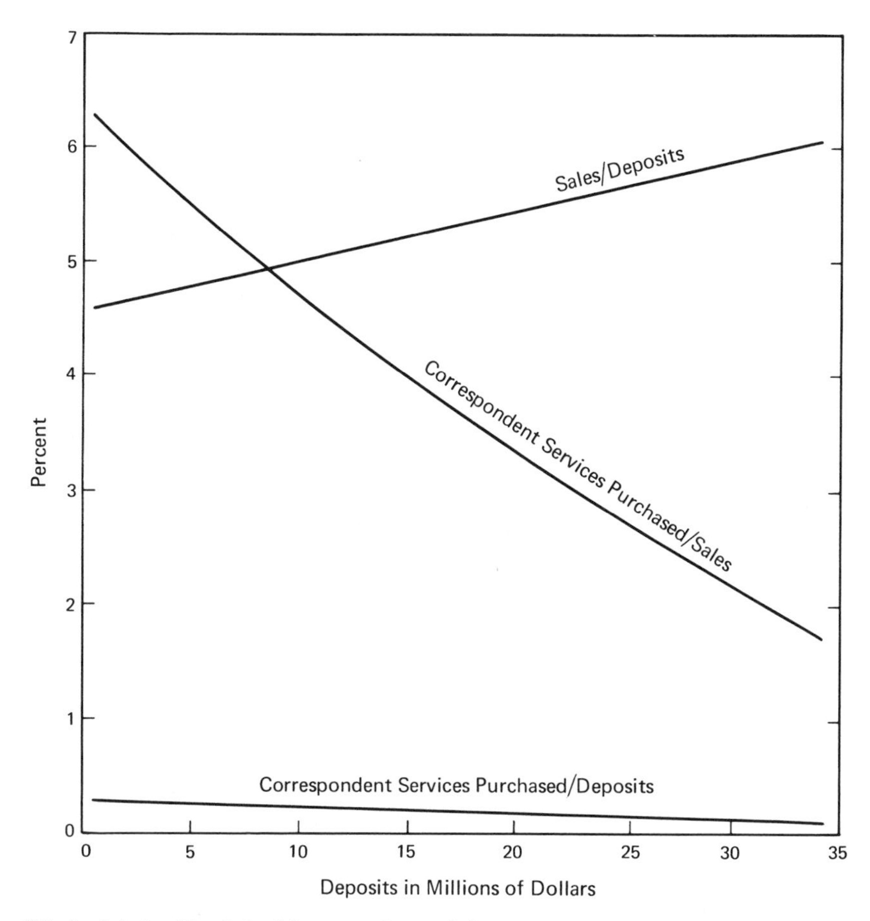

FIG. 2 Relationships derived from equations underlying Fig. 1.

ever, judged to be of relatively minor importance, and the contour of the derived relationship appears quite plausible.

EXPLICIT SERVICE CHARGES VERSUS THE MAINTENANCE OF BALANCES

To this point, the question of why banks apparently prefer to receive and/or make payments for correspondent services in the form of interbank balances has not been considered. If explicit and implicit payments were equal, banks might be expected to be indifferent to the form of payment. However, payment in the form of balances is rather general in banking. Services provided the U.S. Treasury are paid for by maintaining tax and loan account balances, and state and local governments commonly use the same means to compensate commercial banks. The role of compensating balance requirements in connection with loans is also analogous to the part played by interbank balances in connection with correspondent relationships. Thus any explanation of implicit payments in correspondent banking may be expected to have wider relevance.

Any one or a combination of three explanations may account for the use of implicit payments in correspondent relationships. First, the legal prohibition of interest payment on demand deposits exerts an important influence. Since deposits represent a productive input to the individual bank, banks seek to purchase them. Prohibition of interest payments precludes effecting such transactions in the conventional manner—through money payments—and thus banks remunerate their suppliers with services.

A second explanation, suggested by bankers, relates to the importance of deposits, apart from the considerations of short-run profit maximization. Some bankers argue that given the choice between implicit and explicit payments in equal amount, they would prefer implicit payment because it fosters deposit growth. The importance of deposit growth stems from its conventional use as a measure of management acumen. Its use as such may be rationalized by arguing that deposit growth provides a foundation for the future growth of earnings. Banks may even trade off current earnings to achieve a desirable rate of deposit growth, in which case the suppliers of deposits could benefit from the use of an implicit payment system. Correspondent services may be obtained at lower cost to the respondent than would be the case under a system of explicit payments. On the other hand, in the absence of the legal prohibition of interest payment on deposits, interest rates presumably would reflect the special value of deposits to banks.

A third reason for implicit payments may be found in bankers' preference for nonprice forms of competition. It has been argued that unbridled price competition imparts a destabilizing influence to the banking system, and thus has generally deleterious implications for the economy. Setting aside the question of the validity of such arguments, implicit payments can be explained by a general aversion to price competition. Although all three suggested explanations for implicit payments are potentially important, the first—the legal prohibition of interest payment on demand deposits—appears most compelling because of its obvious impact. The actual relevance of the other explanations is more open to question.

Consider the case of nonmember banks where the opportunity cost of maintaining interbank balances is zero, assuming such deposits are used to satisfy legal reserve requirements. If correspondents earn 4 per cent on such deposits, they will be able to provide services worth any amount between zero and 4 per cent of balances and both banks will find the relationship profitable. Assume, for the purpose of discussion, that the correspondent pays the respondent 2.5 per cent—in the form of services—on interbank balances. The respondent is thus earning 2.5 per cent on its legal reserves which, in effect, have no earning power in alternative uses.

The correspondent also finds this arrangement advantageous in that it profits to the extent of the spread between the earning power of the deposits—4 per cent—and the cost of providing correspondent services—2.5 per cent—to its respondent. In highly competitive markets the value of correspondent services would be expected to approximate 4 per cent on balances, while in other circumstances some intermediate value might be arrived at through negotiation. In any case, the value of correspondent services might be expected to remain meaningfully above the zero floor because smaller state banks have the alternative of membership in the Federal Reserve.

The situation of member banks is altered in detail, but remains essentially the same. The difference stems from the fact that interbank balances of member banks serve as secondary reserves and the opportunity cost of maintaining interbank balances thus approaches the yield on highly liquid earning assets, say 3.5 per cent. This means the member respondent must receive services worth in excess of 3.5 per cent on balances to make the correspondent relationship attractive, whereas any nonzero return may satisfy the nonmember respondent. On the other hand, in highly competitive markets all respondents will be offered approximately 4 per cent—the assumed value of such balances to city correspondents—and the member-nonmember distinction will be inconsequential. But if such circumstances do not prevail and correspondents are able to treat different customers differently, the member bank may be able to command a somewhat higher return on its interbank balances.

CONCLUSION

The discussion presented thus far has touched many bases, several of them somewhat technical. In concluding, a few broad generalizations may be useful.

Many students of banking structure have argued the advantages of branch banking by alluding to economies of scale in the production of commercial bank services. Much of the foregoing discussion suggests that correspondent banking is a potentially effective means for circumventing these inherent disadvantages of small-size banking firms. To the extent that correspondent banking is an efficient system for the production and distribution of bank output, the advantages of branch banking attributable to economies of scale may be seriously weakened.

In serving commercial banks, correspondent banking mobilizes interarea flows of capital, other factors of production, and information. It effectively integrates the banking system and in doing this it represents a cogent alternative to branch, group, or chain banking. On the other hand, there is reason to question the viability of unit banking in the absence of well-developed correspondent banking institutions.

TECHNICAL NOTES

1. The sample of banks employed in the regression equations consists of all (602) country member banks in the Kansas City Federal Reserve District with correspondent deposit liabilities of less than $100,000. Earnings data were taken from individual bank Income and Dividend Reports for the year, 1963. Deposits data came from Reports of Condition for year end 1963.

2. The regression equations used in Figure 1 were as follows:

$$C = .2766\,(10^{3}) + .9342\,(10^{-1})\,D - .1744\,(10^{-6})\,D^2$$
$$(.2483\,(10^{3}))\quad(.6770\,(10^{-2}))\quad(.2875\,(10^{-7}))$$
$$R^2 = .4423$$

$$E = .7678\,(10^{2}) + .4567\,(10^{-1})\,D + .4345\,(10^{-7})\,D^2$$
$$(.4816\,(10^{2}))\quad(.1313\,(10^{-2}))\quad(.5575\,(10^{-8}))$$
$$R^2 = .9506$$

where C is demand balances with banks in the United States (excluding reciprocal balances), E is current operating revenue, and D is total deposits. R^2 is the coefficient of determination adjusted for degrees of freedom. Values in parentheses below the regression coefficients are standard errors of the coefficients. Neither intercept is significantly different from zero at the 10 per cent level. They were consequently assumed to be zero in plotting the equations in Figures 1 and 2.

3. The cubic form of deposits was tested as an explanatory variable but its coefficient was not significantly different from zero.

4. The relationship between C/E and D as shown in Figure 2 was derived from the two equations shown in note 2. C/E was also independently regressed upon deposits. The resultant equation was cubic in deposits. C/E fell at a falling rate and then at an increasing rate as deposits grew. This equation indicated C/E was slightly higher at low levels of D and slightly lower at high levels of D than is the case in Figure 2.

The Coming Change in Correspondent Relationships

Paul S. Nadler

As commercial banks learn more about their true costs of operation, one result may well be the reduced importance of correspondent banking.

A lessened reliance on correspondent relationships would come to many as a surprise. For it would appear that large banks are always anxious to develop new correspondent balances, while small banks rely on their bigger correspondents for a vast variety of services.

Yet the available statistics already indicate that the role of correspondent balances in the total banking scene has declined markedly in recent years. While interbank demand deposits were equal to 13.4% of all other demand deposits and comprised 8.9% of all bank deposits at the end of 1947, by the end of last year these interbank deposits were equal to only 10.2% of all other demand deposits and comprised only 5.1% of all commercial bank deposits.

What is far more significant, though, is that large banks may well become less and less anxious and willing to maintain correspondent relationships with smaller banks unless these smaller institutions act to make their correspondent relationship more profitable to the larger banks.

The reasons for the sharp decline in correspondent balances as a percent of total commercial bank deposits are not hard to fathom.

The most obvious reason is that the bulk of bank growth is now in the time and savings deposit area, and smaller banks need far less in the way of correspondent services to handle this time and savings business than they need to process demand deposit transactions. Thus, as bank time and savings deposits have grown, banks have not increased their correspondent balances commensurately with this growth.

DWINDLING BALANCES

But many smaller banks have had other fairly good reasons to reduce the amount of funds they maintain in correspondent balances with larger

Reprinted with permission from *Banking,* Journal of The American Bankers Association, April 1966.

institutions in recent years. Prime among these is the steady rise in the cost of money, which has sharply increased the value of the money left with correspondents. Treasury bill rates for example, never averaged as much as 2% in the 20 years ending with 1955, while new rates average more than double this figure. Thus many smaller banks have decided that they should cut their correspondent balances and put the surplus funds residing in these balances out in earning assets.

As this trend has developed, it has been stimulated further by bankers themselves, by bond dealers, and others who have tried to win the goodwill of smaller bankers by teaching them how to use their excess reserves more profitably. The development of smaller-sized transactions in Federal funds trading has also furthered this trend.

Finally, even the trend of merger among larger banks seen in recent years has lessened the role of correspondent balances. For many a smaller bank has maintained a policy of keeping a fair-sized account in each major bank in the central city of its trading area. Thus when two of these majors merge, the smaller bank's usual reaction has been to maintain one account in the merged bank that is considerably smaller in size than the combination of the two accounts formerly held.

Thus many smaller banks have been paring the size of their correspondent balances, while most correspondents have not been increasing the size of their balances to match deposit growth. Were membership in the Federal Reserve System made mandatory for maintenance of Federal deposit insurance, as some have suggested, this trend would be stepped up enormously. For a good portion of the correspondent balances maintained today comprise the required reserves of nonmember banks. And while these nonmembers would leave something in correspondents were they required to maintain their legal reserves at a regional Federal Reserve bank, the amount that would be maintained would be curbed sharply. But even without this structural change, the trend toward reduction in the percentage of total deposits smaller banks are willing to keep at correspondent banks is bound to continue.

But far more significant to the long-range role of correspondent banking is a second question that is just beginning to come to the forefront. Are correspondent relationships profitable to the larger banks that up to now have so aggressively cultivated them?

UNPROFITABLE RELATIONS

Some top officers of major banks admit privately that they have a number of correspondent accounts that are not profitable. Some have gone so far as to indicate, again in confidence, that once they finish their cost studies and are sure of their figures, they will be willing to drop some of these correspondents if they are not willing to raise the profitability of their accounts to the larger bank.

But far more basic as evidence of the unprofitable nature of many correspondent accounts to the banks that are in the correspondent business are the results of the Survey of Banker Opinion on Correspondent Relations conducted by the Subcommittee on Domestic Finance of the House Banking and Currency Committee under Representative Wright Patman, published in October, 1964. For in it, the overwhelming majority of smaller bankers reported that they were happy with correspondent relationships, but would not be willing to pay a direct fee for the services they now receive.

THE CASE FOR FEES

This is the point that makes the observer question the profitability of correspondent banking to the large bank. For it would appear that the small bank, anxious to maximize its profits, would prefer to pay with fees instead of balances for its correspondent services.

The case is easy to prove. A bank in a smaller city can lend out its funds in loans that yield it net anywhere from 4% to 6% or more after costs. Yet when it leaves this money in a correspondent bank, it is given a credit on it that at best approximates 3.5% or 4%, and this only after 20% or 25% of the balance credit is deducted to cover reserve requirements, cash needs, and other liquidity reserves the larger correspondent must maintain behind the balance.

One would think, then, that a smaller bank would be delighted to leave nothing in its correspondent account, compensating the correspondent with a fee for the services rendered instead of leaving a balance that earns so much less than the bank could earn using the money itself.

The answer to this apparent paradox is that the banks maintaining correspondent balances obviously feel that if a fee system were established, they would have to maintain fully compensatory fees. While now, with a balance system, the balances are negotiable and often can be well below the amount that would be necessary to compensate the correspondent fully for services rendered.

WHAT BANKERS SAY

As it was expressed by one respondent to the Patman survey—from a bank in the $10- to $50-million range:

"Selfishly, because of competition, a cost-conscious country bank can 'underpay' for services rendered, or at least keep costs at a minimum. The eagerness of correspondent bankers for balances causes them to perform many favors and services they might not perform under a fee schedule. We feel also that many services of a somewhat intangible nature, which we now receive, would be discontinued under a fee plan."

And as another banker from an institution of the same size range put it:

"I believe, if explicit fees were charged generally, many small banks with nominal earnings would hesitate to ask correspondents for advice or assistance in various matters, which, in my opinion, would be harmful to the banking system as a whole."

Thus it is not hard to conclude that if many smaller banks feel that their accounts are not profitable to the major correspondents, it will not be long before some of these majors decide that they have little to gain from maintaining such a relationship.

But another trend that may well further a change in correspondent banking is the new approach in banking of buying growth when loan demands are strong. Because of the development of the negotiable time certificate of deposit, the consumer savings certificate, and other time deposit forms that attract money from well outside of a bank's own territory, many banks have found that their growth is limited not by the availability of deposit funds in their communities, but rather by the strength of loan demands. For if loan demands are strong and returns available on lending are profitable, these banks find they can usually attract enough money to meet these demands, simply by making their time certificate interest rates attractive enough and promoting their time deposit business more aggressively.

AN IMPORTANT TREND

This trend could have a considerable impact on the correspondent business; for in many cases the banks that can buy their growth find that the potential for loan demand growth is greatest not in their immediate territories of operation, but rather in the territories served by some of their correspondents.

The result of this could well be a dual trend in correspondent banking. In those cases in which the local correspondent is doing a good job of meeting local loan demands, the major bank undoubtedly will take the viewpoint that there is nothing to be gained by competing in this territory. Thus with the smaller bank generating the loans and the bigger one able to generate the deposits through the practice of buying growth from outside its territory, a natural bond of cooperation in loan participation develops, which should strengthen the correspondent relationship rather than weaken it.

AN ALTERNATE APPROACH

But in those cases where the smaller correspondent is not serving the loan needs of its community, the larger bank may well feel that it is more profitable to have the correspondent's customers than his balances. In this regard this is similar to the switch which commercial banking took from its former posture of being very cautious in soliciting savings deposits for fear of alienating savings bank and savings and loan depositors to its present position of much preferring the funds of the savings institutions' customers to the balances of the savings banks and savings and loans themselves.

In those cases in which the larger bank finds that the smaller correspondent's account is not very profitable or actually generates a loss, there should be even less hesitancy to break the relationship and compete for the former correspondent's loan business.

This trend obviously will not develop overnight. For, in the first place, banks will try to make their correspondent accounts more profitable instead of just breaking the relationship if they see that the current status is unprofitable. In addition, most major banks would move extremely slowly in competing with present or former correspondents for fear of alienating other correspondents whose accounts are profitable.

But already there is considerable evidence of correspondent banks trying to carry water on both shoulders—by catering to their own smaller correspondents at the same time as they try cautiously to win away some of their correspondents' own customers.

The trend toward buying growth makes many a correspondent's territory approachable through the routes of soliciting money into certificates of deposit and of sending loan officers into this territory even though the bank is not allowed to open a branch there. And at the same time, the developing studies on bank costs indicate that many correspondent relationships are far less profitable to the major bank than supposed.

Thus it is not far-fetched to conclude that a major shake-up in the whole practice of correspondent banking is on the horizon.

When it is over, many banks that have relied on correspondents for services they could not really afford may well decide that the merger and holding company routes to obtaining services are more palatable than formerly believed. Others may well develop more cooperative action between several banks to provide on their own some of the services that correspondents now give them.

The result should be, then, even further decline in the relative importance of correspondent balances in the total picture of bank deposits.

But those correspondent relationships that do remain are likely to be less shaky and more profitable.

Sources of Commercial Bank Funds:
An Example of "Creative Response"

This article considers the growing importance of newly innovated sources of commercial bank funds. It thus is concerned with the "creative response"[1] of an industry—in this case, commercial banking—to a new environment in which old or traditional ways of conducting business will no longer produce the same results. In other words, the article examines what banks have done to attract funds in a period when traditional ways proved less than adequate.

Innovation, which is doing something new or doing something old in a new way, arises usually out of need. This is true of innovations in managerial structure, in production, in marketing, and in finance—to mention only a few areas of activity closely associated with the economic process. The case of commercial banking conforms to the pattern of doing something new or doing something old in a new way.

COMMERCIAL BANKING SINCE WORLD WAR II

Since the end of World War II, commercial banks have declined in importance relative to other financial institutions, continuing a trend that originated around the turn of the century.[2] While commercial banks have grown in size and are still the nation's leading financial intermedi-

[1] The term is borrowed from Joseph A. Schumpeter, "The Creative Response in Economic History," *Journal of Economic History,* Vol. VII, November 1947.

[2] See Raymond W. Goldsmith, *Financial Intermediaries in the American Economy Since 1900* (Princeton, New Jersey: Princeton University Press, 1958).

Reprinted with the permission of the Federal Reserve Bank of Cleveland from *Economic Review,* November 1965.

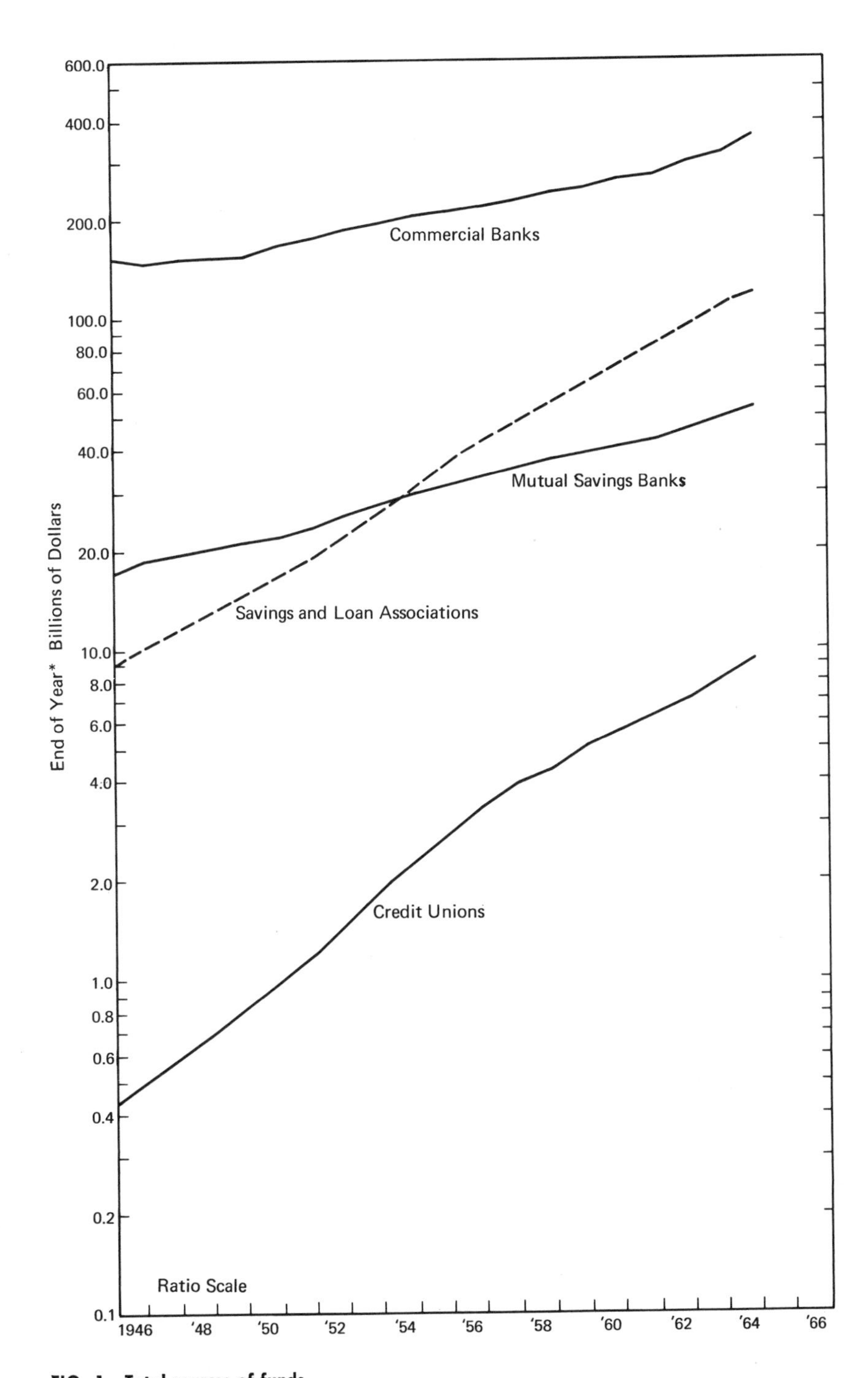

FIG. 1 Total sources of funds.
Deposit-type financial institutions.

* Last call report of year for commercial banks.
Sources of data: Federal Deposit Insurance Corporation; U.S. Savings and Loan League; National Association of Mutual Saving Banks; Credit Union National Association data.

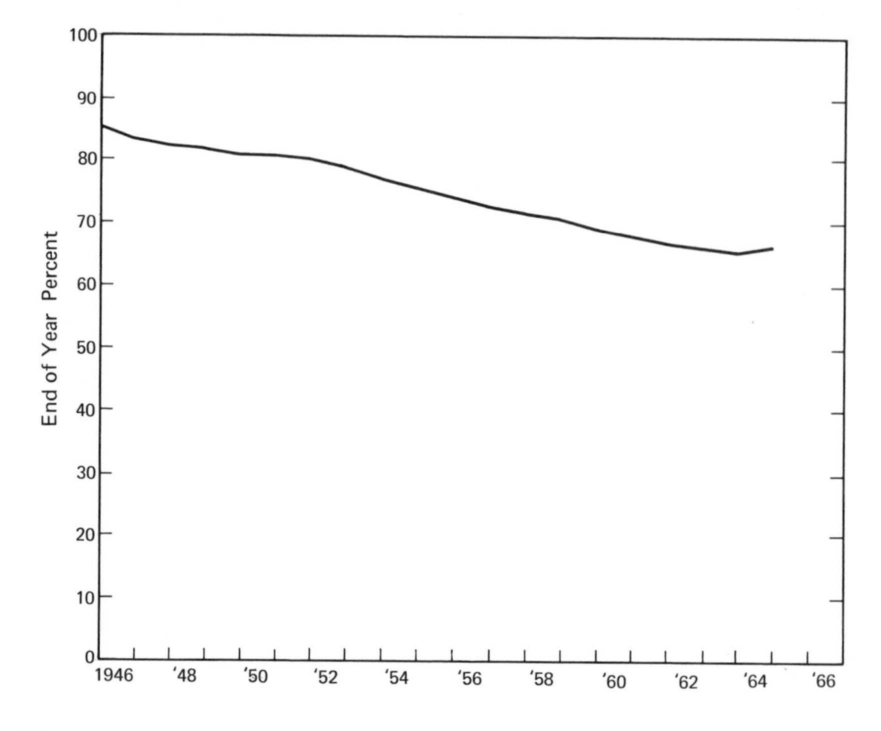

FIG. 2 Proportion of total funds of deposit-type financial institutions accounted for by commercial banks.

Source of data: Federal Deposit Insurance Corporation.

ary, their growth has not kept pace with that of other private deposit-type financial institutions.[3] This is shown in Figure 1. Whereas over the 20-year period since World War II, total sources of funds of commercial banks rose about 120 percent, those of mutual savings banks more than tripled, those of savings and loan associations increased more than twelvefold, and those of credit unions, though still relatively small in absolute size, increased some twentyfold.

Put otherwise, while commercial banks at the end of 1945 had held 86 percent of the financial resources of all deposit-type financial institutions, the share had dropped to 65 percent at the end of 1964. In each year through 1963, as shown in Figure 2, financial resources of commercial banks—the total of liabilities and capital—constituted a smaller proportion of the total resources of all deposit-type institutions. In 1964, however, there was the first sign of a change in this pattern. Thus, in 1964 for the only time since World War II, commercial banks succeeded in maintaining—in fact, slightly improving—their relative position. As a

[3] In this article, commercial banks are compared only with other deposit-type institutions. A broader comparison with nondeposit-type financial institutions, for example, insurance companies and pension funds, would yield conclusions similar to those of this article.

result, at the end of the year, sources of funds of commercial banks comprised a slightly larger portion of the total resources commanded by all deposit-type institutions than at the end of 1963—65.37 percent in 1964 against 65.35 percent in 1963.

The primary factor underlying the relatively poor showing of commercial banks in the postwar period perhaps has been the change in attitude of both businesses and individuals toward holding demand deposit balances. Both have become increasingly aware of the income foregone by holding temporarily idle funds in the form of "money" or, more specifically, as demand deposits; both have correspondingly become increasingly disinclined to do so. This is evidenced, in part, by the rapid growth of other deposit-type claims, which in turn reflects the public's desire to hold liquidity in income earning forms. Thus, as indicated in Figure 3, demand deposit liabilities of commercial banks over the last 20 years have grown at an average annual rate of only 2.1 percent; this contrasts sharply to average annual growth rates of 7.5 percent for time and savings deposits at commercial banks, 6 percent for mutual savings deposits, 14 percent for savings and loan shares, and nearly 17 percent for credit union shares. On the other side of the ledger, and as shown in Table 1, demand deposit and currency holdings of nonfinancial corporations have grown less rapidly than have their holdings of total financial

Table 1 Holdings of Financial Assets by Nonfinancial Corporations

Year	1 *Demand Deposits and Currency (billions of dollars)*	2 *Total Financial Assets (billions of dollars)*	3 *One as a Percent of Two*
1946	$21.2	$ 74.0	28.6%
1947	23.4	81.2	28.8
1948	23.6	86.6	27.3
1949	24.7	90.7	27.2
1950	26.2	107.5	24.4
1951	27.9	116.1	24.0
1952	28.7	122.1	23.5
1953	28.8	125.2	23.0
1954	30.9	130.3	23.7
1955	31.9	147.7	21.6
1956	32.1	153.0	21.0
1957	32.1	158.1	20.3
1958	33.5	170.0	19.7
1959	32.5	183.4	17.7
1960	32.1	191.4	16.8
1961	33.7	208.4	16.2
1962	34.5	224.4	15.4
1963	32.0	241.7	13.2
1964	32.5	260.7	12.5

Source: Flow of funds data, Board of Governors of the Federal Reserve System

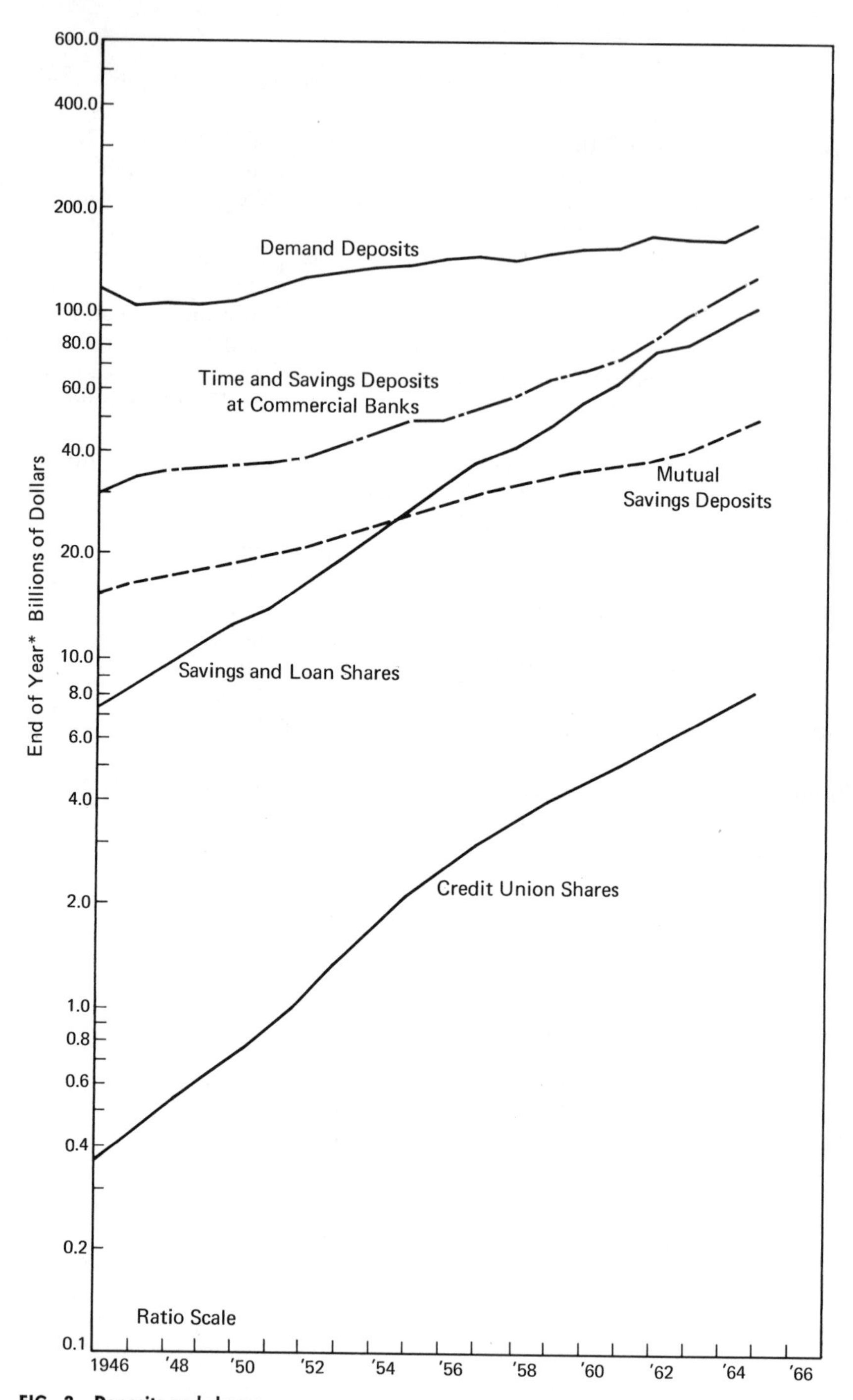

FIG. 3 Deposits and shares.
Deposit-type financial institutions.

* Last call report for commercial banks.
Sources of data: Federal Deposit Insurance Corporation; U.S. Savings and Loan League; National Association of Mutual Savings Banks; Credit Union National Association data.

assets (which include demand deposits and currency). Thus, the ratio of demand deposits and currency to total financial assets of nonfinancial corporations declined from nearly 29 percent in 1946 to 12.5 percent in 1964.

FACTORS ASSOCIATED WITH THE DECLINING DEMAND FOR CASH

The slower growth of demand deposits, reflecting as it does greater reluctance on the part of the public to hold idle money, is due in part to relatively high and generally rising interest rates that have characterized much of the postwar period.[4] An additional influence in this connection has been the absence of severe alternations in the level of economic activity since the end of World War II. Unlike the previous past when financial and industrial crises periodically gripped the nation's economy, the relative stability characterizing the two most recent decades has enabled businesses to plan their financial affairs better and hence to minimize unprofitable idle cash balances. Other factors might perhaps be cited, but whatever the causes of slower growth of demand deposits, commercial banks had to find ways of holding on to existing deposits[5] and of attracting newly generated funds.

TRADITIONAL RESPONSE

Though commercial banks did react to the changing environment, responses—until the past few years—were pretty much along traditional lines. As a general matter, commercial banks tended to limit their competition for loanable funds—to the extent possible under limitations imposed by Regulation Q—to raising interest rates paid on time and savings deposits, and to narrowing the differential between interest rates

[4] Lower and/or declining interest rates would not necessarily reverse the trend. One observer of the financial scene is probably correct in arguing that "once companies and individuals begin to economize on cash and place surplus funds into earning assets, the process is hard to reverse even though the return available from this economizing of cash may decline." See Paul S. Nadler, *Time Deposits and Debentures: The New Sources of Bank Funds* (New York: C. J. Devine Institute of Finance, Graduate School of Business Administration of New York University, 1964), p. 30.

[5] Shifts of funds out of demand deposits and into interest-bearing claims issued by nonbank financial intermediaries do not result in a decline in the demand deposits of the banking system—only a transfer of ownership. But, such shifts create losses for *particular* banks and increase the *volatility* of deposit balances in general. Moreover, if carried to an extreme, commercial banks would evolve into check clearing facilities—not a useless function, but certainly not one that is particularly profitable.

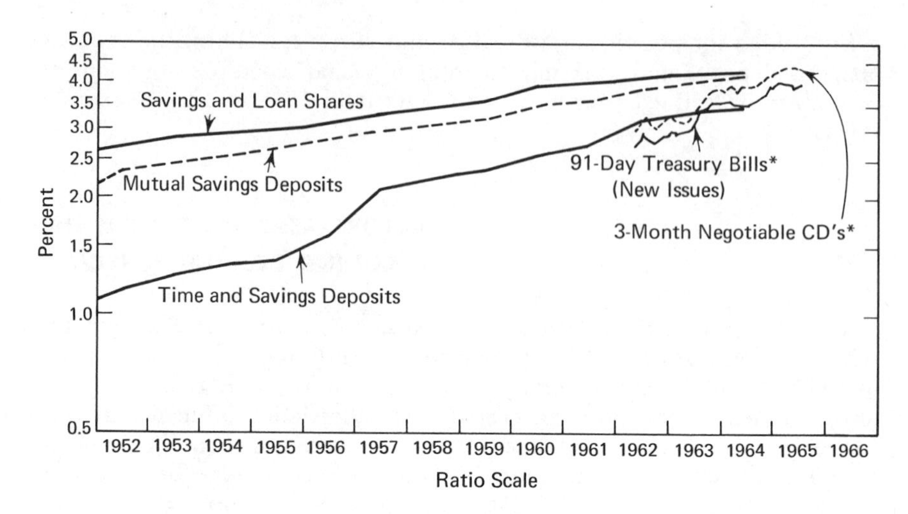

FIG. 4 Selected interest rates.
* *Monthly averages.*

Sources of data: Federal Deposit Insurance Corporation; U.S. Savings and Loan League; National Association of Mutual Savings Banks; Solomon Brothers and Hutzler.

paid on such deposits and on deposit-type claims issued by other financial institutions as well as to advertising. That commercial banks did compete in terms of interest rates is seen in Figure 4. In each year from 1952 through 1964, the effective rate paid on interest-bearing claims issued by deposit-type financial institutions exceeded the rate of the previous year. Commercial banks conformed to this pattern, reflecting both a willingness to compete for funds—albeit along traditional lines—and permissive actions by the regulatory authorities in progressively raising the ceiling on Regulation Q.

Banks were successful, after 1956, in narrowing the unfavorable differential between interest rates paid on their claims and interest rates paid on the claims of major competitors. Thus, whereas rates paid by savings and loan associations between 1952 and 1956 exceeded rates paid on time and savings deposits of commercial banks by more than 1.5 percentage points, this differential had narrowed to about ¾ of a percentage point by the end of 1964.[6]

Commercial banks have also sought to compete in the money market for the highly mobile short-term funds of both corporations and well-to-do individuals. The willingness to compete is also evident from Figure 4, where it can be seen that the rate paid on negotiable time certificates of

[6] Various factors enable commercial banks to compete successfully for loanable funds (particularly long-term savings) despite payment of lower effective rates of interest. One reason, for example, is that only commercial banks offer complete banking services and, hence, convenience.

deposit has tended to be above the bid rate on 91-day U.S. Treasury bills, as well as to correlate closely with variations in that rate.[7]

Thus, as it became increasingly apparent that corporations and individuals were less likely to continue to hold large demand deposit balances, commercial banks attempted, as a second best alternative, to induce such depositors to keep funds on deposit as either time or savings deposits by making interest rates more attractive. In these efforts, particularly in the period beginning in 1957, some success was achieved.[8] Commercial banks were able to retain, often with the same deposit ownership, a portion of the funds formerly held in demand balances that might have sought profitable investment outside banks, as well as to attract a share of newly generated loanable funds.

It is evident from Figure 5, which shows the various sources of commercial bank funds, that total time and savings deposits have increased at a much faster rate since the end of 1956 than have demand deposits—the former increased by 1.5 times as compared with the less than 25 percent increase of the latter. At the end of 1956, demand deposits contributed almost 67 percent of total sources of funds of commercial banks; by the end of 1964 the proportion had dropped to only slightly more than 50 percent. Time and savings deposits, on the other hand, gained in relative importance, rising from less than 25 percent to 37 percent over the same period.[9] No particularly pronounced changes in the magnitudes of bank capital and other miscellaneous liabilities appeared in this period; at the end of 1956, the two components combined accounted for

[7] The behavior of commercial banks in setting interest rates for different forms of deposits is rather interesting, and reveals a keen understanding of the advantages of money market segmentation. It is apparent from Figure 4 that the secondary market rate paid on three-month negotiable CDs has moved up considerably faster than the rate paid on total time and savings deposits. Moreover, the former rate has moved much more in sympathy with money market rates than has the effective rate paid on all time and savings deposits. The major portion of time and savings deposits is held by individuals as long-term savings. Though such savings are by no means insensitive to relative interest rate differentials and levels, they are thought to be less sensitive than the short-term idle funds of corporations and well-to-do individuals. Thus, rather than competing for the marginal liquidity of such spending units by raising interest rates across-the-board, commercial banks have issued negotiable CDs in large denominations, especially for acquisition by this segment of the market.

[8] From 1936 through the end of 1956, maximum interest rates payable on commercial bank time and savings deposits under Regulation Q remained unchanged. As of January 1, 1957, maximum interest rate ceilings were raised on all types of time and savings deposits, excepting 30- to 89-day time deposits. This action by the regulatory authorities was initiated in recognition of the general rise in interest rates beginning in 1951.

[9] These percentages are for *total* demand and *total* time and savings deposits, as reported on bank balance sheets. The proportions thus differ from those usually derived from adjusted deposit data. Both sets of data, however, reveal similar patterns over time.

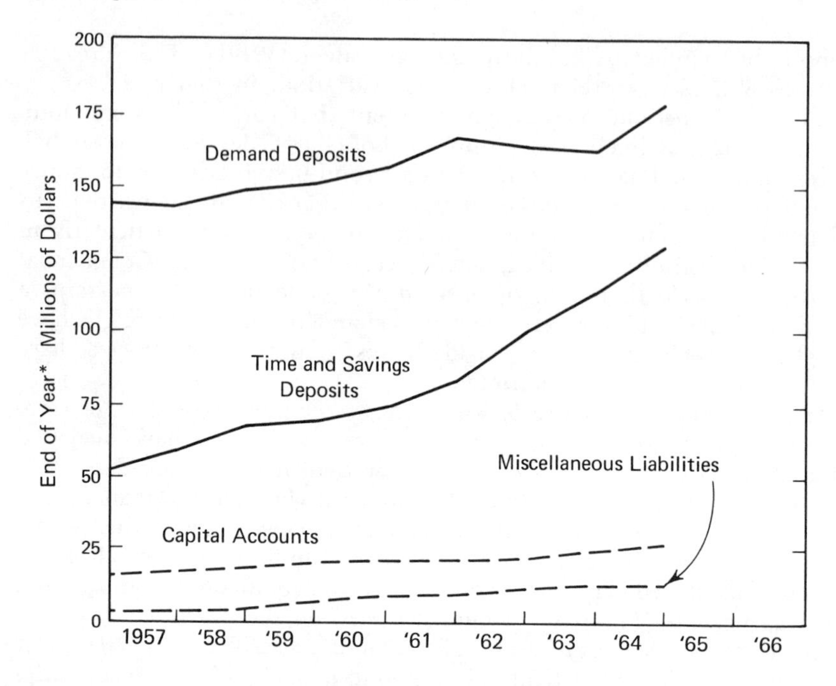

FIG. 5 Sources of commercial bank funds.

* Last call report of year for commercial banks.
Source of data: Federal Deposit Insurance Corporation.

9.1 percent of total sources of funds of commercial banks as compared with 11.2 percent at the end of 1964. However, recent innovations affecting these sources of funds have potentially important implications for the future, which are discussed later.

CREATIVE RESPONSE

To date, the 1960's have seen commercial banks become considerably more aggressive in their competitive efforts. This has been made possible in part by the greater leeway given by the monetary authority to commercial banks in the setting of interest rates.[10] But, in addition, commercial banks have found new ways of competing for funds—ways which likely will play a major role in determining the fortunes of commercial banking in coming years.

Prior to the early 1960's, commercial banks, as a general matter, apparently had been content to attract funds from traditional sources and by

[10] Permission to raise rates payable on various types of time and savings deposits has been granted in every year since 1961. Thus, changes in maximum rates payable under Regulation Q were made effective as of January 1, 1962, July 17, 1963, and November 24, 1964. As of this writing, there has been no change in 1965.

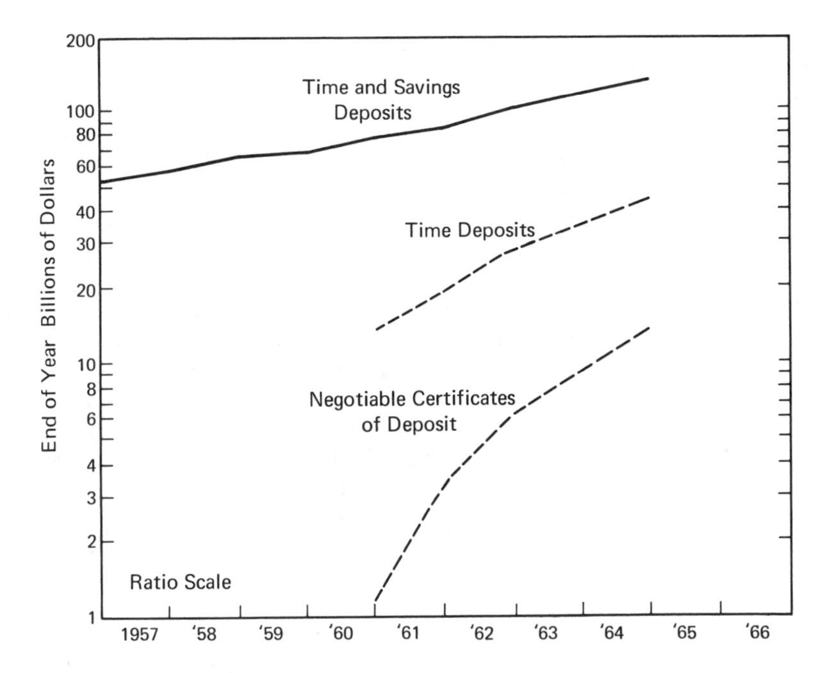

FIG. 6 Time and savings deposits of commercial banks.

Sources of data: Board of Governors of the Federal Reserve System and Federal Deposit Insurance Corporation.

traditional means, with rising interest rates as the primary lure. The past four years, however, have witnessed a considerable change, with innovation now playing a dominant role in terms of both characteristics of claims issued by banks and the markets to which these claims are meant to have appeal.

Most important thus far of the debt instruments recently introduced by commercial banks—at least in terms of magnitude—is the negotiable certificate of deposit. In sharp contrast to the past when many banks discouraged or refused corporate-owned time deposits,[11] negotiable CDs were issued primarily to halt the movement of demand deposit funds from large commercial banks by corporate money managers into investment in various money market instruments, for example, Treasury bills, commercial paper, and bankers' acceptances. Certificates of deposit were not unknown prior to 1961, when leading New York City banks announced that they would offer such instruments to both corporate and noncorporate customers and a leading Government securities dealer indicated that it would maintain a secondary market for such instruments. But, as seen from Figure 6, negotiable CDs totaled only slightly in excess

[11] A view in the past often was (and in some cases still is) that the buildup of interest-earning time deposits owned by corporations would be at the expense of demand deposits which earn no interest.

of $1 billion at the end of 1960. By the end of 1964, this almost insignificant figure had grown to more than $12.5 billion—by August of this year to over $16 billion.

Negotiable CDs clearly have grown considerably faster than the total of time and savings deposits. While at the end of 1960, negotiable CDs constituted just 1.5 percent of total time and savings deposits, by the end of 1964 they accounted for almost 10 percent. Of the $54-billion increase in time and savings deposits between the end of 1960 and the end of 1964, negotiable CDs contributed more than one-fifth. Since negotiable CDs are a form of time deposit (as distinct from savings deposits [12]), their increase has contributed far more significantly to the growth of time deposits. And it is the time deposit component in recent years that has evidenced most of the growth recorded in the total of time and savings deposits. From the end of 1961 to the end of 1964, time and savings deposits together increased by about 55 percent. Time deposits alone, however, expanded about 2.3 times. The growing volume of negotiable CDs accounted for almost 45 percent of the nearly $26 billion increase in time deposits over the period.

The appeal of negotiable CDs reflects in part their attractive yields; it also reflects their marketability, something the traditional time deposit lacked. However, while having much appeal to money managers, negotiable CDs are not necessarily as pleasing to bankers. For one thing, CDs tend to be highly sensitive to interest rates—to the extent that adverse differentials between interest rates paid on CDs and on other money market instruments could cause a loss of CDs and, hence, a source of funds to the banks involved.

Interest rate considerations aside, there also exists the possibility of holders failing to renew maturing CDs, for example, because holders may want back their funds for working capital purposes. This is not a surprising situation in that, in many cases, CDs represent *temporarily* idle funds which in former years might have contentedly remained in demand balances. Negotiable CDs are therefore a potentially volatile source of funds, in contrast to the traditional savings, or even time, deposit. In this respect, CDs bear a strong resemblance to demand deposits.[13] Moreover, not only must legally required reserves and adequate capital be kept against CDs (as in the case of other deposits), but bankers may often feel queasy about investing such funds in high-yielding though relatively illiquid assets. In short, negotiable CDs can easily become a rather volatile and expensive source of funds.

The issuance of negotiable CDs has probably been the most widely

[12] Time deposits are generally held by businesses and well-to-do individuals, and include: time deposits open account, time CDs (negotiable and non-negotiable), and other special accounts. Savings deposits, as evidenced by the ownership of a passbook, represent generally the savings of the public-at-large.

[13] See George R. Morrison and Richard T. Selden, *Time Deposit Growth and the Employment of Bank Funds* (Association of Reserve City Bankers, 1965), Chapter III.

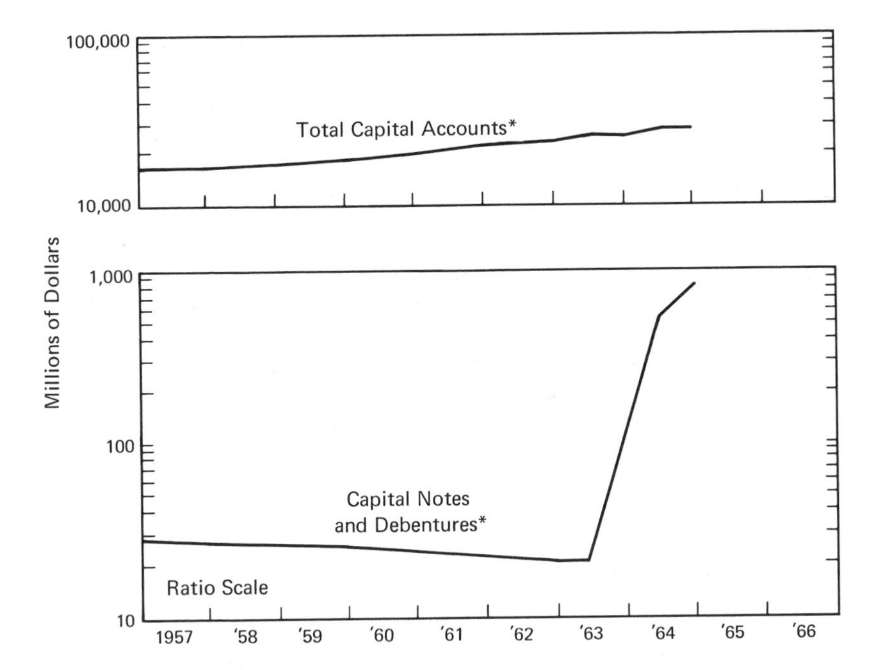

FIG. 7 Capital accounts of commercial banks.

* End of year through 1962; semiannually beginning 1963.
Source of data: Federal Deposit Insurance Corporation.

discussed aspect of the renewed vigor with which commercial banks have sought to strengthen their commanding position as a financial intermediary. Of less quantitative importance thus far—but also possessing significant implications for the future—are new sources of funds showing up in the capital and miscellaneous liability accounts of commercial banks. Of particular interest are subordinated debentures and capital notes, and more recently unsecured short-term promissory notes, which were first issued in September 1964 by The First National Bank of Boston. As seen in Figure 7, the outstanding volume of subordinated debentures and capital notes rose from a level of only $21 million in mid-1963 to over $800 million at the end of 1964. In relation to total bank capital of nearly $28 billion at the end of 1964, $800 million is an inconsiderable amount. Yet, in the absence of regulatory restraints, there is reason for believing that the total could increase sharply and to significant proportions.

From a bank's point of view, debentures and capital notes have much to recommend as a source of funds. To the extent that they substitute for additional sales of common stock, and to the extent that the rate of interest on these funds is less than the rate of return on invested capital, present stockholders stand to benefit from higher earnings per share and possibly higher market values of their equity holdings.[14] But, aside from use as a substitute for the issuance of additional common stock, unsecured debentures and capital notes may also substitute for and/or supplement deposits (demand and time and savings) as a source of loanable funds to commercial banks.

Compared with negotiable CDs, for example, debentures and capital notes possess several distinct and widely accepted advantages. First, neither debentures nor capital notes require the maintenance of legal reserves, while as a deposit liability, CDs require such reserves. Second, debentures or capital notes do not require supporting equity capital or, at least, not to the extent that CDs or the more traditional deposit liabilities would require it. Third, neither debentures nor capital notes are subject to a Federal Deposit Insurance Corporation assessment; as a form of time deposit, CDs are subject to a 1/12 of one percent annual assessment. Finally, because funds secured through debentures and capital notes are likely to remain for a relatively long period of time, there is less need for maintaining secondary reserves, such as Treasury bills and other low-yielding though highly liquid assets. Thus, nearly all the proceeds from debentures and capital notes can be placed in loans and longer maturity investments.

In the absence of regulatory restraint, it is likely that unsecured short-term notes will become an increasingly important source of funds for commercial banks. Having some of the advantages of debentures and capital notes, short-term notes, in addition, are not burdened with similar marketing problems.[15]

CONCLUDING COMMENTS

Having said this, however, it should be remembered that, if not handled properly, that is, with full appreciation of the costs and risks involved, these "new" sources of funds could present serious problems to commercial banks.[16] Thus, it should not be surprising that the super-

[14] For discussion and illustration of this, see Nadler, *Time Deposits and Debentures: The New Sources of Bank Funds,* pp. 20–24.

[15] On August 26, 1965, the Banking Department of the State of New York gave state chartered banks permission to offer non-negotiable promissory notes (in amounts exceeding $1,000,000) to corporate customers. As of this writing, six large New York banks have issued such notes.

[16] Acquisition of substantial amounts of loanable funds through the issuance of capital notes and debentures commits the issuing bank to fixed interest payments over extended periods of time. Should market rates of interest subsequently decline, the bank's earning power may become jeopardized. An additional source of possible difficulty arises from the relatively high interest rate paid on these sources of funds. At, say, a 5 percent rate of interest on debentures, proceeds from this source could hardly be placed in shorter-term loans and investments. Thus, it might become necessary to place these funds in longer-term and less liquid loans and investments. At some point the desire for profit might conflict with prudent behavior. For addi-

visory authorities have demonstrated prudent caution in evaluating such sources of funds. Nevertheless, the fact that new sources of funds have been "innovated" does suggest that commercial banks are seriously seeking to revitalize their position as a financial intermediary. The ultimate success of any single innovation is perhaps not important. What is important is that creative innovation has been reintroduced to commercial banking. And this virtually guarantees that the business of banking will never again be the same—as it probably should not since change happens all the time in the various segments of U.S. business and financial enterprise.

tional discussion see L. Wayne Dobson, *The Issuance of Capital Notes and Debentures by Commercial Banks* (Kentucky Bankers Association, 1965), pp. 22–26.

Compensating Balances*

Jack M. Guttentag and Richard G. Davis

Many banks expect business customers to hold minimum average balances as a condition for extending loans or lines of credit. There are some indications, moreover, that the practice of requiring such "compensating" balances has become more widespread during the past decade. One result of this development has been an increased interest in the effects of compensating balance requirements on the loan volume and interest earnings of individual banks as well as on the general cost and availability of credit throughout the banking system. Another result has been the growth of a financial device, known as "link financing."

CHARACTERISTICS AND IMPORTANCE OF BALANCE REQUIREMENTS

Compensating balance requirements are usually expressed as a percentage of the line of credit extended. In a survey of 100 large banks

* This article is reprinted—with certain revisions required to bring it up to date as of mid-1964—from the December 1961 *Monthly Review*, issued by the Federal Reserve Bank of New York.

taken in 1958 by the Robert Morris Associates, the great majority of banks requiring compensating balances reported requirements in that year of 10–20 per cent of the line of credit.[1] The specific percentage varied from bank to bank, and often from borrower to borrower. In almost all cases the required volume of deposits is defined in terms of average balances held over a period, so that required balances may also serve to meet customer working balance needs.[2]

While it is impossible to estimate the dollar volume of deposits held by business borrowers as compensating balances, the 1958 survey indicated that over 70 per cent of the banks covered made such balances a condition for extending lines of credit to all business borrowers. Other banks required them against lines of credit in most but not all cases and, for a few banks, balances were required on lines of credit granted only to particular types of borrowers, such as sales finance companies. Compensating balance requirements do, however, tend to be considerably more common among large banks than among small ones, and among large rather than small borrowers.

Sometimes balance requirements against lines of credit are raised when the line is in use, while in other cases the balance requirement does not change when the line is activated. Actual balances in such cases may, indeed, be at their *lowest* level when the credit line is being used most fully, the small balances at such times being offset by higher balances during periods when the line is being used less intensively or not at all. Where loans are made to borrowers who had not previously been required to hold a balance against their line of credit, or who had not previously had a line of credit at all, balance requirements frequently become effective at the time the loan is made. The lending bank may, however, not ask for a compensating balance if the borrower had voluntarily carried balances with it in the past—or gives strong promise of doing so in the future.

This underscores the important fact that compensating balance requirements often reflect an informal understanding in which exact percentages are not discussed, rather than a hard and fast agreement that spells out the obligation of the borrower in precise detail. If the customer, for example, voluntarily holds balances in excess of those the bank would ordinarily require, the subject of a compensating balance is not likely to be brought up.

Informal and flexible arrangements are common where there is a continuing relationship between the bank and its customer. Compensating balances and credit lines may be merely one aspect of such a relationship; the bank often performs various services for the customer, in addition to extending credit, and perhaps the customer will steer other business (that

[1] F. P. Gallot, "Why Compensating Balances? Part II," *Bulletin of the Robert Morris Associates,* August 1958, pp. 309–319.

[2] See George Garvy, *Deposit Velocity and Its Significance,* Federal Reserve Bank of New York, November 1959, pp. 29–37.

of its own customers or subsidiaries, for example) to the bank. Where such relationships are mutually satisfactory over the long pull, the exact nature of the customer's obligation with respect to the level of his balance may never be explicitly spelled out.

From the standpoint of the borrower, compensating balances may be viewed as something of an informal "commitment fee," i.e., as the price he pays for the bank's commitment under the line of credit to extend a loan when needed. At the same time these balances may also serve to compensate the bank for other services. The cost to the borrower of maintaining balances for these purposes largely depends on whether the balances needed exceed those the customer would voluntarily hold to carry on his business, even in the absence of any requirement.

Comparison of the 1958 Robert Morris survey with a similar survey taken by that organization in 1954 suggests that banks were tending to extend compensating balance requirements to a wider group of business borrowers. There are indications that the practice became even more widespread after 1958. The 1958 survey indicated, moreover, that the requirements had been raised since 1954 and were being enforced more vigorously. Customer failure to fulfill requirements is usually met, in the first instance, with persuasion. If this does not work, the bank may have recourse to higher interest rates, reduction of credit lines, or even outright cancellation of borrowing privileges, depending upon the persistence of the deficiency, the customer's current and potential value to the bank, and the general state of credit conditions.

EFFECT ON DEPOSITS AND CREDIT

Banks generally look at compensating balances as an aspect of bank-customer relations—indeed, as one means of fostering such relationships and thereby encouraging borrowers to use various banking services. Some banks also feel that compensating balances can moderate fluctuations in deposit balances and that, in the event a loan goes into default, such balances might offset part of the loss.

Much of the interest in the effects of compensating balance requirements, however, has centered on their influence over the volume of deposits, lending capacity, and the effective interest rate on loans. From the standpoint of the individual bank, compensating balance requirements can increase both deposits and loans, and thereby swell interest earnings. These requirements, however, actually reduce the volume of withdrawable funds which the bank can make available to borrowers because part of the bank's funds are tied up as required reserves held against borrowers' compensatory deposits.

These points are illustrated by the example in Table 1.[3] Assume that

[3] For simplicity, the example assumes that requirements are based on the loan amount rather than the line of credit. The alternative assumption leads to the same results.

Table 1 Balance Sheet of Individual Bank

No Compensating Balances Required			
Assets		*Liabilities*	
Required reserves	$ 210	Initial deposits	$1,050
Credit	840		
	$1,050		$1,050

Compensating Balances Required			
Assets		*Liabilities*	
Required reserves	$ 250	Initial deposits	$1,050
Credit	1,000	Deposits held as compensating balances	200
	$1,250		$1,250

a bank obtains a deposit of $1,050 from the public and that it must hold 20 per cent of this amount, or $210, as required reserves. The remaining $840 can be made available as loans to borrowers who, we assume, immediately withdraw these funds to make payments. But if the bank requires compensating balances of 20 per cent it can, based on the same $840, extend $1,000 in loans because the balance requirement assures the bank that only $800 will actually be withdrawn. (The bank must hold the rest of the $840, or $40, as required reserves against the $200 in deposits maintained by the borrower as a compensating balance.) The $1,000 in loans represents a $160 increase, compared with the case where no compensating balances are required, and interest earnings are correspondingly higher. At the same time, however, the amount of withdrawable funds is reduced from $840 in the no-requirements case to $800 when balances are required, the difference being equal to the additional required reserves that must be held against the compensating balance.

Although the individual bank can increase its deposits by requiring compensating balances, the ability of the banking system as a whole to create deposits is limited by total reserves, which are not influenced by balance requirements. However, to the extent that compensating balance requirements tend to concentrate deposits in city banks, which have higher required reserve ratios, total deposits may tend to be somewhat reduced. On the other hand, in so far as balance requirements reduce the day-to-day volatility of deposits, they may make some banks willing to remain more fully invested than otherwise, thereby tending to increase deposits.

Aside from these possibly minor influences, compensating balance requirements have no effect on total deposits. A bank that increases its own deposits by requiring compensating balances reduces deposits of other banks by the same amount. This is obviously the case where the borrower obtains the compensating balance by withdrawing funds deposited in other banks. But it is also the case where the compensating balance is obtained directly from the lending bank as part of the loan, as illustrated in the table. In the example, the $200 compensating balance absorbs $40 of reserves that otherwise would have been available to support $200 of deposits by credit expansion elsewhere in the banking system.

RELATION TO WORKING BALANCE NEEDS

Where the borrower must hold balances that cannot be withdrawn, it might be concluded that the loan amount (or line of credit) overstates the actual volume of funds that can effectively be used. By the same token, it may seem that the effective interest rate (i.e., the interest payment figured as a proportion of usable funds) is higher than the contract rate. Even in cases where such conclusions do hold, the higher cost would have to be set against the value to the customer of the informal guarantee of loan accommodation under the line of credit, as well as the value of any other bank services rendered to him.

But even aside from these collateral benefits, the compensating balance requirement may not increase the effective cost of credit to the borrower. Most business borrowers have substantial working balance needs. They must maintain an average level of deposits sufficient to bridge day-to-day gaps between payments and receipts as well as to meet those special contingencies (emergencies and opportunities) that require immediate cash. Actual balances held for this purpose may fluctuate markedly, but since compensating balance requirements are usually stated in terms of average balances over a period, they serve in part, at least, to satisfy working balance needs. Where required balances are equal to or less than the average balances borrowers would hold to meet working balance needs, the requirement does not reduce the effective availability of funds to the borrower, nor does it mean that the effective interest cost of credit to him is higher than the contract rate.

Thus, in the example cited above, a borrower who seeks to hold working balances of $200 is not adversely affected by the $200 balance requirement. The balance requirement merely obliges him to hold his working balance at the lending bank rather than elsewhere. From the point of view of the lending bank, the arrangement assures a continuing bank-customer relationship. The customer's deposits add to bank earnings, and may encourage the bank to offer him a larger loan or lower contract rate than it offers to nondepositors. (The latter, in fact, may not obtain accommodation at all.) Indeed, where a potential borrower with heavy working balance needs does not already have a compensating balance arrangement with his bank, another bank might be able to solicit his business by offering a relatively low contract rate of interest on condition that the borrower transfer a balance large enough to meet that bank's balance requirement. Where borrowers already have a compensating balance arrangement that is reflected in loan rates lower than those charged to nondepositors, the scope for this inducement is of course limited.[4]

When balance requirements exceed the borrower's working balance needs, however, the requirement does force him to pay interest on balances he does not need. Thus, if the borrower in the example above has working balance needs of only $100 but is nevertheless obliged to hold $200 of his $1,000 loan as a compensating balance, he is provided with only $900 of effective funds, and the effective rate of interest he pays rises correspondingly. (If the borrower uses his line of credit only part of the time but must hold average balances that are $100 higher than those he needs over the full year, the effective rate he pays is still higher.)

In cases of this type, the effective yield to the bank theoretically could be raised and, at the same time, the effective cost to the borrower reduced by an appropriate combination of reduced balance requirements and increased contract rates of interest. The potential benefit arises from the elimination or reduction of the required reserves that must be held against the compensating balance. The customer may of course feel that he receives full value for these balances in the form of "commitment insurance" and other bank services. Nevertheless, in principle, direct payment for these services could be beneficial to both parties, since it would eliminate the reserve requirement against the compensating balance.

For example, if the recipient of the $1,000 loan in the compensating balance case shown on the table needs no working balances at all so that the loan provides him with only $800 of funds that he can use effectively, he would be just as well off with a loan of $800 at a contract interest rate one-fourth higher and no required balance. The bank, however, would be better off in the latter case, because its interest earnings on this specific loan transaction would remain the same while $40 of required reserves would be "freed" and could be used to make additional loans. In principle, this benefit could be shared between borrower and lender, although in practice much depends on the relative bargaining positions of the two parties.

The burdensomeness of compensating balance requirements where they exceed borrower working balance needs may account for the fact that balance requirements are sometimes waived or set at comparatively low levels for certain types of borrowers, such as builders, whose normal balance needs are small; in such cases, the lower requirements may be offset by higher contract rates of interest. Indeed competition may exert pressure toward keeping requirements low in cases where working balance needs are relatively small just as it encourages the development of compensating balance arrangements where such needs are heavy.

Nevertheless, in some cases, compensating balance requirements in excess of customer working balance needs do, for various reasons, persist. Banks may have a special incentive to maintain compensating balances

[4] See Donald R. Hodgman, "The Deposit Relationship and Commercial Bank Investment Behavior," *Review of Economics and Statistics,* August 1961, p. 262.

in order to solidify bank-customer relations, from which they often obtain collateral advantages. Compensating balances, moreover, may be administratively the most convenient way of compensating the bank for services, despite the added cost to the bank of holding reserves against idle deposits. Some banks, furthermore, may strive to make their deposits as large as possible, even if this causes some reduction in earnings—especially when the impact on earnings is not clearly visible. In addition, balance requirements may be rendered inflexible by the bank's desire to maintain uniformity of requirements or contract rates of interest among different borrowers of the same general type. Finally, the upward adjustments in the contract rate needed to offset any reduction or elimination of compensating balances may be restrained in some cases by legal or traditional ceilings on contract interest rates. If borrowers are generally satisfied with their banking relationship, competitive pressures that might otherwise overcome some of these obstacles and spark downward adjustments in requirements may not develop.

How important are cases where compensating balance requirements exceed borrower working balance needs? The necessity felt by many banks to educate their customers to an acceptance of compensating balances, as well as the problems sometimes encountered in enforcing the requirements, strongly suggests that it is more than an occasional and isolated phenomenon. It is probable that the importance of such cases grew during the middle and late 1950's in line with the long-term uptrend in contract rates of interest and parallel development in other aspects of the lender-borrower relationship reflecting the final working-off of swollen wartime liquidity positions. Indeed, a higher incidence of compensating balance requirements in excess of working balance needs may have been partly responsible for the growth during the early 1960's of a new device for financing these requirements known as "link financing."

LINK FINANCING

While many variants of link financing exist, the general nature of this technique may be illustrated by the following example: A borrower receiving a $100,000 loan is required by the bank to keep a compensating balance of 20 per cent (or $20,000) but wishes to withdraw the full amount of the loan to make payments. Both the borrower and the bank may be satisfied if the borrower can find a supplier of funds, such as an insurance company, mutual fund, or pension fund, that will deposit $20,000 of its own money in the borrower's bank—such deposits typically taking the form of time certificates of deposit. In this way, the lending bank obtains the compensating balance of $20,000, the borrower gets the use of the entire $100,000 loan, and the supplier of deposits receives a certificate of deposit on which it receives interest paid by the borrower.[5]

[5] Some cases have been reported where the supplier has provided deposits equal to the full amount of the loan, rather than merely the compensating balance.

In some cases, the supplier may subsequently sell part or all of his time certificates to other investors. Finance companies have been important users of link financing, but the technique has been employed by construction and manufacturing firms as well. Some link financing deals are arranged by middlemen who have been quick to discover a profitable brokerage opportunity. These brokers may sometimes obtain funds for an individual borrower from several participating suppliers (frequently in units of $5,000).

The supplier of deposits in a link financing deal is paid by the borrower, but he may, in addition, receive interest on the certificate of deposit directly from the lending bank. The fact that the total return from both sources has generally exceeded the legal maximum that banks are permitted to pay on time deposits has perhaps been the major inducement to the flow of funds into this market. In cases where the deposit is noninterest bearing, the payment by the borrower normally exceeds the legal maximum rate on time deposits.

Although link financing requires the borrower to make a supplemental payment to the supplier of the compensating balance, it may nevertheless be the least expensive means for the borrower to obtain use of the full amount of funds he requires. Even if the bank is willing to increase the size of the loan by an amount sufficient to cover the balance requirement, the added charge could exceed the cost to the borrower of obtaining the deposit through a link financing arrangement. Where the bank is unwilling to increase the size of the loan, the only alternative to link financing may be even more costly borrowing from other nonbank sources. Link financing can thus reduce, but cannot eliminate, the cost imposed by compensating balance requirements in excess of working balance needs.

From the standpoint of the lending bank, a compensating balance in the form of a time certificate has the advantage of reducing the volume of required reserves that must be held against the deposit. On the other hand, some banks express opposition to link financing on the ground that it does not encourage close bank-customer relations.

COMPENSATING BALANCES DURING THE BUSINESS CYCLE

There is considerable evidence that compensating balance requirements are responsive to cyclical changes in general monetary conditions. Thus in periods of declining interest rates, when money is plentiful and banks are seeking to expand loans, banks often reduce compensating balance requirements as one more way of making borrowing more attractive and meeting competition. Similarly, during periods of stringency, pressures may be generated to raise balance requirements. In the 1958 study referred to above, slightly over half the bankers interviewed stated that they adjusted their policies in the light of general monetary conditions, and effective flexibility may be even more widespread. Even a bank which aims at a fixed ratio of compensating balances to lines of credit, regardless of monetary conditions, may enforce the policy more vigorously in periods of rising interest rates and loan demand than in periods of comparative slack. Such variations in the vigor of enforcement may indeed provide a more flexible means of adjusting to changing market conditions than changes in nominal requirements or in contract rates.

Cyclical flexibility in the application of compensating balance requirements thus can be a mechanism through which changes in the cost and availability of credit are transmitted to the market for business loans. On the availability side, increases in balance requirements or in the vigor of enforcement tend to immobilize a larger part of loans and deposits in cases where required balances already equal or exceed working balance needs. On the cost side, increases in the required balance ratio will raise effective interest rates, over and beyond increases in contract rates, to borrowers with small working balance needs. It is impossible to estimate the quantitative significance of the cost and availability effects of cyclical shifts in compensating balance policies, but they may have a definite importance. One study of finance company borrowing suggests that decreases in compensating balance requirements between 1953 and 1954 may have reduced borrowing costs by about as much as reductions due to declines in the contract rate of interest itself.[6]

CONCLUDING COMMENT

When the effects of compensating balance requirements are taken into account, cyclical swings in effective bank interest rates and credit availability are larger than is indicated by conventional statistical measures. This does not imply, however, that these swings in effective rates and availability have been larger than they would have been in the absence of compensating balance requirements. In its conduct of monetary policy, the Federal Reserve System takes into account all influences bearing on the supply of credit that are outside the System's immediate control, of which compensating balance requirements is one. Changes in the supply of credit from this and other sources that are inappropriate to the prevailing economic situation may therefore be neutralized by offsetting adjustments in monetary policy.

[6] See Robert C. Holland, *Bank Lending to Finance Companies, December 1951–June 1956,* unpublished doctoral dissertation, University of Pennsylvania, 1959.

A Test of the Deposit Relationship Hypothesis

Neil B. Murphy

INTRODUCTION

In a recent article, Donald R. Hodgman set forth a framework for analyzing commercial bank lending behavior which emphasized the relationship of customers to their banks as both depositors and borrowers.[1] Specifically, Hodgman links the borrower's contract rate of interest to the profitability of his deposit account, i.e., banks compete for profitable deposit customers by offering the customer a rate which is lower than the comparable open market rate (adjusted for risk). Hodgman uses the terms *deposit relationship* and *customer relationship* to describe this behavior.[2] He argues that compensating balance requirements, the prime rate convention, and provision of services below cost may be viewed as a systematic, rational attempt by commercial banks to maximize long-run profit under existing institutional arrangements when viewed from the perspective of the customer relationship.

Davis and Guttentag (D–G), on the other hand, have argued that there is not necessarily any relationship between granting of concessions on loan rates to profitable deposit customers and other commercial banking practices, such as the granting of lines of credit, the prime rate convention, compensating balance requirements, and provision of services.[3] Nevertheless, their model accepts the rate concession hypothesis.

Neither Hodgman nor D–G have attempted to test this hypothesis

[1] Donald R. Hodgman, "The Deposit Relationship and Commercial Bank Investment Behavior," *Review of Economics and Statistics,* XLIII (August 1961), pp. 257–268.

[2] In his *Commercial Bank Loan and Investment Policy* (Urbana: Bureau of Economic and Business Research, University of Illinois, 1963), Chapters 9–12, Hodgman has a more comprehensive treatment of this concept.

[3] R. G. Davis and J. M. Guttentag, "Balance Requirements and Deposit Competition," *Journal of Political Economy,* LXXI (December 1963), pp. 581–585.

Reprinted with permission from the *Journal of Financial and Quantitative Analysis,* March 1967.

empirically. There are several reasons why it has been difficult to do so: (1) Commercial banks understandably do not provide information concerning their individual customers, (2) loan agreements have many provisions such as maturity terms, repayment terms, collateral, etc., which in effect cloud the possible relationship of loan rates to deposit levels, (3) the relationship between bank and customer in many cases is multidimensional, and provision of services such as lines of credit (deemed very important by D–G [4]) and transactions, advisory and informational services (emphasized by Hodgman [5]) clouds the effect of deposit levels on loan rates, and (4) the notes of business customers have varying levels of quality, and the open market rate for their notes would be very difficult to estimate. Data provided by a set of customers to which these objections do not apply provide the basis for a test of the deposit relationship hypothesis accepted by both Hodgman and D–G.

THE DATA

Massachusetts towns provide a convenient set of commercial bank customers for a test of the deposit rate hypothesis for the following reasons:

1. Massachusetts towns generally have to issue tax anticipation notes during the course of the year due to the nature of their receipt and expenditure patterns.[6] Commercial banks usually purchase these notes. Therefore, these towns are both borrowers and deposit customers.
2. Commercial banks bid on these anticipation notes. Thus, the banks provide no lines of credit to the town.
3. The anticipation notes of the towns have identical terms (except for maturity) and tend to be standardized as to quality since they are certified by the Bureau of Accounts of the State Department of Corporations and Taxation.[7]

Fortunately there is an open market rate published weekly.[8] We may then compare observed rates received by a sample of Massachusetts towns

[4] *Ibid.*, pp. 582–583.

[5] D. R. Hodgman, *Commercial Bank Loan and Investment Policy,* pp. 165–168.

[6] See N. Murphy, "Cash Management in State and Local Government," *New England Business Review,* June 1966.

[7] For a more comprehensive discussion of the quality of Massachusetts town revenue anticipation notes, see Richard E. Bennink, "Temporary Loans to Massachusetts Municipalities in Anticipation of Revenue," Unpublished Thesis, Stonier School of Banking, Rutgers University, June 1953, pp. 10–15.

[8] Advisory Section of the Government Bond Division, Morgan Guaranty Trust Company of New York, "Domestic Money Market Run-Down," published weekly. Actually this rate is an offer rate (price) and is generally below (above) the bid rate (price). For a more complete discussion of the series and the market, see Morgan Guaranty Trust Company of New York, *Money-Market Investments: The Risk and the Return,* 1964.

with the published open market rate. For this purpose, a survey of 30 town treasurers was undertaken for the summer of 1965.[9] Although there is no rating as such for tax anticipation notes, the towns chosen were limited to those with Aa or Aaa Moody Bond ratings on the premise that this was the only information available to open market purchasers and that the notes of these towns were most similar to those traded on the open market. Treasurers were asked to state the rate which they received on their anticipation notes, the term of the note, the dollar amount of the note, and the type of deposit relationships with the purchasing bank. All 30 treasurers surveyed replied, and there were 34 usable observations.

THE MODEL

Since the town treasurers are required to solicit bids,[10] the model is in the form of bank offer function. The dependent variable of the model which was tested is the rate of interest paid by the town on its tax anticipation note. Independent variables are the open market rate, the "closeness" of the deposit relationship, and the size of the note. The open market rate represents the opportunity cost of bidding on the town's note, i.e., the bank could purchase an asset with similar characteristics and receive the open market rate. As the open market rate rises, the opportunity cost rises as does the rate which the bank will bid. This rate was adjusted for a maturity to match that of the observed town note in the following manner: The open market rate is quoted for 90-day term to maturity intervals, (90, 180, 270, etc.). Let rd_t be the open market rate quoted at the nearest Friday to the observed town note issue with t indicating the 90-day interval immediately below that of the observed town note maturity. M is the term to maturity of the note issue. Then

$$r_o = rd_t + \frac{M - t}{90} [rd_{t+1} - rd_t]$$

This assumes a linear term structure, but in the cases under observation there was usually a constant basis point difference between the 90-day intervals up to 270 days.

Two basic types of deposit relationships were revealed in the survey:

1. The bank which purchased the note was also that bank which provided all the depository services needed by the town.

[9] The survey requested that the treasurer supply this information for the note issue closest to August 1, 1965. The responses ranged from 15 days prior to that date to 10 days after. The sample is treated as a cross-section.

[10] After certification by the Bureau of Accounts of the Commonwealth's Department of Corporations and Taxation, the treasurer notifies by telephone those banks which have previously expressed an interest in bidding. Bids are then mailed to the treasurer.

2. Although the town did not keep its working balances at the purchasing bank, the proceeds of the note issue were held at the purchasing bank while expenditure of the proceeds took place, thus spreading the bank's reserve drain over the expenditure period. This arrangement is not uncommon when the town maintains its working balances at a smaller local bank which does not purchase anticipation note. Massachusetts law limits the amount of the balance which may be kept at any bank depending upon the level of the bank's capital, and some towns must place temporary excess deposits with larger banks. The bank which bids on notes might also consider the possibility of obtaining these temporary deposit balances in formulating their bids.

We shall consider the first type as a "closer" relationship which is valued more highly by the bank and reflected in its bid.

The size of the note is considered a proxy for the magnitude of the deposit relationship, i.e., towns that borrow large amounts maintain larger balances. This analysis implicitly assumes that the loan/average deposit ratio is invariant across towns, or that any variation is inconsequential. This unfortunately is a limitation of the analysis, but the form of the data precluded explicit consideration of this point.

One non-price characteristic not standardized by the choice of borrowers is the maturity of the note. Therefore, the term-to-maturity of the observed town notes was included as an independent variable. We expect that banks have, *ceteris paribus*, a preference for shorter maturities and that an increase in maturity will have a positive influence on the rate bid by the bank.

We shall use the following notation:

Dependent variable:

r_b = the rate bid by the bank and paid by the town on a tax anticipation note.

Independent variables:

r_o = open market rate
N = size of the tax anticipation note
R = type of deposit relationship, 0 for the "closer" relationship, 1 for the "maintenance of proceeds" relationship
T = term to maturity of the note, in days

$$(1) \quad r_b = f(r_o, N, R, T)$$

$$\text{where } \frac{\delta r_b}{\delta r_o} > 0, \quad \frac{\delta r_b}{\delta N} < 0, \frac{\delta r_b}{\delta R} > 0, \frac{\delta r_b}{\delta T} > 0.$$

Since r_o is the same for all banks in cross-section, it may be removed as an independent variable and the equation may be recast in the following manner:

(la) $r_o - r_b = d = \phi(N,R,T)$

$$\frac{\delta d}{\delta N} > 0, \ \frac{\delta d}{\delta R} < 0, \text{ and } \frac{\delta d}{\delta T} < 0$$

EMPIRICAL RESULTS

Multiple regression analysis was applied to the survey data for the following equation:

$$d = \alpha + \beta_1 N + \beta_2 R + \beta_3 T$$

Table 1 shows the results of the multiple regression when run in logarithmic form.

Table 1

	Variable	*Coefficient*	*t Value*
	N	.1207	1.6289
	R	—.0968	—2.0404
	T	—.2675	—1.7980
$R^2 = .2347$			
$n = 34$			

The signs of the coefficients are consistent with the deposit relationship hypothesis, and the coefficient of the deposit relationship variable is significant at the 5 percent level.

SUMMARY AND CONCLUSION

The deposit relationship hypothesis suggested by Hodgman and accepted by his critics (D–G) was seen to be one that would be difficult to test due to heterogeneity of loan terms, quality of borrower notes, and other customer characteristics. A set of customers which seemed to satisfy the requirements for a test was surveyed for rate, note size, type of deposit relationship, and maturity. A bid rate model was formulated and tested. The results suggest that the deposit relationship hypothesis was useful in explaining the variation in rate received from commercial banks by a sample of Massachusetts towns during the summer of 1965.

However, we must note that the coefficient of determination is not too large, indicating that there is much more work to be done in explaining commercial bank price behavior. This low R^2 is not surprising in view of the size of the sample and the lack of dispersion in the dependent variable which had a coefficient of variation of only .3312. Also, the use of a cross-section for a single period does not allow us to infer anything about the relative importance of the deposit relationship in influencing bank behavior over the cycle. The results of the analysis, however, suggest that non-price terms and deposit relationships are of sufficient importance in explaining the determinants of commercial bank pricing behavior to warrant further, more comprehensive investigation. Cross-section studies including borrower characteristics, non-price loan terms, cost considerations, and bank characteristics would seem to be a minimal requirement for meaningful results.

3

Bank Capital:

Reconsiderations and Innovations

Bank capital has been a subject of extensive re-examination and innovation during recent years. Professors Robinson and Pettway provide a comprehensive analysis of the subject in their recent study *Policies for Optimum Bank Capital,* of which the summary section is reproduced as the first reading—which considers the function of bank capital, the problem of its measurement, and procedures individual banks should use to make optimal bank capital decisions.

A significant innovation has been the accelerated use of bank debt capital. The article by Paul F. Jessup outlines the background of this instrument and analyzes its implications for bank managers, depositors, investors, and supervisory authorities.

Because of its direct relationship to retained earnings, a bank's dividend policy is a major variable in its capital structure decision. In the third reading, E. Sherman Adams uses a sample of banks and utilities to analyze the association between dividend payout and price-earnings multiples. His statistical evidence suggests that banks—and their shareholders—would benefit from higher dividend payouts.

Policies for Optimum Bank Capital:

Summary

Roland I. Robinson and Richard H. Pettway

1. During the century and a half for which United States banking statistics are available, the capital of banks has grown less rapidly than their assets and liabilities. Thus, the relative amount of bank capital has persistently declined. The logical inference is simple: if capital were only barely adequate in the past, then either it is less than adequate in the present or the relative need for capital has declined. Since instability marred the history of banking in many earlier periods, it would have been hard to have argued that past banking capital was excessive. Therefore, the only logical grounds on which present safety can be rationally assumed is that the relative need for banking capital has declined.

2. The question of capital adequacy has recently received renewed attention because commercial banks have become more aggressive, growth-minded institutions—and they have also become less liquid.

3. The function of bank capital is that of absorbing short and intermediate term losses resulting from events that managerial foresight cannot be reasonably expected to anticipate; a margin of safety that, preferably, would allow a bank to continue operations without loss of momentum and, at least, would buy time in which a bank could re-establish its operational momentum. If proper liquidity policies are pursued so that banks are not forced to liquidate good, but illiquid, assets under pressure and at unfavorable times, then the risks to be covered are those which cannot be anticipated by actuarial or other probability methods. Some such risks can be covered by insurance; defalcation, for example. Many of the "losses" suffered by banks can be so anticipated —most loan losses and even those associated with short-term swings in business conditions. The type of losses for which capital protection is needed are those that cannot be anticipated: expropriation of foreign property, uninsurable disasters in the area in which a bank operates, and lapses of managerial judgment.

Reprinted with the permission of the Association of Reserve City Bankers, Chicago, from *Policies for Optimum Bank Capital,* February 1967.

4. A bank needs capital to cover the hazards it faces as an individual bank; banks could not be expected to have enough capital to cover national hazards such as those that would be experienced in an attack upon the nation by nuclear weapons. Nor should banks be expected to have capital to cover gross errors in official judgment such as marked the banking difficulties of the Great Depression. Banks must be prepared for recessions, but it is not necessary that they compound this need by assuming that such recessions will be aggravated by uninformed public economic policy.

5. Since capital is needed to cover the hazards that cannot be anticipated, it follows that capital adequacy cannot be measured; it cannot be reduced to a formula; the only way in which it can be approximated is by the judgment of persons with mature financial experience. The honest label for this is "subjective" judgment.

6. The test of capital adequacy for a bank is not only the judgment of bankers themselves but also the judgment of their customers with money and credit availability at stake; also the judgment of bank supervisors as the agents for the general public interest.

7. Since direct measurement of bank capital adequacy is logically impossible, only indirect evidence can be marshalled. Such evidence as could be assembled in this study, mainly the judgments of the second group mentioned above in (6), gave no hint of bank capital inadequacy. This essentially negative finding, however, does not prove adequacy. This evidence was mainly relevant to larger banks; the capital position of small banks was not tested.

8. Although direct evidence on the point could not be marshalled, the relative need for bank capital probably has declined. Fiscal and monetary policy are better equipped to deal with economic instability, and managerial methods of dealing with risk have been improved. However, new hazards may be encountered, even if they cannot be clearly discerned. World political instability could have drastic economic effects on the United States; technological revolution is not always beneficial to every segment of the economy.

9. Although no evidence of inadequacy was detected, the decline in relative bank capital protection is likely to continue unless some most unusual and unanticipated changes in conditions should occur. Even though indirect, testing should be continued; individual banks need to review their capital position regularly by application of such tests as are relevant. The public authorities probably will have to continue to take an interest in the problem, at least with respect to smaller banks.

10. Individual banks need a capital policy which, as a minimum, should embrace the following elements:

a. A bank should not only have enough capital to cover unanticipated losses but also enough more to keep on functioning without loss of institutional momentum.

b. Since profits are, and almost certainly will continue to be, the primary source of capital additions, a bank should aim to maximize the rate of return on its capital and not its size.
c. A bank should shape its financial policies so as to minimize its cost of capital and cost of funds. An approximate test of minimization of funds cost is whether a bank is failing to secure deposits or paying a higher price for deposits than it would have to pay with more capital.
d. A bank should balance the profits in all special operations (trust departments, foreign operations, EDP services, even bank buildings themselves) against the cost of the added equity and debt capital required for such operations. This evaluation of capital expenditures parallels good practice in non-financial business.
e. The most important part of an individual bank's capital planning is its dividend policy. The evidence seems clear and unmistakable that bank share prices are influenced by dividend pay-out. If a bank retains earnings to increase its rate of capital growth, it increases its cost of external equity capital. Except for banks in areas of exceptionally fast growth, bank stocks have been considerably less than star price performers in post-war equity markets. It is not clear that different dividend policies would have improved the performance, but a general re-examination of dividend policy seems indicated. Rather than follow a median dividend policy, an individual bank may have to go to one or the other extremes: retain a larger part of earnings with consequent damage to its stock prices; or pay out rather generous dividends with the hope that such pay-outs will be more than returned in higher share prices when external equity financing is undertaken.
f. A bank should raise new capital externally only when it is possible to improve, or at least to maintain, the rate of return on existing equity capital. Another way of stating this rule is that a bank should raise equity capital only when it can be employed at a rate of return equal to or in excess of the cost of equity capital to that bank. The same rule should be applied to debt capital. During 1964 and 1965, when most capital notes and debentures were sold, they qualified under this rule. The sale of such obligations has since slackened, suggesting that this rule is already being followed by most banks.

11. The standards developed by the public authorities for screening or evaluation of bank capital adequacy cannot be said to have produced useful results. The public interest in banking safety would be discharged better if attention were focused on quality of bank management. As suggested above in (10a), rational bank managers would want at least as much as and possibly more capital than merely that required for public safety; they would want to be sure of more than barely covering losses; they would prefer to be able to keep operational momentum. The public interest requires no more capital than indicated by this standard. Negatively, it can be said that the public authorities should not press

for added bank capital unless an adequate return can be earned on it. If an adequate return can be earned from added capital, then a bank itself would have reason to add capital from external sources voluntarily.

12. Earnings have priority as a banking problem over the capital problem. The social optimum is reached when the marginal returns to capital are equalized among all companies and industries. That point has not yet been reached by commercial banking as an industry, and the attainment of it should be a major objective, not only of individual banks, but of the industry as a whole.

Bank Debt Capital:

Urchin of Adversity to Child of Prosperity*

Paul F. Jessup

Beginning early in 1963, banks have been introducing increased amounts of debt instruments into their capital structures. In less than two years, over $700 million in capital notes and debentures have been issued. Not only is this use of debt capital a major shift from past policy, it has broad implications for the future.

A variety of banks have issued such capital notes and debentures. The largest issue of $100 million was that of the Bankers Trust Company of New York City, the ninth largest bank in the nation. At the other end of the spectrum was an issue of $300,000, placed privately by a small bank ($13 million in deposits) in Tennessee. In addition to the increasing use of such instruments, new innovations are being introduced. For example, in the past year several banks have chosen to sell *convertible* capital notes. It seems certain that the present trend toward bank debt capital will continue—and probably accelerate. Why has this method of bank financing recently become popular? To answer this question it is necessary to consider recent developments influencing bank capital requirements. Then one must look at the various factors influencing the

* This reading has been slightly abridged from the original article.

Reprinted with permission from *The Bankers' Magazine,* Summer 1965.

decision as to the "best" method of raising new capital. Having considered this general framework, this article analyzes the recent issues of capital notes and debentures. In conclusion, attention is focused on the probable impact on such individuals and groups as: bank customers, investors, shareholders, and the supervisory authorities.

HISTORICAL BACKGROUND OF BANK SENIOR CAPITAL

Senior capital (debt instruments and preferred stock) was seldom used by American commercial banks until the onset of the Depression. Typically banks were capitalized only with common stock. With the spreading bank failures in the early 1930's, the Reconstruction Finance Corporation (RFC) was established as a government corporation to lend to banks, the loans to be secured by sound—if illiquid—assets.[1] Despite this initial assistance, many banks continued to find their capital impaired because of decreasing asset values and the shifting standards of the bank examiners.[2] In 1933 further action was taken when the Emergency Banking Act authorized the RFC to purchase preferred stocks of banks. A subsequent amendment to this Act also permitted the RFC to purchase bank capital notes and debentures, subordinated to deposit liabilities. To permit this Act to be implemented, most states proceeded to authorize their state banks to issue preferred stock and/or debentures.

Thus the use of senior securities in bank capital structures developed during a period of economic crises and emergency measures. Given these conditions, the concept of such senior securities became associated in the minds of many people with bank "weakness"; and most bankers hastened to eliminate such securities from the capital structures of their banks. Contributing to this trend was the attitude of the bank supervisory authorities. For example, in 1954 the Board of Governors of the Federal Reserve System denied the request of a member bank to issue senior capital.[3] The Office of the Comptroller of the Currency also discouraged such new issues. From a peak of nearly $1,000 million in 1934, the amount of such senior securities rapidly declined so that by 1950 there was less than $100 million outstanding, and by 1960 less than $50 million. These few remaining issues were primarily in the states of Minnesota, New Jersey, and New York.

[1] Charles M. Williams, "Senior Securities—Boon for Banks?" *Harvard Business Review*, July–August 1963, p. 83.

[2] Donald P. Jacobs, *The Impact of Bank Examination Practices*, Committee on Banking and Currency, U.S. House of Representatives, 1964.

[3] Cited by Herbert Bratter, "Debentures: A New Way to Raise Bank Capital," *Banking*, February 1964, p. 59.

BANK CAPITAL REQUIREMENTS IN RECENT YEARS

During recent years, total bank assets have been increasing, requiring increased capital accounts just to maintain a similar ratio of capital accounts to total assets. Given the bankers' aversion to senior securities, capital accounts have been increased through retained earnings and occasional sales of additional common stock.

However, not only have bank assets been increasing, there have been important *changes* in bank assets and deposit liabilities. Inspection of Table 1 suggests several such important changes.

While demand deposits have only slightly increased since 1958, there has been a major increase in time deposits. Many of these time deposits have been attracted by the higher rates of interest which banks offered after the limit under Regulation Q was increased from 3 to 4 per cent. In addition to these higher rates, banks have more aggressively sought time deposits by their recent emphasis on negotiable certificates of deposit. Thus one may argue that many of these time deposits are "interest

Table 1 Selected Assets and Liabilities of All Member Banks [1]
(Average in billions of dollars)

	1958	*1959*	*1960*	*1961*	*1962*	*1963*
Total Assets	194.9	201.3	207.2	221.8	239.0	254.0
Total Loans[2]	82.4	89.1	97.7	102.1	111.4	124.1
Commercial and Industrial	37.1	36.1	38.1	39.7	42.1	45.3
All Other	45.2	52.9	59.6	62.3	69.3	78.8
Total Investments	67.2	66.9	62.7	69.0	74.9	77.6
U.S. Government Obligations	51.5	50.4	46.5	51.2	53.0	50.9
State and Municipal Securities	12.5	13.6	13.8	15.4	18.9	23.2
All Other	3.2	2.8	2.5	2.5	2.9	3.6
Cash and Due from Banks	41.5	41.5	43.7	45.1	46.6	45.6
Total Deposits	175.8	180.8	185.8	197.3	211.7	223.8
Demand	125.1	126.7	129.8	133.6	137.4	137.7
Time	50.7	54.1	56.0	63.7	74.3	86.1
Capital Accounts	15.1	15.9	16.8	18.0	19.2	20.4
Ratio of Cash and U.S. Government Securities to Total Assets	48	46	44	43	42	38
Ratio of Capital Accounts to assets other than Cash and U.S. Government Securities	15	15	14	14	14	13

[1] Figures exclude deposits, loans and investments at foreign branches.
[2] Net after deduction of valuation reserves.

Sources: Rows 1–14 reprinted from *Bank Stock Quarterly*, June 1964, p. 8, published by M. A. Schapiro and Co., Inc. Row 15 calculated from above data by author.

sensitive" and perhaps more volatile than the present aggregate of demand deposits.

To be able to earn more in order to meet these higher interest costs on time deposits, banks have been shifting their asset structures to include more higher-yielding loans and investments. Table 1 points out the moderate increase in commercial and industrial loans, while all other loans (such as consumer credit and loans on real estate) have almost doubled since 1958. In a similar manner, investments in U.S. Government securities have remained virtually the same since 1958, while holdings of state and municipal securities—with their special tax features—have almost doubled.

A further indication of these changes is provided by the ratios presented in Table 1. The ratio of cash and U.S. Government securities to total assets has declined steadily from 48 per cent in 1958 to 38 per cent in 1963. This suggests that "risk assets" (defined as assets *other than* cash and U.S. Government securities) have increased more rapidly than total assets, thus raising the question of adequate liquidity. Similarly the ratio of capital accounts to assets other than cash and U.S. Government securities has declined from 15 per cent to 13 per cent, thus raising the question of capital adequacy. Of course, such general trends and ratios cannot measure unequivocally a need for increased bank capital, but they do raise serious questions about a need for additional capital in the present banking structure.

Recently an increasing number of metropolitan banks have added to their capital accounts by means of sale-and-leaseback arrangements. By selling its depreciated buildings to another owner at market value, a bank may then increase its capital accounts by the difference between the sale price and the depreciated book value of the property. At the same time as the sale, the bank signs a long-term lease for the continued use of the property. A further refinement of this technique is to set up a wholly-owned subsidiary, which in turn may raise the purchase price by selling long-term securities.

THE COMPTROLLER'S RULING OF DECEMBER 1962

It has been pointed out how senior capital of banks was associated with the distress financing of the 1930's. Despite this background and prevalent attitude, the Commission on Money and Credit, in its report of 1961, recommended the exploration of two suggestions—bank authorization to issue debentures subordinated to the claims of the depositors, and issuance of preferred stock. Shortly afterwards, the Advisory Committee on Banking to the Comptroller of the Currency reported that "there is no sound reason why national banks should be deprived of any legitimate capital-raising method that is available to corporations generally." [4] The Committee further recommended that national banks be permitted to issue capital notes and preferred stock. This recommendation related well to Mr. Saxon's general concepts of greater flexibility and competition in national banking. On December 28, 1962, the Comptroller of the Currency published new rulings permitting national banks to issue convertible or non-convertible capital debentures, subject to his approval.[5]

It has already been pointed out how increased bank capital seemed advisable by 1963. This ruling of the Comptroller provided the impetus to a major reappraisal of senior securities in bank capital structures. On December 28, 1962, the nation's insured commercial banks had $21 million outstanding in capital notes and debentures. By June 30, 1964, this figure had increased to $521 million; and currently it exceeds $700 million.

Not only has the issuance of capital notes and debentures become increasingly evident during the past two years, the trend could readily accelerate. As a rough measure of the *possible* growth of these debt instruments, one can consider the Comptroller's ruling that capital notes "shall not exceed an amount equal to 100% of the bank's unimpaired paid-in capital stock plus 50% of the amount of its unimpaired surplus fund." It may be assumed that many state banks will seek similar limits from their state supervisory authorities.

As of December 20, 1963, the Federal Deposit Insurance Corporation reports that all insured commercial banks had aggregate common stock of $7,283 million and an aggregate surplus of $12,163 million.[6] *If* these banks were to issue capital notes to their assumed legal limits, these outstanding notes could amount to $13,365 million.[7] Of course this example suggests only the short-term maximum amount, and it disregards such important variables as actual capital needs, the marketability of large amounts of such capital notes, and the time periods involved. Nevertheless this calculation does suggest the major potential of these bank debt instruments.

[4] Cited by Alfred C. West, "Senior Capital Financing by Commercial Banks," *Bankers Monthly Magazine,* May 15, 1964, p. 38.

[5] Title 12—Code of Federal Regulation—Section 14.5: (a) It is the policy of the Comptroller of the Currency to permit the issuance of convertible or non-convertible capital debentures by national banking associations in accordance with normal business considerations.

[6] *Annual Report of the Federal Deposit Insurance Corporation,* December 31, 1963, p. 143.

[7]

100% of banks' unimpaired paid-in capital stock:	$ 7,283
50% of their unimpaired surplus funds:	6,082
Total (millions)	$13,365

ALTERNATIVE METHODS OF RAISING NEW BANK CAPITAL

Capital accounts have been increased principally through retained earnings. In this way, bank management has followed a policy similar to that of many major corporations which have emphasized self-financing. With this capital, the managers should try to maximize the return on shareholders' equity within the context of an acceptable degree of "risk." At times, however, some bank managers may judge that their present capital is "fully employed" and that their banks' growth potential requires additional sources of capital. It is then that the managers must consider the best method of raising this new capital.

Until the Comptroller's recent ruling about capital debentures, those banks which required additional capital have usually secured these funds by selling new shares to the bank's stockholders.[8] Of course if a shareholder fails to subscribe for the additional shares to which he is entitled, then his proportionate interest in the bank's future earnings is reduced. This consideration tends to penalize those individual shareholders who are not able to subscribe to their additional shares at the time of the offering.

A further problem involved in selling additional common shares is when the market value of a bank's stock is below its book value. In the case of most expanding banks, such a relationship is not likely to be the case; but for smaller, closely-held banks it may be that additional shares would have to be sold below book value. In such a case, those shareholders who do not subscribe for additional shares not only have their proportionate ownership of the bank reduced, they are selling their right in the bank's earning power to other shareholders at less than current value (as measured by book value).

In addition to the preceding problems of the possible "dilution" of a shareholder's equity in the bank, there is the further consideration of possibly introducing senior capital and thus trading on the shareholders' equity. In this way management may be able to increase the earnings of the bank's owners—the common stockholders. Not to do so may indeed be a "cost" to these shareholders in that their equity might have greater earning power through the introduction of such senior securities.

It has been pointed out that bankers were reluctant to issue preferred stock because of its association with the bank problems of the 1930's. Another reason why banks have issued very little preferred stock in re-

[8] "All national banks and probably the great majority of state-chartered banks must issue pre-emptive rights to shareholders upon sale of additional common stock because each holder must have the opportunity to retain his pro rata voting rights after such sale." Source: "Convertible Capital Notes for Bank," *Bank Stock Quarterly,* September 1964, pp. 6–7.

cent years is because dividends on such stock are payable from net income after taxes, in contrast to debt instruments wherein the interest is paid before federal income taxes. The only significant preferred stock issued by a bank in recent years was the $20,000,000 in 4.60% cumulative preferred ($100 par) issued by the Franklin National Bank (Mineola, New York). At the time of this offering in September 1962, *The Commercial & Financial Chronicle* observed that "since the 1930's, there has not been a public sale of preferred stock by any major bank in the United States, although several bank holding companies have issued preferred stock." [9] After this successful offering, several other banks did sell small amounts of preferred stock in 1963.

Although there have been these few issues of preferred stock, it has been primarily to debt instruments that banks have turned since the Comptroller's ruling and the subsequent reconsideration by many bankers of their capital accounts. The issuance of capital notes and debentures avoids *dilution* of shareholders' equity—although it may reduce the *return* on shareholders' equity in the short run. In the longer run it will almost certainly increase the return on shareholders' equity, because such senior capital usually introduces favorable leverage. Table 2 presents examples of this leverage phenomenon.

Of course the illustrations of Table 2 rest on several assumptions, such as: (1) the amount which the bank can earn on its total capital before income taxes; (2) the rate of interest on the debentures; and (3) the effective rate of Federal income tax. Each bank must consider these variables as they apply to its particular circumstances. For example, other factors being equal, a bank which (1) earns more than this assumed rate of return, (2) obtains a lower interest cost, and (3) pays a higher rate of income tax, would find the issuance of debt capital even more attractive than suggested by Table 2.

Most banks have been able to sell their non-convertible capital notes and debentures at an interest cost of between 4½ and 5 per cent. As noted, however, this interest cost is deductible before Federal income taxes. Another cost advantage of such debt capital for Federal Reserve member banks is that no additional subscription to Federal Reserve Stock is necessary, as it would be if this new capital were in the form of common or preferred stock. Selling costs of such debt issues (particularly private placements) are less than they would be for an offering of a comparable dollar amount of common stock. In addition, the subsequent handling costs are likely to be less than they would be for an equity issue with its attendant dividend handling and transfer costs.

That many banks are issuing such debt instruments as a source of capital alternative to subscription offerings of common stock is reflected in the fact that almost all of these banks have had such subscriptions in the past decade. Indeed, many banks have offered to sell additional

[9] *The Commercial & Financial Chronicle,* October 1, 1962, volume 196, number 6199, p. 1345.

Table 2 Hypothetical Example of Leverage Effect of Debenture Capital

(Dollar figures in millions)

A	B	C	D	E	F	G
Debt Ratio	*Total Capital*	*Debentures*	*Shareholders' Equity*	*Net Income before Federal Income Tax* [1]	*Interest on Debentures* [2]	*Net Profit after Interest*
0	$100	$—	$100	$15.0	$—	$15.0
20%	125	25	100	18.8	1.3	17.5
33%	150	50	100	22.5	2.5	20.0

H	I	J
Federal Income Tax [3]	*Net Profit after Tax*	*% Return on Shareholders' Equity*
$6.0	$ 9.0	9.0 [4]
7.0	10.5	10.5
8.0	12.0	12.0

[1] Assumes that the bank can earn 15 per cent on its total capital before Federal income taxes. In 1963 insured commercial banks in the United States earned an average 14 per cent before such taxes.
[2] Assumes an interest rate of 5 percent for the debentures. This is in accord with such interest costs on bank debentures to date.
[3] Assumes an effective Federal income tax rate of 40 per cent. In 1963 insured commercial banks in the United States paid an effective tax of 33 per cent.
[4] This accords with the fact that in 1963 insured commercial banks in the United States earned about 9 per cent after taxes on their shareholders' equity.

Source of 1963 data for insured commercial banks: *Annual Report of the Federal Deposit Insurance Corporation,* December 31, 1963, pp. 152–153.

shares to their stockholders in two, three, or even four of the past ten years.

In addition to considering such debt instruments as a source of additional bank capital, one may also view such capital notes and debentures as a source similar to long-term deposits. In other words, one might compare them to long-term certificates of deposit with a fixed maturity. Viewed in this way, one may observe additional cost savings to the issuing bank. First, for member banks there is not the reserve requirement with the Federal Reserve. This requirement is currently 4 per cent for time deposits. Second, because these debt instruments have fixed maturities, there is not as great a liquidity need for secondary reserves—often low-yielding assets—as there would be in time deposits. For the same reason of the fixed maturity, one can therefore invest these funds in longer-term, higher-yielding assets. Some banks may indeed "hedge" all or part of these new funds by investing them in high-yielding assets which will mature at times appropriate for the servicing of this long-term obligation. Third, since these funds acquired through the sale of capital notes are not deposits, there is not the added insurance cost payable to the Federal Deposit Insurance Corporation. As a final point, the cost of placing and handling these funds is likely to be less than it would be if these funds were acquired through additional time deposits.

As a source of capital or as a source of funds comparable to long-term deposits, the sale of capital notes may permit bank management greater flexibility. The fixed maturity enables bank management to plan ahead for that particular date, often by means of scheduling asset maturities and making sinking fund payments. If it is found after the issuance of debt instruments that the additional funds are not all necessary, the bank may have such options open to it as increased sinking fund purchases or a call of the notes. It is much less easy to retire "excess" common stock, and the bank may be less able to influence its time deposits (although it can usually do so by changing its level of interest rates when it is below the legal maximum).

By selling capital notes to raise bank capital, the Comptroller has ruled that national banks may include such notes "as part of the total capital funds for the purpose of computing loan limits."[10] However, this ruling applies only to general loans because the Board of Governors of the Federal Reserve System has ruled that under the Federal Reserve Act, capital notes and debentures do *not* constitute a part of a bank's capital stock or surplus.[11] Under the Act this restriction applies to: loans to affiliates, securities purchases, investments in bank premises, loans secured by stock or bond collateral, deposits with nonmember banks, and bankers acceptances, as well as provisions that limit the amount of paper of one borrower that may be discounted by a Federal Reserve Bank for any member bank.

For groups which control banks, the issuance of capital notes may well be an attractive method of securing additional capital without diluting their control. The investor in such capital notes becomes a creditor of the bank, but he receives no voting rights. This factor of control may be particularly important in those cases where the control is by families or holding companies.

GENERAL CONSIDERATION OF RECENT ISSUES OF CAPITAL NOTES

Having considered the reasons why such issues of capital notes and debentures have recently become popular, it is instructive to look at the general features of those issued recently. Table 3 presents the significant features of 54 such recent issues of debt capital. These 54 issues, totaling

[10] *Years of Reform: A Prelude to Progress.* Reprinted from the 101st Annual Report (1963) of the Comptroller of the Currency, p. 19.

[11] *Federal Reserve Bulletin,* January 1964, pp. 9–10.

Table 3 Selected Provisions of 54 Issues of Bank Debt Capital

	Amount (millions)	Term (years)	Rate of Interest
Bankers Trust Co. (N.Y.C.)	$100	25	4½
Crocker-Citizens National Bank (San Francisco)	100	25	4.60
Wells Fargo Bank (San Francisco)	50	25	4½
	25.3	25	3¼*
United California Bank (L.A.)	35	25	4½
Franklin National Bank (Mineola, N.Y.)	30	25	4¾
Manufacturers National Bank of Detroit	25	25	4.65
Mercantile Trust Co. (St. Louis)	25	20	4.60
Union Bank (L.A.)	25	25	4⅝
Central National Bank (Cleveland)	20	25	4¾
Citizens & Southern National Bank (Savannah)	20	25	4⅝
First National Bank in Dallas	20	25	4½
Meadow Brook National Bank (Jamaica, N.Y.)	17.5	25	4.85
First National Bank of Atlanta	16.9	25	3½*
First Union National Bank of North Carolina	15	25	4⅞
Mercantile National Bank at Dallas	15	25	4¾
Western Pennsylvania National Bank (Pittsburgh)	15	25	5
Valley National Bank of Arizona (Phoenix)	13.7	25	3½*
First Western Bank & Trust Co. (L.A.)	12.5	25	4⅞
First National Bank (Miami)	10	25	4.70
First National Bank & Trust Co. of Tulsa	10	25	4⅝
Lincoln Rochester Trust Co. (Rochester, N.Y.)	10	25	4.70
Liberty National Bank & Trust Co. (Oklahoma City)	8	25	4¾
City National Bank (Beverly Hills)	7.5	20	4⅞
Security National Bank of Long Island (Huntington, N.Y.)	7.5	25	4¾
First National Bank of San Diego	6	25	4.7
Security Trust Co. of Rochester (N.Y.)	6	25	4.8
LaSalle National Bank (Chicago)	5	25	4.75
Northwestern Bank (North Wilkesboro, N.C.)	5	20	5
Peoples Trust Company of Bergen County (Hackensack, N.J.)	5	20	4⅞
United States National Bank of San Diego	5	20	4⅞
Exchange National Bank (Chicago)	4	23	5
Central Trust Co. (Rochester)	3.5	25	4⅞
Central Valley National Bank (Oakland)	3.5	20	4⅞
Central Bank & Trust Co. (Denver)	3	20	5¼
Deposit Guaranty Bank & Trust Co. (Jackson)	3	25	4½
First National Bank at Orlando	3	25	4.8
Michigan Bank N.A. (Detroit)	3	25	5⅛
Texas Bank & Trust Co. (Dallas)	3	25	4¾
Bank of Commerce (N.Y.C.)	2.5	15	5
Commercial Bank of North America (N.Y.C.)	2.25	7	5¼
American National Bank of Maryland (Silver Spring)	2	20	5
American Security Bank (Honolulu)	2	20	5¼
First National Bank (Mansfield, Ohio)	2	20	4⅞
Oakland Bank of Commerce	2	25	4⅞
Rockland National Bank (Suffern, N.Y.)	2	20	4⅞
McDowell National Bank (Sharon, Pa.)	1.5	20	5⅛

Table 3 (Continued)

	Amount (millions)	Term (years)	Rate of Interest
Bank of Buffalo (N.Y.)	1	20	5
Clarendon Trust Company (Arlington, Va.)	1	10	4¾*
Exchange Bank (Santa Rosa, Calif.)	1	20	5.10
First Bank & Trust Co., N.A. (Fords, N.J.)	1	10	5
First National Bank (Niles, Mich.)	1	15	5
Hightstown Trust Co (N.J.)	0.5	20	4⅞
San Fernando Valley Bank (Pacoima, Calif.)	0.5	10	5†
First Farmer & Merchants National Bank (Columbia, Tenn.)	0.3	15	5

* Issue with a conversion feature.
† Conversion feature. Also, for the first five years, interest will be payable in common stock at rate of one share for each $250 note, and in cash thereafter at 5% a year.
Source: *Moody's Banks & Finance*, 1963, 1964.

$714 million, are the great majority of such issues through October 15, 1964. The size of the issues has ranged from $100,000,000 to $300,000. Only three issues exceeded $50,000,000; and half of the issues were for $10,000 000 or less.

Nearly all of these issues have a term of 20 or 25 years. There is a clear tendency of the larger issues to be of a longer maturity than the smaller issues (under $3,000,000), many of which are for 20 years or less. The point should be noted that many issues are scheduled to mature in 1988 and 1989. If, in the next few years, many banks also issue capital notes with maturities in 25 years, there will be a cluster of such debt instruments maturing around 1990. Although the operation of sinking funds and call provisions will retire or refinance many of these issues before their scheduled maturities, this fact that many are scheduled to mature around 1990 should be recognized by the issuing banks and the monetary authorities.

The rates of interest paid on the non-convertible issues range between 4½ and 5 per cent. There is an evident tendency of the larger issues to have been placed at rates nearer 4½ per cent.

From the information which is available, it seems that most of the issues have provisions for sinking funds and call provisions. These call provisions frequently come into effect only after several years from the date of issuance, and they usually provide for this call at a declining premium.

The indenture provisions of these issues usually provide that the capital notes are subordinate to the bank's obligations to its depositors and other customers. For example, the Bankers Trust issue specifies that "the capital notes will be subordinated in all respects to prior payment in full of the bank's obligations to depositors, its obligations under bankers' acceptances and letters of credit, its obligations to any Federal Reserve Bank, and (except as to any funded debt) its obligations to its creditors, whether now outstanding or hereafter incurred." [12]

[12] *Moody's Bond Survey*, December 16, 1963, p. 281.

Most of these recent issues set limitations on the bank's creation of further debt, often permitting such additional debt only if it is on parity with, or subordinate to, existing capital notes. Frequently there are also provisions which establish dividend restrictions, default rights, and modification of indenture procedures. The majority of these issues were placed privately—public offerings being made only in the case of the largest issues. Such private placements often can be made at lower selling costs to the issuing bank. In nearly all cases, the private placements have been with institutional investors such as insurance companies, pension funds, and trusteed funds.

GENERAL CONSIDERATION OF THOSE BANKS RECENTLY ISSUING CAPITAL NOTES

Table 4 shows a breakdown of the issuing banks by size of bank, measured by total assets. To date most of the capital note issues have been sold by the larger banks. However, given this precedent, it is reasonable to expect many more banks of less than $100 million in total assets to sell capital notes and debentures in the near future. These will probably be sold through private placements.

Table 5 lists the issuing banks of the 54 issues studied by type of bank (national or state) and by location.

The information suggested by this table has major implications for the nation's "dual banking system." Many states prohibit the issuance of capital notes and debentures by their state banks. As pointed out in Table 5, national banks have recently issued capital notes in states currently—or recently—prohibiting the issuance of such securities by the state banks. If these securities appear to favor the national banks in such states, the state bankers and supervisory authorities are likely to want changes in the state law. In this manner, such states as Arizona, Michigan, North Carolina, and South Carolina have acted recently to authorize

Table 4 Banks Issuing Capital Notes
(by size of bank)

Total Assets December 31, 1963 (millions)	*Number of Banks*
$1,000 or more	8
500–1,000	9
100– 500	24
50– 100	7
25– 50	3
10– 25	2
under 10	1
Total	54

Table 5 Banks Issuing Capital Notes
(by type of bank and location)

National Banks State	Number of Issuing Banks	*State Banks* State	Number of Issuing Banks
California	5	California	7
New York	4	New York	7
Michigan [b]	3	New Jersey	2
Florida [a]	2	Colorado	1
Georgia [a]	2	Hawaii	1
Illinois [a]	2	Mississippi	1
Ohio	2	Missouri	1
Oklahoma [a]	2	North Carolina [b]	1
Pennsylvania [a]	2	Tennessee	1
Texas [a]	2	Texas	1
Arizona [b]	1	Virginia	1
Maryland	1		
New Jersey	1		
North Carolina [b]	1		
Total (14 states)	30	(11 states)	24

[a] States in which state banks *may not* issue capital notes and debentures.
[b] States which have *recently permitted* their state banks to issue capital notes and debentures.

their state banks to issue debt capital.[13] It may well be that such state laws should be changed, but one must recognize that the impetus for such changes evolves largely from a ruling by one individual, the Comptroller of the Currency. His decision to permit national banks to issue debt capital is causing many states to grant the same permission to their state-chartered banks.

As considered earlier, the use of debt instruments is particularly appropriate when a controlling group of bank stockholders wants to raise additional capital without decreasing its control of the bank. Of the 54 banks which have issued capital notes or debentures, 7 are controlled by holding companies.

THE USE OF CONVERTIBLE CAPITAL NOTES

So far five banks have issued convertible capital notes. As pointed out in Table 6, two of these five banks are controlled by holding companies.

The three largest issues were sold at an interest cost of 3¼ to 3½ per cent. To have sold nonconvertible notes may have meant an interest cost of 4½ to 5 per cent. This is rather evident in the case of the Wells Fargo Bank. This bank issued some nonconvertible notes at the same time that it issued the convertible notes. Both issues were identical in such features as: maturity, call provisions, subordination, additional debt limitations,

[13] *Bank Stock Quarterly,* June 1964, p. 6.

Table 6 Banks Issuing Convertible Capital Notes

Name of Bank	Amount of Capital Notes (millions)	Rate of Interest	Conversion Price	Approximate Bid Price on Stock at Time of Issue	Bid Price on Notes[1]
Wells Fargo Bank	$25.3	3¼	60	52	106¼
Valley National Bank of Arizona	13.7	3½	85	73	109½
First National Bank of Atlanta	16.9	3½	75	64	108
Clarendon Trust Company [2]	1.0	4¾	50	N.A.	N.A.
San Fernando Valley Bank [2]	0.5	5 [3]	12½	N.A.	N.A.

1 As of September 18, 1964.
2 Bank controlled by a holding company.
3 For first five years, interest will be payable in common stock at rate of one share for each $250 note, and in cash thereafter at 5% a year.

and dividend restrictions. However, the bank was able to sell the convertible issue at an interest cost of 3¼ per cent, while the nonconvertible issue was sold at an interest cost of 4½ per cent. Thus, it seems that the selling of convertible notes enables the issuing bank to get a noticeably lower interest cost.

Another factor to be considered, however, is the selling costs of a convertible issue in contrast to a nonconvertible issue. Most banks must issue to their common stockholders pre-emptive subscription rights if convertible notes are issued. With this procedure there is a greater risk due to possible market fluctuation of the share price, and so the charges of the underwriters of a convertible issue are likely to be higher than they would be if it were a nonconvertible issue—and particularly if it were a negotiated private placement of such a nonconvertible issue. Also the subsequent handling costs would probably be less if the nonconvertible issue were placed with several institutional investors.

Table 6 also shows how the three major banks were able to set a conversion price of almost 20 per cent *above* the market price of the stock at the time the notes were being issued. To have sold common stock to raise this additional capital, the banks would have had to set the subscription price *below* the current market price.

Given these variables of interest costs and administrative costs, bank management may want to issue convertible notes if it believes that this additional capital is to be permanent rather than temporary. This is not to say that the bank could not "turn over" such long-term debt by refinancing it as it approaches maturity. But management may feel more comfortable by not having to be concerned with such refinancing, and so prefer the issuance of convertible notes. Such a procedure does provide certain benefits. In contrast to a current sale of common stock, the convertible notes are likely to be sold at a premium above the market price of the stock. Similarly, immediate dilution of earnings per share is avoided. As the bank profitably uses these additional funds, its earnings per share and book value should increase.

These favorable factors should lead to a higher market valuation of the common stock, and as this market price exceeds the conversion price the convertible notes will gradually be converted into common stock. Given an increased market valuation of the shares through the following years, the bank can usually force the conversion of the notes before maturity. This "forced conversion" might be achieved by such methods as a call or a dividend policy on the common stock such that the holder of the notes could secure a larger rate of return on his investment by converting to the common stock. In view of these benefits a bank may secure by issuing convertible notes, there are likely to be more bank borrowings of this type in the next several years.

BANK CUSTOMERS AND CAPITAL NOTES

The introduction of a moderate amount of capital notes or debentures into a bank's capital structure may be beneficial to its customers.

For the depositors, these debt instruments are clearly subordinate to their deposits. These senior securities are part of bank capital, and this additional capital provides more "staying power" for bank management in the event that certain assets become criticized by the bank's examiners. Other things such as asset holdings being equal, a bank depositor is more secure in the bank which has the larger capital accounts in relation to total assets.

While adequacy of the bank's capital is an important measure of the safety and liquidity of a depositor's money, the depositor is further protected in today's economy. The advent of the Federal Deposit Insurance Corporation enables the depositor to "insure" the liquidity of his deposit to the legal limit. The Federal Reserve System is committed to a sound monetary system, and hopefully will be able to prevent a recurral of the banking débâcle of the 1930's. Similarly bank examinations by the supervisory agencies are to help protect depositors. These institutional safeguards continue with the advent of debt instruments as part of bank capital.

In addition these supervisory authorities can influence the issuance and servicing of such capital notes and debentures. For example, the optional call provisions and optional sinking-fund payments of the Bankers Trust 4½% Capital Notes, due 1988, are subject to the approval of the New York Superintendent of Banks. In a similar way, the Financial Code of the State of California provides for supervision of capital notes and debentures by the Superintendent of Banks of the State of California.[14]

[14] "Section 662 of the Financial Code of the State of California provides that no payment may be made on account of principal of any capital notes or debentures unless following such payments the aggregate capital, surplus, undivided profits, capital notes and debentures of the bank equal such aggregate on the date of original issue

As considered above, the introduction of a reasonable amount of such debt capital should not reduce—but rather increase—the protection of a bank's depositors. Borrowers from a bank with a larger capital base may find such a bank more "aggressive" in its lending policies. A bank with a smaller capital base, other things such as deposit liabilities being equal, is likely to hold more of its assets in liquid securities than in loans. Furthermore, a bank management willing to innovate and experiment with such new techniques of raising capital is likely to be a management which is similarly alert to developing trends and opportunities in other types of banking services.

As a further point to consider, it may be that in the longer run the use of bank debt capital will contribute to a reduction in the cost of some services. The successful use of such debt capital will enhance profitability, and this may encourage banks (or force them through competition) to pass on part of these savings in their "cost of capital" to their customers.

INVESTORS AND CAPITAL NOTES

To date, most of the capital notes and debentures have been privately placed with institutional investors. However, with increasing amounts of these securities being offered, it is important that more investors be aware of the rapid developments in this new form of capital securities.

The three largest issues of capital notes have been offered to the public.[15] The interest yield, around 4.5 per cent, was similar to the yield on other high-grade taxable bonds. For example, during the first half of 1964, corporate bonds rated Aaa yielded about 4.4 per cent, and public utility bonds yielded around 4.5 per cent.[16]

The usual indenture provisions which are to help protect the interests of investors in these debt instruments have already been mentioned. Of particular importance to investors are the restrictions on a bank's creating additional capital debt—especially any such debt which would rank above the outstanding capital notes or debentures. Similarly, the role of the bank supervisory agencies in controlling the issuance and handling of these debt instruments serves to protect the interests of the investors.

The fact that most of these issues to date have included sinking funds and call provisions permits bank management to be flexible in the servicing of these obligations. Significantly the optional call provisions usually provide for an early call only at a premium. This is meant to

---

of the capital notes or debentures or as may be otherwise authorized by the Superintendent of Banks of the State of California." Source: *Moody's Bond Survey,* August 24, 1964, p. 556.

[15] Bankers Trust Co. 4½% due 1988
Crocker-Citizens National Bank 4.60% due 1989
Wells Fargo Bank 4½% due 1989

[16] *Federal Reserve Bulletin,* October 1964, p. 1298.

discourage the early refinancing of such capital notes and debentures in the event that interest rates should fall shortly after the issuance of these obligations. For a similar reason, there is at times a period of non-call provided for by some of these issues.

Table 7 outlines the pro forma capitalization of three major banks at the time each issued some capital notes. It can be seen that for these banks, the capital notes accounted for about 25 to 35 per cent of their total capital accounts. This is similar to almost all the other issues of capital notes and debentures, in that these outstanding debt instruments generally have not exceeded one-third of the pro forma capitalization. The fact that the national banks have not sold issues as large as they could under the Comptroller's ruling suggests that they consider these initial debt instruments to be trial offerings, in order to evaluate their impact. It further suggests that these banks have additional flexibility to sell more issues if their initial offerings are considered to be successful.

Of interest to investors in debt instruments is the question of interest coverage. In calculating the "interest cover," some analysts do not include interest on time deposits as a fixed obligation of the bank. While this cost is indeed somewhat flexible in the intermediate-term, it seems advisable to look at the interest cover of these bank capital notes taking into consideration the interest paid on time deposits. In addition, investors in such bank debt instruments must take into consideration such variables as: the amount and trend of time deposits in general and for that bank in particular; the degree of flexibility the bank may have in altering its interest payment on time deposits; and the probable actions of the Federal Reserve and state authorities if the banks should find themselves in a "squeeze" on interest rates.

Also important are the debtor bank's other fixed obligations, such as mandatory sinking fund payments and rental payments under long-term

Table 7 Pro Forma Capitalization of Three Banks Issuing Capital Notes

	Bankers Trust Co.		Crocker-Citizens National Bank		Wells Fargo Bank	
	Dollar Amount (millions)	Percent of Total	Dollar Amount (millions)	Percent of Total	Dollar Amount (millions)	Percent of Total
Capital notes	100.0	23	100.0	33	75.3 [a]	25
Capital stock	90.9 [b]	21	94.1 [c]	31	88.7 [d]	29
Surplus	161.0	37	82.4	27	91.3	16
Undivided profits	82.4	19	25.5	9	50.8	16
Total	$434.3	100	$302.0	100	$306.1	100

[a] Aggregate capital notes (convertible and nonconvertible) due September 15, 1989.
[b] Represented by 9,087,248 shares ($10 par) as of September 30, 1963.
[c] Represented by 9,407,120 shares ($10 par) as of December 31, 1963.
[d] Represented by 8,871,567 shares ($10 par) as of June 30, 1964.

Source: *Moody's Bond Survey:* December 16, 1963, p. 281; March 23, 1964, p. 834; August 24, 1964, p. 557.

leases. For example, in the case of the Bankers Trust Co., there is a mandatory annual sinking fund requirement (1964 through 1987) of $4,000,000; and "the bank's maximum annual rentals on property leases extending beyond September 30, 1966, net of maximum annual rentals received under subleases thereof, totaled $4,141,350 as of September 30, 1963." [17]

While considering such preceding factors as protective provisions, capital structure, and "interest coverage," the investor must also carefully analyze the quality of the bank's management. Where an issue provides a conversion privilege, the investor must evaluate this instrument as a means to participate in the bank's earnings growth. Another factor to be considered by the investor is the probable secondary market for an issue of capital notes, in the event that the investor decides to sell this security before it matures.

STOCKHOLDERS AND CAPITAL NOTES

As already discussed, a bank's issuance of debt capital enables it to secure additional capital without diluting the stockholders' equity. Similarly, viewed as a long-term deposit with a fixed maturity, it permits an able management to secure additional funds which it can then invest or lend. In this way, these senior securities can increase the bank's profitability and also the return on shareholders' equity.

However, a bank's shareholders must recognize that these debt instruments are obligations which must be serviced. It has been discussed how competent bank management has the flexibility to service moderate amounts of such debt through such procedures as sinking funds, optional calls, and planned reserves through "hedging." An implication of these procedures is that bank management will declare only modest cash dividends on the common stock in order to accumulate retained earnings to service the debt.

The issuance of such debt capital need not reduce the market's valuation of the bank's common stock. In fact, the reverse is more likely to occur. If a bank's management is able to use these new funds effectively, it should add to the earnings potential of the common stock. In this event, investors in bank shares may well place an increased valuation on shares in aggressive banks which have introduced senior securities into their capital structures.

Of course this does not preclude possible "leverage in reverse," whereby a bank fails to use such new funds efficiently and thus reduces the return on shareholders' equity. (Even worse, it may be that a bank should fail to meet its interest obligation on such debt capital.) But this situation suggests a management which has failed to acquire suitable assets with

[17] *Moody's Bond Survey*, December 16, 1963, p. 281.

its new capital. Such a situation could occur, but it assumes poor bank management; and this can occur even without senior securities in a bank's capital structure. Similarly, such economic conditions may occur which jeopardize bank assets which had previously seemed sound; but this implies inadequate bank supervision and inadequate monetary policy. This, too, could occur; but also it could occur without the existence of bank debt instruments. In summary, the use of senior securities by banks has many merits; but it could lead to abuses. To avoid the latter requires careful judgment on the part of bank management, investors, and the supervisory authorities.

THE SUPERVISORY AUTHORITIES AND CAPITAL NOTES

The supervisory and monetary authorities have an important interest in this recent introduction of debt instruments into the capital structures of commercial banks.

The use of such debt capital should hasten a re-examination by supervisory authorities as to what constitutes "adequate capital" for banks. The Comptroller's Office has recently reconsidered the concept of "capital adequacy ratios"; but this question deserves further study among the supervisory authorities and students of banking.

The bank supervisory authorities have a major responsibility in regulating the issuance and use of capital notes and debentures. Important questions must be considered: What will be the general impact of these debt instruments on the banking community? Why does a particular bank want to issue such securities? Are there proposed issues which are intended to ensure continued control of a bank for a particular group where a broader ownership might better serve the public interest? Is this the best way for a particular bank to raise new capital? Will the management use these funds well, and will it be able to service such debt capital efficiently?

Furthermore, state authorities must re-examine other facets of such bank debt capital. As noted, many states continue to prohibit their banks from issuing such securities. With national banks now permitted to use debt capital, state banks may be placed at a competitive disadvantage.

The Federal Reserve must be aware of the changes in bank structure evolving from this use of debt capital. Where such capital notes are being used as a form of long-term certificate of deposit, there is no reserve requirement. This suggests possible slippage factors in monetary policy. The use of this debt capital requires adequate bank profits to service such obligations. The monetary authorities must recognize this implication for their policies, and it may even force them to place undue emphasis on this impact of their policies at times when other goals should be emphasized. In other words, there may be new constraints on the necessary flexibility of monetary policy.

If properly used, bank debt capital promises to benefit both bank depositors and stockholders. However, because of the importance of banking to the American economy, failure to understand the many implications of the trend in bank debt capital could be detrimental to the longer-term best interests of the banking industry and the public. For this reason the banking community and its regulatory agencies must carefully study this major development in contemporary banking.

Are Bank Dividend Policies Too Conservative?

E. Sherman Adams

After all, there is such a thing as being excessively conservative, even in banking. So we venture to pose the question: Are commercial banks paying out too small a portion of their current earnings in dividends?

This is a question that deserves careful reexamination today by bankers and bank directors. In the judgment of some analysts, a significant liberalization of bank dividend policies might enhance the aggregate market value of outstanding bank shares to the extent of hundreds of millions of dollars.

Some of the points put forward on either side of this question are quite venerable, but others are new. And even the old arguments need to be reappraised in the light of present-day circumstances.

It should be recognized at the outset that bank dividend policies reflect a large element of tradition, which some persons, I suppose, might less respectfully call inertia. In any event, the dividend policies of most banks do not often change very noticeably. Over the past four years, a representative list of leading banks paid out, on the average, 45% of net operating earnings in cash dividends. For the preceding four years, the ratio was 46%. For the past 15 years, the ratio has averaged 46%. These figures would seem to reflect considerable adherence to traditional payout policies.

This does not mean that these policies are necessarily wrong, of course, but it does suggest that they might be. There may be merit in maintain-

Reprinted with permission from *Banking,* Journal of The American Bankers Association, November 1967.

ing some consistency in a bank's payout policy over the years, but only if that policy still makes sense in today's world.

It should be emphasized that this article does not attempt to deal with all of the many factors that a bank must consider in connection with its dividend policy. Instead, attention is focused primarily on just one factor—the effects of payout policy.

No attention is given to the controversial subject of stock dividends, not because the author thinks that stock dividends have no merits, but because, as a practical matter, most banks are not going to use them and consideration of them here might be more confusing than helpful.

We shall examine two main questions:

(1) Is the case for conservative bank dividend policies as persuasive as it was years ago?

(2) What benefits might accrue if banks were to move toward more generous payout policies?

A NEW DEVELOPMENT

On the first of these questions, one significant new development is that debt financing by commercial banks has now become respectable. Previously there were only two important sources of bank capital: Retained earnings and the sale of new stock. Of these two alternatives, the former was by far the more advantageous from the standpoint of protecting a bank's earnings per share, and this was always the clinching argument for accumulating as much capital as possible from retained earnings by adhering to a low dividend payout policy.

Now there is a third source of bank capital, and one that is even more advantageous, namely, the issuance of capital notes or debentures. To be sure, this new vehicle is not a panacea. A bank cannot expand its indebtedness indefinitely. Also, there could be prolonged periods when market conditions would make banks reluctant to sell capital notes—the past year, for example.

It is plain, nevertheless, that over the years commercial banks will be able to go considerably further with debt financing than they have to date. So far, less than 2% of all commercial banks have issued any debt capital, and even for those that have, the average ratio of debt as a percentage of capital funds is less than 25%. For the banking system as a whole, debt issues constitute only about 6% of total capital.

How much higher this percentage will eventually go, no one can say. Even today, many bankers and bank supervisors would not be concerned to see debt capital comprise up to one-third or more of the capital funds of well-managed banks. And views on this may tend to become even more lenient as debt financing becomes more prevalent.

Most bankers do not yet think of debt as being a permanent part of a bank's capital structure. To be sure, they long ago abandoned the expectation that governments would retire their debts, and they are thoroughly accustomed to seeing indebtedness persist on the balance sheets of their corporate customers. Their attitude has even softened considerably toward continuous borrowing by consumers. For that matter, they are quite used to carrying large debts themselves under the more appealing name of deposits. But they have not yet come to regard debt capital as performing a continuing role in their capital setup. They still think of it as something temporary, something to be retired before too long and presumably replaced with equity capital.

Despite this attitude, they have shown little reluctance about using debt financing whenever the price is right. The volume of this financing has apparently abated over the past year or so because of its increased cost, but when interest rates subside, it can be expected to expand again.

Moreover, it seems safe to predict that when banks start retiring their presently outstanding debt capital, they will replace it with new. A particular issue of capital notes may be temporary, obedient to its sinking fund provisions, but in all probability the existence of debt in bank capital structures will not be.

It seems clear, therefore, that debt financing will be an important alternative source of bank capital over the years ahead. This injects a major new consideration into the formulation of dividend policy. For most banks, the chief argument for a low payout policy is less compelling than it used to be.

WHAT BENEFITS?

We come now to the second main question: What benefits might result from more liberal dividend policies?

Some shareholders would doubtless like larger dividends simply because they regard increased income as being a fine thing. But from the standpoint of most shareholders, the problem is more complicated than that. It is a question of weighing the comparative benefits that might flow from alternative uses of the bank's earnings: Retention to augment capital or the payment of higher dividends. What payout policies would bring maximum benefits to shareholders not only in terms of income, but also in terms of the market value of their holdings?

The crucial question here is what effect more liberal dividend policies would have on the level of bank stock prices. Indeed, the whole case for such policies rests primarily on the thesis that they would bring about an appreciable improvement in quotations for bank equities.

Market price is a matter of great significance to all bank shareholders, including those who have no intention of selling their holdings for a long time to come. Whenever a bank has occasion to issue new stock, the price-earnings ratio at which its outstanding shares are quoted is a major determinant of the cost of acquiring new capital and it therefore importantly affects the amount of dilution of per-share earnings that is entailed. Market price is also an important factor in acquisitions, with similar effects on dilution of earnings.

Let's start with the basic fact that the price of almost every stock is influenced to either a greater or lesser degree by its cash dividend rate. At one extreme are some exceptionally high growth-rate stocks, like IBM, Xerox, and Avon Products, whose prices appear to be affected hardly at all by their low payout ratios—though it is noteworthy that even these companies do pay cash dividends. And at the other extreme are stocks that are purchased primarily for income and sell largely "on a yield basis." Most stocks, including the great majority of bank stocks, are somewhere between these extremes.

In days of yore, many large holders of bank stocks had little interest in cash dividends. Indeed, some wealthy investors had no need for additional income and favored low payout policies for tax reasons. From their standpoint, it made sense for a bank to reinvest its earnings directly for the benefit of the stockholders rather than have the Treasury take a big tax bite out of higher dividends. These investors tended to regard book value as a significant indicator of the "intrinsic value" of their bank stocks and preferred to see a rise in book value than a larger dividend.

But wealthy individuals are relatively far less important today as holders of bank stocks. Individuals of more moderate means and institutional investors have become far more important. These investors have little interest in a stock's book value but they are very much interested in dividends and market price. It is the attitude of these investors that determines the average price-earnings ratio of bank stocks as a group.

In short, dividends may weigh considerably more heavily than formerly in the thinking of investors and potential investors in bank stocks. The problem is to evaluate just how important this factor is today and also how much more significant it might become in the future if banks were to liberalize their payout policies.

Good evidence on this is not easy to come by; it has to be dug out. There are of course many different factors that affect the prices both of individual stocks and various categories of stocks. The problem is to isolate the influence of the factor of dividend policy as it now applies, or might apply in the future, to bank stocks as a group.

REVEALING COMPARISON

It is revealing to compare bank stocks with public utility stocks. These two groups differ in a number of important respects, but they are widely regarded by investors as being similar from the standpoint of several fundamental investment characteristics. In general, on the basis of the record, both afford promise of moderate, relatively stable growth in earnings and in dividends over a period of years. The remarkable parallel between the price movements of leading bank and utility stocks over the past decade is shown in Figure 1.

In comparing these two groups, the most striking differences are that banks have a much lower average payout ratio than utilities and they also consistently sell in the market at a lower price-earnings multiple. For example, over the past six years, the average payout ratio of a representative list of leading banks was 45%, whereas the average ratio for the stocks comprising Standard & Poor's public utility index was 67%. For the same period, the average times-earnings multiple at which the bank stocks were quoted was 15.6, whereas the average multiple for the utilities was 20.1.

These facts suggest the possibility, of course, that banks' lower payout ratio might be a major reason for their lower price-earnings multiple. But these few figures alone cannot be regarded as any real evidence that such a causal relationship actually does exist. The correlation between payout ratios and price-earnings ratios may be coincidental. Completely different factors could conceivably be responsible for all of the disparity in the price-earnings multiples.

Several possible factors might be cited. It could be plausibly argued, for example, that for various reasons investors are more confident that utilities will enjoy greater and steadier growth in per-share earnings from year to year. Over the past several years, some investors have been con-

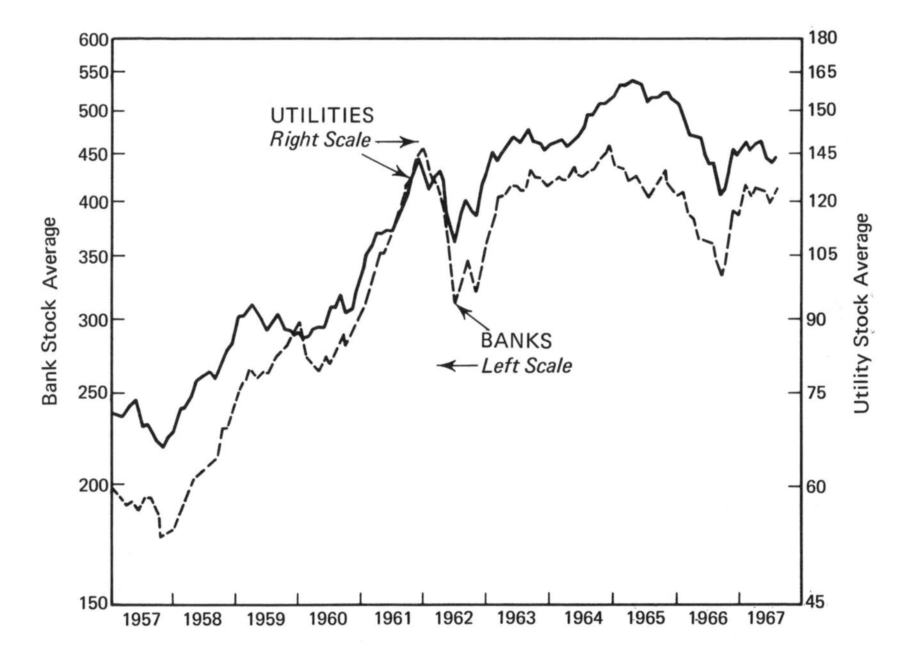

FIG. 1 Parallel action of bank and utility stocks.

Sources: Dow-Jones Utility Average; Keefe, Bruyette and Woods Bank Stock Index.

cerned about the squeeze on bank profit margins and the decline in bank liquidity. These fears were partly responsible for the poor performance of bank stocks in 1965 and the first nine months of 1966, as shown in Figure 1.

In addition, there are more well-known and actively traded utilities than bank stocks and, as a result, they receive more attention from brokers and analysts and enjoy a broader following among investors. Some investors find the outlook for bank stocks difficult to analyze. There are many utility stocks you could buy for long-term investment almost with your eyes closed, whereas with bank stocks there is a wide assortment of unforeseeable developments that might affect them adversely over the coming years. And many investors are mindful of Murphy's Law; to wit, that if anything can go wrong, it will.

This is no mean array of alleged advantages for the utilities. Do they perhaps account for all or almost all of the disparity in the price-earnings ratio of utilities versus banks? Or is there room left for dividend payout as a really significant causal factor?

WHAT THE DATA REVEAL

We can get at this question by examining regional data. Both banks and utilities are affected by the economic and population trends in the regions in which they operate and, by comparing companies in the same region, the influence of other factors can be seen more clearly (Table 1).

Presented here is a summary of pertinent statistics for lists of representative utilities and bank stocks in four broad regions: Eastern, Southern, Central, and Western. The lists of stocks used for this exercise and some of the data relating to them were supplied by David C. Cates, Manager, Bank Stock Department, Loeb, Rhoades & Co. The purpose here is to examine the *percentage differentials* in the payout ratios, price-earnings ratios, and growth in earnings per share of these groups of stocks.

Take the figures for the Western Region. For three representative Western utilities, the average payout ratio in 1966 was 59%, and for three leading Western banks, the average ratio was 46%. The differential between the two was 13 percentage points. In other words, the payout ratio of the utilities was 28% higher than that of the banks. This we refer to as the "percentage differential."

Similarly, the average price-earnings ratio of the utilities was 32% higher than that of the banks, and the increase in earnings per share during 1961–1966 was 40% greater for the utilities than for the banks.

These three percentage differentials of the Western utilities over the Western banks—28%, 32%, and 40%—are all roughly comparable in size. Looking at these figures alone, we cannot say what the causal relationships are. It could be that the higher price-earnings multiple of the utilities reflects their higher payout ratio. But not necessarily. It could

Table 1 Factors Affecting Price-Earnings Ratios

Comparison of the percentage differentials in the dividend payout ratios, price-earnings ratios, and growth of earnings per share of representative bank and utility stocks by regions.

	Average payout	*Price-earnings ratio*	*Increase in earnings per share 1961–66*
Western region			
A. Utilities (3)	59%	15.0	42%
B. Banks (3)	46%	11.4	30%
C. Differential (A minus B)	13	3.6	12
D. Differential (C as % of B)	28%	32%	40%
Eastern region			
A. Utilities (4)	74%	15.4	30%
B. Banks (4)	50%	10.9	34%
C. Differential (A minus B)	24	4.5	—4
D. Differential (C as % of B)	48%	41%	—12%
Southern region			
A. Utilities (5)	60%	21.6	59%
B. Banks (6)	37%	14.1	59%
C. Differential (A minus B)	23	7.5	0
D. Differential (C as % of B)	62%	53%	0
Central region			
A. Utilities (7)	68%	15.9	47%
B. Banks (7)	40%	10.6	46%
C. Differential (A minus B)	28	5.3	1
D. Differential (C as % of B)	70%	50%	2%
All regions			
A. Utilities (19)	65%	17.2	45%
B. Banks (20)	42%	11.8	42%
C. Differential (A minus B)	23	5.4	3
D. Differential (C as % of B)	55%	46%	7%

Payout ratios are based on 1966 earnings and cash dividend payments. Price-earnings ratios are based on 1966 earnings and average of high and low market quotations in 1966.

be instead that their faster earnings growth is mainly responsible. Or it could be some of each. By themselves, these three percentage differentials prove nothing.

But look now at the data for the Eastern Region. There the percentage differentials of utilities over banks are higher both for payout ratios and for price-earnings multiples. In this region, however, the banks actually achieved a better average increase in per-share earnings over the past five years than the utilities. In other words, there is good correlation here between payout and price-earnings ratios, but the factor of earnings growth does not correlate at all.

Looking at the Southern and Central Regions, we find the same pattern as in the East. In both the Southern and Central Regions the percentage differentials of utilities over banks are higher than in the East for both payout ratios and price-earnings multiples, but in both of these regions there were almost no differentials in the growth of earnings. Again, payout and price-earnings correlate and earnings growth does not.

The percentage differentials shown in the table are presented graphically in Figure 2. Here you can see at a glance the close correlation between dividend payout and price-earnings ratios and the absence of correlation of earnings growth. The correlation between the dividend payout and price-earnings ratios is summarized in simplified form in Figure 3.

This is simply a plotting of the percentage differentials for these two factors for the four regions and combined. The close correlation of these differentials is indicated by the fact that when they are plotted in this kind of a chart, they are practically in a straight line. The nearness of all the plottings to the so-called "line of regression" indicates how closely correlated these factors are.

In the language of the statisticians, the coefficient of correlation for these differentials is .95, which is a very high degree of correlation for factors of this kind. Perfect correlation would be indicated by a coefficient of 1.00, a score rarely encountered in the real world.

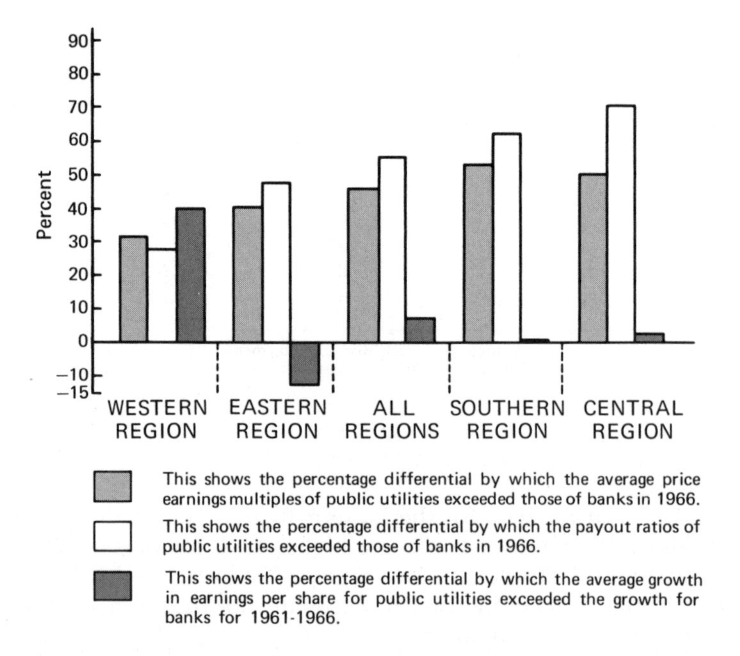

FIG. 2 Factors affecting price-earnings ratios.

OTHER EVIDENCE

Applying the same method, we also computed correlation between the percentage differentials for price-earnings ratios and growth of earnings per share. The coefficient of correlation of these two factors is not just zero; it is actually negative.

As a check on this whole exercise, similar computations for the same lists of utilities and bank stocks were made for an earlier date, using 1965 instead of 1966 figures for earnings, dividends, and market prices and taking 1959–1965 rather than 1961–1966 as the period for measuring the increase in earnings per share. Using these earlier dates, the correlation coefficient for payout and price-earnings ratios was .97, even higher than for 1966, and there was again a negative correlation between price-earnings and earnings growth.

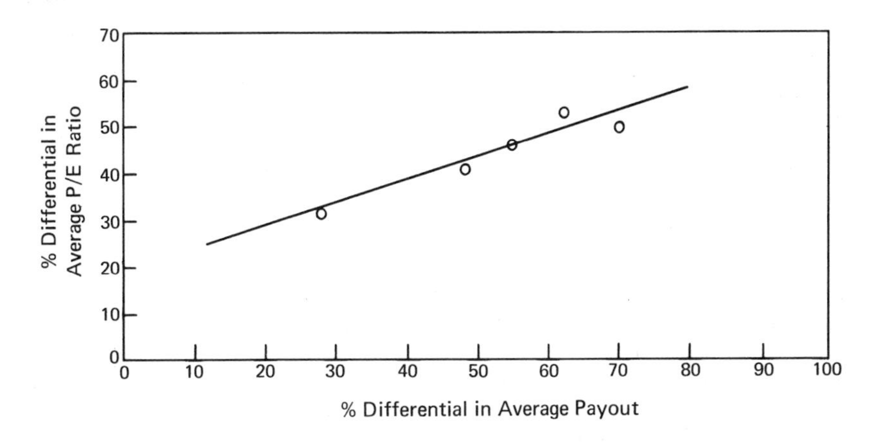

FIG. 3 Close correlation of payout and price-earnings.

These findings may not be absolutely conclusive, but they are certainly impressive. They lend considerable support to the thesis that one of the main reasons why utilities as a group enjoy substantially higher price-earnings ratios than banks is because of their more liberal dividend payout policies.

The implication is that if banks as a group were to move up to an appreciably higher average payout ratio, this would probably be reflected in a significant enhancement of the market value of outstanding bank stocks. Indeed, one could make a strong case that if banks were to start moving steadily toward higher payout ratios, they would deserve to sell at a considerably higher price-earnings ratio than at present because they have so much room for future dividend increases.

BENEFITS TO ONE BANK

It does not follow, of course, that the stock of any one particular bank would be correspondingly benefited if it alone adopted a higher payout ratio. This is quite a different question and one on which we need to look at different evidence.

Again the problem is to isolate the influence of payout policy from other factors. To do so, we tabulated payout ratios and price-earnings multiples for 1966 for the 50 largest commercial banking organizations whose shares are actively traded. We then put them into four groups on the basis of their payout ratios: Those that paid out more than 55% of net operating earnings in dividends, those that paid from 50%–55%, then 35%–49%, and below 35%. Here are the results:

Payout ratios	No. of banks	Average payout ratio	Average price-earnings ratio
Over 55%	4	61%	15.0
50%–55%	11	51	12.2
35%–49%	27	43	11.7
Under 35%	8	31	11.3

As you can see, there is clearly a correlation here between payout ratios and price-earnings multiples. Indeed, the coefficient of correlation for these four groups is .83, which is quite high.

Note, however, that more than half of the 50 banks have payout ratios ranging from 35% to 49% and that they have all been put into one large group. The reason is that when you look only at these banks within this broad range, you find little correlation between their payout and price-earnings ratios. Specifically, the coefficient of correlation among these banks as a group is only about .30, which indicates some, but rather poor correlation.

In other words, there is no evidence that if an individual bank were to increase its payout ratio from, say, 38% to 44%, or from 42% to 48%, the price of its stock would necessarily be affected at all. It might be, of course, but the data indicate that for these banks, other factors—future growth prospects, for example—exert more influence on price-earnings differentials as compared with other banks within the same broad payout range.

On the other hand, the evidence does clearly suggest that if a bank is outside this range, then its payout policy is likely to have an appreciable effect on its price-earnings multiple. If a bank now paying out 45% of earnings were to move up to a payout ratio of 60%, this would probably have a favorable effect on its price-earnings multiple.

How much effect? Unfortunately, there are too few leading banks with high payout ratios to provide a good answer. Much might depend on how the change is made. For one thing, investors would undoubtedly be more impressed if they thought the bank intended to adhere to a higher payout policy for a period of years. For example, a bank might announce that it planned, if circumstances permitted, to move steadily in the direction of a 60% payout policy over the next five years. This is hardly to be recommended for every bank, of course, but it would not be imprudent for some. For many banks, the announcement of such a policy would create the prospect of an average increase in the dividend rate on the order of 15% per year. For investors, such a prospect would be most appealing.

There would be far greater impact, of course, if a considerable number of leading banks were to move simultaneously toward higher payout ratios. Perhaps what is needed is an open conspiracy among bankers to become more generous to shareholders. This might be rather hard to put in motion, admittedly, but it is something to think about.

4

Profit Planning and Cost Analysis

The introductory essay by W. O. Pearce summarizes the concept and procedures of functional cost analysis, a program sponsored by Federal Reserve Banks for their members. Information developed by this service can assist bank managers in their profit strategies.

During the postwar years banks have increasingly emphasized installment loans. The second reading questions the profitability of such lending and provides empirical data concerning relationships among revenue, costs, and profitability. Also introduced is the concept of break-even analysis. Robert W. Johnson and Eugene E. Comiskey, the authors of the third reading, further consider the concept of break-even analysis, pointing out fallacies that can arise from uncritical acceptance based on full-cost allocation procedures and recommending use of marginal (incremental) analysis.

The next three readings focus on costs and the potential profitability of bank deposits. The first briefly outlines the relative cost differences between demand deposits and time deposits. James P. Furniss and Paul S. Nadler focus on corporate demand deposits and analyze reasons why banks should re-examine their pricing policies for such accounts and for services provided to corporate customers. The third appraisal examines some variables affecting the profitability of savings accounts and suggests procedures for improving profits in this area.

In addition to its importance for bank management, analysis of bank costs has significance for the formulation of appropriate public policy concerning bank size and structure. Frederick W. Bell and Neil B. Murphy investigate certain banking functions to determine the extent of possible economies of scale. Also considered are the relationships among certain costs and the extent of branching operations.

Functional Cost Analysis:

A Tool of Bank Management

W. O. Pearce

High interest rates on time deposits, rising salary and wage expenses, and increases in other cost factors affecting earnings have made it increasingly difficult for banks to employ available funds in areas that will yield a return large enough to pay the interest and other costs and still produce adequate profits.

For a bank to obtain the total cost or the total income for a year's operation is a relatively simple task. Information in the aggregate such as this does not lend itself readily to analysis by management, however. Before any meaningful evaluation can be made, income and expense figures must be allocated to the proper functions. As a result of these allocations, management can more readily answer such questions as:

What does it cost to maintain demand deposits and time deposits?
Where can expenses be reduced for a particular function if they are considered excessive?
What is the average cost of making a loan?
What is the average cost of processing each loan payment?
Do we have more tellers than are needed for our volume of transactions?
What are the break-even points on our consumer instalment loans?
What is the cost of issuing a certificate of deposit?
What is the officer expense per $1,000 of loans?

FUNCTIONAL COST ANALYSIS

To assist management in answering these and related questions is the overall objective of Functional Cost Analysis, a cost accounting service that eleven Federal Reserve Banks sponsor for the member banks in their respective Districts. Although Functional Cost Analysis has been in existence since 1956, it has grown significantly only in the past three years. In 1964, 279 banks in three Federal Reserve Districts participated in the

Reprinted with the permission of the Federal Reserve Bank of Richmond from *Monthly Review,* November 1967.

program. In 1966, however, 1,022 banks in eleven Federal Reserve Districts took part in the voluntary study.

The program is offered without charge each year to member banks. Even though participating banks are not required to remain in the program in consecutive years, experience has shown that there is very little attrition from one year to the next. One of the advantages of participating in consecutive years is that comparisons are given for each bank with its own year-ago figures. To participate, all a bank must do is fill in the five reporting schedules that are supplied by the Federal Reserve. The time required to fill in the schedules varies, of course, from bank to bank depending on the size, accounting procedures, and operational set up that each bank has.

Functional Cost Analysis has two primary objectives. First it is designed to give an itemized list of the various current income and expense items as they relate to the major banking functions. Also, comparative figures for groups of other banks are provided to aid in the analysis of an individual bank's performance. The uniform reporting of all participating banks makes possible interbank comparisons that are not generally available in any other cost program. Where overall comparisons are made—such as between balance sheets—banks are compared with other banks that have a similar dollar volume of total deposits and a similar percentage of time deposits.

The work schedules are filled out on a calendar year basis and returned to the Federal Reserve Bank for processing in February of the ensuing year. About six weeks later the finished report, consisting of 28 computer printout pages and several printed pages, is mailed to the participating banks. The report gives an analysis of three fund-providing functions, four fund-using functions, and four categories of nonfund-using service departments (Figure 1).

FUND-PROVIDING FUNCTIONS

Demand deposits, time deposits, and net capital funds are considered to be the fund-providing functions. The demand deposit analysis includes a detailed breakdown of the processing, administrative and overhead expenses. This analysis, like all others in the Functional Cost Analysis report, is developed from information supplied to the Reserve Bank on the reporting schedules and includes information such as the average cost of handling a home debit, a deposit, and a transit check. Demand deposits are also segregated into, and an analysis is given for, regular and special checking accounts. Information for determining the average break-even balance on a checking account is also provided. This is expressed as the average annual balance required to pay: (1) the account maintenance, (2) the home debits cost, (3) the transit checks cost, and (4) any added services cost. A deduction is made for any activity income earned on the account.

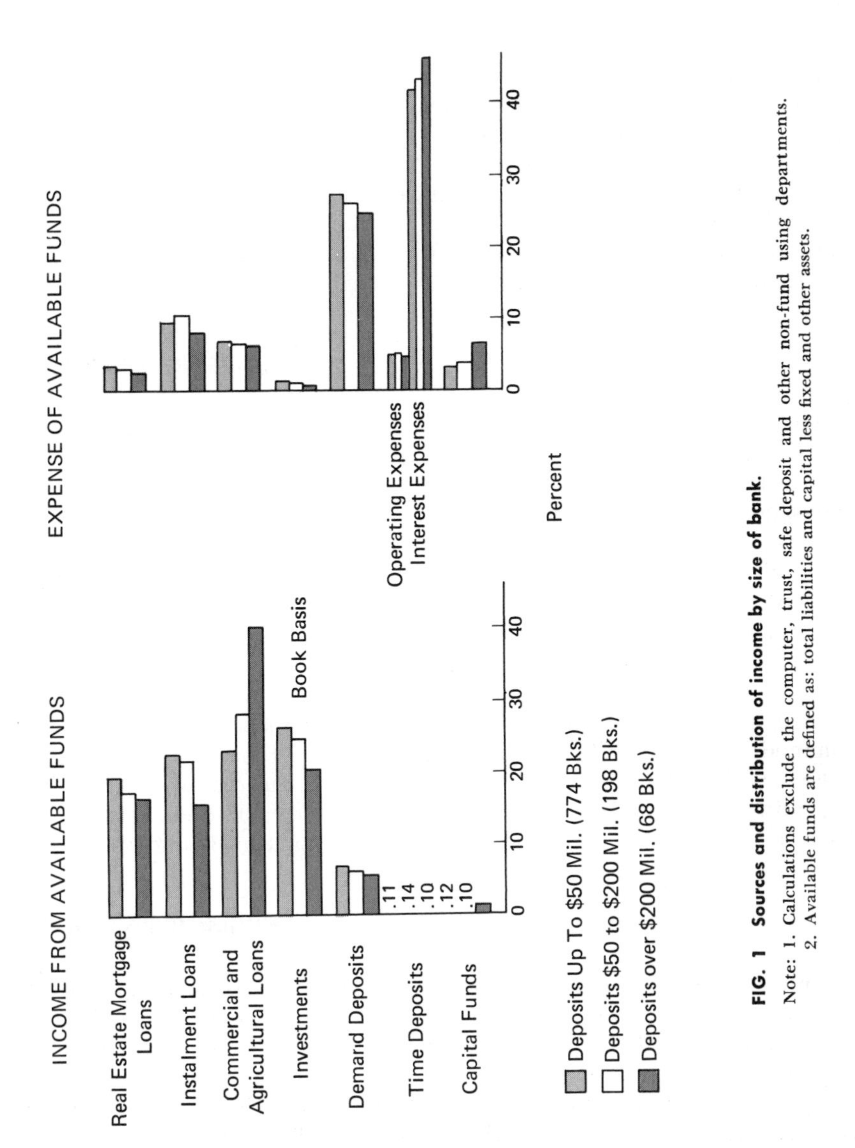

FIG. 1 Sources and distribution of income by size of bank.

Note: 1. Calculations exclude the computer, trust, safe deposit and other non-fund using departments.
2. Available funds are defined as: total liabilities and capital less fixed and other assets.

In addition to the comparisons with its own year-ago figures, interbank comparisons are also given. For the demand deposit function, demand deposits of ten banks—five having a dollar volume of demand deposits just above and five having a dollar volume of demand deposits just below the subject bank—make up the group average.

For the time deposit function, the average cost per transaction of a deposit, a withdrawal, opening an account, and closing an account is given. A separate analysis, complete with information for determining the average annual break-even balance, is given for passbook savings, certificates of deposit, and Christmas and similar club accounts. The group average for the time deposit analysis consists of average time deposits of ten banks with similar dollar volumes.

The third fund-supplying function, net capital funds, consists of capital and valuation reserves plus "other" liabilities and borrowings less fixed and "all other" assets. Federal funds purchased are analyzed as part of the capital funds function.

FUND-USING FUNCTIONS

The fund-using functions consist of real estate mortgage loans, instalment loans, commercial and agricultural loans, and investments (see Figure 1). For each of the fund-using functions, the clerical expense per thousand dollars is given along with such miscellaneous information as the average cost of making a loan, the average cost of collecting a payment, the average volume of loans serviced per person, and the break-even points for the consumer instalment loan function. Gross yield on investments and liquidity loans are included in the analysis of the investment function. Liquidity loans are restricted to Federal funds sold, commercial paper purchased, brokers' loan participations with a correspondent, purchased certificates of deposit, bankers' acceptances and commodity credit certificates of interest.

For each of the fund-using functions, as was the case with the fund-providing functions, a comparison is made with ten other banks that have similar dollar volumes of the particular function being studied.

SERVICE DEPARTMENTS

The computer, trust, and safe deposit functions are service departments that do not use balance sheet funds and are included in the non fund-using section of the report. Interbank comparisons for the computer department are made with ten banks that have a rental expense for computer hardware similar to the subject bank. Comparisons for the trust function are with banks that have similar 5-year average incomes, while total number of boxes is used for selecting group average banks in the safe deposit analysis.

SUMMARY REPORTS

Two reports in addition to those for individual banks are produced by the Federal Reserve. The "National Average" report and the "Performance Characteristics of High Earning Banks" report both contain virtually the same information as the individual bank report except that the "National" report contains average figures for all banks in the program and the "High Earnings" report contains average figures for banks in the top earnings quartile.

A review of all three reports will give a fairly accurate evaluation of how a bank is doing on the national level as well as how it compares with the best earning banks.

While participation in Functional Cost Analysis is limited to Federal Reserve member banks, the "National" and "High Earnings" reports are available free of charge to non-member and non-participating banks upon request.

CONCLUSION

There are many ways of costing a bank. The important thing, however, is that a bank is doing some type of costing. Today banks are offering more and more services to their customers beyond the traditional banking functions of receiving deposits and making loans, and the trend will no doubt continue in the future. It is no secret that banking is becoming more complex and competitive, and the banker that has more detailed and reliable cost and income information has the advantage.

The Federal Reserve's role, so far as Functional Cost Analysis is concerned, is to diagnose—not prescribe. Once a bank has its cost report, it has a medium of unlimited potential as a management tool. The report can be a prelude to budgeting, profit planning or any other use that management can determine with its discerning eye.

Instalment Loans—How Profitable?

Many bankers assume that, since instalment loans have a high gross yield, the way to increase bank earnings is to increase instalment loan volume. This assumption seems valid and in many situations the results justify this premise. However, there are banks that have increased their instalment portfolios without experiencing the increase in earnings they had anticipated.

Reprinted with the permission of the Federal Reserve Bank of Boston from *New England Business Review,* February 1962.

"Why did our anticipation not materialize?" they ask as they follow the charts in the board room. "Instalment volume has increased. The percentage of instalment loans to total assets has increased. But net earnings have not increased proportionately!"

This seeming paradox has confounded some bankers for years and they wonder whether this type of loan warrants the emphasis placed upon it.

To help answer this question the *Functional Cost Analysis* study of member banks, conducted for four years by the Federal Reserve Bank of Boston, was expanded in 1960 to include more information about the instalment loan function. Eighty banks participated in the study of 1960 operations. Neither a high volume of instalment loans nor a high percentage of assets invested in instalment portfolio automatically produced high over-all bank earnings for the banks surveyed. The study also pointed out that large average instalment loan size did not necessarily result in higher instalment earnings.

High instalment loan income is obvious. A 6 percent loan, repaid monthly, generates slightly better than an 11 percent yield. This is because the face amount of the loan is nearly cut in half by monthly repayments, i.e., a $6.00 return on a $100 loan for 12 months is a $6.00 return on an average outstanding of $54.17 per the formula $(N + 1)/2N$ where N is equal to the term of the loan. Thus, $6.00 divided by the average outstanding of $54.17 equals a gross yield of 11.1 percent.

INCOME AND COSTS

But what is sometimes overlooked or even brushed aside are the costs associated with this type loan. Not only do instalment loans require monthly handling but they often require substantial credit investigation and processing time. In addition there are losses associated with instalment loans. Thus, the cost figures must also reflect a portion of the loss inherent in each loan.

The cost of the money used by the department to lend to customers is an additional cost that is frequently overlooked. Unlike the loan companies that depend upon banks and other lenders to provide them with the funds that are in turn loaned to customers, banks obtain the bulk of their investable funds from depositors. As surely as the loan company has to include its cost of borrowing in determining the charge to its customer, so also must the bank include in its cost figures the cost of the funds provided by the savings and demand deposit functions. Only when he includes all costs can the banker soundly price his product.

The 80 banks in this study had volumes of instalment loans ranging from $280,000 to $13,350,000. The ground rules of the study specified that the banks consider the instalment function as a single entity. Thus the functional analysis included any business instalment loans that were processed by instalment personnel. In addition the instalment analysis included the income and expense of any "floor plan" loans handled by the bank, regardless of whether these dealer loans were made and processed apart from the instalment center. Floor plan loans are dealer inventory loans on goods (mainly automobiles) which are generally sold through consumer instalment financing. It was reasoned that the floor plan loans bring in indirect consumer paper and the two types of loans should not be divorced. The low-income high-service costs of floor planning are offset by the high-income low-service costs of purchased paper. Furthermore while the income from various types of instalment loans such as direct, indirect and floor plan, can be indentified in the participating banks, the expenses are not segregated. Thus the entire function was considered in its entirety.

While this approach may be unsophisticated to purists, the information obtained gave these bankers, most of them for the first time, some idea of what their instalment loan costs were. And by providing them with a formula for obtaining break-even points, the analysis enabled them to determine what they were actually earning on individual instalment loans. This points out an important fact—that costs by themselves are of limited value. The real value in cost figures arises when they are associated with income to arrive at a net earnings figure.

DIFFERENCE IN BANK EARNINGS

The wide spread in net instalment earnings was the result of several factors. These included operational differences, loan rate differences and what type of business was conducted, whether wholesale or retail, or so-called direct versus indirect lending.

Figure 1 indicates that as total bank earnings increased earnings from the instalment function increased, suggesting that high instalment earnings make a valuable contribution to total bank earnings. But note that instalment loans as a percentage of total assets vary widely. And while the group of 10 banks with the highest earnings had the highest ratio of assets in instalment loans, the lowest earning group on the left had as high a percentage of instalment assets as the sixth highest earning group.

This suggests that there is more to net upward leverage on earnings than merely the percent of assets invested in instalment loans. This is further affirmed by the fact that the group of banks earning the second highest return had the lowest percent invested in instalment loans. The third line on the chart indicates the volume in dollars. It is evident that the group with the lowest volume average had very high net earnings while groups with high volume average did not always fare as well.

INSTALMENT EARNINGS

If volume and/or percentage of assets invested in instalment portfolio produce such marked variances on earnings and are not by themselves a

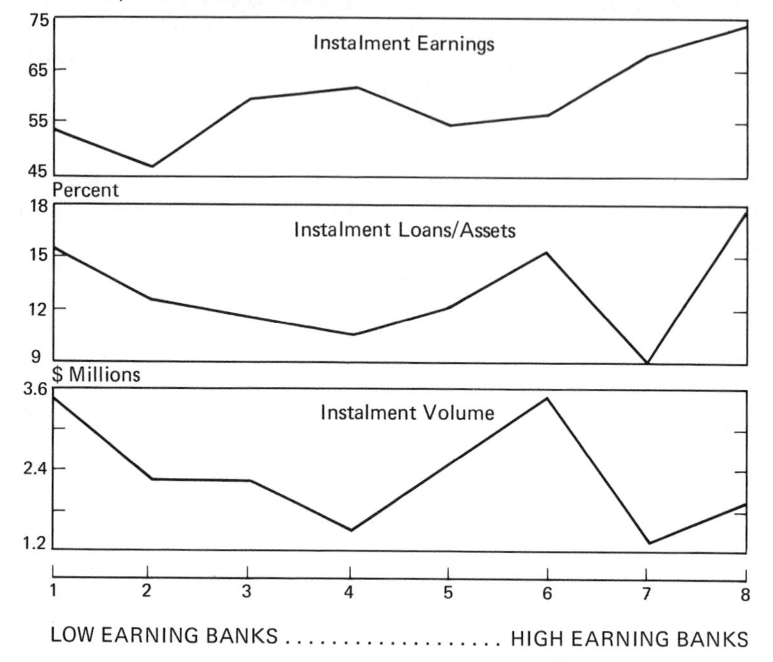

FIG. 1 Instalment loans and bank earnings.
80 New England banks—1960.

guaranty of increased bank earnings the question is then raised, "What does generate the higher instalment earnings that contribute to higher over-all earnings?" To help answer this question we can look at Figure 2, which shows the 80 banks ranged in groups from low instalment earnings on the left to high earnings on the right. It is clear from the top portion of the chart that the best combination of high income and low expense produces the higher earnings for the group on the right. This group reflects a net return of better than twice the return of the lowest earning group. And based on the average portfolio outstanding of $2,285,000 for the 80 banks, the difference in net earnings between the low and high group amounts to $108,000!

Is income or expense the more important factor in attainment of high earnings? Although the chart at first glance indicates that income is the more important factor there is actually only a 3.08 percent difference in income between the high and low groups and a 1.66 percent difference in expense. This does not appear to be much of a spread but it does infer that income offers a greater opportunity for increasing earnings. However, a more appropriate conclusion may be that neither income nor expense has a prior claim on generation of earnings but that it is the

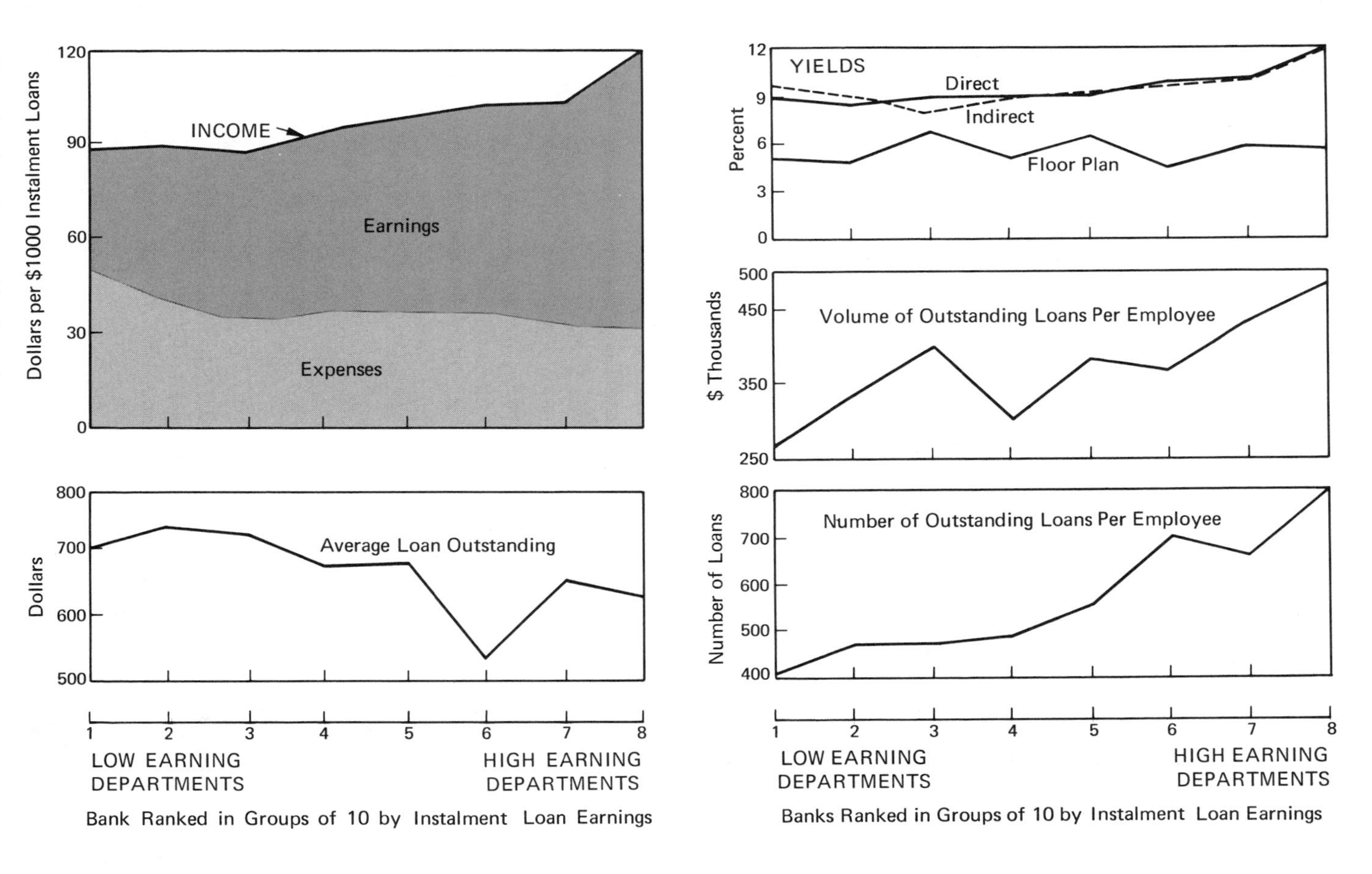

FIG. 2 Instalment loans and bank earnings.
80 New England banks—1960.

trite—but all too true—fact that increased earnings are the result of the most fortunate combination of income and expense.

Ordinarily high earnings are associated with large loans. For the most part, this is true, but large loans themselves will not guarantee a high net yield. Actually loan size, plus yield, plus efficiency (expense control) are the ingredients that will insure high net returns.

The higher earning departments had substantially higher yields but the largest size loan averages are associated with the lowest yields, as shown in the middle portion of Figure 2. This could be the result of competition. This could be the result of volume at any cost. It is evident from other data that the better earning groups had the highest portion of direct instalment loans when contrasted with the lower earning groups. The latter had a greater portion of their portfolio in indirect and floor plan loans. And notwithstanding the fact that the gross yields of the direct and indirect loans are practically identical, floor plan loans, usually associated with indirect paper, have substantially lower yields, which, combined with higher operational and servicing costs, tend to suppress earnings.

It is also clear that higher earnings and low expenses are associated with a high degree of efficiency. The bottom part of the chart indicates that each employee in the higher earning group handled nearly twice the volume and processed twice as many loans as did each employee in the lower earning group.

BREAK-EVEN POINTS

As indicated earlier in this article, the factors making up the total costs of an instalment loan were prepared for each bank to enable them to make up a table of break-even points. These factors included the cost of making a loan, the cost to collect each payment, the loss factor inherent in each loan and the cost of funds supplied them through deposits. Bearing in mind that these are average figures and the data included floor plan and any business instalment loans, it cost the average bank $12.57 to make each loan and 93 cents to collect each monthly payment. Furthermore, there was a loss factor of 17 cents per $100 loaned and a cost of money of $1.71 per $100 loaned.

While it may be argued that there are varying costs in the making of direct versus indirect loans, the simplified approach employed here does not distinguish between them. Even so, if credit checks and investigations are similar for all loans, the acquisition costs will not vary widely. Furthermore, the costs of processing payments, the loss factor and the cost of money ought to be similar. Thus for this size function the value lies not so much in the precise accuracy of the data arrived at but, as in most cost studies, provides management with one additional piece of information from which it can more appropriately and soundly determine future steps to be taken.

The importance of the break-even point table for both direct and indirect loans is obvious. The average bank in the study has to lend $475 at 6 percent for one year before it recovers its costs. How many loans are on the books that were loaned below this break-even point? How many loans now on the books were granted below this amount and at a lower rate? The table now makes it possible for the participating banker to determine where the bank is and where it was with regard to the instalment loans on the books. Where the bank will go and which road it will take in such matters as direct versus indirect paper, changes in operations to reduce costs, revising minimum charges and so forth, will depend on management policy.

Certainly it would be foolhardy for management to base its decision solely on the basis of cost data without regard to community needs, loss leaders desired and competition. But management policy will now be based more on fact than guesswork or suppositions.

In summation, the degree of profitability on the instalment loan function depends not merely on the volume or percentage of total assets a bank has invested or even, in some cases, the size of the various loans. The amount of net earnings contributed to total bank earnings from instalment loans depends not only on an efficiency of operations but also on the mixture of loan sizes, the maturity lengths, the interest rates and the types of loans, whether direct or indirect. This mixture is dependent upon management policy, advertising, promotion, competition and so forth. But before charting a course, navigational hazards must be studied. In the banker's case these hazards are his costs. And the first step to a successful operation and a maximum return is to know these costs.

Breakeven Analysis in Instalment Lending

Robert W. Johnson and Eugene E. Comiskey

For years, practitioners and accountants in the field of consumer instalment credit have been calculating "breakeven loans," that is, the size of credit extension, given a particular maturity and finance rate, at which

Reprinted with the permission of The Administrator of National Banks, United States Treasury, Washington, D.C., from *The National Banking Review*, December 1966.

income and costs are equal.[1] A number of Federal Reserve banks have now joined in this activity as part of functional cost analysis programs.[2] The purpose of this article is to analyze this practice and to discuss a number of related problems.

THE BASIC FRAMEWORK

The first step in functional cost analysis of installment loans is to allocate various direct costs to the instalment loan department. Second, indirect costs such as occupancy, business development, and administration are allocated to the instalment loan activity on the basis of that department's proportionate share of the total direct costs. Direct expenses of the instalment credit departments in the 171 banks studied in 1965 equaled 15.7 percent of the total direct expenses. Thus, 15.7 percent of total indirect costs was charged to the instalment loan activity.

The third step divides total operating costs into two classifications:

(1) Acquisition expense—All costs associated with the successful or unsuccessful effort to acquire instalment loans.

(2) Processing cost—All salaries, supplies, and costs required to service the loans on the books, including any collection effort made.[3]

Acquisition costs are then expressed as cost per loan acquired, and processing costs as cost per payment processed. These cost allocations are summarized in the diagram below.

Two remaining cost elements are expressed as a percent of the average dollar amount of loans outstanding:

(3) Bad debt cost—The average annual losses on instalment loans, net of recoveries, for the preceding seven years are expressed as a percent of the average instalment portfolio outstanding during the year.[4]

[1] M. R. Neifeld, *Trends in Consumer Finance,* Easton, Pa.: Mack Publishing Co., 1954, pp. 95–100; Harold E. Randall, "The Basic Cost Factors in Instalment Lending," *Time Sales Financing,* 13, May 1949, pp. 7–8 and 20–21; Gilbert W. Urban, "Time and Dollar Costs in Consumer Financing," *N.A.C.A. Bulletin,* 36, April 1955, pp. 1063–1068; *Instalment Credit,* New York: American Institute of Banking, The American Bankers Association, 1964, pp. 137–139; Max A. Mitcham, "Eye-Opening Statewide Survey of Bank Costs," *Burroughs Clearing House,* 50, April 1966, p. 39; J. T. Arenberg, "Consumer Credit Net Yields," Arthur Andersen and Co., Subject file AD 7810, Item 20.

[2] The program of functional cost analysis was first developed by the Federal Reserve banks of New York and Boston, and more recently adopted by the Federal Reserve banks of Chicago, Cleveland, St. Louis, Minneapolis, and San Francisco. The data cited in this study for illustrative purposes are from *Functional Cost Analysis: 171 Bank Comparative Study, Deposits up to $50 Million, 1965–64,* subsequently referred to as *Functional Cost Analysis.* This study covers banks in the Boston, New York, and Philadelphia districts.

[3] Instalment Unit Cost Study, General Instructions for Schedule D

[4] Since instalment loans have been rising, this procedure tends to understate the net bad debt percentage.

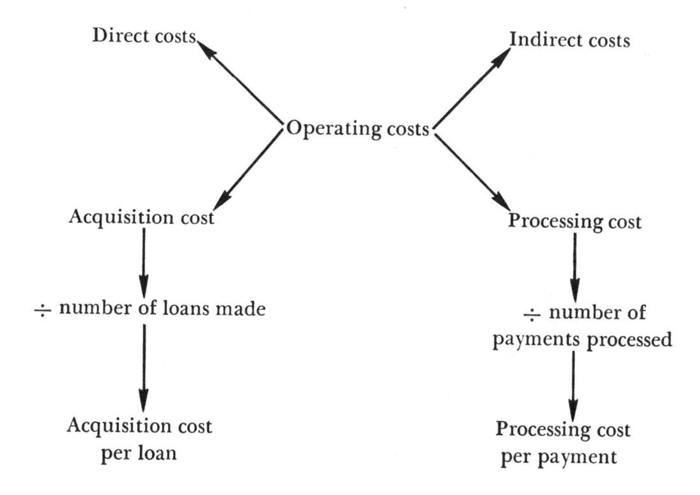

(4) Cost of money—The costs of servicing demand and time deposits (including interest expense), less any service charge income, are divided by total available funds to measure the cost of money as a percent of average dollar outstandings in the instalment loan portfolio.[5]

The four elements, comprising total instalment loan cost and their average values in 1965 for the 171 banks studied, are shown below:

Instalment-Loan Cost	*171 Bank Average*	*Cost Basis*
Acquisition cost	$17.47	per loan made
Processing cost	$ 0.96	per payment processed
Bad debt cost	0.226 percent per year	average instalment portfolio
Cost of money	2.42 percent per year	average instalment portfolio

DEVELOPMENT OF BREAKEVEN LOAN SIZE

Calculation of the breakeven loan size entails the solution of an algebraic expression based on the following components:

C_a = Acquisition cost per loan.
C_p = Processing cost per payment.
C_b = Bad debt cost as percentage per annum of average dollar outstandings.

[5] This procedure appears to be deficient in two respects. "Available funds" is the total of all liabilities plus net worth less fixed and other assets. No charge is made for the cost of equity. In addition, the same rate of charge is applied to the average outstandings in each of the functional areas (and the cost of money then deducted from net earnings). For these reasons, the charge of 2.42 percent to the instalment loan function appears to be low.

C_m = Cost of money as percentage per annum of average dollar outstandings.
C_v = $C_b + C_m$, variable costs as percentage per annum of average dollar outstandings.
i = Add-on finance rate—percent per year of initial unpaid balance.
N = Number of payment periods in the contract.
X = Breakeven loan size.

The breakeven loan size is calculated by equating income to costs and solving for X in the following equation: [6]

$$(1) \quad Xi\left(\frac{N}{12}\right) = C_a + NC_p + \frac{N}{12} \cdot \frac{C_v (N+1) X}{2N}$$

Solving for X, we have:

$$(2) \quad X = \frac{24 (C_a + NC_p)}{2iN - C_v (N+1)}$$

The breakeven loan size for a 24-month loan ($N = 24$) at an add-on finance rate of 6 percent ($i = .06$) can be calculated by substituting the appropriate values in (2):

$$X = \frac{24 [17.47 + (24)(0.96)]}{[(2)(.06)]\, 24 - .02646 (24 + 1)}$$
$$= \$438.24$$

A number of similar calculations are summarized in Table 2.

INTERPRETATION

The following sections discuss the possible uses of breakeven analyses of instalment loans. Although the functional cost analysis program provides no guidelines for bank management, other proponents of the breakeven approach have suggested applications that warrant analysis.[7]

[6] In the last term of the equation, the average dollar outstanding over the life of the credit extension is given by $(N + 1) X/2N$. This is a reasonably accurate approximation under the "constant-ratio method." It understates the average balance slightly, with the result that the breakeven loan is slightly understated as well. A more important problem is the treatment of bad debt expense as directly variable with the size and maturity of loan. Evidence suggests a nonlinear relation between bad debts and maturity.

[7] "Interpretation and application of the findings is (sic) left to the participating bank." *Functional Cost Analysis*, p. 1.

Portfolio Management

The consumer credit department of a commercial bank is essentially involved in portfolio management. The management of the bank must decide the portion of the bank's assets to be committed to that department. But within the department, additional allocation problems occur daily. Decisions must be made on each loan applicant, the types of paper to be purchased, and the sources of instalment paper to be used.

Although a lending officer might reject all loan applicants seeking less than the breakeven amounts, most proponents of breakeven analysis are more circumspect: "As a matter of policy, it is not always possible to operate an instalment credit department and accept only profitable business." [8] Loans are made below the breakeven level to encourage good will, and in the hope that these loans may be enlarged or renewed at a lower acquisition cost. However, a more persuasive argument exists for a policy of accepting loans below the breakeven point.

If loan breakeven analysis is a suitable decision model, it should follow that accepting loans of less than breakeven size would reduce bank profits; that is, the resulting increase in costs (ΔC) would be greater than the increase in revenues (ΔR), with a subsequent reduction in profits (ΔP).

$$(3) \quad \Delta R - \Delta C = \Delta P < 0$$

This is not necessarily the case. As the previous two sections have indicated, breakeven analysis is based upon a total cost concept. The acquisition and processing cost elements include both direct and indirect costs. Indirect costs are largely fixed and, therefore, will be unaffected by the activity of the instalment loan department.[9] Even in the case of the direct costs of instalment lending, fixed cost elements are present in the short run, unless all elements of the department are operating at full capacity during each hour of the day. For example, no wage cost can be directly assigned if an interviewer takes an application for a $300 loan when he would otherwise be idle.

The effect of excluding indirect expenses from breakeven calculations on a 24-month loan for $438 at an add-on rate of 6 percent is shown below. The breakeven loan contributes at least $12.48 to before-tax profits.

[8] *Instalment Credit,* New York: American Institute of Banking, The American Bankers Association, 1964, pp. 138–139. See also Neifeld, *Trends in Consumer Finance,* Easton, Pa.: Mack Publishing Co., 1954, p. 98; and Elmer Grant, "Profit from Installment Credit: Challenge to a Popular Belief," *American Banker,* March 29, 1965.

[9] Where the growth of instalment loan activity would force an increase in indirect costs, such as occupancy cost, the decision to expand should be based on a marginal analysis that includes the added occupancy cost. Breakeven analysis provides no apparent help in this decision.

	Full-cost basis	*Direct-cost basis*
Change in revenue (ΔR)	$52.56	$52.56
Change in costs (ΔC):		
Acquisition	17.47	12.19
Processing	23.04	15.84
Bad debt and cost of money	12.05	12.05
	$52.56	$40.08
Change in profits (ΔP)	$ 0	$12.48

The elimination of all loans below the breakeven point would also serve to raise the breakeven point, since the indirect costs would then be spread over a smaller number of loans. A policy of refusing loan applications below the breakeven points as adjusted sequentially could eventually force the department out of business.

If breakeven analysis does not enable a department to decide whether to accept or reject individual loans, does it provide a guideline for accepting or rejecting certain types or sources of business? It is entirely possible to continue the same type of functional cost analysis by product lines or to allocate costs and revenues to particular sources of instalment paper. In this manner, tables like Table 1 could be developed for appliance paper and automobile paper, for direct versus indirect sources of instalment paper, and even for particular dealers. The result may show that "on the average, no automobile loan of less than $500 will prove profitable for any of the maturity periods shown." [10] Alternatively, it might be discovered that an entire block of business is unprofitable because most of the instalment paper acquired is below the breakeven point.

These conclusions, if based on a full allocation of indirect expenses, are likely to be incorrect for the same reasons explained in relation to accept-or-reject decisions on individual loans. The only way to decide whether to drop a particular source of business is to determine which costs and which revenues will be eliminated. For example, if the funds invested in appliance paper provide a greater addition to profits than if they were invested elsewhere in the bank, then investment should be continued even though most of the paper falls below the breakeven point.[11]

An alternative to rejecting a loan below the breakeven point is to increase the size and/or to lengthen the maturity to raise it above the breakeven level. Although blind acceptance of the breakeven analysis

[10] Gilbert W. Urban, *N.A.C.A. Bulletin,* 36, April 1955, p. 1068.

[11] See *Developing Cost Information on Instalment Credit Operations,* New York: Instalment Credit Committee, American Bankers Association, 1964, pp. 29–32. Accepting a particular block of business on a marginal-cost basis may bring closer the need for additional expenditures on supervision or fixed assets. Marginal cost analysis is deficient in failing to take this fact into consideration.

Table 1 1965 Instalment Loan Breakdown Points for 171 Banks

Maturity (in months)	*Add-on Finance Rate* .04	.05	.06	.07
6	$1,891	$1,344	$1,043	$851
12	1,129	813	635	521
18	890	643	503	413
24	773	559	438	360
30	703	509	399	329
36	657	476	374	307

Source: Adapted from *Functional Cost Analysis 171 Bank Comparative Study, Deposits Up To $50 Million 1965–64,* p. A12.

might well lead to this decision, its merits are doubtful. There are cases where a credit grantor may properly consolidate debts to increase the size of the loan, but he does not need a breakeven analysis to establish the merits of this decision. In other instances, adjusting the size and maturity of a loan merely to place it above the breakeven level often increases the risk of nonpayment. Since breakeven analysis is based upon an average risk, increasing the risk to make a particular loan "acceptable" in relation to the breakeven point may represent poor portfolio management.

Rate making

Breakeven analysis has also served in rate making, justifying the use of minimum fees and increased rates charged on smaller loans.[12] In other instances, the analysis has encouraged bankers to shift consumers from instalment loans to check-credit plans providing a higher rate of charge or lower handling costs.[13] In these cases, breakeven analysis provides more of a goad than a guideline. If rates could be raised to borrowers of small accounts, so that net profits are increased, this could have been accomplished without breakeven figures. The principle of graduated rates has been used in the small loan field by nonbanks for years, but breakeven analysis has been required to inspire banks to follow this example.

In determining the proper level of minimum charges, breakeven analysis often provides misleading information. Consider the full costs of a six-month loan for $100:

Acquisition cost	$17.47
Processing cost (6 × $0.96)	5.76
Bad debt and cost of money (2.646 percent of average balance)	.77
Total	$24.00

[12] Randall, *Time Sales Financing,* 13, May 1949, p. 20.
[13] Grant, *American Banker,* March 29, 1965.

If these are accepted as the assignable costs on this type of loan, an effective annual rate of about 78 percent would be required. From a strictly economic point of view, the issue is not whether this rate is "fair" to consumers or to the bank, but whether this rate would reduce profits by driving many small loans from the bank. This decision is related to the market for this type of loan and to the sensitivity of consumers to the rates charged. It also requires the same type of marginal analysis discussed earlier, and the consideration of questions of public policy.

Expense and income control

A final possible use of the functional cost approach to breakeven analysis is to compare one bank's data with that for all banks in the sample. A banker may compare his cost of making an instalment loan with the average cost of $17.47. Similarly, a banker might find that for all maturities and add-on rates his breakeven loans are higher than the average for other banks.

While such comparisons may be useful as a form of exhortation to reduce costs, they may be misleading as a management tool. The size of the instalment credit department, as well as the size of total deposits, may influence the cost structure. Available studies suggest that cost per loan is inversely related to the number of loans made.[14] Hence, it would be misleading for a bank that made 1,800 instalment loans during the year to compare its average loan costs with the 171 bank average of 2,834 loans per year. Other cost variations are introduced by the types of paper acquired, the source of business (direct versus indirect), and the number of branches in which instalment loans are processed.[15]

The nature of the market served may influence revenues and costs more than the size of the bank. Large banks (deposits over $50 million) are generally located in large cities. The functional cost analysis of 61 banks with deposits in excess of $50 million in 1965 shows that, in comparison with smaller banks, they receive a smaller gross yield on direct instalment loans (8.8 percent versus 9.1 percent) and have a lower percentage of qualified loan applicants (83.1 percent versus 88.9 percent). This is understandable in view of the more intense rate competition and the concentration of low-income groups in metropolitan areas. But a small bank located in a large city is also subject to these economic forces. Other things being equal, it may be more appropriate to compare the urban small bank's average income and expenses with large city banks than with small country banks. In short, comparison of breakeven loans of one bank with average results for a group of banks may obscure more than it reveals.

[14] George Benston, "Economies of Scale and Marginal Costs in Banking Operations," *The National Banking Review*, 2, June 1965, pp. 527–530.

[15] George Benston, "Branch Banking and Economies of Scale," *Journal of Finance*, 20, May 1965, pp. 312–331. Paul F. Smith, *Consumer Credit Costs 1949–59*, Princeton: Princeton University Press, 1964, pp. 79–85.

SUMMARY

Interviews with instalment lenders and review of published statements suggest that calculation and publication of breakeven loan figures are most effective as a goad for management to study the profitability of credit services offered and to reexamine its pricing structures. If this is the only result data on breakeven loans are probably helpful. However, the analysis has suggested that pricing and lending decisions based on breakeven analysis may be incorrect. Correct decisions could be made without the use of breakeven analysis. On balance, the creation and publication of breakeven figures appears to offer a chance for more harm than good.

None of the comments are intended as criticisms of the functional cost analysis program. On the contrary, as a first step toward multivariate cost analysis for commercial banks, the program represents a worthwhile contribution to an industry notably deficient in this area.[16]

[16] For an example of multivariate cost analysis, see Eugene E. Comiskey, "Cost Control by Regression Analysis," *Accounting Review,* 41, April 1966, pp. 235–238.

The Cost of Demand Deposits*

Commercial banks pay interest on savings and on time deposits. They do not pay interest on demand deposits. Because of this an impression exists that the demand deposits are available to banks for them to lend "free of cost."

Such an impression rests upon the misconception that banks incur little or no expense in accepting and servicing demand deposits.

One reason commercial banks can afford to pay interest on time deposits is because the processing and overhead costs of maintaining them

* The data in this article are largely drawn from a study of 1960 functional income and expenses sponsored by the Federal Reserve Bank of Boston and participated in by 80 First District member banks. Their deposits ranged in size from $3.5 million to $50 million.

Reprinted with the permission of the Federal Reserve Bank of Boston from *New England Business Review,* October 1961.

are so low compared with demand deposits. Per dollar of deposits, demand deposit operating expenses are in the range of four times as great as time deposit operating expenses. In the average small-to-medium-sized bank in the First Federal Reserve District even a very modest rate of interest paid on demand deposits would entirely wipe out the operating earnings arising from such deposits. This conclusion is drawn from the 1960 functional cost study sponsored by the Federal Reserve Bank of Boston and participated in by 80 member banks in the deposit range of $3.5 million to $50 million. Average assets of these banks totaled $17 million, and average demand deposits were $10.5 million.

Striking differences exist between demand deposits (checking accounts) and time deposits. The difference between payment and nonpayment of interest has already been cited. A second difference is in their purpose. A time deposit account is an investment made either because the owner is accumulating funds for some specific use or because he is depositing a sum of money pending a more permanent investment. In either case he places the funds at interest in order to have some return on his money.

Indeed, though the depositor may not realize it, as one of the considerations for receiving interest, he gives to a savings bank or to a commercial bank the option of requiring advance notice of withdrawal. In practice this option is almost invariably waived. Nevertheless the fact that it exists is as essential a distinction of a savings account as is the payment of interest. In addition, a withdrawal from a savings account usually involves a visit to the bank.

By contrast, a checking account gives the depositor the advantage of being able to keep his money in a safe place with the unqualified right to withdraw it at will. This he can do without ever leaving his desk.

In addition to holding this option to withdraw his money upon demand, the depositor also gains the opportunity, through the use of checks, of transferring his money by mail in any amount and for any distance. The requirements of paid-in capital and surplus, insurance coverage by the Federal Deposit Insurance Corporation, and the various examination and supervisory policies, are all directed at insuring that the obligation to meet withdrawal on demand is honored.

The alternatives to the use of checks for transferring money would be to make payments, hand-to-hand, using currency; to forward the money by government money order, by registered mail, or by a registered bank check; by forwarding currency by ordinary mail which is certainly not recommended; or finally, in large transactions, by the use of armed guards or armored trucks.

The scope of check writing is best indicated by the fact that annually 14 billion pieces of paper representing $2½ trillion flow through the banking system. It is commonly estimated that 90 percent of the dollar volume of money transfers is by check. Conservative estimates suggest that by 1970 the number of checks will have grown to 22 billion annually.

A third difference between demand deposits and saving deposits is in the expense of handling. The 80 banks in the cost study had an average of nine officers and 46 employees. But of the employees, 10 commercial tellers, four transit-proof clerks and 12 bookkeepers were required to handle the demand deposits. Dollarwise, average total operating expenses (excluding interest paid) for the 80 banks were $460,328; yet of this amount expenses of the demand deposit function were $242,563, of which a third constituted employees' salaries alone.

By contrast these same banks averaged $4.3 million in time and savings deposits which required the services of 2.8 employees. In other words the demand deposit function averaged about 2½ times the dollar volume of the time deposit function but required the services of nine times as many employees.

Conventional cost accounting methods suggest that the cost to a commercial bank of savings and other time deposits (all hereafter referred to as time deposits) comprises the processing and overhead costs of the time deposit function plus interest paid. By the same reasoning the cost to a bank of its demand deposits is the processing and overhead costs of that function less a deduction for any activity charges which have been collected.

In the time deposit function, controls must be maintained and interest must be computed but, relatively speaking, these are neither costly nor complicated operations. A typical transaction in a savings account entails a simple debit or credit, usually made while the depositor is at the teller's window.

Not so with the demand deposits. The American Bankers Association estimates that each home debit (a check charged against a customer's account) involves processing in six different operations. Similarly, each deposit involves four phases of processing; each transit item (a check drawn on a different bank) involves two. Further, each operation requires a system of controls to insure that each check and deposit is handled speedily and accurately.

The relative simplicity of the time deposit function, coupled with the smaller number of transactions, is apparent from the fact that each employee handled an average annual volume of $1,536,000. By contrast, the demand deposit function employees handled an average annual volume of $405,000.

It is obvious that the service which the banks rendered in connection with handling demand deposits was costly. It is logical, therefore, to ask if activity charges were not sufficient to compensate banks fully for the service.

On the average the activity charges of the 80 banks were only 35 percent of the total expenses involved in handling demand deposits. This was just about sufficient to pay the salaries of the 26 people required to process the annual volume of checks and deposits.

The other 65 percent was unrecovered expense which the banks absorbed as the price they paid for acquiring the demand deposits. This includes such direct costs as printing, stationery, postage, equipment, prorated officers' salaries, fringe benefits, and FDIC insurance, and prorated indirect overhead costs including light, heat, rent or occupancy, telephone and the like. Thus, the gross expense of handling demand deposits was 2.31 percent of demand deposits and the net unrecovered expense after allowing a credit for activity charges was 1.50 percent.

A fourth difference between time and demand deposits is their rate of turnover and the consequent necessity to vary liquidity policy for each source of funds. Savings deposits tend to be stable, demand deposits tend to be volatile. In the pool-of-funds concept used in this study 5 pércent of time deposits were held in required reserves and 3 percent were held as working cash. The balance of the time deposits was considered to be invested in the portfolio. The remaining cash and the remaining portfolio were attributed to demand deposits. On this basis cash reserves for the 80 banks averaged 8 percent for time deposits and 25 percent for demand deposits.

In this pool-of-funds concept the rate of portfolio earnings attributed to time and demand deposits would be identical. However, because $92 out of every $100 of time deposits could be invested to generate income and only $75 of each $100 of demand deposits could be so invested, the time deposits were able to out-earn demand deposits by 3.76 percent to 3.03 percent.

Based on each $1,000 of demand deposits, gross expenses on the average were $23.07. When this was deducted from the average gross income of $38.40 it left net earnings of $15.33. A deduction of $6.73 for federal taxes left net current operating earnings of $8.60 after federal and before state taxes. On a percentage basis this was 0.86 percent of demand deposits. This was before payment of dividends to stockholders.

Of course it does not follow that, because the typical demand deposit account yields a small return, this is true of all accounts. Quite the contrary. Large accounts with low deposit turnover can be very profitable. In the postwar period, however, many of the financial officers of large corporations and large municipalities have pulled down their average demand deposits by investing their idle balances in Government securities. This action has increased the turnover of demand deposits and has had a depressing influence on the over-all profitability of the demand deposit function in commercial banks.

The statement is sometimes made that existing legislation forbidding payment of interest on demand deposits should be repealed. Were banks in this study to pay interest on demand deposits they would have to increase service charges proportionately or experience a drop in profits. If interest were set at only 0.86 percent, an added expense at that rate would equal the entire average net operating earnings arising from the demand deposits for the 80 banks in this 1960 study.

Should Banks Reprice Corporate Services?

James P. Furniss and Paul S. Nadler

Banking, potentially one of the fastest growing service businesses in the United States, is coming face to face with a critical problem that is old hat to most industries—namely, how to price and charge for services. Consider:

Banks have traditionally undercharged for most corporate services, offering them at cost instead of charging a price that includes a profit.

To offset this policy, banks have used unrealistically low interest rates in establishing the value of the checking account balances with which corporations pay for most of these services.

Thus by undercharging for services and undercrediting for these demand deposit balances, banks generally have hoped they would make their corporate accounts profitable on balance.

A FRESH LOOK

Now, however, some bankers are beginning to recognize that this traditional policy not only makes many major corporate accounts unprofitable, but also that it is harmful to their growth and erodes their competitive position with nonbanks for certain services.

Consequently, some commercial banks are taking a fresh look at their traditional methods of charging for corporate services. In so doing, they are developing means of compensation that should be more predictable and equitable to both customer and banker alike. Even more important, these new approaches, if adopted generally by banks, should have an impact on the policies of corporate financial officers, the composition of bank deposits, the use of bank services, and the overall relationship between banks and their business customers.

Realism needed

In order to earn a profit on each business account, some banks are now considering offering credit on checking account balances closer to what the corporate treasurer could earn through investment of his excess funds in the money market. Concurrently, these bankers see that they will have to raise their charges for corporate services. By making these two changes, they feel that corporate treasurers will have options which they now do not have. Treasurers with excess money may then use their balances to pay for all account services. Others who temporarily or regularly are short of cash will be able to pay for services of all kinds with a combination of fees and balances.

With this new approach to the value of money in banks, many a corporate executive will then be able to reexamine certain parts of his cash management policies.

To banks generally, this trend eventually will mean some moderation of the pace of increase in the turnover of demand deposits, accompanied by a more rapid growth of demand deposit balances. But far more important, it will mean that the banking business should be able to earn a profit on each of its business accounts.

TRADITIONAL PRACTICE

How did banking get itself into this bind of undercharging for its major services and undercrediting for balances? The answer appears to be that banking originally was aimed at the well-to-do business organization or individual, offering few services in relation to the size of the checking accounts maintained. And because of the relatively modest number of services requested and the high profitability of the balances, banks traditionally offered such "incidental" services without extra charge.

Cost structure

In starting from a policy of offering such services free as a normal part of a banker-depositor relationship, the banker established a tradition that was hard to break, even when the variety and cost of services offered increased to the point at which the balances of many customers were not adequate to compensate for the work done for them by the bank. It was the bank's comptroller who first came to grips with the need for making all accounts pay their own way. And in doing so he looked at each account from the viewpoint of the bank's cost structure. His analysis centered on determining the costs of providing services and on the return that the bank was able to earn on balances left with it.

Thus the bank generally began using the comptroller's cost figures, not prices, when talking with an unprofitable customer. Subsequently, the bank also began providing the customer with a credit for the worth of his account on the basis of the value of money to the bank rather than the value of money in the money market.

In providing earnings credit, the commercial bank applied it only to that part of a customer's deposit which the bank actually could lend out. The bank therefore deducted from balances the amount it needed to meet legal reserve requirements, to maintain reserves of vault cash, and to compensate other banks for clearing checks. This led to the development of an account analysis form (shown in Table 1) which is close to the one generally in use today.

Since this analysis form looks at the corporate account from the banker's viewpoint rather than from that of the customer, the corporate financial officer is asked, in effect, to understand and to worry about the banker's problems. The treasurer will readily accept the fact that the amount of his balance which represents uncollected checks should be subtracted from the book balance of his account.

There is little reason, however, why he should accept the banker's argument that an additional amount of what is left after float should be subtracted to compensate the bank for the reserves it must keep at its Federal Reserve Bank against its demand deposits, for the vault cash it must maintain, and for the deposits it must keep at other so-called correspondent banks to compensate them for their aid in clearing checks and performing other services.

The reserve requirements that banks must meet and the correspondent balances and cash that they must keep are out-of-pocket expense to the banks. They should be of no concern to the corporate officer. In fact, these costs should be part of the price that banks charge to compensate themselves for the services they render, rather than coming as a deduction from the amount of the corporate balance on which credit is earned.

Table 1 A Typical Account Analysis Form

Book balance of all funds deposited by customer	$______
less *float* (amount of customer's checks not yet collected)	$______
Collected balance	$______
less *reserve requirements* (reserves required by state law, Federal Reserve, vault cash, balances kept in other banks, etc.)	$______
Loanable balance	$______
Value of the money for the month based on an earnings allowance of ______% per annum	$______
Costs of services rendered (itemized)	$______
Monthly profit or loss on account to the bank	$______

Table 2 Reserve Requirement Deductions of 37 Major Banks

Number of banks	*Percent of collected balance*
12	16.5%
1	18.0
3	18.5
1	19.5
15	20.0
1	21.5
1	22.0
3	25.0

Survey findings

Yet a study of 37 major banks made in the spring of 1965 showed that the amount deducted under this general category of "reserve requirements" ranged from 16½% to 25% of the collected balance. These reserve requirement deductions from collected balances used in determining the amount of loanable balance are shown in Table 2.

The corporate executive knows that if he cuts his demand deposit balance to an absolute minimum, and chooses the alternative of investing in short-term money market instruments such as Treasury Bills, he will earn a return on every cent invested, not just on his investment minus 16½% to 25%.

Furthermore, an analysis of the earnings allowance (Table 3) offered by the 37 major banks which participated in the 1965 study mentioned above showed a rather low distribution of earnings allowances on the loanable balance at a time when yields on 90-day Treasury Bills fluctuated narrowly around 3.9%.

Thus the corporate treasurer with money in his checking account in excess of the minimum needed to meet bills theoretically had two options in the spring of 1965: (1) he could move his excess funds into Treasury Bills and earn 3.9% on them, paying the banks in cash for checking account services rendered; or (2) he could leave the money in the bank to compensate it for services rendered, and thus reduce or eliminate any service charge assessments.

Table 3 Earnings Allowance Offered on Loanable Funds

*Number of banks**	*Percentage rate*
2	1.8 (lowest offered)
6	1.9 to 2.3
15	2.4 to 2.8
9	2.9 to 3.1
3	3.2 to 3.5
1	4.0 (highest offered)

* Data not available on one bank of the 37 surveyed.

Table 4 Hypothetical Value of Treasurer's Collected Balance in Spring of 1965

In U.S. Treasury Bills (actual value)	3.9%
In bank offering 1.8% after 25% reserve requirement deduction	1.35
In bank with most frequently used rate of 2.6% after 20% reserve requirement deduction	2.08
In bank offering 4.0% after 16½% reserve requirement deduction	3.34

If he made the latter choice, as shown in Table 4, the earnings on his balances in the 37 surveyed banks would have ranged from a 3.34% high to a 1.35% low. Taking the survey's most frequently used rates of a 20% reserve requirement deduction and a 2.6% earnings credit, the corporate treasurer would have earned 2.08% on his balance as opposed to 3.9% in the Treasury Bill market.

On top of this, many corporate treasurers recognize that when they do pare their demand deposits to a minimum and compensate the bank with a fee instead of a balance for services rendered, the fee is usually low because of the bank's traditional practice of costing instead of pricing services. This gives corporate financial officers even more incentive to keep their demand deposits at a minimum.

The banks thus have been facing a dilemma of their own making. Many customers want to use bank services to the utmost. Because customers may not have large demand deposit balances to leave in banks as compensation, or because they may feel they can earn more by investing their cash, they ask to pay for bank services in cash. The result is: some customers cut demand deposits to a minimum and at the same time buy certain bank services at cost.

An analogy might be a railroad charging only 5¢ for a trip from New York to Chicago, hoping to make up losses by charging $50 for a hamburger in the diner and pricing other food comparably. Under such a price schedule, the vice president of operations would undoubtedly have to report to the president, "A lot of people are riding our trains, but nobody seems hungry."

IMPACT ON PROFITS

Banking's practice in this area certainly has had an adverse impact on bank profits. Fortunately for banks, most corporations pay their own way by keeping balances large enough to compensate for the services they use. There are a growing number, however, that resort to the practice of keeping balances low and paying fees wherever possible. Bankers who argue with corporate treasurers to increase balances find themselves having to justify their own costs and abilities to earn money on investable funds, something few other industries must do to obtain compensation.

The net result has been that most banks have a certain number of accounts where profit margins are low or nonexistent. The new account man is often unfairly blamed for this. He has long needed better tools in the form of more realistic prices and earnings allowances on balances. Lacking these, he has a tendency to avoid discussions with certain corporations, hoping against hope that soon there will be a new treasurer or an act of God which will somehow make the account profitable.

The corporate treasurer, on his side, has been highly confused by the tremendous variation between the cost figures and credit allowances of different banks. For example, using as basic reference how many dollars of collected balances a bank requires to support collection of one check per month, the survey of the 37 major banks showed a staggering variation from $8.57 needed in the bank with the lowest balance requirement to $26.66 required in the bank with the highest.

It is small wonder, then, that despite a sincere desire to make his relationship profitable to the bank, the corporate treasurer often finds paring his account markedly the prudent course. Some treasurers frankly admit that they cannot take the figures offered by each individual bank at face value. Rather, they must set up their own objective standards, expecting that if they are reasonable, the bank will accept them no matter what the bank's own cost figures show.

In many instances the treasurer simply uses a trial and error approach —cutting his balances as far as he can and waiting to see the reaction. To illustrate:

A major transportation company, using over 100 banks to collect tariff revenue for it, decided to see what would happen if it cut its demand deposit balance at each bank in half. It did so, and nobody objected. It then decided on a second cut of 50%. At that point, three banks complained. The company adjusted those three balances upward, and left the rest at 25% of the original deposit level—without one word of complaint from the other banks.

Similarly, the treasurer of a national shoe chain shifted his collections from traditional methods to an automatic depository system that quickly removed his funds from collecting banks. Since the treasurer, under the new system, did not maintain any base balance to compensate his banks, one banker after three months called him and asked him to pay service charges. The treasurer replied, "I know that all my accounts were bound to have gone in the red with that change, but I am not going to beg to pay the banks. When bankers have enough guts to ask me, I'll pay service charges—but never balances—because I can earn more with the extra cash than I can get credit for. So far, less than one fourth of the bankers have said anything, so I'm money ahead." [1]

With the initiative left to the treasurer, and with the corporation often better off by cutting balances to a minimum and paying with fees for

[1] Charles Pistor, *The Account Analysis—Boon or Bane to Effective Bank Pricing* (unpublished thesis at the Stonier Graduate School of Banking, June 1964).

the services used, it is small wonder that demand deposit balances have dropped to fairly low levels generally.

DEMAND DEPOSIT TURNOVER

As far as the banking system is concerned, the cost of this reduction in corporate demand deposits becomes even greater than it first seems. When a company cuts its demand deposit to a minimum and invests the rest of its funds in the money market, it is increasing the number of times in any given year that each dollar of its checking account balance is turned over. Although it is using less dollars of demand deposits than before, it is still writing the same average volume of checks.

What makes this so significant to the banking industry is that increased turnover of money can serve as an adequate substitute for a rise in the supply of demand deposit money in financing the growth of the ecenomy. For example, $1 being spent 50 times in a day can finance as much economic activity as $50 turned over only once a day.

The linkage between monetary velocity and the supply of money is provided by the Federal Reserve System. Since the Federal Reserve wants the effective demand for goods and services closely coordinated with the nation's productive capacity and available manpower, it carefully watches the velocity of money. When it sees velocity speeding up, it knows that this is increasing effective demand. The only recourse, then, if the Federal Reserve wants to maintain a stable level of spending in the economy, is to curb the growth in demand deposits—the basic component of the money supply. Doing so offsets the impact of the increase in deposit velocity.

Thus, even though it is to be expected that the money supply—and demand deposits in particular—should grow as rapidly as the economy grows, this has not been the case in the United States, because of the speedup in deposit velocity. Specifically, while the economy, as measured by the gross national product, grew 80% in the decade of the 1950's, demand deposit growth was only 21%. From 1960 to 1964, moreover, when the GNP advanced 24%, demand deposit expansion reached only 12%. The rest of the nation's growth was financed by the only available alternative to demand deposit expansion—increased turnover of deposits.

The practice of encouraging corporate officers to pare demand deposits to a minimum thus leads to a second adverse impact on bank earnings. When the economy's growth is financed by increased quantity of demand deposits, the Federal Reserve is allowing the banking industry to have more raw material for lending and investing on which an income can be earned. But when the economy's growth is financed by augmented deposit velocity instead of growth in deposits, the banks simply get the additional work and expense that increased activity in their checking accounts creates.

COURSE OF CHANGE

It has not been easy for the banking business to do anything to alter the impact of its corporate account analysis policy on bank profits. The individual account officer generally has been trained to judge his success in terms of the size of his customers' balances and the number of accounts he serves. Rare is the bank that has been able to judge its contact officers on the basis of the profitability of these accounts. Cost figures generally have been too inaccurate for fair comparison between two contact officers with different types of accounts and different functions in the bank. And, with poor cost figures, taking corrective action on individual accounts has been difficult.

Moreover, many U.S. banks have continued to be growth oriented instead of profit conscious. Banks generally consider rate of growth the most important measurement of performance. Thus there has been considerable hesitancy to ask unprofitable accounts to leave the bank, even in those instances where the bank knows the account is losing money and it can do nothing to get the corporation to make the account pay its own way.

As for the second adverse impact of its corporate account analysis policy—that of increased deposit velocity slowing demand deposit growth—no one bank can have much impact on deposit velocity. Each individual bank has accepted the reality that demand deposit growth of the banking system as a whole is an outside force set by the Federal Reserve. The banks, therefore, have seen little they could do individually to aid demand deposit expansion, and so they have done nothing much more about it than observe the trend of increasing velocity with regret.

What, then, has been bringing about the gradual change away from costing for services and undercrediting for balances to a system of pricing and full crediting?

Factors involved

Chronologically, probably the first force causing the change in bank corporate analysis has been the steady rise in interest rates on short-term investments that has taken place in the last decade. When interest rates on 90-day Treasury Bills averaged well under 2%, as was the case until ten years ago, it did not pay the corporate treasurer to pare his demand deposit to a minimum. The added return available by open market investment of his surplus funds was simply not large enough to be worth all the effort. Now, with money market rates averaging up to 4% and more at times, paring demand balances and investing the surplus is worth the work involved.

Secondly, banks started to offer their customers a greater variety and quantity of services, especially those produced by electronic data processing equipment. Yet bank officials responsible for providing new and expensive services recognized it would be unrealistic to expect most customers to keep balances large enough to compensate the bank for these services.

For one thing, the corporate treasurer would have had to borrow money in many cases to keep his balance at a satisfactory level. For another, money invested in the operations of the corporation itself would yield better profits than money in the bank or in market securities. Thus bankers saw advantages to offering the corporate customer an option between balances and fees. Doing so not only made it more convenient to buy bank services, but it also gave the customer a new way to afford them. This was a major step toward mixing the balance compensation method with a fee system.

Banking experience with account reconciliation provided further realization that compensation by balances alone had its drawbacks. In the 1950's the idea of banks reconciling corporate checking accounts made sense both to the corporations and to those banks which had new data processing equipment that could do the job more simply, conveniently, and inexpensively than a firm could. At first, this service was offered solely for balances. As more and more banks came to offer it, however, two patterns emerged: (1) some customers started to take it for granted as part of their regular demand deposit accounting and cut their balances back to former levels, and (2) some banks began to offer it "free" as a competitive weapon to pick up new accounts from banks not yet providing the automated service.

Thus much of the banking industry learned the sad lesson that if services are offered, they must be offered on a solid price basis. For once the fee is established, the bank will continue to earn this amount. But when a new service is offered for balances, there is no assurance that the balance will be maintained and that the bank will be adequately compensated for the work it has newly taken on.

PERCEIVED TRENDS

In the provision of new automated services, the banks had to face stern competition from service bureaus and other providers of these services who operated solely in the data processing field. These competitors had to know just what their costs of service provision were and how much profit they had to earn. In competing with suppliers of data processing services, the banks had to offer their services at comparable prices.

And as bank cost-accounting methods and time-study procedures improved, banks found that they would have to determine just what amount of profit their prices should include—something that few banks had truly done much about in years past.

But while the above factors provided the specifics that led to the change brewing in corporate account analysis, two major trends underlie the entire picture.

Profit Emphasis

One trend is the transfer of emphasis from size to profitability as the test of bank performance. With the banking business relying now on interest-bearing time and savings deposits for the bulk of its growth, instead of on interest-free demand deposits, bank costs have soared. And in the ensuing profit squeeze a new emphasis on bank profitability has developed. The growth in the number of professional investors in bank stocks has further accentuated this trend toward profit emphasis. Professional investors are far more interested in the income statement than the balance sheet in evaluating a bank.

Equally significant has been the slow recognition of the dangers inherent in the continuing practice of letting the customer determine the rate and amount of compensation paid for bank services. Prior to now, despite bankers' complaints that the corporate treasurer is a man who pares bank profits to the bone, the banking industry has fared fairly well on its corporate accounts. This situation exists largely because the corporate executive has wanted to keep his bank relationship mutually beneficial, often feeling it is good to have a strong friend in his banker. However, the situation is full of possible danger because the banking industry must count on the good will of the corporate treasurer in making sure that compensation will be adequate. The potential for abuse in this system of compensation is enormous.

The irony of letting the customer know the bank's cost and then imploring him to provide adequate compensation is highlighted by this classic story reported by the president of the Mellon National Bank:

> Illustrative of what I am saying was an experience with one of our customers in connection with some equipment we were putting in one of our large buildings. I should say at the outset that the treasurer of the company had recently asked for a complete account analysis. Subsequently, the president called and said that he hoped we would consider their equipment. I said that there was no question in our minds but that we were going to buy the product. But I told him I thought it would be a good idea if he brought his cost figures over sometime, and he and I would review them together and determine the price.
>
> There was a long silence on the phone, and I thought we were disconnected, and I said, "Hello, are you there?" He said, "Yes, I was just thinking—you must have rocks in your head." I said I didn't think so, that I assumed that this was his company policy because his treasurer asked for all our cost figures, and I naturally assumed that since he apparently was asking for such figures of all his suppliers, he would be glad to give his own to his customers. He said, "You weren't crazy enough to give the treasurer the figures, were you?" [2]

[2] John A. Mayer, "Banking's Future—Bright or Gloomy?" address at the Directors-Officers Conference, Girard Trust Corn Exchange Bank, November 18, 1962, Philadelphia, Pennsylvania.

A change from costing to pricing services would end the bank's reliance on the corporate executive for determination of compensation and would place banking on the same firm price footing as other industries with regard to compensation patterns. For the corporate treasurer, moreover, it would end the pattern of uncertainty and confusion under which he finds he must pay for some services with fees, for others with balances, and under which he finds all too often that the bank's compensation is left to his conscience. It would also end the present pattern under which the more lenient corporate treasurer pays part of the bank costs incurred by the more militant one.

PRICING OF SERVICES

How can bank services be priced under a system of compensation that includes all costs plus a profit?

In the first place, banks generally must recognize that they cannot continue to sweep their pricing problem under the rug by assuming that the undercrediting of balances will produce profits from services that now do not pay their own way. To make the needed changes, though, banks will first have to develop good costing procedures.

Next, banks will have to keep much better track of services rendered, centralizing this information in one place in order to compute the total price of services rendered so that the corporate treasurer will receive one consolidating statement. A single bank officer then can be made responsible not only for the account but also for its profitability. As a by-product, the officer in charge of the account will also be able to see just which bank services the customer is, and is not, using. He then can point out to the business firm just where the introduction of additional bank services could be of mutual benefit.

Another consequence will be that the banks will have to start setting prices on some of the professional services they have been giving away, such as help on plant location, business information, and the like. For other services, bankers may well have to measure their time in much the same way that lawyers keep track of time devoted to specific clients. The bank officer with profit responsibility for the account no longer will be able to rationalize that the bank is being compensated in other ways for the free services being provided.

As for fees established, banking obviously will have to use price schedules similar to those of other industries. Establishment of such schedules generally includes consideration of the following factors:

1. What is the value of the service to the customer? (This sets the top limit on any price.)
2. What are the costs of getting into the business? Are they to be amortized over a short or long time period or not at all?
3. Will the service have a broad appeal, or will it apply only to a narrow group of customers?

4. Are the costs subject to improvement with volume, better systems, and/or new machines?
5. What price is being offered by competitors?
6. Does the bank want to dominate the market? If so, will a lower profit margin discourage competition?
7. Can or should costs be absorbed in other profits attributed to a customer—that is, can the service be a valuable loss leader?
8. Does the service require capital to be tied up in order to make its performance possible? If so, then on what basis should capital costs be included? (In this regard, it can be assumed that every bank would like to earn at least its average rate of return on capital on each service offered, but that if competitive conditions make this impossible, it will accept a lower return on capital.)

CREDITING OF BALANCES

If a bank sells its services for a price that includes a profit, then obviously it must also alter the present arrangement of undercrediting balances and switch to providing full credit for balances based on what the depositor's money would be worth elsewhere. Otherwise the bank will be getting its profits twice: from the service price and from the undercrediting of the balance.

Since banks generally cannot shift from costing to pricing all services at one instant in time, some unusual crediting arrangements have been developed as interim policies. For example:

> One bank continues the traditional policy of using costs for checking account charges. On its lock box collection program, however, it uses prices. Thus it is using a temporary system under which the customer's balance is anaylzed, and a high rate of credit is placed on that part of the balance which is used to compensate for lock box collections.
>
> After the lock box fees have been met, the rest of the balance is provided with a lower rate of credit as an offset to checking account costs. Meanwhile, the bank is scrambling to complete a study of its checking account costs as a basis for establishing firm prices.

Once most services are firmly priced, there is little question but that the balance compensation must be at going interest rates in the money market if further erosion of corporate demand deposits is to be avoided.

This does not mean, of course, that a bank automatically must offer the corporate depositor the same rate as he could earn on Treasury Bills, since the purchase of such bills necessitates the typing up of corporate funds for 90 days. Checking account funds, for example, are available instantly. A better value for checking account money would therefore be the market rate available to the corporate treasurer on a one-day investment.

Corporate options

What is likely, then, is that banks will offer the corporate customer several alternatives as to how he wants his bank balances handled. If the customer is willing to tie up his cash in a 90-day non-interest-bearing time certificate of deposit, for example, then the bank should offer him a credit on the full balance of this certificate at the going rates for 90-day funds. However, if the customer expects that his account will be volatile, and that his balance will fluctuate, he will have the option of maintaining his funds as demand deposits, as at present, and get the one-day rate.

With a choice of options available to him, the corporate treasurer would presumably cease to care whether the charge was in the form of fees or balances for specific services since the expense to him either way would be the same. The bank, too, ultimately would have little reason to care whether its compensation was derived from fees or balances.

A danger for banks does exist in such a compensation policy change in cases where there may be many companies with excess balances which could then be used as compensation for new services. Those customers sitting on idle balances, however, already are sitting ducks for attack from competitive institutions and money market instruments. Recent history shows that big excess balances in banks have been disappearing, so the danger to banking today may be less than it would have been ten years ago.

(See the Appendix for what could be a typical account analysis form of the future—formulated in the customer's terms—which offers market value for balances, and gives the corporate treasurer the opportunity to assign a value to the tasks that would be hard for the banker himself to evaluate, such as locating an office for the firm and assisting it with a sale.)

FUTURE IMPLICATIONS

The eventual adoption of this more realistic approach to corporate account analysis should have major implications for the corporate treasurer, the composition of bank deposits, and the sources of bank profits.

For the corporation

In getting full credit for their bank balances based on today's money market yields, the corporation would have less incentive to move its funds into money market instruments. Of course, the treasurer still would only want to keep enough money in his corporate bank account to pay the costs of the services he uses; any balances left in excess of that amount would earn nothing for him.

However, it is entirely likely that the corporation—while gaining added flexibility in payment method—will find it possible to maintain demand deposit balances at much higher levels than at present and still have every cent of deposit earning as much for the company as it could in the money market.

One touchy problem the banks will face in trying to get a buildup of corporate demand deposits to larger levels, though, is that in many a treasurer's office there is a small staff of men whose main function is the process of cash management. Their success is often measured by how fast they can get money collected, by how low they can pare the company's demand deposits, and by how much added investment return they can earn in the money market.

Thus the reversal of the present trend toward razor's edge cash management will come slowly, if for no other reason than that a science of short-term cash investment has been developed which its practitioners would hesitate to give up. It must be recognized, of course, that the corporate treasurer would only find bank deposits attractive again in comparison with investing surplus funds in money market instruments. The corporation would still have the same incentive as ever to keep the total posture of its liquid assets at a minimum, since money invested in the actual operations of a reasonably profitable firm should earn far more than a similar amount invested in the money market.

In addition, with the new techniques of lock box collection systems, wire transfer of funds, the draft, and the other methods of faster money mobilization that have been developed in recent years, the amount of float in the typical corporate account has been curbed. Today, money due the company is being collected much more rapidly than in the past. Thus the corporation can operate with less cash tied up in demand balances. This reduction is at the expense of banks all over the country that used to have several days' float time on checks sent by their depositors to out-of-town corporations.

Hence the new approach to corporate account analysis will not stop or reverse the trend toward minimizing demand balances. But what can be halted is the additional reduction in demand balances resulting from the present willingness of some corporate treasurers to cut demand deposits even below the minimum level of liquid assets the corporation wants to hold. Further, some cash rich companies may put money back into banks to compensate for bank services which previously were paid for on a cash-fee-only basis.

Under the new account analysis approach, then, the corporation should keep a much larger percentage of its "cash and marketable securities" account in demand deposits and non-interest-bearing time deposits, as long as the bank continues to offer needed services at reasonable prices and to provide competitive yields on deposit funds in the corporation's account analysis. For the corporate executive, then, the new approach to account analysis can lead to a de-emphasis on investing cash and a renewed buildup of bank deposits.

For the bank

This obviously means more demand deposit growth, reduced deposit velocity, and finally even additional demand deposit growth, stemming from the Federal Reserve's allowing more rapid growth in demand deposits to compensate for the slowed growth in deposit velocity.

The bank that offers a large variety of services will find, moreover, that in making demand and non-interest-bearing time deposit balances more attractive as a means of compensating for services rendered, it will reduce its dependence for growth on "hot money" represented by negotiable time certificates of deposit. The bank will be able to obtain more of its growth through demand deposits. Since these deposits will be supporting the costs of new services rendered, chances are they will be more stable than the negotiable certificate of deposit which often is transferred to the bank offering the highest rate. Thus the whole present trend toward dependence on negotiable time certificates as the major source of bank growth will be somewhat modified, if not substantially halted.

Certainly, under the new account analysis approach, the checking account in which there have been juicy balances will tend to decline in profitability as the customer becomes aware of just what his balances are worth to the bank. In the long run, however, this can mean a healthier bank in which every customer pays his own way instead of having a loss customer riding the back of a profitable group.

Ultimately, the customer who is overpaying for services will tend to leave the bank where he is overcharged, or he will curb his balance through increased knowledge anyway.

Pricing all services fairly instead of offering some at cost, coupled with giving realistic earnings credit for checking account deposits, should tend to increase the rate of growth of bank demand deposits. It should bring an end to the present anomalous situation, in which the corporate depositor is confused about how to compensate his bank and about how, on occasion, to dictate his own terms on what he will pay for bank service. Most important, however, a change in banking policy to across-the-board pricing and realistic money values should produce better customer service and a fairer structure of compensation for all corporate customers.

APPENDIX: A FUTURE ACCOUNT ANALYSIS FORM

CORPORATE SERVICE DEPARTMENT

P.O. Box 4899 Atlanta, Georgia 30302

June 3, 1965

To: Joe Jones, Treasurer
ABC Corporation
Anytown, U.S.A.

Period Covered: Month of May 1965

Firm: ABC Corporation

Here is a summary covering the relationship of your firm with this bank for the period shown. Services rendered, cash fees paid and value of funds on deposit with us are shown in the attached lists.

A. *Services Rendered*	
1. Regular Services	$5,450
2. Other Services	
3. Total Services Rendered	$
B. *Compensation*	
1. Cash Fees Paid	800
2. Value of Funds Deposited	2,000
3. Total Compensation	$2,800
C. *Difference* (A minus B)	$

Customer Service Department

Copies: Pete Smith, ABC Corporation, Macon
John Brown, ABC Corporation, Atlanta
Fred Banker, Bank account officer, Atlanta

Remarks:
See my letter of June 3, 1965

Fred Banker

Authors' note: Mr. Banker's letter in this case might explain that the bank had received only $2,800 to cover $5,450 worth of regular services. It might suggest that the firm pay $2,650 in cash for the professional services rendered, plus an increase in demand deposit balances to cover help given in office location and sales assistance. The size of the increase would be based on the company's evaluation of the special services rendered.

A. *Services Rendered*

1. *Regular Services*

   A. *Deposit and Checking Accounts*

________Checks Deposited	$3,000
________Drafts Deposited	
________Lock Box Items	
________Checks Cashed	
________Drafts Handled	
________Wire Transfers	

   B. *Loan Services*

Standby Cost of Loan Line	$1,650
Loan Interest	
Other Loan Fees	

   C. *Other Regular Services*

Trust Services	$ 800
Travel Services	
Computer Services	
Etcetera	
Subtotal	$5,450

2. *Other Services*

   Because of their nature, the value of services shown below is best measured by you in terms of what they have meant to your firm.

1. Locating your office in Macon	$
2. Assisting with the XYZ sale	$
Subtotal	$

3. *Total Services Rendered* $

B. *Compensation*

1. *Cash Fees Paid*

A. Trust fees	$800
B.	
C.	
D.	
E.	
Subtotal	$800

2. *Value of Funds Deposited*

   A. *Deposit and Checking Accounts*

Description	*Book Balance*	*Less Float*	*Collected Balance*	*Valued at*	*Value for Period*
Macon #133	300,000	100,000	200,000	3.9	$ 433
Atlanta #456	600,000	200,000	400,000	3.9	866
Subtotal	900,000	300,000	600,000	—	$1,300

B. *Non-Interest-Bearing Certificates of Deposit*

Description	*Collected Balance*	*Valued at*	*Value for Period*
Due date of			
8/1/65	100,000	4.2	350
10/1/65	100,000	4.2	350
Subtotal	200,000	—	700

3. *Total Compensation* $2,800

Savings Accounts and Commerical Bank Earnings*

Savings deposits have become increasingly important to commercial banks. At the beginning of 1963, the "passbook" type of deposit totaled 107 billion dollars and accounted for 36 per cent of total deposits. As recently as mid-1957, such accounts totaled only 44 billion dollars or 24 per cent of total deposits.

The growth of savings deposits mirrors in part the sizable increase in nearly all kinds of liquid financial assets but also reflects the concerted efforts of commercial banks to acquire such deposits. Banks have raised interest rates paid on savings and spent substantial sums on advertising to bring this service to the attention of potential depositors.

Not all bankers agree, however, that it is profitable to aggressively seek savings deposits, and, of course, it is essential that banks operate profitably if they are to serve their communities effectively.

* This article, including the tables, is based upon a study by Allan R. Drebin, "Savings Accounts and Commercial Bank Earnings," Bureau of Business Research, Graduate School of Business Administration, The University of Michigan, Ann Arbor. Copyright, 1963, used by permission. The study was initiated while Mr. Drebin was a Research Fellow at the Federal Reserve Bank of Chicago. The conclusions, of course, are those of the author.

Reprinted with the permission of the Federal Reserve Bank of Chicago from *Business Conditions,* August 1963.

Answers to the complex and perplexing questions about the profitability of time deposits are difficult for bankers to find and probably are not the same for all banks. The problem is complicated by the fact that banks provide many closely interwoven services, making it extremely difficult to evaluate the costs and returns of any one alone. A change in policy affecting one service is likely to affect costs and returns of other services offered by the bank.

In this study of the profitability of the savings account component of time deposits, a method is suggested that may be helpful to individual banks in evaluating the profitability of savings accounts. In general, the results indicate that several categories of savings accounts may contribute little or nothing to profits and probably are maintained at a loss by many banks. Among these are accounts with small balances, accounts with excessive activity and accounts closed within short periods after they are opened. The study concludes that banks might find it profitable to make special efforts to attract larger, longer-lived accounts and to limit transactions activity in savings accounts.

THE PROFIT CONTRIBUTION

Revenues

Before a bank can determine whether its savings department contributes to profits, the revenues and expenses traceable to the savings function must be established. Because the savings department does not contribute directly to bank revenues, income attributable to savings accounts can be determined only by reference to the earnings of the funds provided from this source. A rate of return must be assigned to the net funds available from the savings department.

While gross returns on any loan or investment can be determined, it is difficult to associate specific assets with funds furnished by savings deposits. Some bankers favor the "pool" approach, wherein all investments are made from a pool of all available funds without regard for their sources. This simplifies accounting, perhaps explaining its popularity, but is not very useful unless it actually corresponds to the investment policy followed by the bank.

Other bankers contend that funds furnished by time deposits are converted to specific types of loans and investments, primarily real estate mortgages, and when all the funds cannot be placed in mortgages, the remainder is invested in tax-exempt municipals with similar maturities.

Any bank can ascribe a suitable earnings rate to the savings function by inquiring into its own investment policies. This rate, multiplied by the dollar amount of funds furnished, provides a figure for gross revenue attributable to savings deposits.

Expenses

Savings department expenses fall into four categories: those proportional to amount of deposits; those depending upon the number of accounts; those varying with account activity, and those related to average account life.

Interest paid on deposits is the largest expense item. Although computed in a variety of ways that may alter the results slightly, interest costs are nearly always proportional to amount of deposits, as are deposit insurance and examination charges.

The other expenses, many of them joint costs, cannot be estimated as easily. Individual banks assign these costs on differing bases, but in general the savings department should shoulder all the direct costs incurred as a result of its operation. The department should share in the "fixed costs" to the extent of benefit obtained from such costs.

Allocation of building expenses and other "fixed costs" to departments is at best a difficult problem. Possibly even more difficult is the evaluation of the impact on other departments of any steps taken to eliminate unprofitable savings accounts.

Although the whole must equal the sum of its parts, the maximization of departmental income is not always consistent with attaining the maximum profit for the entire establishment. In taking steps to maximize profits of the savings department, a bank must consider the over-all effect of such action on its complete banking operation.

AN ILLUSTRATIVE EXAMPLE

A "model" bank based on the actual records of five large banks was used to illustrate the steps which can be taken to help in identifying any unprofitable accounts. Since the model is not based upon a representative sample of banks, it does not permit conclusions as to whether savings accounts are profitable generally. However, it does serve to illustrate some characteristics of accounts which may be generally applicable.

Account size

The size distribution of accounts has an important bearing on profits, since revenues are proportional to amount of deposits while some costs are independent of deposit balances.

Information on distribution of accounts by size was available from two large banks. For these banks, 67 per cent of the total number of accounts had balances of less than 500 dollars, yet these small accounts comprised only 8 per cent of total savings deposits. The remaining one-third of the accounts, with average balances above 500 dollars, included

Table 1 Size Distribution of Accounts

Account size (dollars)	*Accounts (per cent)*	*Deposits (per cent)*
Under 100	43	1
100–500	24	7
500–1,000	11	9
1,000–5,000	18	44
5,000–10,000	3	21
10,000–25,000	1	11
Over 25,000	*	7
Total	100	100

* Less than ½ of 1 per cent.

92 per cent of total savings deposits in these banks. The percentage attributable to each size category is shown in Table 1.

Account activity

An attempt was made to determine whether or not any relation exists between account size and activity. Analysis of a sample of savings accounts at a large commercial bank during a six-month period indicates that small accounts tend to be more active than large ones, as is indicated in Table 2.

Except for the under-100 dollar category, the average number of transactions declined as size of account increased. The higher percentage of inactive accounts in the under-100 category implies a rather high rate of activity among those accounts that had transactions.

More than half of the accounts studied had either one or no transactions in the period, while 7 per cent had 10 or more transactions. The

Table 2 Analysis of Sample of Savings Accounts

		Transactions	
Account size (dollars)	*Number of accounts*	*Average number* (per cent)*	*Accounts idle (per cent)*
Under 100	231	2.79	42.4
100–500	212	3.73	30.6
500–1,000	149	3.27	25.5
1,000–5,000	390	2.68	24.6
5,000–10,000	172	2.37	26.1
10,000–20,000	70	1.77	30.0
Over 20,000	23	1.52	26.0
Total	1,247	2.83	29.6

* In six-month period.

Table 3 Account Mortality—1950–1960

Account size (dollars)	Original accounts		ORIGINAL ACCOUNTS CLOSED					Accounts still open
	Number	Per cent	First six months	Second six months	Second year	Three to five years	Six to eleven years	
			(per cent)		(per cent)	(per cent)		(per cent)
Under 100	795	51	16	10	10	16	16	32
100–500	307	19	10	11	9	19	17	34
500–1,000	117	7	7	3	12	22	15	41
1,000–5,000	281	18	6	10	8	20	18	38
5,000–10,000	57	4	5	11	9	14	26	35
Over 10,000	18	1	6	22	0	6	22	44
Total	1,575	100	12	10	10	17	17	34

latter group accounted for 40 per cent of the total activity, but supplied only 4 per cent of the total savings deposits.

Account mortality

This characteristic was studied because of the cost of opening and closing accounts. A sample of 1,575 accounts opened in January 1950 was studied for the years 1950–60 (Table 3).

The smaller accounts were found to have somewhat shorter lives than the larger ones, but the difference was slight. However, of the accounts in the sample with initial deposits of 100 dollars or less, more than one-fourth were closed within the first year. Unless the average balances were much greater than the original deposits, the bank probably lost money in handling these accounts.

More accounts were closed in the first year than in any other year in all sizes except 500–1,000 dollars, which lost two per cent more accounts in the second year than in the first. The accounts were closed in a fairly regular pattern of progressively diminishing numbers during the 11-year period. The percentage of total accounts in each category at the end of the period was practically unchanged from that at the beginning.

A little more than one-third of the 1,575 accounts were still open when the period under study closed. By assuming that these accounts would be closed at the rate indicated by the experience of the last several years, the average life expectancy of accounts was estimated to be about 12 years.

Interest, the largest element of expense for the savings department, is largely proportional to deposit dollars. If all expenses varied in this manner, then it would be impossible to select any group of accounts as being unprofitable, as long as the whole department was profitable, since revenues also are proportional to deposits. But the study shows that transactions activity, account opening and annual maintenance costs are not proportional to account size. Furthermore, these costs are substantial and, therefore, it is possible that small accounts might not yield enough revenue to cover the costs incurred in servicing them.

In the five large banks for which records were available the following average costs were determined:

to make a deposit	$0.42
to make a withdrawal	0.45
annual maintenance	1.00
to open and close account (combined)	3.00

The earnings on net available funds averaged 4.12 per cent and the effective interest paid on savings averaged 2.80 per cent. There was considerable variation in these costs and returns among the five banks.

IMPROVING PROFITS

In general, a bank's profitability will be enhanced by plans that tend to increase average account balances, to decrease transactions and to lengthen account life, provided these do not also have a detrimental effect on other departments of the bank.

For the model bank—using figures provided by the selected banks for revenues and expenses—it was estimated that the savings department as a whole contributed about 296,000 dollars to the after-tax earnings of the bank. Accounts with balances of less than 500 dollars, however, incurred a loss of about 86,000 dollars. Presumably the bank could realize annual savings of about this amount by requiring a 500 dollar minimum balance, assuming that the personnel, equipment and space devoted to the accounts eliminated by this action could be shifted to other uses or eliminated, and again assuming there would be no adverse effects on other departments of the bank.

However, it is likely that customers whose savings accounts were driven away by this action would also take their credit needs, demand deposits and other possibly profitable banking business to other institutions. It also would tend to eliminate those depositors whose balances grow from modest opening figures to substantial sums.[1]

Commercial banks also hold that they have an obligation to serve the financial needs of the entire community. Elimination of small savings accounts may be in conflict with this "service" concept, even though it might improve a given bank's profits.

[1] Dr. Elmer M. Harmon, vice president, Bowery Savings Bank, New York City, in the *American Banker* last fall, noted that of all depositors with current balances of 10,000 dollars or more, one out of four had opening balances of 500 or less. He further estimated that had the Bowery refused to accept or maintain accounts of 500 dollars or less, it would have 67 per cent fewer depositors and 26 per cent less in deposits.

Direct measures aimed at limiting the number of transactions permitted in individual savings accounts do not appear to be a good answer to the problem of high activity because of the strong possibility of creating ill will. Interest incentives probably would serve this purpose better, but an individual bank may not have much latitude because of competition from other banks and financial institutions.

Reducing or eliminating interest on certain classes of accounts, say, those with balances of less than 500 dollars, might be tried. However, it seems likely that of accounts in the 100–500 dollar range—many, because of their long life and low activity, do contribute to earnings—would shift to institutions offering interest while accounts with balances of less than 100 dollars might be retained since these draw so little interest that it is of minor consequence. In the model bank, interest cost on accounts of 100 dollars and less was only about 36,000 dollars while acquisition, service and maintenance costs were about 162,000 dollars and revenues were about 50,000 dollars.

While the larger accounts tend to be the most profitable, and should be actively sought, they can present problems. Many banks avoid accounts with very large balances, probably because of fears that their liquidity position would be threatened by large, unexpected withdrawals. This problem could be minimized if large accounts were acquired from a variety of sources, thereby providing diversification.

The study of activity and mortality indicates that large accounts may remain open longer and have fewer transactions than small ones, but additional measures can be taken to promote longer life and limited activity. The payment of an interest bonus on the first anniversary of a deposit works in this direction. It might also be helpful to calculate interest by a method which allows little or no interest on balances remaining with the bank for less than six months. Account activity might also be reduced somewhat if interest was computed so as to provide a smaller return on accounts which have high turnover.

Service charges seem to hold the greatest promise for combating transactions activity, allowing the bank to recover deposit and withdrawal costs. A system of service charges should enable banks to pay higher interest rates which would be particularly attractive to the larger and less active accounts. Those whose accounts are profitable would benefit, since the added interest should more than offset service charges. Those whose accounts are not contributing to profits would be charged for the cost of bank services provided for them or would close their accounts.

Economies of Scale in Commercial Banking

Part 1: The Measurement and Impact

Frederick W. Bell and Neil B. Murphy

Much of the controversy over State and Federal banking laws regarding branching, merging, and other regulation stems from differences of opinion about the competitive capabilities of small banks. Does size give large banks an inherent advantage and allow them to operate at lower unit costs? How great are these cost savings?

One way of investigating these questions is to study the production process in commercial banking. Banks hire the services of labor, capital equipment ranging from desk calculators to sophisticated electronic computers, and materials to produce the range of services offered to the public. If a proportional increase in each input results in a greater than proportional increase in output, economies of scale are said to exist. These economies result in lower unit operating costs as the bank grows since fewer inputs per unit of output are needed. For example, a 10 percent change in output is accompanied by a less-than-10-percent change in total costs if economies of scale are present.

An important distinction, however, must be made between methods of expansion. First, a bank with a fixed number of offices or branches may expand its total output. A second way is to add branch offices to handle the additional business.

This article shows that within existing facilities, expanding operations result in significantly lower unit costs. For many banks, however, these savings are offset by the greater expenses of branching operations.

Reprinted with the permission of the Federal Reserve Bank of Boston from *New England Business Review,* March 1967 (Part I).

HOW AND WHAT DO BANKS PRODUCE?

A steel mill's output can be easily defined in terms of physical units of similar products; however, the output of a bank is diverse and consists of a broad range of specialized services. The typical commercial bank is a multi-product firm engaged in servicing demand and time deposit accounts; processing business, installment, and real estate loan accounts; and providing many other services. From a cost standpoint, all these functions or services may be regarded as different products. Thus, a meaningful analysis of bank costs must consider each function separately.

For example, the servicing of demand deposit accounts is a distinct "production line operation." Associated with this function are the receiving and processing of checks, involving sorting, tabulating and many other detailed operations. Tellers, bookkeeping machine operators, and many kinds of equipment are employed to process or "produce" a demand deposit account.

To measure the relation between bank costs and output, data on 283 commercial banks for 1965 were obtained from the Functional Cost Programs of the Boston, New York, and Philadelphia Federal Reserve Districts.[1] This sample represents approximately 20 percent of all commercial banks in the three districts and includes a somewhat higher proportion of intermediate and fairly large banks. Moreover, these banks range from $2.8 to $801 million in assets, indicating a significant dispersion in the scale of operations. As Table 1 shows, cost data for the sample are classified by several functions or product lines. The most important functions are either fund supplying or fund using. What follows is a detailed description of the relations between costs, output, and other factors for the principal fund using and supplying bank functions.

THE DEMAND DEPOSIT FUNCTION

The holding and transfer, on demand, of funds (checking accounts) is a unique and one of the most important products offered by commercial banking. In the *typical* bank, the demand deposit function supplied 48.6 percent of the total pool of funds available for lending and investment.[2] Of all functions, demand deposits is the largest one, comprising approximately 33.7 percent of costs and 51.1 percent of employment.

There are essentially two kinds of demand deposits: *regular* and *special*. Regular checking, which is available at favorable rates when accounts are both active and large, is used primarily by business firms and institu-

[1] See note at end of reading for a detailed description of this program.

[2] Because of wide variation in the size of banks and the related distortion of simple averages, the geometric mean was used to more accurately describe the *typical* bank. See note at end of reading for technical description.

Table 1 Functional Cost and Employment for the Typical Commercial Bank *—1965

Function	*Number of Banks Reporting*	*Direct Cost of Operation*	*Percent of Total Cost*	*Employees*	*Percent of Total Employees*
Fund Supplying					
Demand Deposits	283	$225,360	33.7%	32.4	51.1%
Time Deposits	264	41,230 [a]	6.2	4.2	6.6
Fund Using					
Real Estate Loans	264	28,090	4.2	2.4	3.8
Instalment Loans	272	85,635	12.8	8.3	13.1
Business Loans	282	45,410	6.8	4.2	6.6
Securities	281	8,936 [b]	1.3	0.5	0.8
Overhead					
Business Development	275	28,200	4.2	1.2	1.9
Administration	272	70,105	10.5		
Occupancy and Maintenance	277	91,300	13.7	5.7 [c]	9.0 [c]
Other					
Safe Deposit	265	8,312	1.3	1.1	1.7
Trust Department	217	35,743	5.3	3.4	5.4
Total		668,327	100.0	63.4	100.0

* Derived from a sample of 283 commercial banks in Boston, New York, and Philadelphia Federal Reserve Districts.
[a] Excludes interest costs.
[b] Excludes interest on borrowed money.
[c] Administration and Occupancy figures combined.
Source: Federal Reserve Banks of Boston, New York, and Philadelphia.

tions. Special checking or convenience accounts, where service charges are assessed on a per check basis, are used by individuals who have minimum account activity and usually carry only a small balance. In the typical bank, approximately 60 percent of the total demand deposit accounts are of the regular variety. For each demand deposit account bookkeeping entries are made, statements are prepared and sent out, checks are processed and ancillary banking services are made available such as receiving payments for large business firms.

Statistical analysis of the 283 Functional Cost banks revealed that the total direct cost—such as labor, rentals on equipment, postage and stationery—of servicing demand deposits depends largely on the volume or number of accounts. It was found that a 10 percent increase in the total number of accounts resulted in a 9.1 percent increase in total direct cost, *holding constant all other factors which might influence cost including the number of branch offices.* Thus, economies of scale with existing facilities are significant in the production of demand deposit accounts. These economies, of course, may be restated in terms of the average cost of producing a demand deposit account. A 10 percent increase in the scale of operations with existing branch facilities, as measured by the total number of accounts, will decrease average unit cost by .91 percent.

Figure 1 indicates these relationships. For example, the average annual cost of a demand deposit account for a typical bank handling 1,000 accounts was $35.05, while a bank at a scale level of 50,000 accounts processed the same account for $24.26, holding all other factors constant.

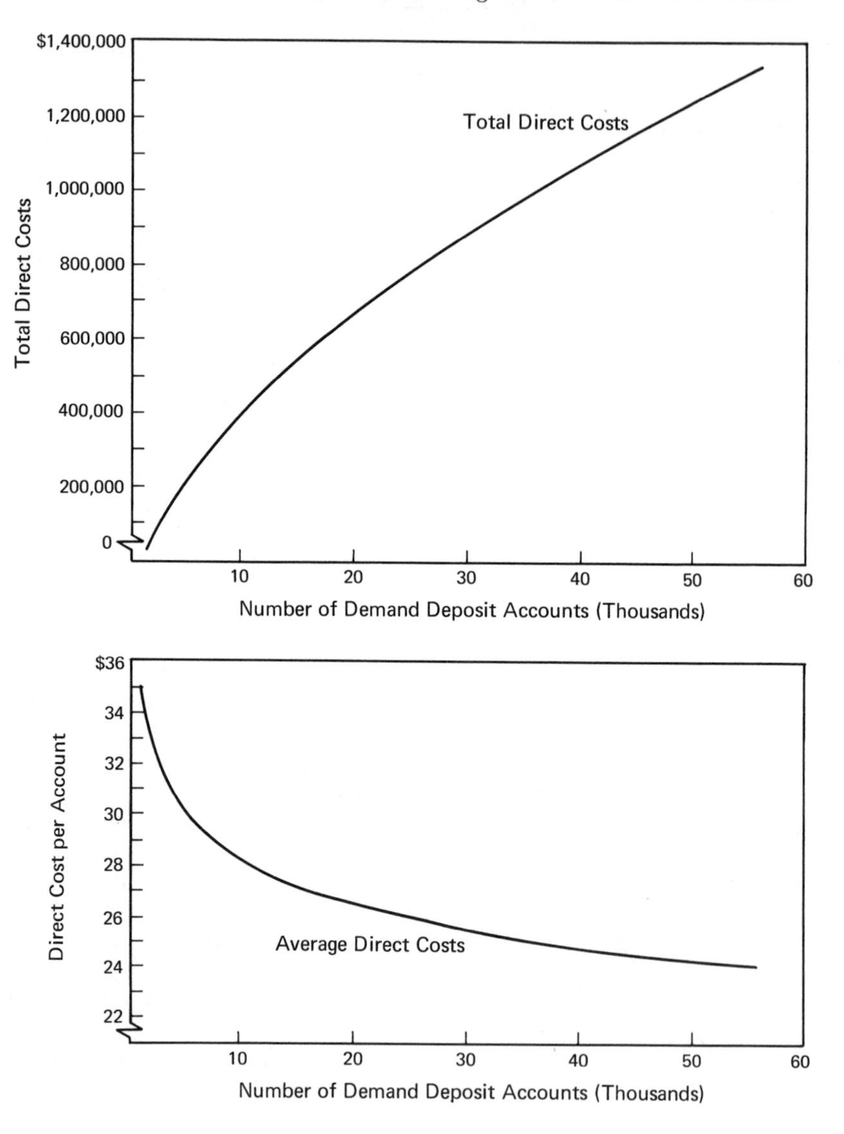

FIG. 1 Relation between total and average direct costs with the number of demand deposit accounts,* annual basis, 1965.

*All other variables which affect costs are held constant at their geometric mean values for sample.

Table 2 Impact on Direct Cost for the Demand Deposit Function of Factors Other Than Scale of Operation—1965

Factor	*Measure*	*A 10% Increase in Factor Will Increase Total Cost by:*
Characteristics of Accounts		
Size	Average Balance per Account	4.0%
Activity	Index of Items per Account *	3.1
Composition	Percent Regular of Total Number of Accounts	2.4
Labor Market		
Wages	Annual Wage per Employee	4.2

* Deposits, withdrawals, and transit items included in index to establish overall activity per account.

Source: Federal Reserve Bank of Boston.

Of course, the nature of the demand deposit account may vary from bank to bank, depending on *average size,* the *percent of regular to total number of accounts,* and *activity.* In analyzing scale economies with a given complement of branch offices, these factors were controlled or held constant since they appreciably influence costs. However, their separate influences may also be evaluated (Table 2). For example, increasing the average size of all demand deposit accounts by 10 percent increased total direct costs by 4.0 percent. This is the case since more services are afforded to depositors maintaining large accounts. Also, since more statements and other services are supplied to those depositors with regular checking accounts, the cost of handling those accounts is higher than for special checking accounts. Thus, a 10 percent increase in the proportion of regular checking accounts to all accounts resulted in a 2.4 percent increase in cost. For example, a commercial bank with approximately 7,800 accounts had an average annual cost per account (both regular and special) of $29.00, a weighted average based on the typical 60 percent proportion of regular accounts. A typical regular account alone cost approximately $34.00 to process while a special cost $22.00. Finally, account activity has an important bearing on costs. Checks processed, deposits, and transit items handled are all measures of activity. As part of this study, an index of activity was constructed and placed on a per account basis. The results show that a 10 percent increase in the activity of all accounts was accompanied by a 3.1 percent increase in cost.

In addition to account characteristics, other factors also influence cost. Annual wage rates varied significantly among banks, ranging from $2,937 to $7,094 per bank employee (including officers). Total wages and salaries amounted to about 66.9 percent of total cost and thus, variations in average wages are important. It was found that a 10 percent increase in the annual wage rate per employee resulted in a 4.2 percent rise in total cost.

BUSINESS LOANS

Business loans, which include all loans except real estate, instalment, and advances of a liquidity type such as commercial paper or call loans to brokers, are a significant aspect of industrial expansion for the economy. They represent a major source of credit for manufacturing, finance, and wholesale trade establishments. For the typical commercial bank in the sample, these loans were about a fifth of all earning assets and represented the most significant source of income. For the typical bank, processing of business loans incurred 6.8 percent of total costs and required 6.6 percent of employment.

The direct cost of the business loan function consists mainly of wages, salaries, and credit reports. These costs are directly related to the loan account, the basic measure of output. Applications must be processed, credit investigations must be made, records posted, notices sent out, and forms prepared.

Statistical analysis revealed that a 10 percent increase in the number of business loans resulted in a 9.2 percent increase in total direct costs, holding constant other factors. Thus, significant economies of scale with a given number of branch offices exist in this fund using function. The result is a decline in average cost per business loan account as the scale of operations is increased. The annual average cost of processing a business loan account for a bank granting approximately 300 loans was $45.88 while a bank with 7,800 loans processed the same account for $34.95 as indicated in Figure 2.

Also, the total cost of producing business loans is appreciably influenced by the size of the loan. Large loans require more extensive credit investigations. Large borrowers are usually large depositors and receive more attention from the loan officer. A 10 percent increase in the size of all business loans resulted in an 8.3 percent increase in total cost (Table 3).

Table 3 Impact on Direct Cost for the Business Loan Function of Factors Other Than Scale of Operation—1965

Factor	*Measure*	*A 10% Increase in Factor Will Increase or Decrease Total Cost by:*
Characteristics of Accounts		
Size	Average Size of Loan Account	8.3%
Riskiness	Interest Rate Charged	9.6
Specialization in Business Loans	Percent Business Loans to Total Loans	—2.0
Labor Market		
Wages	Annual Wages per Employee	2.0

Source: Federal Reserve Bank of Boston.

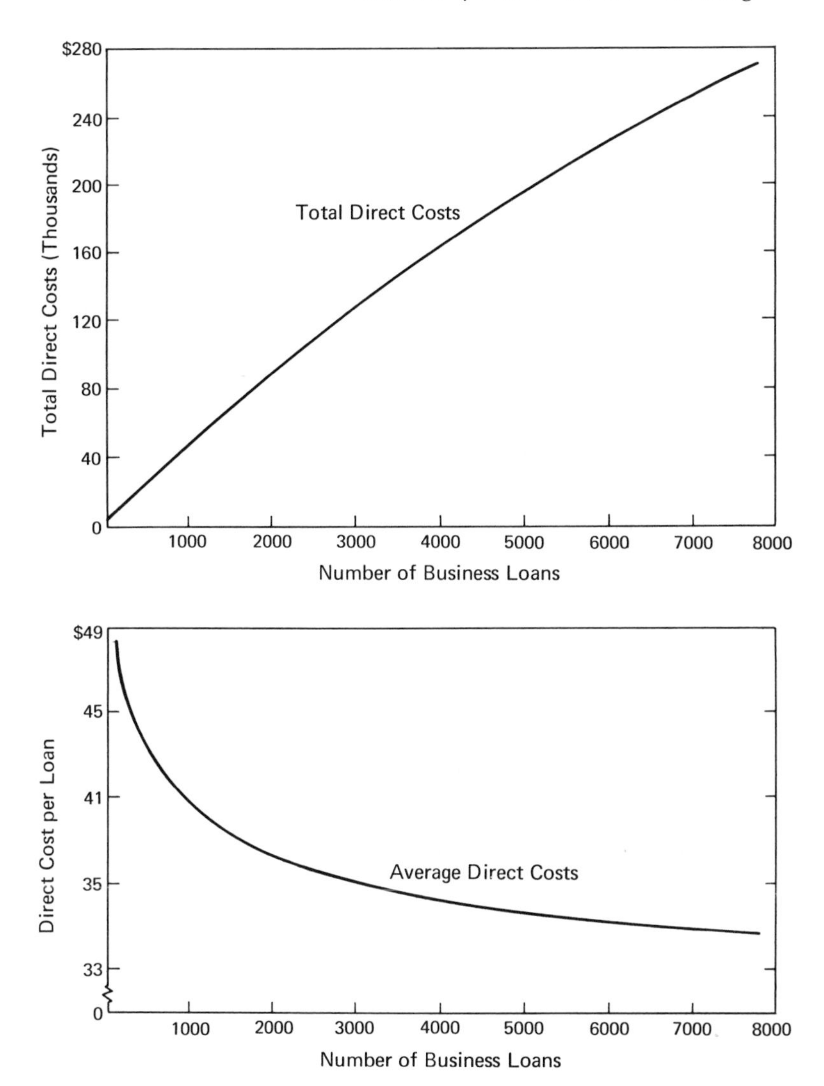

FIG. 2 Relation between total and average direct costs with the number of business loans,* annual basis, 1965.

* All other variables which affect costs are held constant at their geometric mean values for the sample.

Costs are also related to the riskiness of the loan. Extensive credit checks and inventory audits of goods accepted as security for loans will raise costs in handling customers who are relatively poor risks. The bank usually charges a higher rate of interest in these cases. For this reason the rate of interest earned was used as a proxy for the riskiness of the loan. A 10 percent change in the rate of interest on all accounts increased total cost by 9.6 percent. In addition, a bank that specializes in business loans will usually incur slightly *lower* costs of operation, as compared to a bank that distributes its resources among various kinds of loans.

Finally, wage rates varied in the business loan function from bank to bank, ranging from $4,321 to $28,352 per year. A 10 percent increase in the wage rate resulted in a 2.0 percent increase in costs among the banks analyzed.

OVERALL ECONOMIES OF SCALE

Since a sample of banks was used in this study, a natural question is whether the estimates of economies arise from pure chance. That is, are the economies of scale observed in the sample only a chance departure from no economies of scale that exist in the universe of banks in the three districts? Tests show, however, that demand deposits, real estate, instalment and business loans, business development, securities, and trust operations all yield economies that could only have arisen 1 out of 100 times if in fact no economies of scale existed. These seven functions represent 68.3 percent of costs and 82.7 percent of bank employment. Slight economies of scale were also obtained in the case of occupancy and administration.

If the typical commercial bank were to expand all its activities within its existing facilities by 10 percent, total cost would rise by 9.3 percent as indicated in Table 4. Of course, the expansion in the number of demand and time deposit accounts will increase the funds supplied to the various investment and loan functions. In the example, these increased funds will be ample to facilitate the expansion of the fund using functions assuming the bank does not vary its mixture of investments and loans.

THE IMPACT OF BRANCHING

Holding other factors constant, significant economies of scale have been detected in the production of many bank services. As pointed out above, these economies accrue to a banking firm with a fixed number of offices which expands output at each location without adding new branches. However, the method by which the bank expands may have a significant impact on costs. Branch banking is usually more expensive than unit banking since many operations that might be conducted under one roof must be duplicated in each branch. In addition, transportation of checks and more extensive communication make branching more costly. It should be noted that these costs do not include overhead and initial capital expenditures which are obviously higher under branch systems.

Table 4 Impact on Overall Bank Cost of a 10 Percent Increase in the Scale of Operation in Each Function—1965

Function	*Measure of Output*	*Average Cost per Bank before Increase in Scale*	*Percent Increase in Costs*	*Average Cost per Bank after Increase in Scale* [a]
Fund Supplying				
Demand Deposits	Account	$225,360	9.1%	$245,868
Time Deposits	Account	41,230	10.0	45,353
Fund Using				
Real Estate Loans	Account	28,090	8.4	30,456
Instalment Loans	Account	85,635	9.7	93,941
Business Loans	Account	45,410	9.2	49,588
Securities	Value of Securities Portfolio [b]	8,936	8.0	9,651
Overhead				
Business Development	Total Assets [b]	28,200	8.2	30,512
Administration	Total Assets [b]	70,105	9.6	76,835
Occupancy and Maintenance	Total Assets [b]	91,300	9.3	99,791
Other				
Safe Deposit	Boxes Rented	8,312	10.4	9,176
Trust Department [c]	Account	35,743	9.4	39,103
Total		668,327	9.3	730,274

[a] In this example, it is assumed that loan deposit ratios and capital ratios do not change as the bank expands.
[b] Used as proxy for output. (Excludes cash and equipment.)
[c] Some data on Trust Department operations were obtained outside the Functional Cost program.
Source: Federal Reserve Bank of Boston.

Suppose that two unit banks of equal size decide to merge to form a main downtown office and a branch. This merger increases the scale of operations of the demand deposit function for the acquiring bank, thus economies of scale accrue. The volume of demand deposits would increase by 100 percent while total direct cost would rise by 91 percent. However, higher costs associated with branching operations tend to offset the cost savings from increase in scale. Analysis of the functional cost banks revealed that the cost of demand deposits for a main office with one branch would be on the average 6.1 percent higher than for one unit bank handling the total volume at one office. Therefore, total direct cost of demand deposits would rise by 97.1 percent due to the merger. Costs would rise still further if the bank added additional branches. This is illustrated in Table 5 as the number of offices increases to share a fixed expansion in the volume of output.

Higher costs for branching operations were found consistently for practically every function except business development, securities, and trust. Moreover, the analysis revealed that if a bank were to expand

Table 5 The Net Impact of Scale Economies and Branch Banking on Costs —1965

Number of Branches Added	*Cumulative Increase in Costs Due to Branching*	*Increase in Cost Due to Output Expansion of 100 Percent*	*Total Increase in Costs*
1. Demand Deposit Function			
1	6.1%	91%	97.1%
2	12.2	91	103.2
3	18.3	91	109.3
4	24.4	91	115.4
2. Business Loan Function			
1	5.6	92	97.6
2	11.2	92	103.2
3	16.8	92	108.8
4	22.4	92	114.4

Source: Federal Reserve Bank of Boston.

through branching, economies of scale would be largely offset by the additional cost of branching operations for many functions.

THE IMPLICATIONS

The explanation of the variance in cost of production among banks may be a useful guide to an individual bank in comparing its costs to the sample of banks used in this study. Comparison may reveal areas of significantly higher costs that might be explained by inefficient methods or use of equipment.

However, the individual bank cannot ascertain its maximum profit from the information developed here. Maximum profit depends on operating revenue as well as costs. Thus, minimum costs may not yield maximum profit. Only through an examination of the revenue derived from each function and the resulting costs can individual bank policy be formulated. It is hoped that this article suggests some answers to the cost side of the question.

A SPECIAL NOTE

The Functional Cost Program

The Bank Relations Deartments of the Federal Reserve Bank of Boston and the Federal Reserve Bank of New York both embarked on a program of collecting, processing, and editing cost data for smaller commercial banks in their respective districts in the mid-1950's. Realizing that a uniform program would be preferable, the Banks combined the two programs into the present *Functional Cost Program,* initiated in 1962.

At the present time, eleven Federal Reserve Banks sponsor such a program for any member bank with deposits over $3.5 million. Over 100 banks in the Boston Federal Reserve District are expected to participate this year. The national total will exceed 1,200.

This program is a co-operative venture between the Federal Reserve Banks and the participating member banks. The methods and procedures for defining bank functions and allocating cost and revenue are developed by the Federal Reserve Banks and periodic workshops are held to discuss the allocation procedures and methods to assure comparable and uniform reporting. The Reserve Banks provide the participating banks with schedules and worksheets. The schedules are returned to the Reserve Banks and are processed, edited, and summarized. The participating banks receive their own report together with a comparison of their results with those of a group of similar size banks.

The program produces a valuable management tool for the participants while at the same time providing the Reserve Banks with a wealth of data which can be utilized better to understand and serve the banking system.

The Typical Bank

The size of any bank function may be expressed in terms of costs, number of accounts, or employment. Frequency distributions of the numbers of banks were plotted using these measures of size. The distributions were not normally clustered around the simple arithmetic average. A number of large banks in the sample made the arithmetic average much too high and consequently an inadequate representation of the typical bank. The geometric mean has the advantage of eliminating this bias. It can be defined as the following:

$$M_g = \sqrt[n]{X_1 \cdot X_2 \cdot X_3 \ldots X_n}$$

$$\text{or } \operatorname{Log} M_g = \frac{\operatorname{Log} X_1 + \operatorname{Log} X_2 + \operatorname{Log} X_3 + \ldots \operatorname{Log} X_n}{n}$$

Where n is the number of observations and X_1 through X_n are the observed sample values. Frequency distributions of logarithms of the various measures of bank size were symmetrically distributed about the logarithm of the geometric mean. Therefore, this measure reflects the central tendency of the sample and is a superior measure of the typical bank.

Part 3: The Overall Impact of All Cost Factors

Part 1 of this series showed that in commercial banking, expansion of output with no change in the number of offices would reduce unit costs.[1] Apparently, therefore, size gives large banks an inherent advantage. But when the net effect of all cost factors is considered, do large banks actually have lower unit costs than small ones? Although large banks enjoy economies of scale, they also tend to engage in branching operations to meet the local demand for banking services. This article shows that the higher costs of branching usually offset the economies of large size. In addition, where large banks are located in areas with high wage rates, these higher costs also counteract savings resulting from size. The overall effect of these cost factors is, as might be expected, reflected in differences in service charges between areas.

BANK SIZE, WAGE LEVELS, AND BRANCHING STRUCTURE

To determine the role of wage levels and branching structure in offsetting economies of scale, the characteristics of the account—the basic unit of output—were held constant while the labor market and organizational structure varied. For example, to examine the demand deposit and business loan functions, the 283 Functional Cost banks located in northeastern United States were classified as large or small banks. Banks were considered small when the number of their accounts was less than the geometric mean while banks with accounts numbering more than the geometric mean were classed as large. For the demand deposit function, the average size of the regular account, the mix of regular and

[1] The second article showed that economics of scale present in the demand deposit function were attributed, in part, to the use of different kinds of equipment as the size of the bank increased. In the other functions, or product lines, economies of scale were primarily due to specialization of labor.

Reprinted with the permission of the Federal Reserve Bank of Boston from *New England Business Review,* June 1967 (Part III).

Table 1 Impact of Scale, Wage Levels and Branching Structure on Cost per Demand Deposit Account *—1965

Factor	*Small Banks* [2]	*Large Banks* [3]	*Increase or Decrease in Cost per Account*
Scale of Operations (Number of Accounts)	3,735	18,470	$—4.36
Annual Wage per Employee [1]	$4,633	$ 4,739	+.27
Number of Branches	1.12	9.	+5.04
Estimated Average Cost per Account	$28.47	$ 29.42	$ +.95

* The average size of regular accounts, the mix of regular and special accounts, and the activity per account held constant for each group.
[1] Includes officers.
[2] All banks below geometric mean of the number of accounts.
[3] All banks above geometric mean of the number of accounts.

special accounts, and the activity per account were held constant for each group. In this way, the relation between average direct cost and bank size was measured for the "typical account" in large and small banks. In analyzing cost differentials between large and small banks, wage differences had only a very slight influence, as Table 1 shows. The major increases arose from branching costs. Large banks had on average nine branches each, while small banks had just over one each. The added costs of branching raised costs of large banks by $5.04 for each account.

Of course, the economies of scale that large banks enjoy act to offset these increased costs. The average number of accounts for large banks was 18,470 while small banks held an average of 3,735. As a result of the increased number of accounts, costs per account in large banks were reduced by $4.36. Thus, for the demand deposit function, the net effect of branching, wages, and economies of scale was a $.95 higher cost per account in large banks than in small for the sample on which this study was based.

In analyzing the business loan function, the average size of the loan account, risk, and the extent to which banks specialize in business loans were held constant for each group of banks. Here again the average direct cost per account was related to the total number of accounts, wage levels, and bank structure. The results showed that in business loans, as in demand deposits, the difference in wages between large and small banks was very slight, but the increased number of branches for large banks raised cost per account by $5.50 (see Table 2). However, large banks held an average of 2,960 business loan accounts, compared with 630 accounts in small banks. Because the greater number of accounts led to economies of scale for large banks, the net effect was that average cost per business loan account was $.48 higher in large banks. Thus, the branching structure largely offsets economies of scale. The same pattern was found for instalment and real estate loans.

It should be emphasized that the higher costs of branch operations do not imply that they are inefficient. The added costs result from providing

Table 2 Impact of Scale, Wage Levels and Branching Structure on Cost per Business Loan Account *—1965

Factor	*Small Banks* [2]	*Large Banks* [3]	*Increase or Decrease in Cost per Account*
Scale of Operations (Number of Accounts)	630	2,960	$—4.85
Annual Wage per Employee [1]	$8,263	$8,084	—.17
Number of Branches	1.67	9.49	+5.50
Estimated Average Cost per Account	$37.82	$38.30	$ +.48

* Average size of the loan account, risk, and the extent to which banks specialize in business loans held constant for each group.
1 Includes officers.
2 All banks below geometric mean of the number of accounts.
3 All banks above geometric mean of the number of accounts.

locationally convenient banking services. For the consumer, the convenience and the saving of time, parking, etc., probably offset any added costs due to branching.

COST FACTOR BY AREA: NEW HAMPSHIRE VERSUS BOSTON BANKS

While wage differentials between the average of large and small banks were very slight, substantial differences were apparent between banks in high and low wage areas. In such comparisons, the labor market as well as bank structure and scale level had an appreciable impact on costs. For example, the 16 New Hampshire banks in the Functional Cost sample averaged less than one branch per bank. (Until very recently, the state had prohibited branching.) On the other hand, the 13 sample banks in the Boston Standard Metropolitan Area had an average of 6 branch offices. The Boston banks are also larger and operate in an area of higher wage rates. Hence, as a result of both higher wage rates and branching costs, unit costs of Boston banks—despite economies of scale—were higher than those of New Hampshire banks, as Table 3 shows.

Table 3 Impact of Scale, Wage Levels and Branching Structure on Cost per Demand Deposit Account *—1965

Factor	*New Hampshire*	*Boston SMSA*	*Increase or Decrease in Cost per Account*
Scale of Operations	4,801	9,605	$—1.83
Annual Wage per Employee	$4,518	$4,931	+1.02
Number of Branches	.75	6.3	+3.16
Estimated Average Cost per Account	$26.83	$29.17	$+2.34

* Account characteristics held constant.

Table 4 New England Areas Ranked by Various Cost Factors for Demand Deposits

(From highest to lowest)

Bank Size (Number of Accounts)	*Wage Level (Average Annual Wage per Employee)*	*Number of Branches*	*Average Cost Per Account*
Connecticut	Boston	Maine	Connecticut
Boston	Connecticut	Connecticut	Massachusetts *
Maine	Massachusetts *	Boston	Boston
Massachusetts *	Vermont	Massachusetts *	Vermont
New Hampshire	New Hampshire	Vermont	Maine
Vermont	Maine	New Hampshire	New Hampshire

* Excluding Boston.

Some large banks operate in areas of low wage rates which aid in offsetting branching costs. For example, compared with sample banks in other New England states, Maine banks are relatively large, have the lowest average wage level for the demand deposit function, but the highest number of branches. Thus, scale economies and low wage rates offset costs of branching. Table 4 shows a ranking of the New England areas by various cost factors.

In general, wage differences are more important between areas than between averages of small and large banks. Small banks, however, do not incur great branching expenses, which counterbalance the absence of large economies of scale. As a result, differences in unit costs are minimized between large and small banks.

SERVICE CHARGES AND COST FACTORS

The factors determining bank costs have an important bearing on prices charged for banking services. To examine the impact of the various cost factors on pricing, this Bank made a survey of service fees charged by New England banks on demand deposit accounts. Service charges and functional cost information were compared for 92 banks. Statistical analysis showed the following: *With the account characteristics, wage rates, and number of branches held constant,* large banks charged slightly lower net service fees.[2] A 100 percent increase in the number of accounts would lower service charges slightly—by 3 percent. Moreover, holding all other cost factors constant, high wages increased the rates for service charges. Thus, a 10 percent increase in wages resulted in a 2 percent rise in service charges. Finally, with all other cost factors

[2] Net service fees (or charges) equal the combined effect of monthly maintenance charges, fees for checks, deposits, and transit items less earnings allowances on account balances.

held constant, branching systems charged higher service fees than unit banks. Thus, as expected, higher cost factors led to higher service charges.

In general, branch banks that are small and pay high wage rates have high service charges. Large unit banks with low wage rates charge low rates for service. Of course, many banks are large branching institutions in high wage areas. These factors are offsetting and tend to equalize both average costs and service charges among areas.

Figure 1 shows the relation for New England areas between net cost (i.e., the effects of scale economies, branching, and wage levels) per demand deposit account and annual service charges, with the characteristics of the account held constant. Although the annual average cost per account appears greater than the service charges, banks also receive earnings from their invested balances which are not included here.

Table 5 shows that the annual service charges on a typical account (i.e., average activity and balance) range from $20.00 in New Hampshire to $22.30 in Connecticut, a difference of 11.5 percent. Similarly, cost per account rose from $26.83 in New Hampshire to $30.24 in Connecticut, an increase of 12.7 percent. In both cases, economies of scale tend to lower costs and service charges, while high wage levels and branching tend to raise them.

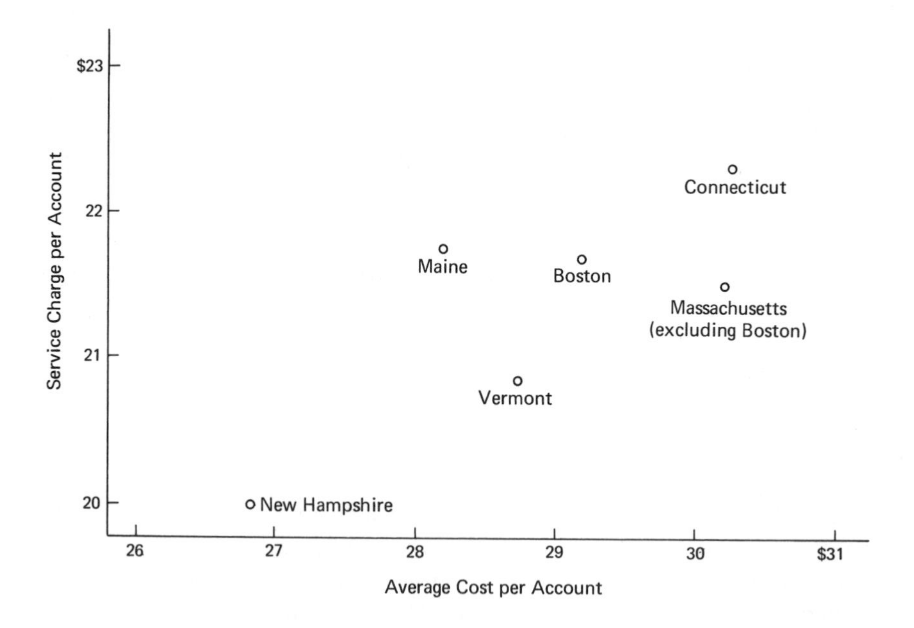

FIG. 1 The relation of service charges to average cost for a typical demand deposit account,* 1965.
Various New England areas.

*Constant activity and average balance.

Table 5 Impact of Scale, Wage Levels and Branching on Costs and Service Charges per Demand Deposit Account *—1965

(New Hampshire versus Connecticut)

	COSTS				SERVICE CHARGES			
Factors	*New Hampshire*	*Connecticut*	*Increase or Decrease in Cost per Account*	*Percent Increase or Decrease in Cost per Account*	*New Hampshire*	*Connecticut*	*Increase or Decrease in Service Charge per Account*	*Percent Increase or Decrease in Service Charge per Account*
Scale (Number of Accounts)	4,801	11,715	$—2.39	—8.9%	4,801	11,715	$ —.64	—3.2%
Wage Levels (Average Annual Wage per Employee)	$4,518	$ 4,922	+1.01	+3.8	$4,518	$ 4,922	+.37	+1.9
Branching (Number of Branches)	.75	6.6	+4.79	+17.8	.75	6.6	+2.57	+12.8
Estimated Average Cost per Account	$26.83	$ 30.24	$+3.41	+12.7	$20.00	$ 22.30	$+2.30	+11.5

* Average balance = $2,467.
Activity: checks = 174;
deposits = 31;
transit items = 22.

These characteristics result from averages of regular (primarily, business) and special (primarily, individual) demand deposit accounts.

It must be remembered that consumers in high cost areas are not necessarily at a disadvantage. As previously mentioned, higher costs may result from branch operations which provide locationally convenient services. Also, consumers living in high wage areas usually receive larger salaries. These factors may reduce and help equalize consumers' real cost of banking services between areas. Any remaining real differential in the cost of banking services probably arises from the size of the bank and consequently, economies of scale.

CONCLUSION

In evaluating the overall difference in bank costs between large and small banks, economies of scale must be considered in conjunction with the extent of branching operations. Differences in wage levels also become important when comparisons are made between banks in different areas. In high wage areas, pay rates and branching tend to offset economies of scale. However, these economies are significant for large banks; in their absence, costs would be much higher.

5

Computers and Management Science

Powerful new tools have become available to assist bank managers in their decision making. Computer capability can extend beyond mechanization of paperwork and routine processing of data; it can be an important adjunct to analysis and decision making in banks. The relationship between computers and modern analytical techniques is presented in the introductory article, which surveys the development of management science in banking. In this article Frederick S. Hammer defines the concept of management science and demonstrates its general applications in various areas of bank management.

The authors of the second article outline the ways in which they have applied linear programming techniques to a model of bank asset management, and they show how such a model can be used to test policy decisions.

Two readings are concerned with bank lending policies. As banks have moved increasingly into instalment lending, they have been developing and refining techniques of credit scoring. Various features of such techniques are examined in the articles by Robert A. Morris and H. Martin Weingartner.

Management science techniques have been applied to other areas of bank operations and decision making. Four papers outline such applications in the areas of: portfolio selection in trust departments, branch bank location decisions, efficient lock-box systems, and appropriate allocation of tellers in relation to customers' arrival and waiting times.

The concluding article outlines a model for optimal management of bank assets. This model is comprehensive in its identification of many variables and constraints and in its specification of important interactions and feedback mechanisms. The model is further dynamic in that its planning horizon consists of a sequence of linked time periods. In conclusion, the authors demonstrate why their model is an important tool for facilitating understanding and communication.

Management Science in Banking

Frederick S. Hammer

In the past 20 years or so, a number of major revolutions have occurred in the perspectives and tools of bank management. Analysis and data have begun to replace hunch and memory in the management process. The computer revolution, on which much has been written in recent years, furnishes one example of these upheavals. The use of management science as an aid in management decision making is another.

Although management science has barely reached voting age, the wide range of problems to which it has been applied fruitfully is quite impressive. Industry has used it in marketing (for sales forecasting, and in the design of advertising programs), in manufacturing (for production scheduling and inventory control), in personnel (for determining salary schedules and hiring-firing guides), in engineering (to design maintenance and replacement policies and for identifying malfunctioning areas in a productive process) and in finance (for determining risks inherent in investment proposals and in evaluating alternative financing schemes).

BANKING APPLICATIONS

In recent years, talk of the management sciences has begun to permeate the conversation of bank management. Spurred by its successes in other applications, bankers have begun to wonder if its approaches and techniques might also prove amenable to banking problems. Some tentative effort has been expended. Although still in its embryonic stages, these early applications of management science indicate that its future in banking is extremely promising. This promise exists in spite of the widespread misunderstanding concerning its nature, the kinds of problems to which it might be applied, and the difficulties which may be encountered when attempting to establish a management science facility.

Thus, let us first explore the nature of management science in an effort to outline briefly its character and scope. We will discuss some of the

Reprinted with permission from *Bankers Monthly,* national magazine of banking and investments, November 15, 1964.

reasons why banking was not among the pioneers in adapting this new technique to its purposes and indicate some problem areas in banking to which management science has been and is being applied. Finally, some potential difficulties posed by this management technique in banking will be discussed.

WHAT IS MANAGEMENT SCIENCE

Over the past two decades, a wide range of definitions have been proffered by writers on the subject in an effort to elucidate succinctly the essence of management science. One conclusion which will most probably emanate from such study is that the various definitions are sometimes vacuous, often contradictory, and almost always arguable. One reason for the semantic difficulties in finding an appropriate definition is that management science is more a methodology than it is a distinct, classifiable body of knowledge. Let us then, discuss some of the more important characteristics of the management sciences.

Four prominent characteristics of the analytical approach brought by this technique to problems are: 1) it is usually heavily *quantitative* in its orientation, 2) a *systems approach* is often involved, in which attention is focused on the interactions existing between related components of the general problem, 3) it is quite *selective* in its use of specific techniques to be invoked in a particular situation, and 4) major emphasis is given to the construction of explicit *models* of the problem at hand.

The notion of a model is a critical concept in management science. Models are abstractions of a real situation, in which unimportant details are omitted and only the important relationships are stressed. We all understand and appreciate the usefulness of *physical* models (such as model airplanes or an architect's model of a building which is not yet constructed), *pictorial* models (such as maps and organization charts), and *verbal* models (such as that which we use when attempting to describe to someone else something with which we are familiar.) In addition, most of us are acquainted with Einstein's fundamental equation of relativity, in which the energy associated with matter is related to its mass and the velocity of light ($E = mv^2$). Similarly, the equation $d = Vt$ relates the distance traveled (d) to velocity (V) and time elapsed (t). These two equations are *mathematical* models. They express unique relationships between variables and omit other details which, while present, are unimportant.

THE VALUE OF A MODEL

Management science deals with such mathematical models. By constructing a mathematical model of a system, several advantages accrue to the problem-solver. First, the assumptions underlying the situation are made explicit, instead of being vaguely buried in an executive's head. Second, by systematically altering these assumptions, one can test the sensitivity of the results to different decision rules. In this manner the importance of changes in the structure of the problem can be evaluated.

Third, an explicit model can be broken down into its components, and these can be investigated independently. Then, by re-combining the parts, one can study the interactions which occur. It is not unusual to find that the best solution to the overall problem involves strategies for the component sub-systems which are inconsistent with optimal achievement of their individually perceived objectives. Finally, explicit models can be easily communicated to others who understand the language. Semantic difficulties are thereby avoided and further development by others encouraged.

Thus, models usually involve a systems approach and quantitative orientation. However, the specific techniques used in the management sciences are quite varied. Methods of formal mathematics and statistics are employed, as well as general concepts provided by economic theory, particularly in the area of micro-economics (i.e., the study of management decisions, as opposed to analysis of the broad economic aggregates of the national economy).

BANKING'S SLOW AWAKENING

It is worthwhile to mention here that management science does not, of necessity, have anything to do with a computer. The approach is quite general, and a large proportion of problems attacked successfully by this technique have had nothing at all to do with computers. Of course, to the extent that large amounts of data must be processed or large-scale simulations must be made, the computer obviously becomes a valuable and sometimes essential tool.

Having briefly indicated the widespread growth of management science in industry and the nature of its approach, let us examine why banking has become interested in the field only recently. I think we can isolate several reasons for banking's slow awakening.

First, the organizational theorists' notion of innovation in a benign environment is relevant. During the war and the boom which followed, the economy was extremely liquid, deposits were easy to come by, and profit experience was quite satisfactory. After the Federal Reserve removed the "peg" from interest rates in 1951, it took time for excess liquidity to contract and, even then, the increase in rates compensated for the loss of investable funds. Thus, since high performance was the rule, there was no pressure to search for new approaches.

With the tightening of money, the advent of fierce competition, and the recessions of 1954 and 1958, this situation changed. Innovation is stimulated by environmental changes which make existing procedures unsatisfactory. Still, it takes time to change managerial criteria, and in the light of past traditions, this was especially true in banking.

Another reason for the slow introduction of management science can be explained in terms of lack of visibility. Traditionally, bank staffs did not include people with training which allowed either appraisal or even contact with the newly developing techniques. Bank economists represented the only possibility for this linkage, but for the most part these individuals were business economists of the traditional school, not the mathematically oriented theoreticians who were the early contributors to this new field.

Finally, regarding computers, only recently has bank expertise advanced and idle machine time expanded to the point where the management scientist could be provided with access to this important tool. Banks were not slow in turning to computers for their data processing work. Yet, the nature of their management problems hampered early analysis through the computer.

NEW METHODOLOGIES

Early applications of management science dealt with systems involving physical items. In contrast, banking business in general deals with dollars. These dollar flows are connected to a host of "free" services; they derive their basic impetus from decisions made by customers responding to their own environments; they are sensitive to decisions of the public authorities, and are related ultimately to ebbs and flows in the pace of economic activity. Changes in these factors can be measured and forecast, at best, only imperfectly. The task of evaluating the effects of these changes on a systematic basis has only begun.

It is important to note that the conditions which hindered recognition of management science by banking have today been substantially reversed. As already mentioned, the benign environment has vanished and, with the consequent "adjustment of criteria," bank management is eagerly searching for new methodologies. The increasingly technical nature of many industrial loans, the attempt to apply statistical tools to economic forecasting, and the inevitable introduction of programmers with a mathematical bent which accompanies computer installations have influenced the large banks to add engineers, statisticians, and mathematicians to their staffs. The once-lacking communications link with management science has thus been established.

A CHANGING ATTITUDE

Perhaps research on banking problems has been stimulated by the growing disillusionment of academic economists with fiscal policy as well as a renewed interest in monetary theory. The relationships between financial institutions and monetary policy, the changing nature of the financial environment, the role of commercial banking in economic growth—topics such as these have become extremely popular among economists. It is a short next step to research into the problems of bank management. In addition, there has been a growing realization among bankers that their problems are too complex to handle on a totally intuitive basis and that, at worst, not much can be lost by giving the new approaches a try.

That management science has capitalized on these developments and is beginning to exert its presence in banking is no longer subject to doubt. The increasing vitality of its activity is attested to by the pronouncements and actions of management, by the number of new groups being established in banks across the country, and the expanding list of problems on which research is being conducted in virtually every area of banking.

Let us review briefly some of the banking problems on which research has been and is being conducted. I include examples in each of five major departments of a bank—operations, banking, bond, trust, and general management.

1. OPERATIONS

Within the operations department, the best known research is probably that published by the NABAC Research Institute on commercial teller operations. This study was devoted to increasing the efficiency of teller scheduling so that costs could be lowered and customer service improved. Attention has also been given to the routing and scheduling of messengers on their calls among branches and between branches and the head office. Several studies have been instigated in which the nature of costs underlying banking operations have been examined, in an attempt to isolate critical areas in which improvements might be introduced.

2. BANKING

In the banking department, management science has been used to optimally locate lock-box cities for a bank's customers. Some longer term research is being done on the identification of factors underlying customer's decisions to allocate deposits between banks. In the installment loan area, studies have been completed on the determination of suitable weights to be used in numerically scoring loan applications and on finding the optimal manner in which defaulted payments should be pursued.

3. BOND

The bulk of research on the problems of the bond department is being done in the area of Municipals. Here, management science is helpful in identifying the best possible coupon schedule to be used by an underwriter when bidding for a new issue. In addition, these techniques are being used to price large municipal portfolios, an otherwise difficult problem, given the "thinness" of the market and the dependence of price on the size of one's holdings and the kind of coupons attached to the bonds. Several projects have been undertaken in an effort to identify and better understand the causal forces being exerted when changes occur in the term structure of interest rates. Studies of this type are important for both trading purposes and proper management of an investment portfolio.

4. TRUST

For the trust department, much work is being done both in the academic world and within banks on the twin and allied problems of security analysis and portfolio selection. The literature in these fields is growing daily, and virtually all management science groups in banking are actively investigating this area. (See "Computers in Investment Analysis and Research," *Bankers Monthly Magazine,* September 15, 1964.) In addition, a study was completed in which the portfolio selection process of a trust officer was simulated in detail. This kind of research may prove useful as a starting point when attempting to improve a decision-maker's method of approach. Although they are difficult to execute, studies of this type may grow in importance as our sophistication concerning decision making processes increases.

5. GENERAL MANAGEMENT

One of the primary problems with which general management is concerned is that of asset management. Various econometric forecasting schemes are being studied which, hopefully, can be integrated into the planning process inherent in this area. In addition, several financial institutions are investigating attempts to optimally select investment portfolios, given prior expectations on loan demand, liquidity needs, and changes in the structure of yields. Management games provide still another example of management science applications in banking. While the banking games presently available have been of only limited effectiveness for teaching purposes, they have proven an excellent vehicle for introducing computers to those who have had no previous acquaintance with what these machines can do.

This inventory is not meant to be an exhaustive survey, but is merely suggestive of a list which can be extended easily. However, note that much of the work is still in process, which again indicates the embryonic nature of management science in banking.

POTENTIAL DIFFICULTIES

For those contemplating the formation of a management science group in their own banks, there are several potential difficulties which should be considered carefully beforehand. First, staffing such a group may require drastic review of existing personnel policies. For one thing, good management scientists are expensive. They are highly trained in mathematics, statistics and economics, with an ability to communicate with and elicit information from non-technical people in the bank. The field is new enough so that the supply of analysts has not yet caught up with the demand for them. Consequently, salary levels are higher for such people than might ordinarily be expected.

In addition, standards concerning the primary loyalties of those hired may have to be revised. Technicians usually possess a professional, as opposed to banking, orientation. This is a desirable characteristic, and should be encouraged. Thus, they will participate in the meetings of professional societies, publish papers, and exchange views with other analysts. While some of the results of their work must be withheld for competitive reasons, development of general problem-solving techniques should be communicated. Much progress, both for internal groups and the discipline in general, comes about through dialogues of this kind.

A BROAD APPROACH

Another potential difficulty may be encountered through the systems approach taken by management science. One implication of this approach is that models will often be constructed which cut across hierarchical and departmental structures. It is not unusual to find the ramifications of a study extending well beyond the seemingly small problem areas originally attacked. Unless handled properly, significant human relation problems may result, along with insurmountable resistance concerning utilization of the project's results.

Computers, basically acquired for data processing purposes, sometimes stand idle a significant proportion of the time. Since this new technique often uses computers, it may be hoped that a management science group can utilize this idle time at little incremental expense to the bank. Unfortunately, while this logic is sound, its application may be more difficult than realized.

When studies require the use of a computer, usually large-scale, scientifically-oriented, flexible computer systems must be employed. The programming systems commonly used for data processing purposes are not those which are most efficient for the purposes of management science. Computer options such as double precision subroutines, floating point facility, and macro programming languages, which are not usually included in systems designed for data processing, are almost a necessity for these advanced applications. Hence, significant changes may have to be introduced in the design of a computer installation before such projects can proceed.

RESEARCH-ORIENTED

A final problem may be posed by the long lead times often required in management science studies. Due to the significant investment involved in organizing such a group, it is natural that management look for this investment to pay out as quickly as possible. However, it is important to recognize that projects undertaken by management science involve *research*. As such, it is impossible to predict just what blind alleys and unforeseen confrontations will be encountered when the Pandora's box is opened. Conversely, however, the results of a study often provide numerous insights to side problems which more than justify the original effort. The point is that research takes time, and too much cannot be expected too quickly.

Thus, management science is firmly establishing a toehold in banking. Its methodology has been found useful in numerous instances, and the areas to which it is being applied are expanding rapidly. Where management invests the time and effort to properly support this activity and keep abreast of its findings, significant dividends can be received. But the cooperation and support of management is virtually a prerequisite for these results. Only as management recognizes its indispensable role in a management science program, can the full benefits be exploited.

A New Tool for Bank Management:

A Mathematical Model in Banking

Robert H. Waterman, Jr., and Robert E. Gee[1]

It is generally known that banks are among the forerunners in the use of data processing equipment. Large banks have their own computers, and computer centers are being set up in many cities to serve smaller banks. Computer use, however, is usually limited to routine data processing and demand deposit accounting. Computers are seldom used by bankers as an aid to decision-making.

A commercial bank has several objectives, but these are often conflicting. For instance, management would like to maximize profits, but realizes that safety and service to the community are objectives also—objectives which don't always work toward highest profits. To further complicate matters, the bank must operate under a host of legal and policy restrictions. As a result, the problem of how best to invest a bank's funds is complex and subject to a great deal of judgment.

One approach to reducing the complexity of this problem is the use of a technique called linear programming. Linear programming is a systematic way of finding the best course of action when many variables and many conditions must be taken into consideration. Stated another way, it is an approach to maximizing an objective which is subject to many restrictions. In the case of a bank, the objective is profit. The other objectives mentioned—safety and community service—are part of the

[1] Credit is also due Dr. Leonard Marks, Jr., of the Stanford University Graduate School of Business Administration faculty and Messrs. John Raventos, Michael O'Shea, and Donald Reid, all Stanford Business School graduates, who participated in the project.

Reprinted with permission from the *Bulletin* of Robert Morris Associates (which in September 1967 became *The Journal of Commercial Bank Lending*), January 1963.

network of restrictions, for these are indeed factors which may restrict profit. General economic conditions, legal constraints, and bank policies make up the balance of the restriction network.

A linear programming model has several advantages, other than profit maximization, for a bank's management:

1. Construction of the model gives the bank additional insight into its everyday operations.
2. The model gives the bank management a way of testing and quantifying the effects of policy decisions.
3. The portfolio designed by the model gives the bank a way to set goals and a way to evaluate performance.
4. The model lends itself to an effective technique for planning future investments in the face of uncertainty.

Linear programming has been used successfully in such diverse problems as gasoline blending, cattle feedlot operations, production scheduling, and branch store location. How did its application to banking come about?

In the spring of 1961, a group composed of students and faculty from Stanford's Graduate School of Business Administration met with the officers of a large bank with many branches. The meeting's purpose: to find new uses for the bank's computer. As a result of the meeting, a study was initiated, to be made by the students with the aid of the faculty and the bank. Objectives of the study were: (1) to observe present methods used by banks in making investment decisions, (2) to explore various mathematical aids to decision making, (3) to select a mathematical aid and actually test it, and (4) to evaluate the capabilities and limitations of the method selected.

Linear programming was selected as the mathematical aid most applicable. Once the linear program was devised, it was actually applied to successive six-month intervals of bank data, representing the past decade of bank operation. For each year tested, profit before tax was improved by at least 4 per cent and as much as 14 per cent—an over-all average of about 10 per cent improvement.

Now, let's retrace our steps to see how this tool was developed.

BUILDING THE MODEL

A familiarity with the workings of and assumptions built into the linear program will be helpful to you in judging the usefulness of the banking model. The best way to give you this familiarity, assuming you are not a mathematician, is to trace for you the building of the L.P. (linear programming) model.

Developing a portfolio breakdown for the model

The first step was to choose a logical portfolio breakdown; where should the line be drawn between various loan and bond categories? A serious danger arose here—the tendency toward oversimplification. Distortions introduced in the simplification process could destroy the value of the L.P. model. On the other hand, the model could not be made overly complex without encountering a serious lack of available data. With these limitations in mind, the portfolio breakdown shown in Table 1 was chosen. (The word "portfolio," as we used it, refers to all earning assets and cash; it was not used to refer strictly to securities.)

The basis of the L.P. model—bank profit—is simply the sum of dollar amounts invested in each category (the x's) times the effective interest rate on each category. (More about effective interest rates later.) Such non-earning assets as cash have an effective rate of zero.

Developing the restrictions placed on the model

If no restrictions were placed on the system, profit maximization would be simple—place all funds in the category with the highest interest rate. This not being so, the next step, then, was to reduce bank policies, practices, and legal restrictions to quantitative terms which could be handled by the computer.

Table 1 Portfolio Breakdown

(In the Linear Program the x's Correspond to the Dollar Amount in Each Funds Category)

Commercial Loans:
- Unsecured loans—x_1
- Secured loans—x_2
- Auto loans—x_3
- Other consumer credit loans—x_4

Real Estate Loans:
- FHA and VA loans—x_5
- Conventional and interim real estate loans—x_6

Government Bonds:
- Due within 1 year—x_7
- Due within 2 to 5 years—x_8
- Due over 5 years—x_9

Other bonds:
- Municipal bonds—x_{10}
- All other bonds—x_{11}

Other Assets:
- Bank buildings and equipment—x_{12}
- Interest uncollected—x_{13}
- Cash and due from banks—x_{14}

An example of a restriction embodying bank policy and practice is the one placed on total loans. The bank has kept total loans at the level of roughly 60 per cent of total deposits—never exceeding 65 per cent or dropping below 55 per cent. This restriction could be translated easily into algebraic form and incorporated into the model.

Another restriction—an obvious one—was that the bank could invest no more than the total funds available. In other words, the sum of the x's (dollar amounts in each funds category) had to equal the total monies available for investment.

Within the loans category itself, other constraints were set. For instance, auto loans—a form of commercial loan—had to be kept in balance with other forms of installment loans.

In all cases restrictions were set to reflect policy or practice as closely as possible, and most restrictions took the form of limits or boundaries; in other words, the funds in a certain portfolio group could not exceed or be less than defined percentages of other portfolio groups. Within the bonds, portfolio relationships were affixed among the governments themselves and between the governments, municipals, and other bonds. Bank premises and equipment were related to surplus and retained earnings, and interest uncollected and other assets were related to total loans. To meet secondary reserve requirements, government bonds due within one year were related to deposit fluctuations and anticipated loan demand.

A problem of special concern was what restriction to place on cash. Since cash is a non-earning asset, it would be most profitable to have as little as possible on hand, but from the standpoint of safety, customer service, and legal requirements, an adequate supply of cash to meet demands is required. To be conservative (and to expedite construction of the model) it was decided that cash plus due from banks could never drop below a fairly high percentage of total deposits. Refinement of this restriction would have led to a lower, but safe, amount of cash, and this would have led to higher profits.

Proceeding in this fashion, a total of 23 restrictions were developed. Although the restrictions certainly did not exhaust all possibilities, they were believed to be complete enough to form the basis for a workable solution. The need for other restrictions, or need for change in existing restrictions, would become apparent as the model was used, and restrictions could be introduced or changed with little difficulty. Incidentally, this flexibility is a major advantage of an L.P. model, as shall be seen later. Whenever there was uncertainty about the adequacy of a particular restriction, it was made sufficiently conservative to dissipate what could be expected to be the bank's fears about safety.

Determining the effective rates of interest

"Effective" rates of return on each funds category have been discussed but not yet defined. Gross interest rates could not be used in comparing profit alternatives because some funds categories are more expensive to service than others. "Effective" interest rates, then, were used. Effective rates are the gross rates less the direct costs [2] of servicing and handling a particular funds category. For example, at one time the prevailing gross rate on unsecured commercial loans was 5.51 per cent. The cost of servicing unsecured commercial loans, as estimated by the bank, was roughly 1.50 per cent of the amount invested in this category. Therefore, for this time period, the effective interest rate used in the model was 4.01 per cent.

Gross rates of interest were derived both from the *Federal Reserve Bulletin* and estimates by the bank's officers. Direct costs were estimated by the bank's accounting department.

Although cost and interest rate estimates should be as accurate as possible, they need not be exact. A close estimate, not being exact, may cause some deviation from the true optimum allocation. The bank must use these figures, or similar figures, however, in evaluating investment decisions without linear programming, and using close estimates with linear programming can only lead to better results.

USING THE MODEL

Once the data and constraints were gathered, the model was applied, as noted earlier, to successive six-month periods of data from December 1950 through December 1959. Results of application to a 5-year period ending December 1959 are shown in Table 2.

Table 2 Results of Applying the Model to Past Data

Period	*Per Cent Profit Improvement*
12/54 to 6/55	9.9%
6/55 to 12/55	10.6
12/55 to 6/56	13.6
6/56 to 12/56	9.6
12/56 to 6/57	NA*
6/57 to 12/57	10.2
12/57 to 6/58	9.5
6/58 to 12/58	NA*
12/58 to 6/59	3.7
6/59 to 12/59	8.9

* Not available due to difficulty in properly defining the constraints.

[2] In the accountants' language, the costs of servicing an account which can be expressed as a percentage of the total invested in that account are called "direct costs." Direct costs vary directly with dollars invested in an account; indirect costs, certain kinds of overhead, would exist whether or not money is invested.

SETTING GOALS AND TESTING PERFORMANCE

The question which occurs immediately is: could the bank actually have made all the dollar adjustments indicated by the L.P. model in each funds account, especially in the loans accounts, within the six-month period? And the answer is: probably not. This is not, however, a serious drawback for two reasons. First, the optimal funds distribution gives the bank valuable goals and, at the same time, a measuring stick against which it can test performance. For example, total FHA and VA loans as a percentage of total real estate loans was optimal at 40 per cent; the actual percentage has trended downward from 67 per cent to 52 per cent. While there is indication from the downward trend that the bank recognized an advantage in a lower ratio, the model stressed this advantage and made it concrete.

Of course, in the above example, the constraint may have been inadequate, or a faulty estimate of interest rates could have led to the low optimal percentage. The point is that the second advantage of a model of this kind is that it gives the bank a better idea of the kinds of information needed in the future. It is a circular process since the model both gives the bank goals and leads the bank in search of better information on which to base the goals.

Testing policy decisions by varying a constraint

The most important advantage was the way the model could be used to test policy decisions. The first constraint mentioned was that total loans must be less than 65 per cent of total deposits. Suppose the upper limit were reduced to 60 per cent, as the result of a bank policy decision to cut back total loans outstanding relative to deposits.

Such a change was effected in the L.P. model for the six-month period ending December 1959. The ultimate result of this change in input to the model was a drop in the optimized ratio of total loans to total deposits. The resultant redistribution of funds caused a net profit increase of 2.5 per cent. The negative effect, however, of reducing total loans outstanding would have been a loss in borrower goodwill. Knowing these things, the loan officer could ask himself: "Is the loss of borrower goodwill worth this short run profit increase to our bank?" If it is, the bank would want to lower its total loan limit.

Working with policies and restrictions in this manner, the bank can produce quantitative measures of the effects of various policy decisions.

Projecting the L.P. model into the future

Thus far the model has been used only on past data. The model is of real use only if it can be used on the combination of total funds available and interest rate structure as it would be sometime in the future, say six months hence. This is because once the optimum allocation of funds is designated by the model, it takes time to redistribute the funds, especially within the loans categories.

But projection is subject to uncertainty. What if the interest rates are not predicted accurately? Suppose predictions were made assuming prosperity and a change in the economy occurs? This dilemma can be resolved using the L.P. model, the computer, and an injection of probability theory.[3] The technique was actually tested on a simplified example, but limitations in the scope of this article prevent complete description of the technique.

Briefly, this is what is done: interest rates and total funds available to the bank are forecast for assumed states of the economy in six months—prosperity, recession, etc. The L.P. model is used to calculate profit under each assumption. A probability of occurrence is assigned to each assumption. (The banker must forecast anyway if he is to plan, and in forecasting he assigns probabilities, although this assignment may be implied rather than stated explicitly.) Expected profits are calculated under each assumption. If the expected profit is highest under a plan for recession, the banker would allocate funds in accordance with the model and his forecasted interest rates assuming recession. Capital investment decisions, whether to buy bonds now or wait, can be facilitated using a similar technique.

The manager need not be too accurate in his estimates of probability, although it may at first seem so. A calculation for a simple example shows that the manager's estimate of probability for the events prosperity and recession can vary by 10 to 20 percentage points before the manager would change his attitude and plan for prosperity. Because the manager can calculate the probabilities at which he would change his decision to plan for a recession and plan for prosperity, he can know how accurate his forecasts must be. Granted, if he is near this "breakeven" point, his forecasts must be more carefully made.

CONCLUSION

The linear programming model, and its use with probability theory, is an analytical tool which the banker can bring to bear on the complex process of investment decision-making. It is no panacea. Mathematically, it is fairly complex, and it is limited in that many factors cannot easily be reduced to mathematical terms. In spite of its limitations, however, it gives the bank manager new insight into his bank's operation. Like any model or analytic tool, it can never represent the total picture; but, like any model or tool, it adds a new dimension to the user's thinking—addi-

[3] The probability theory used here is called Bayesian statistics; it was written up in *Business Week,* March 24, 1962, p. 54.

tional perception. It gives the banker a frame of reference in which he can pull together many diverse ideas; in doing this it paves the way for more sophisticated portfolio management.

Credit Analysis:

An O.R. Approach

Robert A. Morris

In this era of the charge account, you—or the members of your family—can probably walk into a department store; choose a television set, suit, or electric razor; tell the sales clerk to "charge it please"; and walk out loaded down with bundles.

All this will have been accomplished without any exchange of money—at least until the bill arrives the following month.

This privilege has been conferred upon you only as the result of a rigorous screening which has established your presumed reliability in meeting that payment. You are what is known as a "convenience customer"—it is merely more convenient for you to use a charge account than pay cash for many of the items you buy. Typically, your accounts will be held with the large and lavish metropolitan stores—the Marshall Fields, the Altmans, the Woodward and Lothrops.

However an entirely different form of credit has undergone spectacular growth in the past two decades. This form of credit is characterized by the presumed inability of the debtor to meet the obligation at the moment the debt is incurred; one spends money that literally isn't there.

The historic prototype of this type of credit is the home mortgage. (One can speculate as to the growth of home ownership in this nation if it had been limited to individuals who could pay cash.) Not long ago the home mortgage stood virtually alone on the "time payment" credit scene.

In 1945 consumer credit, excluding home mortgages, stood at $5½ billion. In these days of "E-Z Terms" that figure has exploded to $85 billion; its dominant element has been the financing of automobile purchases.

Reprinted with permission from *Management Services,* a publication of the American Institute of Certified Public Accountants, March–April 1966.

As the amount of money involved in the time payment loan has shrunk from the many thousands of dollars involved in the home mortgage to the smaller amounts involved in the small loan or merchandise credit, the profit potential inherent in each loan has dwindled. This has created a need for a means of credit control that is less costly than the procedures used in mortgage financing—but still effective.

To solve this problem we have adapted some of the basic techniques of operations research. This article describes the application of these techniques to mass consumer credit operations, particularly to the screening of credit applications.

The "mass consumer credit" operations which we will speak of here will be loans in the $10–1,000 range; in the specific case of auto loans, the upper figure may be several thousands. These are referred to here as "mass" operations inasmuch as they depend upon the servicing of a large volume of smaller credit contracts.

The companies with which we have dealt represent a broad spectrum of industries, having in common a heavy involvement in credit and collection activity. The five principal industries for which we have provided this specialized operations research service are mail order houses, finance companies (small loan, auto, and sales financing), utility companies, credit card operations, and retailers (chain and local department stores, specialty stores, etc.).

CONSUMER CREDIT PROBLEMS

Management has by now become somewhat accustomed to the use in business decision making of various mathematical, statistical, and other scientific techniques (generally described as operations research). Principal areas of application include production and inventory control, marketing research, and distribution systems.

It is somewhat more difficult to see how such a mathematical approach might be effectively utilized in the consumer credit area. In the "mass consumer credit" operations considered here, we are dealing with a large number of people and are interested in the performance of aggregate groups. The essential problem is to determine the "riskiness" or "risk level" of any single individual; for this purpose, individuals may be assigned to "risk pools," a concept similar to that used by the insurance industry. With this in mind it becomes possible to talk about a certain percentage incidence of collection problems, or the residual portion of good, paying accounts.

PROBLEM CATEGORIES

Credit problem areas may, for the purposes of discussion, be broken down into three categories. Although these are interconnected within the context of a credit operation, it will be useful to consider them separately. These are, in reverse chronological order:

1. The collection of delinquent accounts
2. The control of individual account purchase activity, i.e., the setting of loan maximums or credit limits
3. The risk appraisal of new credit applications and the decision to grant or deny credit.

Under any credit granting system it may be reasonably anticipated that there will be some customers who will not pay their bills on time. For these customers it becomes important to determine the best and most economic manner of securing payment.

First, one must determine the proper sequence of approaches to use in "breaking" a customer; the techniques one might use would include reminders, soft letters, hard letters, phone calls, telegrams, field visits, attorney's letters, collection agencies, etc. The proper sequencing and "tone" of these collection techniques might be likened to a series of moves in a chess game.

Second, and equally important, one must decide when to quit the game. The above activities all have expenses connected with their use; there comes a point in the pursuit when the expected return from continuing the game is less than the expected cost of continuing.

This problem is amenable to a mathematical approach. Inasmuch as it has been considered at length elsewhere,[1] we will not focus attention on this problem in this article.

CREDIT LIMITS

While some customers are obviously justified in being granted high credit limits, many customers have to be carefully contained in order that they do not overextend themselves and become collection problems. From the viewpoint of sales, it is of paramount importance that the good risk be allowed to purchase goods (or borrow) in a relatively unrestricted fashion. A balance between sales promotion and credit costs and losses must be struck.

In addition to the problem of initially assigning credit limits, one must also be concerned with the subsequent changes in these limits in relation to the account's purchasing activity and to its payment patterns.

The determination of initial limits is largely dictated by the risk level of the individual. The subsequent dynamic alteration of this limit is a somewhat complex problem and will not be treated in this article.

[1] Dr. T. E. Caywood, "The Use of Mathematical Techniques to Improve Credit Operations," *Management Controls,* September, 1964.

APPRAISAL OF APPLICATIONS

The obvious fundamental question in the appraisal of a credit application is whether the individual concerned will meet his payments. This is the "risk" inherent in granting credit.

Typically, in the past, credit managers have used a completely subjective approach to this problem. The key elements in this area have been "experience" and "judgment."

This "human" approach has a number of weaknesses. First, human beings are, of course, subject to their own "biases and prejudices," which are not always substantiated by the facts. Secondly, subjective decision making has certain deficiences with regard to management control and record keeping. Thirdly, judgment and experience must be slowly developed in new personnel in an environment where the results of a decision are quite slow in becoming apparent—and quite often are never even communicated back to the original decision maker. Finally, in a situation of great expansion in credit volume, the few truly talented people find themselves greatly overburdened; this situation is aggravated when some form of decentralization is present.

In the past decade or so some companies, wholly or increasingly involved in the consumer finance area, have recognized these problems and have attempted to turn their operations toward a more quantitative and measurable basis. It is the fundamental quantitative assessment of risk with which this article is primarily concerned.

NUMERIC SCORING SYSTEM

The quantitive technique by which we have measured risk is commonly called a "pointing plan" or "pointing scheme" or "pointing system." The use of this technique is to provide a numeric measure of the risk of an individual. Pointing schemes provide a set of number scores which may be applied to an individual applicant so as to place him in a distinct risk classification. They may be thought of as "score cards," for an individual is credited with a certain number of points for each of his personal characteristics; the point total places the applicant into a risk category with other applicants achieving the same total. The actual numeric value of the point total is a direct indication of the risk to be associated with that value.

The use of pointing schemes is simple and highly efficient; it is much like grading a multiple-choice examination and may be employed by relatively untrained personnel. For example, assume we have a 36-year-old married truck driver. He may receive 4 points for his age, 3 points for being married, and 2 points for being a truck driver, achieving a total of 9 points. The actual points awarded are integers of low value for ease of calculation; they may easily be added in one's head. The maximum total may range from 15–60 points; choice of scale is largely a matter of convenience. The number of factors actually considered by a working plan may vary from about seven to fifteen. Such a scheme is called a "linearly additive scheme," for each category is considered separately and merely added to a total.

The actual point score total places the individual in a risk classification; individuals then become associated with this classification. One will then speak of a "19-pointer" or a "26-pointer" rather than a "marginal" risk or a "fairly good" risk; the numeric designation is a more precise way of communicating, bringing into mind a category with very definite risk characteristics.

Such pointing schemes can separate applicants into highly differentiated categories when constructed properly. On one end of the pointing scale one may find applicants with only 1 chance in 1,000 of becoming charge-offs; at the other end the chance may be 1 in 3.

POINTING PLAN CONSTRUCTION

The operational simplicity of a pointing scheme belies the complex statistics required in its creation.

For the technically minded, the technique is that of the discriminatory analysis model where the hypothesis is not of full rank. The model is a subset of analysis of variance theory, which is in turn part of the broad topic of linear regression theory.

The actual system is based upon the "correlation" between the historical loss experience of the client's credit operation and the personal characteristics of individual applicants. In the first stages of implementation

Table 1 List of Credit Factors in Relative Order of Importance

1. Type of Neighborhood	15. Finance Company Reference
2. Time at Address	16. Time at Previous Job
3. Occupation	17. Number of Rooms
4. Time at Job	18. Jeweler Reference
5. Telephone	19. Type of Merchandise
6. Bank Account	20. Total Indebtedness
7. Marital Status	21. Down Payment
8. Number of Dependents	22. Type of Store
9. Amount of Income	23. Time at Previous Address
10. Living Status	24. Length of Terms
11. Source of Additional Income	25. Furniture Store Reference
12. Department Store Reference	26. Automobile
13. Company Region	27. Total Number of References
14. Amount of Additional Income	28. Other Business References

of such a system a moderately large sample of applications is collected, perhaps several thousand each of (1) accounts which have performed well, (2) accounts which have been written off as losses, and (3) applications which have been rejected.

The information about each individual account will minimally contain the information that has been historically required on the credit application. In addition, one may add a number of economic measures, e.g., contract type and terms; account performance information; collection activity; interest paid, accrued, or returned; terminal account balance; life of loan; losses incurred; etc. One may also add a digest of information obtained from a credit bureau on the applicant, where such information has been recorded.

The problem then narrows down to determining which factors are useful in distinguishing good risks from bad risks. As in most large-scale statistical and mathematical calculation today, computing machinery is required.

Table 2 Account Performance Information by Category within Factor

Factor and Category	*Average Collection Cost*	*Number Charge-off Rate*	*Average Profit*
Type of Neighborhood			
Best	$ 3.76	4.8%	$ 18.03
Good	5.76	8.1	10.42
Fair	9.07	17.3	3.01
Poor	11.46	21.7	—1.02
Military Base	8.46	16.4	3.47
Time at Address			
0–6 Months	9.26	17.3	2.46
7 Months to 1 Year	8.76	14.6	3.91
1 Year to 2 Years	7.42	12.1	5.86
2 Years to 3 Years	6.91	9.8	8.92
3 Years to 5 Years	5.89	8.1	10.50
5 Years to 7 Years	5.53	6.5	12.79
7 Years and Over	4.24	5.9	15.96
Telephone			
Yes	5.37	6.8	12.79
Nearby or Neighbor	9.18	16.9	3.17
None	8.69	14.2	4.02
Bank Account			
None	8.62	13.7	4.00
Name Only	6.81	9.7	8.82
Checking	5.81	7.3	11.02
Savings	6.63	8.2	8.67
Checking and Savings	5.42	6.8	13.01

The end result of this "number juggling" is the creation of a set of pointing scores which are "best" in separating the good accounts from the poor ones. A number of technical difficulties, including correction for the biases introduced by rejecting some applicants, factor classifications, interval determination, structural weaknesses in the mathematical model, etc., will not be discussed in this introductory article.

Effort is then expended in creating a simple and workable scheme for actual use in the field. Many applications contain literally dozens of factors, and one must choose only the most important in order to keep the final system as simple as possible. It is therefore necessary to determine the relative importance of the factors.

Everything one knows about an applicant, which may include credit bureau information, neighborhood assessment, etc., may be thought of as a "box" of information. All we really want out of the box is that portion which will enable us to measure the risk of the individual; the remainder might serve other purposes for the company, e.g., the collection process. By considering the factors in combination it is possible to determine what is "new and unique" about each factor in contributing to our knowledge; we wish to omit all redundancies. Typically, out of a list of thirty factors, for instance, the top eight to twelve will statistically represent virtually all the information contributed by the "boxful" we started with. Table 1 shows a typical list of factors in their relative order of importance.

Table 2 illustrates how accounts might perform within four highly indicative factors. Note that this exhibit is drawn from a study that included economic information. It is immediately obvious that certain application characteristics suggest a very poor payment history, while others point to a very good history.

THE USE OF POINTING SCHEMES

We have, to some extent, discussed how one would actually use a pointing scheme. Their use requires little or no subjective judgment. Two of the factors in Table 1—type of neighborhood and occupation—might be subject to some judgment. Zoning maps or directories of occupational listings can be used to minimize this effect. The calculation of a point total for an applicant is a relatively simple matter; the technique is designed for use by clerical personnel.

In Table 3 a typical—but fictitious—pointing plan is presented. This plan consists of nine factors, with the possible total point score ranging from 0 to 41. The majority of the applications will fall between 15 and 30 points. In this scheme high scores correspond to good credit risks and low scores to poor credit risks; one can easily define it the other way. The reader might enjoy "pointing up" himself.

Table 3 Nine-Factor Pointing Plan

Points	Factor
Type of Neighborhood	
7	Best
5	Good
3	Fair, Military Base
0	Poor
Time at Address	
0	0–6 Months
1	7 Months to 1 Year
2	1 Year to 2 Years
4	2 Years to 5 Years
6	5 Years or More
Occupation	
0	Unemployed, Relief
5	Pension, Retired
4	Professional, Managerial, Clerical
2	Salesman
3	Non-Seasonal Skilled
2	Non-Seasonal Semi-Skilled and Unskilled
2	Seasonal Skilled
1	Seasonal Semi-Skilled and Unskilled
Time at Job	
0	0 Year–1 Year
1	1 Year–2 Years
2	2 Years–5 Years
3	5 Years–8 Years
4	8 Years or More
Telephone	
0	None or Nearby
4	Yes
Bank Account	
0	None
3	Name Only
4	Checking or Savings
3	Checking and Savings
Marital Status	
1	Single Male
3	Single Female
4	Married
0	Divorced or Separated
2	Widow
Number of Dependents	
1	0
2	1
3	2
1	3
0	4 or More
Amount of Income Per Week	
0	\$0–\$50
1	\$51–\$70
2	\$71–\$90
3	\$91–\$110
4	\$111–\$130
3	\$131–Over

Table 4 provides a pertinent summary of the operation of a typical (fictitious) pointing scheme. What is given is the actual average account performance at each point level (or risk pool). In addition, the number of applications normally experienced at each point level is given, commonly called the "risk distribution." The information consists of average total purchases, service charges, and collection costs. In addition, the total dollars written off in that category (or risk pool) has been averaged across all members in that category and is designated as "Amount Charged Off"; the percentage of accounts in this point value category that may be expected to be charged off is indicated as "Percentage Accounts Charge-off." From these figures it is possible to derive the average profit to be associated with any particular point value. The profit figure also includes a merchandise (or net finance) margin and the usual credit department revenues and costs (including account acquisition costs and cost of capital).

Table 4 Summary of Average Account Performance by Point Value

Point Value	Frequency	Total Purchases	Service Charges	Collection Cost	Amount Charged Off	% Accounts Charge-off	Profit
36	2	240.37	36.90	3.15	.00	.0	50.26
35	18	236.42	34.07	4.17	.00	.0	47.26
34	27	227.96	35.26	5.16	.00	.0	47.19
33	38	237.43	33.27	4.92	.00	.0	42.47
32	61	218.76	31.49	4.07	.00	.0	38.42
31	93	221.43	32.91	5.97	.46	.3	41.06
30	127	219.81	30.19	5.06	1.01	.7	37.19
29	186	201.47	30.21	4.98	.97	.9	38.47
28	201	207.96	29.47	6.01	1.43	1.2	41.27
27	248	193.87	28.87	6.91	1.20	2.1	32.58
26	308	179.08	26.49	7.01	2.01	2.9	30.96
25	369	181.18	28.51	7.23	2.86	4.6	28.76
24	401	176.91	25.37	6.98	4.01	7.6	30.91
23	437	163.87	23.90	7.43	3.91	9.8	20.96
22	517	171.43	22.47	6.03	6.21	12.0	12.46
21	486	141.26	19.38	8.91	8.17	15.1	8.26
20	400	163.91	21.43	10.17	10.02	17.1	5.47
19	307	138.87	19.71	11.17	12.19	20.9	3.26
18	226	127.42	17.03	13.32	15.01	23.2	1.07
17	173	121.98	16.70	11.46	16.15	27.6	–1.42
16	143	100.41	15.91	12.59	17.18	30.1	–6.41
15	108	112.96	13.83	13.98	18.42	38.7	–8.01
14	76	97.16	14.96	14.32	21.03	40.6	–12.43
13	22	81.43	13.71	15.26	23.71	53.2	–15.27
12	14	69.40	10.93	17.01	26.90	70.1	–20.19
11	8	73.90	12.14	18.96	38.70	100.0	–30.91
10	4	62.14	10.40	19.47	41.90	100.0	–41.06

In this table, one can readily observe that 23 points or above represents an extremely desirable application. A point score of 17 or less is clearly undesirable. The mid-range category, 18–22, may be considered as marginal in value. For this middle 39 per cent of the applications, more extensive investigation seems warranted as well as the judgment of the more expert credit personnel.

THE VALUE OF POINTING SYSTEMS

Such schemes, developed through elaborate mathematical and statistical procedures, do not provide a panacea. At best, the scheme is designed to process a large proportion of the volume at a low error rate. Such schemes provide for the rather routine disposal of from 60 to 85 per cent of all applications.

The actual employment of a pointing system by any given company may serve manifold purposes.

1. A first purpose might be to minimize the amount of investigation activity required by disposing of a large portion of the applications rather routinely, as indicated above; in addition, such schemes provide a method for standardization.

2. A second typical purpose is to contain and reduce actual losses in order to improve the profitability of the overall operation. It has been our experience that, with the assistance of such a system, charge-off losses may be reduced by from 10 to 35 per cent without a material decrease in credit volume. When a slight reduction in volume is desired or warranted, the reduction will be greater—in some cases, 60 per cent loss reductions have been effected. The amount of improvement will, of course, depend upon the efficiency of the operation prior to the introduction of these techniques. While we would not rank these schemes on a par with a very seasoned and expert credit man, such schemes do work about as well as a good credit man. For the booming company having difficulty in maintaining high standards of excellence in staffing its credit department, such schemes may prove to be extremely useful.

There are other substantial benefits that accrue from the use of these schemes, including:

3. The focusing of problem applications upon experienced personnel: Recall that these schemes will generate a "marginal risk" in the mid-range; it is here that the system operates as a lens to focus the expertise of the better credit people upon the tougher "problem applications."

4. The training of new personnel: These schemes essentially summarize the history of the company's loss experience in simple form.

5. They provide for the constant monitoring and control over the risk grade of incoming accounts, a feature not possible under a subjective system. For a multi-location user, these schemes allow one to measure the "average risk level" and "risk distribution" of the credit offerings at each location. Differences in the risk quality of offerings are immediately apparent.

6. These schemes provide for effective management control over the general risk level at which the firm will operate. It is much more precise to issue instructions in terms of "Raise the minimum score from 17 to 18" rather than "Tighten up a bit." The former procedure allows one to calculate in advance the impact of this directive upon volume and losses.

7. Such schemes provide for the identification of weak elements in the overall credit operation. No longer can the branch rely upon excuses of "poor offerings," etc. Each location has a measurable risk situation with which it must cope; those who fare badly are immediately recognizable.

8. The sample taken for purposes of credit evaluation provides a marketing panel as well; these samples provide a "profile" of the characteristics of the credit consumer.

While the most obvious benefits of these systems are in the measurable reduction in dollar losses (and perhaps investigation costs), oftimes the more indirect benefits of placing the credit operation of the company on a sound, quantitative basis—and much more amenable to management's control—may be equally important.

It might be added that there is some temptation to use a scheme created for a competitor or another industry. Every scheme we have created has been done on an entirely individual basis; there is no "package program." While the next man's scheme may provide some improvement for your own situation, it will generally provide only a fairly efficient system for your own operation. All the advantages of having the scheme "sharply tuned" to your own operation will be lost. As a management tool, the ancillary information provided in the study report is additionally required if intelligent use is to be made of the system. For an operation of even small to moderate size, the difference in efficiency between the "borrowed" plan and the custom plan is easily great enough to pay the costs (and learning experiences) of developing your own.

OTHER APPLICATIONS

The use of this discrimination modeling approach may well grow beyond its current use in credit and marketing. Such techniques are already being used to predict whether a prisoner will "jump bail" when released. Research is under way on using such systems in the granting of auto insurance. For industries with high training costs and turnover such a technique might well be used to separate out the "short-termers."

In merchandising and retailing one might construct pointing systems to predict who might be the hardware buyer, or camp equipment buyer, at whom special promotions should be directed. Retailers under pointing systems are pressing these developments, inasmuch as the detailed information collected on each account provides a very natural lead-in to promotional and marketing activities.

Automated credit bureaus, recently discussed in this magazine, are under development. The techniques discussed here may very well allow the bureaus to supply prediction indicators as well as raw data from their files.

To summarize, credit activities have provided businesses with a profitable venture as well as a tremendous selling tool. When issuing credit on a mass basis, it is necessary to find a fast, efficient, objective, and controllable method of screening applications. It is our belief that the system described here meets these requirements and provides the most effective means for taking the guesswork out of credit.

Concepts and Utilization of Credit-Scoring Techniques

H. Martin Weingartner

Credit as a way of life in the United States is a fact that carries with it special implications for financial institutions. Not only business, but the consumer has come to depend on the availability of credit for the purpose of decoupling the rigid relation between income and expenditure, to allow him to spend in anticipation of income, and to satisfy wants as well as to take care of needs before the means are in hand. With the rise in respectability of credit for consumption has also come substantial growth of a new type of business for banks—the large volume, small size consumer loans. Although these take a variety of familiar forms, making of direct cash loans, purchase of sales finance paper from dealers, or extension of "lines of credit" for consumption, relative to other bank assets they represent an entirely different distribution of account sizes and require different methods for the process of credit selection and control.

Under these circumstances it is natural that consumer credit should be one of the first areas of application of operations research within the financial industry. Although methods of accomplishing these tasks were suggested already in 1941 in studies by the National Bureau of Economic Research and sponsored by the commercial banking industry, application of statistical techniques to credit selection did not make headway until electronic computers became available. Since then, credit screening procedures based on actuarial methods have been put into operation not only by banks, but also by firms in the sales finance, small loan, and gasoline industries, as well as by mail order houses and retail stores.

HOW IT WORKS

Granting credit to consumers is complex because it requires, in effect, a forecast of the behavior of the borrower—his willingness as well as

Reprinted with permission from *Banking*, Journal of The American Bankers Association, February 1966.

ability to repay. Credit scoring is a technique to aid in making this forecast. For each applicant a score is arrived at by weighting his attributes in a predetermined way, e.g., by giving a certain number of "points" for being a home owner, plus an additional number for being married, etc.

The total number of points is the score of the applicant, and this is used in the following way. If the score is low, no further analysis is made and the application is turned down. If the score is high, a check is made to verify the accuracy of some of the information to see, for example, whether the time at his present job or address was truthfully reported. A quick check for consistency is also made to ensure that factors not included in the score do not change the over-all picture. If no adverse information is turned up, the application is approved.

If the score falls between "low" and "high"—limits carefully determined at the start—the application is subjected to more careful verification and review by experienced credit analysts who consider all the information available about an applicant, and occasionally ask for more. In the case of cash loans or consumer lines of credit, the score is also used to set limits on the initial amount which may be advanced to the customer.

Since the total number of applications requiring intensive study is reduced usually to fewer than half the original number, the quality of the decisions made for applicants in the "gray area" is dramatically improved, and the total time taken by the process is shortened, reducing the number of trained personnel required for the department.

The development of the scoring system can logically be separated into two parts, the derivation of the weights assigned to attributes of applicants, and the determination of the cut-off scores for acceptance or rejection. Since there are no known laws of social science which enable one to predict credit behavior, actuarial methods are used to evaluate experience with a variety of customers. Although it is highly desirable to obtain a sample of accounts on an experimental basis and to evaluate the outcome after a sufficient amount of time has elapsed, the time lag necessary for completion of the analysis generally precludes this approach. Instead, a scientific sample of past applications is obtained giving approximately equal representation to accounts which have paid off satisfactorily, and which are classified as "good," and accounts which were charged off, the usual definition of a "bad" account. Depending on the nature of the loan this requires locating the original applications for loans made from one to two years prior to the time of the analysis. The information on the applications plus any other borrower characteristics recorded at that time are coded for machine processing.

OBTAINING THE WEIGHTS

The actual statistical analysis performed to obtain the scoring weights is quite complex. The most commonly used method for purposes of credit applications is the linear discriminant function which fortunately can be determined by use of the more common linear regression analysis, a set of procedures which has been programed for most medium and large scale computers.

Application of these methods culls the attributes which are useful for the purpose of discriminating between good and bad accounts and also obtains the weights to be applied to the attributes selected. It also takes into account the inter-relationships between variables as when, for example, age and time at job are correlated.

The procedure is, however, far less mechanical than this outline indicates. At every step checks are made and interpretations sought, and the inclusion or exclusion of factors is considered in the light of requirements for an operational system. In this way, the variables included are assured to be meaningful and the number of items which comprise the final scoring system is kept under control.

Setting the minimum acceptable score may best be explained by use of a simplified example. In the graph is shown the proportion of each of good and bad accounts having a particular score or higher. Suppose that, among applicants generally, good accounts outnumber bad ones by a ratio of nine to one, so that out of 1000 applicants, on average 900 may be expected to be good, 100 to be bad. Suppose further that, on the average, a bad account which is accepted results in losses, both direct and indirect, of $9 for every $1 a good account produces. Keeping these figures in mind it is possible to calculate the following from Figure 1. Because of random variation between accounts, it may be expected that some good

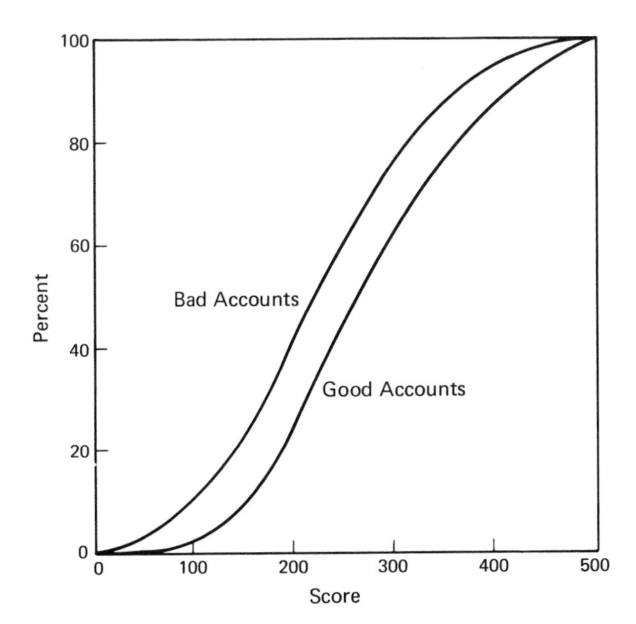

FIG. 1 Cumulative distribution of credit scores for a population of good and bad loans.
Percent of good and bad applicants having a given score or less.

applicants score below many bad ones, i.e., that separation between good and bad loans will be far from perfect. According to Figure 1, a cut-off of 150 means a rejection of 22% of the bad accounts as opposed to 8% of the good ones. Compared with acceptance of all applicants, a cut-off at 150 would result in an increase of $126 for every 1000 accounts, computed as follows. Elimination of 8% of the good accounts would mean loss of 8% of 900, or 72 good accounts; at $1 per good account this is $72. Avoidance of 22% of bad accounts would mean 22% of 100 or 22 fewer bad accounts, which is 22 times $9 or a $198 net gain. This is clearly an improvement over no screening at all. However, setting the cut-off at 180 would result, for this example, in a further increase in profit of $18 per 1000 accounts over the profit from a cut-off of 150. At 180, the proportions of good and bad accounts eliminated are 16% and 32% respectively. This represents 8% more of the good ones and 10% more of the bad accounts. In terms of accounts per 1000 applicants, it is an increase of 72 good and 10 bad accounts. The result is a loss of income of $72 (72 times $1) from not accepting good accounts versus avoidance of $90 (10 times $9) in losses on bad accounts. The 180 cut-off is therefore an improvement over a 150 cut-off. Increase of the cut-off to 200 produces no increase in profit in this example. With total rejections of 24% of good, 40% of bad accounts, the increase in rejections represents 8% of the good accounts as compared with 8% of the bad. In dollars this is 72 accounts times $1 or $72 of lost income versus 8 accounts times $9 or $72 in losses avoided. The benefits from this increase in the cut-off just balance the costs. Any further increase would mean lower total profits. Hence, the best cut-off here is 200 points. In actual practice, the computations are altered to allow for specific treatment of the "gray area" which is subject to review by experts, and for the setting of loan limits to correspond to scores.

NECESSARY TO PERFORM A SERIES OF TESTS

Before the scoring system can safely be put into operation, a series of tests must be performed. At the time the initial sample of accounts is obtained, a number of loans is segregated for test purposes. Once the scoring weights and cut-off are provisionally determined, they are applied to the hold-out sample for validation. Next, accounts currently delinquent are scored to see whether they include a fair proportion of low scores. Finally, especially in a multi-branch operation, one or more branches are selected for a field trial for the purpose of training as well as for ironing out difficulties that arise.

The by-products of credit scoring come close to rivaling its main function in importance. First, by including credit scores in reports, management obtains a running barometer of the quality of credit granted, and of the quality of applications turned down. Such information permits monitoring and changing, when necessary, over-all policy with respect to consumer loans. In addition, it enables management to make better forecasts of future write-offs. In multi-branch operations it helps to oversee decentralized operations and identify weak spots early. Second, a credit scoring system helps in training new credit personnel by systematically displaying the factors considered in judging credit, and associating credit performance with these factors.

Research under way and already completed indicates substantial advances over what has been reported here. A separate but related problem is to predict profitability of individual accounts, not just whether they are likely to be charged off or not, and to base selection of applicants on profit. A further refinement ties credit selection to credit control, allocating effort more appropriately, and identifying accounts which are most likely to respond to collection efforts of various kinds. Continuous monitoring of accounts by computer to locate potential problems is also supplemented by the initiation of corrective steps by computer.

Lest these ideas sound uncomfortably close to 1984, it is useful to be reminded that here as in other applications of operations research to business problems, it is the teaming up of computers and mathematical or statistical methods with investigators who bring insights from the problem area itself that spark the successful solutions.

Portfolio Selection: A Heuristic Approach*

Geoffrey P. Clarkson and Allan H. Meltzer

INTRODUCTION

The problem of selecting a portfolio can be divided into two components: (1) the analysis of individual securities and (2) the selection of a portfolio or group of securities based on the previous analysis. Up to now, the

* The research was supported by grants of the Graduate School of Industrial Administration, from the school's research funds and from funds provided by the Ford Foundation for the study of organizational behavior.

The authors gratefully acknowledge assistance furnished by the trust department of a local bank. Without the kind co-operation of the investment officer and other officials of that department, this research would have been impossible. Their comments on an earlier draft of this paper were most helpful in eliminating ambiguities.

Reprinted with permission from *The Journal of Finance,* December 1960.

majority of writers have focused on the first part of the problem and have developed several, well-accepted methods of analysis.[1] Little attention has been paid to the second phase of the problem. It is to this second part of the portfolio selection process that this paper is principally devoted.

Recently a normative approach to portfolio selection for a particular kind of investor has been proposed by Markowitz.[2] He defines a decision problem (in this case the selection of a set of securities), assumes a decision function, and observes the behavior which the system generates when inputs are varied. In his analysis, Markowitz shows that, for given securities, a rational investor can determine the "efficient" set.[3] To obtain an optimal portfolio from the efficient set, additional assumptions are required: namely, a Markowitz investor must choose that combination of mean and variance which provides maximum utility. But, whatever form the decision function takes, it must be such as to make its mathematical representation tractable and soluble.

A positive theory of portfolio selection does not yet exist. Such a theory must describe and predict the investment behavior of individuals under uncertainty. Whether one constructs a positive theory or compares the results of a normative theory with existing procedures, knowledge of actual behavior is a prerequisite. Since neither a theory nor an adequate description of the selection process is available, the aim of this paper is partially to fill both gaps.

The focus of our study is the investment of trust funds held by banks. We view this process as a problem in decision-making. A heuristic[4] model, written as a computer program, simulates the procedures used to assign accounts to a common trust fund or to select particular portfolios. The analysis is based on the operations at a medium-sized national bank (with trust assets approximately equal to the average for all national banks). The decision-maker of our problem is the trust investment officer;[5] our simulation asks the computer program to select a portfolio based on information available to the investment officer at the time his decision is made.

This approach is related to the traditional literature of financial analysis and portfolio selection. Like the traditional approach, it is based on rules of thumb (heuristics) which guide the decision-maker from the

[1] B. Graham and D. Dodd. *Security Analysis* (3d ed.; New York: McGraw-Hill Book Co., Inc., 1951), is an example of one of the more comprehensive works in this area.

[2] H. Markowitz, *Portfolio Selection* (New York: John Wiley & Sons, 1959).

[3] *Ibid.* Portfolios which provide the maximum return for a given variance are "efficient."

[4] Heuristics are important, as they often lead us quickly to solutions which we would otherwise reach much more expensively by analytic techniques. For a more extensive discussion of heuristic programs see—H. A. Simon and A. Newell, "What Have Computers To Do with Management?" (RAND Publication P-1708 [May 21, 1959]).

[5] It should be noted carefully that our results reflect the behavior of one investor and hence may not describe the general case.

original input of information about the client, the securities markets, and the economy to the choice of particular portfolios. But, unlike that approach, the rules must be completely specified, unambiguous, and capable of being refuted by empirical tests. When the rules for processing information (or heuristics) yield results consistent with those obtained by human subjects, the model is said to have "simulated" the decision process; the set of heuristics (or simulation model) has "predicted" the behavior of the subject.[6]

Even if the model fails to predict, simulation provides valuable information about the decision process in the form of a step-by-step record of the procedures used. Sources of error can frequently be identified and eliminated. In this way, the model, through a series of successive tests, can be designed to approximate the behavior of the subject or subjects.

Simulation accommodates both the inductive and the deductive approach. One may simulate the process used by a number of individuals and attempt to generalize the results. Alternatively, one can construct a model and test it against a wide variety of observed behavior. The latter approach has been used in this paper.

Simulation need not involve a computer, just as addition does not require an adding machine. The advantage of the computer is its ability to solve complex problems more accurately. Moreover, the computer permits the addition to the simulation program of as many mechanisms as are interesting and important, subject only to the speed and storage capacity of the computer. Thus, by using the computer, one can move farther away from an assumed decision function and focus on the actual operations performed by a decision-maker.

The next section briefly describes some recent developments in the theory of human problem-solving. The third section discusses the application of problem-solving to the trust investment decision. We then describe the computer model which selects the assets to be held in particular accounts. The results of some of the tests of the model are shown in the appendix.

COMPUTERS AND THE THEORY OF HUMAN PROBLEM-SOLVING

Recent interest in the theory of human problem-solving[7] has focused on the computer programing of mental processes. Most of this work has been directed toward developing an understanding of the operations

[6] For a more complete discussion of the theory and technique of simulation see the symposium on simulation in the December, 1960, *American Economic Review.*

[7] This section is largely based on A. Newell and H. A. Simon, *The Simulation of Human Thought* (RAND Corporation, June, 1959).

performed in thinking; some recent work has focused on the application of these techniques to industrial or business problems.[8]

Basic to these studies is the assumption that thinking processes can be isolated as well as identified and that they can be represented by a series of straightforward mechanical operations. This is not to say that thought processes are simple and easy to represent but rather that they can be broken down into their elemental parts, which, in turn, consist of collections of simple mechanisms. These operations are written as a set of statements and rules which, when coded in computer language, become a computer program. The program is tested by running it on a digital computer, and, as in the more familiar case of mathematical theory, the logical consequences of the initial conditions are derived by performing the operations according to the specified rules.

In an actual simulation the derived computer statements are compared with the output of human subjects who have verbally reported (in detail) their thought processes and decisions. If the humans and the computer use similar processes, the computer is said to have successfully simulated the behavior of the humans. Moreover, if this occurs, the computer program is sufficient to account for the "observed" behavior.

It must be remembered, however, that computers are neither necessary nor sufficient devices for building heuristic models. A human can replace the computer and perform each operation as directed by the program. But humans are inefficient at this task and are usually replaced by digital computers.

One particular characteristic of computers, called "transfer" or "branching," is essential to the study of problem-solving and information-processing. Conditional transfer operations permit a program to choose between alternatives and/or follow strategies.

As a hypothetical example, in a problem-solving context, consider the following translation problem: [9] The computer is supplied with a Russian-language dictionary, a program, and a Russian story. The program specifies that symbols representing Russian words be read and that the

[8] For examples, see the following: L. A. Hiller, Jr., and L. M. Isaacson, *Experimental Music* (New York: McGraw-Hill Book Co., Inc., 1959); A. Newell, J. C. Shaw, and H. A. Simon, "Empirical Explorations of the Logic Theory Machine," *Proceedings of the Western Joint Computer Conference,* February 26–28, 1957, pp. 218–230; A. Newell, J. C. Shaw, and H. A. Simon, "Chess-playing Programs and the Problem of Complexity," *IBM Journal of Research and Development,* No. 2 (October, 1958), pp. 320–335; E. A. Feigenbaum, "An Information Processing Theory of Verbal Learning" (unpublished Ph.D. thesis, Carnegie Institute of Technology, 1959); J. Feldman, "An Analysis of Predictive Behavior in a Two-Choice Situation" (unpublished Ph.D. thesis, Carnegie Institute of Technology, 1959); and F. M. Tonge, "A Heuristic Program for Assembly Line Balancing" (unpublished Ph.D. thesis, Carnegie Institute of Technology, 1959).

[9] While this is not the process followed by most translation programs, it is illustrative of the economies inherent in conditional transfer operations.

corresponding English words be printed out. The program finds a word in the Russian story. It is instructed to *search* through a list of commonly used words (or dictionary), until it finds symbols identical with the symbols it is using to represent the Russian word. The conditional transfer operation specifies that (1) if the symbols are identical, replace the Russian symbols with the corresponding English symbols and transfer to the next word (set of symbols) in the story, then repeat the process for the next Russian word in the *story,* but (2) if the symbols are not identical, transfer to the next Russian word in the *dictionary*.

Three points are worth emphasizing. First, the program is iterative, i.e., it uses its operations repetitively to process different pieces of information or to solve quite separate problems. During the processing, it sorts information, retaining those parts which are useful, discarding the irrelevant. Second, the program is capable of modifying the "dictionary" or lists. Frequently used "words" may be separated, to narrow future search activity in the interests of economizing time. Third, the hypothetical program described above is general. Any type of list could replace the Russian dictionary as an input without necessitating modification of the search-compare-transfer operations.

While the general processes which the computer follows remain unchanged, each successful simulation must recognize the constraints which arise within the context of the particular problem. These constraints restrict the program to those processes that are consistent with the operations performed by humans engaged in similar tasks. In the translation example, a constraint might call for initiating search by looking at the first letter of the word; in searching a list of Treasury notes, the computer might first consider their yields or maturities.

In our work, a list of common stocks becomes the basic list of the problem—i.e., the dictionary. The goals of the client and the amount of money to be invested represent the Russian story of our example. And conditional transfer operations allow the program to follow the strategies of portfolio selection.

When the constraints which arise in the choice of portfolios are imposed on the general theory of human problem-solving, a theory of portfolio selection emerges. The following section describes the constraints and the resulting theory.

SIMULATION OF THE TRUST INVESTMENT PROCESS

An investor is confronted with a large assortment of information which he may use in making decisions. There is a wide variety of data, past and current, on the operation of firms and the market valuation of their stocks. There are many published predictions about the present and future state of the general economy, the stock market, and particular industries and firms. There are legal restrictions and the desires of clients to be considered when an investor acts in an agency or fiduciary capacity. These factors, when evaluated and combined with an investment policy, ultimately result in a decision to buy specific quantities of particular stocks and bonds.

An investor choosing a portfolio is processing information: he sorts the useful from the irrelevant and decides which parts of the total information flow are most important. As we have seen, the theory of human problem-solving was built to handle problems of this type. The postulates of the theory particularly relevant for our purposes are that the following exist:

> (1) A control system consisting of a number of *memories,* which contain symbolized information and are interconnected by various ordering relations. . . .
> (2) A number of *primitive information processes,* which operate on the information in the memories. . . .
> (3) A perfectly definite set of rules for combining these processes into whole programs of processing. From a program it is possible to deduce unequivocally what externally observable behavior will be generated.[10]

In the portfolio selection problem, these postulates consist of (1) The memory, i.e., lists of industries each of which has associated a sublist of companies. The memory also contains lists of information associated with the individual companies.[11] (2) Search procedures for selecting a portfolio from the information stored in the memory. These function in a manner similar to the traditional clerk who prepares lists of stocks suitable for current investment by scanning a master list. (3) A set of rules or criteria which guide the decision-making processes by stipulating when and how each primitive process is to be used. The set of rules constitutes the processing program for an individual investor. It might be compared with the heuristics of the traditional "expert," but, as noted, there is an important difference—the program must be unambiguous.

Like any problem-solving program, the simulation of the portfolio selection process relies principally on this set of basic operating rules. The rules are specified in advance and may be modified by the outcome of specific decisions. In particular, the record of past successes, failures, and the processes involved in each are stored in memory. The program

[10] A. Newell, J. C. Shaw, and H. A. Simon, "Elements of a Theory of Human Problem Solving," *Psychological Review,* LXV (1958), 151 ff.

[11] Investors categorize companies by industry. Not all investors may associate identical companies with a given industry, but the process of classification by industry remains invariant as the primary basis for listing companies in the memory. The information associated with each company also varies among investors, but each has a list of attributes and values stored in memory (e.g., growth rate, dividend rate, price, price/earnings ratio, expected earnings, expected yields, etc.).

modifies its behavior by eliminating such unsuccessful procedures. In this sense it learns from its past experience.[12]

In common with other heuristic programs, the process is iterative. Lists of industries and companies are searched for particular attributes; sublists are created, searched, and again divided. For example, to obtain a high-growth portfolio, the list of companies stored in memory is searched to obtain shares with the desired characteristics. Additional criteria are employed to narrow (or expand) this list. Further search and matching against desired criteria yield the specific selection of stocks to buy.

Like the investor it simulates, the computer stores the final result (list) for future use. When the same problem recurs, the entire search process need not be repeated. The list may be judged by present criteria, accepted, adapted to new conditions, or completely rejected. In the latter event, the computer would use a conditional transfer operation to renew search activity until a new list had been formed.

Within this general framework, the problem of constructing a model of investment behavior becomes a problem of uncovering the basic rules (operations) which lead to a decision to purchase particular securities. The following procedure was used to obtain these data: First, the trust department of a local bank was observed by attending committee meetings called to review past and future decisions. Interviews were then conducted with departmental officers to obtain a better understanding of the lines of authority. From these procedures it became apparent that the investment officer was the primary locus of all decisions relevant to the choice of portfolios.

Interviewing as a technique provided helpful background information. However, as portfolio selection has a well-developed lore, this technique failed to separate the relevant from the irrelevant criteria.

Second, the history of several accounts was examined. Naïve behavioral models were constructed to approximate the recorded behavior and to help uncover those processes which appeared to be invariant between accounts.

Third, and most important, the investment officer was asked to permit "protocols" to be made of his decision processes.[13] To accustom the sub-

[12] For a complete discussion see G. P. E. Clarkson and H. A. Simon, "Micro-Simulation: The Simulation of Individual and Group Behavior," *American Economic Review*, December, 1960.

[13] A "protocol" is a transcript of the verbalized thought and actions of a subject when the subject has been instructed to think or problem-solve aloud. Thus the transcript is a record of the subject's thought processes while engaged in making a decision. Since a protocol is a detailed description of what a person does, it avoids some of the problems inherent in interview and questionnaire techniques, which ask the subject to state his reasons for behaving as he does. For further discussion see Newell, Shaw, and Simon, "Elements of a Theory of Human Problem Solving," *Psychological Review*, LXV (1958).

ject to verbalizing his procedures, the first case was based on an account with which he had dealt before. Artificiality was introduced into the description of the beneficiary and the past history of the account. Successive protocols recorded the investment officer's decision processes for accounts which arose in the course of his work. The decisions made during these problem sessions determined the particular securities which were purchased for these accounts.

From these protocols a program of the investment decision process was built. As yet, the number of protocols is insufficient to answer all the problems that are raised in writing such a program. But our experience has shown that programing focuses our attention on precisely those details for which our specific knowledge is weakest. To date, there are still large gaps in our understanding of the decision-making process, especially in the areas of goal formation [14] and the association of particular industries with particular goals. Also the selection process which determines the particular company and the number of shares to be purchased has not been completely determined. However, an adequate amount of information has been gathered to program a substantial part of the portfolio selection process.

THE PORTFOLIO SELECTION PROCESS

This section describes the step-by-step simulation of the trust investment process in a medium-sized bank. At present we are directly concerned with the way in which common stocks are chosen for individual portfolios. The selection of bonds and preferred stocks has not yet been explicitly considered.

The investment officer's behavior can be described by a flow chart (Figure 1) detailing the sequential pattern followed in the decision-making process. Each of the elements in the flow chart requires a specific decision by the investment officer. Although the model operated with a basic list of eighty stocks, specification of the goal of the account (step 2) eliminates securities inconsistent with the goal and reduces the list to approximately thirty stocks.

The model was required to predict the portfolios for two accounts with different goals. That is, operations 6–9 were performed as directed by the program. The output was compared with the investment officer's recorded decisions. The results are shown in the appendix.

The descriptions which follow detail the processes used. Translated into symbolic form, they become the computer program.[15]

[14] E.g., the precise way in which a "growth account" differs from an "income account."

[15] The program was written in an information-processing language IPL-V (Newell and Simon).

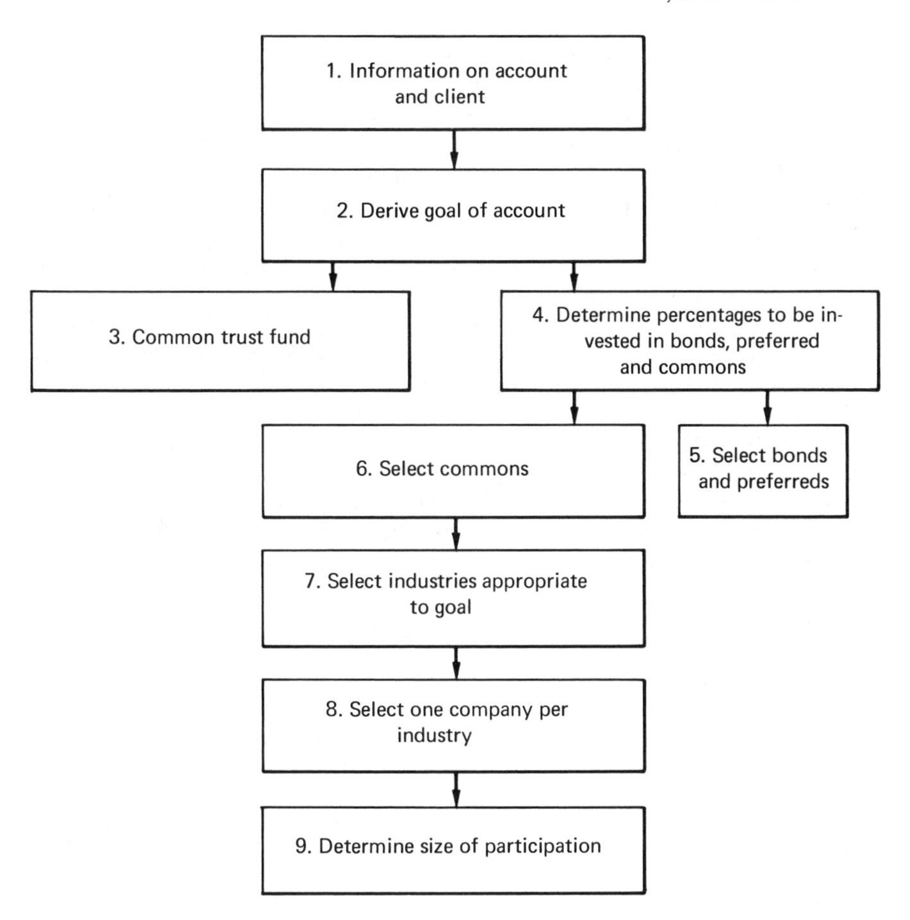

FIG. 1

Information on account and client

There are two basic sources of information on each account: the administrative officer's interviews with the client and the written record, containing a copy of the legal instrument (often a will) setting up the trust.[16] From the accumulated data and the subjective impressions of the administrative officer, the investment officer proceeds to step 2: formulating a concept of what the client wants the trust to do, i.e., the goal of the account. Before transforming this concept into a goal (or investment

[16] In most cases, this contains information about the beneficiaries, the investment powers of the bank, what is to happen to the principal, what should be done with the income, etc. From these sources he also gets information on the beneficiaries' age, marital status, number and age of dependents, place of legal residence, income tax bracket, and status and age of future beneficiaries, if any.

policy) for the account, the investment officer must choose between two courses of action. Conditional transfer operations direct the program to (1) invest the assets in the common trust fund (C.T.F.),[17] (2) set up an individual portfolio for the account.

The bank prides itself on the "individual" investment service which it offers to its customers. Thus there are clear preferences for setting up individual accounts whenever the size of the account permits. The following rules (or procedures) guide the decision to invest the assets in the common trust fund:

a) All "legal" [18] trusts are eligible for investment in C.T.F. The funds of beneficiaries who have waived legal requirements are not so invested.

b) All legal trusts which have less than $*K* [19] in assets are automatically placed in the C.T.F.

c) Legal trusts greater than $*K* may or may not be placed in C.T.F., depending on the goals of the beneficiary. However, as noted, no account may participate for more than $100,000. Thus, in the range between $*K* and $100,000 the decision will be determined by the goal of the account. If the client has goals consistent with expected C.T.F. results and does not have assets which permit the purchase of five common stocks in round lots, C.T F. is indicated, and the process ends.[20]

The investment of assets in the C.T.F. is an all-or-none decision. But all legal accounts greater than $100,000 [21] and all accounts which are not

[17] The common trust fund was established to provide a medium for the collective investment of trust funds held by the bank in a fiduciary capacity. Investments are restricted to those considered legal for investment in Pennsylvania. Under Federal Reserve Board regulations, no account may participate for more than $100,000. Under Orphan's Court rulings, not more than 10 per cent of the fund may be invested in securities of any one corporation, with the exception of direct and guaranteed obligations of the United States government. In addition, the fund may not own more than 5 per cent of any one class of stock of any corporation or have the amount invested in common stocks exceed one-third of the total investment in the fund.

[18] " 'Legal investment' statutes fall into two general categories: (1) those that restrict all or part of the investments to specific investments or specific classes of investments, and (2) those that limit investment in non-legal securities to a given percentage of the account or fund. The statutory limitations on investment in non-legal securities range from 30 per cent to 50 per cent of the market value (in one state, inventory value) of the fund" ("Survey of Common Trust Funds, 1958" *Federal Reserve Bulletin,* May, 1959, p. 477). Many people, when setting up the trust relation, specifically waive these investment restrictions. Thus "legal" refers to situations in which the investment officer must comply with these investment restrictions.

[19] To protect the bank's anonymity, the precise dollar values are not revealed. Nationally, the average C.T.F. participation is approximately $22,000 (*Federal Reserve Bulletin,* May, 1958, p. 537).

[20] This problem and many of those which follow clearly lend themselves to "conditional transfer" operations in computer terminology.

[21] As yet, we have not programed the heuristics underlying the choice of the C.T.F. portfolio. As noted above, we are concerned here only with explaining the mechanisms underlying the decisions on common stocks for individual accounts.

of a fiduciary nature have their own portfolios. The minimum size for these accounts depends on the asset composition. For accounts with participation in bonds, as well as common stocks, a minimum of $\$1/2K$ is required; if the account participates only in common stocks, a minimum of $\$0.4K$ is required. Smaller accounts are refused or placed in C.T.F. The funds of very small accounts are deposited in a savings bank.

Derive the goal

For all portfolios not invested in C.T.F., the investment officer must formulate a goal. Data previously collected are transformed into an investment policy that approximates his perception of what the client wants. The number of possible combinations is very large. But the goal he decides on must lie somewhere along a continuum between the extremes of growth and income. The bank's records indicate that accounts are categorized into four or five classes: pure growth, growth with some income, income with some growth, and income alone.[22]

Determine percentages to be invested in bonds, preferreds and commons

The main function of the program is to select the particular common stocks to be held in any given account.

In legal trusts, the maximum amount that can be invested in common stocks is 33⅓ per cent.[23] In trusts where the legal requirements are waived or do not exist, this decision is left to the investment officer. Except under unusual circumstances, such as a statement that the entire fund be placed in commons, the amount invested in commons ranges between 40 and 65 per cent.[24]

[22] A growth account is roughly defined as one in which the monetary value of the assets appreciates at an average rate of 10 per cent per year for a five-year period. In an account seeking current dividend and interest income, a minimum yield of 4–4½ per cent is expected. In a mixed growth and income account, a capital appreciation of 5 per cent combined with a dividend of 3–4 per cent is customary.

The goal of an account is determined from the initial data in the following manner. Data on the client: lawyer, high current income, high tax bracket, no pension on retirement, married with no children, desires security after retirement, earnings to be reinvested. The goal of growth with current income as a secondary goal is indicated for the present. Income will be emphasized after the client has retired and is in a lower income tax bracket.

[23] This figure is determined by Pennsylvania state law (Act. No. 340 of 1951) and is the amount designated by the state as constituting a "prudent investment." The prudent-investment criterion limits banks, in practice, to choosing securities which, if preferred stocks, have paid dividends for 16 years and which, if commons, have had positive earnings and have paid dividends in 12 out of 16 years. A list of securities meeting these requirements is prepared by the Pennsylvania Bankers Association.

[24] It is abundantly clear from the protocols that the process involved in choosing government bonds is similar to the one described for common stocks. Under present

Select industries appropriate to goal

Despite the large overlap between industries, the investment officer associates a set of industries with each goal. These are chosen from a previously selected "preference list." [25] A one-to-one correspondence between goal and industry does not exist. But each goal invokes a search of the preference list (memory), which leads to the selection of a particular list of industries. The length of the list depends on the size of the account, since each industry is represented only once in any given account. Thus the association of industries with goals narrows the search for appropriate securities to a much shorter list.[26]

Select companies

Once an industry has been selected, the company to be chosen for participation is picked by the following series of conditional transfer operations. Companies are examined on the following criteria: (i) subject to tax in Pennsylvania, (ii) legal in Pennsylvania, (iii) current uncertainty, (iv) growth, (v) yield, (vi) expected earnings, (vii) past earnings, (viii) expected dividends, (ix) expected price-earnings ratio, (x) past price-earnings ratio, (xi) amount spent on expansion and/or research and development.[27] The first three criteria are used in an absolute manner to reduce the lists further:

---

market conditions, it appears to consist of selecting the highest yield from a table listing short-term governments. Hence it is a search procedure using established processes within a given memory.

[25] The preference list is the investment officer's working list of stocks. This list of approximately 80 stocks is categorized by industry. The investment officer refers to it on every selection that he makes. The preference list is designed to cover various economic situations. Although it is re-examined every three months, few changes are made. We take the list as given.

[26] The investment officer's rule of thumb seeks to spread risk by diversification. But, as Markowitz (*op. cit.*, p. 109) has shown, when the returns on securities are correlated, this may not be accomplished if the amount which the client deposited is relatively small.

Further recording of protocols is expected to specify the selection process that associates particular industries and particular goals. However, it is clear that this association depends on the characteristics of the goal and the general characteristics of the companies within each industry. Some industries contain companies which vary only slightly in their individual characteristics, e.g., banks or utilities. Others, like oils, are more heterogeneous, i.e., appear on several lists.

[27] Large current expenditures on plant expansion and/or research and development will lower current dividends while raising expectations of future earning power. For companies heavily dependent on the discovery products, e.g., chemicals, drugs, and office equipment, the amount spent on research and development is used as an indicator of the company's intention to continue developing new and profitable products.

Rule a: If the beneficiary is a resident of Pennsylvania, reject all stocks which are subject to personal property tax in Pennsylvania.

Rule b: If the trust is a legal trust, reject all stocks which do not have legal status in Pennsylvania.

Rule c: Reject further purchases of stocks in which there are "current uncertainties." The investment officer would not buy du Pont stock pending the court's decision on what they are to do with their holdings in General Motors. During the Middle East crisis of 1958, international oil companies were labeled "current uncertainties."

The next two criteria (iv and v) are used in a somewhat similar manner. If the goal is growth, all stocks which do not meet minimum growth criteria are rejected. Similarly, if income is desired, low-yielding stocks are rejected.

The rest of the criteria are used in a relative manner. A rough simulation has been achieved by matching the remaining companies on these criteria and seeing which has the most points in its favor. To do this, the program sets up a three-valued scale for each criterion (low = 1, medium = 2, high = 3) and makes binary choices by subtracting the value of a particular criterion of one company from the value of the same criterion for the other company. The result of any one comparison will be a positive, negative, or zero number. All the remaining criteria are matched in this manner, and the resulting scores are added algebraically to yield a unique value for the particular comparison. Since one company's criteria are always subtracted from the other's, a positive sign on the summation will denote that the first company is chosen; a negative sign, the second company. In the case where the sum is zero, no choice has been indicated.[28]

An example will clarify this process. Assume that a portfolio of high-yield stocks is required and that the selection process has reached the point where it is starting to select stocks on the basis of attributes vi through xi. At this point the choice lies between Company A and Company B. Since we are considering only attributes vi through xi, let their values for Company A be given by the vector (3, 3, 1, 3, 3, 2) and for Company B by the vector (2, 3, 1, 3, 2, 2). As mentioned above, the selection process consists of subtracting the values of the attributes of Company B from the values of the similar attributes of Company A. In this case the result of this subtraction yields a vector whose values are given by the following six numbers: 1, 0, 0, 0, 1, 0. Since the algebraic sum of

[28] More recent protocols suggest an alternative selection routine, which lists all the companies in a preference order on the two basic criteria of growth and income. For the goal of growth or income the program would take the first company on the growth or income list and check through each of the remaining criteria to see whether it met a specified standard or not. If it did, the company would be accepted, and search in that industry would terminate. If it did not, the first company would be interchanged with the second company on the list, and the test would be repeated. Changes in suitability occur because the stored data on price, income, earnings, dividends, etc., are kept up to date.

these numbers is positive, Company A is selected. If more alternatives are available, a transfer operation directs the program to match Company A against the next alternative.

Determine the size of participation

The investment officer divides the accounts into two classes. For accounts with less than $\$5/8K$ to invest in commons, his rules are as follows:

a) Given the amount to be invested and the number of participations, determine the average amount which can be invested in each company.

b) Divide this average amount by the current price of the stock to obtain the number of shares which can be purchased.[29]

c) Since each purchase may be slightly over or under the average dollar amount to be spent, maintain a continuous count of "funds remaining" figure and not the average number.

In accounts with more than $\$5/8K$ to invest in commons, a different procedure is used. Once the amount to be invested and the number of participations are determined as above, the minimum round lot is purchased for each company that is selected. Again a "funds remaining" account is kept to determine the size of the last participation.

CONCLUSIONS

In recent years new techniques for the study of human problem-solving have been developed. Of these, the simulation of individual behavior is most apposite to the study of problems of choice under uncertainty. Application of this technique has been facilitated by the use of digital computers capable of storing and processing large blocks of information.

This paper proposes the use of simulation as a basis for studying portfolio selection. Clearly, the choice of securities by individuals or their agents is an application of the theory of decision-making under uncertainty. We contend that focusing on the decision-making process per se is a more appropriate technique for dealing with this problem than those which, though mathematically more elegant, either (1) lead to non-testable implications or (2) rest on probabilistic assumptions.

Building computer programs focuses attention on areas of least knowledge. Moreover, since computer statements must be operational, hypotheses advanced must clearly specify assumptions about the mechanisms at work.

Using information recorded from "protocols," we programmed portions

[29] If this number of shares is 90 or greater, 100 shares (a round lot) are purchased; if less than 90, but greater than 10, the number is reduced to its nearest multiple of 5, and that number of shares is purchased; if less than 10 but greater than 5, 10 shares are purchased; if less than 5, 5 shares are purchased. Note, however, that, in general, this process will not lead to selection of a portfolio which is "Markowitz-efficient."

of the decision rules employed by a trust investment officer. The program was tested by two simulations, and, although such small samples are never conclusive, we believe that the results strongly indicate the potential power of the theory as a predictor. (A crude test for "goodness of fit" is shown in the appendix.)

Future work will be directed at discovering the rules that are used in the formation of goals, in the association of industries with goals, and on parts of the present program that are not yet fully defined. As programs are added, we expect to generate more of the recorded behavior. We suggest that in this way a descriptive theory of portfolio selection can be developed to serve either (1) as a predictor of investor behavior or (2) as the basis for a theory of optimal portfolio selection.

APPENDIX

RESULTS OF SIMULATION OF ABC ACCOUNT, 7/7/58

Description of Account:

1. Agency account
2. Revocable
3. Goal of account: high growth with little or no concern for income; fluctuations in principal not a problem
4. Investment restrictions: not a legal trust, hence not restricted to legal list; donor stated that all assets were to be invested in common stocks
5. Amount available for investment in common stocks: assumed to be given

The *program* selected the following portfolio for the ABC Account:	The portfolio selected by the investment officer on 7/7/58 was:
85 shs. Monsanto Chem. comm.	80 shs. Monsanto Chem. comm.
10 shs. I.B.M. comm.	10 shs. I.B.M. comm.
50 shs. Continental Oil comm.	45 shs. Continental Oil comm.
45 shs. Owens Corning comm.	50 shs. Owens Corning comm.

The funds remaining figure was too small to generate new activity.

RESULTS OF SIMULATION OF XYZ ACCOUNT, 3/28/58

Description of Account:

1. Agency account
2. Revocable
3. Goal of account: high income and stability of income
4. Investment restrictions: not a legal trust, hence not restricted to legals
5. Amount available for investment in common stocks: assumed to be given

The *program* selected the following portfolio for the XYZ Account:	The portfolio selected by the investment officer on 3/28/58 was:
100 shs. Philadelphia Elec. comm.	100 shs. Philadelphia Elec. comm.
100 shs. Equitable Gas comm.	100 shs. Equitable Gas comm.
60 shs. Socony Mobil Oil comm.	50 shs. Socony Mobil Oil comm.

Risk Analysis and Branch Bank Location Decisions

Kalman J. Cohen

Risk analysis simulation is an approach to capital budgeting which has been operational for several years in a number of major industrial firms. While it is a technique which is readily transferable to many problem areas in banking (i.e., situations in which a decision is required about a major commitment of funds, the returns on which are fraught with uncertainty), this paper specifically discusses its applicability to branch bank location decisions. In this context, risk analysis simulation can be considered to be a procedure for quantifying and measuring the extent to which uncertainty is present in the determination of the rate of return anticipated from the establishment of a proposed branch bank.

PROFITABILITY OF BRANCH

The profitability of a future branch bank depends upon such factors as the market potential of the area it services, the share of this potential market actually tapped by the bank, the total amounts of the bank's deposits and its mix between demand and time deposits, the earnings yield realized and the expense ratios incurred by these deposits, the deposit growth rates that will materialize, and the magnitude of the initially required investment. Until now, most sophisticated bankers would do their utmost to make the "best possible estimate" of each of these critical factors, and then use the resulting numbers to compute the rate of return that was to be anticipated if the branch were actually opened. This procedure unfortunately ignores the fact that each "best possible estimate" of any critical factor is itself only one point in a range of possible values that this factor may assume, and it thus may lead to an erroneous viewpoint about the degree of reliance which should be placed on the com-

Reprinted with permission from *Banking*, Journal of The American Bankers Association, February 1966.

puted rate of return. In particular, the fact that proposed branch X has an anticipated rate of return of 15% per year while proposed branch Y has an anticipated rate of return of 20% per year does not necessarily imply that Y is a better investment than X, since the uncertainties surrounding the "best possible estimates" of the critical factors associated with Y may be much greater than the corresponding uncertainties for X's critical factors.

The technique developed in this paper for coping with the problems of uncertainty employs computer simulation and Monte Carlo analysis to generate the entire probability distribution of the anticipated rate of return on a prospective branch bank. This distribution is implicit in the estimates of the many critical factors upon which the branch's profitability depends, when these estimates are themselves realistically regarded as probability distributions rather than as "best possible" single values. Once the distribution of the anticipated rate of return is obtained, meaningful probability statements can be made concerning such important questions as the chance of loss, the range of likely outcomes, etc. Accordingly, a more comprehensive understanding of a proposed branch's risk can be obtained.

Let us start by considering how we might compute the anticipated rate of return for a proposed branch bank on the assumption that we can make accurate forecasts of all the relevant factors. An outline of the procedure that could be employed is shown in flow chart form in Figures 1 and 2. According to Figure 1, the average levels of demand and time deposits in the branch during the first year of its life are determined by the demand and time deposit potentials in the total market area served by the branch and by the share of deposit potential initially obtained by the branch. While it would be possible to explain how the market potentials for demand and time deposits and the initial share of market realized by the branch are determined, this has not been done here in order to avoid detail.

After the first year of the branch's life, its deposits are computed by applying some particular growth rate to the preceding year's deposits. The initial growth rate is generally the highest that will be experienced during the entire lifetime of the branch. After the branch reaches maturity, its deposits will grow at the average rate experienced by the bank as a whole. Between the initial year and the time when the branch matures, its deposits will grow at successively decreasing rates.

Each year, the revenues generated by and the current costs incurred in the branch depend upon its levels of demand and time deposits. The particular earnings, yields and expense ratios applied to the deposits vary from year to year as the general level of interest rates changes. Thus, Figure 1 shows the prime rate of interest each year affecting the revenues and current costs of the branch. Since the prime rate changes infrequently, the level in any one year generally depends upon its level in the preceding year. The final factor which affects current costs is the annual rent.

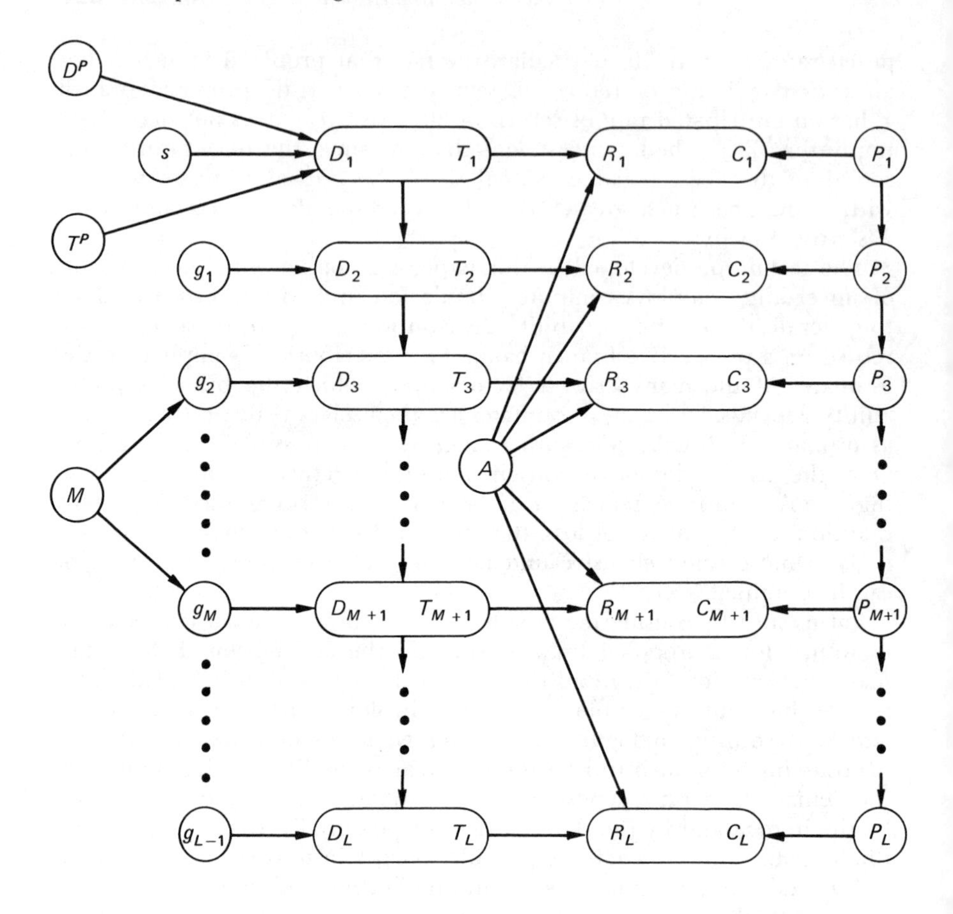

FIG. 1 Generate deposits, revenues, and current costs.

(The following key refers to Figures 1 and 2.)

$t =$ year of branch operation ($t = 0, 1, 2, \ldots L$)
$L =$ lifetime of the branch in years
$C_o =$ initial outlay required to establish branch
$C_t =$ current costs (not including depreciation) of operating branch in year t
$D_t =$ average level of demand deposits in branch in year t
$T_t =$ average level of time deposits in branch in year t
$D_p =$ demand deposit potential for the branch
$T_p =$ time deposit potential for the branch
$A =$ annual rental cost for the branch
$s =$ share of deposit potential initially realized by the branch
$Dg_t =$ actual growth rate in the branch's demand deposits in year t
$Tg_t =$ actual growth rate in the branch's time deposits in year t

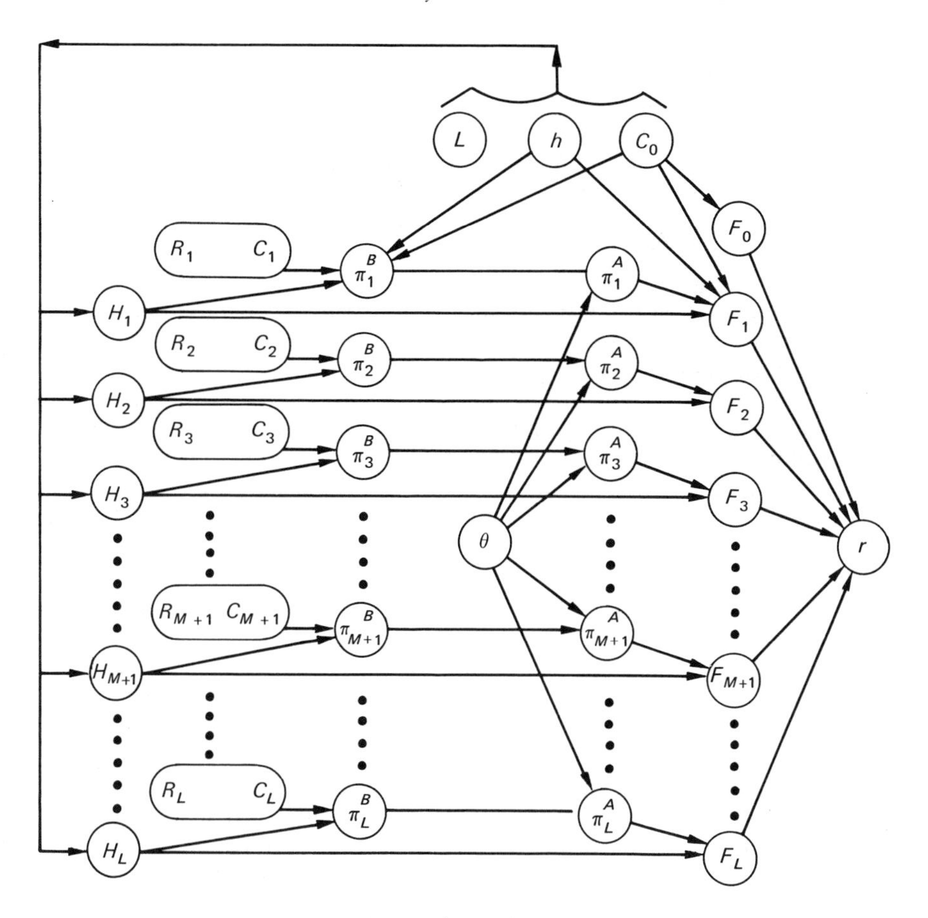

FIG. 2 Generate profits, net cash inflows, and rate of return.

M = number of years required for the branch to reach maturity
p_t = prime rate of interest in year t
r = rate of return of the branch over lifetime (L)
F_t = after-tax cash inflow from branch in year t
θ = marginal tax rate on corporate profits
R_t = annual revenues for branch in year t
$B\pi_t$ = before-tax profits of the branch in year t
$A\pi_t$ = after-tax profits of the branch in year t
h = fraction of the initial outlay required to establish the branch that is depreciable (the remainder of the initial outlay being expensed in the first year)
H_t = depreciation charges for the branch in year t

The annual revenues and current costs of the branch which have been determined in Figure 1 are repeated in Figure 2. The difference between the revenues and current costs, reduced by the amount of depreciation charges, determines the branch's profits before taxes each year. During the first year, a fraction (1-h) of the initial investment outlay is written off as a current operating expense, further reducing the initial year's profits before taxes. The depreciation charges each year depend upon the magnitude of the initial investment outlay, the fraction of it which must be depreciated rather than expensed, and the lifetime of the branch. Once the profits before taxes are known, the relevant marginal corporate income tax rate is applied to determine the branch's profits after taxes each year. All non-cash charges (depreciation each year and the fraction of the initial investment outlay that was expensed during the first year) must be added back to the profits after taxes to generate the net after-tax cash inflows of the branch each year. Since the total investment outlay is considered to be a cash outflow (a negative net cash inflow) at the time the branch is established, the portion of the initial outlay that is tax deductible as a first-year expense should not be treated as a first-year cash outflow.

The rate of return of the branch, which is a time value of money concept, is defined as that discount rate which equates the present value of net after-tax cash inflows to zero. Once the rate of return of a proposed branch has been computed, as shown in Figure 2, it is then used as a figure of merit in determining whether or not to establish the branch.

We have now considered in some detail how one could compute the rate of return on a proposed branch bank assuming that all relevant factors can be accurately forecasted. In reality, however, it is clear that this assumption of perfect forecasts is a gross simplification. There are inevitably many critical uncertainties involved in attempts to predict the relevant aspects of the future. In most cases, we can at best generate reliable forecasts that take the form of probability distributions, rather than the form of single values known with certainty.

The risk analysis simulation technique has been designed to start from the premise that most forecasts can meaningfully be made only in the form of probability distributions. The "bell-shaped" curve illustrates one way in which we can represent as probability distributions our forecasts of most of the factors relevant to the profitability of a proposed branch bank. These are the same factors assumed to be known with certainty in Figures 1 and 2. The illustrative results discussed below assume that we can accurately forecast only three of the relevant factors: The lifetime of the proposed branch; the marginal tax rate applicable to corporate profits; and the annual rental of the branch. The predictions for the other relevant factors upon which the rate of return of the proposed branch depend are various types of probability distributions.

In risk analysis simulation, we use an electronic computer to generate a realized value from each of the probability distributions for the underlying factors. Once these specific numbers have been generated, then the

Table 1 Differences in the Definitions of Branches C and D

Variable	*Normal distribution parameters*	*Branch C*	*Branch D*
Initial investment	μ	$ 100,000	$ 200,000
	σ	$ 10,000	$ 20,000
Demand deposit potential	μ	$7,500,000	$7,500,000
	σ	$2,250,000	$1,500,000
Time deposit potential	μ	$2,500,000	$2,500,000
	σ	$ 750,000	$ 500,000
Share of deposit potential	μ	20%	25%
	σ	5%	6.3%

rate of return is computed in the manner already shown in Figures 1 and 2. The process is then repeated, and the computer generates another set of realized values from each of the probability distributions for the underlying factors, and once more a rate of return is computed as in Figures 1 and 2. This is done a large number of times; in the illustrative results described below, it has been done 250 times for each of the proposed branch locations. As a result, we obtain not just a single number which is alleged to be the rate of return on a proposed branch, but, rather, a whole distribution of rates of return for any branch. In effect, this distribution of rates of return shows the probability that any specified rate of return will be achieved if the branch is established.

For four hypothetical branch bank locations (A, B, C, and D), the distributions of rates of return generated by risk analysis simulation are shown in Figure 3. Let us now turn to a more detailed analysis.

Branch C versus Branch D. *Both of these prospective branches have the same certainty-equivalent rate of return: 17.2% per year. Their definitions differ only along the dimensions shown in Table 1.*

The frequency distributions for both branches (see Figure 3 and Table 1) show a great deal of variability in rates of return, with the rates of return for Branch C being more variable than the rates of return on Branch D. Comparison of the cumulative distributions (see Figure 4) shows that Branch C is a less conservative investment than Branch D; i.e., Branch C is more likely to generate a high rate of return than Branch D, but Branch C is also more likely to generate a loss or a low rate of return than Branch D.

Although the choice between C and D would appear to be a matter of indifference based upon the certainty-equivalent rates of return, risk analysis simulation shows that the prospective outcomes differ significantly, although neither branch dominates the other irrespective of the risk preferences of management. Thus, a conservative management would be inclined to prefer Branch D, while a venturesome management would be inclined to prefer Branch C.

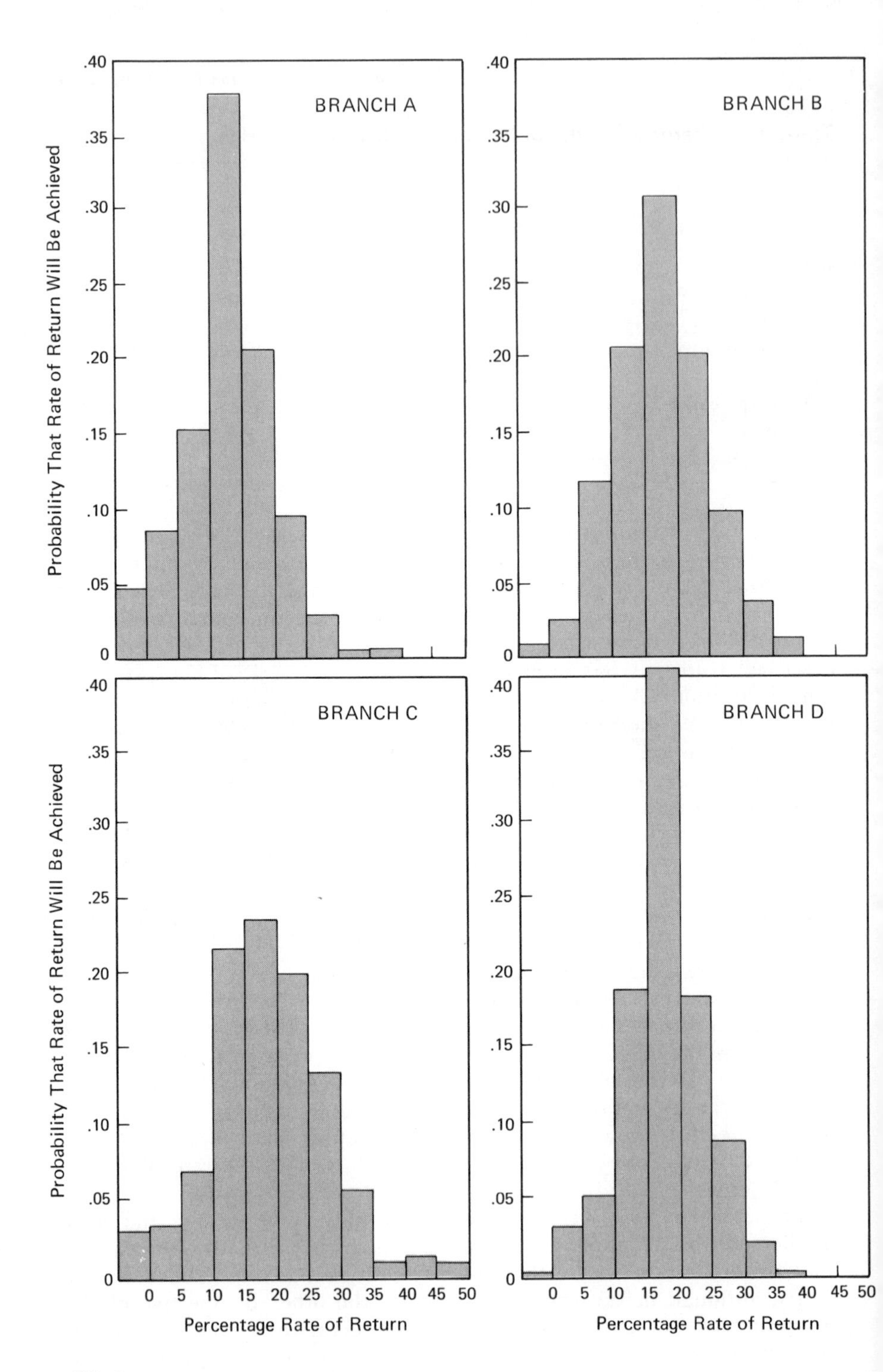
BRANCH A
BRANCH B
BRANCH C
BRANCH D
Probability That Rate of Return Will Be Achieved
Probability That Rate of Return Will Be Achieved
.40
.35
.30
.25
.20
.15
.10
.05
0
0 5 10 15 20 25 30 35 40 45 50
Percentage Rate of Return
Percentage Rate of Return

FIG. 3

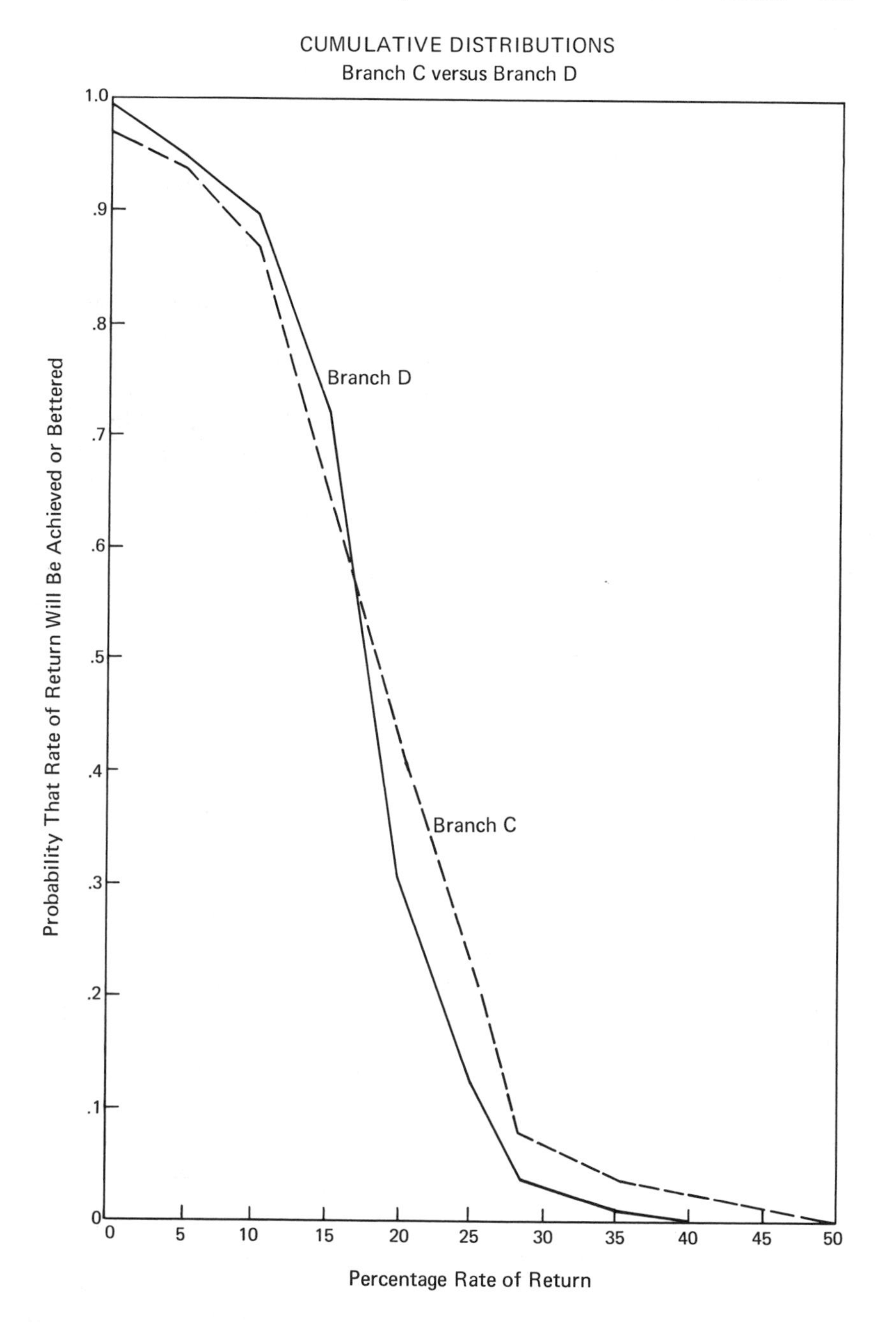
CUMULATIVE DISTRIBUTIONS
Branch C versus Branch D
Probability That Rate of Return Will Be Achieved or Bettered
Percentage Rate of Return
Branch D
Branch C
1.0
.9
.8
.7
.6
.5
.4
.3
.2
.1
0
0
5
10
15
20
25
30
35
40
45
50

FIG. 4

Branch A versus Branch B versus Branch D. *These three situations should be regarded as being mutually exclusive possibilities for the establishment of a single real branch. They differ only in that each has a different distribution of initial investment outlays, to which there corresponds a different distribution of share of deposit potential initially obtained (Table 2). In particular, the definitions of these three cases differ only along the dimensions shown below.*

The certainty-equivalent rates of return are 10.9% for Branch A; 17.2% for Branch B; and also 17.2% for Branch D. The frequency distributions for all branches show a great deal of variability in rates of return, with the rates of return for Branch B being the most variable. Comparisons of the cumulative distributions show that Branch A is clearly dominated by both B and D (Figure 5). This means that there is a greater probability that any given rate of return will be achieved by B and by D than by Branch A. Hence, Branch A is not as good an investment as either Branch B or Branch D, regardless of management's degree of risk aversion. Note, however, that neither Branch B nor Branch D dominates the other. Branch D is a somewhat more conservative investment than Branch B; i.e., Branch D is less likely to generate a high rate of return than Branch B, but Branch D is also less likely to generate a loss or a low rate of return than Branch B.

Thus, comparisons based upon risk analysis of prospective branches A, B, and D, which represent mutually exclusive alternatives, show that A is the worst possible choice; the choice between B and D depends upon the risk preferences of management. Thus, even though Branch D requires a much greater initial investment outlay than Branch B, a conservative management should prefer D to B, while a venturesome management would be inclined to prefer B.

All this assumes, of course, that management is basing its branching decisions on rate of return on investment as a criterion, rather than using rate of deposit growth as a criterion. Although I feel that bank management should behave in this manner, the results of some research being conducted jointly with Professor Samuel R. Reid raise serious doubts about whether bank management actually does behave in this manner.

Many banking situations occur in which a decision is required about a

Table 2 Differences in the Definitions of Branches A, B, and D

Variable	*Normal distribution parameters*	*Branch A*	*Branch B*	*Branch D*
Initial	μ	\$ 75,000	\$ 100,000	\$ 200,000
investment	σ	\$ 7,500	\$ 10,000	\$ 20,000
Share of	μ	15%	20%	25%
deposit potential	σ	3.7%	5%	6.3%

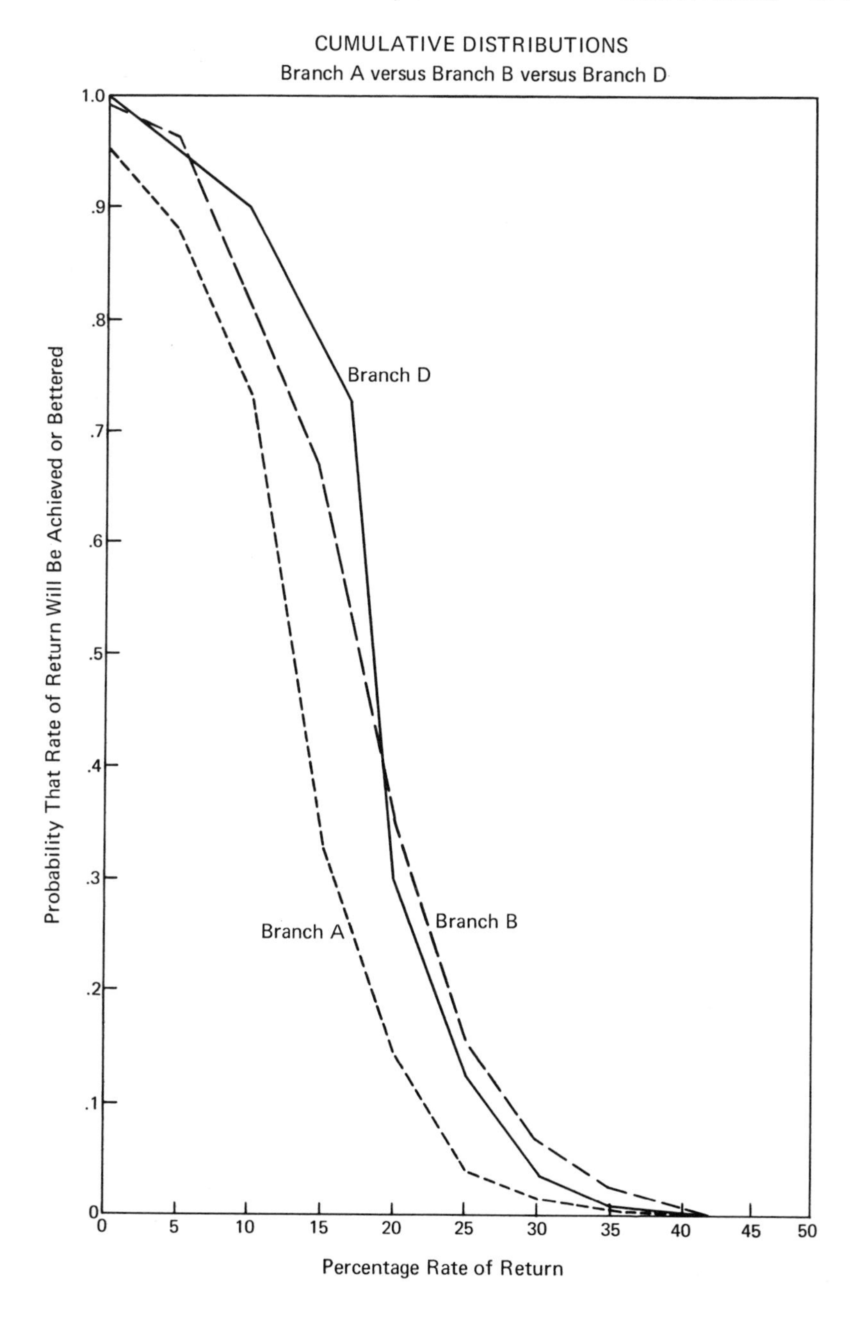
CUMULATIVE DISTRIBUTIONS
Branch A versus Branch B versus Branch D
Probability That Rate of Return Will Be Achieved or Bettered
Percentage Rate of Return
Branch A
Branch B
Branch D
1.0
.9
.8
.7
.6
.5
.4
.3
.2
.1
0
0
5
10
15
20
25
30
35
40
45
50

FIG. 5

major expenditure of funds, the returns on which are highly uncertain. The following examples are illustrations of representative banking problems to which the risk analysis technique can be applied.

(1) When examining a potential new branch, many of the relevant factors on which ultimate profitability depends can only be estimated within some perceived margins of error.

(2) The costs, savings, and service benefits from a large installation of data processing equipment can be estimated only with great uncertainty.

(3) The effects of alternative promotional expenditures on bank profitability can at best be described in terms of subjective probability distributions.

(4) The prospects inherent in potential bank merger possibilities depend on a number of highly uncertain political and economic forces.

(5) In analyzing the credit-worthiness of a proposed term loan, the banker must consider the wide range of possible outcomes associated with the customer's investment project.

(6) Some banks undertake a limited number of potentially profitable, but highly risky, equity-type foreign investments under the provisions of the Edge Act.

In all these situations, the risk analysis simulation procedure can be employed. Usual analyses ignore the problem of uncertainty and assume that all relevant variables can be accurately forecasted. In contrast, the risk analysis technique, by providing an understanding of the entire probability distribution of returns, is conducive to better decision-making.

Analysis of Lock Box Locations

Robert L. Kramer

Utilizing the computer to produce an efficient lock box arrangement can substantially increase the availability of funds for a bank's commercial customers. A lock box, of course, is a post office box address to which a company asks its customers to send their remittances. The mail received at such a box is picked up at frequent intervals by the company's bank,

Reprinted with permission from *Bankers Monthly,* national magazine of banking and investments, May 15, 1966.

which then processes the checks and presents them for clearing through the Federal Reserve System or a local clearing house.

This procedure results in earlier presentation of the checks for payment by the drawee banks and thus increases investible funds for the corporation. The design of an optimum lock box arrangement, particularly one involving several cities, is a very complex process, one which can utilize the speed, flexibility and accuracy of the computer.

SAVINGS SOURCES

The resultant savings (or earnings) from this more rapid availability of money stems from the following sources:

Improved mailing times. Lock boxes are usually strategically located in major cities, whereas the customer's office may be in a town with less frequent mail service. Furthermore, the lock box city may be closer to the bulk of the depositor's customers than is the company's own office, even if that office is located in another major city.

Improved processing times. When customers send checks directly to the company, it must record, endorse, and further process the checks before depositing them in the bank. This added step in the collection procedure creates a delay of anywhere from ½ day to several days before the checks are entered in the clearing channels.

Improved clearing times. Many Federal Reserve cities have local clearing houses which provide same day availability of funds for checks drawn on local banks when they are presented before a specified deadline. Also, clearing times between Federal Reserve branch cities is normally faster than between a country point and a Fed city. Since lock boxes are seldom located in a non-Fed city, improved clearing time is a virtual certainty.

Thus, the advantage of a lock box to the depositor is the consequent earlier availability of funds, meaning the company will require less working capital. For example, if a corporation has average daily receipts of $1 million, an improvement of two days in availability will provide an average of $2 million more money.

BANK CHARGES

The improvement will be greater for: 1) larger companies, 2) companies with less-favorably located offices, and 3) companies with larger average remittances. The size of the remittance is important in that the banks generally charge for this service on the basis of the number of checks passing through the box annually. The charge may be in the form of a fee, or in the compensating balances created by the lock box activity (credit being given at a specified interest rate on the average balance maintained at the bank by the depositors.) Of course, the rates and forms of these charges and credits vary from bank to bank.

For very large companies with customers scattered over a wide geographic area, it is often worthwhile to use several lock boxes in different cities. It becomes a complex problem to determine how many such locations should be used and in which cities lock boxes should be established. A computer program has been prepared at Bankers Trust Co. to assist in the selection.

SIMULATION APPROACH

The basic approach of the program is to simulate the mailing, processing and clearing times for a number of alternative single-city or multi-city lock box plans, using a representative sample of the depositor's receipts. No random element is introduced other than that inherent in the selection of the sample. Thus, the computer compares what would have happened to typical checks under each of the several plans tested, including the company's present system, under identical conditions.

The sample must provide at least the following information for each check: postmark date, postmark location, amount of check and drawee bank location. The actual date of receipt by the depositor is an optional requirement. Samples usually consist of at least one week's receipts, and often those for a month or more, with the number of checks involved often ranging from 100 to 10,000.

The movement of each item is then simulated from the postmark date until the time the funds become available to the depositor. This requires the following additional data: 1) a table of mailing times from all points to each of the Federal Reserve branch cities, 2) a table showing the time required for a check drawn on banks in each Federal Reserve branch city or country point to clear, when presented to the Federal Reserve Bank in each branch city, and 3) a record of holidays falling within the sample period, as well as any other non-working dates for both the banks and depositors. (Many lock boxes operate on a six day week, rather than the normal five day business week.)

The final items of input data include a description of the present system and a list of the lock box plans to be evaluated. The latter can specify exactly which cities shall be included in the plan, or simply provide a list of potential lock box cities and allow the computer to select the best arrangement from among them, taking into account any stated restrictions.

HEURISTIC PROGRAMMING

One technique which can be used to provide solutions to problems such as these is heuristic programming—a combination of mathematics and logic in the form of a set of decision rules. The evaluation of lock box plans involves such decision rules at two points in the typical simulation, selecting the cities, and determining the arrangement for customer remittances.

The first heuristic programming model, the Optimum Cities Selector, is used to determine which cities will be included in a lock box plan. For example, the computer may be asked to select the five most desirable cities for such a plan from a list of 10 potential locations. In this instance, there are more than 250 such combinations possible. To simulate each of these and then compare the results would be both time-consuming and expensive. In many cases, the programming model reduces the number of simulations required to only one, that involving the optimal set. Rarely would the number of simulations performed in this example exceed five or six. (This step is unnecessary, of course, when the cities to be included have been specified in advance.)

The Lock Box Plan Definition Generator, a second heuristic programming model, is used for every plan. Given the list of cities in a lock box arrangement, the decision still remains as to where each customer is to send his remittances. This is done on a geographical basis, i.e., all customers in one set of cities, states, or regions of the country send their checks to one lock box, while those in other locations send to other boxes. Before the movement of each check can be simulated, its mail destination must be specified. The decision rules perform this task.

Given this data, the computer adds to the postmark date of each item the mailing, processing, and clearing times for the plan under consideration. It accumulates this information for all checks in the sample. All available evidence indicates that the heuristics used in the Bankers Trust program provide solutions at or near the optimum.

INFORMATION PROVIDED

The results of each simulation provide the following information:

The distribution of times from postmark date to availability of funds for investment. This shows the total number of items and the total amount becoming available during each succeeding number of days after the postmark date, and their respective cumulative percentages.

The grand totals, and average time to availability.

The saving (in days) over the present system, and the equivalent increase in investible funds provided by the lock box plan (see Table 1).

Additional tables showing the distributions of mailing times and clearing times (see Tables 2 and 3).

The lock box plan definition, showing for each origin, the mailing destination specified by the computer (see Table 4).

The typical analysis performed for a depositor involves evaluating from five to 15 plans, ranging from one-city plans to those involving five or six cities, some of which are specified by the input and some are computer generated.

ELECTRONIC LOCK BOX ANALYSIS FOR XYZ CORPORATION

Table 1 Elapsed Time from Postmark Date to Availability of Funds for Investment

Days	*Amount*	*Cumul. % of Total*	*Items*	*Cumul. % of Total*
1	88599	1	7	1
2	640081	10	26	6
3	1795883	34	99	25
4	1884712	59	147	53
5	1808640	84	146	80
6	902854	96	78	95
7	309510	100	26	100
Totals	7430279		529	

Average time to availability 4.16 days Increase in investible
Saving over present plan 2.05 days funds $447710.

Table 2 Mailing Times

Days	*Amount*	*Cumul. % of Total*	*Items*	*Cumul. % of Total*
1	3015693	41	170	32
2	2752395	78	242	78
3	1335387	96	105	98
4	320008	100	11	100
5	6796	100	1	100
Totals	7430279		529	

Average mailing time 1.86 days
Saving over present plan 0.99 days

Table 3 Clearing Times

Days	*Amount*	*Cumul. % of Total*	*Items*	*Cumul. % of Total*
0	217363	3	13	2
1	916007	15	47	11
2	4493971	76	302	68
3	501296	82	52	78
4	834551	94	76	93
5	467091	100	39	100
Totals	7430279		529	

Average clearing time 2.30 days
Saving over present plan 0.06 days

Table 4 Times for Availability, Mailing, and Clearing for Each City in Plan

City	Days	*Availability* Amount	Cumul. %	*Mailing* Amount	Cumul. %	*Clearing* Amount	Cumul. %
LOUISVILLE							
	0	0	0	0	0	128444	4
	1	0	0	256188	8	475152	20
	2	198906	6	2112008	77	1766763	77
	3	330736	17	671589	99	320996	88
	4	1359685	62	18731	100	166077	93
	5	790648	87	6796	100	207880	100
	6	200110	94	0	100	0	100
	7	185227	100	0	100	0	100
Totals		3065312		3065312		3065312	
Averages		4.33 days		2.15 days		2.18 days	
NEW YORK							
	0	0	0	0	0	88919	2
	1	88599	2	2759505	63	440855	12
	2	441175	12	640387	78	2727208	75
	3	1465147	46	663798	93	180300	79
	4	525027	58	301277	100	668474	94
	5	1017992	81	0	100	259211	100
	6	702744	97	0	100	0	100
	7	124283	100	0	100	0	100
Totals		4364967		4364967		4364967	
Averages		4.04 days		1.66 days		2.38 days	

This sample lock box plan includes the following cities: New York and Louisville. It is the best two city plan devised from these potential cities: New York, Chicago, Los Angeles, Louisville, and Dallas.

(Note: The "present plan" referred to in Tables 1–3 was also analyzed on the computer. It included one day for extra processing by the depositor. Thus, the 2.05 day saving shown in Table 1 includes the .99 days from Table 2, and .06 days from Table 3, and elimination of the 1 day processing time.)

FINAL SELECTION

The basic decision criterion is the increase in investible funds provided by each plan. However, the arrangement providing the largest increase in such funds may not necessarily be the best one to implement. While it is usually true that more cities in a plan will provide a greater increase in available funds, the magnitude of this advantage may not be enough to justify the opening of an additional account and the added administrative costs. There is also the intangible factor of bank relationships which must be considered. Measured solely by quantitative factors, Chicago may appear to be the midwestern city best suited for inclusion in a certain lock box plan, but the company may already have major banking connections in Detroit. This existing relationship will be enough to offset a small advantage in favor of Chicago, but not enough to cancel a large difference. Of course, the definition of "small" and "large" are difficult to quantify. Thus the final selection depends heavily on judgmental factors and the recommendation is made by banking officers who are familiar with the depositor's situation.

The computer program provides the following advantages for both the bank and the depositor:

Better analysis. The program gives more accurate estimates of the advantages of lock boxes than was possible using "seat-of-the-pants" methods. It also evaluates a vastly larger number of alternatives than could be done by human calculation.

Faster analysis. Once the sample data is received, even the largest depositor's problems can be analyzed in a few weeks. Smaller runs have been completed in a matter of days. These times include input preparation and report preparation, with computer time accounting for only about 15 minutes to two hours of the total.

Better presentations. The computer output is designed to be included in the presentation of the proposed plan to the customer. It helps him understand how and where the lock box plan will make money for the company, and it makes the banker's job easier and his discussion more effective.

The Use of Mathematical Models in the Analysis and Improvement of Bank Operations

Richard A. Byerly

Mathematical models

If the management of a bank wished to determine the effects of changing the bookkeeping system in demand deposit accounting from one type to

Reprinted with the permission of the Bank Administration Institute (formerly NABAC Research Institute), Park Ridge, Illinois, from *NABAC Research Bulletin,* May 1960.

another, and from the second to a third type of system, the most dependable results might be obtained by actually changing the systems and observing the outcome. The disadvantages of this approach are obvious.

If bank management wishes to determine the best way to schedule a line of commercial tellers at various levels of activity, experienced judgment or "cut-and-try" are the principal aids.

If it were possible to set up a model of any banking function that could be manipulated to produce desired answers faster, surer, and without disrupting daily operations, management would have gained a technique of considerable aid in decision-making.

Mathematical models can be constructed to do these things.

The idea behind the design and use of mathematical models is by no means new, although it has developed very rapidly during the last few years. Formulas for computation of compound interest are small examples of mathematical models. Formulas for the amortization of premium or discount on bonds are models—so are formulas for the depreciation of assets, which follow the actual depreciation of assets with some degree of accuracy.

If telephone companies assumed that every subscriber made a call simultaneously, not recognizing the fact that calls are made at random and are of random duration, the switchgear required would be many times the present complement of equipment. Mathematical models based on studies of the random behavior of telephone subscribers are used to determine realistically the required equipment.

Whenever a process can be represented with an acceptable degree of accuracy by mathematical formulas, the behavior of the process under all sorts of conditions can be examined rapidly and economically by manipulating the formula as opposed to changing the process or disrupting it in any way.

This idea has been exploited by toll road authorities to determine the number of toll stations that must be manned to meet given traffic conditions. It has been used by large retail stores to determine the necessary docking facilities for a fleet of trucks arriving and departing at random. It has been used by airlines, railroads, and the military departments of the government.

It has not been adapted to the analysis of banking operations heretofore, because of the absence of some basic information, primarily performance standards. With the development of industry-wide standards by the NABAC Research Institute, the use of the concept became possible for the first time.

The first model

On May 6, 1960 the Trustees of the NABAC Research Institute witnessed the first use of a mathematical model in the study of bank operations. An electronic computer (IBM card-650) was programed to perform as if it were a portion of a bank—in this instance, a group of savings tellers servicing the requirements of customers. The participants in this demonstration could open or close windows at will; customers appeared and were serviced when a teller was available, or waited in line until their requirements could be fulfilled. The computer calculated the time customers had to wait, and the number of customers waiting at any time. It determined the amount of time the tellers were busy servicing customers, and the time they were not so occupied. Many other factors were calculated as well. No one could predict when a customer would arrive, or what he would require in the way of service.

The computer in effect "rolled dice" to determine when the random arrivals of customers would occur, and what their requirements might be. This process, called "Monte Carlo," is the key to analyzing situations of this type, where random behavior is part of the problem. The manner in which it works is outlined in the following description of the teller model.

LINES OF CUSTOMERS WAITING FOR SERVICE—AN EXAMPLE

Introduction

In perhaps no other area of bank operations does the conflict between sheer efficiency of operation and requirements of good customer service on day-to-day public relations exist as in the teller operation. Here the teller *is* the bank to many customers. Talk of good service is proved or disproved at this point. Here management policy decisions relative to customer service have a direct and measurable impact upon costs of operation.

In the final analysis, management's goal is to provide the best service at the least cost. Service and costs must be kept in proper balance. A decision to cut customers waiting time at the teller window by increasing the number of tellers will raise costs. Conversely, a decision to eliminate a window to reduce costs will add to customer waiting time and inconvenience.

In the past, management has had to be content pretty much with experience and a trial-and-error method in determining the optimum point of balance between desired service and costs. For any point in time management could say there were the right number of tellers or there were too few or too many. But by this time it would be too late to correct a situation that had passed.

Management has needed a tool to predict with a high degree of accuracy what the needs of today and tomorrow will be before they become history. Specifically, management needs answers to questions such as these:

1. On an average day, how long will customers have to wait for service, if at all?

2. Will queues (waiting lines) build up? How long will they be? When do they occur?
3. What happens to service on a peak or very busy day?
4. What happens to service when a window is temporarily closed, e.g., for lunch?
5. How much would service be improved if an additional window were opened during certain periods of the day?
6. During what hours or periods can a window be closed without permitting the building up of queues of unacceptable length? How would this affect the efficient utilization of tellers?
7. How long is the maximum wait of a customer likely to be?
8. How much time are tellers likely to be busy servicing customers and for how much time are they not so occupied?
9. What would be the effect on servicing time of changing from a dual to a single system?
10. What would happen to servicing time if reference to balance and signature cards were eliminated?
11. If volume would double in the next few years, how many windows would be required to provide service at least equivalent to that given now? When is it likely that each additional window would be needed as volume grows?

A model cannot be expected to predict precisely how events will occur, and, of course, cannot produce results of greater validity than that of the data with which it is supplied. A mathematical model can, however, answer questions such as the foregoing with a degree of precision that is sufficient for planning and decision making purposes.

An illustration from a hypothetical bank

For purposes of illustration, a hypothetical banking situation has been established. Since the manipulative process is far too lengthy to perform manually in more than a limited way the situation has been kept simple. The situation is similar to the "bank" demonstrated to the Institute Trustees using an electronic computer.

Only one alternative out of many hundreds is examined: the effect of closing one or two windows during slack and peak hours.

The following outline gives a step-by-step explanation of the process in general terms, followed by the results of the examination of the hypothetical bank's performance with the data supplied in Table 1.

While any of these factors can be varied at will, and additional ones added, this situation will serve to illustrate the method of "turning the bank on" and observing customers being waited on by the three tellers.

Outline of the process

The flow-chart (Figure 1) illustrates the Monte Carlo technique in general outline.

Table 1 Hypothetical Bank "A"

1. Number of Savings Tellers		Three
2. Types of System		Unit (Single)
3. Bank Hours		9 a.m. to 3 p.m. = Six Hours
4. Expected Number of Transactions for the Day		600
5. Expected Hourly Distribution of Transactions:		
9 a.m. to 10 a.m.	60	
10 — 11	30	
11 — 12 noon	60	
12 noon — 1 p.m.	180	
1 p.m. — 2	90	
2 — 3	180	
Total	600	
6. Types of Transactions, and Expected Distribution by Types:		
Transaction		
Basic Deposits	100	
Basic Deposits—Cash Back	50	
Special Deposits	75	
Christmas Club Payments	150	
Total Deposits		375
Basic Withdrawals	50	
Special Withdrawals	25	
Total Withdrawals		75
Cashed Checks	150	150
		600

Box 1 of the flow chart indicates that the factors known about the hypothetical bank are tabulated (or put into the computer). The tables of standards applicable to the unit system are at hand, or in the computer, as well as other tables of a mathematical nature necessary for the solution of the problem.

Box 2 indicates the process by which the arrival times of customers is computed. The Monte Carlo process comes into play in this operation, as explained in the following section.

When this process is completed, the probable arrival times of the 600 customers are tabulated, assuming that they arrive 60 the first hour, 30 the second hour, etc., as shown in Figure 1, but otherwise completely at random.

Box 3 indicates the assignment to each customer of a "name tag," again using Monte Carlo, so that each customer is assigned a transaction code at random, except that the percentage of each type of transaction to the total is maintained (for example, there will be approximately 100 basic deposits, etc.).

At this point the time when each customer will arrive is known, and his requirements are specified.

Box 4 indicates that the time required to service the individual's needs must be determined.

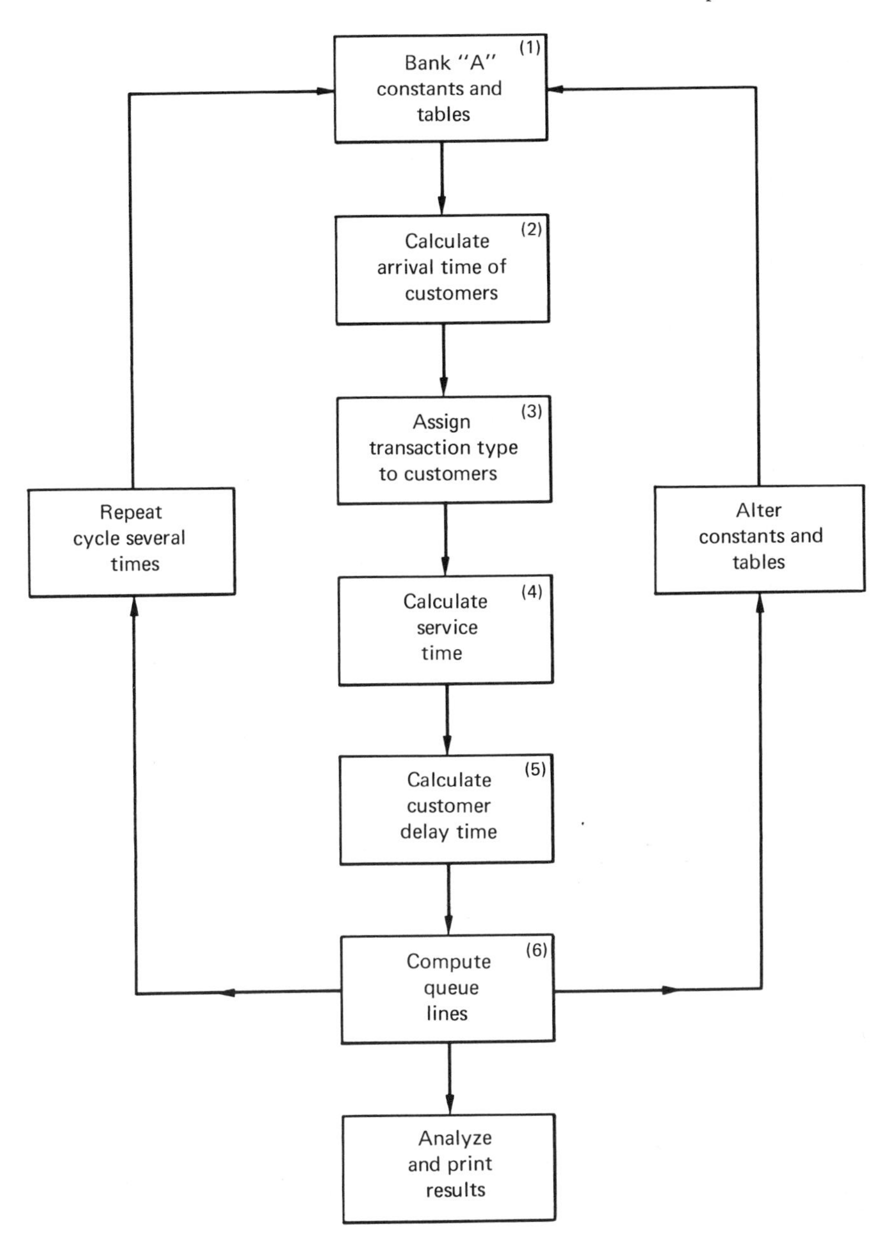

FIG. 1 Monte Carlo flow chart.

A special comment is called for in connection with the use of forthcoming Institute standards in this type of process. For customary purposes to which standards are to be put, the single value of a standard is appropriate. In the problem under consideration, however, *variations in servicing time* are very important. Therefore, the constant factor given as a standard is not sufficient. If a teller performed the same function in exactly the same time in each instance, queues might not form as they do. It is quite likely that the occasional very slow performance of an operation has an appreciable effect upon queuing up at a window.

For this reason the complete *array* of servicing times observed in Institute field studies will be used in the example from which random samples will be drawn, thus including times approaching the standard, but also including faster and slower times in the proportion that they were actually seen to occur.

An array of observations with the related standard is illustrated in Figure 2. The standard is 34.0 seconds, but it can be seen that 10.3% of the time a servicing time of 45 to 50 seconds was observed, for example. The determination of servicing times takes all such variations into account.

At this point the 600 customers are "tagged" for arrival time, transaction type, and time required to handle their requirements.

Box 5 indicates that a "Customer Delay Time" is to be determined. Since the forthcoming standards represent only the element of time from the moment a teller receives documents or instructions from a customer until the second the transaction is completed, the time required for the customer to depart from the window must be considered. This factor is also determined by a Monte Carlo selection of random delay times.

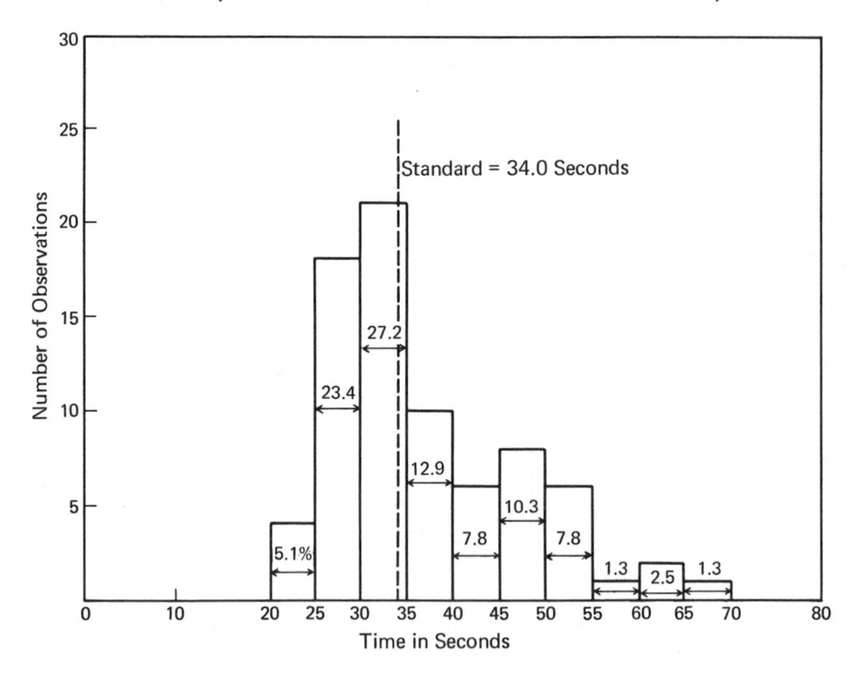

FIG. 2 Basic deposits.

Box 6 indicates that the process can now begin, by assigning customer 1 to window 1. In other words, the bank is opened for business, customers arrive in the predicted fashion, and queues may or may not form, depending upon volume, servicing time, etc.

The Monte Carlo process

The Monte Carlo process referred to in preceding paragraphs is the key to the solution of many queuing problems. In concept, it is a very simple device, although the theoretical basis for its use is mathematically involved.

The principle behind the method can best be explained by an illustration. Suppose that the immediate problem is that of assigning transaction type to the 600 customers appearing at the hypothetical bank. The number of expected transactions has been set forth and the distribution by seven types of transactions has been assumed. Therefore, the ratio of the number of each type of transaction to the total can be determined, as shown in Table 2.

The objective at this point is to assign a transaction type to each customer in a completely random fashion and yet to maintain the distribution of transactions according to proportions established.

This is easily accomplished by means of a table of random numbers. Such a table supplies a large quantity of 5-place numbers equally distributed from 00000 to 99999 with no pattern or order whatever. Therefore, if numbers are read from such a table, they will automatically fall in one of the seven number groups indicated in the "5-place numbers" column and thereby designate a transaction type to be assigned to each customer as he appears. The number of transactions selected for any particular group will obviously be approximately proportional to the ratio designated for that group. For instance, any number selected which falls in the number group 25001–37500 will designate a type 3 transac-

Table 2

Transaction Type	*Number Assumed*	*Ratio to Total*	*Cumulative Ratio*	*5-Place Numbers in Group*	*Type*
Basic Deposits	100	.16667	.16667	00000–16667	1
Basic Deposits—Cash Back	50	.08333	.25000	16668–25000	2
Special Deposits	75	.12500	.37500	25001–37500	3
Christmas Club Payments	150	.25000	.62500	37501–62500	4
Basic Withdrawals	50	.08333	.70833	62501–70833	5
Special Withdrawals	25	.04167	.75000	70834–75000	6
Cashed Checks	150	.25000	1.00000	75001–99999	7
		1.00000			

Table 3

Random Number from Table	Transaction Type Selected	Customer Number
53219	4	1
01932	1	2
95010	7	3
22789	2	4
etc.	etc.	etc.

tion. This number group contains 12.5% of all the numbers between 00000 and 99999 and therefore about 12.5% of all transactions will be type 3, as specified. In Table 3, a portion of a table of random numbers is shown, just as it would be used in the Monte Carlo selection of transaction types.

This process is continued until all 600 transactions have been "tagged" or identified by type. The totals are compared with the specified percentages to be sure that they do not depart materially from the pre-established specifications.

The column headed "5-place numbers in group" in Table 2 is called a "distribution function." Applying random numbers against some kind of distribution function constitutes the Monte Carlo process. In the investigation of waiting lines in savings teller operations, distribution functions will be used for selecting servicing times from the arrays of observed performance, for determining the random arrival times of customers, and for customer delay times.

In a computer operation, these distribution functions and the table of random numbers are stored in the computer and the process proceeds at electronic speeds, making it possible to examine any aspect of the situation rapidly. Operating conditions can be changed at will.

Calculation of arrival times

Random arrivals of customers, random arrivals of trucks at a receiving dock, and other similar phenomena have been found to follow a common type of distribution function. While it would be interesting and possibly profitable to study and record in detail the actual arrival of customers at a real teller window it is unlikely that the results would differ substantially from those derived from the usual distribution function. This function is called the "Poisson'" function.

In the hypothetical bank it is necessary only to know or assume the number of persons who can be expected to arrive in a given time period in order to develop a detailed schedule of random arrival times for the customers. This has been done by stating that 60 customers can be expected to appear during the first hour, 30 the second hour, and so on. These assumptions can be modified in any way desired. Once suitable

Table 4 First Hour—60 Arrivals Expected

Customer Number	*Time Between Arrivals (Sec.)*	*Time When Customer Arrives (Sec. from Starting Time)*
1	39	39
2	63	102
3	37	139
4	72	211
5	1	212
etc.	etc.	etc.

assumptions have been made, the Monte Carlo method is used in conjunction with the arrival function to estimate time between arrivals.

During the first hour, for example, since 60 customers are expected, the average arrival rate is 60 per hour. From this average rate the appropriate distribution function is determined, random numbers are selected and arrival times set down as shown in Table 4.

Servicing customers

If the foregoing procedure has been fully carried out, in effect a table has been produced containing the time of arrival of each of the 600 customers, a transaction type, and a time required to execute each transaction based on the standard array of service times. This table could be prepared in the form of Table 5.

Following this procedure, the customer delay time is determined from an appropriate distribution function. In the interests of simplicity, this step has been omitted from the example.

All that now remains to be done is to assign the customers to one of the three tellers, if one is not occupied, and otherwise to form a queue or waiting line. An illustration of how this may be done is given in Table 6.

Table 5

Customer Number	*Time of Arrival (Sec. from Starting Time)*	*Transaction Type*	*Service Time (Sec.)*
10	396	7	16
11	403	4	11
12	595	5	43
13	613	1	32
14	656	1	39
15	693	4	29
etc.	etc.	etc.	etc.

Table 6 Partial Table of Customer Arrivals, Servicing, and Queues
(Hour 4—180 Arrivals)

Window 1			Window 2		
Customer Number	Arrival Time (Sec.)	Departure Time (Sec.)	Customer Number	Arrival Time (Sec.)	Departure Time (Sec.)
161	3233	3314	162	3262	3301
			165	3301	3360
166	3314	3383			
168	3337	3383			

Window 3			Queue				
Customer Number	Arrival Time (Sec.)	Departure Time (Sec.)	Customer Number	Arrival in Queue (Sec.)	Assigned to Window (Sec.)	Waiting Time (Sec.)	Number in Queue
163	3270	3286	164	3272	3286	14	1
164	3286	3320	165	3276	3301	25	2
			166	3277	3314	37	3
			167	3285	3320	35	4
167	3320	3364					
etc.							

Table 6 is simply constructed by assigning a customer to any window that is open when he arrives. If no window is open, he goes into the queue and waits until a window is available. His departure time is determined by adding his servicing time to his arrival time. For example, when customer 165 arrived at 3276 seconds from the beginning of the hour, all three windows were busy. Window 1 was occupied by customer 161, window 2 with customer 162, and window 3 with customer 163, and customer 164 was ahead of customer 165 in the queue. Customer 165 then waited 25 seconds until window 2 completed his transaction with customer 162, when he was then accommodated in 59 seconds.

For purposes of simplicity, it is assumed that a customer will go to any open window, or to the shortest line, or move from a queue to the first open window. Therefore, for all intents and purposes of this example, there is only one queue from which customers are assigned to the first open window.

Analysis of results

Without further consideration of the technicalities of the process, the results of the operation of the model can be analyzed.

Based upon the facts given in establishing the model, the following questions can be answered. Following this analysis, the system can be changed in any way desired and comparative results determined.

1. What is the total time devoted to servicing customers?
2. What is the total time during which tellers are not servicing customers?

3. How are these two time factors distributed for each hour of the day?
4. What is the length of the longest line of waiting customers?
5. What is the longest wait of any customer? What is the average waiting time of customers who must wait in line?
6. What is the average time for each type of transaction? What is the maximum time? The minimum time?

Table 7 shows the results of making such an analysis of one trial day's operation of the model bank and the answers to the foregoing questions. (More than one run is necessary to produce results of maximum reliability. Table 7 is illustrative only.)

Analyzing the impact of changed circumstances

The next steps in the procedure involve changing the suitation in any manner desired in order to evaluate the impact of the change. For example, stipulated lunch hours for each of the three tellers can be inserted into the problem, and the queues, waiting time, etc., evaluated. Or one window may be closed permanently to see whether the waiting lines and times become excessive or another window may be opened to determine the extent to which service is improved. The number of anticipated transactions can be doubled or tripled, or altered in any way, and the effects estimated.

One interesting alternate is that of examining a complete change of system, from a dual to a unit system, for example. Manual examination of the many alternatives is prohibitively lengthy, and therefore only one alternative has been examined in this article, and that for purposes of illustration only.

Hour 2 is a slack period. Can it be handled with only one teller without creating undue waiting time?

Hour 4 is a busy period. What is the effect of operating with only two windows open to the public?

Table 8 summarizes the results of operating the "bank" in this manner.

During hour 2 it is obvious that the customers can be satisfactorily accommodated with only one window open, since only 8 of them wait for service at all, and then only 14.3 seconds on the average. The maximum wait of 31 seconds does not seem to be too much of a delay to consider the service to be very good. The percentage of time the tellers devote to service is more reasonable.

Essentially the same overall service is given during the fourth hour with three windows open. While more customers wait, the average wait is only 14.4 seconds, and the maximum is 43 seconds. However, if one window is closed, the average wait is nearly one minute, and the maximum is three minutes. 131 People out of 180 must wait at least some measurable period of time. While the utilization of personnel for accommodating customers is much higher, of course, service suffers considerably.

Table 7 Summary of Hourly Arrivals

Hour	Number Arrivals	No. Type Arrivals 1	2	3	4	5	6	7	No. of Customers Who Wait	Max. Wait (Sec.)	Longest Queue	Total Wait (Sec.)	Avg. Wait (Sec.)	Service Time (Sec.)	Non-Service Time (S.)	% Utili-zation
1	60	18	3	2	19	3	1	14	1	11	1	11	11	1580	9220	14.6%
2	30	6	2	5	7	1	1	8	0	0	0	0	0	957	9843	8.9
3	60	12	4	5	17	4	3	15	1	15	1	15	15	1606	9196	14.9
4	180	21	16	17	45	13	17	51	49	43	4	705	14.4	5637	5163	52
5	90	17	6	12	18	8	2	27	5	32	2	94	18.8	2168	8632	20.1
6	180	21	16	17	45	13	17	51	49	43	4	705	14.4	5637	5163	52
Totals	600	95	47	58	151	42	41	166	105			1530	14.6	17585	47217	26.9%
% of Totals		15.8	7.8	9.6	25	7	6.8	27.6								

	1	2	3	4	5	6	7
Average Time per Type (in seconds)	33	48.3	61.3	15.6	41.7	57.5	14.7
Maximum Time (in seconds)	47	66	99	33	59	98	35
Minimum Time (in seconds)	17	17	18	4	13	30	4

Table 8

	Hour 2 (30 Customers)		Hour 4 (180 Customers)	
	3 Windows Open	*1 Window Open*	*3 Windows Open*	*2 Windows Open*
Number of Customers Who Wait	None	8	49	131
Longest Queue	None	1	4	7
Total Waiting Time	None	114 sec.	705 sec.	6991 sec.
Average Wait	None	14.3 sec.	14.4 sec.	53.4 sec.
Maximum Wait	None	31 sec.	43 sec.	154 sec.
Total Service Time	95 sec.	957 sec.	5637 sec.	5637 sec.
Total Non-Service Time	9843 sec.	2643 sec.	5163 sec.	1563 sec.
% Utilization of Teller Time	8.9%	26.6%	52.2%	78.3%
Number of Tellers	3	1	3	2

Summary

It must be borne in mind that the foregoing example is illustrative of a method. Almost any degree of refinement may be introduced that promises to produce valuable results. For instance, if the length of maximum acceptable queue lines is pre-established by bank management, or the maximum permissible waiting time is decided upon in advance, a computer can be programmed to open additional windows automatically when these limits are reached, and to close them when the circumstances no longer prevail, thus effectively scheduling tellers for specific situations. In the model run on the IBM 650 computer, participants in the demonstration opened and closed windows at will, and observed the effect of their actions on service and teller utilization.

In presenting this new and somewhat complicated technique to NABAC Research Institute member banks, the difficulties faced by individual banks in applying it are recognized. Plans are being evolved that promise to bypass these difficulties. . . .

Considerable work remains to be done in refining the present model, and in developing models for other areas of bank operations. The significance of the technique is such, however, that member banks should be informed of its adaptation to Institute research. While the good judgment of skilled operations personnel in individual banks will always provide the best decisions, this method will provide much new information upon which to base decisions.

The cooperation of the International Business Machines Corporation in programming the model on extremely short notice and in furnishing the computer is gratefully acknowledged. Both IBM and the Institute recognize that any electronic computer can be programed in a similar fashion.

Linear Programming and Optimal Bank Asset Management Decisions

Kalman J. Cohen and Frederick S. Hammer

Those interested in the application of analytical techniques to management decision problems recently received a severe jolt from a series of research reports investigating the use by management of Operations Research models. The impact of this research is perhaps best indicated by Churchman's findings that of all the articles published in the first six years of the professional journal *Operations Research,* "in no case was there sufficient evidence that the recommendations derived from O.R. projects were fully accepted and carried out by management." [1]

Many reasons can be advanced to mitigate the force of this finding. For example, it can be argued that since successful research usually provides competitive advantages to management, many firms will prohibit the dissemination of results of such projects. In addition, since the probability of successful implementation of a model can be expected to be inversely related to the model's complexity and degree of abstruseness, and since the editors of professional journals tend to possess a bias in favor of abstract complexity, it can be argued that it is precisely those models with less practical usefulness which are included in the professional literature. Nonetheless, Churchman's findings are still disturbing and have led to increased debate about whether the burgeoning literature in the area of analytical methods has really represented "management science fiction," not actual and potential management practice.

The results reported in this paper are in strong contrast to Churchman's findings. This paper describes an important and yet complex analytical model developed by the Management Science group at Bankers Trust Company. This model has for several years been an operational

[1] C. W. Churchman, "Managerial Acceptance of Scientific Recommendations," *California Management Review,* Vol. 7, No. 1 (Fall 1964), p. 33.

Reprinted with permission from *The Journal of Finance,* May 1967.

tool in the asset management process. Thus, those interested in the financial applications of analytical techniques can take heart in the fact that at least one situation exists in which complex models are being practically and usefully implemented.

The first section of this paper provides a brief statement of the nature of asset management problems faced by bankers. This section also describes and criticizes one pseudo-analytical technique now enjoying widespread discussion and popularity in banking. A description of the complex linear programming model used to make asset management decisions is contained in the second section. The model is described in terms of its constraints, its criterion function, and the nature of its intertemporal characteristics. In the third section the paper concludes with a discussion of the model's data requirements, the results it provides and their applications, and a brief discussion of its experience at a major commercial bank.

ASSET MANAGEMENT AND ASSET ALLOCATION

The central problem of asset management revolves around the bank's balance sheet. How *large* should its total assets be? This is equivalent, of course, to asking how *large* should its total liabilities and capital accounts be. What should the *composition* of these assets, liability, and capital accounts be?

It is well known that a bank can usually increase the yield on its earning assets by reducing their liquidity. One of the fundamental aphorisms of asset management, however, is that a bank should not merely attempt to maximize short-run yield. Under normal economic conditions, to do so would require lengthening the maturity and increasing the default risk of the earning asset portfolio. Such actions would eventually result in the bank's inability to meet its loan demand and deposit withdrawals and, perhaps, even in its insolvency. On the other hand, any bank which maintains an excessively liquid earning asset portfolio is unnecessarily forgoing many profitable opportunities. It is thus inviting potentially destructive competition to enter its market. Finding an appropriate balance between profitability, risk, and liquidity considerations is one central problem in asset management.

The optimal balance between these factors cannot be found without considering important interactions that exist between the structure of a bank's liabilities and capital and the composition of its assets. The fact that bankers pay attention to such simple and naive rules of thumb as the ratios of loans to deposits, capital to risk assets, and mortgages to savings deposits indicates their awareness of the interactions which exist among these various accounts. The capital adequacy criteria that have been devised by various bank regulatory agencies attempt to reflect these interactions in a more comprehensive manner.

The yield, liquidity, and risk implications of asset management decisions are usually reflected not only in the current time period, but also throughout a long future. To the extent that bankers are interested in increasing their earnings, it is important that they consider the long-run implications of their actions. Today's asset management decisions create tomorrow's problems as well as tomorrow's opportunities. Thus, one must consider potential loan demand, future deposit levels, and the interest rates or yields that will exist over the course of a planning horizon, as well as any impending changes in the legal and economic environment in which the bank operates. In devising a tool to assist in asset management, it is consequently important that the dynamic elements inherent in the problem be explicitly incorporated. It is obviously true that the future cannot be predicted with complete certainty. This is, however, no excuse for ignoring the future in an ostrich-like fashion.

Thus, asset management decisions in a commercial bank can be viewed as focusing upon two major problems. *First,* in order to accommodate the many and complex interactions which exist between the appropriate balance sheet categories, the nature and magnitude of the trade-offs which exist between yield, liquidity, and risk considerations must be assessed. *Second,* the short-run versus long-run implications of various decision alternatives must be evaluated and decided upon.

Because asset management represents the most pressing problem routinely faced by senior bank executives both in terms of time devoted to this area and its potential impact on bank profitability, it is not surprising that a wide variety of techniques have been suggested to help management in this area.[2] To a large extent, these techniques represent nothing more than a cataloguing of traditional rules of thumb, tempered by the non-operational observation that such rules must be continually modified by ill-specified quantities of "management judgment."

An attempt at greater rigor is represented by the operational technique of Asset Allocation. This technique rests on the basic assumption that investments in the various asset categories should be directly related to the sources from which these funds were obtained. The fundamental criterion used to earmark funds is that the velocity (i.e., turnover rate) of the source of funds dictates the appropriate maturity of asset supported. Thus, for example, relatively stable funds (e.g., savings deposits and capital funds) can be invested in longer-term, higher-yielding assets (e.g., municipal bonds) while demand deposits, which are subject to greater fluctuations, are matched with cash and short-term loans.

Asset Allocation can be severely criticized along a number of dimensions.[3] For example, the belief that available funds should be used to support assets appropriate to the velocity of these funds mistakenly over-

[2] See, for example, Part II in *Analytical Methods in Banking,* edited by K. J. Cohen and F. S. Hammer (Homewood, Illinois: Richard D. Irwin, Inc., 1966).

[3] K. J. Cohen and F. S. Hammer, eds., *Analytical Methods in Banking,* pp. 45–53 and 108–111.

looks the important difference between the *volatility* of any particular dollar of deposit and *minimum amounts* and *stability* of these deposit balances. In addition, by sole attention on velocity as the relevant criterion for earmarking funds, Asset Allocation implicitly assumes that sources of funds are determined independently of their uses. Thus, the dynamic feedback links which characterize current loan decisions and future deposit flows are ignored. For these and many other reasons, Asset Allocation is a deficient tool that leaves much to be desired as a management decision aid. Clearly, an improved and more sophisticated device is needed.

A suggested alternative is discussed in the balance of this paper. Some of the concepts and relationships of the model to be presented are based on an earlier paper by Chambers and Charnes [4] that, in part because of its technical nature, has remained relatively obscure to the banking community. Besides elaborating extensively upon the embryonic and insightful ideas contained in the Chambers-Charnes paper, the present model contains a host of other considerations which play a critical role in the asset management process. In an effort to make this model more accessible to the non-mathematically oriented reader, the present paper does not utilize any mathematical symbolism.[5]

THE MODEL

The asset management model under discussion is couched in a linear programming format. Linear programming can be viewed as a technique for maximizing a linear criterion function subject to a set of linear constraints. One of the important benefits derived from formulating problems in this manner is that computationally feasible algorithms exist which guarantee the generation of optimal solutions. The present model will be described in three stages: intra-period constraints, inter-period considerations, and the criterion function.

Intra-period constraints

The linear programming model for asset management is intertemporal in nature. It determines a sequence of balance sheet positions over a multi-period planning horizon; this sequence is optimal, given the bank's initial balance sheet position and its economic forecasts over the horizon. In each period within the planning horizon, there are a variety of constraints which must be observed. The general form of these intra-period constraints, which essentially are the same within each planning period, is discussed in the present section.

[4] K. J. Cohen and F. S. Hammer, eds., *Analytical Methods in Banking,* Chapter 4.

[5] A more detailed and mathematical explanation will be contained in a forthcoming publication.

Risk Constraints: Examiners' Criteria for Balanced Portfolios

It is widely recognized that traditional measures of bank safety, e.g., the capital to risk asset ratio, are virtually worthless as operational tools.[6] It is clear, for example, that the risk inherent in bank assets should be measured along a continuum instead of a simple dichotomy between non-risk (i.e., cash and short-term governments) and risk (i.e., all other) assets. In addition, the use of this ratio as a measure of capital adequacy does not consider the impact upon bank safety of the structure and stability of its deposits, the nature of its trust operations, etc. Thus, a more comprehensive measure of capital adequacy and safety should be employed.

Such a measure has been provided by the examiners of the Board of Governors of the Federal Reserve System. The concept underlying the examiners' criteria is a complicated leverage restriction that combines a capital adequacy test with a liquidity test. These criteria become more restrictive as the need for potential liquidity becomes greater—i.e., as assets become less current, liabilities become more current, or trust operations become relatively larger. In this respect, the examiners' criteria are more comprehensive than the ratios and rules of thumb usually employed by bankers to gauge safety and liquidity.

It is important to note that the examiners' criteria are not rigid legal restrictions which must be met by a bank at all times at any cost. These criteria have evolved out of years of experience in banking. They are (perhaps unduly) conservative; a bank which satisfies these criteria is unlikely to become financially insolvent.

A bank's score, as calculated by the examiners' criteria, is a ratio comparing actual capital funds to the amount of capital "required" against the bank's portfolio. In essence, capital requirements are levied in three stages. *First,* capital requirements are levied directly against assets. In the event of forced liquidation, some assets usually must be sold for less than their book value. The capital required to support these potential losses is assigned according to the inherent risks of these assets, as evaluated by the examiners.

Second, for any given asset structure, potential liquidity may increase (according to the examiners' criteria) as the bank's liabilities become more current. To the extent that liquidity against potential fluctuations in deposits must be provided by longer-term assets, additional capital requirements are imposed.

Finally, capital requirements are levied against a bank's trust operations. Substantial capital losses can be incurred if a bank is proven negligent in the management of its fiduciary activities.

These various considerations can be expressed in mathematical terms.

[6] See, for example, the *Annual Report* of the Federal Deposit Insurance Corporation for the year 1945, pp. 7–10.

Although the constraints themselves interact non-linearly, a series of mathematical transformations can be employed which make it possible to express the examiners' criteria as a set of linear relationships. Thus, the powerful technique of linear programming can be utilized.[7]

As originally specified by the examiners, these criteria incorporate a severe degree of conservatism—a degree that would not be tolerated by the management of any aggressive commercial bank. Thus, even though the *form* of the constraints may be sensible, the specific *numbers* employed by the examiners should be modified to fit both the economic circumstances and management policies of a particular bank.

Funds Availability Constraint

In expressing all but a few of the model's constraints, it is most natural to regard balance sheet variables as average stocks over a planning period. It is obvious that a sensible planning model must explicitly specify that the balance sheet balance, i.e., that on average total uses of funds equal total funds available.

To this point, the framework suggested by Chambers and Charnes has been followed in that the only constraints they employ are the risk and funds availability restrictions discussed above. The present model departs from the Chambers-Charnes framework both by adding many additional types of constraints (as discussed below) and in employing more realistic assumptions concerning the implied pattern of cash flows through time. Both the present model and that of Chambers and Charnes are intertemporal in nature—they include several time periods within their planning horizon. This is necessary because, as indicated above, future requirements must be taken into account when making current decisions concerning the balance sheet position. Thus, given the set of expected interest rates, loan demands, and deposit levels used as inputs, the optimal solution obtained from the linear programming model determines a sequence of balance sheet positions that the bank should try to obtain over the planning horizon.

Since each succeeding balance sheet in the sequence is generally different from the preceding one, it is necessary to make some explicit assumptions concerning the pattern of cash flows involved in making the transition from one position to another. Chambers and Charnes assume that all flows occur instantaneously at the start of a planning period, i.e., that the desired average balance in a particular category is identically equal to the spot balance of that category at every instant within each planning period. Clearly, this assumption is unrealistic.

In an attempt to incorporate greater realism concerning the cash flow pattern, the present model assumes that cash flows occur at a constant rate within a planning period. A diagram can be usefully employed to illustrate the ways in which the assumptions of the present model differ from those employed by Chambers and Charnes.

[7] See Chambers and Charnes, in Cohen and Hammer, eds., *Analytical Methods in Banking,* Chapter 4.

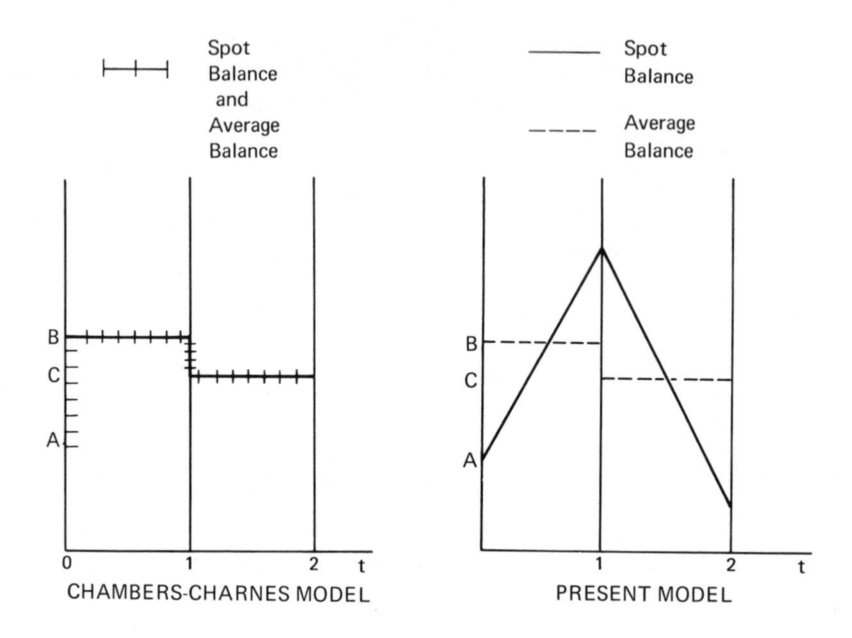

FIG. 1 Spot and average balances.

For illustrative purposes, Figure 1 depicts a two-period planning model. Assume initial stocks are at level A and it is desired to achieve *average* balances of B and C in periods 1 and 2, respectively. Panel (a) of Figure 1 indicates the cash flow pattern assumed by Chambers and Charnes. Thus, desired levels B and C are achieved instantaneously at the beginning of the relevant period. In contrast, the assumptions of the present model are indicated in panel (b). Beginning at point A, the model assumes that the net increase in this particular balance sheet category occurs at a constant rate of 2(B-A) per period during period 1 and the net decrease occurs at a rate of 2(C-B) during the second period.

These assumptions, of course, are relevant only for those stocks which cannot in fact be adjusted instantaneously in banking, i.e., most loan accounts and certain categories of investments and deposits. Of course, for certain instantaneously adjustable items like daily assets (loans to government dealers, Federal funds sold, etc.), the Chambers-Charnes assumptions remain relevant. In addition, the realities of the marketplace will restrict the maximum rates at which the levels of various balance sheet categories can be altered.

Because of these assumptions concerning the cash flows, it is clear that although *on average* the balance sheet will balance within each period, it is not necessary that this relationship hold for every instant of each period. Thus, in moving from one balance sheet position to another, if changes in *sources* are preponderantly in instantaneously adjustable categories (e.g., Federal funds bought) and changes in *uses* are in assets which take longer to adjust (e.g., commercial loans), the implied *spot* balance sheets at the beginning and end of the planning period will not necessarily balance.

In practice, of course, a bank's balance sheet will always balance. Since the present model is intended for intermediate and longer-range planning purposes, and not day-to-day decision making, the unrealism of the implied spot balance sheets is of trivial importance. The actual adjustment mechanisms utilized by a bank in daily operations do not occur at a constant linear rate. The assumptions employed in the present model are not meant to be accurately descriptive. Clearly, any degree of realism in this respect can be incorporated into the model by appropriately shortening the durations of the planning periods utilized. In formulating any model, however, one must inevitably abstract away a large amount of inessential detail. This model is intended for planning purposes; thus, the exact rate at which day-to-day flows occur is essentially irrelevant. Hence, the assumptions employed in the present model serve as an effective compromise between the unrealism of the Chambers-Charnes flow assumptions and the impracticalities of completely accurate description.

Policy Considerations

There are many time-honored and well-established heuristics used to gauge bank safety and liquidity, e.g., the ratios of governments to assets, capital to risk assets, loans to deposits, etc. Sophisticated observers have long realized that each of these heuristics involves only a limited, narrow view of the overall portfolio balance problem. These rules of thumb are superseded by the more comprehensive measure of the Federal Reserve Board of Governors examiners. Nonetheless, so long as such heuristics remain in vogue, bank management must be sensitive to possible adverse reaction by stockholders, depositors, and others to balance sheet positions which imply ratios which greatly deviate from "accepted" ranges.

Policy constraints can easily be added to express these conventional measures. The minimal required values of these ratios would be set at the outside perimeters of what is deemed by management as acceptable. The dual variables obtained in solution to the linear programming problem are especially pertinent in evaluating the impact of limited constraints of this type. If the duals indicate that the opportunity cost of these restrictions is unduly high, management may well wish to re-evaluate the necessity of adhering closely to policy restrictions of this type.

Since the market for certificates of deposit is of relatively recent origin, bankers may not yet be confident of the extent to which this money market instrument can be relied upon as a source of funds in all economic climates. Thus it is not clear *ex ante* whether under particular economic conditions it will be possible to increase the stock of these funds, or even to roll them over as outstanding certificates mature. Hence, as a policy matter, management may wish to avoid placing undue reliance upon this particular source of funds.

Policy constraints of this type can be expressed in either of two ways: (a) as a maximum percentage of total deposits, or (b) as an absolute dollar limit. Obviously the force of this constraint can be modified from period to period within the planning horizon to reflect management's expectations concerning changes in the state of monetary conditions over the planning horizon.

Market Restrictions

The policy constraints outlined immediately above are internally generated. In addition, a set of restrictions must be imposed to reflect the limitations on a bank's freedom of action which arise from the economic and institutional realities of the marketplace.

LIQUIDITY BUFFER As already indicated, the linear programming model assumes that deposits are expressed as average balances over a planning period. It is clear, of course, that actual deposits will fluctuate from day to day within a planning period. These fluctuations are consistent with the model's implicit assumption that the average levels of deposits are accurately known. For planning purposes, some minimal liquidity buffer of cash and near-cash items must be provided. This buffer will be utilized in making the daily adjustments required by these fluctuations in deposits. Such considerations are incorporated by a constraint which requires that on average some minimal amount of cash, daily assets, and readily marketable investments be held throughout the planning period. This minimal amount, of course, depends upon the magnitude of the day-to-day swings expected in deposits.

LOAN DEMAND Under normal economic conditions, there is a limit on a bank's ability to make at prevailing market terms loans of a particular type and quality. Thus, the rate at which the bank can make new loans of various types is constrained to be no greater than the forecasted demand for them. In a tight monetary environment, of course, it may appear that the bank can make all the new loans for which resources can be mustered, i.e., that loan demand for the bank is far higher than funds available. In these circumstances, these demand constraints become redundant, and the rate at which the bank makes new loans is determined through interaction with other parts of the model.

DAILY LIABILITIES There are many types of daily liabilities, each of which can be used only to a limited extent as a source of funds. Constraints must be added to the model to represent these limitations. For example, through its experience and contacts in the marketplace, a bank may believe that there is an absolute maximum dollar amount of Federal funds that it can buy at any one time. Similarly, it is possible to borrow either from the Federal Reserve System or under repurchase agreements only to the extent that suitable securities are available as collateral.

DAILY ASSETS Some types of daily assets and daily liabilities are dealt with in the same market. For example, a bank may feel that in order to maintain its market position as a net purchaser of Federal funds, it must also sometimes be active as a seller. Under these conditions, the minimal amount of Federal funds sold can be expressed as a linear function of Federal funds bought—a constraint that can easily be incorporated.

PLEDGED ASSETS Many depositors (especially public authorities) require a bank to maintain collateral against their deposits in the form of specific types of assets. Thus, the minimal amounts held of the appropriate assets must be related to the volume of relevant deposits.

CASH Because of legal reserve requirements, float considerations, and correspondent bank relations, the bank must maintain a minimal level of cash. This minimal level, of course, is related both to the size and composition of its deposits.

SELLING CONSTRAINTS The maximum rate during a period at which a bank can sell any type of security or marketable loan must be related to the amount available for sale at the beginning of that period. Hence, a series of upper-bound constraints is added to the model. Note that sales (no matter when they occur) can be permitted only out of stocks held at the beginning of the planning horizon. To show that this formulation implies no loss in generality, assume that instead of purchasing securities of desired maturity, it is more profitable to buy instruments of longer-than-desired maturity and resell these in a later period within the planning horizon. Even though the present model focuses solely on asset management considerations in determining the desired maturity structure, if a bank wished to exploit the profit potential inherent in its yield expectations, it could establish a trading operation to do so. This linear programming model is intended, however, for planning rather than trading purposes. Thus, its major intent is to provide management with insight into the desired size, composition, and maturity structure of its balance sheet position over the planning horizon. The desirability of trading operations is more appropriately determined by other devices.

Inter-period considerations

Thus far the constraints of the model have all been couched in terms of variables pertaining to a *single* planning period. It is understood, of course, that a similar set of intra-period constraints exists for *each* period within the planning horizon. In order to link the variables pertaining to *different* time periods, one must explicitly indicate how balance sheets depend upon both initial stocks and decisions made in earlier periods within the planning horizon. To do so, there are at least three major considerations: intertemporal links, endogenous changes in capital, and loan-related feedback mechanisms.

Intertemporal Linkages

It should be noted that for any given balance sheet category, as many as four different concepts may be required to define its average balance: the spot balances at the beginning and the end of a period, and its rates of purchase and sale within that period. Observe that the stock at the beginning of a period is precisely the same as the corresponding ending stock of the previous period. Then invoking the assumption of constant flow rates within a single period, the intertemporal relationships between opening stocks can easily be expressed.[8] Given this definition of opening and closing spot balances, the average balance of that item can be defined as the arithmetic mean of the two. For those balance sheet categories which are disaggregated into multiple maturity classes, the definition of the end-of-period spot balance must incorporate the run-out into shorter maturity classes and the run-in from longer maturities. This can easily be accomplished by assuming exponential flow rates from one maturity category to the next. The parameters describing these exponential flows depend upon the relative lengths of both the maturity classes and the time periods.

It is not at all necessary, of course, to divide the planning horizon into time periods of equal length. It becomes increasingly difficult to forecast the economic climate the further into the future one looks. In addition, management is more interested in greater detail concerning near-term activity than it is about actions which will occur only in the longer-term future. Thus, it may be useful to utilize relatively short time periods in the early stages of the planning horizon, and longer stretches of time in the later periods.[9] Since flow variables in the model are expressed as annual rates, the lengths of the planning periods themselves become parameters in the intertemporal links.

Endogenous Changes in Capital

It should be clear that the amount of available capital funds during any period depends in part upon decisions made in both the same and preceding periods within the planning horizon. Changes in capital occur as (a) interest is paid and received, (b) securities are traded at capital gains or losses, (c) expenses are incurred for promotional efforts aimed at changing the bank's loan and deposit market shares, (d) dividends are declared, etc.

Since considerations such as these are an integral part of the bank's asset management problem, decisions concerning the relevant variables must consider the trade-offs involved between induced changes in the volume of capital funds (i.e., in the constraint matrix) and present and future yields (i.e., in the criterion function) generated by these variables. Thus, changes in capital which occur for reasons such as those enumerated above should be explicitly included in the model. Each of these factors can be easily accommodated, thereby allowing their effects to be included when determining optimal asset management decisions.[10]

[8] As previously indicated, rates of purchase and sale are not relevant for such stocks as daily assets and daily liabilities, since these are assumed to adjust instantaneously.

[9] For example, if five planning periods are to be employed stretching over a four-year horizon, one might usefully regard the first two periods as each being three months long, the third period as six months long, the fourth period as one year long, and the fifth period as two years long.

[10] It should not be assumed, of course, that these considerations imply that future levels of capital funds can be precisely forecasted. On the contrary, changes in capi-

The endogenous changes in capital mentioned above can be incorporated in the intertemporal link defining capital funds. For example, the capital at the end of a period will depend upon the interest received and interest paid on the various assets and liabilities held by the bank in that period. For this purpose, the relevant interest rates must be on an after-tax basis, net of marginal processing costs, marginal default losses, etc. Similarly, realized capital gains or losses will, on an after-tax basis, also affect the bank's capital.

To the extent that promotional expenses (e.g., advertising, give-aways, etc.) affect the bank's loan and deposit market shares, the determination of desired levels of these expenses falls within the purview of asset management. If the way in which these expenses affect the relevant market shares is both understood and can be expressed linearly, these relationships can be added to the model and the optimal level of these expenditures determined endogenously.

Capital funds are reduced when dividends are paid. If the value of dividends to stockholders is known, the imputed yield can be assigned to the dividend variable in the criterion function. In this case, the model can be used to determine the optimal dividend level. This approach is overambitious at present, given the unfortunate state of financial theory. Thus, for now a more pedestrian approach will be employed. This requires adding constraints describing the bank's dividend payout policy. Such an approach allows the model to reflect the impact of dividends paid on future available capital funds.

It should be realized that these endogenous changes in capital are not incorporated merely in homage to the fetish of precise forecasts. The amounts of capital actually available to the bank at future times will depend heavily upon exogenous factors which cannot be predicted perfectly. In evaluating the yield-risk trade-offs of a given decision, however, it is essential that its impact on future capital funds be made explicit. Thus, endogenous changes in capital are included in the model in order to extend the comprehensiveness of the interactions considered in making present asset management decisions.

Loan-Related Feedback Mechanisms

Bankers often make loans at contract rates which are less than the market rates of interest obtainable on alternative investment instruments (e.g., tax-exempt municipal securities). Clearly this is not necessarily an irrational action on the part of the banker. To the extent that a present loan makes available both present and future deposits, it generates re-

---

tal will occur for various reasons exogenous to the model. For example, changes in fees and commissions received from trust operations and bond trading activities can at best be forecasted imperfectly. Since these other functions are basically independent of asset management, their effect on capital funds can be included in forecasts made externally and supplied as input to the model. Thus, the overall estimates of capital funds used in each of the model's periods are only forecasts based upon the bank's best expectations.

sources which sustain additional earning assets. Thus the present value of the stream of future income earned on these assets should be considered as an increment to the present value of the contract interest earned on the loan. Evidently, in the banker's judgment, the implied "imputed rate" is more than enough to overcome the stated differential in the contract rates. This phenomenon must clearly be considered by the model in determining optimal asset management decisions. Three ways of attempting to do so will be discussed.

First, it is possible exogenously to determine the pace at which the bank will make new loans in the future. Utilizing this forecast, the upper-bound constraint on loan demand is converted to an equality constraint. The model can then be used to structure the maturity and composition of the investment portfolio and sources of funds in a way which permits the bank to meet all of its desired loan volume. While this approach has the virtue of simplicity, it fails to consider the trade-offs that exist between loans and other asset management alternatives. This approach will undoubtedly become less satisfactory given the accelerating proliferation of new dimensions in asset management thinking.

A second and more satisfactory approach is to estimate the magnitude of the "imputed rates" on loans, and then to add this imputation to the loan interest rate in the criterion function. If the imputed rates are accurately chosen, this technique is capable of producing reasonable approximations to the optimal asset management decisions. Such an approach, of course, is not without its limitations. At best, even if the *correct* imputed rates were known, this method will inevitably introduce some distortions into the implied intertemporal funds flows. A more serious drawback, however, is the fact that these imputed rates cannot be determined without an adequate understanding of the underlying dynamic feedback effects related to the loan decision. To the extent that a bank explicitly possessed this understanding, a more precise third mechanism can be employed.

This third approach consists of incorporating the loan-related feedback mechanisms into the intertemporal constraints of the model. To the extent that a bank does better or worse than its competition in meeting its loan demand, it will gain or lose market share as a result. These changes in market share will occur both for loans and for deposits. If the form of these feedback effects is linear, they can be included in the constraints of the model.

Criterion functions

The various types of intra-period constraints and intertemporal linkages which comprise the model have been discussed above. It is left to specify the criterion function that will be used, i.e., to define the goals that the bank is striving to maximize by its asset management decisions during the planning horizon.

Rather than delineating a single criterion function that must be used, three possible choices will be discussed: [11]

(1) maximize the value of the stockholders' equity during the final period of the planning horizon;
(2) maximize the present value of the net income stream plus realized capital gains (and losses) during the planning horizon; and
(3) maximize the present values of the net income stream plus realized capital gains (and losses) during the planning horizon plus the present value of the stockholders' equity during the final period of the planning horizon.

It will be seen that while arguments can be advanced for each of these criterion functions, the authors generally favor the third alternative.

Maximize Horizon Value

There are two major reasons for considering this criterion function. First, it avoids the necessity for determining a rate at which to discount monetary receipts and disbursements which occur during various time periods. The difficulties associated with choosing the proper discount rate are well known and need not be belabored. Second, this criterion implies a willingness to sacrifice current income if so doing will lead to a higher value of stockholders' equity at some future (but not too far distant) date. This can be easily illustrated.

Consider the two alternative growth paths shown in Figure 2. Suppose that a "conservative" bank policy would result in the stockholders' equity growing along path A, whereas an "aggressive" bank policy would result in growth along path B. The selection of growth path A or B depends entirely upon how long one must wait for the two growth paths to cross at time t^*. Thus, if the first criterion function is utilized, the length of time represented by the model's planning horizon—at best an ill-specified notion to the ordinary banker—will have an inordinately severe impact on the implied asset management decisions.

Maximize Present Value of Net Income

There are three general reasons why the second criterion function might be preferred to the first:

(a) not all earnings opportunities are explicitly incorporated as decision variables in the linear programming model;

[11] With respect to each of these criterion functions, there are two points to be noted. First, the question of possible dilution effects on stockholders' equity from new stock issues can be handled by selective reruns of the model. Professor W. W. Cooper, of Carnegie Institute of Technology, has suggested that the solution on a per share basis may be directly obtained by formulating the criterion function in linear fractional form, i.e., as a ratio of two linear functions of the decision variables. (See A. Charnes and W. W. Cooper, "Programming with Linear Fractional Functionals," *Naval Research Logistics Quarterly,* Vol. 9, Nos. 3 and 4 (Sept.–Dec., 1962), pp. 181–186.) Second, it is assumed throughout this section that endogenous changes in capital are incorporated into the constraints of the model.

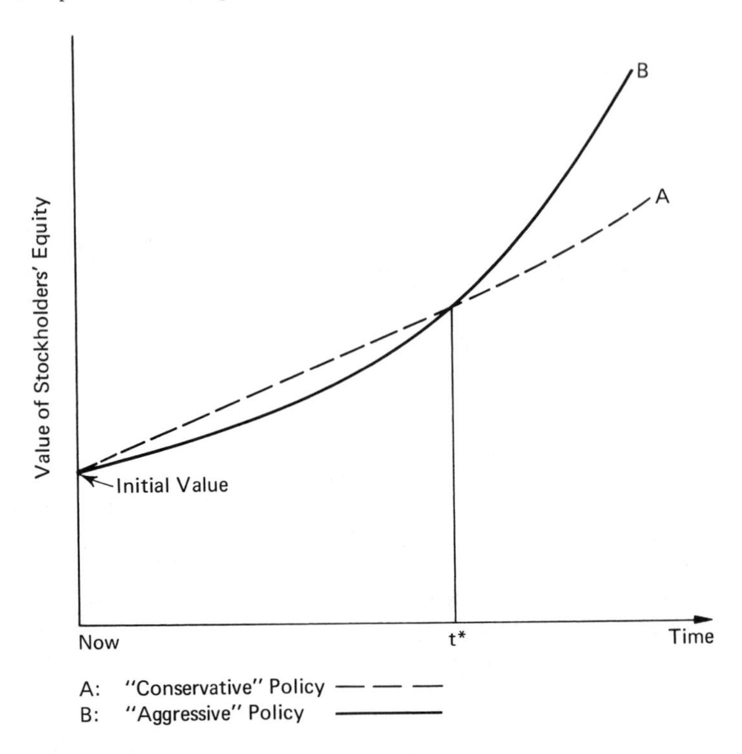

FIG. 2 Alternative growth paths.

(b) increasing degrees of uncertainty are implicitly attached to more distant forecasts; and

(c) it is felt that shifts in the time pattern of the net income stream will affect the market's valuation of the bank's stock.

For any of these reasons, most bankers would prefer the second (maximize present value of net income) criterion to the first. This choice, however, immediately leads to a problem: what discount rate should be employed in computing present values?

The optimal solution generated by the linear programming model can be highly sensitive to the discount factor used. This is easily seen in terms of Figure 2. If future income is discounted at a very high rate, then this second criterion will prefer growth path A to growth path B; if future income is discounted at a very low rate, growth path B will be preferred to growth path A.

Conceptually, the most plausible candidates for determining the proper discount rate are: (a) the bank's cost of capital, (b) the rate at which the stock market implicitly capitalizes net income in determining the market value of the bank's stock, or (c) management's subjective time rate of preference for net income.

Most modern economists would agree that on a theoretical basis, the bank's cost of capital should be used. There is a practical drawback in so doing, however, since few economists agree on an operational procedure for determining this rate.

In lieu of this, it may be somewhat easier operationally to estimate the implicit rate at which the stock market capitalizes the bank's net income. It may be possible to determine this rate using econometric techniques when a suitable bank equity valuation model becomes available. It should be noted, however, that employing any such rate implicitly assumes an acceptance of the "traditional viewpoint" that, within conventionally accepted limits of leverage, raising additional debt capital does not change the cost of equity.

Finally, if no more objective basis for determining the proper discount rate can be agreed upon, one can always fall back upon management's subjective time rate of preference for net income. Some clever interviewing is clearly required in order to obtain consistent agreement concerning this rate. In the absence of consensus, the model can be rerun to determine the sensitivity of the implied optimal decisions to the choice of discount rate.

Maximize Present Value of Net Income Plus Terminal Valuation

The third possible criterion function is essentially a combination of the preceding two, and hence much of the foregoing discussion remains applicable. In order to understand the reason for adding terminal valuation to the second criterion function, note that it is really only the optimal decisions for the first period that must be known. These are the only decisions that can be immediately implemented.

The phrase, "optimal first period decisions," must be interpreted, however, as the first step in a plan that is optimal in a long-run sense. Later time periods are included in the planning horizon only because we do not know how to modify the criterion function to reflect the consequences of present decisions on future opportunities. If these consequences were understood, they could be explicitly incorporated within the criterion function. This would enable one to deal with a sequence of a single-period models to generate a path of decisions which is optimal in the long run.

The value of T in a T-period model should be chosen where the set of first-period decisions becomes insensitive to further increases in T. By adding the terminal valuation of the stockholders' equity [12] to the second criterion function, it is possible to obtain with only T periods the same first-period decisions that would be made if net income were

[12] In practice, this terminal valuation utilizes the market values of the balance sheet categories; these market values are based on the interest rates projected for the final period of the horizon.

discounted over a longer time horizon. By not including valuation, one implicitly assumes that stocks held at the end of the planning period are worthless.

IMPLEMENTATION AND IMPLICATIONS

As indicated in the opening paragraphs of this paper, the model described in the preceding section was developed and applied at Bankers Trust Company. It is now an operational tool in the asset management process. This section will discuss some of the considerations involved in implementing such a model and the nature of the results obtained.

Transformation to computational form

In actual practice, a bank will utilize one of the available computer algorithms for linear programming to obtain solutions to the asset management model. Unfortunately, the model as described above includes many concepts and variables which do not appear in banking vernacular. In order to simplify both the construction of the linear programming model and the interpretation of its solution, supplementary computer programs are specially written. These programs contain the transformation rules to convert statements of the problem in banking language to formulations which are computationally more efficient. These programs also convert the outputs of the linear programming algorithm into reports containing terminology and format with which bankers are readily familiar.

Data requirements

Five different types of data are required as input to the model. First, the bank's *initial balance sheet* at the beginning of the planning horizon must be categorized into the same degree of detail with respect to type and maturity as is used in expressing the constraints and the criterion function of the model. In principle this presents no difficulty; in practice, however, it may require the collection of data which are not routinely generated. The necessity of supplementing the bank's ordinary data processing system in this manner points out once again the advantage provided by an analytical model in pinpointing the types of data relevant for management planning and decision making.

Forecasts of future *interest rates* over the planning horizon represent the second major type of required input data. These interest rate forecasts must be made for the various types and maturities of relevant assets, liabilities, and capital items. These forecasts enter the model both directly (as revenue inflows and expense outflows) and indirectly (as the major determinant of capital gain and loss factors). There are at least two ways of forecasting interest rates: from subjective judgments on the part of management or designated experts, and by utilizing econometric techniques. In the latter case, if one accepts the validity of either the expectations hypothesis or the liquidity preference theory, the term structure of interest rates presently observed in the market can be used to forecast future yield curves.

A third major data input to the model are forecasts of future *loan demand.* As discussed above, these will ultimately be transformed into flow rate form. In practice, the natural tendency of the banking community is to conceive of loan demand in terms of stocks rather than flows. In order to convert this type of "stock" thinking into the relevant "flow" form, it is necessary to understand the nature of the underlying dynamics. This understanding cannot be obtained from data normally available. Information must be collected on the rates at which new loans are made and maturing loans are repaid. Finally, the forecasts of future loan demand which are used as input to the linear programming model should incorporate the implicit assumption that the bank's loan performance during the planning horizon will exert a neutral effect upon its market shares. Proper allowance for these market shares being altered by the loan-related feedback mechanisms should already be reflected in the model's constraints.

Fourth, forecasts of future levels of *deposits* within the planning horizon must be made. These forecasts should also assume neutral effects on market shares of loan performance.

The final type of input data consists of forecasts of the *exogenous variables* affecting funds availability, capital requirements, etc. Even though asset management plays a focal role in the bank, the model's decision variables exclude some activities. Because these excluded areas may influence the bank's capital and funds available, the one-way effects of these exogenous variables must be represented.

Economic considerations indicate that the various types of input data discussed above are highly interdependent. The covariabilities inherent in economic variables must be realistically embodied in the forecasts if the model is to produce sensible asset management results. It should be noted that the input data to the linear programming model should *not* be seasonally adjusted. To the extent that there are recurrent seasonal patterns, however, these should be utilized in the forecasting process.

Nature of results

One of the major benefits of analytical models of the type presented here is that sensitivity analyses are easily performed. Thus, the extent to which the indicated asset management decisions are sensitive to possible forecast errors can be discovered by systematically altering inputs and rerunning the model. In this way, management attention can be focused upon the critical variables, thereby sharpening understanding of the uncertainties which exist. When traditional asset management methods are employed, a considerable amount of executive attention is devoted to endless and heated debates concerning the effects of possible future economic developments. Whether different assumptions about the course of the economy really imply different current actions can be readily assessed through comparative runs of the linear programming model. Thus, one of the important contributions of the model stems from its ability to indicate the crucial factors upon which management attention should be focused. It thereby helps to avoid unnecessary floundering upon the sea of uncertainty concerning factors which in the last analysis are essentially unimportant.

Two major categories of output are produced by the linear programming model: (a) the direct values for the decision variables, and (b) the dual solution. The direct solution can easily be transformed into a sequence of balance sheet positions for the bank throughout the planning horizon. Major attention, of course, will be focused upon the target portfolios indicated for the first period, for these are the factors utilized in determining the bank's present asset management posture. While the implied decisions for a later period within the planning horizon are of less immediate use, they still may provide valuable insights for longer-range planning purposes.

Perhaps of even greater importance is the information provided by the dual solution to the model. The dual solution indicates the incremental benefits associated with a marginal relaxation of any of the model's constraints. Thus, by suitable utilization of the dual variables, one can determine the marginal rate of return on capital, the maximum interest rate one can pay for additional certificates of deposit, the opportunity costs associated with various management policies, and so forth.

Experience with the model

Since everyone thinks in terms of his own ill-specified and implicit model, a common basis for understanding and communication often does not exist unless it is supplied by an explicit analytical model. When attempting to reach asset management decisions through conventional procedures, the opinions of the most forceful, rather than the most insightful, speakers often carry the day. One of the major contributions provided by a model like that presented above is the concrete way in which it exposes assumptions employed about the banking environment, the inter-relationships among relevant variables, and the forecasts of future economic conditions. Thus, a common frame of reference is established for all participants in asset management meetings. It can be observed that this is a major, although perhaps subtle and unheralded, advantage of implementing such a model in a bank.

An additional subtle advantage of the model is that it makes operational the concept of a "target portfolio," i.e., of an "ideal" balance sheet toward which the bank should strive. The existence of target portfolios can usefully serve as guiding principles in the day-to-day decisions of line managers. Without these targets, short-run decisions will instead be made on an *ad hoc*—and possibly inconsistent—basis. Hence, the use of the model in a bank helps substitute rational planning for the traditional "fire-fighting" procedures utilized by bank managers.

Another use of the output provided by the linear programming model is as an important component in a responsibility accounting system. Since for this purpose marginal, rather than average, valuations are required, the information provided by the dual solution to the model is immediately applicable in the design of such a system.

Perhaps the most important strategic use of the model, however, is in generating new portfolio strategies which would otherwise have gone unnoticed. As already indicated, the dual solution to the model can be used to determine the marginal rate of return on capital. Both in an illustrative example provided by Chambers and Charnes and in at least one dramatic instance in actual practice, the indicated marginal rate of return on capital was far higher than expected. At the margin, earnings on capital can arise from two different sources. First, a direct return stems from investing the additional capital in earning assets. Second, an indirect return arises when additional capital permits shifts to take place in the planned composition of assets. Funds which otherwise would have been invested in lower-yielding, more liquid assets will instead be switched into higher-yielding, less liquid alternatives. This secondary effect will arise when the risk constraints (i.e., the capital adequacy criteria) are binding. In practice, it is often found that this secondary (recomposition) effect contributes far more to the magnitude of the marginal yield on capital than does the direct (investment) effect.

The secondary effect must also be considered when attempting to determine the costs associated with foreseeable reductions in sources of funds, e.g., losses of deposits or retirement of capital notes. The level of planned assets must be reduced to meet the anticipated net decrease in liabilities. Both direct and secondary costs are incurred when planned holdings of assets must be curtailed.[13] The direct costs include both the opportunity loss from the reduced income stream and the net capital loss associated with sales of assets. In order to obtain an optimal portfolio balance, however, it may also be necessary to reconstitute the asset mix. Thus, secondary costs are incurred to the extent that the yield on the asset portfolio is thereby changed. If one employs the "imputed rate" approach discussed above to incorporate into the linear programming model the effects of loan-related feedback mechanisms, the imputations used should reflect both the direct and secondary cost components.

In summary, this paper describes an important new tool now available for bank asset management. The linear programming model includes comprehensive risk constraints, various policy considerations, economic

[13] Each component of cost, of course, may be either positive or negative.

and institutional realities of the marketplace, and a variety of different dynamic effects which must be considered in order to make optimal asset management decisions. Conceptual problems concerning the formulation of the bank's goals are considered. The paper concludes with a discussion of some important implications of the model and the way in which it has been successfully implemented and utilized by the management of a major New York commercial bank.

Linear Programming and Optimal Bank Asset Management Decisions:

Discussion

H. Martin Weingartner

Messrs. Cohen and Hammer are to be congratulated for they have not given us the usual kind of progress report but the report of an *implemented* decision model. Thus they have presented a model which has been accepted and used by the top management of a bank, and this is a noteworthy accomplishment. To achieve it they have had to work with and educate the management of a non-technical firm, and to learn from it those rules and constraints which serve until a more fundamental understanding of the complex economic environment of the business is attained. In my remarks I wish to point out or emphasize some of the features which this audience might otherwise overlook, and also, without detracting from their paper, to suggest problems and methods for dealing with them.

The asset management problem encompasses and integrates almost the full range of decisions faced by a bank's top management. To develop a cohesive corporate strategy for resource allocation requires pulling together the ramifications of the alternatives for each of the components: commercial loans, installment credit, trust department operations, the

Reprinted with permission from *The Journal of Finance,* May 1967.

investment portfolio and levels of demand and time deposits. To capture the interrelationships in committee is virtually an impossible task.

Use of a formal model in this application has a number of non-economic advantages. In building the model each department of the bank brings to bear its expertise on only those aspects it is qualified to handle. This activity is substantially decentralized, as is also the forecasting function, which can similarly be performed by each department for its own variables. Further, obtaining an optimal decision involves application of the model and there is no need to second-guess the purely logical process of deduction. Once the structure has been agreed upon, only the question of the model's applicability needs to be raised and that only under unusual circumstances. The model thus serves as a powerful device for communication. When decisions are agreed upon by the members of the asset management committee, the assumptions regarding the component parts are all "on the table," and there is a more nearly common understanding of the problem and its solution by all the participants.

It may be useful to focus on some problems or questions concerning the structure of the model for asset management insofar as it can be inferred from this non-technical description. The basic set of constraints on resource allocation arises from legal regulation and supervision of all commercial banks except those state banks not insured by the FDIC. (These excluded banks are few in number and may be disregarded here.) The legal provisions relating to bank solvency and liquidity take the form of laws and regulations which govern individual or sets of related transactions such as the limit on loans to any single borrower, and other rules which apply to categories of bank assets. Some of these are mandatory, such as the allowable ratio of mortgage loans to deposits while others (such as tests for liquidity) are qualitative in nature and are enforced mostly by persuasion through exercise of the supervisory function over bank managements by these regulatory agencies. The tests for liquidity in particular (which are reduced to a set of "scores"), are used in the model for stating limits on the composition of the bank's total asset portfolio.

The criteria for liquidity and capital adequacy of the Federal Reserve were first applied to the bank asset management problem by Chambers and Charnes [1]. As pointed out by them, these measures are only "aids to the exercise of judgment, to be tempered by consideration of the quality of a bank's management, the importance of its trust department and the nature of the community in which it operates"; nevertheless, they use them as "a statement of the limits of what is regarded as good banking practice." [1]

Cohen and Hammer observe that these criteria are too conservative and in any case not mandatory, and so to offset this condition, they utilize the constraints only after substituting their own set of coefficients. The question, nevertheless, remains whether tests improvised for control pur-

[1] See [1] pp. 394–395.

poses in bank supervision have the appropriate *form* for use in planning. Admittedly, their use may only serve during an intermediate phase, until more appropriate constraints can be formulated. If this is so, a minor question arises as to whether the constraints are potentially violated to a substantial extent between those future dates on which they serve as constraints. More important, however, it may be more appropriate to express them as chance constraints,[2] in which case it is not necessary that they be planned to hold with certainty, but rather only with a specified (presumably high) probability.

In general, the model does not explicitly provide for the problems of uncertainty. Presumably this difficulty is handled only on an interim basis by use of general sensitivity analysis, which is a computationally difficult stop-gap. For example, the model is probably sensitive to forecasts of interest rates and loan demand, among other variables. Lacking certainty equivalents for these requires compensating explicitly for forecast errors and the evaluation of risk in terms of the consequences if forecasts are not met.[3] Even as it stands, the model requires rules to determine when recomputation is called for. When the environment changes continually, it may not be adequate to run the model only at stated intervals. Although at each recomputation only the current variables must be implemented while those with future dates can be reconsidered before they become current, the implied zigs and zags still could be potentially costly since the model does not explicitly value stability, or, alternatively, the cost of making adjustments is not part of an explicitly dynamic formulation.

A final point concerns the alternative objective functions used by Cohen and Hammer with their model. Their somewhat apologetic tone is understandable both because of the difficulty in getting their points across to management, and in terms of the problems of measuring the appropriate discount rate for evaluating future benefits. As an alternative in this situation they might consider using what have been called "position constraints" [4]—minimum conditions imposed by an ongoing firm to express its ability to survive or other constraints that enable it to grow in the future. These can be handled parametrically as, for example, in [5], or in ways similar to lexicographic utility functions as in [6].

While some of these and other modifications may already be on the way this model, which has been applied to a decision problem by a large bank, is clearly a formidable accomplishment.

REFERENCES

1. D. Chambers and A. Charnes, "Inter-Temporal Analysis and Optimization of Bank Portfolios," *Management Science,* Vol. 7, No. 4 (July 1961), pp. 393–410.

[2] See e.g., [2] or [4].

[3] On incorporation of risk in a related application, see for example [3].

2. A. Charnes and S. Thore, "Planning for Liquidity in Financial Institutions," *Journal of Finance,* Vol. 21, No. 4 (December 1966), pp. 649–674.
3. A. S. Kahr and C. R. Wolfe, "Normative Analysis for Selection of Commercial Bank Investments," paper presented at the San Francisco Meeting of the Econometric Society in December 1966.
4. R. Byne, A. Charnes, W. W. Cooper and K. Kortanek, "A Chance-Constrained Approach to Capital Budgeting," paper presented at the San Francisco Meeting of the Econometric Society in December 1966. [Graduate School of Industrial Administration, Carnegie Institute of Technology, Management Science Report No. 95.]
5. H. M. Weingartner, "Criteria for Programming Investment Project Selection," *Journal of Industrial Economics,* Vol. 15, No. 1 (November 1966), pp. 65–76.
6. J. Encarnacion, "Constraints and the Firm's Utility Function," *Review of Economic Studies,* Vol. 31 (April 1964), pp. 113–120.

6

The Regulatory Framework: Implication and Innovations

Banks operate in a regulatory environment that has evolved through time—often in response to crises in American banking. The resulting patchwork of various restrictions and regulations has constrained the flexibility and innovative possibilities of bank managers.

The first two articles are provocative analyses of important regulations and their implications for bank management and public policy. Almarin Phillips demonstrates how effective competition in banking is constrained by regulatory actions and attitudes and also by institutional and behavioral patterns of bankers. He then advocates important changes in regulatory policy to stimulate more effective competition in banking. The article by Donald Jacobs analyzes the background and implications of the existing regulatory framework and contrasts this framework to a prototype of a minimally regulated banking system.

Two related articles by the Federal Reserve Bank of Chicago consider the question of competition in banking. The first examines the issues involved while the second surveys recent empirical studies that have attempted to measure possible relationships between banking structure and performance. Findings of such studies are important for public policy and bank management strategies.

Changes in banking structure are closely associated with public policy toward bank mergers. Legislative actions and legal decisions in this area have been very controversial in recent years. The article by Edward G. Guy surveys the issues involved in recent bank merger legislation.

Extensive regulatory supervision of bank portfolio policies is often justified as necessary to ensure sound banking and to protect depositors. However, these objectives are largely served by the deposit insurance program of the Federal Deposit Insurance Corporation. In a stimulating essay, Thomas Mayer proposes a graduated deposit insurance plan and contends that adoption of such a plan would reduce the need for regulatory controls.

The concluding sequence of articles and policy statements outlines the rise and demise of short-term promissory notes as a source of funds for banks. This episode dramatically demonstrates how banks must anticipate and adapt to a continually changing regulatory environment.

Competition, Confusion, and Commercial Banking*

Almarin Phillips

The recent interest in competition in the commercial banking industry is a strange turn of events. Not long ago it was customary to refer to banking as one of the "regulated" industries—an industry in which competition had to be restricted by public authority to preserve the liquidity of the payments mechanism and to provide safety for depositors. Competitive (or antitrust) policy, it was thought, had very limited applicability to banking because of its regulated character.[1]

Rather suddenly, competition in banking has emerged as an ostensibly relevant public policy consideration. What some have regarded as a "wave" of mergers and holding company formations is in part responsible.[2] Fears of monopoly and of a substantial lessening of competition have arisen with regard to an industry which hitherto few had regarded

* This paper was prepared while the author was serving as a consultant to the Banking Markets Unit, Division of Research and Statistics, Board of Governors of the Federal Reserve System. The paper is not an official project of that Unit and the views expressed are those of the author. Thanks are due to Tynan Smith, George R. Hall, and Robert C. Holland, all of the Board staff, and to James R. Schlesinger for many helpful comments.

[1] See, for example, Adolf A. Berle, "Banking Under the Antitrust Laws," *Columbia Law Review,* vol. 49 (1949). As recently as 1959, Carl Kaysen and Donald F. Turner classed commercial banks among those industries for which conventional antitrust policy was inapplicable. See their *Antitrust Policy: An Economic and Legal Analysis* (Cambridge, Mass., 1959), pp. 42–43, 291. For a brief discussion of regulations, see *National Banks and Future,* Report of the Advisory Committee on Banking to the Comptroller of the Currency (Washington, 1962).

[2] The recent "wave" has been an increasing one. In the 1940's, the average annual number was 81. For the period 1950–1959, the average number was 150. Since the passage of the Bank Merger Act of 1960, the rate has been about 160 per year. These rates, however, are far below those of the late 1920's. See Charlotte P. and David A. Alhadeff, "Recent Bank Mergers," *Quarterly Journal of Economics,* vol. 69 (November 1955); *Annual Report of the Comptroller of the Currency* (Washington, 1960); *Annual Report of the Federal Deposit Insurance Corporation* (Washington, 1960, 1961, 1962).

Reprinted with permission from *The Journal of Finance,* March 1964.

as competitive in the first place. Congress responded with the Bank Holding Company Act of 1956 and the Bank Merger Act of 1960. The Department of Justice has brought Sherman and Clayton Act charges, and the courts—*because* of the regulations rather than *irrespective* of them—have found that commercial banking is to be treated as any other industry under the basic antitrust laws.[3]

In this paper, I shall argue on the one hand that commercial banking markets are typically not competitive enough to assure the efficient social performance of the industry. Evidence will be offered to demonstrate certain inefficiencies of the present banking structure which suggest the need for more intensive competition.

On the other hand, it will be contended that the existing complex of public policies with respect to banking, given the character of the industry, makes it quite impossible to achieve through conventional antitrust policies a type of competition which would be conducive to significantly improved performance. Public regulation and private organizational and institutional market characteristics make the performance of the industry insensitive to differences in market structure. As a result, orthodox policies aimed at maintaining or increasing competition by controlling the banking structure—as, for example, by preventing mergers—verge on the metaphorical "tilting at windmills." The performance of the industry will not be much affected by such policies so long as the regulatory and institutional characteristics remain unchanged.

The performance of banking markets could be improved, however. To achieve this, the most important changes in public policy would involve a relaxation of regulations and supervision to encourage more freedom of decision-making for *individual* banks, and to permit market forces to reward efficiency and to penalize inefficiency. The prohibition of such private competitive restraints as are inimical to the efficient functioning of the industry is also in order.

Paradoxically, it appears that, while the prevention of mergers cannot do much to maintain or increase competition, the increase in market rivalry signaled by changes in market organization would *foster* mergers and other types of consolidations. One of the virtually certain results of policies aimed at improving performance would be a slow but significant reduction in the number of banks in the country. This reduction in number would reduce the amount of inefficiency in banking but, because of the oligopolistic and locally-monopolistic structure of banking markets, because of remaining regulations, and because of the private organization of the industry, active price competition cannot and likely should not be achieved.

[3] *United States v. Philadelphia National Bank*, 374 U.S. 321 (1963). In addition several Sherman Act cases alleging conspiracy in restraint of trade have been brought.

THE EVIDENCE OF INADEQUATE COMPETITION

Competition is desirable because of its effects on market performance and the allocation of scare resources. Bankers, as is true of other businessmen, will not be persuaded by the academic scribbler who charges that competition does not prevail.[4] For to them—understandably—competition appears primarily as rivalry with other banks and financial institutions and in concern over profits, market shares, and growth. The relationship between competition and efficient resource allocation is not their concern.

Assessing the degree of competition in a specific industry is typically difficult. With respect to commercial banking, however, the evidence is unusually persuasive, attesting really to the effectiveness of public policy in preventing the types of competition which would produce bank failures and market instability. Thus, the principal evidence consists of: (1) the low failure rate and general stability in the structure of the industry; (2) the persistence of firms of less than the optimal scale; and (3) price performance which is inconsistent with the results of multilateral market competition.

Stability of the banking structure

During the ten years 1953–1963, there were only 91 voluntary bank liquidations and suspensions in an industry composed initially of about 14,000 firms.[5] Some of the liquidations may not have reflected adverse operating results. During the same period, there were 1,669 bank disappearances through mergers and absorptions, a small portion of which may have been motivated by "failing firm" considerations, but most of which occurred for other reasons. Thus, the rate of forced withdrawal from the banking industry has been remarkably low compared with other industries characterized by a large number of geographically dispersed firms.[6] Banking has either been blessed with exceptionally able management which has prevented withdrawals due to shifts in market conditions, inefficiency and management errors or, more likely, has been afforded some shelter from dynamic market forces. Bank failure, in itself, is of course not a goal of effective competition, but the risk of failure and, often, a turnover of firms are concommitants of competition. The

[4] For example, see the discussion of competition in *The Commercial Banking Industry,* American Bankers Association (New York, 1962), Ch. 1.

[5] "Changes in Banking Structure, 1953–1962," *Federal Reserve Bulletin* (September 1963).

[6] The rate of failure—and of new entrants—of retail and wholesale firms are many times this rate. For all industrial and commercial firms the failure rate is about 60 per month per 10,000 concerns.

higher bank failure rates prior to recent decades—and prior to extensive regulation and supervision—illustrate this point.[7]

The low failure rate is especially interesting in view of the size distribution of banks. Of the 12,933 insured commercial banks in existence at the end of 1962, 7,370 of them had total deposits of less than $5,000,000.[8] At the other extreme, only 314 banks had deposits of more than $100,000,000; 64 had deposits of over $500,000,000. The size distribution is highly skewed.

The same sort of distribution exists in many local and regional markets. In Chicago, for example, there were 154 banks in 1960, with the largest three having 48.1 per cent of total deposits. Similar figures for New York are 51 banks and 49.0 per cent; Philadelphia, 21 banks and 63.7 per cent; San Francisco, 18 banks and 50.6 per cent.[9] In these cities—and in many smaller ones—small banks frequently operate side-by-side with larger ones without apparent tendencies for the larger to force the smaller from the market. Larger banks, even without economies of scale, must possess some potential competitive advantage because of their greater assets and advantageous cross-elasticity of demand relationships. It would be expected, in other words, that without private or public sanctions moderating and rationalizing price rivalry, or without product differentiation sufficient to accomplish the same thing, there would tend to be more failures, especially among the smaller firms.

Scale economies

In effectively competitive markets, firms of less or greater than optimum scale are forced to make scale changes or to fail—though not necessarily in a short period of calendar time. It has become a commonplace, but certainly not an empirically proven fact, that there are economies of scale in banking.[10] In view of the conceptual difficulties involved in defining bank output, in treating product-mix and in separating the effects of branch and holding company operations in measuring scale, it is unlikely that the precise extent of these economies will be unearthed for some time to come. Nonetheless various estimates suggest that the economies are substantial up to at least $5,000,000 in deposits, and then perhaps plateau over size ranges up to the very largest of banks.[11] If it is

[7] Anticipating a later argument, the consequences of these failures raise questions as to whether competition can be tolerated in banking.

[8] *Annual Report of the Federal Deposit Insurance Corporation* (1962), p. 134.

[9] Data developed in the Banking Markets Unit, Board of Governors of the Federal Reserve System, based on the principal county (or counties) of the cities, not on the entire S.M.S.A.

[10] David A. Alhadeff, *Monopoly and Competition in Banking* (Berkeley, 1954); Lyle E. Gramley, *Scale Economies in Banking* (Kansas City, 1962). But see also Paul Horvitz, "Economies of Scale in Banking," an unpublished paper for the Committee on Money and Credit, which questions the existence of economies of scale.

[11] David A. Alhadeff, *Monopoly and Competition in Banking*.

true that economies extend only to the $5,000,000 deposit size, there would remain some 57 per cent of all commercial banks of less than optimal scale. If the economies extend to larger sizes, the percentage is even higher.

Such global figures may be misleading. In the first place, as of the end of 1962, 7,705 banks outside of metropolitan areas operated in one-bank towns.[12] Many of the smaller-than-optimum banks are found in this group. In some one-bank towns, the breadth of the market may be so restricted that the optimum scale cannot be achieved. Second, since the economies (or diseconomies) of branching operation and of the scale of branches are unknown, it could be argued that many of these small banks are still the most efficient of the alternatives practically available, and that no lack of competition is indicated.

This counter argument is not entirely convincing. While the breadth of the market in many towns may preclude even a single bank of optimum scale, competition would allow no more than one such bank. Yet, at the end of 1962, 1,800 banks operated in two-bank towns and 362 banks operated in three-bank towns.[13] Many of these banks are smaller than the apparent optimum, and market forces which foster the growth of one of them at the expense of the others are rarely observed. In addition, the fairly rapid development of branch operations in the wake of legislative changes in states such as Virginia and New York, and the premiums paid for the acquisition of small banks, especially where *de novo* entry is barred, are evidence that, at least in some types of operations, branch banking is more efficient than is unit banking.

Price behavior

For some industries, the behavior of prices is used as a prime indicator of the degree of competition. To be useful for this purpose, price data on individual transactions are typically necessary and very little of this sort of data is available for banks. The Federal Reserve's *Business Loan Surveys* of 1955–1957 and its quarterly *Survey of Short-Term Business Loans* contain limited data on interest rates charged on individual commercial loans, but no full scale analysis of the competitive implications of these surveys has been released.[14] For rates on other types of loans, and for rates paid on time deposits, for checking account service charges, and other miscellaneous prices, all one has for individual banks is published announcements—from which there are frequent deviations—and collected personal experience.

With these caveats, what can be said? First, it can be observed that

[12] "Changes in Banking Structure, 1953–1962," *Federal Reserve Bulletin* (September 1963).

[13] "Changes in Banking Structure, 1953–1962," *Federal Reserve Bulletin* (September 1963).

[14] Reference is made below to some unpublished studies.

individual banks charge different rates to different customers for what seem to be the same type and size of loan. These may be due in part to different risk factors and to other dimensions of the product being sold—the type of collateral, the timing of repayments, the amount of compensating balances required, etc. One gains the suspicion, however, that these factors would not account for the existing variance in rates,[15] and that the bank and individual customers are, in fact, in bilateral rather than openly competitive bargaining postures. The customer with the greater alternatives, including the alternative of not borrowing because of his excellent financial standing, is apt to get lower rates than the customer with fewer or no alternatives. To the extent that this is true, the bank can, within limits, operate as a discriminating monopolist.

The alternatives available to buyers would certainly be greater were they willing and able to "shop" among banks and other financial institutions for the best terms. If this occurred in substantial proportions, the variance in rates charged by individual banks for particular types of loans would tend to be small and there would tend to be only small differences in rates among banks in the same market. In other words, the monopoly power of sellers is inversely related to the ability of customers to "shop."

The data on interest rate variations within and among banks are indicative, yet not proof, of very little actual "shopping" by bank customers. To some extent it may be necessary for the bank-customer relationship to be a continuing one, but it also seems obvious that banks discourage their customers from seeking alternative sellers in ways which lower the effective cross-elasticity of demand among banks.[16] As a result, different banks in the same city are able to charge different rates for ostensibly identical loans. Price competition, which tends to generate uniform prices for the same product in a given market, is not very strong.

It is arguable that the lack of competition displayed by interest rates is a result of structural problems in the industry. With the conventional hypotheses of market theory, one would anticipate that rates would be somewhat lower and possess less variance in markets in which the number of banks is large, no one bank is of dominant size, and the distribution of size is not highly skewed. One might also conjecture that unit banks offer more attractive rates than do branch system and holding company banks if these forms of organization create or are associated with monopoly power.

There is little to support such hypotheses in banking markets. In a study of short-term loans to business by large banks in 19 major cities, the Banking Markets Unit, Board of Governors of the Federal Reserve

[15] For example, rates charged on business loans of $1,000–$10,000 by a single bank at a given time ranged from 5 to 6.5 per cent according to the FRB quarterly *Survey of Short-Term Business Loans.*

[16] Cf. "Maintaining an Effective Bank Relationship," a speech by Charles A. Agemian before the 1963 Eastern Area Conference of the Financial Executives Institute reported under "Required Reading," *American Banker* (August 5, 6, and 7, 1963).

System, has failed to find that market structure variables are associated with interest rates in any significant way. For small business loans ($1,000–$10,000)—a type of lending for which there are few alternatives outside of commercial banking—interest rates were found to vary significantly by the region of the country in which the cities covered by the study were located. After accounting for the regional effect, there was a slight but significant tendency for the rates charged by individual banks to decrease as the share of the market possessed by the bank increased.[17] The number of banks in the markets, the size of the largest bank, and the proportion of the market accounted for by the three largest banks, all possessed no explanatory value, even when checked for interaction effects.[18]

For large business loans ($200,000 and more), total variance in rates was found to be as large as that for the small loans. The regional influence was still significant—casting doubt on the idea that a truly national market exists for such loans. The larger banks tended to charge slightly but significantly lower rates than did the smaller banks. As with the small loans, the number of banks and the proportion of total deposits held by the three largest banks were not significant. There was no evidence that banks in a branching system charged rates different from those of unit banks.

[17] This may well be due to the larger banks selecting the higher quality loans.

[18] Mr. Frank Edwards, using data from the 1955 *Business Loan Survey,* reports a statistically significant but absolutely very small positive relationship between interest rates and concentration for 1955. Data for 1957 do not confirm this relationship. His study uses the average rate paid on business loans, including term loans, by city by asset size class of borrower as the dependent variable in a multiple correlation test. The study by the Banking Markets Unit uses the average rate paid on short-term business loans by bank by city. Variance in rates among banks within a city is thus included in the latter, but not in the Edwards study. It is possible that it is the inclusion of inter-bank as well as inter-city variances which causes concentration ratios to fail the tests of significance in the Banking Market Unit study. If this is the reason for the difference in findings, the conclusions based on total variance including inter-bank, intra-city variance seems to be the better. Edwards argues that the null results for 1957 are due to a "ceiling effect" which reduces total variance during periods of high interest rates. This argument would be as valid for 1960, the time of the FRB study, as for 1957.

It is interesting to note that the Supreme Court, in *United States v. Philadelphia National Bank,* was willing to conclude from simple and untested structural hypotheses that performance improves as the number of banks increases. "Specifically, we think that a merger which produces a firm controlling an undue percentage share of the relevant market and results in a significant increase in the concentration of firms in that market, is so inherently likely to lessen competition substantially that it must be enjoined in the absence of evidence clearly showing that the merger is not likely to have such anticompetitive effects." The Court, relying on Kaysen and Turner, *Antitrust Policy: An Economic and Legal Analysis,* and others, observed that "[C]ompetition is likely to be the greatest when there are many sellers, none of which has any significant market share." (374 U.S. 321, at 363).

Finally, in a smaller and admittedly less reliable study of small banks in several Minnesota towns, the Banking Markets Unit inquired into differences in interest rates depending on whether there were one, two or three banks in the town. The results indicated that the number of banks was unimportant in explaining rates charged even after the effects of loan mix, bank size, city size, level of income, and rate of change in city size and income were removed.[19] Interest rates paid on time deposits did not vary significantly with the number of commercial banks, but did tend to be higher in towns in which savings and loan associations were large relative to commercial banks. While neither rates charged nor rates paid varied significantly with size of bank, net earnings per dollar of earning assets tended to increase slightly as the size of banks increased. Net earnings per dollar of earning assets tended to decrease as the number of banks increased, implying—since neither rates charged nor rates paid varied significantly with number of banks—that the competition associated with numbers of banks may result in higher costs rather than lower prices.

PUBLIC REGULATION AND PRIVATE RATIONALIZATION OF COMPETITION

The apparent lack of strong price competition, the continued existence of many banks of less than optimal scale and the insensitivity of market performance to market structure are not difficult to explain. They arise because of a vastly complex system of public regulation and supervision working in conjunction with a well-developed, yet generally informal, private market organization.[20] Most of the public regulation appears in the guise of instruments designed to protect the safety of banks and the liquidity of the payments mechanism—that is, to prevent bank failures and banking practices which might lead to failures. Much, but not all, of the private rationalization of competition is a side effect of certain cooperative arrangements among bankers—clearing houses, loan participations, and correspondent relations, for example—which add to the efficiency of the system. The point is not that there are conscious efforts to arrange conspiracies in restraint of trade, but rather that public regulation has the express purpose and private organization has the necessary effect of producing essentially non-competitive results.

Since public regulation is not pervasive of all facets of bank operations, and the private organization is typically informal, their restraining effects may not be obvious in those market areas in which the number of banks is reasonably large and there is such a lack of concentration that the

[19] This is contrary to the findings of Irving Schweiger and John S. McGee, *Chicago Banking* (Chicago, 1961).

[20] See Donald R. Hodgman, *Commercial Bank Loan and Investment Policy* (Champaign, Illinois, 1963), pp. 158–160, for a similar view.

possibility of strong leadership is absent. As already noted, however, a substantial portion of all commercial banks operate in communities in which there are no more than three banks. The relevant market of some of these banks undoubtedly extends to areas outside their own communities, thus making the effective number of banks in the market larger than the community count of banks indicates. Still, to the extent that the geographic market for any bank service contains only a small number of sellers, conventional oligopoly theory is relevant. Without formal agreement and without direct communication concerning prices to be charged and market areas and customers to be served, tacit understandings quite similar to those which would be achieved by overt agreement are apt to arise. In the case of banks, the tacit understandings—which, parenthetically, may not be consciously recognized as such by the participants—are abetted by public regulation and supervision which helps to assure that no individual bank will behave in a way which would have a strong competitive impact on others.[21]

Public regulation

Very little of the public regulation of banks positively requires identical pricing. The most obvious instances relate not to output prices—rates charged—but to the prices paid for inputs—rates paid for funds. Here regulations require that no interest be paid on demand deposits and establish an upper limit to interest paid on time deposits. Until recent years, the latter was low enough so that the maximum rate was also typically the actual rate, though this is no longer so generally true.[22]

Control of input prices may have profound effects on the degree of competition for output. There have been numerous instances in industrial markets in which an anti-competitive pricing system for output developed and was maintained through the control of input prices. The crux of the *Socony Vacuum* case[23] was that major oil companies agreed to purchase "hot oil" and gasoline refined from this oil in an effort to prevent some of themselves and independent, non-integrated, companies from having significantly different costs. Without the condition of equal costs, the tacit agreement to follow the output price leadership of Standard of Indiana tended chronically to breakdown. Other cases in which cost identity was important in rationalizing output competition

[21] See Donald R. Hodgman, *Commercial Bank Loan and Investment Policy,* pp. 116–135, 159–160, for an excellent discussion of the "administered" and oligopolistically set New York prime rate and its effects in restraining competition. See also David C. Motter, "Bank Mergers and Public Policy," *National Banking Review,* vol. 1 (September 1963), p. 96, especially fn. 23.

[22] See Caroline H. Cagle, "Interest Rates on Time Deposits, Mid-February 1963," *Federal Research Bulletin* (June 1963).

[23] *United States v. Socony-Vacuum Oil Co.,* 310 U.S. 150 (1940).

can be found in the beet sugar,[24] milk distribution,[25] and cigarette[26] industries.

In banking, it would be unwarranted to conclude that the regulation of interest paid on deposits creates a tight system of collusive output prices. However, they have—purposely—been instrumental in the general moderation of competition. The regulations prevent considerable price competition for funds, both among banks and between banks and other financial institutions. One consequence has been the prevention of what would otherwise have been a form of cost-increasing rivalry for funds and, for this reason, the erection of a protective shield for the less efficient and often smaller banks. In addition, the lack of competition for funds has been an important ingredient in eliminating cost differences which, especially in local markets, would be apt to get translated into more active competition in the output market. Banks, being unable to attract customers by paying higher rates on deposits, have had no alternative but to use non-price forms of rivalry. The resulting product differentiation—based on location, convenience, advertising, loan accommodations, etc.—have likely reduced the desire and ability of customers to shop among banks. The expenses involved in advertising and the proliferation of branches may in some instances have resulted in higher bank operating costs than would prevail with more rate competition. Moreover, since even the most aggressive banks have been restricted in their ability to use deposit rates as a competitive weapon, tacit understandings to compete only with non-price techniques are made more viable. In short, the regulations tend to create more identical "value systems" among banks and, hence, to prevent the outbreak of open price rivalry.[27]

Similar tendencies for an identity of value systems arise from other aspects of regulation. Only a few of the regulations go directly to prices and terms for deposits and loans. Most have a more subtle effect. Limitations on mortgage lending and ownership of stocks, along with supervisory rules governing the risk asset ratio, standards for lending, and for accounting procedures, make for similar asset compositions and for similar views with respect to "sound" banking practices. Bankers, that is, are encouraged to conform to an established and, in many respects, non-competitive pattern of market behavior.

Finally, state and Federal regulations prevent various forms of entry into the markets of existing banks. Whether nationally or state chartered, banks cannot establish branches across state lines even though the economic market does not accord with these political boundaries. With

[24] *Mandeville Island Farms, Inc. v. American Crystal Sugar Co.,* 334 U.S. 219 (1948).

[25] *Pevely Dairy Co. v. United States,* 178 F.2d 363 (8th Cir. 1949).

[26] *American Tobacco Co. v. United States,* 328 U.S. 781 (1946).

[27] For a more complete discussion of the role of differences in costs and other aspects of "value systems" of firms on competition, see Almarin Phillips, *Market Structure, Organization and Performance* (Cambridge, Mass. 1962), pp. 32–40.

respect to both entry by new banks and entry by existing banks through merger or *de novo* branching, the "adequacy" of the existing banks to meet the convenience and needs of the market is considered. The question of convenience and needs of a market very often reduces to the question of whether existing banks would be injured if they shared their market with another, not to whether there are economic reasons for the establishment of a new bank. These regulations facilitate tacit market sharing and reduce the likelihood that "maverick" bankers—those who might upset the status quo of a market—will enter.

The entry problem is a more difficult one in banking than in other industries, however. Entry performs its valuable role in allocating resources efficiently because of its effects on long-run supply. While in local markets a new bank may increase supply and tend to force down prices (if the new bank does not adopt the same non-competitive behavior of the existing banks), in the aggregate the total supply of bank credit is loosely fixed by monetary authority. For the entire economy, more banks do not mean a larger total supply in the same sense as is the case in other industries, or in the same sense as they do for local and regional bank markets. Rather, if the number of banks increases and supply of bank credit is fixed, the size of the average bank decreases and, assuming the existence of scale economies, the system moves away from the most efficient allocation of resources. If the competitive force of new entrants is to be relied upon to achieve efficiency, free entry in banking must take the two-way meaning attached to it in competitive theory—freedom of entrance and freedom of exit (failure or forced disappearance through merger). Forced exit, of course, is precisely what regulation and supervision, including restrictions on entry, are designed to prevent. As a result, the banking structure has responded very slowly to inefficient operations and to geographical shifts in demand.

Private organization

Public regulation is not the only source of rationalized competition among banks. It may not be even the primary source. The rationalization which comes from the organizational and institutional aspects of banks themselves is more difficult to see but probably no less important.

The informal organization of oligopoly in local markets was mentioned above. There are also several more formal types of horizontal relations. Of these, the clearing house is the most familiar. Its function of clearing balances is a necessary one, but one which does not require either the ownership of or active participation in the clearing house by the member banks. The functions beyond those of clearing which are performed are something of a mystery to any save the members, but no one would be surprised if matters such as hours of business, service charges on checking accounts, and perhaps even interest rates charged and paid, were occasionally discussed.

Commercial banking, as other industries, has its trade associations—local, regional, state and nationwide bankers associations. These associations undoubtedly perform valuable informational and educational services. They also provide a forum for communication among bankers and an opportunity for those high in the organizational hierarchy—the leaders of the industry—to make known their views on sundry subjects. This sort of communication can hardly result in formal conspiracy among bankers; there are too many members in the group, the subject matter is too complex, and the disciplinary power is too weak. Still, the associations have their purpose. When problems arise, established channels of communication are available. And communication, especially when it comes from those at the top of a power hierarchy, tends to facilitate conflict resolution. Perhaps a great deal should not be made of this, but competition is a form of conflict and, in the present context, conflict resolution is a form of restraint on competition. If nothing more, the communication makes it easier to know what is expected of a "good" banker; easier to conform to "sound" banking practice.

In addition to horizontal relations there is in the organization of banking an explicit vertical relationship among banks. It is found in correspondent banking. It is well-recognized that a system of vertical affiliations among firms may restrain competition. This is probably one effect of correspondent banking, but the restraint is perhaps a mild one. Unlike resale price maintenance, in which the vertical relations may operate in a manner identical to that which would occur with full, horizontal agreement among distributors, correspondent relations exert a less obvious influence. There is no commodity flowing from the correspondent to corresponding bank which is resold. And it is general practice that the several banks in one community correspond with different banks in others.

The correspondent system tends to pyramid from a large number of banks in small cities and towns upward to a smaller number of banks in a few larger cities and upward again to a small number of banks in one or a few financial centers. Detailed knowledge of the full role played by correspondent banks is lacking and generalizations are hazardous. It is known that corresponding comprises much more than a holding of deposit balances and a clearing operation. Services and information flow from correspondents to the corresponding banks, in a direction opposite to that of the deposits. These often include advice with respect to portfolio, credit advice, and a sort of management consulting service. There are, in addition, loan participations which alter the otherwise vertical relation to a horizontal one.

To reiterate, this does not completely foreclose competition. But, as argued above, the banks in each of the cities involved have an implicitly recognized community of interest which arises from their horizontal and frequently oligopolistic market relations. Even while banks in one town generally correspond with different banks in the city at the next level up, the horizontal relations at each level are such as to produce substantial uniformity of behavior. The correspondent relations provide another system of communication among banks and easy access to information which allows and encourages all the banks in the system to conform to established modes of behavior.

The unique combination of formal and informal organization in commercial banking—partly associated with public regulation and supervision and partly with private, institutional arrangements—explains the lack of competitive market performance and the failure of that performance to vary with the market structure. This organization is by far the most pervasive factor in determining performance. "Good" banking practices are equated with "quiet," non-price forms of rivalry in the view of both bankers and the regulatory agencies.

IMPROVING COMMERCIAL BANKING PERFORMANCE

It would be possible and, within limits, it probably is desirable to improve the performance of commercial banking markets. It appears, however, that the role of conventional antitrust policy—the prevention of mergers and combinations in restraint of trade—in achieving this result is an extremely limited one, because of the continuing necessity for some public regulation and supervision and also because of the impossibility of altering substantially the oligopolistic structure of the typical banking market.

The most obvious need for public intervention is to preserve the liquidity of the money supply which, in the absence of deposit insurance, requires supervision and regulations to prevent bank failures. With deposit insurance, the liquidity of the payments mechanism depends not on the liquidity and solvency of the banks themselves, but rather on the liquidity of those to whom the banks owe debts—the depositors—which it is the function of the insurance to maintain. Nonetheless, deposit insurance does not make possible the elimination of bank regulation and supervision. If the insuring agency did no more than examine banks for the purpose of discriminating in premiums on the basis of risk, *de facto* regulations would continue to exist. Moreover, given the highly leveraged position of bank capital and the liquidity of bank liabilities, continued supervision and regulation will be necessary to prevent systemic failures and their generally disrupting influence.

Regulation, then, will continue, but the nature of regulation requires modification. If it is accepted that the organization, rather than the structure, of the industry is the controlling variable in determining performance, it follows that the primary means of altering performance is through changing the organization, especially that part which emanates from regulations.

The most important single policy would be to permit freer entry. This would involve making new charters available on a less restrictive basis than is done on the current "needs and convenience" criterion, removing arbitrary limitations on *de novo* branching and branching by merger, and ending the prohibitions against branching over state lines. Efficient independent banks and those smaller banks which offer differential services for which there is market demand would not be forced from the market by these changes. Inefficient banks would have to improve their efficiency, merge, or fail; the market power of locally monopolistic or oligopolistic banks would be effectively constrained.

The elimination of restrictions on interest rates paid on deposits would be another important step. This, especially if accompanied by steps to equalize the reserve requirements of all banks, regardless of size,[28] would remove what amounts to protective subsidization of smaller banks. In addition, bank supervision could be modified to permit banks greater freedom in establishing their own credit and risk standards. Increased price competition would not likely arise from permitting banks to experiment with new types of credit or to specialize in particular lines, but there would be encouragement for a constructive type of non-price competition. Competition through advertising, promotion, and location would to some degree be supplanted by competition through new and improved loan and deposit services.

The removal of interest rate restrictions and the relaxation of regulations would also tend to reduce the number of banks. The increased cost of funds, while good for the industry as a whole and its relations with other financial institutions, would tend to increase operating costs. Some banks, because of the cost increase and because of management errors in the extension of credit, would experience operating difficulties; some would fail, perhaps to be absorbed by another bank or to be succeeded by a new firm.

These are not small changes in policy. Accomplishing them would require the establishment of a *national* policy for what should be a *national* industry. Uniform chartering and branching policies, uniform and less compulsory supervisory standards, uniform reserve requirements and free interstate banking would spell the end of the dual banking system as is now exists. Moreover, while the social benefits appear to merit such changes, they are radical enough to suggest that they should be accomplished in small steps over a period of years. The opposition of bankers to the proposals probably is assurance that no change will be rapid!

Finally, some sort of antitrust policy would still be necessary. While clearing houses, loan participations and correspondent relationships are necessary to the industry, there is no obvious reason why other horizontal and vertical combinations in restraint of trade should be accorded special Sherman Act exemption. That is, the private organization of the industry should be left intact except where it has no purpose other than

[28] Including for this purpose interbank deposits and vault cash in reserves.

to restrain trade. A necessary caution here is that the sometimes extremely difficult distinction must be made between those kinds of cooperative endeavors which are necessary because of the character and structure of the industry—and, hence, are "reasonable" restraints—and those which are unnecessary and operate to the detriment of society. This calls for the antitrust standard used by Judge Medina in the *Morgan* case [29] rather than the usual *per se* procedures for restraint of trade cases. Too, it should be recognized in antitrust proceedings that the classical type of atomistic competition cannot be made to prevail in banking markets. The most that can be sought is oligopolistic competition for differentiated products, constrained by freedom of entry and the ability of existing banks to innovate.

Similarly, while legislative barriers to mergers should be removed to encourage competition, competitive policy for the industry should, at the same time, include the prohibition of mergers and holding companies which may tend to lessen competition substantially. This is a difficult standard to apply, however, and even when enforcement is in the antitrust agencies—as it should be—rather than lodged with regulatory authorities, there is danger that the policy could evolve into the protection of small and inefficient competitors rather than a policy to promote competition.[30] An extremely strict merger policy would make it difficult to realize scale economies and the benefits of freer entry.

[29] *United States v. Morgan*, 118 F. Supp. 621 (S.D.N.Y. 1954).

[30] It can be argued that the trend of enforcement of the amended Section 7 of the Clayton Act has already turned in this direction. In particular, see *Brown Shoe v. United States*, 370 U.S. 294 (1962). *United States v. Philadelphia National Bank*, 374 U.S. 321 (1963) may have similar overtones despite the testimony of small bankers that they favored the merger. A more competitive market environment could easily alter their views.

The Framework of Commerical Bank Regulation:

An Appraisal

Donald Jacobs

In the hundred years since the passage of the National Currency Act substantial changes have occurred in the regulatory atmosphere surrounding commercial banking. On the whole the movement has been toward increased regulation, with the greatest impetus coming during periods of crisis. At the present time, changes in the bank regulatory apparatus and process are widely discussed, although no crisis has occurred since the depression of the 1930's. The absence of crisis should permit a more judicious appraisal of proposed changes in the regulatory structure.

In any economy some industry structure will evolve. Wherever consideration is given to any form of public control or public action, the issue arises as to whether the social benefits will exceed the social cost. This paper is concerned with regulations aimed at the operations of commercial banks, which, like other private business concerns in a free enterprise economy, are profit motivated. Regulations designed primarily to facilitate monetary policy are excluded from consideration. Such regulations are promulgated on a basis significantly different from the operational regulations under consideration.[1]

In the first section of this paper a prototype of a minimally regulated

[1] The mechanics of bank supervision are also omitted from this discussion. Admittedly, the supervisory apparatus for administering regulation is an important element in an evaluation of the framework. But that analysis is beyond the scope of this paper. For a discussion of the interaction between bank supervision and monetary policy, see G. L. Bach, "Bank Supervision, Monetary Policy, and Government Reorganization," *Journal of Finance,* IV, December 1949.

Reprinted with the permission of The Administrator of National Banks, United States Treasury, Washington, D.C., from *The National Banking Review,* March 1964.

system is developed. In the second section the rationale for regulation and the present regulatory structure are described. In the third section the current structure is compared to the minimally regulated system in an attempt to determine whether any parts of the present system are unnecessary. Branching restrictions, which are excluded from the second and third sections, are discussed and evaluated in the fourth section. The concluding section analyzes prospects for regulatory change.

THE FRAMEWORK OF A MINIMALLY REGULATED BANKING SYSTEM

The establishment of a perfectly competitive banking industry would require free entry into banking, including the establishment of branches as desired by the firms in the industry. No territorial limitations would be placed on branches. No control would be exercised over portfolio decisions, or bank operations. No overt capital requirements would be established.

If there are substantial economies of scale in banking, a competitive structure would not be viable, or it would be inefficient. Either a race for optimal size would result in some number of survivors less than that necessary to maintain competition, or the firms would engage in some form of collusion out of fear of the results of "cutthroat competition." [2] Neither result would lead to the "socially best" price.

Two studies bearing on economies of scale in banking have recently been published.[3] Both, utilizing multiple regression techniques, concluded that costs per dollar of assets fell as banks increased in size. Both of these important studies, however, assume that banks of all sizes service the same types of customers and make the same types of loans. Large banks, however, produce a substantially different product than do small banks. For example, many large banks have extensive tax departments and foreign departments, and supply correspondent services to small banks. Federal Reserve surveys show that large banks handle deposits and loans of a much greater average size than do small banks. Since the business of a small bank is different from the business of a large bank, the regression studies do not shed light on the question of economies of scale. The question of economies of scale is not whether large banks conduct their business more cheaply than small banks conduct theirs, but rather whether large banks conduct the business handled by small banks more economically than do the small banks. Therefore, the answer to this essential question has not been given by these studies.

[2] This statement is predicated purely on economic theory. If it is assumed that anti-trust policies are applied, the results will be less certain, since they will be determined by the form of the legislation and the manner in which it is enforced.

[3] Lyle E. Gramley, "A Study of Scale Economies in Banking," Federal Reserve Bank of Kansas City, November 1962; and Irving Schweiger and John S. McGee, "Chicago Banking," *The Journal of Business,* XXXIV, July 1961, pp. 203–366.

A recent study of banking in New England, using accounting data for unit banks, and for branch banks and unit banks which had been merged and converted to branches, concluded that for very small operations branches and unit banks have about equal costs, but, "in the case of moderate size banking offices, a branch can be operated at a somewhat lower cost than a unit bank, but the amount of saving is not as great as many proponents of branch banking have assumed." [4] This study was primarily aimed at comparing the operation of branch and unit bank structures; it does, however, offer suggestive evidence on economies of scale in banking.

One observes that in England and Canada, where nationwide branch banking is allowed, the commercial banking system is dominated by a few nationwide branch systems. This evidence might be construed as proof of the existence of economies of scale in banking, but it is certainly not conclusive. It is quite possible that inadequate monetary policy and the absence of deposit insurance were more important than economies of scale in causing the emergence of a small number of branch systems in these countries.

Another piece of evidence which may be taken to indicate economies of scale in banking in the United States is the wave of bank mergers in the period since the end of World War II. But other factors, such as management succession problems and the imperfect market for bank securities, are often said to be the overriding motive for recent bank mergers. Also, the possibility of lessened competition as a motive for mergers should not be overlooked. This is especially significant in view of the restrictions on new bank entry.

If banking is not characterized by declining costs as the scale of enterprise increases, it is possible, in theory, to maintain an unregulated competitive banking structure which will provide an efficient amount and allocation of resources devoted to banking services. However, free entry into the banking business and the abolishment of all regulations would not, alone, maintain the viability of such a system. Depositors are not in a position to evaluate the risk of loss of deposits as a result of the lack of capital or the loss potential of a bank. In the absence of deposit insurance, a market structure with large numbers of banks could not be maintained, because depositors would seek out the protection of prestigious banks. A new, unknown entrant would have a difficult time.[5]

[4] Paul M. Horvitz, *Concentration and Competition in New England Banking,* Research Report to Federal Reserve Bank of Boston, #2, 1958, pp. 119–128.

[5] It is often said that smaller and/or newer firms in any industry are in some degree at a competitive disadvantage as compared with larger and/or established firms in the industry. Market preferences built through time and cost of capital are usually mentioned as the major factors underlying this competitive disadvantage. This, however, does not preclude the establishment of a competitive industry. The validity of the need for an insuring agency to establish a competitive banking structure rests on a belief that there is much greater competitive maneuverability in the production and sale of most other products, compared to competition to attract deposits.

An institution such as the Federal Deposit Insurance Corporation is thus needed for the maintenance of a large number of banking institutions.

With deposit insurance, the majority of depositors can be largely indifferent to the strength of a bank's capital and management. However, without some controls, under deposit insurance a strong incentive would exist for persons with high risk preferences to go into the banking business. As bankers, they could operate with very high leverage, that is, with low capital-to-asset ratios. With a small amount of capital they could undertake high risks and, therefore, high-yield lending opportunities. If the loans paid off, they would receive handsome rewards. If losses occurred, they would lose the small amount of capital invested; but most of the loss would be borne by the insuring agency.

At present, insured commercial banks pay to the Federal Deposit Insurance Corporation a flat fee based on deposits. If this method of charge were used in the context of a system of free entry and no regulation or capital requirements, a bank with low capital and a high portfolio risk could be given a chance of gain without commensurate risk. Under such a system the insuring agency would have to be given some power to control risk exposure of its reserves, a power which at a minimum would require control over ratios of capital to risk for insurance eligibility.[6]

To summarize, if substantial economies of scale exist, a competitive banking system could not be established without regulation. Even if economies of scale do not preclude an unregulated system, the nature of the products and services performed by banks requires deposit insurance, in order that banks of various sizes may compete effectively in the same market. A viable banking system with a minimum amount of regulation would necessarily include some portfolio and/or capital-on-entry regulations to protect the solvency of the insurance fund.

It should be pointed out that at the present time the regulatory authorities do not consider the solvency of the insurance fund to be a major justification for these regulations. The regulations deemed necessary for the minimally regulated system now exist. Should the rationale presently used to justify these regulations be abandoned, the regulations would either be kept in use to protect the insurance fund or one of the consequences outlined above would occur.

THE PRESENT FRAMEWORK OF REGULATION

The underlying economic reasons for regulation of banks are twofold: to protect depositors; and to insure the economic well-being of the com-

[6] Probably the most elegant method for handling this problem in a free enterprise economy would be to make the insurance fee a function of the ratio of capital relative to risk exposure in the asset portfolio. This would make the basic decisions on capital structure, cost of capital, and capital budgeting the same in banking as it is in other industries.

mercial banking system, and hence of the economy at large.[7] Both of these basic purposes are, of course, closely intertwined.

Large depositors may be able to assess the adequacy of the protection offered by the equity of a bank. Small and medium size depositors ought not to be under the dictum of "investor beware." They do not generally have the time or the ability to assess adequately the risk of loss in banks of varying financial strength. Jeopardy of loss would cause small depositors to seek alternative places to hold their funds, an activity which would entail a large social loss.

A healthy commercial banking system is necessary for a well functioning economy. Commercial banks are the major medium through which money transfers are made. Such an agency is needed to facilitate the rapid, low-cost transfer of money. Commercial banks hold a large part of the liquidity of the nation. Should the banking system fail or falter, these liquid assets would be wiped out or impaired. Also, banks, in conjunction with other financial agencies, play an important role in the financial markets. Commercial lending to small and medium-sized firms is often considered to be their most important function. Banks are not alone in this area of lending activity, but they occupy a central and predominant position.

The economic importance of a healthy banking system and the need to protect depositor funds was vividly demonstrated by the events of the early 1930's. Depositor runs on banks and inadequate aid from the Federal Reserve to bolster bank liquidity needs led to a large decline in the money supply and much hoarding of cash reserves.

From the end of June 1929, to the end of June 1933, the number of commercial banks declined 43%, from 24,970 to 14,208; total deposits declined 35%, from $49.4 billion to $32.1 billion; and capital accounts declined from $8.8 billion to $6.3 billion, or 28%.[8] Serious concern arose over the ability of the commercial banking industry to perform efficiently, or even survive.

Rebuilding the capital position of commercial banks and ending the danger of rapid deposit withdrawals were the two major problems facing the banking authorities. However, the belief that "over-banking" was a major contributing factor to the serious plight of the commercial banking industry provoked regulations beyond those needed to deal with the capital and deposit withdrawal problems. Banking had been a heavily regulated industry even in the 1920's, but the regulatory apparatus was much expanded during the 1930's.

[7] These reasons do not encompass restrictions on branching, which are discussed in the fourth section. Moreover, the emphasis here is on the word "economic." Many presently existing regulations and supervisory controls are aimed at non-economic problems. For example, restrictions against self-dealing on the part of bank management is not dictated by economics, but rather by considerations of "equity."

[8] *All Bank Statistics, United States 1896–1955,* Board of Governors of the Federal Reserve System, Washington, D.C.: page 37.

To deal with the problem of bank runs, a federal program of deposit insurance was instituted.[9] The introduction of deposit insurance has had the desired effect. Of course, this does not mean that all possibility of large scale deposit runs has been eliminated; but in the 30 year period since the introduction of deposit insurance this phenomenon has been virtually non-existent.

Increasing the capital of banks is largely a problem of profitability, for if banks are profitable they can both sell stock when necessary and increase capital through earnings retention. Bank profitability is largely a function of the demand for funds. But, because the demand for bank credit is relatively inelastic with respect to interest, when interest rates are low, bank profitability is low, and when interest rates are high, bank profitability is high. It must be remembered that during the 1930's low interest rates prevailed. Therefore, under normal circumstances, low bank profitability was to be expected. This fact heightened the problem of rebuilding bank capital accounts.

Many regulations affect bank profitability, but most of these regulations also have other effects. Many existing regulations imposed originally as an aid to profitability are now retained and thought necessary to serve other regulatory purposes.

For convenience of discussion the existing regulatory framework may be divided into two broad categories: regulations governing entry; and regulations concerned with managing the operation of the going concern. The latter category may be further divided into two major parts: regulations influencing portfolio management; and regulations dealing with deposit acquisition.

Let us first consider the regulations governing entry. To start a bank, a charter must be obtained. These are coveted documents. Under the dual banking system that has evolved in the United States, bank charters are granted by authorities in each of the 50 states; in addition, the Comptroller of the Currency issues charters for national banks.

The 51 bank chartering authorities operate with varying regulations and use different tests and procedures in determining whether a charter is to be issued. For example, before a charter is issued for a new national bank, the Comptroller of the Currency conducts an exhaustive investigation into the background and financial position of the organizers of the proposed bank, the present banking facilities available to potential customers of the proposed bank, and the probable public need and acceptance of a new banking institution in the area. A bank examiner from the Comptroller's staff is charged with investigating in the locale of the proposed bank, and with drawing specific conclusions about the following factors: ". . . the potential of management, earning and deposit forecasts, public need, capital adequacy, location and the general com-

[9] The history of state insurance plans and proposals for federal insurance are described and analyzed in the 1950, 1952 and 1953 *Annual Report,* Federal Deposit Insurance Corporation, Washington, D.C.

petitive climate in which the new bank would exist." The Comptroller states that this last factor, competitive climate, is given much weight in deciding whether a charter will be issued.[10] Other chartering authorities follow similar investigatory procedures, but most probably use a much less elaborate process. The weight given to the various factors also varies among chartering authorities.

Restriction of entry can be assumed to affect commercial bank profitability. The fewer new entrants in any given area, other things being equal, the higher will be the income of existing banks. Tightening of entry restrictions in the 1930's was probably strongly influenced by the desire to raise profitability. In recent years, with the rise in bank earnings, this motive has substantially lessened, and other effects deemed desirable by the regulatory authorities have gained in relative importance. The various investigations carried out by the Comptroller's office and other bank chartering authorities suggest a concern that a new bank might lessen, rather than increase, competition; or that competition might be intensified to the point where an existing bank would fail; or that the quality of bank assets in the area would deteriorate because of increased competition.

In competing for deposits, banks operate subject to a ceiling on rates they may pay on time and savings accounts, and they are prohibited from paying interest on demand deposits. Restriction of interest payments on deposits was meant largely to lower operating costs and so to increase profitability. The prohibition of interest payments on demand deposits does have this effect. Even though services are given in lieu of interest, some depositors do not use all of the value of the imputed interest.

The connection between costs and profits is not at all clear in the case of the ceiling on time and savings deposits. The ceiling lowers the interest cost on whatever deposits there are in banks. Strong competition from other financial intermediaries uninhibited by interest ceilings, however, may cause commercial banks to lose substantial amounts of potential deposits. Thus, the effect on profits depends upon the marginal cost of acquiring additional funds and the marginal revenue to be gained from the use of these funds.

In addition to their effect on profitability, restrictions on interest payments are believed to affect portfolio decisions. Higher interest costs, some authorities believe, prod bankers into making riskier, higher-yield loans and investments in order to offset the higher costs. Thus, this set of regulations is partly aimed at reducing the risk of a deterioration in the quality of bank assets.

Bank investment and loan portfolio decisions are directly circumscribed

[10] Conflict of Federal and State Banking Laws, Hearings Before Committee on Banking & Currency, statement by James J. Saxon, Comptroller of the Currency, May 3, 1963. Pages 281–330 of these hearings contain a description of the procedures and policies followed by the Comptroller with regard to bank branching and chartering.

by a large number of regulations. Among the more important of these are the regulations on the maximum loan to any one borrower relative to bank capital, the prohibition of equity investments, and the restrictions on the amount which may be invested in mortgages and other types of long-term debt instruments. Moreover, the banking acts of the 1930's substantially reduced the power of banks to operate in the capital markets. The broad prohibition on investment banking functions previously performed by commercial banks is an important aspect of this reduction in operating discretion.

It is difficult to rationalize clearly the purposes of individual portfolio restrictions. In part they contain vestiges of supervisory concern over bank liquidity; in part they are aimed at controlling the quality of assets held; in part, also, there is some belief that they aid profitability. In general, these regulations act to lower risk exposure and so reduce losses on loans and investments.

In a free enterprise economy, risk taking must be adequately compensated or capital will not be channeled into risky endeavors. There is no reason to believe that bankers are endowed with below average business ability. Hence, restricting the freedom of bankers to undertake risk should cause both a reduction in average income after provision for losses, and also a reduction in the variability of income. The main effect of portfolio regulations, therefore, is to reduce bank failures, but at the expense of lower average bank profits.

To summarize, there is a clear rationale for regulating commercial banking. But the present structure of regulation is also a reflection of the problems encountered by the banking system during the 1930's. The scope of competition has been reduced. This has had an uncertain overall effect on bank income. Some regulations tend to increase income while others tend to lower income. The only valid generalization is that the possibility of bank failure has been substantially reduced and is much lower than would be true in a minimally regulated system.

AN EVALUATION OF THE REGULATORY FRAMEWORK

Public regulation may be justified in a free enterprise economy either because competition cannot be sustained where costs decline as the size of firms increases, or because goals other than economic efficiency are deemed more important. In appraising the present regulatory framework two important questions must be answered. First, are the objectives underlying these regulations desirable? Second, if the objectives are desirable, are the present regulations necessary to bring them about? There is almost universal acceptance of the objectives of depositor protection and the maintenance of the economic well-being of the banking industry. This section is therefore devoted to an analysis of the need for the existing structure of controls.

Even in a minimally regulated system, deposit insurance would be needed to help equalize the ability of new and/or small banks to compete with large and/or established banks for deposits, and thus maintain a sufficient number of banking units to keep the industry competitive. Moreover, some portfolio and capital regulations would be necessary in order to protect the insurance fund, if a flat insurance fee on deposits were used. Beyond that, the major question is whether the present structure of controls is needed, in order to prevent a greater volume of bank failures than is socially acceptable. To rationalize fully the present regulatory system, one must assume that banking is inherently an extremely competitive business, and that bankers, if allowed to compete freely, would operate at prices which would cause many bank failures.

An important element in the present regulatory rationale is the belief that a state of "overbanking" developed during the 1920's, and that this led to a deterioration in the quality of bank assets. The quality of credit is an illusive concept. Measured *ex-post* by losses on loans negotiated during the latter part of the 1920's, there is no doubt that credit quality deteriorated. The quality of credit is, however, largely determined by ensuing business conditions. Had business conditions remained stable after 1929, and had banks not been subjected to forced liquidation because of deposit runs, bank losses would certainly have been substantially less. A large part of the problem in which the commercial banking industry found itself in the 1930's was a result of large scale deposit runs on banks. If banks had been supplied with the liquidity to meet the deposit drains, bank failures would surely have been very drastically reduced. The question as to whether credit quality, measured *ex-ante*, did in fact deteriorate has not really been answered.

Portfolio regulations aimed at reducing the income variability of commercial banks and restrictions on bank entry are sometimes defended on the ground that they reduce resource waste which would occur because of the entry and destruction of firms which find that they cannot operate successfully. It has been argued that bank failure is socially more costly than is the failure of other types of enterprise. The failure of a bank causes losses to depositors as well as to stockholders. It makes the depositor distrust banks and therefore impairs the check mechanism. This depositor mistrust is transmitted and felt by all banks in the community. In addition, rapid turnover of operating banks, it is believed, would cause costly disruptions of established borrowing channels.

This line of reasoning had much to commend it in the past. Failure of a bank in a community often resulted in heavy deposit withdrawals at other nearby banks. However, the introduction and success of deposit insurance has greatly reduced, if not entirely eradicated, the transmitted effects of bank failure. With deposit insurance the effect of failure in banking is much the same as in other industries. Resource loss due to incorrect forecasts or changed consumer tastes is generally experienced in competitive industries. Knowledge of the future is never perfect. The usual evaluation is that the benefits brought about by the competitive drive in the industry more than compensates for the losses.

An answer to the problem of the disruption of borrowing relationships between banks and businesses is less certain. The question of whether it is socially more costly to replace suppliers of bank funds after failure of the bank with which relations are established than it is to replace suppliers of other factors of production after a failure of an established supplier is an empirical question. The answer is not certain.

A further major question to be faced, if a large part of existing regulations were dropped, is: Would banking attract sufficient capital to perform adequately its necessary functions? Annual rates of return to equity in commercial banks, private electric utilities, and all manufacturing corporations for the period 1947–1961 are shown in Table 1. Until 1958, the return to bank capital averaged just under 8 percent; but from 1958 to 1961 the return to bank capital rose to an average of almost 9 percent. Until 1958, utility earnings averaged 2.5 percent more than bank earnings; since 1958, increased bank earnings have reduced the differential. Earnings on capital in manufacturing were substantially above returns on banking in the 1950's; however, manufacturing profitability has fallen in recent years and in the last four years has been on a par with returns in banking.

These aggregate data, however, are not wholly reliable for our purpose. The following factors distort the comparisons: accelerated depreciation taken by utilities and manufacturing companies; valuation reserves set-up by banks; and the general inflationary conditions during many of the

Table 1 Annual Rates of Return on Common Equity in Commercial Banking, Privately Owned Utilities and All Manufacturing Corporations, 1947–1961

Year	Commercial Banking [1]	Electric Utilities [2]	All Manufacturing [3]
1947	8.0	10.3	15.6
1948	7.3	9.9	16.1
1949	7.8	10.6	11.7
1950	8.3	10.6	15.4
1951	7.6	9.6	12.4
1952	7.9	10.3	10.3
1953	7.7	10.3	10.5
1954	9.1	10.6	9.9
1955	7.6	11.0	12.6
1956	7.5	11.1	12.3
1957	8.0	11.0	11.0
1958	9.3	11.0	8.6
1959	7.7	11.2	10.4
1960	9.6	11.3	9.2
1961	9.0	11.2	8.8

Source: 1. *Annual Reports*, Federal Deposit Insurance Corporation.
2. *Statistics of Electric Utilities in the United States*, Privately Owned, 1961, Federal Power Commission, Washington, D. C.
3. *Quarterly Financial Report*, for manufacturing companies, Federal Trade Commission, and Securities and Exchange Commission, Washington, D.C.

years covered. Nonetheless, it seems probable that, even considering the relative safety of investment in bank capital, bank profits have not been out of line with profits in other private businesses. These data are not conclusive, since it is possible that profits above the competitive level exist in banking, but are taken "in the quiet life."

Restrictions on entry, the prohibition and ceiling on interest payments on deposits, and other regulations which affect profitability have certainly not led to extraordinary rates of return on capital in banking. The greater competition which would occur if entry became freer and interest restrictions were rescinded would most certainly lower rates of return and thus intensify the problems of the bank supervisory authorities in coercing banks to maintain adequate capital accounts.

It is impossible to predict how many new banks would be formed if barriers to entry were dropped, or what the long run effect on profits would be if interest restrictions were removed. The data on relative profitability of banks and other businesses, however, suggest that there would not be a substantial rush of new firms into banking. Moreover, banks would enter in the areas where opportunities are greatest, which is exactly where new entry is most desirable. Leaving aside questions of fiduciary responsibility and the character of new applicants for bank charters, which ought to continue to be guarded, we can summarize the economics of entry as follows: If the rate of return is low in an area, no new bank will seek to enter. Restrictions on entry in these cases are redundant. In areas where the rate of return on capital is high, entry restrictions may impede the free flow of new capital. At best, the economic effects of entry restrictions are redundant; at worst, they are harmful.

An additional difficulty in assessing the profitability of an unregulated commercial banking system is to gauge the depressing effect of the present portfolio restrictions. It is difficult to determine how much income is foregone because of these restrictions, but there is much room for attracting business away from other financial intermediaries. With a heightened competitive stature the aggregate income of commercial banks could probably increase substantially.

Regulations which inhibit competition and therefore raise bank profitability could be defended on the ground that a well functioning healthy commercial banking system provides large external benefits. If this were true, the competitive pricing system would not provide the socially desirable quantity of banking services. This same argument of external benefits can be made for almost any basic industry. It is difficult to judge whether or not banking provides a markedly larger amount of external economies than other industries. However, if it is desirable to increase the quantity of capital in banking because of external benefits, above that which would be provided in a minimally regulated system, bank profitability could be changed without affecting bank market conditions.

In large measure, the overall profitability of the commercial banking industry is determined by the actions of the monetary authorities. Federal Reserve monetary policy is dictated by business conditions, but the actual monetary tool used to carry out policy is determined by the Federal Reserve. Raising reserve requirements and selling bonds through open market operations may have similar monetary effects, but different effects on profitability. Higher reserve requirements would have a more adverse effect on bank profits than would the sale of bonds; and, conversely, lower reserve requirements would have a more favorable effect on bank profits than would Federal Reserve purchases of bonds. It is possible, therefore, substantially to increase the profitability of the commercial banking system through appropriate Federal Reserve action. The socially desirable quantity of capital could be attracted to banking without the need for regulations which tend to inhibit competition.

It should be emphasized that this suggestion does not call for any interference with the conduct of monetary policy. The monetary effect is the same; only the tool is changed. Moreover, great caution should be exercised not to assure profits to any level of capital investment in banking.

To summarize, assuming a presumption in favor of minimum regulation in a free enterprise economy, and given the belief that it is desirable to regulate banking to the extent necessary to achieve depositor protection and to guarantee a healthy, viable banking system, there is reason to believe that the present regulatory structure is more restrictive than necessary. The indicated direction of change should be toward easing the regulatory environment in which banks operate.

REGULATION OF BRANCHING

The rationale for bank regulation discussed above does not explain the restrictions imposed on branching. This part of the regulatory apparatus dates back to the demise of the Second Bank of the United States. The closing of the Second Bank of the United States has been attributed largely to rivalries between states and regions. Western states were fearful that Eastern interests would control the Bank and that funds would flow to the large financial centers of the East. Prohibition of branching across state lines, it was assumed, would keep control of the financial resources of the state in local hands, and would speed up development.

Certainly this prohibition had the effect of maintaining local control, but it may have slowed growth and development of the Western states. These states were large importers of capital, and the prohibition of interstate branching probably impeded the free movement of capital. Through time, however, with the relative increase in the wealth of the West, the development of a national capital market and the extensive correspondent relationships that developed between banks in all parts of the country, the adverse significance of this restriction has been diminished, if not eliminated.

Branching restrictions within states were motivated by many of the same fears that motivated interstate branching restrictions. The development of large accumulations of capital in a few hands was generally feared. Moreover, the rural areas tended to mistrust urban interests.

At the present time, a widely diverse set of regulations formulated by each state are binding upon both state and national banks domiciled within the state. A bank may not branch over state lines.[11] As shown in Table 2, sixteen states permit statewide branching; twenty states permit branch banking within limited areas; eleven states prohibit branching entirely; and three states have no legislation regarding branch banking.

The desirability of branching restrictions depends on the costs relative to the benefits which accrue from the restriction. The potential cost would be the resource waste resulting from the loss of size efficiency, if economies of scale do exist. The potential benefits would be the benefits derived from local control over banking facilities, and the possibility of greater availability and lower cost of bank credit to small and medium size businesses.

In appraising branching restrictions under the present regulatory framework, additional complicating factors must be considered. The lifting of restrictions on branching would not change the existing restrictions on entry into banking. The data in columns 1 through 4 in Table 2 show changes in the number of banks from 1946 through 1961, grouped by the degree of branching restrictions. These data show that the wider the branching privilege, the greater is the reduction in the number of banks. This relationship results from two factors: the greater number of mergers, and the lower number of new bank formations, where branching restrictions are less severe.

The requirements for starting a new bank are more difficult to meet where branch banking is permitted. Opening a branch in a new location does not normally require the parent bank to acquire additional capital. Even considering only out-of-pocket expenses, a branch might lose money for years but still be kept in operation if long-run prospects seemed favorable. When the area has grown sufficiently to support a unit bank, the branch is already in existence and incorporators may not be able to show need for a new bank. The impact of these facts on new bank formations is shown by the data in column 5 of Table 2. There is little doubt that the number of new banks is affected by branch restrictions, and that, all other things being equal, tightening branching restrictions leads to a larger number of new bank formations.

The incentive to merge is much greater where branching is permitted. Where branches are allowed, a merger usually results in an additional

[11] The bank holding company could be considered not to conform to this pattern. But banks controlled by holding companies are individually organized, capitalized and staffed with officers. Legally and, it is argued by students of bank holding companies, operationally, these banks do not operate as one branch system. See Gerald C. Fischer, *Bank Holding Companies,* New York: Columbia University Press, 1961.

branch. In a unit banking state, on the other hand, a merger between two banks requires the closing of one of the banks. Customers of the closed bank might find it desirable to transfer their accounts to another more convenient bank. The surviving merged bank can, therefore, expect to lose a sizable portion of the deposits of the merged institutions.[12] Thus the amount that can be paid profitably for a bank in a merger transaction under branching restrictions is smaller, because of the greater expected loss of deposits, and because after the merger no banking value remains in the second location.

Wider geographic branching privileges lead to a smaller number of banks; but, as can be seen from columns 7, 8 and 9 of Table 2, the opposite relationship holds with regard to the number of offices. The wider the branching privilege, the greater the number of banking offices. It is not clear, however, whether competition is heightened by the existence of more units or more offices.

The extent to which economies of scale characterize banking is another important question. If costs continue to decline as banks become very large, then wide branching privileges would result in a strong push toward concentration of banking assets. Under these conditions, increased branching privileges would lead to a sharp increase in merger applications.[13]

If economies of scale do not exist or are of limited significance, branching restrictions might be dropped or loosened. The important parameters here are the total size of the commercial banking industry, the minimum number of units necessary to give reasonable assurance of effective competition, and the size of banks when costs start to turn up.

On the other hand, much additional research is needed to quantify some of the arguments which are presented in defense of the continuance of branching restrictions. Research results would be extremely desirable to answer questions such as the following: What differences are there in the lending activities and other banking actions between unit banks and branch systems? Is there any economic or social value to local control over banking? Are branch managers less interested in community affairs than unit bank officers?

Surveys of loan portfolios of commercial banks indicate that large banks make a large fraction of their loans to large businesses, while small banks

[12] Mergers, where the absorbed bank becomes a branch, may also lead to deposit loss. When two large banks are merged, some duplicated lines of credit of large concerns and duplicated correspondent balances might be lost. When a large and small bank or two small banks are merged, some customers may not want to deal with the resulting bank and branch. This type of business loss could occur in any merger. But the location problem exists only in unit bank states.

[13] It is too early to assess fully the impact of the recent decision of the Supreme Court to restrain the Philadelphia National Bank from merging with the Girard Trust. But, the concentration guidelines set in the case suggest that the growth of concentration through merger could be largely contained if existing antitrust legislation were strongly enforced.

Table 2 Changes in the Number of Commercial Banks, Banking Offices and New Bank Formations, by States Grouped by Branching Restrictions, 1946 and 1961

States Permitting Statewide Branch Banking	(1) Number of Banks 1946	(2) Number of Banks 1961	(3) Absolute Change in Number of Banks 1946–61	(4) Percent Change in Number of Banks 1946–61	(5) Total New Bank Formations 1946–61	(6) Number of Banking Offices 1946	(7) Number of Banking Offices 1961	(8) Absolute Change in Number of Banking Offices 1946–61	(9) Percent Change in Number of Banking Offices 1946–61
Arizona	10	11	+1	+10.0	4	48	194	146	+304.2
California	207	117	—90	—43.4	88	1065	1941	876	+82.3
Connecticut	123	63	—60	—48.8	6	213	283	70	+32.9
Delaware	39	20	—19	—48.7	0	56	75	19	+33.3
Idaho	47	32	—15	—32.1	13	91	120	29	+31.9
Louisiana	155	192	+37	+23.9	43	218	374	156	+71.6
Maine	64	46	—18	—28.1	3	165	184	19	+11.5
Maryland	170	132	—38	—22.4	9	291	385	94	+32.3
Nevada	8	7	—1	—12.5	2	24	50	26	+108.3
North Carolina	227	163	—64	—28.2	5	389	702	313	+80.5
Oregon	70	48	—22	—31.4	28	146	252	106	+72.6
Rhode Island	23	9	—14	—60.9	0	73	92	19	+26.0
South Carolina	149	144	—5	—3.4	28	148	302	154	+104.1
South Dakota	169	174	+5	+2.9	14	213	237	24	+11.3
Vermont	72	52	—20	—27.8	0	98	84	—14	—14.3
Washington	122	89	—33	—27.0	42	240	381	141	+58.8

States Permitting Branch Banking within Limited Areas									
Alabama	219	238	+19	+8.6	39	241	330	89	+36.9
Arkansas	219	237	+18	+8.2	28	238	288	50	+21.0
Georgia	316	420	+104	+32.9	82	345	482	137	+39.7
Indiana	488	441	–47	–9.7	19	568	763	195	+34.3
Iowa	649	673	+24	+3.7	41	813	851	38	+4.7
Kentucky	390	351	–39	–10.0	17	421	510	89	+22.1
Massachusetts	187	166	–21	–11.2	29	558	573	15	+2.7
Michigan	434	373	–61	–14.1	42	630	993	363	+57.6
Mississippi	203	193	–10	–4.9	9	255	335	80	+31.4
New Jersey	348	244	–104	–29.9	14	509	696	187	+36.7
New Mexico	44	57	+13	+29.5	17	50	114	64	+128.0
New York	672	388	–284	–42.3	12	1560	1842	282	+18.1
North Dakota	151	156	+5	+3.3	6	175	186	11	+6.3
Ohio	674	576	–98	–14.6	26	842	1257	415	+49.3
Pennsylvania	1016	671	–345	–34.0	14	1145	1320	175	+15.3
Tennessee	294	294	0	0	17	358	526	168	+46.9
Utah	59	50	–9	–15.3	12	71	127	56	+78.9
Virginia	315	302	–13	–4.1	27	392	606	214	+54.6
Alaska	19	14	–5	–26.3	9	18	41	23	+127.8
Hawaii	9	7	–2	–22.2	4	53	103	50	+94.3

Table 2 (Continued)

States with No Legislation Regarding Branch Banking	(1) Number of Banks 1946	(2) Number of Banks 1961	(3) Absolute Change in Number of Banks 1946–61	(4) Percent Change in Number of Banks 1946–61	(5) Total New Bank Formations 1946–61	(6) Number of Banking Offices 1946	(7) Number of Banking Offices 1961	(8) Absolute Change in Number of Banking Offices 1946–61	(9) Percent Change in Number of Banking Offices 1946–61
New Hampshire	64	73	+9	+14.1	6	122	77	—35	—31.3
Oklahoma	383	387	+4	+1.0	22	383	388	5	+1.3
Wyoming	55	55	0	0	7	55	55	0	0
States Prohibiting Branch Banking									
Colorado	142	166	+24	+16.9	36	142	166	24	+16.9
Florida	184	315	+131	+17.1	172	185	324	139	+75.1
Illinois	871	973	+102	+11.7	184	869	980	111	+12.8
Kansas	614	590	—24	—3.9	34	613	593	—20	—3.3
Minnesota	677	688	+11	+1.6	42	636	695	59	+9.3
Missouri	596	622	+26	+4.4	49	596	625	29	+4.9
Montana	110	122	+12	+10.9	19	110	122	12	+10.9
Nebraska	409	420	+11	+2.6	37	417	421	4	+1.0
Texas	851	1017	+166	+19.5	237	857	1013	156	+18.2
West Virginia	180	181	+1	+0.5	14	181	181	0	0
Wisconsin	552	564	+12	+2.2	22	705	720	15	+2.1

Source: Branch restriction format, *Banking Concentration and Small Business.* A Staff Report to the Select Committee on Small Business, December 1960, page 35.
Columns 1 through 4—*Federal Reserve Bulletins,* February 1962, p. 237 and June 1947, p. 752.
Column 5—State bank data supplied by banking departments of the various states. National bank data supplied by the Comptroller of the Currency.
Columns 6 through 9—*Polk's Bank Directory,* March 1961 and March 1947.

make a large fraction of their loans to small businesses. Since restrictions on branching lower the average size of banks, there is a question of whether the removal of these restrictions would adversely affect the ability of small and medium sized businesses to get bank financing.

The Horvitz study of the structure of banking in New England examined this question and concluded:

> . . . there is some evidence to support the view that branch bank lending policy is impersonal in the sense of not taking account of the individual element in the lending process to the same extent as unit banks. This is seen in the relatively small number of unsecured loans made by branch banks to small borrowers. We have also seen that as far as interest rates are concerned, small borrowers are likely to be better treated by the small unit bank than by the large branch bank. A reasonable conclusion from this evidence is that small borrowers are harmed rather than helped when the unit bank in their community is replaced with a branch of a large bank.[14]

The quotation above refers to commercial borrowers. Branch banks, Horvitz states, "are usually much better set for personal loans than unit banks." It should also be noted that Horvitz in his final analysis concludes in favor of branch banking for New England.

Without further research no general conclusion seems warranted. It is clear, however, that if restrictions on branching are changed, restrictions on entry ought to be changed concurrently. Continued restrictions on entry argue in favor of continued branching restrictions, because the heightened incentive to merge in areas where branching is permitted could in time cause too drastic a reduction in the number of competing banks, if charters for new entry were not easily granted.

The question of whether, and to what extent, to change branching restrictions is probably the most important among those facing the bank regulatory authorities. Changes in branching restrictions could have more far reaching effects on the structure of the commercial banking system than any other regulatory change under consideration.

FORCES OF CHANGE

There is reason to believe that the banking community may be relied upon to press for needed changes in the regulations governing bank operations. These regulations tend to inhibit the ability of banks to compete with other financial intermediaries. As a consequence, forces are set in motion which will help to alter these regulations in a socially desirable direction.

This is not true, however, of entry restrictions. There is reason to believe that changes within the banking system which have occurred since the early 1930's, as a result of deposit insurance and more knowledge

[14] Horvitz, *Concentration and Competition in New England Banking*, p. 170.

and ability to act on the part of the Federal Reserve, may have made entry restrictions unnecessary or less necessary.

However, neither bankers nor the majority of the bank regulatory bodies strongly desire to ease entry restrictions. Bankers cannot be expected to agitate for an easing of these restrictions. It is only natural for a businessman to abhor additional competitors. On the bank supervisory side, the job of the regulatory authorities is eased by restrictions on entry; fewer bank failures are encountered, and it is easier to coerce existing banks to increase capital when this seems desirable. Moreover, uncertainty exists as to what will happen to the rate of return if a policy of easy entry is instituted. Also, the increase in competition and other public benefits to be gained from an additional bank in an area is open to much conjecture. Hence, for the most part the banking authorities cannot be expected to ease restrictions on entry into banking as quickly as is socially desirable. Thus, if entry restrictions are to be changed, the impetus must to some extent come from outside the industry.

This latter point is probably the strongest argument in favor of the dual banking system. Under a dual banking system, two chartering authorities can be approached to allow a bank opening in any geographical location. If the state authority is very restrictive, banks may be chartered by the Comptroller, and vice versa. The constraint will come from the least restrictive agent. It is interesting to observe how this has worked in the 1946–1961 period. During this period, 581 new state banks and 203 new national banks were opened. New national banks exceeded state bank formations in only seven states. It is difficult to generalize from available data, but they do suggest that the Comptroller has been more stringent than most state authorities on new entry during this period. Recent statements of the present Comptroller indicate that the Comptroller's office will be less restrictive in granting new charters in the future. These statements are borne out by the record. In his first eighteen months in office, Comptroller Saxon has issued more than four times the number of new bank charters that were issued by his predecessor, Comptroller Gidney, in his last eighteen months in office; 187 granted by Saxon, versus 45 granted by Gidney.

Disagreements over branching restrictions have been almost wholly intramural affairs within the banking community. The general public has been almost totally unconcerned. The academic community has, in general, been in favor of the extension of branching privileges, but has not been overly active in pushing its opinions. This may be fortuitous. Academic opinion has probably been substantially influenced by comparisons with other businesses where branching privileges are freely exercised. In those businesses, however, new firms are also free to enter any market. In banking, entry is restricted. As has been shown, wide branching privileges and restricted entry tend to lower the number of banking units. In time, this could lower the number of competing banks to the point where active competition was precluded.

The question of bank branching is too important economically to allow the decision to be made by heavily vested interests. Research on this question is vital. Moreover, the results of such research must be made influential in the decision-making process.

Competition in Banking:
The Issues

Larry R. Mote

In an economy characterized by private property and production for profit, competition among buyers and sellers has long been considered a prime prerequisite of economic efficiency—efficiency in this context being construed to include both the maximizing of output for any given resource used and the allocation of resources among all possible uses such that total production is maximized.

So strong has been the American belief in impersonal market forces to set prices and guide production, as opposed to joint decisions among producers or the decrees of government boards, that our country early put on the books the strictest and most comprehensive antitrust legislation in the world. The basic statutes are the Sherman Act of 1890 and the Clayton and Federal Trade Commission Acts of 1914.

To be sure, it has long been recognized that the technologies of some industries preclude primary reliance upon competition to guide investment, production and pricing. In these so-called "natural monopolies," such as the production and distribution of electric power and other "public utilities," the discipline of the marketplace has been replaced by the deliberations of public regulatory agencies.

Still other industries, although not considered natural monopolies, have been acknowledged as greatly affecting the public interest. Because the failure or other malfunctioning of an individual establishment in these industries has been deemed to have adverse effects on the economy over and beyond the injury accruing to the firm's stockholders, public regulation has been imposed in order to assure that certain minimal

Reprinted with the permission of the Federal Reserve Bank of Chicago from *Commercial Banking: Structure, Competition and Performance,* August 1967.

operating and fiduciary standards are met. Of the industries accorded such treatment, commercial banking is both the most prominent and the most heavily regulated.

WHY BANKS ARE REGULATED

Demand deposits of commercial banks provide the primary means of payment and are the major component of the money supply. Furthermore, banks, while presumed by the public to be safe depositories, typically have liabilities that are very large in proportion to their capital and consequently could provide an attractive temptation to gambling by reckless entrepreneurs. These facts alone would suggest the desirability of regulation to assure the liquidity and solvency of commercial banks.

In addition, historical experience provides dramatic, if superficial, evidence for the view that permitting banks to engage in unrestrained competition may lead to disastrous results. The evils of the past—specifically, the chaos and instability that attended the era of "free banking" between 1837 and 1863, the large numbers of bank failures in the 1920s and the banking collapse and economic depression of the early 1930s—have sufficed to convince most people that some measure of Government intervention is not only desirable but an absolute necessity.

The Federal and state governments have responded to this apparent need by constructing over the years a highly detailed and extensive system of commercial bank regulation that includes specific lending and borrowing restrictions, usury laws, ceilings on rates that banks may pay on time deposits, the prohibition of interest on demand deposits, capital and management requirements for the establishment of new banks, geographical restrictions on branching, requirements for periodic publication of statements of conditions and examinations by public officials.

WHY COMPETITION IN BANKING?

Since official regulation imposes numerous limitations on the activities of banks, vigorous competition among banks may appear both superfluous and inconsistent. After all, one may ask, is not the public's interest in having quality services provided at reasonable prices protected in banking through public regulation, as it supposedly is in the case of electric utilities and transportation? The answer, clearly, is in the negative.

Although commercial banks are subject to a great number of specific regulations limiting the scope of their activities, a broad range of discretion still remains open to them. As far as their lending and investment activities are concerned, banks retain the prerogative of emphasizing particular kinds of loans (for example, business, consumer, agriculture and mortgage loans) and of setting prices for these loans at whatever levels they choose, subject only to the ceilings on some types of loans established by state usury laws. Thus, there is ample room for the play of competitive forces to establish the actual levels of charges.

The scope for nonprice competition in banking is even wider. The services provided in conjunction with the bank's lending and deposit business provide a variety of opportunities for nonprice maneuvers designed to win new customers and retain old ones. It is the incomplete nature of regulation which, while imposing definite constraints on each bank's choice of alternative policies, nevertheless permits a wide latitude for the exercise of individual discretion that makes possible a meaningful role for competition in banking. This is the consideration that lay behind the Supreme Court's dictum in *U.S. vs. Philadelphia National Bank* that the regulated character of banking "makes the play of competition not less important but more so."

CHANGING VIEWS ON COMPETITION

Interest in banking competition has intensified in recent years. After virtually ignoring the commercial banking industry for many years, the Justice Department brought suit in the late 1950s in a number of cases involving clearinghouse agreements to set uniform service charges. In more recent years, despite a long and widely held belief to the contrary, the courts have ruled that the antitrust laws apply to acquisitions and mergers in banking as well as in other areas.

It may appear rather anomalous that the Federal Government, having established a superstructure of regulation designed at least in part for the purpose of limiting competition in banking, now undertakes to restrict banks' actions which might tend to reduce competition. The issue is further confused by the fact that the Office of the Comptroller of the Currency and the Department of Justice—two agencies of the Federal Government—have been on occasion cast in the roles of opposing parties in recent bank merger cases. It would be inaccurate to portray these events as reflecting merely a jurisdictional dispute between Federal agencies. Instead there appears to be a growing conviction on the part of public officials and bankers alike that a reevaluation and revision of policy may now be in order—though there is little agreement on specific issues.

Until recently students of banking were generally agreed that competition was not only less essential in banking than in most other industries but in many circumstances inherently destructive. However, new evidence and reexamination of old arguments now suggest that competition in banking may not have been the culprit it has been painted to be in bringing about the financial crises of earlier days. The banking troubles of the era before 1863 are now considered to have been more the result of the absence of a uniform national currency than of excessive competition or the lack of detailed controls over banking. This deficiency was remedied by the passage of the National Banking Act of 1863, which substituted national bank notes for the bewildering variety of state bank issues then in circulation.

Similarly, the periodic epidemics of bank failures of the late nineteenth and early twentieth centuries, as well as the striking and unprecedented attrition of banks in the decade following World War I, appear to have had their roots more in cyclical factors and secular changes in transportation and agriculture than in any inherent tendency toward destructive competition in banking. Even the banking debacle of the early 1930s is no longer uncritically viewed as the inevitable result of imprudent banking practices attributable largely to excessive competition for deposits. On the contrary, all of these instances of injury to the banking system—and in most cases, to the economy as well—are now generally agreed to have had their major cause in developments much broader than local competition and often far removed from the sphere of individual bank management.

Today, there exist numerous safeguards against any widespread and self-reinforcing epidemic of bank failures. To the extent that violent cyclical fluctuations in aggregate economic activity may have been responsible for the waves of bank failures in the past, the announced readiness of the Federal Government and the Federal Reserve System to take whatever fiscal and monetary measures are required to maintain a high and growing level of income and employment serves as protection against similar future disturbances. To the extent that bank failures were the result of "runs" on banks occasioned by general fears on the part of the public of the inability by banks to redeem their deposits for currency, Federal Deposit Insurance and the readiness of the Federal Reserve to act as the lender of last resort appear to afford a sufficient remedy. Although the evidence is not unequivocal on each of these points—and even though all are agreed that supervision remains a necessary means for promoting good bank management and ensuring the safety of depositor's funds—there seems little doubt that competition can safely play a more important role in banking than has until recently been deemed prudent.

One piece of evidence for this conclusion is the fact that regulation frequently has been unsuccessful in suppressing competition even where it has undertaken to do so. For example, the attempt to reduce interbank competition by erecting strict legal barriers to entry has been at least a major contributing cause to the rapid and continuing growth of such nonbank financial intermediaries as savings and loan associations, a growth that has brought with it increased interindustry competition.

Similarly, the attempt to relieve effects of unduly severe competition among banks by prohibiting them from paying interest on demand deposits has been only partially successful at best. Far from eliminating competition, the prohibition simply caused banks to substitute less overt but nonetheless vigorous nonprice rivalry for the rate competition that previously existed. In effect, "interest" on demand deposits continues to be paid through an earnings credit offset to deposit service charges and numerous "free" services, all dependent largely on the size of the average balance and the number of transactions associated with each account. On the other hand, the depositor has been deprived of the option of being paid in cash.

CHANGES IN NUMBER OF BANKS

While much of the recent interest in competition in banking has been focused on the system of bank regulation as presently constituted, expressions of concern have also been voiced concerning the merging and branching activities of the banks themselves. Despite virtually uninterrupted prosperity and population growth in the postwar period, the decline in the number of commercial banks in the United States that began in the 1920s continued until very recently (Figure 1).

After a small immediate postwar rise from 14,011 in 1945 to 14,181 in 1947, the number declined steadily, reaching a low of 13,427 at the end of 1962. Since then the number of banks has increased slightly to 13,784 in November 1966. The net decrease of 227 banks since World War II—an average of about 10 a year—is small compared to the rate that prevailed throughout the generally prosperous 1920s when the average net annual attrition exceeded 700. However, in contrast to the earlier period when a significant part of the attrition resulted from bank failures and voluntary liquidations, virtually all the recent decline has been the result of mergers and acquisitions that have absorbed formerly independent banks.

NUMBERS AND COMPETITION

To many observers this decrease in the number of banks provides evidence that the availability of alternative sources of supply of banking services, and hence the vigor of competition, is undergoing a decline. This conclusion is based on the theory that the chances of collusion are less and the likelihood of independent rivalry greater when sellers are many than when they are few.

However, in evaluating the effect of the decline in the number of banks, it must be noted that all of the more than 13,000 banks in the United States do not compete in a single, nationwide market. A relatively few giant banks do operate in what is loosely referred to as the "national banking market"—the market for the loans and deposits of the largest corporations that have banking connections throughout the country.

But it is a widely acknowledged fact that, for most bank customers, the national market is segmented by the real and psychic cost of distance into

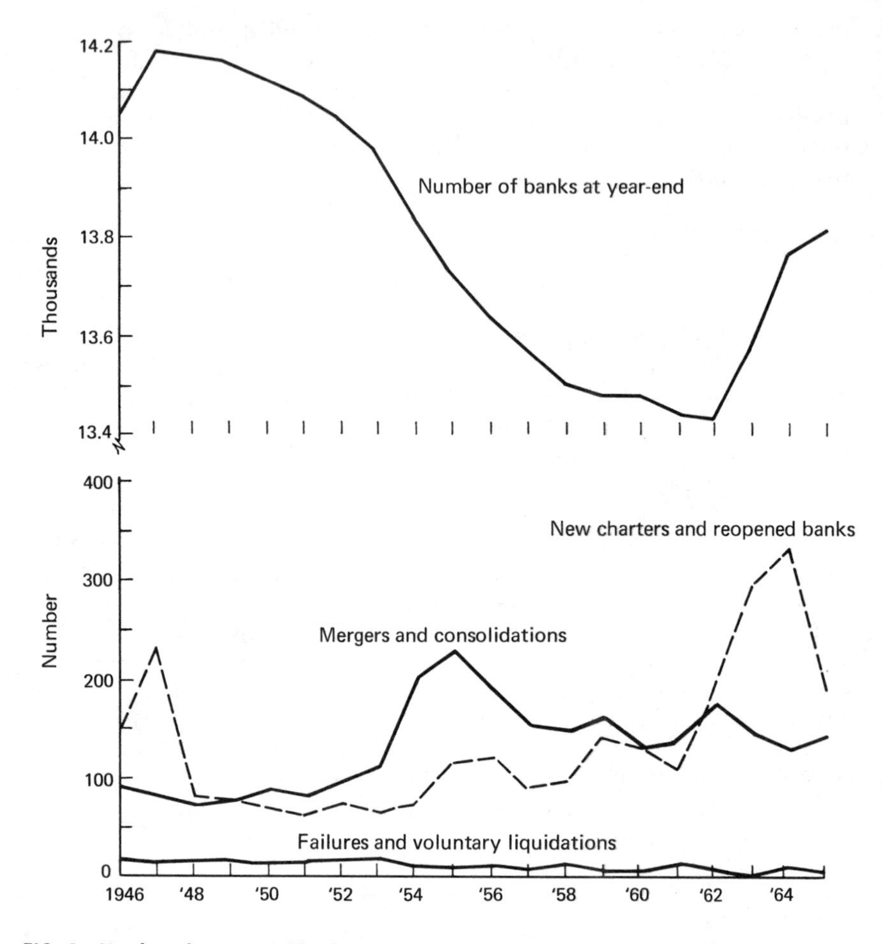

FIG. 1 Number of commercial banks rises in recent years following many years of decline.

relatively narrow regional and local submarkets. For this less mobile majority of customers, the most relevant consideration is the number of independent banks within the confined area in which their reputations are known and in which they find it practicable to seek accommodation. This number of banks, however, is not deducible from a knowledge of how many banks there are in some broader area, such as the state.

Although states which permit branch banking have experienced deep declines in the number of banks, it does not necessarily follow that significantly fewer different banks are represented in individual communities in these states than in those that prohibit branch banking (see Table 1). This apparent contradiction is explained by the great expansion in the number of branch offices during the past several decades. Similarly, even when mergers have decreased the total number of banks in the country and the number of alternatives available to customers in par-

Table 1 Increased Number of Branches More Than Offsets Decline in Number of Banks

State Classification*	CHANGE, 1946–64					
	Banks		Branches		Banking offices	
	Number	Per Cent	Number	Per Cent	Number	Per Cent
Branch banking						
Statewide	–323	–23	3,922	24	3,599	118
Limited	–979	–15	6,097	290	5,118	60
Unit banking	1,018	17	338†	148†	1,356	21
Total	–284	–2	10,357	260	10,073	56

* Includes 50 states and District of Columbia.
† Includes offices that do not offer a full line of banking services. In addition, a few full service branches that were established before legal prohibitions of branching or after removal of such prohibitions are included.
Source: U. S., Comptroller of the Currency, *Annual Report 1964* (Washington, 1965).

ticular local markets, they may have added to the number of effective competitors in the markets serving large- and medium-sized corporate customers by permitting the merging banks to attain the minimum size required to operate in these markets.

CONCENTRATION IN BANKING

Concomitant with the decline in the number of banks, the average size of bank and the percentage of banking resources concentrated in the hands of a relatively few large banks have increased in many broad areas of the country. Concentration in this sense is often considered to have a potentially adverse effect on competition because, however large the total number of banks in a market, if one or a few of them control most of the total supply, they will be able to influence prices strongly.

Available data on concentration of deposits in major metropolitan areas indicate that concentration levels were generally higher in the early 1960s than a decade earlier. On the other hand, they appear to have been lower than in the prewar year of 1939. It is necessary, however, to take account of important interarea differences. For the period 1960–64 increases in concentration have been typical in metropolitan areas in states where statewide branching is prevalent (see Table 2). In metropolitan areas where restricted branch banking is the rule, increases and decreases were about equally frequent. Decreases predominated in these areas where unit banking was the most common form of bank organization.

Some would interpret these figures as demonstrating that unit banking is more conducive to competition than branch banking. However, inasmuch as concentration and changes in concentration have significance for competition only in relation to specific product markets and partic-

Table 2 Metropolitan Areas in Statewide Branch Banking States Show Greatest Increases in Concentration

*SMSAs including reserve cities**	Percent of total deposits held by three largest banks		
	1960	*1962*	*1964*
Branch Banking			
Statewide			
Baltimore	59	73	72
Los Angeles	78	75	71
Portland, Ore.	87	90	89
San Francisco	60	79	77
Seattle	68	72	72
Limited			
Atlanta	72	75	74
Birmingham	93	93	97
Boston	79	83	83
Buffalo	77	93	95
Cincinnati	82	84	84
Cleveland	78	77	76
Columbus	88	87	93
Detroit	78	76	74
Indianapolis	97	96	96
Louisville	68	76	76
Memphis	93	93	93
Nashville	89	92	93
New Orleans	85	80	79
New York	49	53	54
Philadelphia	64	62	64
Pittsburgh	82	83	81
Richmond	80	78	73
Toledo	90	88	88
Washington, D.C.	74	75	73
Unit Banking			
Chicago	48	53	52
Dallas	80	79	76
Denver	69	68	68
Fort Worth	77	76	73
Houston	60	59	64
Jacksonville	79	75	72
Kansas City, Mo.	63	61	58
Miami	41	43	40
Milwaukee	68	67	66
Minneapolis	60	62	60
Oklahoma City	70	72	71
Omaha	82	80	79
St. Louis	52	50	48
San Antonio	67	64	62
Tulsa	81	79	76

* Metropolitan areas of Reserve Cities having populations in excess of 400,000 as of April 1, 1960.
Source: Federal Deposit Insurance Corporation, *Annual Reports.*

ular groups of customers, such a conclusion follows only if certain conditions are satisfied. Among these is the rather crucial assumption that metropolitan areas serve equally well as approximations to local banking markets under both branch and unit banking. To the extent that locational convenience serves to restrict the practicable range of alternatives of some customers to an area smaller than the whole metropolitan area, concentration in unit banking areas is understated by the measure used here. A more important qualification is that competition has not been shown to depend in any simple and reliable way on the degree of concentration in bank markets.[1]

PUBLIC POLICY TOWARD BANK MERGERS

In deciding whether to approve or disapprove a particular application to merge, the appropriate regulatory agency must arrive at a judgment concerning the probable effect of the merger on the public interest. The fundamental questions that must be answered include the justification of the consolidation in terms of economies of scale or the ability of a larger bank to render better, cheaper and more complete banking services and its effect, via changes in the number and size distribution of banks, on the competitive relations among the remaining firms. It is over answers to these questions that much of the interagency conflict has arisen.

For example, advantages in the form of lower operating costs have often been advanced as a major factor in bank mergers. Yet, available empirical studies tend to indicate that such economies may be quite modest—at least when the differences in output mix between large and small banks are taken into consideration, as they must be.

A second argument in support of mergers emphasizes the ability of a bank with greater resources to hire better management and to utilize more fully the services of a large number of specialists. This argument appears to have fairly general validity as indicated by both casual observation and a number of recent studies. Large banks generally do offer a broader variety of services than is obtainable at small banks in the same locality. But whether this constitutes a net advantage is not immediately obvious. It must be determined first whether a decrease in the number of alternative sources of banking services is adequately compensated by the availability of a number of special, but infrequently utilized, services that only large banks can supply.

BRANCH BANKING

Any discussion of the relative merits of large and small banks must include consideration of the advantages and disadvantages of branch

[1] These and other measures of the degree of competition are discussed in *Commercial Banking: Structure, Competition and Performance* (Federal Reserve Bank of Chicago, August 1967), pp. 22–27.

banking. One of the major advantages claimed for branching is that it is often the quickest way a bank can grow to large size. Also, since the full resources and facilities of the bank can be made available to the customers of each branch, branch banking provides a means of bringing a fuller range of banking services and larger lending capacity to individual communities.

The still unresolved issue of branch banking underlies one of the oldest and most vitriolic controversies in American banking. It involves questions both political and economic in character. Without evaluating the merits of the arguments, it may be noted that the unit-branch issue is an inseparable part of the larger public debate over competition in banking reviewed above.

The precise relationship between branch banking and banking competition is a matter of dispute. A number of economists, bankers and public officials maintain that branching is an essentially procompetitive form of banking that facilitates the penetration of additional banking markets and brings to bear the force of potential competition in even the smallest and most isolated communities. Other students of banking hold that branching is a monopolistic device whose prime purpose is to eliminate competition. Which characterization is the more accurate may depend as much on what one understands by competition as on the objectively determinable facts of the case.

It is hardly open to serious doubt, for example, that some portion of the criticism of branch banking is of a protectionist nature, more concerned with preserving locally owned unit banks than with fostering vigorous interbank rivalry. Independent bankers frequently feel themselves threatened by the presence of a nearby office of a large branch bank.

On the other hand, it is not always easy to distinguish in practice between the protection of competitors and the preservation of competition. One reason is related to the difference between the incentives required to induce merger and those required to induce *de novo* establishment of a new bank or branch. It appears easier for two existing banks to come to terms on a merger agreement which has as one of its "fringe benefits" the elimination of competition than it is for a potential entrant into the banking field to obtain financing and run the regulatory gauntlet required to obtain a charter for a new bank. As was indicated above, it is in those areas where the possibility of operating an acquired bank as a branch maximizes the incentive to merge that the disappearance of banks and the concentration of banking have proceeded most rapidly. This pronounced assymmetry between merger and entry is the primary reason why branching via merger, which *ipso facto* involves the elimination of an independent source of supply, may have adverse and irreversible effects on competition. It is also one of the considerations that prompted Congress in 1950 to strengthen the Clayton Act and to pass the Bank Merger Acts of 1960 and 1966.

It might still be maintained, on the other hand, that *de novo* branching could have nothing but beneficial effects on competition. Its immediate effect is always to introduce a new competitive force into a banking market or submarket. When, for example, a branch bank sees a potentially profitable location for a banking office and opens a branch there—perhaps years in advance of the time when it would have been profitable to organize a new unit bank—it clearly benefits the community to have banking facilities where none existed before or would otherwise have existed for a considerable period of time. Whether this is a net gain in the long term depends on the potential benefit to the local populace of having an independent source of supply of banking services when it would become feasible to open a new unit bank.

Where banks find it easy to establish branches within a local banking market they may—and often do—anticipate profitable locations and saturate entire areas with branches, thereby largely foreclosing future entry by competitors. In this they may be inadvertently aided and abetted by the regulatory agencies which, though reluctant to grant a new charter that could conceivably result in "overbanking," are usually willing to rely on the applicant's judgment regarding the prospective profitability of a new branch.

At a theoretical level a good case can be made for removing all geographic restrictions on branching, while simultaneously discouraging concentration in particular local banking markets. However, this would require a uniform national policy with respect to branching and the chartering of new banks, a development not now on the horizon. Legislation regarding branching traditionally has been left to the states. Nevertheless, the competitive environment created by state branching restrictions is clearly one of the many factors that must be taken into account in Federal Agency decisions governing mergers.

CONCLUSION

There exists a great deal of uncertainty at the present time as to the proper public policy toward competition in banking. Ideally, policy should undertake to foster a degree of interbank rivalry that assures that consumers will be provided bank services of high quality at minimum cost, without sacrificing the private and public benefits of large-scale production or the regulatory aim of ensuring the liquidity and solvency of the banking system. The extent to which these goals can be realized simultaneously and even the direction in which policy should move to approach them as closely as possible is still imperfectly understood. However, a start toward collecting and interpreting the data that would permit a more objective basis for deciding these issues has been made. . . .

Competition in Banking: The Evidence

Larry R. Mote

Certain aspects of recent controversy over the role of competition in banking were discussed in general terms in the preceding article. In banking as in baking, however, the proof of the pudding is in the eating. The present article, therefore, undertakes to describe the actual results achieved in the marketplace, as gauged by prices charged and paid and services rendered, under alternative banking structures.

Studies of structure and performance in banking markets have been handicapped both by data difficulties and by the impossibility of holding "all other things equal" when seeking to measure the effects of specific factors present in different market situations. Nevertheless, by cross classification of the data and the use of multiple regression analysis, it often has been possible to isolate the more important and consistent relationships and to shed light on certain of the issues.

Summarized here are the major results of a generous sample of research efforts that have been undertaken in the past two decades. These are listed below together with their reference numbers. (See Bibliography.)

It deserves stress that the conclusions indicated by these studies are suggestive rather than final. In some instances, clear inconsistencies are revealed in the results. Complete consistency in the findings could scarcely be expected simply because of the widely diverse samples of banks and bank markets studied and the possibilities that some of these were not representative of all banks. Where all but one or two of several investigators report similar findings, the relationship found by the majority may still be a valid one, but it should be studied further before being accepted as conclusive and providing a basis for generalization.

THE EFFECTS OF BANKING CONCENTRATION

With these reservations in mind, we proceed to present the available evidence. Among the structural characteristics of banking markets most

Reprinted with the permission of the Federal Reserve Bank of Chicago from *Commercial Banking: Structure, Competition and Performance,* August 1967.

frequently alleged to have an effect on performance are the number and size distribution of banks and other financial institutions. There is a presumption—partly based on experience in other industries and partly derived from economic theory—that the smaller the number of independent sellers in a particular market or the greater the concentration of business in the hands of a few, the lower is likely to be the quality of the product or service and the higher the price.

Several analysts have attempted to determine the relationships, if any, between concentration—generally measured as the percentage of total deposits in a given banking market accounted for by some small number of banks—and various measures of banking performance. Other things equal, it would be expected that interest rates on loans should be higher, interest rates on time deposits lower, the ratio of time to total deposits lower and pretax earnings on assets higher in markets where concentration is high than in those with greater diffusion of "market power."

In addition, it has been suggested that concentration would be likely to result in less activity in the form of direct lending and more in purchases of securities, which would be reflected in a lower loan to deposit ratio than would otherwise prevail. The number of banks in the market, on the other hand, would be expected to be related to measures of performance in a manner opposite to that premised for concentration.

Results of four published studies [5, 6, 7, 13] and two preliminary studies that examined the relationships between concentration and performance are generally consistent with expectations. The inconsistencies are so few and tentative as to be attributed reasonably to chance characteristics of the data. The one exception concerns the relationship between interest rates on business loans and concentration.

Although three of the four studies [5, 6, 13]—including a major research effort that utilized extensive data from the Federal Reserve's 1955 and 1957 surveys of business loans [5]—found a direct relationship, another study [7] utilizing many of the same data came to the conclusion that "no easily identifiable relationship exists between concentration ratios and the level of interest rates charged by commercial banks on business loans."

According to the author of this research paper [7], intercity variation in loan rates is better explained by regional differences in such factors as the rate of change of employment, bank operating expenses and competition from nonbank financial institutions. He further contends that the direct or positive relationship between concentration and loan rates found by the earlier studies is a spurious result, ascribable to the pronounced but misleading correlation between concentration and the true explanatory factors.

The technical nature of these questions precludes any attempt here to demonstrate which of the conflicting results should be accepted. Suffice it that competent scholars have been unable to reach agreement on this issue on the basis of the data currently available. Nevertheless, this still unresolved controversy serves to illustrate the dangers of accepting the results of any one study as conclusive, especially in the absence of thorough familiarity with the data and methods employed in the analysis. But with the possible exception of interest rates on business loans, the evidence so far available is consistent with the view that differences in the degree of banking concentration may be responsible for at least a part of any differences observed in performance in banking markets.

THE NUMBER OF BANKS

The results of two published studies [12, 13] and two preliminary studies that examined the effects on performance of the number of banks in the market are also generally in accord with theoretical expectations. As with concentration, the most important inconsistencies concerned interest rates on loans. Two of the studies found a positive relationship between number of banks and loan rates—that is, the greater the number of banks the *higher* the level of loan rates—and two found the "expected" negative relationship. In all four studies, average loan rate was measured as the ratio of interest received on loans during the year to total loans outstanding, recorded either as of a given date or as the average of two or more dates during the year.

Such a gross measure is, of course, open to many objections, particularly that it glosses over differences in the makeup of credit demand and resulting bank-to-bank variations in loan composition. The distortion caused by the use of such a measure of the interest rate on loans would tend to be smaller for large samples and for samples consisting of banks that are alike in as many characteristics as possible. For this reason, the negative relationship between the number of banks in individual market areas and average interest rates on loans found in a study [13] of 672 banks in Iowa is more persuasive than the contrary result reported on the strength of an analysis [12] of 106 one- and two-bank towns throughout the country. At the same time, the highly localized character of the Iowa sample makes any generalization to conditions elsewhere hazardous; a preliminary study at the Chicago Federal Reserve Bank of 413 Indiana banks under somewhat less uniform conditions yielded generally inconclusive results.

A second unpublished paper, which examines the relationship between loan rates and changes in the number of banks in Indianapolis in the postwar period, lends further support to the view that interest rates on loans tend to vary inversely with the number of competing banks. As for the relationships between the number of banks and other performance variables—specifically, interest rates on time deposits, ratios of loans to assets, time to total deposits and pretax earnings to assets, and service charges on demand deposits—none of the four studies contradicts the conjectures made above although in a few cases the data also fail to give them positive support. Importantly, however, of the four foregoing studies only the one for Iowa reported relationships that were "significant" in the statistical sense that the results might not reasonably have occurred by chance.

Additional evidence is offered in two other bank studies, one in New York state [15] and the other in the Chicago area [19]. The former found some tendency for rates on new car loans, conventional mortgage loans and small business loans to be higher and rates paid on savings deposits to be lower in upstate New York towns with only one banking office than in towns with two or more offices. On the other hand, service charges on checking accounts were generally lower in the one-bank towns. The Chicago study found that interest rates on automobile loans tended to be lower in suburbs having larger numbers of banks. The samples in both of these studies, however, were relatively small and the results are therefore only tentative.

The findings reviewed thus far generally conform with expectations. This is not true, however, of the results of a number of other studies that have been made. An example is furnished by investigations of the effects on bank behavior ascribable to the presence of nonbank financial institutions.

COMPETITION FROM THRIFT INSTITUTIONS

Students of banking and bankers alike are aware that, although commercial banks offer checking deposit services that are unique, they face strong "outside" competition in the supply of other financial services. This is particularly true for savings. The savings and time deposits offered by commercial banks compete with mutual savings bank deposits, savings and loan association and credit union shares and other highly liquid financial assets.

The intensity of such competition has been in sharp focus during the recent "rate war" between the banks and savings and loan associations and had been evident in the earlier dramatic rise in commercial bank time and savings deposits following the revision of Regulation Q in 1962. Nevertheless, evidence so far examined indicates that the presence of a thrift institution in a community has no systematic influence on the rates paid by commercial banks on time deposits.

Of three studies that examined this question [12, 13, 18], only one—which looked at unit banks in Minnesota—supports what would be expected on a priori grounds, namely that the additional competition afforded by the presence of a nonbank financial institution would raise the interest rates on time deposits paid by commercial banks. The Iowa study [13] found no such relationship and the previously mentioned study of 106 unit banks [12] showed results precisely opposite to what would appear plausible.

The evidence regarding the effect that the presence of a thrift institution has on the ratio of commercial bank time deposits to total deposits and total local savings (savings held in local institutions) relative to population or income is more clear-cut. Both the study of Iowa banks [13] and that of the 106 unit banks located throughout the country [12] found that the ratio of commercial bank time deposits to total deposits tends to be lower in those communities where a nonbank thrift institution is present, indicating that to some degree commercial bank and other savings are substitutes.

A related finding is the conclusion of a follow-up study [14] of the same Iowa counties included in study [13]. This study was supplemented by an analysis of data for 48 states and showed that the volume of local savings at banks and thrift institutions combined—both in the aggregate and per capita—is larger, the greater is the proportion of local "deposits" held by the nonbank institutions. Similarly, a study of large metropolitan areas found that savings are greater relative to income in areas with mutual savings banks [19]. On balance, this evidence, if not that relating to time deposit interest rates, confirms the existence of considerable inter-industry competition between commercial banks and thrift institutions.

BRANCH BANKING AND PERFORMANCE

Perhaps the most controversial issue in American banking history and one on which feelings have been stronger than any other concerns branch banking. While much of the emotion surrounding discussion of this subject is undoubtedly attributable to aspects of a noneconomic nature, much of the writing and debate have focused upon purely economic considerations. Certain of the claims and counterclaims made over the years regarding the economic effects of branch banking have recently been subjected to the impersonal assessment of statistical analysis.

Seven studies [2, 6, 10, 12, 16, 19, 20] comparing bank performance in unit and branch areas reveal only one clear-cut contradiction: one [12] found interest rates on time deposits to be higher in branching areas while another [6] found them to be lower.

Of 12 other measures of performance, six were observed to be generally more favorable to bank customers in branch banking areas than in unit banking areas. The ratios of time to total deposits and loans to assets were higher under branch banking as were personal savings relative to income and the number of banking offices relative to population. At the same time, interest rates on mortgage and unsecured instalment loans were lower.

The six remaining measures of performance, on the other hand, were more favorable in unit banking areas. Interest rates on business and new car loans, the average return on all loans, the ratio of net current earnings both to assets and to capital and service charges on checking accounts were all lower in unit banking areas. However, the lower earnings to assets and earnings to capital ratios of unit banks are to be viewed as advantageous to consumers only insofar as they reflect competitive pricing in the market, which is already partially taken into account in the measures of time deposit and loan interest rates. If the lower earnings rates of unit banks are the result of inefficiency—that is, higher unit costs for a given package of services—they may actually be detrimental to the interests of consumers in the long run by leading to a deterioration in the quality of service.

The observed relationships may be due to factors other than the prevalent form of banking organization. In particular, branch and unit banking follow fairly definite geographic patterns in the United States, suggesting that regional differences in demand or in the character of state bank regulation could have pronounced effects on bank performance that may not properly be attributed to organizational characteristics. It may be useful, then, to look at the results of seven studies [1, 2, 6, 12, 15, 19, 21] that have compared the performance of unit and branch banks *within* branch banking states.

A comparison of these findings again illustrates the extent to which the results of individual studies have occasionally differed on particular questions. The only results not contradicted by at least one of the seven studies are that branch banks generally have higher net current earnings relative to capital and higher loan to asset ratios than unit banks in the same state. The latter finding has been reported with unvarying regularity.

Inasmuch as loans bear greater risks than Government securities, the reduction in risks attributable to the geographic and industrial diversification of lending enabled by branch banking would be expected to result in higher ratios of loans to deposits and loans to assets; competition may or may not be an important factor in accounting for them. These ratios, in turn, are important in accounting for the higher earnings rates of branch banks.

Somewhat less thoroughly documented, but still worthy of consideration is the finding reported in two recent contributions [6, 12] that ratios of time to total deposits are lower for branch banks than for unit banks in the same states. Also receiving support from two studies [15, 21] is a tendency for service charges on checking accounts to be higher at branch banks. But while the latter finding simply confirms what was learned in the comparisons between branch banking and unit banking areas, the former flatly contradicts the reported results of the inter-area comparisons.

What at first glance seem to be inconsistent conclusions are in fact two valid aspects of the relationship between branch banking and the ratio of time to total deposits. Although branch banking areas typically have higher time deposit ratios than unit banking areas, unit banks within the branch banking areas surpass branch banks in their proportion of time to total deposits. If, as has been tacitly assumed here, the time to total deposit ratio reflects competitive forces—in the sense that vigorous competition for deposits will result in some demand deposits being bid away to the interest paying time deposit categories—then the interarea comparisons suggest that deposit competition is keener in branch banking areas.

This interpretation, however, may attribute to branching laws the influence of regional differences in saving habits or other factors. Similarly, the generally higher interest rates paid on time deposits and higher ratios of time to total deposits of unit banks within branch banking areas lend themselves to various interpretations. They might mean, among other things, that unit banks in branch banking areas must resort to rate competition to make up for the greater locational convenience offered by branch systems.

ENTRY BY BRANCHING

A distinctive type of comparison between branch and unit banking was the before-and-after study carried out in Nassau County, New York [17]. This examined the effects of New York state's Omnibus Banking Act of 1960, which opened suburban counties to branches of the New York City banks. The findings for Nassau County were as follows: Somewhat surprisingly, the aggregate rate of return to capital in banking did not fall in the years immediately following entry, possibly because of the strong and growing demand for banking services during the period in question. On the other hand, there was a "significant increase in number of offices and number of banks per submarket," a reduction in instalment loan interest rates and a gradual increase in interest rates on time and savings deposits.

But although these results strongly suggest that benefits are to be derived from liberalization of branching laws and subsequent entry by branching, the study deals only with the immediate, short-run effects of such a move. It tells nothing about the potential long-term influence of big city branches on competition in the suburbs, nor does it adequately isolate the influence of liberalizing the branching law from that of the extraordinary growth and economic change in Nassau County in affecting the measures of bank performance used. Nevertheless, the figures presented are sufficiently impressive to make a strong *prima facie* case that the change in banking law favorably affected the price and quality of banking services in Nassau County.

BRANCHING BY MERGER

A final type of study bearing on the merits of branch and unit banking looks at the changes in lending behavior and pricing policy that occur when a unit bank becomes, through merger, a branch of a larger bank. Two studies [12, 15]—which utilized similar questionnaires—purport to shed some light on this area of banking controversy.

The results of the two studies are striking in their agreement. In only one of 17 measures of performance is any inconsistency evident; this disagreement concerns service charges on regular checking accounts. Whereas the New York state study [15] found that mergers generally led to reduced service charges, the other study [12]—which surveyed all national banks that acquired other banks through merger in 1962—reported that service charges were usually raised. With respect to every measure but two—service charges on special checking accounts under two alternative assumptions regarding activity and average balances—the effects of mergers were generally favorable to consumers. After merger, interest rates on savings deposits were higher; interest rates on 24-month new car loans, 15-year conventional mortgages and unsecured small business loans were lower; secured and unsecured lending authority of the chief lending officer was greater; maturities on car loans and conventional, FHA- and VA-mortgage loans were longer, and maximum amounts on car loans and all three types of mortgage loans were greater. Thus, the quantitative measures of bank performance relied on in these two surveys failed to discern any of the noncompetitive results that opponents of branch banking and mergers often allege to be inherent in multiple office banking.

Closer examination, however, reveals that the results reported are at best misleading and at worst potentially dangerous. It would be absurd, for example, to use them as a guide to future policy, for the favorable effects found to accompany most of the mergers are themselves partly the result of the discretion exercised by regulatory authorities in the past in deciding which mergers to permit. This is less true of the New York study [15], which examined mergers that occurred from 1951 to 1961 when little public control was exercised over bank mergers. Nevertheless, the bias imparted by the selected nature of the samples studied cannot safely be ignored.

Even if it is the case that mergers are, on balance, beneficial to consumers, this would not be grounds for giving blanket approval to all branching by merger. Both studies found some mergers to be detrimental to the public interest. The emphasis must continue to be on strengthening the ability to identify in advance, for purposes of prevention, those mergers that would be likely to have adverse effects on bank customers.

BRANCH LENDING POLICIES

Certain other charges against branch banking receive support from the studies cited. The New York state study [15] found that the out-of-town branches of branch banks were less willing to make small (less than $25,000) unsecured loans than were unit banks. This was evidenced by the greater volume, whether measured by number or dollar amount, of unsecured loans relative to deposits at unit banks. The same phenomenon was observed several years earlier in a study of New England banking [10].

Often voiced in conjunction with the charge that branches tend to have much more impersonal lending policies than unit banks is the argument that branch banking is undesirable because it drains some localities of funds and lends them elsewhere. The charge receives support from the New York finding that branches showed a much greater dispersion of loan to deposit ratios than did unit banks, clearly indicating that some branches were primarily deposit collecting agencies, whereas others were primarily loan outlets.

Although the evidence apparently bears out the factual basis of these two charges, it has nothing to say about their logic. Their underlying premise—the notion that deposit funds generated locally should stay at home—has little to recommend it, either as banking practice or public policy. It amounts to a contention that the interests of bank borrowers and depositors perfectly coincide, which is not generally true.

Any attempt to limit the lending activities of banks to a specified geographic area or otherwise to favor local borrowers would be almost certain to divert bank credit into less profitable channels. This, in turn, would reduce the earnings from which depositors can be paid for the use of their funds and introduce a distortion in the allocation of society's resources.

BANK SIZE AND PERFORMANCE

An additional characteristic of banks that may be systematically related to bank performance is absolute size, measured in terms of assets or deposits. The studies that have been made of the influence of this factor fall into two broad categories: first, studies of economies of scale [1, 3, 8, 9, 11, 19] and, second, studies of the price, quality and availability of banking services at banks of different sizes [2, 4, 6, 12, 19, 21].

Studies in the first category are concerned with finding which size of bank is most "efficient"—that is, which scale of production results in minimal costs per unit of output. Although several of these studies are the products of imaginative and laborious research, none of them satisfactorily comes to grips with a major conceptual problem—namely, the specification of just what it is that banks "produce."

Banks of different size and location offer diverse combinations of services that cannot readily be measured with a common yardstick. The failure to solve this problem in an adequate manner—a failing of which most investigators in the field are fully aware—robs their quantitative findings of much significance. In fact, since most studies arbitrarily measure bank output in terms of the dollar value of assets and since it is well established both that larger banks in general make larger loans than small banks and that costs per dollar are regularly lower for large than for small loans, these studies embody a systematic bias in the direction of overstating the relative efficiency of large banks.

Despite this, a finding common to almost all of the studies was that the greatest part of the potential savings due to size may be realized by banks with no more than 10 million dollars in deposits. When output is measured by the number of loans or deposit accounts rather than the dollar volume, as in a recent study of the costs of a sample of New England banks [3], the results are even less favorable to large size. Extremely moderate economies of scale were reported for each of six separate bank activities for which cost to output relationships were estimated.

Another interesting attempt to measure economies of scale defined bank output as the yield weighted sum of 16 earning asset categories [9]. The study found that average costs of banks in the Kansas City Federal Reserve District decreased up to a deposit size of about 300 million dollars, then began to increase. In sharp contrast to the conclusion reached in a study of all member banks in 1959 [11] that branch offices were more expensive to operate than unit banks of the same size, it was reported by the Kansas City study that merging unit banks into a branch system would reduce costs even if the output of each office remained unchanged.

At the present time—given the conflicting results, inadequate data and imperfect methodology of extant studies—there is no firm basis for judgment on which size of bank is most efficient. In all probability this will depend on the composition of the services rendered so that at best there may be only an optimal distribution of sizes of banks, rather than a single optimal size for all banks.

The influence of size on other banking performance variables has been the subject of several studies [2, 4, 6, 12, 19, 21]. At first glance, the results seem to be entirely in favor of size. Not only do larger banks pay higher average rates on savings, but they charge lower average rates on loans, have higher ratios of time to total deposits and— despite this price situation, which would appear to be unfavorable to bank profits—they end up with higher net current earnings relative to both assets and capital. The problem, similar to that encountered in studies of economies of scale, is that the effective rates of interest were computed as the ratios of total interest income on loans to total loans and total deposit interest paid to total time deposits (except for the Chicago area study [19], which gives the quoted rates on specific types of loans).

It is well known, however, that large banks have a larger share of their assets in large, low-cost, low-risk loans to major corporations on which interest rates charged are relatively low. Similarly, large banks normally have a much larger share of their time deposits in large denomination certificates of deposit, which entail little administrative expense and generally command higher interest rates than are paid on regular savings accounts. For this reason the findings presented contain a pronounced bias and must be regarded as possessing only limited validity.

Some additional insight into the relationship of size to banking performance is shed by a recent questionnaire survey of 2,650 commercial banks [21]. Using cross-classification tables to sort the separate influences of bank structure (branch versus unit), size and location (city versus other), the authors concluded that "size is what matters in the provision of banking services, not location, and not structure."

Thus, larger banks more frequently made automatic allocations from depositors' demand deposits to their savings accounts; maintained Christmas Club programs, and provided trust services, parking facilities, drive-in windows, special checking accounts, data processing, payroll and locked box services, foreign exchange, revolving credit and safe deposit boxes. On the other hand, charges on regular checking accounts were found to be generally lower at small banks than at large banks.

But although the authors concluded that "banking services definitely increase with bank size," they hastened to add that "where small banks are less apt to provide the service than large ones . . . usually it is because there is little demand for this service by the customers of the smaller banks."

POLICY IMPLICATIONS

No attempt has been made in this article either to present every detail of each study or to survey more than a small sample of recent research in the general area of banking markets. Nevertheless, most of the major empirical studies that deal directly with banking competition have been included so that the results presented are biased to only a minimal degree by selective omission. If the findings are taken at their face value—which, as has repeatedly been indicated, is very hazardous—they would seem to suggest the desirability of a public policy toward banking structure that discouraged concentration, encouraged new entry, liberalized branching and permitted banks to grow to large size, either by merger or through internal growth.

That these immediate goals in many market situations would be mutually contradictory follows as a matter of arithmetical necessity. These contradictions—apparently inherent in a society where technological advantages of size exist side by side with an economic system that relies on competition to prevent exploitation of consumers and the stagnation of industry—are the essence of the problem faced by the public agencies entrusted with channeling the evolution of the banking system along those lines most conducive to the public interest.

Valuable as they are as a start toward providing a factual basis for decisions bearing a crucial impact on the quality and prices of banking services today and in the future, empirical studies like those summarized above can provide only part of the answers to questions involving fundamental value judgments. There is the possibility that particular changes in the banking structure may have much more pronounced effects on some classes of bank customers than on others. There is also the fact that bank performance, far from being uniquely determined by bank size or structure or even the intensity of external rivalry, depends heavily on the qualities of individual bank managements and personnel—factors that are not easily reducible to terms suitable for statistical investigation.

Imperfect knowledge, nevertheless, is greatly to be preferred to total ignorance. If the great amount of effort currently being expended on research in the field of banking markets and banking competition yields nothing else, it will have been worthwhile if it dispels some of the prejudices and preconceptions that have marked discussion of these subjects in the past.

BIBLIOGRAPHY

1. Alhadeff, David A. *Monopoly and Competition in Banking.* Berkeley: University of California Press, 1954.
2. Anderson, Bernard Eric. "An Investigation into the Effects of Banking Structure on Aspects of Bank Behavior." Unpublished Ph.D. dissertation, Ohio State University, 1964.
3. Benston, George J. "Economies of Scale and Marginal Costs in Banking Operations," *National Banking Review,* II (June 1965), 507–549.
4. Carson, Deane, and Cootner, Paul H. "The Structure of Competition in Commercial Banking in the United States." *Private Financial Institutions.* (Commission on Money and Credit, Research Studies.) Englewood Cliffs: Prentice-Hall, 1963, pp. 55–155.
5. Edwards, Franklin R. *Concentration and Competition in Commercial Banking: A Statistical Study.* Research Report No. 26, Federal Reserve Bank of Boston, 1964.
6. Edwards, Franklin R. "The Banking Competition Controversy," *National Banking Review,* III (September 1965), 1–34.
7. Flechsig, Theodore G. *Banking Market Structure & Performance in Metropolitan Areas.* Washington: U.S. Board of Governors of the Federal Reserve System, 1965.
8. Gramley, Lyle E. *A Study of Scale Economies in Banking.* Kansas City, Missouri: Federal Reserve Bank of Kansas City, 1962.
9. Greenbaum, Stuart I. "Banking Structure and Costs: A Statistical Study of the Cost-Output Relationship in Commercial Banking." Unpublished Ph.D. dissertation, Johns Hopkins University, 1964.
10. Horvitz, Paul M. *Concentration and Competition in New England Banking.* Research Report No. 2. Boston: Federal Reserve Bank of Boston, 1958.
11. Horvitz, Paul M. "Economies of Scale in Banking." *Private Financial Institutions.* (Commission on Money and Credit, Research Studies.) Englewood Cliffs: Prentice-Hall, 1963, pp. 1–54.
12. Horvitz, Paul M. and Shull, Bernard. "The Impact of Branch Banking on Bank Performance," *National Banking Review,* II (December 1964), 143–188.
13. Kaufman, George G. "Bank Market Structure and Performance: The Evidence from Iowa," *Southern Economic Journal,* XXXII (April 1966), 429–439.

14. Kaufman, George G. and Latta, Cynthia M. "Near Banks and Local Savings," *National Banking Review,* III (June 1966), 539–542.
15. Kohn, Ernest. *Branch Banking, Bank Mergers and the Public Interest.* Albany: New York State Banking Department, 1964.
16. Kreps, Clifton H. Jr. "Character and Competitiveness of Local Banking: A Summary." Unpublished paper, Federal Reserve Bank of Richmond, 1965.
17. Motter, David C. and Carson, Deane. "Bank Entry and the Public Interest: A Case Study," *National Banking Review,* I (June 1964), 469–512.
18. Phillips, Almarin. "Competition, Confusion, and Commercial Banking," *Journal of Finance,* XIX (March 1964), 32–45.
19. Schweiger, Irving and McGee, John S. *Chicago Banking, The Structure and Performance of Banks and Related Financial Institutions in Chicago and Other Areas.* Chicago: University of Chicago, Graduate School of Business, 1961.
20. Wallace, Richard S. "Banking Structure and Bank Performance: A Case Study of Three Small Market Areas." Unpublished Ph.D. dissertation, University of Virginia, 1965.
21. Weintraub, Robert and Jessup, Paul. *A Study of Selected Banking Services by Bank Size, Structure, and Location.* U.S. Congress, House Committee on Banking and Currency, 88th Cong., 2d Sess., 1964.

The Applicability of the Federal Antitrust Laws to Bank Mergers

Edward G. Guy

To what extent should the antitrust laws apply to bank mergers? After extended committee hearings, Congress has found it desirable to legislate for the second time in six years an answer to this question. Public Law 89–356, amending the Bank Merger Act of 1960, was signed by the President on February 21, 1966. This article reviews briefly some of the pertinent background and sets forth the principal provisions of the new legislation. For brevity, the term "merger" will be used to include con-

Reprinted with the permission of the Federal Reserve Bank of New York from *Monthly Review,* April 1966.

solidations, acquisitions of assets, and assumptions of deposit liabilities as well as mergers.

PRE-1960 BACKGROUND

Prior to 1960, controls over bank mergers were incomplete, and ineffective with respect to the competitive aspects involved. There were gaps in the controls exercised under the banking statutes by the Federal banking agencies (the Comptroller of the Currency, the Board of Governors of the Federal Reserve System, and the Federal Deposit Insurance Corporation). Mergers in some cases could be effected without obtaining Federal approval, and even in those cases where approval was required the statutes prescribed no standards by which the appropriate Federal banking agency was to be guided in determining the significance to be attributed to the anticompetitive effects of a proposed merger.

Moreover, the antitrust laws had apparently provided no solution. There was little experience by which to judge the usefulness of the Sherman Act in dealing with bank mergers. Section 1 of that act prohibits unreasonable restraints of interstate trade or commerce,[1] and Section 2 prohibits monopolizing and attempts to monopolize any part of such trade or commerce.[2] No bank merger case under the Sherman Act had come before the United States Supreme Court, and the thrust of that act in the regulated field of banking had yet to be authoritatively determined. In addition to the apparent ineffectiveness of the Sherman Act, it was understood, by probably every responsible Government official who took a position on the question between 1950 and 1960, that Section 7 of the Clayton Act, as amended in 1950,[3] prohibiting specified corporate acquisitions where the effect "may be substantially to lessen competition, or to tend to create a monopoly," would not apply to the usual method of merging banks through asset acquisitions.[4]

[1] Section 1 of the Sherman Act, 15 U.S.C. §1, provides in part: "Every contract, combination in the form of trust or otherwise, or conspiracy, in restraint of trade or commerce among the several States, or with foreign nations, is declared to be illegal. . . ."

[2] Section 2 of the Sherman Act, 15 U.S.C. §2, provides in part: "Every person who shall monopolize, or attempt to monopolize, or combine or conspire with any other person or persons, to monopolize any part of the trade or commerce among the several States, or with foreign nations, shall be deemed guilty of a misdemeanor. . . ."

[3] Section 7 of the Clayton Act, as amended in 1950, 15 U.S.C. §18, provides in part: "No corporation engaged in commerce shall acquire, directly or indirectly, the whole or any part of the stock or other share capital and no corporation subject to the jurisdiction of the Federal Trade Commission shall acquire the whole or any part of the assets of another corporation engaged also in commerce, where in any line of commerce in any section of the country, the effect of such acquisition may be substantially to lessen competition, or to tend to create a monopoly."

[4] This understanding was due, in part, to the terms of Section 7. As amended in 1950, Section 7, by its literal terms, reached acquisitions of corporate stock or share

The legislative history of the Bank Merger Act of 1960 leaves no doubt that the competitive effects or possible antitrust implications of bank mergers were the major reasons prompting adoption of that act. It was emphasized that competition is an indispensable element to a strong and progressive banking system. These considerations, as well as the important gaps that existed prior to 1960 in the Federal law governing bank mergers, were stressed as the reasons why legislation was necessary.

THE BANK MERGER ACT OF 1960

The Bank Merger Act, as enacted on May 13, 1960, required the Comptroller of the Currency, the Board of Governors of the Federal Reserve System, or the Federal Deposit Insurance Corporation—depending on whether the resulting, acquiring, or assuming bank was to be a national bank (or a District of Columbia bank), a state member bank, or a nonmember insured bank—to pass upon applications for mergers. In so doing, the following six so-called banking factors were to be considered: (1) the financial history and condition of the banks involved, (2) the adequacy of their capital structure, (3) their future earnings prospects, (4) the general character of their management, (5) the convenience and needs of the community to be served, and (6) whether the corporate powers of the banks were consistent with the purposes of the Federal Deposit Insurance Act. In addition, the responsible agency was required to take into consideration "the effect of the transaction on competition (including any tendency toward monopoly)." The Bank Merger Act provided that the responsible agency "shall not approve the transaction unless, after considering all of such factors, it finds the transaction to be in the public interest." The Bank Merger Act thus made the "public interest" the ultimate consideration with regard to bank mergers. Although the responsible agency "in the interests of uniform standards" was required, except in a case involving the probable failure of one of the banks, to request reports on the competitive factors from the other two banking agencies and from the Attorney General, these reports were merely advisory. The final decision as to whether the proposed merger was in the public interest was to be made by the responsible agency on the basis of a balancing of the competitive factors and the so-called banking factors. The Senate defeated a proposed amendment which would have made the competitive factors controlling.

Although the Bank Merger Act was silent as to the applicability of the

---

capital by any corporation engaged in commerce and acquisitions of corporate assets but only by corporations "subject to the jurisdiction of the Federal Trade Commission." Since bank mergers were not considered as being accomplished through stock acquisitions and since banks were not subject to the jurisdiction of the Federal Trade Commission, it was understood that Section 7 did not apply to the usual method of merging banks.

antitrust laws to a merger approved by the responsible banking agency, it was generally understood that Congress intended that the banking agency's decision on a proposed bank merger would be determinative. A recent report of the Senate Banking and Currency Committee states that at the time the Bank Merger Act was passed "it was clearly expected that the decision of the responsible Federal banking authority . . . would be final and conclusive."

Accordingly, it seemed with the passage of the Bank Merger Act in 1960 that that act was to be the paramount statutory provision governing bank mergers. But then came the *Philadelphia* and *Lexington* cases.

In 1963, the United States Supreme Court held in *United States* v. *Philadelphia National Bank et al.*[5] that the proposed merger of The Philadelphia National Bank and the Girard Trust Corn Exchange Bank of Philadelphia, which had been approved by the Comptroller of the Currency under the Bank Merger Act, would violate Section 7 of the Clayton Act, as that section was amended in 1950. The understanding that such section did not apply to bank mergers accomplished through asset acquisitions was thereby laid to rest.[6] In the following year, the United States Supreme Court in *United States* v. *First National Bank & Trust Co. of Lexington et al.*[7] held that the consummated merger of First National Bank and Trust Company of Lexington, Kentucky, and Security Trust Company of Lexington, which had been approved by the Comptroller of the Currency under the Bank Merger Act, constituted a violation of Section 1 of the Sherman Act. In effect, these decisions meant that bank mergers approved by the appropriate Federal banking agencies under the Bank Merger Act were not rendered immune from challenge under the antitrust laws, and that in antitrust suits bank mergers would be measured solely by the standards of the antitrust laws unencumbered by the standards of the Bank Merger Act. In his *Philadelphia* dissent, Mr. Justice Harlan said, "The result is, of course, that the Bank Merger Act is almost completely nullified; its enactment turns out to have been an exorbitant waste of congressional time and energy." Many Congressmen agreed with this position.

Thus, the Federal law applicable to bank mergers had turned out to be quite different from the law as it was generally thought to be upon the enactment of the Bank Merger Act. Moreover, since there was no applicable statute of limitations, mergers approved under the Bank Merger

[5] 374 U.S. 321 (1963).

[6] In his majority opinion, Mr. Justice Brennan concluded that Congress intended the 1950 amendment to give Section 7 of the Clayton Act a reach which would bring mergers within its scope. Although the literal terms of the section would appear to limit its coverage, as noted in n. 4, *supra,* the stock-acquisition and asset-acquisition provisions, *read together,* were viewed as reaching mergers which, Mr. Justice Brennan said, fit neither category perfectly but lie somewhere between the two ends of the spectrum. So construed, Section 7 was held to embrace bank mergers.

[7] 376 U.S. 665 (1964).

Act, and mergers consummated prior to its enactment, were potentially vulnerable to antitrust attack.

The *Lexington* case not only demonstrated the potential thrust of the Sherman Act in the merger area, but also involved the difficult problem of divestiture since in that case, unlike *Philadelphia,* the merger had been consummated prior to the United States Supreme Court decision. Following the *Lexington* decision, the United States District Court for the Eastern District of Kentucky ordered the consolidated bank to create a separate institution that would be the competitive equal of the former Security Trust Company. The divestiture problem gained wide recognition when the District Court for the Southern District of New York held in *United States* v. *Manufacturers Hanover Trust Company* [8] that the consummated merger of Manufacturers Trust Company and The Hanover Bank, approved by the Board of Governors of the Federal Reserve System under the Bank Merger Act, violated Section 1 of the Sherman Act and Section 7 of the Clayton Act.

THE NEW LEGISLATION

In an effort to clarify the applicability of the antitrust laws to bank mergers, the Senate, in the first session of the current Congress, passed S. 1698. This bill would have exempted past approved and consummated bank mergers from antitrust attack, including those as to which antitrust suits were then pending. The bill would have required that future bank mergers not be consummated until thirty days after the date of approval by the appropriate banking agency under the Bank Merger Act. If the Attorney General did not institute an antitrust suit during the thirty-day period, the merger could be consummated and thereafter would be exempt from attack under the antitrust laws. If an antitrust suit were instituted during the thirty-day period, however, the bill would not have changed the apparent rule of the *Philadelphia* case to the effect that, in an antitrust suit involving a merger approved under the Bank Merger Act, the merger would be measured solely by the standards of the antitrust laws.

In contrast, the legislation, as modified by the House Banking and Currency Committee and enacted this year, establishes identical standards to be applied by the Federal banking agencies in approving merger applications and by the courts in judging such proposed mergers in antitrust suits brought by the Attorney General (other than under Section 2 of the Sherman Act). This new legislation, in amending the Bank Merger Act of 1960, is designed to accomplish the following:

1. A proposed merger "which would result in a monopoly, or which would be in furtherance of any combination or conspiracy to monopolize or to attempt to monopolize the business of banking in any part of the

[8] 240 F. Supp. 867 (S.D.N.Y. 1965).

United States" [9] may not be approved by the responsible Federal banking agency. The responsible agency, however, may approve a proposed merger "whose effect in any section of the country may be substantially to lessen competition, or to tend to create a monopoly,[10] or which in any other manner would be in restraint of trade," [11] but only where it finds that the "anticompetitive effects of the proposed transaction are clearly outweighed in the public interest by the probable effect of the transaction in meeting the convenience and needs of the community to be served." In making its determination, the responsible agency is, "in every case," to consider "the financial and managerial resources and future prospects of the existing and proposed institutions, and the convenience and needs of the community to be served"—this language revises the language of the six so-called banking factors of the Bank Merger Act of 1960.

2. The responsible banking agency, before acting upon a proposed merger, is required to request reports on the competitive factors from the other two agencies and the Attorney General, except that reports may be dispensed with where immediate action is necessary to prevent the probable failure of one of the banks involved. The reports must be furnished within thirty days of the request but, where an emergency exists requiring expeditious action, the reports must be furnished to the responsible agency within ten days. As under the Bank Merger Act of 1960, these reports are not binding upon the agency responsible for approving the merger.

3. An approved merger may not be consummated before the thirtieth day following the date of approval by the responsible banking agency, except that this period would be shortened to five days in those cases found by the responsible agency to be emergencies requiring expeditious action, and an approved merger could be consummated immediately in order to prevent the probable failure of one of the banks involved. The Attorney General, who is to be immediately notified of approval by the responsible agency, can institute an action under the antitrust laws arising out of the merger, but only if he commences the action prior to the expiration of the prescribed waiting period. The House Banking and Currency Committee Report indicates that these prescribed time limitations do not relate to antitrust actions brought under Section 2 of the Sherman Act, and such actions may be brought at any time. In an antitrust action brought by the Attorney General within the prescribed period, the court would "review *de novo*" the issues presented, but would be required to apply standards "identical" with those to be applied under the new law by the responsible banking agency in approving the merger. The merger could not be consummated after such suit is commenced unless the court otherwise specifically orders. In such suit, the Federal banking agency concerned and the state bank supervisory agency having

[9] Compare Section 2 of the Sherman Act, *supra* n. 2.

[10] Compare Section 7 of the Clayton Act, as amended, *supra* n. 3.

[11] Compare Section 1 of the Sherman Act, *supra* n. 1.

jurisdiction within the state involved may appear as a party and be represented by counsel. The House report indicates that this provision would even permit the appropriate state bank supervisory agency to present its views in a case involving the merger of two national banks.

4. The following bank mergers are, in effect, exempt from any attack under the provisions of the antitrust laws, other than under Section 2 of the Sherman Act:

(a) Future mergers approved under the new law as to which the Attorney General does not institute suit prior to the expiration of the prescribed waiting period.
(b) Past mergers consummated before June 17, 1963, the date of the *Philadelphia* decision, and not as yet unscrambled pursuant to final court order.
(c) Past mergers consummated on or after the date of the *Philadelphia* decision and before enactment of the new law, except those as to which suits have been brought before enactment.

These provisions exempt, except as to Section 2 of the Sherman Act, some 2,200 bank mergers consummated since 1950 (including over 700 approved under the Bank Merger Act of 1960) which might otherwise continue to be, at least potentially, vulnerable to antitrust attack. Among those so exempted are the three pre-*Philadelphia* mergers as to which antitrust suits were then pending in the courts, involving Continental Illinois National Bank and Trust Company of Chicago (Illinois), First Security National Bank and Trust Company of Lexington (Kentucky), and Manufacturers Hanover Trust Company (New York). The *Manufacturers Hanover* action was terminated on March 7, 1966, and the *Continental Illinois* action was terminated on March 11, 1966. With respect to the *Lexington* case, it has been reported that the Justice Department is considering pressing for a favorable decision under Section 2 of the Sherman Act. (The Government had alleged violations in that case under both Section 1 and Section 2 of the Sherman Act, but the United States Supreme Court decision was based solely on Section 1.) These provisions do not exempt the three post-*Philadelphia* cases pending in the courts, involving Crocker-Citizens National Bank (California), Mercantile Trust Company National Association (Missouri), and Third National Bank in Nashville (Tennessee); and, in these suits, the new bank merger standards are to be applied.

5. Pre-enactment merger applications, which were withdrawn or abandoned as a result of objection or suit brought by the Attorney General, may be reinstituted and are to be acted upon in accordance with the new law.

The standards imposed by the new law have been praised, on the one hand, as providing certainty, uniformity, and promptness in the resolution of antitrust questions involved in bank mergers, and condemned, on the other hand, as vague and uncertain.

It would seem that the new law is intended to modify the application by both the courts and the Federal banking agencies of the antitrust laws to future bank mergers. Ultimately, of course, it will be up to the courts to resolve the extent of this modification; some clarification should be forthcoming in the cases now pending in the Federal courts.

A Graduated Deposit Insurance Plan*

Thomas Mayer

The most acceptable justifications for the extensive supervision exercised over commercial banks, savings banks and savings and loan associations, are the prevention of financial panics and deflation and the protection of depositors.[1] The proposal made here would accomplish these tasks with less government control than is currently required. Like most government regulations, bank and savings and loan regulations at present substitute the government's discretion for market processes. By contrast, the plan proposed here uses a market system analog for exercising control.

II

The first and minor part of the plan is to locate all bank supervisory work in the FDIC (and all savings and loan supervisory duties in the FSLIC) so that any asset permitted by the FDIC would be a bankable asset. The major part of the plan deals with the enforcement mechanism. In effect, the safety of most bank deposits is, at present, guaranteed by

* The author is indebted for helpful criticism at various stages to Carl Brehm, Frank Child, Robert Einzig, Edward Ettin, Thomas Gies, Ira O. Scott, Jr., Eli Shapiro, W. Paul Strassmann, and Clark Warburton, who, of course, are not responsible for any remaining errors.

[1] See T. Mayer, "Is the Portfolio Regulation of Financial Institutions Justified?" *Journal of Finance* (May 1962), 311–317.

the FDIC. Regulations of asset quality therefore protect, not so much the depositor as the FDIC.[2] This suggests that instead of attempting to prevent bank failures we should try to maintain the solvency of the FDIC's guarantee fund. This can be done in several ways. One is our present system of preventing banks from holding unsafe assets, another is to allow banks to hold risky assets, but to vary the FDIC insurance premium accordingly.

Such a scheme of varying the insurance premium could take several forms. On the one hand, it could consist of no more than an arrangement whereby banks and savings and loan associations would have to meet present requirements of asset quality in all but one aspect, say the holding of some common stock, or holding more mortgages than presently allowed, and would then be charged a higher insurance premium to compensate the FDIC and FSLIC for the greater risk. On the other hand, numerous classes of asset safety could be established with a different insurance premium for each class. The problems of establishing such classes are discussed in the following section. It would, of course, not be necessary to establish risk classes embracing all types of risk, banks could still be prohibited from buying some assets which are too risky. Hence the scheme is not as radical as it may appear at first. Moreover, for the somewhat similar problem of capital adequacy a broadly similar scheme already exists. Thus the Federal Reserve Bank of New York, in evaluating capital adequacy, classifies bank assets into six risk classes and assigns to each class a specific minimum capital requirement. Similarly, the Federal Home Loan Bank Board uses the volume of risk assets held by savings and loan associations as one of the criteria for determining the Federal insurance reserve account.[3]

The main advantage of a fully graduated deposit insurance plan is, of course, that it would introduce the price mechanism into the insurance system; each institution could then accept risk until the marginal cost of risk (measured by the extra insurance premium) is equal to the marginal benefit (measured by the rate of return). If the insurance premium is set correctly it would induce the optimal degree of risk taking.[4] Just as a life insurance company will insure individuals in risky occupations at above

[2] There are two qualifications. First, deposits above $10,000 are not fully insured. But this is only a minor qualification because in most cases, by rescuing banks prior to actual failures the FDIC in effect protects all deposits fully. Second, there are a few uninsured banks and this proposal would not apply to them.

[3] Risk assets are defined as total assets minus cash, government obligations, Federal Home Bank stock, prepaid FSLIC premiums and 60 per cent of insured and guaranteed loans, See Howard D. Cross, *Management Policies for Commercial Banks* (Englewood Cliffs, New Jersey, 1962), 169 ff.; Federal Home Loan Bank Board, *Amendment Relating to Required Amounts and Maintenance of Federal Insurance Reserve,* FSLIC-1,712 (Dec. 30, 1963) and FSLIC-1,709 (Dec. 27, 1963).

[4] One cannot tell how much additional risk financial institutions would be willing to take were they allowed to do so, but present regulations clearly reduce risk taking to some extent below what it would be in a free market.

standard rates the FDIC and FSLIC could insure deposits at above average rates.[5]

A second, though less important advantage of this proposal is that making insurance regulations more flexible might induce a number of uninsured institutions to join the FDIC and FSLIC. This is quite unimportant in the commercial banking field, where nearly all banks are already insured, but among mutual savings banks and savings and loan associations uninsured institutions account for a somewhat greater proportion of total assets. Of course, many of them might refuse to join the FSLIC in any case.

A graduated insurance system could operate in several ways. One would be to insure not deposits directly, but rather, to insure the assets held by the institution. This system has a major disadvantage; it provides insurance not only to the depositor, but also bank stockholders, and stockholders should be left to look after themselves.

Although the insurance should therefore safeguard deposits rather than assets, the insurance rates charged would still have to depend upon the types of assets held. One way of classifying assets for this scheme would be to examine each specific asset, much as a banker does in choosing his portfolio. But this would be very expensive since it would in effect mean duplicating the bankers' work. It is therefore preferable to set up fairly broad asset classes. To set the system up one could take the presently operating system as a base and add one or several "surcharge" classes. Banks and savings and loan associations would then be allowed at a "surcharge premium," to hold presently proscribed assets, for example mortgages with a very high loan-to-value ratio, or to exceed present limitations upon the volume of specific assets they may hold.[6] Since the probability of failure depends not only upon the riskiness of assets, but also on the capital ratio, this factor could be taken into account in setting the premium. One crude rule of thumb would be to set the surcharge premium not on the basis of the proportion of deposits invested in risky assets, but on the proportion (or multiple) of capital held in risky assets.

The main difficulty is estimating the correct premium for each risk, since risk of failure cannot be properly estimated from the law of large numbers. Moreover, there are many examples of assets whose safety, or lack of safety, was not realized until the acid test of the depression. But if the risk premium is set too high, the plan may still be superior to the present system and at the worst would be equivalent to it. This is so

[5] A counter analogy would be establishing variable premiums for fire insurance depending upon the type of structure, with abolition of building codes pertaining to fire hazards. But this analogy is not valid. The reasons why such a scheme would be unacceptable are first, that it would create a danger for the whole neighborhood and second, that it would risk human life; neither of these points applies to deposit insurance. Incidentally, the existence of different rates for different types of buildings does introduce an element similar to the scheme here proposed.

[6] This assumes that the alternative to the proposed system is simply the present one, and not a realization of standards under the present system.

because the present system in effect imposes an infinite premium on certain portfolios. If instead the premium were, say, one per cent, whereas it should be one-half per cent, the FDIC would be better off than it is at present (because the premium would exceed the additional losses), as would those banks willing to hold these portfolios at a one per cent premium.

If the surcharge premium is set too low there are two types of disadvantages. First, banks and savings and loan associations, at least in the short run, are given a windfall profit, and second, there is too much risk taking.[7]

The difficulty of discriminating between assets is not a peculiarity of the proposal. The present system of dividing assets into permitted and proscribed classes also faces this problem. To be sure, it requires the setting up of only two classes whereas the proposal would require at least three classes. But a mistake made under the present system may perhaps do more damage than an equivalent mistake under the proposed system. This is so because the present system, by prohibiting some asset acquisitions imposes what, in effect, amounts to an infinite surcharge premium on some assets, while the permitted assets carry an extremely low premium.[8]

In addition to the problem of determining the correct surcharge premium, there are four other disadvantages of the plan. First, there is the cost of setting up and administering the system. But these administrative costs may perhaps be not much greater than they are under the present system. Since a decision under the present two-category system carries much more weight than a decision under a multiple-category system, it presumably also requires more work in making a decision. There is even one situation in which the proposed plan could have a negative cost. Suppose that financial institutions press the regulatory authorities for permission to hold certain assets; allowing them to do so at a higher insurance premium may well be a compromise which saves administrative costs.

Second, banks and savings and loan associations may be reluctant to hold more risky assets than they presently hold, particularly if these assets are officially labeled as more risky. If so, the work of setting up the scheme would be wasted.

Another problem is that the scheme requires that commercial bank regulation authority be concentrated in the FDIC, a proposal which has been argued pro and con on its own merits.[9]

[7] There is, however, an arbitrary element in bank profits in any case due to different impacts on bank profits of open market operations and reserve requirement changes.

[8] Strictly speaking, this is not correct since a bank can become a nonmember noninsured bank and savings and loan associations, too, can leave the FSLIC.

[9] See G. L. Bach, "Bank Supervision, Monetary Policy and Government Reorganization," *Journal of Finance* (Dec., 1949), 269–285; C. C. Warburton, "Coordinating Monetary and Bank Supervisory and Loan Agencies of the Federal Government," *Journal of Finance* (June, 1950), 148–169.

Third, a much more fundamental problem is created by the fact that since prices do not equal marginal costs and resource allocation is not perfect in all other sections of the economy, it does not necessarily follow that setting prices of risk taking for the financial intermediaries equal to marginal costs would improve resource allocation.[10] This is a weakness of all piecemeal schemes to improve resource allocation.

[10] R. G. Lipsey and R. K. Lancaster, "The General Theory of Second Best," *Review of Economic Studies,* No. 63 (1956–1957), 11–32.

Short-Term Notes and Banking Competition

A new avenue of obtaining funds for lending and investing was unveiled last September when a Boston commercial bank announced its intention to borrow funds by issuing short-term promissory notes, generally in denominations of $1 million or more. This step was one of a series of moves banks have taken in the postwar period in response to intensifying competition, such as raising their interest rates and broadening their services.

THE BUSINESS OF BANKING

Banks are generally classified as service businesses, providing such financial services to the community as check clearing, investing, and lending. To its management, however, a bank appears much like a trade concern. Management sees its main function as one of first buying, or collecting funds, and then selling these funds at a profit through lending and investing. As competition among banks and other financial institutions has intensified since World War II, bankers have acquired sharper pencils to calculate the costs and profits involved in this money business.

"THE GOOD OLD DAYS"

In some ways, the early postwar years were "the good old days" for banking. Inflows of funds were abundant at little or no cost. The average

Reprinted with the permission of the Federal Reserve Bank of Boston from *New England Business Review,* December 1964.

rate on time deposits was about 1 percent, demand deposit levels were high, and if additional funds were needed banks could liquidate part of their huge portfolios of government securities at a price supported by the Federal Reserve. There was comparatively little demand for loans because most businesses and consumers had sizable holdings of liquid assets. All in all, the banking life was pleasantly tranquil.

NEW DEVELOPMENTS IN THE POSTWAR PERIOD

But this life was artificial and could not last too long. Competition in the financial area began here and there, with the most marked surge shown by savings and loan associations. These associations found that many consumers wanted to become home owners and were willing to pay attractive rates of interest for mortgage loans. The associations also found that they could attract a virtual flood of savings by paying rates only a little higher than those paid by other institutions. So they began to serve both home buyers and savers and as a result had a phenomenal growth. Mutual savings banks pursued a similar course. Thus, savings associations and savings banks preempted almost all the savings side of banking.

Another postwar development affecting banks was the re-emergence of monetary policy operations by the Federal Reserve System in 1951. The System no longer was willing to accept all government bonds offered to it at par. This led to a decline in bond prices, higher interest rates in the money markets, and some restrictions in the availability of bank credit.

At about the same time treasurers of large business corporations began to be aware of lost income which was represented by their large demand deposits. They found out that a demand deposit level only one-half as large as what they were carrying was often enough for their payment needs. The remainder could be invested in Treasury bills to yield extra income. This led to a liquidation of some demand deposits at commercial banks and a slower growth in the total. With the time deposit area being largely taken over by the thrift institutions, overall bank deposits were rising quite slowly. This served to restrict the availability of lendable funds.

Still another postwar change affecting money business was the growth in the issuance of commercial paper, mainly directly-placed paper by sales finance companies. These firms were able to borrow funds from the public through commercial paper at rates 1 to 2 percentage points below the prime loan rates of commercial banks during most of the postwar period up to 1963. Corporate treasurers began to invest their excess demand deposits in this commercial paper and not only reduced the growth of lendable funds of banks but actually began, in effect, to compete in the business loan area. Thus, banks were subject to some pressure from both the source and the use of funds sides.

These activities tending to impinge on banks' business were carried on by corporate treasurers who handled large deposit balances. The small individual depositor usually did not have a balance large enough to enter the financial markets for Treasury bills or other instruments. But even though this small depositor kept his whole balance at the bank, his account was generally not as profitable as the large corporate account. The handling costs of a check are the same whether it is for $10 or $10,000, but the investment and loan income from a large deposit balance is, of course, many times greater than that from a small balance. Cost studies of banks show that small demand deposit accounts tend to generate little or no profit to the bank even if a 10 cent charge per check is imposed. Almost all of a bank's profits come from the larger accounts. Thus, the most profitable segment of banks' business is affected when corporate treasurers draw down their companies' accounts for direct investment in government securities or commercial paper.

STEPS TO MEET COMPETITION

In 1961 banks moved aggressively to meet the rising competition in their business by issuing negotiable certificates of deposit [C.D.] on a larger scale. These certificates, which represent time deposits held in the issuing banks, can be sold through securities dealers if the holder corporation (that is, the time depositor) wishes to "cash in" his time deposit before its maturity date. These negotiable certificates provided corporate treasurers with a short-term investment outlet for their temporarily idle demand deposits. For the corporate treasurer these certificates served as a substitute for Treasury bills, commercial paper, and other short-term money market instruments. At the same time, they kept deposits in the bank although in the form of time, rather than demand, deposits.

Time deposits are a more expensive source of funds than demand deposits so the shift toward time deposits increased bank expenses. The spread between the cost of bank funds and the rate earned on loans has declined. As shown in Figure 1, the spread between the rate paid on 6-month C.D.'s and the prime loan rate has declined substantially since 1961. While the prime rate has remained at 4½ percent over this period, the 6-month C.D. rate has risen from about 2¾ percent in early 1961 to 4 percent in late 1964 (Figure 2). The earnings spread between C.D.'s and 3-year municipals has been much more satisfactory, however. The yield on these medium-term municipals has risen along with the yields on comparable maturities of Federal obligations, so that the spread now is actually somewhat greater than in 1961.

Another problem encountered by banks in their competition for time deposits was the interest ceiling imposed by the Board of Governors of the Federal Reserve System under Regulation Q. On 6-month certificates of deposit, for example, this ceiling was 3 percent during the 1957–1961

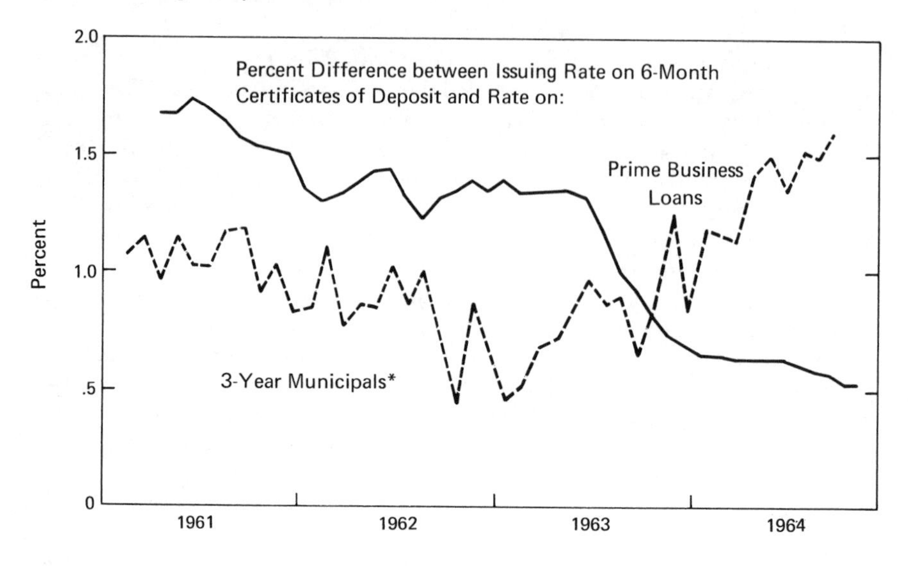

FIG. 1 Earnings spread on bank funds.

*Municipal yields are averages of new AAA, AA, and A rated issues. These yields were doubled for comparability with taxable yields.

period, 3½ percent from January 1, 1962 to July 17, 1963, and 4 percent up to November 1964. During each of these periods, competition tended to push rates up against the ceiling. Last November 24 the ceiling was raised to 4½ percent for maturities of 90 days or more.

When rates on certificates of deposit reach the ceiling, the leading money market banks mainly in New York City, are able to take many accounts away from other slightly smaller banks. These other banks often have to pay a slightly higher rate for negotiable certificates of deposit than do leading money market banks whose certificates have a somewhat greater marketability. When the ceiling is reached by money market banks, the smaller banks no longer have any leeway for paying a slightly higher rate. When a certificate of deposit comes due, they are in danger of losing this deposit to the large banks.

One method of obtaining protection against deposit losses when rates reach the Regulation Q ceiling is to issue unsecured negotiable short-term notes. These notes perform the same function as negotiable certificates of deposit in that they are both used by banks for acquiring funds, but there are several differences. Short-term notes have the following unique characteristics:

1. Classified as borrowings, not deposits.
2. Not subject to Regulation Q.
3. No reserve requirements.
4. Not covered by deposit insurance and therefore do not have insurance premiums assessed against them.

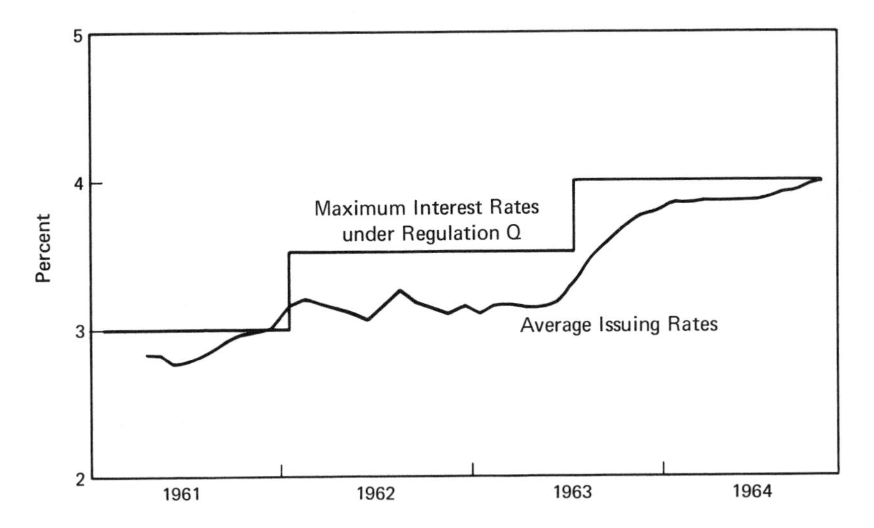

FIG. 2 Average and maximum interest rates on 6-month certificates of deposit.

These differences result in both advantages and disadvantages for the bank issuing short-term notes rather than certificates of deposit. First, some banks are quite conscious of their relative size as measured by deposits. Since notes are borrowings, they do not contribute to the deposit size of the bank, and thus might be viewed as a disadvantage. In addition, some banks are sensitive about the size of their borrowings.

The other three differences favor the issuance of notes. Exemption from Regulation Q is a definite advantage when interest rates are near the ceiling. The absence of reserve requirements makes short-term notes about 16 basis points (0.16 percent annually) more profitable to the bank, if the stated interest rate is the same as in a certificate of deposit. Moreover, avoidance of the deposit insurance premium reduces the cost of a short-term note about 3 basis points.

Deposit insurance is not very important for either certificates of deposit or short-term notes because currently only the first $10,000 is covered. These instruments are typically issued in $1 million amounts. Short-term notes are also generally considered to have an equal claim with deposits against bank assets if a bank were to go into liquidation. In other words, they are not subordinated claims.

The lower net cost of short-term notes than of certificates of deposit amounting to 19 basis points raises an interesting competitive situation. Will the two instruments be issued and traded in the market at identical interest rates, which allow the banks to keep the net cost saving of 0.19 percent? Or will the investors, mainly corporations, get a higher yield on notes, making the net cost of the banks equal on the two investments? What is probably most likely is that some intermediate position will be reached with the banks and short-term note investors sharing in this "extra" gain.

With short-term notes being somewhat more profitable than certificates of deposit, it might be expected that they would largely tend to displace certificates of deposit. But this will not be the case evidently because their issuance is limited, in the case of national banks, to an amount equal to capital stock plus 50 percent of surplus. If state banks were generally subject to some similar limit, the maximum value of short-term notes that the Nation's 100 largest banks could issue would total about $8–9 billion. Negotiable certificates of deposit currently total almost $13 billion.

But banks may not even issue these notes to the allowable limit. They would probably choose to hold a reserve of unissued note capacity for periods of need, such as when the Regulation Q ceiling prevents effective competition by certificates of deposit. Some banks may also want to reserve some borrowing capacity for the possible issuance of long-term subordinated debentures. These debentures are considered as part of the capital base in the case of national banks. As such, they can be issued instead of stock to build up the capital position of banks. Because of income tax considerations, debentures are a much less expensive source of "capital" than are capital stock issues.

Even though it is 3 months since the first issuance of short-term notes, not many banks have participated as yet in this market. The total amount outstanding has been estimated currently as somewhat less than $200 million. The growth has been much slower than that of certificates of deposit in 1961 when they began to be actively used.

One important reason for the slow growth of short-term notes is that the New York City banks have not yet entered this market. There is some doubt as to whether they are legal under New York State law. These banks may wait for the law to be amended.

NEW ENGLAND OPINIONS

A survey of attitudes among New England bankers showed the following:

1. Generally the larger the bank, the more active the interest in short-term notes. But few intend to use them soon, although several have obtained authorizations from their boards of directors.
2. The more active the bank in issuing certificates of deposit, the more interest it had in the possibility of using short-term notes.
3. Almost all banks surveyed viewed the notes as defensive instruments. They would issue notes only when they could not retain an account by use of certificates of deposit. For example, they expected to use these notes if the Regulation Q ceilings prevented them from competing through certificates of deposit. They also foresaw the possibility of using these notes for special cases which would leave the regular structure of rates on certificates of deposit unchanged.

Several technical factors exist which will tend to dampen the growth of short-term notes. The Internal Revenue Service has ruled that borrowed funds may not be invested in securities which are exempt from Federal income taxes. If it were apparent that a bank was investing funds secured via short-term notes in tax-exempt obligations of state and local governments, the Internal Revenue Service would declare the interest income of such securities subject to the corporate income tax.

In most New England states, municipalities and other local governments are allowed to invest their treasury funds only in U.S. Government securities or bank deposits. Since short-term notes are not deposits, these localities cannot purchase them, but must use certificates of deposit instead.

The raising of rate ceilings under Regulation Q in late November may also serve to limit the use of short-term notes somewhat. Prior to November 24, the ceiling on certificates of deposit with maturities of less than 90 days was 1 percent. Short-term notes were likely to be issued to investors who did not want maturities of as long as 90 days. But since the ceiling on maturities below 90 days is now 4 percent, notes are less likely to be needed. But there may be some use of notes in maturities of less than 30 days. Under Regulation Q, deposits with a maturity of less than 30 days are classified as demand deposits and no interest may be paid on them.

Policy Statements on Unsecured Negotiable Notes

[The following excerpts from the *Federal Reserve Bulletin* indicate a major shift in position from 1964 to 1966.]

ISSUANCE OF UNSECURED NEGOTIABLE NOTES BY MEMBER BANKS[1]

In response to questions with respect to the applicability of the Board's Regulation D (Reserves of Member Banks) and Regulation Q (Payment of Interest on Deposits) to unsecured negotiable notes issued by member commercial banks as a means of obtaining funds, the Board of Governors has stated that, since such notes constitute borrowings, they are not subject, under present law and regulation, to the interest rate limitations or reserve requirements prescribed for deposits by the Board.

The legality of the issuance of notes of the type referred to must be determined in the light of applicable Federal and State laws, and it is assumed that any bank borrowing by means of such notes will satisfy itself that their issuance is authorized. Borrowings of this type would, of course, be so identified in financial statements and call reports and added to all other borrowings in the application of statutory or other limitations on the total amount of debt a bank may incur. Any liabilities thus incurred by a bank would increase the necessity for maintaining an adequate cushion of liquidity and equity capital.

• • •

PROMISSORY NOTES AS "DEPOSITS"[2]

The Board of Governors, effective September 1, 1966, has amended Regulations D and Q by inserting a new paragraph (*f*) in section 204.1

[1] *Federal Reserve Bulletin,* September 1964, p. 1137. Reprinted with the permission of the Board of Governors of the Federal Reserve System.

[2] *Federal Reserve Bulletin,* July 1966, pp. 963, 979. Reprinted with the permission of the Board of Governors of the Federal Reserve System.

and section 217.1, respectively, of such Regulations. This new paragraph defines deposits as including certain promissory notes in order to bring short-term bank promissory notes and similar instruments under the regulations governing reserve requirements and payment of interest on deposits. Paragraphs (*f*), (*g*), (*h*) and (*i*) of section 204.1 have been redesignated as paragraphs (*g*), (*h*), (*i*) and (*j*), respectively. The text of this new paragraph is as follows:

(*f*) *Deposits as including certain promissory notes.* For the purposes of this part, the term "deposits" shall be deemed to include any promissory note, acknowledgment of advance, due bill, or similar instrument that is issued by a member bank principally as a means of obtaining funds to be used in its banking business, except any such instrument (1) that is issued to another bank, (2) that evidences an indebtedness arising from a transfer of assets that the bank is obligated to repurchase, or (3) that has an original maturity of more than two years and states expressly that it is subordinated to the claims of depositors. This paragraph shall not, however, affect the status, for purposes of this part, of any instrument issued before June 27, 1966.

• • •

(2) The Board acted to bring shorter-term bank promissory notes and similar instruments under the regulations governing reserve requirements and payment of interest on deposits. This action would not apply to Federal funds transactions, interbank borrowings, transfers of assets with agreements to repurchase, or bank notes for capital purposes that have a maturity of more than two years and are subordinated to claims of depositors. The action will become effective September 1, 1966, and will apply to all promissory notes covered by the action that are issued on or after June 27, 1966, and are outstanding on or after the effective date. Promissory notes and other instruments of the type covered by the action have come into use only in the last few years, and the volume outstanding is small. The purpose of the Board's action is to prevent future use of these instruments as a means of circumventing statutory and regulatory requirements applicable to bank deposits.

7

International Banking: A New Frontier

As discussed in *Banking Goes International,* the postwar period has seen an expanding role of the dollar—and American banks—in international finance. Furthermore, this reading outlines the significant interactions among the American balance of payments, the Voluntary Foreign Credit Restraint program, the developing Euro-dollar market, and postwar activities of American banks abroad.

"The biggest growth area of U.S. banking today is not in the U.S. but overseas." This is the opening statement of the selection by Jeremy Main, which analyzes the motives for American banks' overseas expansion. He develops an important concept: that international activities are believed to contribute to increased profitability of a *bank system*. This article further considers the alternatives involved in an American bank's decision about whether to expand abroad by means of branches or correspondent participations.

The article by Fred H. Klopstock, detailing the increasing activity of American banks in the Euro-dollar market, suggests the banks' motives and outlines the use of Euro-dollars in various strategies of bank management. Interrelationships among liquidity management, loan opportunities, and competition for deposits are illustrated in this reading. Also recognized are the ways in which elements of the regulatory environment —such as Regulation Q, reserve requirements, and administration of the Voluntary Foreign Credit Restraint program—stimulated the Euro-dollar activity of American banks.

Banking Goes International

Commercial banks in the United States had almost 12 billion dollars of credits outstanding to foreigners at the end of 1966—a fivefold increase within the last ten years. At the same time the number of foreign branches of American banks increased from 115 to 264, and the assets of these branches amounted to 9.1 billion dollars at the end of 1965.

These figures reflect the tremendous expansion of foreign activities of American commercial banks and the "coming of age" of the United States as a center of international banking and finance.

BACKGROUND OF THE DEVELOPMENT

For centuries, international banking was dominated by European banking houses. This tradition dates back to the twelfth century when the money lenders of Lombardy (an area in northern Italy) became engaged in financing foreign trade. Then followed the development of private banking houses in Florence, Genoa and Venice and thus, up to the mid-sixteenth century, Italian banking reigned supreme over international finance. In the latter part of the sixteenth century, the center gradually shifted to the Low Countries—Belgium and Holland. First, Antwerp and, then, in the early seventeenth century Amsterdam became the international financial centers. With the establishment of the Bank of England in 1694, Britain gradually became the focal point of international finance and retained its supremacy until World War II.

United States banks did not engage in international activities in any significant way until 1914. Prior to that time, national banks were prohibited from establishing foreign branches and from accepting bills of exchange; thus they were largely precluded from financing international commercial transactions. Only a modest amount of international banking business had been carried out by private, unincorporated banks and by state chartered banks.

The passage of the Federal Reserve Act in 1913 opened the door to the expansion of the American banks into the international field. Banks were permitted to accept bills arising from international transactions, and any bank with capital and surplus of 1 million dollars or more was authorized to establish branches abroad. However, although the legal door was open,

Reprinted with the permission of the Federal Reserve Bank of Chicago from *Business Conditions,* April 1967.

expansion was slow in coming. It was only through vigorous efforts on the part of the Federal Reserve to promote an acceptance market that the volume of trade financing by American banks gradually increased. Total volume of acceptances grew to an estimated 250 million dollars in 1916 and rose further to 1 billion at the end of 1919.

The establishment of foreign branches by American banks also developed slowly. During the three years following the passage of the Federal Reserve Act, only one national bank established branches abroad. To facilitate the expansion, the Federal Reserve Act was amended in 1916 to permit investment by national banks in corporations engaged principally in international or foreign banking. However, no provision was made for Federal chartering and only three "agreement corporations" were state chartered in the two years following the amendment.[1]

To provide additional inducement for American commercial banks to expand into export and capital financing, Congress passed a law in 1919 (commonly known as the Edge Act after its sponsor, Senator Edge of New Jersey) authorizing the Federal Reserve Board to charter and regulate corporations established ". . . for purposes of engaging in international or foreign financial operations." Initially, two types of corporations were permitted to be established by Regulation K of the Board of Governors: banking corporations and financing corporations.[2] They were authorized to:

—buy and sell spot and future foreign exchange
—receive checks, bills, drafts, acceptances, notes, bonds, coupons and other securities for collection abroad
—buy and sell securities for the account of customers abroad.

Moreover, the banking corporations were authorized to hold demand and time deposits of foreigners and were permitted to acquire equity investment in foreign corporations engaged in banking.[3] The financing corporations, while not permitted to accept deposits, were empowered to invest in foreign corporations other than banks.

The 1916 and 1919 legislation—together with rapidly growing foreign trade and investment—finally provided the impetus for the expansion of American banks into international banking in the following decade. By

[1] The name "agreement corporations" arose from the provisions of the amendment requiring each corporation to "enter into an agreement" with the Federal Reserve Board regarding the type and manner of activities.

[2] In September 1963 Regulation K was revised and the distinction between the two types of corporations eliminated. Existing Edge Act financial and banking corporations were permitted to merge all functions into one corporation.

[3] In 1966, legislation was passed allowing national banks with capital and surplus of 1 million dollars or more to invest, upon the approval by the Board of Governors of the Federal Reserve System, an amount not exceeding 10 percent of their paid-in capital and surplus in the stock of foreign banking corporations, thus opening a more direct route to such investment.

1920, American banks had established 181 offices abroad, and by 1929, 18 agreement and Edge Act corporations were formed. However, the worldwide depression that hit in 1930 brought the expansion to a standstill. Throughout the depression-ridden Thirties and the war-torn Forties, the number of foreign branches and Edge Act corporations declined. By 1945, there were only 78 offices of American banks operating abroad, and only two Edge Act corporations had survived.

After the war and up to the late Fifties, the expansion proceeded at a very slow rate. Although the dollar had emerged in the postwar period as a key currency, and dollar exchange was in short supply throughout most of the world, various restrictions placed by individual countries on the convertibility of their currencies made it difficult for American banks and corporations to extend credit to foreigners. The shortage of dollars to finance the imports and capital needs of the world was met largely through U.S. Government aid programs.

The massive flow of goods and services that the United States assistance made possible produced spectacular results. By 1958, a number of industrial countries of Western Europe reached levels of prosperity and eco-

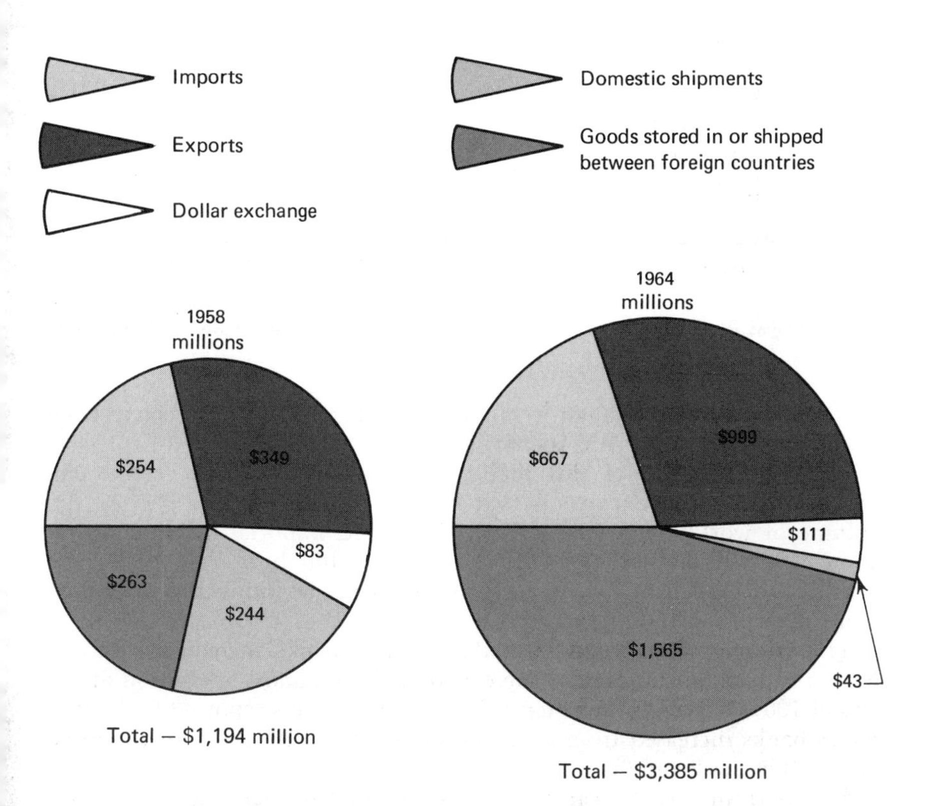

FIG. 1 Foreign trade financing by United States banks increases in early Sixties.

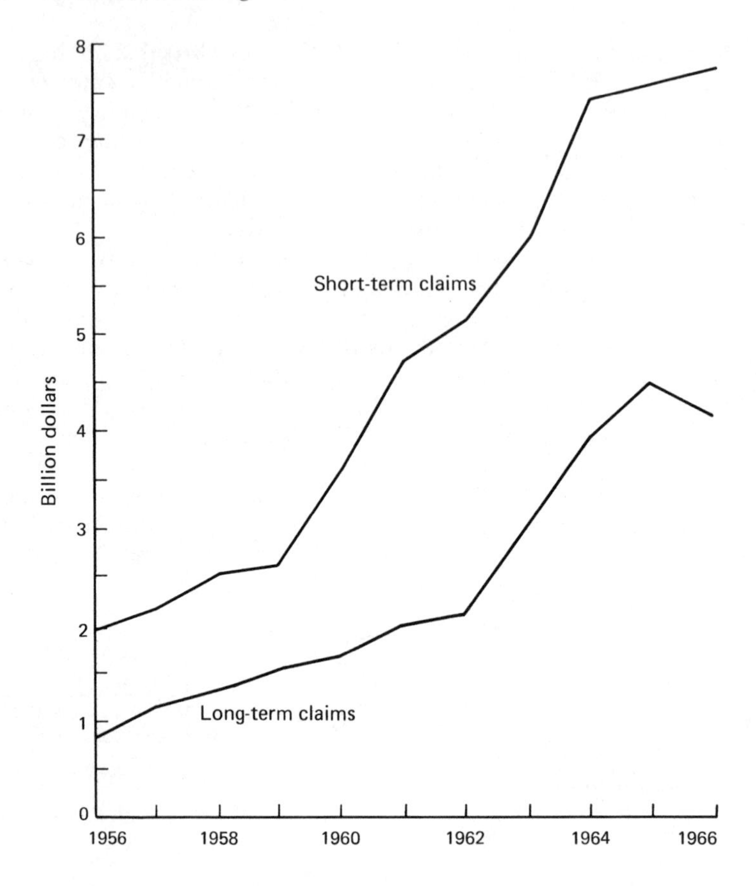

FIG. 2 Claims on foreigners reported by United States banks increased rapidly in the early Sixties.

nomic stability high enough to enable them to establish free convertibility of their currencies into the dollar.

With the removal of this major impediment, American banks embarked upon rapid expansion that reached its climax by 1964. As the volume of world trade (as measured by world imports) increased from about 100 billion dollars in 1958 to about 160 billion in 1964, the financing extended by American banks—directly or indirectly—increased more than proportionately.

The volume of acceptances made by these banks increased from 1.2 billion dollars outstanding at the end of 1958 to almost 3.4 billion at the end of 1964 (Figure 1). Short-term claims on foreigners reported by United States banks increased from 2.5 billion dollars to 7.9 billion in the same period (Figures 2 and 3).

As American corporations undertook to establish manufacturing facilities closer to their markets abroad, United States banks expanded their network of foreign branches in order to provide their customers with the

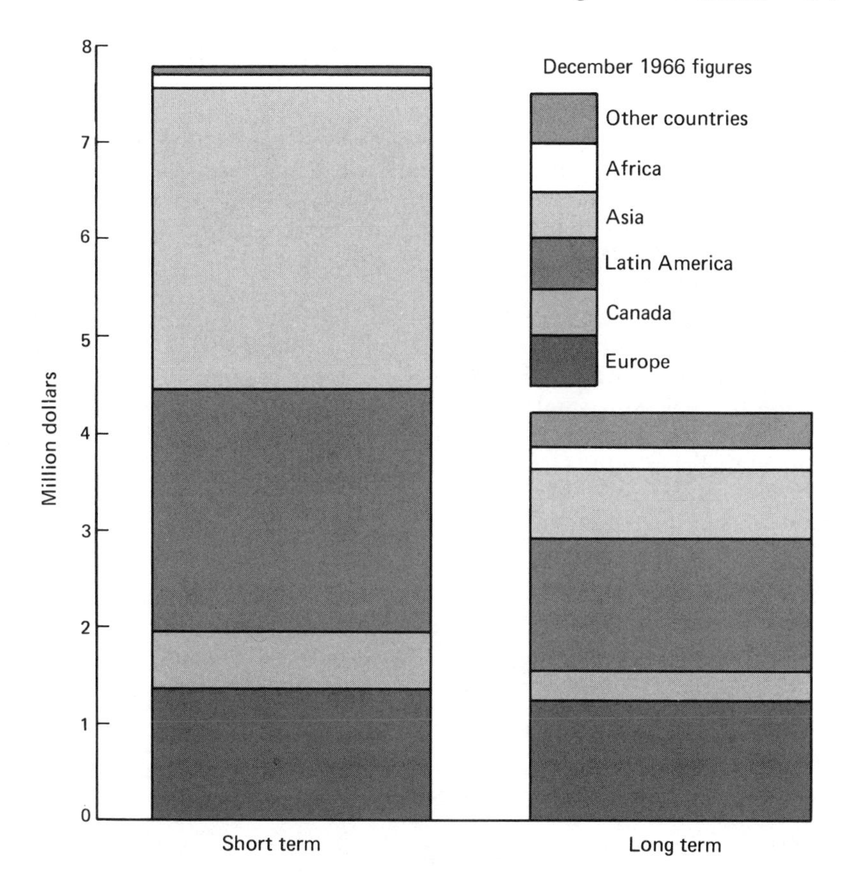

FIG. 3 Wide distribution of United States banks' claims on foreigners.

variety and quality of services they were accustomed to at home. By the end of 1964, American banks were operating 181 branches in 45 foreign countries with total assets of 6.9 billion dollars.

The growth was not limited merely to the expansion of traditional banking activities. Between 1958 and 1964 the number of Edge Act and agreement corporations rose from 8 to 38, and through these, an increasing number of United States banks entered new areas of foreign activities —equity financing. The banks, either in association with local firms abroad or, in some instances, in association with U.S. Government lending agencies, have made equity investment in foreign manufacturing, mining and public utility industries.

ENTER: THE DEFICIT

Expansion of foreign activities by American banks in the late Fifties and early Sixties coincided with unfavorable developments in the United

States balance of payments. Since 1950, the United States balance of payments was in deficit in all years except 1957. Throughout most of the Fifties, this deficit was viewed by all countries of the world as a favorable development not only because it represented net additions of goods, services and capital to the war-depleted world supplies, but also because it enabled war-torn countries to acquire dollar exchange.

By the late Fifties, however, the attitude of the major countries of the world toward the United States deficit began to change. The flow of private United States capital (including bank credit), particularly to Western Europe, rose rapidly under the impetus of free convertibility and profit opportunities arising from the establishment of the European Common Market. Although the United States continued to realize an increasing surplus in goods and services accounts, this was not sufficient to offset the rising deficit in the capital accounts (Figure 4). Consequently, the overall balance of payments deficit widened. Confronted with heavy inflows of dollars into their treasuries, a number of countries began to convert accumulated dollars into gold.

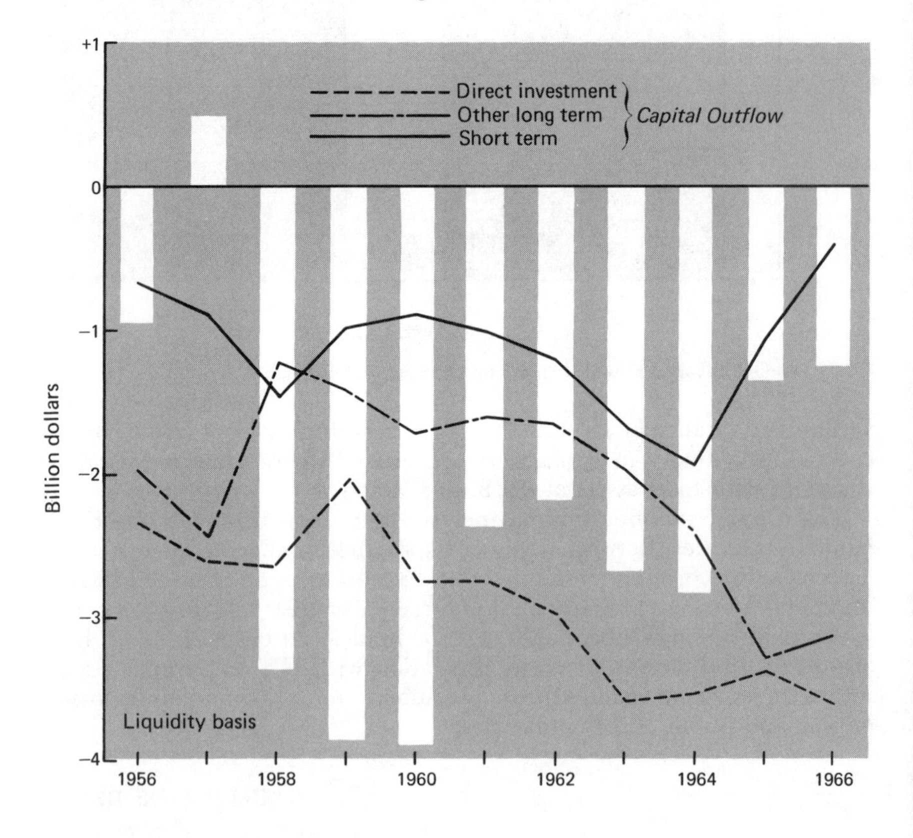

FIG. 4 Capital outflows play a dominant role in the United States balance of payments deficit.

Faced with these developments, the U.S. Government undertook various measures to reduce or eliminate the deficit. Overseas procurement for military purposes was restricted to items for which prices were far below those for domestically supplied goods. Foreign aid was increasingly "tied" to procurement in the United States.

These measures notwithstanding, the United States deficit continued at a high level. Therefore, in 1963 the President proposed a tax on purchases of foreign securities by United States residents. Its purpose was to "equalize" the cost of long-term capital financing between the United States and other developed countries, thereby reducing the incentive for capital outflow via purchases of foreign securities.

The Interest Equalization Tax (IET) appeared to have been highly successful in accomplishing its objective: sale of new issues of foreign securities in the United States dropped from a 1.8 billion dollar annual rate in the first half of 1963 to a 660 million annual rate in the second half.[4] Although securities sales rose somewhat in 1964, this was primarily the result of increased borrowing by countries exempt from the Interest Equalization Tax. Overall, the net outflow of United States capital through the transactions in foreign securities was reduced from 1.1 billion dollars in 1963 to 677 million in 1964.

But while foreign securities sales in the United States declined, foreign lending by United States banks increased. Outstanding loans to foreigners rose by 1.5 billion dollars in 1963 and 2.5 billion in 1964 and continued to rise rapidly in the early weeks of 1965. To deal with this problem, the President, on February 10, 1965, announced extension of the Interest Equalization Tax to bank loans of over one year maturity and a Voluntary Foreign Credit Restraint (VFCR) program to reduce bank lending abroad. Under this program, the banks were requested to limit the extension of credit to foreigners during 1965 to 105 percent of the amount outstanding at the end of 1964. The banks were further asked to give priority to credit used in financing United States exports and that extended to developing countries.

These measures, no doubt, have greatly impeded foreign activities of American banks.[5] However, recognizing the importance of achieving balance in international payments, the banks have shown an overwhelmingly favorable response. The heavy outflow of banks' funds experienced in 1964 was reversed, and by mid-1965 the accounts showed a net reduction in outstanding foreign loans (Figure 5).

During 1965, banks contributed substantially to the improvement in

[4] Although the measure was not enacted into law until 1964, the original request by the President—and the ultimate enactment—called for retroactivity to the date of proposal, July 18, 1963. Thus the restraining effect of the tax was felt in late 1963.

[5] Originally, the 1965 extension of IET to bank loans was thought to be applicable to loans made by foreign branches of United States banks. Therefore, the tax acted as an impediment to long-term lending by United States-based banks—as well as by their branches abroad. However, in 1967 Congress passed legislation explicitly exempting foreign branches from the tax.

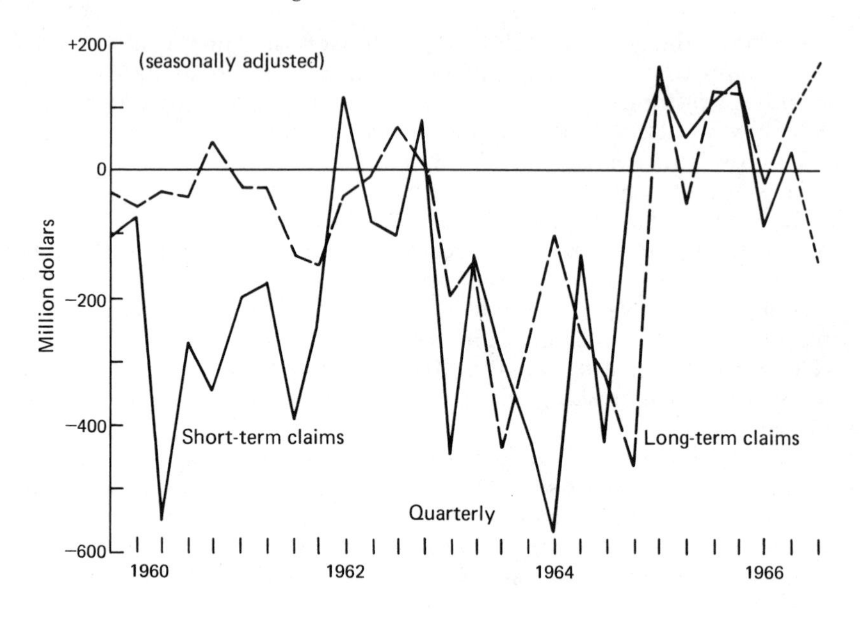

FIG. 5 Bank lending to foreigners reverses sharply in 1965.

the nation's balance of payments position. Yet, the deficit, although cut from 2.8 billion dollars in 1964 to 1.3 billion in 1965, still remained at an uncomfortably high level. Thus, the Government found it necessary to extend the VFCR program through 1966. The banks were asked to restrain expansion in foreign credits so that the amount outstanding at year-end would not exceed 109 percent of the amount outstanding on December 31, 1964 (Table 1).

The 1966 program, combined with general monetary restraint imposed to combat domestic inflationary pressures, produced a 260 million dollar net reduction in foreign credits of commercial banks in 1966.

In December 1966, in view of the still unsatisfactory balance of payments situation, the Administration announced extension of the VFCR program for another year. The 1967 foreign credits ceiling for commercial banks was retained at 109 percent of the 1964 base, and each bank was asked to limit the use of its leeway available on October 1, 1966, to not more than 40 percent before March 31, 1967, not more than 60 percent before June 30 and not more than 80 percent before September 30, 1967. In addition, banks were requested to expand nonexport credits to developed countries by not more than 10 percent of the October leeway.

EFFECTS OF THE RESTRAINT PROGRAM

In terms of the immediate balance of payments considerations, the VFCR program has apparently been highly successful. Although the

Table 1 Foreign Credits of United States Banks

	December 1965	March 1966	June 1966	September 1966	November 1966	December 1966: 1966 Guide-line [1]	December 1966: 1967 Guide-line [2]
Number of reporting banks	161	161	161	159	156	148	148
			(million dollars)				
Total foreign credits subject to ceiling	9,652	9,367	9,429	9,142	9,303	9,496	9,496
Target ceiling	9,973	10,076	10,179	10,290	10,375	10,360	9,640
Net expansion of credit since December 1964	156	–134	–77	–369	–200	–3	–3
Net leeway for expansion within target ceiling	319	709	751	1,148	1,072	864	144
Banks in excess of target ceiling							
Number of banks	35	22	24	13	20	18	51
			(million dollars)				
Net reduction in credit necessary to achieve target	114	18	26	17	30	31	155

[1] Target ceiling was generally 109 percent of December 1964 base.
[2] Target ceiling was generally the amount outstanding on September 30, 1966, plus 40 percent of the difference between that amount and 109 percent of the December 1964 base.

United States deficit continued to be large in 1966 mainly because of what appears to be a temporary deterioration in trade surplus (see *Business Conditions*, January 1967), the position of the dollar in the exchange markets has improved considerably. This improvement was reflected in the *surplus* of 271 million dollars in the United States balance of payments on the official transactions basis during 1966—as opposed to a deficit of 1.3 billion in 1965.[6] This surplus meant that the dollars accruing to foreigners during 1966 as a result of our "liquidity deficit" did not flow into "official" hands and thereby become a direct claim on United States gold.[7] Partly because of this, the outflow of gold

[6] The balance on the official reserve transaction basis is computed by summing the changes in liquid and nonliquid liabilities to foreign official holders, changes in the United States holdings of official reserve assets consisting of gold, convertible currencies and the United States gold tranche position in the International Monetary Fund.

[7] The balance on the liquidity basis equals the balance on the official transactions basis plus changes in liquid liabilities to all other foreigners minus certain nonliquid liabilities to foreign official institutons.

from the United States in 1966 amounted to only about a third of the large outflow in 1965.

American banks played an important role in this improvement, not only through their performance within the framework of the VFCR program, but also through their activities and those of their foreign branches in the Euro-dollar market.

During 1965—the first year the VFCR program was in operation—the total deposits of overseas branches of member banks of the Federal Reserve System increased 1.8 billion dollars or 36 percent. Almost the entire increase—1.69 billion—was accounted for by a gain in time deposits, believed to be mostly the so-called Euro-dollars. The gain in deposits enabled the branches to increase their loans outstanding by 1.4 billion dollars or 43 percent, in the same period. This development reflected, to a considerable extent, the impact of the Government's balance of payments program under which United States companies were urged to finance the operations of their foreign subsidiaries from foreign sources—and a shift to foreign branches of some bank loans which, in the absence of the voluntary foreign credit restraint effort, might have appeared on the books of the head offices of these branches (Table 2).

In 1966, this development intensified considerably. The branches, being increasingly hard-pressed for funds, began to bid more actively for Euro-dollar deposits, and some banks issued negotiable dollar-denominated certificates of deposit in London in order to obtain funds. As the demand

Table 2 Overseas Branches of Member Banks of the Federal Reserve System, December 31, 1965

	England	*Continental Europe*	*Latin America*	*Far East*	*Other*	*Total*
Number of branches *	21	21	88	50	31	211
Assets			(million dollars)			
Cash	877	301	175	76	81	1,510
Loans	2,020	664	465	866	595	4,610
Due from head offices and branches	1,083	198	131	359	224	1,995
Other	277	191	107	399	13	987
Total	4,257	1,354	878	1,700	913	9,102
Liabilities						
Demand deposits	520	488	425	293	338	2,069
Time deposits	3,193	461	226	652	422	4.954
Due to head offices and branches	315	247	131	396	138	1,227
Other	229	158	96	354	15	852
Total	4,257	1,354	878	1,700	913	9,102

* Includes branches in the Commonwealth of Puerto Rico and overseas dependencies of the United States. Includes assets and liabilities in United States dollars and all other currencies.

for funds—and thus the competition for Euro-dollars—intensified, the rate of interest paid on such deposits continued to climb.

The increasing interest rate made it progressively more attractive for foreigners receiving dollar payments to place them in the Euro-dollar market rather than to convert them into their domestic currencies and invest them at home (Figure 6).

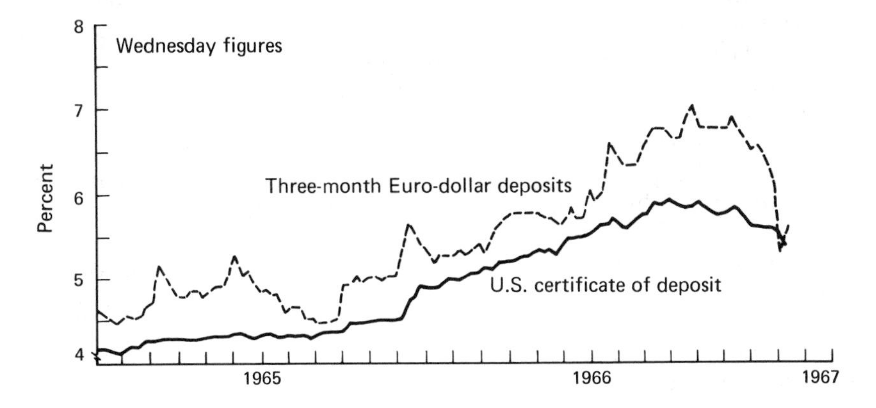

FIG. 6 Euro-dollar rate shoots up.

With this increasing flow of funds into the Euro-dollar market, deposits in the branches of American banks in England—the center for the Euro-dollar market—increased by more than 1.7 billion dollars in the first nine months of 1966. As in the past, these funds were used partly to accommodate the loan demand by what were formerly foreign customers of the home offices. During 1966, however, these funds were used increasingly by the home offices of United States banks to help meet their strong loan demand at home. As monetary restraint in the United States intensified, the banks turned increasingly to the Euro-dollar market to supplement their reserve position; Euro-dollar deposits obtained by branches abroad were channeled to their home offices. This process accelerated in the latter part of the year when the liabilities of United States banks to their foreign branches increased sharply from 1.8 billion dollars at the beginning of July to more than 4.3 billion in mid-December.[8]

[8] This inflow of funds did not, in its entirety, represent a net addition to reserves of the United States banks because the Euro-dollar deposits that their branches acquired were mostly funds held by foreigners as deposits in banks in the United States. As these deposits were "withdrawn" by the foreigners, "redeposited" in branches abroad and subsequently "returned" by them to the home offices, the United States banks were, in effect, merely exchanging one type of deposit liability (i.e., that to foreigners) for another (i.e., that to their foreign branches). A small net addition to reserves nevertheless, did occur because the banks are not required to hold reserves against liabilities to their foreign branches (as opposed to the 16½ percent reserve require-

While somewhat complicating the management of domestic credit policies of the Federal Reserve, these developments had a twofold beneficial effect. First, the increasing supply of dollars made available to the branches of the American banks abroad had enabled them, to the extent that these were used to make loans abroad, to fill the "financial vacuum" created by the reduction in foreign lending by United States banks in response to the VFCR program. Second, by offering rates high enough to attract Euro-dollars, the banks prevented these funds from ending up in foreign official holdings and thus, from possibly becoming a direct claim on United States gold. This latter aspect of the foreign operations of American banks contributed significantly to the strengthening of the dollar in the exchange markets in 1966.

In its initial phase, the development of international activities of American banks centered on the eastern seaboard, particularly New York. Until the late Fifties, only a few Midwest banks maintained a foreign department, and even in cases where such a department existed, its operation was largely limited to small amounts of foreign trade financing for domestic customers. However, certain developments in the late Fifties greatly influenced the rate of expansion of Midwest banks into international banking.

ACTIVITIES OF DISTRICT BANKS

The opening of the St. Lawrence Seaway in 1959 was perhaps the most important of these developments. The Seaway permitted exports originating in the "land locked" Midwest to move directly to Canadian ports and to the Atlantic Ocean on oceangoing vessels. The waterborne exports originating in the ports of the Seventh District increased from 1.7 million tons in 1955 to more than 4.3 million tons in 1964; imports increased in the same period from 1.7 million tons to more than 8.8 million. Exports of manufactured goods originating in the five states of the Seventh District increased 18 percent between 1960 and 1963.

In 1963, such exports totaled 3.7 billion dollars and accounted for about 23 percent of United States exports of manufactured goods. Of the total exports of machinery, the five District states' share was more than 41 percent in 1963. In agriculture, 44 percent of total feed grain exports and 50 percent of total soybean exports in 1964 originated in the Seventh District states. Of the total volume of 6.2 billion dollars of United States agricultural exports in 1964, 21 percent originated in the Seventh District.

The increasing importance of the Midwest in United States foreign trade helped to boost the activities of banks in financing that trade. For

---

ment for reserve city banks against all, including foreign, demand deposits), and because some foreign deposits were official deposits originally held with the Federal Reserve.

example, the volume of bankers acceptances originating in the Seventh District increased from 23 million dollars outstanding at the end of 1958 to more than 191 million dollars at the end of 1966, and the District's share in the total outstanding increased from less than 2 percent to more than 5 percent. The acceptances based on exports rose from about 5 million dollars to more than 31 million dollars in the same period.

The most significant increase, however, has occurred in acceptances based on goods stored in, or shipped between, foreign countries and those based on creation of dollar exchange. While at the end of 1958 such acceptances amounted to about 2.6 million dollars (less than 1 percent of the national total), at the end of 1966 these amounted to almost 127 million (or more than 7 percent of the total). From this evidence, it appears that the Midwest banks are becoming increasingly engaged in international finance.

While the Seaway opened the door for expansion of foreign trade financing by District banks, the development of the multinational, American-based corporation in the late Fifties and early Sixties provided additional opportunity for enlarging their international operations. The Midwest corporate giants have participated heavily in the foreign investment boom of recent years. Many of them established new subsidiaries and manufacturing branches in foreign countries, particularly in Western Europe. A recent survey [9] shows that 21 percent of the total expansion of foreign facilities undertaken by United States firms between July 1960 and June 1965 originated from four states in the District; more than 10 percent originated from the Chicago metropolitan area alone!

With the internationalization of their operations, the corporations' credit needs became increasingly international in nature. The Midwest banks responded by establishing Edge Act banking corporations and branches abroad. In 1960, none of the District's banks operated a branch abroad, and none had established an Edge Act corporation.[10] By the end of 1966, the District banks had established six branches and six Edge Act corporations, and numerous representative offices and foreign-correspondent relationships were enlarged. Through their Edge Act corporations, the banks also have acquired financial interests in a number of foreign banks, enabling them to utilize established banking facilities abroad to serve their customers' needs directly.

For many of the District banks, the inception of the VFCR program was a severe blow to their plans for foreign expansion (Table 3). A number of them had only begun to lay a foundation for what appeared to be

[9] Booz, Allen & Hamilton, Management Consultants, *Five Years of New Foreign Business Activity of U.S. Firms.*

[10] The first Midwest bank to participate in foreign branch banking was Corn Exchange National Bank of Chicago—one of the five original founders of the American Foreign Banking Corporation of New York. The Corporation was established as a New York State chartered company in 1917 and eventually operated 21 branches in Central and South America and the Far East. It was liquidated in 1925, shortly after the Corn Exchange National terminated its existence in late 1924.

Table 3 Foreign Credits of Banks in the Seventh Federal Reserve District

	December 1965	April 1966	September 1966	December 1966
Number of reporting banks	17	20	20	21
		(million dollars)		
Total foreign credits subject to ceiling	900	878	820	985
Target ceiling	979	1,000	1,010	1,029*
Net expansion of credit since December 1964	—33	—55	—113	+50
Net leeway for expansion within target ceiling	79	122	190	44*

* Based on 1966 guidelines.

a substantial increase in international activities. Thus, their performance in conforming to the guidelines has been all the more remarkable.

A LOOK TO THE FUTURE

The expansion of American banks into international finance was slow in coming. Long after the United States, through the development of its tremendous industrial base, became a key force in the world economy in the Twenties, American banks still played only a small role in the international scene. The stormy weather in the international financial relationships of the Thirties and Forties provided little incentive for expansion during that period. But once having taken the step, the American banker with proverbial Yankee ingenuity, has introduced fresh approaches to many aspects of international banking.

Further expansion in the near future most likely will continue to be impeded by the troublesome United States balance of payments. But once this problem has been resolved, the United States banks will have an almost unlimited potential for growth in the international area, both in their role as financial intermediaries for the channeling of savings into productive investment and in their role of providing a broad array of financial and related services—roles they have performed so effectively for the American economy.

The First Real International Bankers

Jeremy Main

The biggest growth area of U.S. banking today is not in the U.S. but overseas. In a great burst of expansion, our banks have set up branches and associations all over Europe, they have moved into Latin America and Africa, and they have established footholds in the old trading cities of Asia. The fever has caught not only the giants, who tirelessly proclaim their new international character in their advertising, but some smaller banks as well. Wherever they go, their aggressiveness and ingenuity have quickened competition in banking, stimulated new kinds of capital markets, shaken the sluggish Old World banking communities out of their complacency, and opened the eyes of businessmen abroad to the possibilities of using money more productively.

The expansion overseas is also creating the first truly international networks of banks. It has become a cliché in banking circles to say that "the only really European banks nowadays are American." The big British clearinghouse banks have networks with thousands of branches, but their operations are pretty much confined to their home islands, the sterling area, and the Commonwealth. The powerful and prestigious German, Dutch, and Belgian banks have rarely ventured beyond their national frontiers; instead they have developed their own tidy local clienteles, leaving business in other places to other bankers and settling international transactions through clubby, noncompetitive arrangements. The cliché, then, is all too true: in most of the major cities of Western Europe, only the First National City Bank, the Bank of America, the Chase Manhattan, and Morgan Guaranty are operating as if Europe really were what Europeans like to think it is—a single economic community.

The overseas expansion of U.S. banking is, of course, a logical consequence of the prior expansion of American corporations, and of the predominant role of the dollar in financing the world's trade. The U.S. banks were long absorbed in their own growth at home, and it is only in

Reprinted from the December 1967 issue of *Fortune* Magazine by special permission;

the last decade that they have pushed abroad in a big way. In those ten years, deposits in the foreign branches of New York banks have risen from $1.35 billion to $9.5 billion; lately they have been growing at a rate seven times greater than deposits at home. At Manufacturers Hanover, foreign business has increased from 10 percent to 25 percent of total business.

In the same decade, the number of overseas branches of American banks has more than doubled, to a present total of about 280. First National City, the most ambitious of the expansionists, is on the average now opening one overseas branch every fortnight—one a month in Argentina alone, where it believes the regime of General Juan Onganía has created an especially favorable environment for investment.

HIDDEN PROFITS

Banks naturally look upon their opportunities overseas somewhat differently than do industrial corporations. They cannot hope to storm the entrenched markets of native banks. Nor do they expect a particularly high rate of profit. Banking in Europe is not inherently more profitable than in the U.S.; the spread between what a bank pays for money and what it can charge a borrower is about the same. The banks going abroad do not even insist upon substantial earnings from every branch. The aim, rather, is to build up a system whose intertwined operations will improve the bank's over-all earnings. The profits of a particular branch do not necessarily reflect its contribution to the system. It may, on occasion, have to make an unprofitable loan to please a client whose gratitude will result in more business for another branch or for the home office. Moreover, when a branch makes a loan to a foreign subsidiary of an American corporation, the parent company is often required to place sizable compensating balances with the bank's home office; these deposits add up to a significant amount of money.

Customarily, banks publish consolidated statements that do not break out the figures for foreign operations—but sometimes they drop a hint. Three years ago, Chase Manhattan disclosed that 14 percent of its net profits came from foreign business, and that percentage has certainly risen since. Manufacturers Hanover says that the profits of its international division have more than doubled in the last five years, which probably means that earnings have kept pace with the division's growing business.

WHERE THE SEX APPEAL IS

While it is hard to get a line on foreign contributions to earnings, it is clear that no major U.S. bank could have decided *not* to go abroad. A bank that is not on the scene when one of its big U.S. corporate clients comes along with a foreign project may lose that client's business at home to a competitor that is overseas. Conversely, a bank that has offices in the major financial capitals has the chance of winning new clients, not only abroad, but at home too.

"It is the foreign facilities that have the sex appeal in this banking game," says Walter Page, vice president in charge of the international division at Morgan Guaranty. "You have a wider, more imaginative possibility of doing something for a company in the foreign field than in the domestic. This is the area that can get you a closer, more exclusive relationship with your American client." Morgan Guaranty doesn't boast about its clients, but Page believes, for instance, that it was able to move up from No. 2 bank for a major U.S. chemical company to No. 1 because of services it performed for the company in Canada, Venezuela, and Germany—particularly in supplying inexpensive medium-term credit at better terms than foreign banks could provide.

It was because First National City has such ample foreign facilities that it was able to acquire Samsonite, the Denver luggage manufacturer, as a customer. Until 1964, Samsonite had hardly any dealings with Citibank, but then it went overseas and set up subsidiaries in four European countries, in each of which, as it happened, there was a Citibank branch. The company turned to Citibank for its foreign banking. Unlike giant corporations, which already know their way around the world, a medium-sized enterprise like Samsonite particularly needs the help of a banker when it goes abroad for the first time. Samsonite is impressed by the services Citibank performs for it: e.g., rapid money transfers (when money is moved in Europe through several banks the transfer can take days, but Citibank's network provides same-day service), credit-rating information, news of government regulations, help on collection problems.

Another force propelling the banks overseas has been the U.S. balance-of-payments deficit—or, more precisely, the controls on the outflow of capital from this country. Under the voluntary foreign-credit restraints invoked in 1965, banks in effect pledged to limit the volume of credit that they extended abroad to 105 percent of the 1964 amount (the limit has since been raised to 109 percent). Corporations also "voluntarily" pledged to curtail their direct foreign investments. The restraints cut off U.S. corporate subsidiaries abroad from their sources of capital back home just when their expansion was at a peak. The subsidiaries therefore had to find their short- and medium-term money locally, which gave the foreign branches of U.S. banks a new and vital function. (The interest equalization tax of 1963 drove the long-term bond market as well to Europe.)

At the same time, the balance-of-payments restraints made life more complicated for those branches. While their lending opportunities multiplied, they (like their customers) found themselves cut off from their natural source of funds—their home offices. They too were forced to raise money locally. The difficulty was that overseas branches do not attract stable local deposits, which are the normal basis of a bank's lending power. Individuals and companies in, say, France or Britain simply do not leave their money with an American bank. And U.S. corporate subsidiaries are not much help, for they tend to be short of cash and have little money to deposit. "This is the source of money that eludes us all," says Barry Sullivan, the Chase Manhattan manager in London.

A DEEP POOL OF USEFUL DOLLARS

Consequently, the branches have had to go into the money market and "buy" the funds they need. Fortunately they have found an ample if expensive source of supply in the Eurodollar market, which is still another byproduct of the balance-of-payments deficit. Its size and usefulness have grown far beyond what seemed likely in the late 1950's, when dollars began piling up in European bank accounts. These dollars, which stayed either in European-owned banks or in the foreign branches of American banks, have become a profitable, regulation-free international money pool, almost a new international currency. The owner of a Eurodollar can turn it in for the equivalent in his own currency—or, if he is an American, he can repatriate it to a bank account at home. But there is an advantage in holding the money as Eurodollars, for these, unlike dollars that are held in the U.S., can be invested in foreign bonds or can earn a tidy interest in time deposits or even as call money abroad.

Since the U.S. payments deficit lingers on, and Eurodollars are attractive to hold, the pool keeps growing. Four years ago the highest estimate of its volume was $3 billion. "It is now a $15-billion market," says Richard Vokey, the Citibank manager in London, "and the turnover, the velocity, have really accelerated in the last four years. It's fantastic." The American branches have become the most aggressive bankers in Europe in using the Eurodollar pool. They use it in a number of ways, ranging from two-day call money (at 4 percent lately) to one-year time deposits (at 5¾ percent). Since there are no reserve requirements on Eurodollars, the banks have 100 percent of their money working for them all the time.

Last year Citibank introduced Eurodollar certificates of deposit in London, first in the thirty, sixty, ninety, and 360-day varieties, and later on three-year terms. The interest on these C/D's is usually a shade lower, about ⅛ of 1 percent, than on ordinary time deposits. The C/D's caught on immediately. When Citibank introduced three-year certificates in London, they were quickly grabbed up. Success attracted imitators, and now European banks are issuing C/D's too. Britain's Midland & International Banks Ltd. has sold $20 million in five-year certificates. All together, more than $350 million worth of C/D's are now out in Europe.

During the great 1966 credit squeeze, the Eurodollars held by overseas branches were a big help to U.S. banks at home. As their own lending resources ran low, they called in Eurodollars from their branches, which simply transferred the money home, charging the home offices the interest rates they were paying for it—4 to 5½ percent, depending on the maturity. At one point last December the amount loaned by branches to their parents in the U.S. reached $4.3 billion. When the crisis passed, demand eased suddenly, and banks began moving money back to Europe. The Eurodollar rate fell by two percentage points on one-month money in one week, and after a while the total of Eurodollars on loan to the U.S. eased back to $3 billion. This fall, in anticipation of another credit squeeze, transatlantic borrowing rose again to $4 billion. The availability of these Eurodollars to American banks when credit is tight at home has become a major reason for having a branch in London, the center of Eurodollar trading.

THE MEN BEHIND THOSE DIRECTOIRE DESKS

As suppliers of bank credit to foreign business, American banks overseas do not yet loom very large. They lend mainly to U.S. corporations and a few large foreign companies with multicontinental operations, and—so they swear—they do not try to steal local business from local banks. The Bank of America may be the biggest bank in the world, but in Paris, where its branch has assets of $200 million, it is a very small fellow indeed compared with the Banque Nationale de Paris, whose assets totaled $5.6 billion a year ago.

Nevertheless, the American branches are making an impact that is way out of proportion to their size. They have brought over a radically different philosophy of lending, which collides head on with the notions that have long prevailed in Europe. Traditionally, Continental bankers waited for borrowers to come to them. As one American banker puts it, "They just sat behind those Directoire desks, under those soft chandeliers, and made sure their pulse beat was slow and steady." A company had to make a good case before it got any money, and it had to satisfy the bank's rigid and exacting standards. In some instances the bank would require that the company set aside—in effect freeze—certain assets as collateral, or issue new shares pledged to the bank.

As a consequence, companies tended to go to the banks only as a last resort, with a hat-in-hand sort of feeling. It was a matter of pride not to borrow. The head of one good-sized European company recently told an American banker, "I'm proud to say we've been in business for twenty-five years and never made a bank loan." The American was appalled, not so much by all that good business he imagined the banks had missed, but by the opportunities the businessman himself must have passed up.

It is in combating such attitudes, and exporting their own more aggressive notions about banking's proper role, that the U.S. banks have had their greatest impact on Europe. They start with the conviction that a loan is a productive instrument. They achieve rapport with a potential client, get to know his business, demonstrate what borrowing will do for him, tailor their lending to his requirements. They have a concept of "credit-worthiness" that contrasts sharply with the one that has long dominated European financial thinking. European bankers have usually been "asset lenders"; they would go around a company's plant, kick the walls, look at the deed and the mortgage, and then, on the basis of the physical assets, make their decision about how much to lend and on what conditions. American bankers look at cash flow and lend on prospects.

The ideas coming across the Atlantic are beginning to have an effect on European bankers. Some are merely disturbed and irritated, but some are starting to change their own approach. The constructive reaction is summed up by Jean Reyre, president of the aggressive Banque de Paris et des Pays-Bas: "The growth of American banks is an excellent thing for the European banks. They were resting a bit after the war. But they have been shaken up by the Americans. Obviously this is not very pleasant, but the lesson is a very good thing."

LOANS THAT ARE NO LONGER NAUGHTY

American bankers are joining energetically in the exploitation of one great gap in European corporate financing. Until fairly recently, the medium-term loan—say, of three to five years—was a rarely used device. Says Walter Wriston, president of Citibank and former head of its international department, "European bankers thought medium-term credit was naughty." In any event, there was little demand from business for medium-term loans. As long as companies could ride on comfortable profit margins, they met their longer-term needs out of their cash flow. When that was impossible, they would either float a bond issue or use endlessly renewable short-term credit; British business, in particular, relied on the good old overdraft, the "never-never" loan, whose great disadvantage was that it might get called in suddenly when there was a squeeze on credit.

But conditions have changed. Profit margins have thinned just at a time when industry has developed a voracious need for capital to finance large-scale expansion. So the prejudices against medium-term borrowing have broken down. "This market is insatiable," says Chauncey Schmidt, manager of the London branch of the First National Bank of Chicago. "It was untapped until the last twenty-four or thirty-six months." James Phelan, Chase Manhattan's manager in Paris, says, "Medium-term financing is probably the most profitable thing we do." He cites the fact that rates on a five-year loan run to 7 percent or better, compared to the 4.5 percent the bank gets for discounting prime commercial paper. Of course, Chase has to pay a lot, at various rates, to get the money, but by making a blended cost estimate, the bank figures it gets a 1 percent spread.

The American banks have their hands full meeting the demands of U.S. corporate subsidiaries, which want their medium-term loans in large packets. Five-year loans of $5 million to $10 million are normal, and there have been much larger ones. For example, General Motors borrowed a reported $40 million for its plant in Antwerp, and Caterpillar Tractor took $50 million in two loans for its Belgian operation. These were too big for one bank alone, so several American and Belgian banks joined forces.

Banks are also making alliances on a more permanent basis. International consortia, specifically set up for medium-term financing, are springing up all over the place. Irving Trust and the First National of Chicago have joined a consortium known as the International Commercial Bank, which also includes the Hong Kong & Shanghai Banking Corp., Commerzbank of Düsseldorf, and the Westminster Bank of London, which initiated the idea. W. F. Graff, senior vice president of Irving Trust, says the arrangement has enabled his bank to hold onto business it might otherwise have had to forgo. If one of its American clients wanted a $15-million, five-year loan for overseas expansion, Irving Trust could no longer supply the money from the U.S. because of the balance-of-payments restrictions, nor could its London branch take on that much of a commitment. But now the London office could take $5 million of the $15 million and place the rest with the other members of the International Commercial Bank.

Bank of America has joined a similar consortium, the Société Financière Européenne, which was sponsored by the Banque Nationale de Paris and includes Barclays Bank, the Banca Nazionale del Lavoro of Italy, the Dresdner Bank of Germany, and the Algemene Bank of Holland. Two other medium-term consortia have been formed without American members: a British Commonwealth group known as MAIBL (Midland & International Banks Ltd.) and a team of British and Continental banks known as the European Bank for Medium-Term Development.

All these groups represent an impressive mobilization of banking power, but they have yet to prove their success. Some Americans in Europe think they just won't work well. They point out that loan applications have to be passed on by too many people, making the process too slow and cumbersome. Moreover, each consortium member will be thinking first of his own bank's business, making for a good deal of internal tension.

"WE COMPETE AGAINST THE WORLD"

There is no visible limit yet to the growth of American banking overseas. Each gloomy prediction that one market or another is about to be saturated proves false as the volume and scope keep widening. The real question is the best strategy for overseas expansion. The basic choice is between opening branches and competing aggressively and obtrusively and building up foreign business by walking in softly and making alliances and other arrangements with local banks.

The biggest U.S. banks, not surprisingly, are the most vigorous branchers. First National City now has 146 foreign branches; says President Wriston: "We compete against the world." Bank of America has sixty branches and Chase Manhattan, forty-five. Morgan Guaranty's Paris branch, elegantly ensconced on the Place Vendôme, is the oldest in Europe; it was established ninety-nine years ago (when the bank was known as Drexel Harjes & Co.). Morgan has five others in Europe. By now, Citibank and Bank of America are penetrating into what might be termed secondary banking markets. The former opened a branch this year in Piraeus, Greece, and the latter in Munich, Marseille, and Birmingham.

The advantages of the multibranch strategy are plain enough. The branch is under the tight control of headquarters. If New York, for example, wants to make a marginal loan overseas to please a client at home, it can order the branch to do so, but it could not make a correspondent bank do so. Citibank's Richard Vokey maintains, "Our selling point is the network. It's the biggest jump we have on the competition. Some banks do well with the correspondent, but it's not like calling my buddy, Paul Austin, our branch manager in Milan. I have known him for years. He's been to my house. I've been to his. We use the same words to mean the same thing."

As the branch network gets bigger, it has more to offer a client. This was illustrated recently by Citibank, which has been negotiating a complex credit arrangement in Europe that only a bank with a widespread, efficient network could consider handling. Perkin-Elmer, the Connecticut-based manufacturer of optical and scientific instruments, was looking for a blanket credit covering the short-term and medium-term needs, in local currencies, of its European subsidiaries in seven countries. The company found that only Citibank, with branches in all seven countries, could handle the loan.

One disadvantage of branches is that they are expensive to maintain, and this may be the real reason why banks with lesser resources prefer other strategies. But some of these banks insist that they are mainly concerned to avoid being abrasive competitors. Boasts John Andren, a vice president of Manufacturers Hanover: "We're the largest bank in the world *not* competing with foreign banks." Manufacturers Hanover's policy is to have representative offices all over Europe. These offices can conduct no banking on their own, but they can scout for business to send home. It is an inexpensive but limited way of operating. Irving Trust, on the other hand, carries on its activities abroad through a network of correspondent foreign banks. But a bank has no authority over a correspondent and is dependent on its good will. Furthermore, American businessmen on the scene like to deal with an American bank.

Those who oppose branching and prefer to ally themselves with foreign banks contend that these banks bring in a lot of business while aggressive branching invites retaliation by foreign banks and government authorities. They argue that *any* bank overseas depends on the good will of the banking community it enters. However, there is as yet no evidence that branching has led to any damaging retaliation.

Whatever plan a bank may follow anywhere else, it always has a branch in London if it goes abroad at all. London is the ticket of admission to international banking. London has an ample and flexible capital market and the British extend a welcoming hand to everyone. For foreign banks there are no reserve requirements or restrictions on interest rates, which makes London the natural center for Eurodollar trade. Thirteen American banks now have London branches. Some of the bigger banks have two, one in the City and one in the West End. A few have been there for decades, but most are newcomers. Continental Illinois and the First National of Chicago have opened branches in the last five years. Crocker-Citizens National Bank of San Francisco plans to have a branch next year and half a dozen others are following.

AN EXPERIMENT IN BRUSSELS

Branches of U.S. banks anywhere abroad always have trouble pulling in local deposits. To overcome that difficulty, some banks have turned to the "participation," which means purchasing an interest in an existing foreign bank. With a participation, a bank buys instant liquidity and need not build up deposits laboriously from scratch.

Although Chase Manhattan has well-established branches in lots of places, four years ago it paused to think about expansion abroad and decided to go into participations. Chase has begun on a small, rather experimental scale. In 1965 it paid $5,400,000 for a half interest in the $80-million Banque de Commerce in Brussels. The other half is owned by the Banque de Bruxelles, Belgium's second largest. While ownership is shared, Chase, in effect, controls the management. The joint venture is still small, but it is growing; profits rose from $193,000 in 1965 to $422,000 in 1966. The idea is that Chase brings American customers to the Banque de Commerce, which if it cannot handle the loan by itself, can fall back on the much greater resources of the other part owner, the Banque de Bruxelles.

Those familiar with the venture scent the possibilities of trouble. In making the deal, one of the main objectives of the Banque de Bruxelles was to avert having Chase as a competitor. But the Belgians fear it hasn't worked out that way at all. They think Chase is using the Banque de Commerce to entice international clients away from the Banque de Bruxelles. One problem for Chase is that the Banque de Commerce is not easily identifiable to American clients as an American bank. In fact, its premises look like an old European meat market, but they are soon to be redecorated.

Bankers Trust of New York has long followed the participations route. Apart from the indispensable London branch, Bankers Trust relies entirely on minority participations, of which it has seventeen in Europe and Africa. Bankers Trust's problem is that, for the most part, its share of the joint venture is too small to give it real leverage in the management. To acquire that leverage in enough banks to form a network would be too expensive a proposition.

No matter how they choose to operate abroad, all American banks are facing an acute shortage of manpower. An officer at Manufacturers Hanover says the only thing that is stopping his bank from opening more representative offices is that it cannot find the people to staff them. The predicament is widespread. In recruiting people abroad, one solution is to make foreign employees part of an international bank staff, eligible for top jobs if they are agreeable to being transferred from country to country. Chase, Citibank, and Bank of America are all working toward a sort of stateless management abroad.

Another personnel problem arises in controlling and checking distant bank offices that are working under conditions unfamiliar to the management back home and are often staffed by people little known at home. Citibank has learned the hard way. There was the famous 1965 case of the foreign-exchange trader in Brussels who lost the bank $7 million. Another Citibank trader in Milan made a $700,000 mistake and one in Lebanon simply absconded with Citibank funds. The bank has tightened its supervision of traders.

IF THE PAYMENT DEFICIT ENDS

It is ironic that the great international expansion of American banking has taken place while its base of operations, the American capital market, is largely cut off from the rest of the world. The restrictions that were put in effect because of the balance-of-payments deficit both cause American banks to set up in business abroad and prevent them from throwing the full weight of their resources overseas. Presumably, one day the balance of payments will be set right, and bankers like to speculate on what will happen then.

Foreign bankers wonder if they will not face a far more dangerous competitive threat from the U.S., a threat that might have to be countered by their own governments. American bankers think that some of their foreign activities might be repatriated. The likeliest outcome in the long run, however, is that international banking and international money markets will keep growing, and that U.S. banks will be in the forefront of that growth.

Euro-Dollars in the Liquidity and Reserve Management of United States Banks

Fred H. Klopstock

During the last decade, the large commercial banks in the United States have exhibited a remarkable degree of imagination and initiative in broadening their access to pools of liquid funds. Their success in attracting corporate and institutional balances through the issue of negotiable certificates of deposit (C/D's) is a case in point. Other examples are their issue of "consumer" investment certificates and the flotation of unsecured notes and debentures in the capital market. More recently this increased readiness of banks to rely on what has become known as "liability management" in the adjustment of liquidity and reserve positions has been demonstrated by their large-scale use of balances acquired through their overseas branches in the Euro-dollar market. The overseas branches became active in this market soon after it emerged in the late 1950's, and have gradually become the most important participants. But only since the midsixties have several of the major United States banks employed large amounts of Euro-dollar balances for adjustments of their money positions in response to changing needs for funds, and more and more banks have opened overseas branches to gain access to the Euro-dollar market.

For some of the large money market banks, Euro-dollars have now become a major source of funds for loans and investments; in certain instances, the head office's dollar liabilities to overseas branches exceed or closely approach its outstanding C/D's. Altogether, liabilities of American banks to their overseas branches are now in excess of $6 billion. It is true that this total includes some funds that do not originate in the Euro-

Reprinted with the permission of the Federal Reserve Bank of New York from *Monthly Review,* July 1968.

dollar market, but on the other hand the United States banks' use of Euro-dollar balances in the management of their portfolios is not limited to the amounts reported as liabilities to their branches. For example, they may use such balances for transfers of loans to overseas branches; or they may conserve head-office resources by referring some loan demands to their branches for financing with Euro-dollars; and those that have no branches overseas may sell loans to foreign banks or borrow from foreign banks directly. The following pages examine the institutional and economic background of the practice of using Euro-dollars in portfolio management, a practice that has greatly increased during the last two years.

THE EURO-DOLLAR MARKET AS A SOURCE OF FUNDS FOR UNITED STATES BANKS

The Euro-dollar market, which centers on London with links in several other major financial centers in Western Europe and elsewhere, is a telephone and telex network through which many of the world's major banks bid for and employ dollar balances. By a generally accepted definition, Euro-dollars come into existence when a domestic or foreign holder of dollar demand deposits in the United States places them on deposit in a bank outside the United States, but the term also applies to the dollars that banks abroad acquire with their own or foreign currencies and then employ for placement in the market or for loans to customers. Compared with other markets used by American banks for adjusting their liabilities, the Euro-dollar market possesses distinctive features which both add to and detract from its usefulness as a source of funds.

By far the greatest merit of the market from the viewpoint of United States banks is that it offers the possibility of obtaining balances that are not subject to the regulatory restrictions applicable to demand and time deposits. Unlike United States banks, the overseas branches may pay interest on dollar call deposits and on time deposits with maturities of less than thirty days. Thus, United States banks can gain access, through the overseas branch route, to sizable amounts of funds that they are precluded by various regulations from acquiring directly from foreign depositors. In addition, balances payable at overseas branches are not subject to Regulation Q rate ceilings, a factor of great significance when rates for money market instruments in the United States or Euro-dollar rates rise above the ceiling rates payable on deposits. And, finally, branch balances placed in head offices are not subject to member bank reserve requirements or to the fees of the Federal Deposit Insurance Corporation (FDIC). Indeed, especially during periods of tight money, the differential between Euro-dollar rates and time deposit rates in the United States tends to reflect this saving.

Another advantage of the market is its broad scope. Actual and potential Euro-dollar sources are diverse and widely dispersed geographically.

They include countless banks and corporations in many parts of the world as well as monetary authorities and international financial institutions. When conditions in some countries restrict offerings by suppliers, conditions elsewhere typically free more resources for Euro-dollar placements. Monetary authorities and international institutions may add to their offerings when commercial banks and corporations pull back theirs. In short, there is a high degree of supply flexibility in the Euro-dollar market.

It must not be thought, however, that the market is always a stable source of funds for United States banks. On the one hand, there may be problems of oversupply—because of relative ease in the money markets of major supplier countries or because foreign customers' demand for loans has been weak or their established credit lines have been filled. At such times the branches will quote defensively, but even so some of them tend on occasion to take in sizable balances from day to day, as they are loath to refuse offerings by correspondent banks and corporations among their established customers that habitually lay off temporarily excess dollar balances with them. Several of the branches of major banks are in effect the residual takers of foreign banks' liquidity reserves, which tend to converge upon them largely in the form of call deposits. If these balances cannot immediately be employed abroad, the respective head offices tend to use these balances as an alternative to Federal funds purchases. Under such conditions, branch deposits in head offices may rise above the targets set by the money-desk or portfolio-management departments.

On the other hand, there are occasionally supply stringencies, notably during periods of heavy seasonal pressures. Moreover, restrictive monetary policies in major supplier countries may reduce offerings by foreign banks. Individual branches may then be unable, at a given rate, to replace maturing deposits. If such deposits account for a sizable proportion of a branch's aggregate balances, its deposits at the head office may drop off sharply, to be built up again when the branch has been authorized to offer more competitive rates. Timing is often important, as other branches and other banks abroad may absorb early in the day major portions of the funds offered. It is true that central banks have increasingly been prepared to supply funds to the Euro-dollar market when it is exposed to pressures, but there are still occasions when the branches are forced to withdraw balances placed in their head offices, thereby forcing the latter to seek additional funds in the United States money market.

At times, the demand for Euro-dollars for use in foreign money and loan markets is so pressing that rates rise to levels that are out of line with those quoted in markets for comparable funds in the United States, thereby inducing the head offices not to renew maturing deposits. This situation is subject to reversal, because the head offices normally absorb so large a proportion of aggregate Euro-dollar deposits that any reduction of their takings will tend to bring rates down. In any event, Euro-dollar rates, especially those for call money and other short-dated funds, which are less suited than the more distant maturities for use in commercial loan markets abroad, are highly sensitive to conditions in the United States money market.

It is true, of course, that banks must allocate a major part of their branches' aggregate Euro-dollar resources to the loan and investment transactions of the branches themselves. The banks cannot disregard the demand for branch loans that comes from the affiliates abroad of important head-office accounts. And the branches must accommodate their own customers with whom they have developed close deposit and loan relationships. But the needs of the branches themselves do not appear to have restricted head-office use of the market for its own requirements. The head offices can almost always obtain additional balances in the market, at a price, if they are pressed for funds. The market has proved to be highly interest-rate elastic, and thus, as rates escalate, offerings rise at a very rapid pace. This was demonstrated during the credit crunch in the summer and fall of 1966, when United States banks by raising their bids pulled very large additional amounts into the market. The Euro-dollar pool is not inexhaustible, but it can be replenished by a large variety of funds held in several types of assets and currencies. Therefore, relatively small shifts from other uses within and to the Euro-dollar market can satisfy a rise in the demand for funds.

There are some negative aspects of the Euro-dollar market from the viewpoint of money position management. The market is far away, and because of the time difference between London and New York (not to mention Chicago or San Francisco) opportunities for immediate and direct head-office communication with it is confined to a few hours during the morning. Moreover, due to the settlement and clearing periods involved, several days pass before a head-office decision to take on Euro-dollars is reflected in available funds in the banks' reserve accounts. Meanwhile, conditions in domestic money markets may have changed significantly. Closely connected with the distance factor is the problem of adequate information. Because of the diverse conditions prevailing in the several major areas where dollar supplies originate, it is not always easy for the branches to obtain accurate knowledge of prospective market factors that might affect rates and amounts offered. And, in turn, head-office money position managers have not always found it easy to convey to their London offices their exact needs in terms of amounts and maturities, since their desire to draw on the market is partly conditional on the rates at which balances in various maturity sectors become available, and the rates change in response to market conditions.

The large banks with overseas branches differ greatly in their appraisal of the merits of the market as a source of funds for head-office use. A few banks look upon the market as one of their preferred methods of portfolio adjustment and have made very heavy use of it almost continuously. For most large banks, however, Euro-dollars appear to be only a second choice. Several of these banks have used the market on a substantial scale solely during periods of severe reserve pressure.

By far the largest part of branch placements with head offices is held in

New York, but several banks in other financial centers also absorb relatively sizable balances from their branches. A few New York banks—and several banks elsewhere that have only recently opened overseas branches—have not yet made any large-scale use of Euro-dollar deposits.

The banks differ substantially in the proportion of their branches' aggregate dollar resources that they take into their own positions. At present, almost half of the branches' aggregate dollar balances, excluding interbranch deposits, are held in head offices, but for the branches of a few banks the figure is in excess of 60 per cent while for others it is below 40 per cent.

The bulk of Euro-deposits taken for head-office use is obtained through branches in London. These branches are, of course, a conduit for funds from many parts of the world. In fact, some banks have instructed their branches in other Euro-dollar centers to redeposit excess dollar balances in London offices. United States banks also obtain sizable funds directly from their Paris branches and, to a lesser extent, from their branches in Nassau. Direct placements in United States head offices by branches elsewhere are generally quite small.

MAJOR HEAD-OFFICE USES OF BRANCH BALANCES

Conceptually, the funds of overseas branches in head offices may be separated into three main categories: (1) balances borrowed by the head offices on a more or less continuous basis for the purpose of enlarging the banks' reserves, (2) balances acquired for short-term adjustments of reserve positions, and (3) working or operating balances to accommodate adjustments between head-office and branch accounts. The boundaries between the three categories are, at least for some banks, somewhat blurred; often the same balances serve all three functions, and clearly, whatever their maturity or the ultimate objective of their acquisition, they all add to the resources of the borrowing banks. Apart from these three categories, Euro-dollars are also used by foreign banks and overseas branches for the purchase of loans from United States banks and to finance loans that otherwise would have been made directly by American banks.

Continuous borrowing for enlarging reserves

The major motive of United States banks in using Euro-dollar funds has been to obtain balances for enlarging or maintaining their credit potential. In their efforts to locate and solicit additional loanable funds, the banks have become increasingly attracted by the continuous availability in the Euro-dollar market of very large amounts of funds in a broad maturity range. Although a large part of these funds are call and short-dated deposits, experience has demonstrated that over extended periods even the call component remains quite steady in the aggregate. Thus the presence in, or availability to, the Euro-dollar market of very large interest-rate-sensitive funds provides the banks with an attractive alternative means of meeting demands on their liquidity positions and adding to aggregate deposit stability.

Rate advantages explain, of course, much of the heavy use of Euro-dollar deposits. During recent years, they have been for extended periods less expensive, or at least not more expensive, than domestic deposits. Even when rates in the Euro-dollar market are nominally higher than those in the C/D market, it may be advantageous to increase holdings of branch balances, relative to sales of C/D's, because of their exemption from reserve requirements and FDIC fees. A further saving associated with the acquisition of branch balances arises from technical factors. When a bank obtains Euro-dollar balances from its branch, it may benefit from reduced reserve requirements, while clearing the transaction, for at least one day—and for more if the date of the acquisition is followed by a holiday or a weekend. The reason is that the check received by a bank in connection with the transfer of a Euro-dollar deposit acquired by its branch increases cash items in the process of collection, which are deductible from demand deposits in computing reserve requirements even though the branch balance does not add to deposits subject to such requirements. This saving arises only if the Euro-dollar deposit is repaid by a so-called "bills payable" check. Outstanding checks of this type need not be included in deposits subject to reserve requirements in contrast to checks issued by banks for purposes other than borrowings. The initial saving would cancel out at maturity of the funds if they were repaid with a check not exempt from reserve requirements.

As noted, the head offices may stand ready to accommodate important suppliers, even if Euro-dollars are offered at rates somewhat above those quoted for comparable domestic funds. Generally, the large banks are very much aware of the advantages of regular contacts and dealings in the market. Some of them have concluded that a continuous readiness to accept large amounts irrespective of immediate needs permits the overseas branches to improve their feel of the market and their information on prospective trends. Moreover, if needs for overseas balances are less urgent at a particular time, they may well rebound in the not too distant future. Keeping a hand in the market makes it a more reliable source of funds. In short, a number of United States banks believe that complete withdrawal from the market when domestic funds can easily be substituted for Euro-dollars would not serve their longer run interest, and on occasion they have been quite willing to pay a price, albeit small, for continued participation.

The head offices issue directives to the branches concerning the amounts they wish to take and the rate limits, either for specific maturities or for a "package" of maturities. During periods of rapidly mounting or declining pressures, head-office instructions to the branches regarding targets and rates are often changed from day to day. If money market conditions in the United States are relatively stable, the directives are issued for extended and sometimes indefinite periods ahead. Because the rising yield curve for Euro-dollar deposits often makes the more distant maturities too expensive relative to C/D rates for corresponding maturities, there is a tendency for head offices to concentrate on the shorter maturities among the balances that branches tap in the Euro-dollar market. Moreover, substantial offerings in the market generally carry short maturities. On occasion, the banks have instructed their branches to reach out for rather distant maturities, so that the banks' loan and investment portfolios can be financed on a more secure basis. Sometimes, the banks acquire longer term Euro-dollars from their branches and invest them in liquid assets in order to maintain a comfortable cushion against the possibility of losing C/D money if open market rates should exceed the Regulation Q ceilings.

Borrowing to finance weekend reserve positions

United States banks seldom use Euro-dollar balances for specifically adjusting day-to-day cash and reserve positions except over weekends. The Euro-dollar market is generally not suited to immediate reserve adjustment needs. One reason is the distance factor: In the morning hours, London time, when the branch officers would need to obtain indications of immediate head-office needs in the light of current offerings, United States banks have not yet opened for business; by noon, New York time, when the evolving cash needs of banks are becoming evident, the London market is closing up shop. Of still greater significance is the fact that the normal delivery period for Euro-dollars is two days, and even if arrangements can be made early in the morning London time to acquire dollars for same-day delivery in New York, these balances become available as bank reserves in Federal Reserve accounts only the next day (see below). Moreover, banks find it difficult to estimate changes in reserve positions for more than a few days in advance. For these reasons, banks generally consider the Federal funds market far superior to the overnight sector of the Euro-dollar market for very short-term adjustments of reserve positions. Yet, a few banks appear to be quite prepared for a variety of reasons to make continuous use of overnight deposits as a substantial core of relatively low cost funds.

An important use of the Euro-dollar market as a tool of short-term reserve management is for the financing of weekend reserve positions. In fact, most of the banks with branches employ overnight deposits each Thursday as a partial substitute for Federal funds purchases on Friday. Because of New York check-clearing practices, overnight borrowing in the Euro-dollar market value-Thursday for repayment on Friday can serve as bank reserves for three days—from Friday through Sunday. Euro-dollar transactions are generally settled through checks on New York banks. Unlike Federal funds transactions, which are recorded in Federal

Reserve accounts immediately, these checks must pass through the New York Clearing House, and it is not until the following business day that they become balances in the Federal Reserve accounts of member banks. Thus, a check drawn on bank A and deposited on Friday in bank B in repayment of a Euro-dollar deposit does not draw down A's reserves until Monday; the same applies if the check is deposited on the day before a holiday.

These weekend and holiday clearing delays are reflected in the rates that head offices must pay for Euro-dollar balances. For a one-day Euro-dollar deposit on Thursday, a United States bank in need of funds to meet its reserve requirements will be willing to pay a rate close to three times the anticipated Federal funds rate on Friday; and it will pay a corresponding multiple when the settlement date for these overnight balances precedes any other period when the New York money market is closed for one business day or longer. Thursday-Friday transactions have become so common that the rates have adjusted themselves almost fully to the anticipated Federal funds rate on Friday. Nevertheless, the banks continue to have their London branches engage in these transactions on a large scale—often for purely defensive purposes—because any bank that does not bid for overnight dollars offered value-Thursday is likely to suffer sizable losses in its Federal Reserve account as other American banks take advantage of the Thursday deposit offerings.

The money-desk managers of United States banks that wish to acquire Thursday-Friday money must make their basic decisions on amounts and rates at the end of the preceding week, or at the latest on Monday, on the basis of projections of supplies and rates in the Federal funds market the following Friday. Within limits further adjustments can be made on Tuesday or Wednesday, but the bulk of the available funds has been spoken for by that time. Actual conditions on Friday may well be and often are different from those projected. By Wednesday, however, the money-desk manager knows the amount of Euro-dollar overnight deposits that will be available on Friday, and in the light of this information he can adjust his Federal fund and dealer loan operations during the closing days of the week.

No statistical information is extant on the volume of Thursday-Friday transactions by the overseas branches of United States banks. Aggregate branch balances in their head offices tend to increase on Thursday by amounts in the $100 million to $300 million range, depending in part on conditions in the Federal funds market. But the overall volume of Thursday-Friday transactions is in excess of this range, which does not reflect balances that mature or are called on Thursday and are placed again for one day.

There are other categories of Euro-dollar deposit transactions that take advantage of the delay in the clearing of checks in New York. For instance, a foreign bank may accept an overnight Euro-dollar deposit on Thursday and make arrangements to sell the resulting Federal funds on Friday through its United States correspondent. For foreign banks, however, such transactions are less attractive than direct dealings with American banks' overseas branches, and have come into disuse with the branches' increasing activity in the Thursday-Friday market on behalf of their head offices.

In addition, use of the foreign exchange market to take advantage of the United States check-clearing procedure is quite common. For instance, a foreign bank, using a foreign currency, may purchase dollars in New York value-Thursday for resale value-Friday. Although the dollars it buys and sells are not "good money" until the following business day, the foreign currency is immediately available to the buyer for investment, because in foreign financial centers checks deposited before a designated hour are cleared the same day. Thus on Friday, when its Thursday dollars become available as "good money," a foreign bank can put them to weekend use in the Federal funds market and also use its Friday repurchase of local exchange for payments needs or for investment over the weekend in a foreign market. Of course, a bank engaging in such a transaction forgoes earnings on Thursday. Or a United States bank buyer of foreign exchange value-Friday can employ the funds abroad over the weekend and also retain its weekend use of the dollars with which it paid for them, since the check deposited for the settlement of the transaction is not debited against its reserve account until Monday. These and similar operations have been reflected in spot and forward exchange rate distortions and erratic flows of funds from foreign money markets.

Operating balances of branches

The third type of liabilities to overseas branches consists of balances carried with head offices for operating purposes. This item has no direct relationship to the branches' overall dollar liabilities. Actually there may be no necessity for a branch to carry an operating balance in its head office if it is authorized to overdraw its account at its head office in case of need, or if the various components of its assets carry maturities of the same length as those of its corresponding deposit liabilities. Moreover, branches are ordinarily able, at a price, to obtain additional balances in foreign currency deposit markets. But the voluntary credit restraint program has made it undesirable for head offices to expose themselves to sudden branch overdrafts for meeting deposit liabilities that cannot be replaced at the time of maturity without costly rate sacrifices. Some branches have been willing to build their asset portfolios on deposits that carry somewhat shorter maturities than loan and deposit placements abroad: it is not easy, and is at times impossible, to match dollar loans to corporations with dollar deposits of similar maturities. Branches also need operating balances to discharge obligations under letters of credit and to take care of a variety of payments orders by customers, and they need contingency reserves in view of their large outstanding loan commitments.

Dollar balances at head offices have on occasion served also as contingency reserves for the branches' deposit and loan operations in sterling. Because of the swings in confidence in the pound, sterling deposits have typically been short dated. On the other hand, the branches' commercial loans in sterling—made both to United Kingdom firms and to European affiliates of United States corporations—are usually for extended periods. At times, though less so recently, the branches have preferred to draw down and convert their dollar balances at head offices in lieu of meeting their sterling liabilities through other more costly portfolio adjustments.

Euro-dollar financing of loan transactions

There is, finally, the special category of Euro-dollar transactions represented by head-office loan transfers to branches. To some extent these entail the sale of outstanding loans under repurchase agreements. Such sales appear to arise mainly from efforts of head offices to maintain their outstanding claims below the quota ceilings set by the voluntary credit restraint program. The sales wipe out any simultaneous increase in branch placements in head offices that have resulted from branch acquisitions of deposits abroad for the specific purpose of purchasing the loans, but the head offices obtain funds for further loans. Of course, the head office does not acquire additional funds if the loan is paid for out of existing branch deposits. In that case the head office reduces its outstanding loans and its liabilities ("due to" branches) by the same amount. Its overall balance sheet thus contracts.

The large banks do not appear to have employed repurchase agreements with branches as a device for obtaining funds for additional domestic loans. Those banks that have considerable credit leeway under the restraint program have made several sizable sales of loans to branches. Under these circumstances, however, the purpose appears to have been to enable individual branches to acquire earning assets with funds that they had taken in to accommodate important nonbank accounts on their books.

Of greater importance than such sales, in terms of dollar amounts involved, are loans made by branches to meet loan demands on their head offices. For these loans to head-office customers the branches employ deposits obtained in the Euro-dollar or other foreign currency deposit market. It is, of course, possible that a branch would have increased its Euro-dollar liabilities even in the absence of this particular loan demand and would have placed additional balances in its head-office account.

It should be mentioned again that many United States banks without branches sell substantial amounts of their foreign loans to foreign banks under repurchase agreements, primarily in order to hold their foreign claims below the credit restraint program ceilings; the foreign banks finance these loan purchases largely with Euro-dollars. And there are indications that an increasing number of banks without branches have made arrangements to borrow Euro-dollars directly from foreign banks. These two types of transactions are analogous to, and have the same liquidity and reserve effects as, the corresponding transactions between head offices and their overseas branches.

HEAD-OFFICE USE OF BRANCH BALANCES, 1964–1968

Before 1964, relatively few of the banks with overseas branches made much use of the Euro-dollar market for their head-office operations. Not until the summer of that year did aggregate head-office liabilities to branches remain continuously above $1 billion. Through most of 1965, they were substantially below $2 billion, as shown in Figure 1. The majority of the banks with branches apparently preferred other options for obtaining funds, either because of cost considerations or because head-office portfolio managements had not yet developed a close liaison with overseas branch managements.

During the first half of 1966, as Federal Reserve pressures on the banks' reserve positions mounted, borrowings gradually increased and the aggregate due to branches approached the $2 billion level. The increased

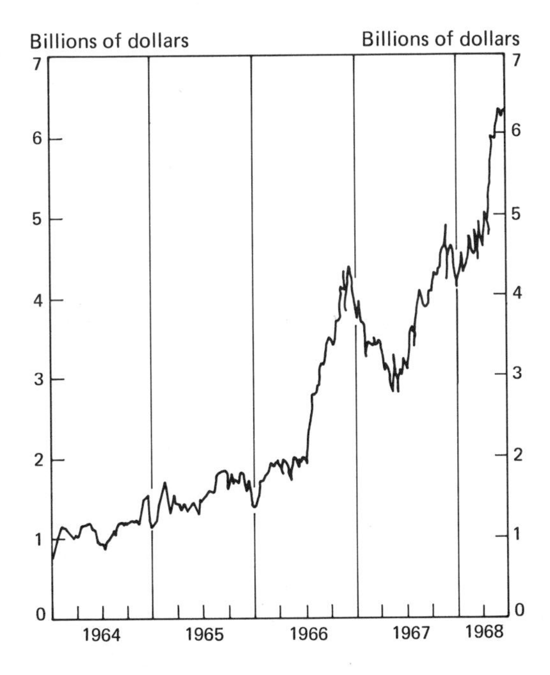

FIG. 1 Liabilities of United States banks to their foreign branches.

Source: Board of Governors of the Federal Reserve System.

resort to the Euro-dollar market during this period represented primarily an attempt to obtain resources over and above those available in domestic deposit markets and thereby to lessen susceptibility to reserve pressures.

Toward the end of June 1966, the pace of borrowing through branches quickened even more. The large money market banks then used the Euro-dollar market to cushion the effects of another weapon in the Federal Reserve's armory of credit control—administration of Regulation Q. With the Reserve System using Q as a deliberate means of reducing the rate of credit expansion, the banks were virtually priced out of the national C/D market. But about four fifths of the loss in outstanding C/D's suffered during the summer and fall of 1966 by the twelve banks with overseas branches was offset by increased Euro-dollar takings from branches. Euro-dollars at that time were in ample supply, partly because of large-scale shifts of funds out of sterling into dollars. By mid-December, aggregate redeposits in head offices, which had then reached $4.3 billion, amounted to substantially more than half of the twelve banks' outstanding C/D's, compared with less than one fifth in mid-1966.

Thus, during the summer and fall of 1966, Euro-dollar balances played an important role in banks' efforts to meet loan demands and commitments, offset losses of other resources, and reduce the need to liquidate securities at distressingly low prices. Moreover, the banks were then experiencing an increase in demand deposits relative to time deposits, and the resultant effects on required reserves were cushioned by the acquisition of balances not subject to reserve requirements.

Late in 1966 and early in 1967, when a large movement of foreign funds into the London money market coincided with a considerable easing of money market conditions in the United States, the use of branch balances by head offices fell rapidly, and by May 1967 it had dropped by about $1.5 billion from the peak level reached in December 1966. The figure then began to rise, however, and in November 1967 it began to exceed the amount outstanding during the 1966 credit crunch. During the short span of six months beginning in the middle of May 1967, aggregate borrowings from branches rose by about $2 billion.

This 1967 surge of branch deposits occurred in a market atmosphere quite different from that prevailing in the second half of 1966. During the latter part of 1967 the demand for business loans was relatively weak. The Federal Reserve supplied bank reserves quite liberally until late in the year, and banks were able to make considerable progress in improving their liquidity positions. There was little, if any, need to reach out for funds in Europe to compensate for shortages of funds in the United States. It appears, therefore, that there was a fundamental change in the banks' attitude with respect to taking Euro-dollars from their branches. Before the summer of 1966, several of them approached the Euro-dollar market with some hesitation, looking on it merely as a marginal source of funds. In general, they discovered the market's full potential only after having been virtually forced into it. As they became familiar with its breadth and depth, they lost their skepticism and came to regard the market as another normal source of funds to be tapped whenever the price was right.

Other factors also contributed to the surge in the use of Euro-dollars during 1967. Foreign investors shifted substantial amounts of their short-term sterling investments into the Euro-dollar market in response to the Middle East crisis in June and the weakening of sterling in the fall of 1967 prior to its devaluation. In addition, market relationships had been established, with considerable effort, and the banks desired to maintain them. Several felt that a withdrawal from the market because domestic funds could be easily substituted for Euro-dollars would not serve their longer run interest, even if continued participation sometimes involved a rate sacrifice.

In the spring of 1968, as money market conditions in the United States tightened, aggregate balances held for overseas branches passed the $5 billion mark, and toward the end of June they amounted to more than $6 billion. Sizable dollar losses by the Bank of France contributed importantly to Euro-dollar availabilities during the closing weeks of the month.

IMPLICATIONS FOR MONETARY ANALYSIS AND POLICY

United States banks' initiative in attracting hitherto untapped liquid funds—their gradual shift from a passive to an active role in acquiring funds through incurring liabilities—has raised important issues for monetary analysis and policy. And their recently increased use of balances obtained by the overseas branches from foreign sources has added to both the number and the complexity of the issues with which analysts and policy makers need be concerned. The success of the banks' efforts to acquire additional funds abroad has implications that touch on many aspects of the financial mechanism, including the country's balance of payments, the distribution of bank reserves and the banks' response to reserve pressures, the foreign ownership of United States money market instruments, and monetary policy.

One of the major consequences of the vast increase in the intermediation of overseas branches for head-office account has been a sizable substitution of United States bank liabilities to their branches for foreign central bank holdings of United States money market assets, and with it an improvement in the United States balance-of-payments position as defined on the official reserve transactions basis. To the extent that foreign-owned dollar balances are placed with United States banks instead of being used in foreign deposit and loan markets, the dollar supply offered on foreign exchange markets abroad is reduced, and thus also for the time being the potential offerings of dollars to foreign monetary authorities. Those authorities' holdings of dollars may even decline, as foreigners' demand for dollars to deposit in the Euro-dollar market may cause central banks to supply dollars to their exchange markets. Since foreign central banks tend to invest the bulk of their dollar holdings in United States Treasury securities, either a diversion of potential dollar balances from monetary authorities or a diminution of their existing holdings occurs largely at the expense of foreign official investments in Treasuries. Moreover, the retention or expansion of dollar balances in the hands of private holders benefits the official reserve transactions balance of the United States. However, some foreign central banks may suffer unwelcome losses in their own reserves as a result of developments in the Euro-dollar market. And if they take monetary action in an effort to reduce the outflows of funds, rates in their own money markets may escalate to levels that are undesirable for domestic reasons.

These substitutions and balance-of-payments effects are also likely to occur when central banks decide on their own initiative for reasons of domestic or international monetary policy either to deposit funds in the Euro-dollar market or to enter into swap transactions with their commercial banks. Especially if attractive swap rates are available, foreign commercial banks will make substantial use of such facilities and convert large amounts of domestic-currency assets into dollar balances. Such injections of foreign official funds into the market often add significantly to supply availabilities and tend to reduce upward pressures on Euro-dollar rates or even to lower rate levels. As a result, United States banks are likely to take on larger Euro-dollar balances through their branches than they would have acquired in the absence of these official injections of funds. Thus, the monetary reserves of foreign central banks are channeled through the Euro-dollar market to United States banks, and this country's official reserve transactions balance is thereby improved.[1]

The transformation of demand deposits into branch balances in head offices does not change United States banks' total reserves, but it does reduce the level of their aggregate required reserves, since overseas branch balances in head offices are not subject to reserve requirements. This fact has to be taken into account if, as is often done, current changes in bank credit are estimated on the basis of changes in deposits subject to reserve requirements. Moreover, the banking system as a whole can carry a somewhat larger amount of earning assets on the basis of a given amount of reserves. Since the banks that obtain balances from their branches typically are in a net reserve deficiency position and tend fully to employ available funds, their additional reserves are likely to be reflected immediately in a bank credit increase or reduced borrowings from other sources

[1] Some branch funds in head offices may originate in shifts of private foreign investments from the New York money market to the Euro-dollar market. In that event, the official reserve transactions balance would not be improved. But the evidence indicates that such shifts are not likely to occur when rates in the New York money market are relatively high. And when money market rates in this country are low in relation to Euro-dollar rates, the banks have little incentive to increase their liabilities to their branches.

rather than in larger excess reserves. In other words, these banks' acquisition of reserves through the Euro-dollar operations of their branches increases the utilization of the banking system's reserve base, as do Federal funds purchases from those banks that are less fully invested.

The banks that have direct access to the Euro-dollar market through their foreign branches are in a position to increase their share in total member bank reserves. If they were to abstain from absorbing Euro-dollar balances, most of the underlying funds would be invested by foreign central banks in the United States money market and would therefore be more widely dispersed throughout the banking system. Of course, to the extent that foreign central banks place their dollar gains in time deposits with American banks, these balances would be largely held with the same banks that acquire funds through their branches. To be sure, banks without branches may borrow Euro-dollar balances from foreign banks, and such borrowings are also exempt from Regulation Q ceilings and reserve requirements. But the branch route to Euro-dollars is more convenient and, in the long run, probably less expensive. Moreover, it allows access to a much larger volume of funds than banks can or would wish to secure through borrowings abroad. And only the larger banks in the United States have the credit standing that would enable them to obtain sizable dollar balances from foreign banks.

For individual banks with overseas branches, the availability of still another liability market of great breadth provides additional elbow room for portfolio and reserve adjustments. Inasmuch as the Euro-dollar market is subject to influences emanating from prevailing climates in foreign money markets, its supply-demand balance at any one particular point in time may differ greatly from that in the New York money market. Money market tightness here may be accompanied by relative ease in the Euro-dollar market. United States banks that find it undesirable or are unable to liquidate securities at such times, or are unable to add to their outstanding C/D's because of interest rate limitations by the Federal Reserve, may find a ready alternative source of funds in branch balances. But, even in the absence of pressure or regulatory interference in domestic money markets, access to Euro-dollars offers additional opportunities to minimize portfolio adjustment costs—as does resort to the national C/D market. Moreover, the very knowledge that they are able to fall back on the Euro-dollar market, and to use it in addition to or as an alternative to other liability markets, may induce portfolio managers to carry larger amounts of loans relative to aggregate deposits, and fewer liquid assets relative to aggregate assets, than they would otherwise consider prudent.

Monetary policy has had to take into account the buildup of overseas branch deposits in United States banks, and now continuously weighs the various implications and consequences of current and prospective changes in these placements. During periods of balance-of-payments pressure, the effect of branch deposits in head offices on the net demand for the dollar in foreign exchange markets is, of course, a matter that deserves particular attention. Nor can policy makers overlook the ways in which their decisions are transmitted through branch operations in the Euro-dollar market to foreign money markets and reflected in foreign monetary reserve changes, notably in countries that are under balance-of-payments pressure themselves. Now that banks in this country have become a major receptacle for the liquidity reserves of foreign commercial banks, the United States authorities have added reason to take an interest in foreign money market conditions. Similarly, they have additional reason to concern themselves with the Euro-dollar operations of those central banks that use the market as a major channel for making adjustments in their own monetary reserve positions. Indeed, prospective developments in the Euro-dollar market are now regularly discussed at the monthly meetings of central banks at the Bank for International Settlements (BIS) in Basle. The Federal Reserve's interest in the market is also demonstrated by the fact that Reserve credit has repeatedly been provided to the market through activation of the System's swap line with the BIS which now amounts to $1 billion. Under this arrangement the BIS can draw dollars from the Reserve System for placement in the Euro-dollar market.[2]

On the domestic side, the Federal Reserve System must be concerned with the redistribution of reserves arising from the access of banks with overseas branches to balances that other banks find it difficult or impossible to attract. It must also take into account shifts in the banks' aggregate demand for reserves as they acquire reserve-exempt balances. Furthermore, it must make allowance for the increased ability of the money market banks—the major source of business loans to large corporate borrowers—to fall back on the Euro-dollar market whenever the interest rate ceilings impair the banks' ability to obtain funds in the national market for C/D's. Indeed, now that some of the major commercial banks in the United States look beyond this country's borders for funds with which to make adjustments in their liquidity and reserve positions, a new and significant dimension has been added to central banking in the United States.

[2] For a description of these operations, see Charles A. Coombs, "Treasury and Federal Reserve Foreign Exchange Operations," this *Review* (March 1968), pages 38–52.

8

Frontiers of Bank Management:

"The Checkless Society"

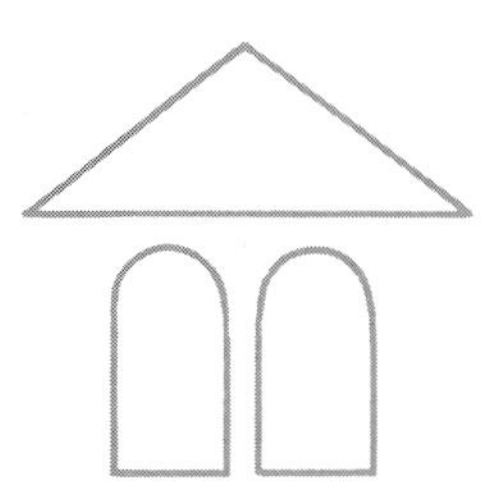

Preceding articles have demonstrated the rapid pace of change confronting bank management. The readings in this section indicate an *accelerated rate of change* in the payments mechanism—with attendant implications for bank management and public policy.

Since discussions of payments mechanisms frequently refer to giro systems, the first reading briefly outlines the nature of giro transfer mechanisms in other countries and relates the concept to advances in communications technology and possible changes in the American payments system. The conclusion of the first reading leads directly to the second article, in which Governor Mitchell of the Federal Reserve System suggests how sophisticated computer systems are likely to transform the payments system and thus affect banking functions and structure. This theme is further developed in the concluding article by R. L. Kramer and W. P. Livingston, who point out that while a nationwide computer information network is now technologically feasible, various obstacles remain, in the form of technical problems and existing attitudes. They also examine the implications of the checkless society for various individuals and groups and provide some time estimates of the evolution toward a "checkless society."

The Giro, the Computer, and Checkless Banking

A speedy and efficient payments system is essential to the functioning of a modern economy. In the United States and England, as in most of the Anglo-American world, most payments are made in currency and coin or by checks drawn on commercial banks. While this system has functioned remarkably well over the years, the growing volume of payments promises to create serious problems in the transportation and processing of checks. The cost to the public of operating the check clearing and collection system is estimated at about $3.3 billion annually, and this cost is almost certain to increase as the volume of payments increases. Moreover, while the check payments system is quite accurate, the growing cost and sometimes considerable delays in collecting checks impairs the usefulness of checkbook money as a medium of exchange.

Some informed observers predict drastic changes in the payments system of the United States in the coming years. These changes would almost eliminate checks and greatly reduce the use of currency. In the payments system envisaged, the average United States citizen may pay his monthly bills to the doctor, the utility company, the mortgage company, and others, not by mailing checks to each of them but by instructing (perhaps by telephone) the bank holding his deposit account to transfer specified amounts from his account to the accounts of designated payees. He may receive his salary payment in the form of a notice from his bank that the amount has been added to his account. When his wife goes shopping, she may make payment by using a special telephone arrangement to instruct a bank's computer to transfer the appropriate amount from the family bank account to that of the store.

These and even more dramatic changes in the payments system may result from combining modern electronic data processing techniques with the so-called "giro transfer" system which has been used in some continental European countries for years but which has been largely untried in the United States. The giro system has characteristics that make it particularly suitable for the use of computers, although it does not require their use. In fact, the European systems operated effectively for many years without computers. A brief description of the giro transfer system may indicate some of the possibilities inherent in it.

Reprinted with the permission of the Federal Reserve Bank of Richmond from *Monthly Review*, April 1966.

NATURE OF GIRO TRANSFER SYSTEMS

The giro system possesses a number of fundamental characteristics in common with the check payments system. Basically it involves deposit balances held by individuals and businesses with some institution and systematic arrangements for the transfer of these balances from payer to payee. It differs from the checking system chiefly in the manner of effecting these transfers. Under the familiar checking system, the payer delivers to the payee a written order, i.e., a check, directing the institution holding his account to pay a certain sum of money at sight. The check may pass through numerous hands, and through two or more banks and/or a clearing house, before it is presented to the drawee bank. In the typical giro transaction, the payer delivers to the drawee institution an order directing it to transfer a specified sum from his account to that of the payee and to advise the payee of the transfer. Thus giro transfers are more direct and involve both less time and less paper handling than ordinary check transfers.

Giro transfers are simplest when both the payer and the payee have accounts at the same institution. They can be made to work with comparable efficiency, however, where the payer and the payee use different institutions. Numerous institutions, for example, may be members of a common giro system which incorporates arrangements for automatic transfers between member institutions as well as for transfers between the customers of these institutions. Such arrangements exist today in some European countries. It is reasonably clear that existing facilities for clearing checks between banks in this country could easily be converted into an effective giro system embracing most, or even all, banks.

As they stand today, the giro systems abroad center around a variety of institutions. Some are operated by the postal service, some by central banks, and some by commercial banks. Others center around facilities provided by savings banks, by municipalities or by credit cooperatives. In some European countries, as many as four or five separate giro systems operate side by side.

The postal giro is perhaps the most important of the giro systems found in the continental European countries. In many of these countries, commercial banks cater primarily to business and industrial accounts and do not, as a rule, offer the special individual checking account services so common in the United States. The postal services of these countries, with their numerous offices, quite naturally became involved in transfers between individuals, and the postal giro was largely an outgrowth of these circumstances. Postal giros offer nationwide coverage, but it should be noted in this connection that equally extensive coverage is possible, and in some countries already exists, under giros operated by systems of private commercial banks.

Foreign giro systems provide an efficient, convenient, and inexpensive payments system not only for individuals but for many businesses as well. This method of payment is particularly attractive to insurance companies, public utilities, mail order houses, and other businesses regularly receiving large numbers of remittances. These organizations are saved much of the work and expense of handling and banking large quantities of checks and currency, and they may well receive credit for funds sooner than if checks were used. For those who must make regular remittances, such as mortgage payments or insurance premiums, it is frequently possible to arrange for automatic transfer of specified amounts at regular intervals.

INTEROFFICE TRANSFERS

Giro systems usually have numerous offices scattered over wide geographical areas. This is particularly true of the postal systems. Accordingly, regional offices are usually maintained for centralized record keeping and for making interoffice transfers. Figure 1, which is based on the Japanese postal transfer system, shows how funds may be quickly transferred over considerable distances through the use of regional transfer centers.

In the Japanese system, all post offices handle transfer transactions, but 28 regional transfer offices maintain records of individual accounts and actually effect the transfers. A person desiring to open an account applies to any post office, pays a small fee, and upon approval by the regional transfer office an account is opened in his name at that regional

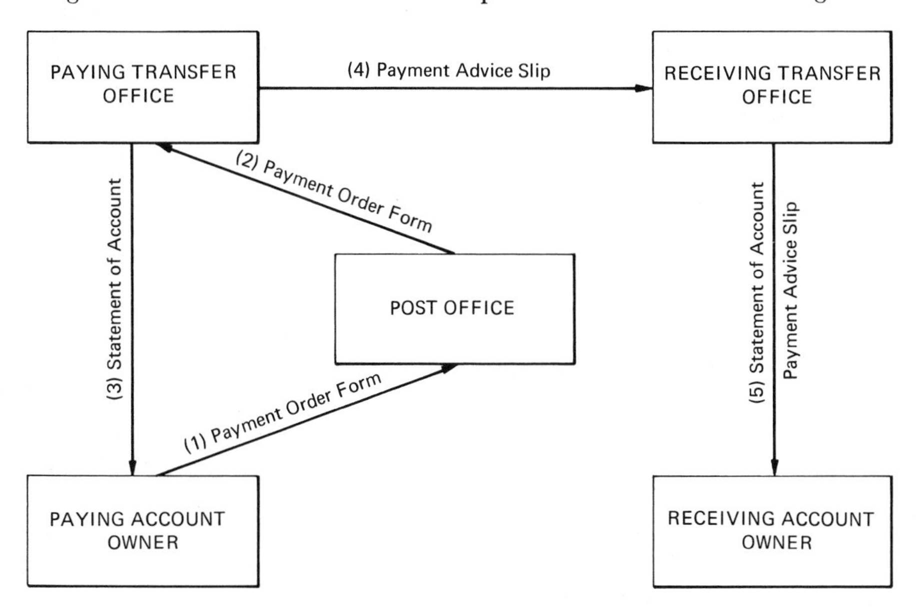

FIG. 1 Interoffice transfer in the Japanese postal giro system.

office. He may make deposits to the account by filling out a form and paying in the amount (plus a fee) to a post office. The post office then sends a copy of the form to the regional office and the amount is credited to the individual's account. The regional office then sends the owner a statement of account together with the original deposit slip.

Figure 1 illustrates how transfers are made between accounts held in different regional transfer offices. In the first step, the payer submits a regular payment order form to his post office, stating the amount of the payment and the name and account number of the payee. The post office forwards the payment order to the payer's regional transfer office, which deducts the amount from his account, sends him a new statement of account, and forwards a payment advice to the payee's regional office. The payee's regional transfer office adds the amount to the account of the payee and sends him a copy of the payment advice form together with a new statement of his account. If time is an important consideration, the payer may request a telegraphic transfer.

Commercial bank giro systems vary greatly, with particular organizations determined primarily by the size and structure of the banking system and by the degree of centralization desired. In most cases there are few problems involved in handling transfers between branches of a single bank, although the exact procedure may depend upon the organization and accounting system of the bank. But methods of effecting transfers between offices of different banks are greatly influenced by the degree of centralization. The most highly centralized systems have common central institutions that manage the entire giro service as well as the funds deposited in individual accounts. On the other hand, some systems have no central institution at all, and each branch receiving a giro order is responsible for making transfers to other banks and branches that may be involved. In these systems, transfers between banks may be settled through correspondent balances or through clearing house settlements.

The organization of the Swedish Bank giro falls somewhere between these extremes. All commercial banks in Sweden contribute to a central giro institution located in Stockholm, but individual accounts are kept at branch offices and sums deposited are administered by these offices. The central institution settles transactions between banks and maintains central offices, but it does not control the money it handles. There is a daily settlement between the central institution and each bank that is a member of the system.

CHARGES FOR GIRO SERVICES

Charges for giro services vary from country to country and from system to system. The proposed charges for the British Post Office giro, which is now in the process of being established, are probably representative of charges by postal giro systems generally. In the British system, there will be no charge for regular transfers of funds such as those described above. Deposits by an account holder to his own account will also be free, but deposits by non-account holders will involve a fee of about ten cents. Fees on withdrawals by account holders or on cash payments to third parties will depend upon the amounts involved, with payments over 50 pounds to cost about 28 cents. Postage to the giro will be free.

Because many transactions are free and only nominal fees are charged on some others, income from charges is expected to cover only a relatively small part of the operating costs of the British system. Interest is not paid on deposits, however, and it is hoped that the investment of accumulated funds will provide sufficient income to cover the difference between charges and costs. Whether this hope will be realized will depend to a considerable extent upon the number of users of the system, the average size of the accounts, and the activity in the accounts.

ELECTRONIC DATA PROCESSING

Advocates of the development of a giro transfer system for the United States base their arguments chiefly on the grounds that this system possesses characteristics which make it particularly suitable for the use of electronic data processing equipment. Unlike check payments systems, transactions in the giro system take place entirely within the individual bank, or if more than one bank is involved, entirely within the banking system. Thus, when a depositor instructs his bank to make payment to another giro account holder, his bank receives all the information needed to complete the transaction—the identification of both the payer and the payee, the amount to be paid, and the time at which payment is to be made.

Proponents of the giro system maintain that the entire transfer process could be handled almost instantaneously by computers. The payer's instructions to his bank could be fed into the bank's computer and if both the payer and payee are depositors of that bank the computer could perform all of the operations necessary to make the transfer, including the printing out of confirmation to the payer and advice of payment to the payee. If the payer and payee have accounts at different banks, the computer at the payer's bank could perform the operations necessary for its records and transmit the information to the second bank's computer, either directly or through a central institution, and settlement between the banks could be made as described above.

Although the transition to a completely computerized giro transfer system undoubtedly would not be without its pain and problems, the development of such a system appears to be entirely within present technical capabilities. Banks already make extensive use of data processing equipment in their operations, and a push-button type of telephone has been developed which permits a customer to communicate directly with his bank's computer. . . .

Making use of the push-button telephone, the housewife of the future may pay the family bills at any time of day or night simply by tapping out instructions to her bank's computer. She may ascertain her account balance by making inquiry of the computer and the information will be provided to her in spoken form. When shopping, she may use a card obtained from her bank which, when inserted in the store's special telephone, will permit her to make payment by instructing the bank's computer to transfer the proper amount to the store's account. Or she may obtain a credit card from her bank which would permit purchases to be charged to a convenience or installment credit account at her bank, thereby eliminating the necessity of opening charge accounts at numerous establishments and carrying a large number of credit cards.

A GIRO SYSTEM FOR THE UNITED STATES?

Despite these apparent advantages, it is still questionable whether the United States will ever have a fully developed giro transfer system. Arguing against such a development is the absence of most of the conditions that brought about the establishment of such systems in other countries. Commercial banks in this country have provided an efficient payments system and, unlike those in some countries, they have actively sought the accounts of small depositors.

Some elements of the giro system have already been adopted in this country. An increasing number of businesses are processing payrolls by instructing their computers to instruct their bank's computers to reduce their accounts and to credit their employees' bank accounts. Banks are already making limited use of the cards described above. The American Bankers Association has conducted seminars dealing with the possibilities of an automated payments system and is sponsoring research efforts along the same lines.

But the full development of the system envisaged would be a lengthy and costly process. The characteristics of the special telephone which make it adaptable for communication with business machines would necessitate major modifications in telephone central offices before these could be made available to the general public. Costs of data processing equipment would be substantial, not to mention the problems of obtaining competent personnel to operate this equipment. In addition, many serious technical problems doubtless would arise during the period of transition. Finally, the transition would inevitably encounter numerous obstacles posed by legal and customary technicalities involved in settling transactions.

But the ultimate benefits might more than offset these costs. In the words of George W. Mitchell, Member of the Board of Governors of the Federal Reserve System, "In the modified giro system . . . there will be no check sorting and re-sorting, no shipment of checks from bank to bank or bank to customer, no storage requirements for checks, no kited checks, no checks returned for insufficient funds, and no float." These are substantial benefits indeed.

Governor Mitchell believes that the adoption of some form of computerized giro system is inevitable and that it will occur much sooner than most observers expect. In any event, possibilities for significant economies have been opened up by the rapid technological advances of recent years. These possibilities create a standing incentive for commercial banks to make important changes in the payments services they offer to the public.

Effects of Automation on the Structure and Functioning of Banking

George W. Mitchell

The commercial banking system in the United States owes its existence to its ability to render for all sectors of the economy a unique and pervasive service; namely, the movement of money. This transfer of funds between debtor and creditor, buyer and seller, citizen and government, employer and employee—in fact from anyone with a balance in a bank to any identifiable payee—is ever ready, safe, and convenient.

Banks consummate money settlements through an elaborate clearing system for transferring deposit balances from one account to another in the same bank or in different banks.[1] The principal tool used is the ordinary check. The mechanical and institutional channels by which 60

[1] Commercial banks also have an important function to perform in the only alternative procedure for settling the economy's accounts; i.e., by the use of coin and currency. They maintain at significant cost local reservoirs of cash for the use of their business and individual customers who can withdraw amounts and denominations when required and return to the pool unfit or excess holdings.

Reprinted with permission from *The American Economic Review,* May 1966.

million checks daily find their way physically, and with appropriate accounting entries, from any one to any other among 70 million accounts is vastly more complicated than might be thought. It achieves a high degree of ultimate accuracy considering its predominant dependence on manual processing. The service is far from instantaneous, however, being no faster than present-day methods of transporting checks in considerable bulk about a city or throughout the country.

In the aggregate, the annual cost of operating the present check and settlement system for the entire country can be estimated at about $3.3 billion. Some of this cost is borne by the Federal Reserve System, some is paid in the form of service charges assessed on the account of the payor, and some is "clipped" from the face of the check instrument itself and charged the payee when nonpar banks are involved. However, the bulk of the total cost is absorbed by the commercial banks themselves to attract balances that can be invested in interest-earning assets.

Given the cost and time pressures inherent in the present check settlement system, it is not surprising that the initial bank efforts to exploit the infant prodigy of electronic data processing have been aimed mainly at lowering the per-item handling cost and speeding up the performance of old-style check collection. This is constructive, so far as it goes, but it falls far short of the potential transformation of banking services rendered possible by automation. Laying aside all the undoubted strains and pains of the transition, it is practical to envision the advancement of the state of the art to a point that will permit—and perhaps almost force—radical change in banking structure and functions. This state will be reached within the discernible future, probably much sooner than most of us expect.

By that time, I expect, check usage as we know it will have largely disappeared, and the intricate process of settlement and deposit accounting will be carried on concurrently at and between 250 or so computer centers located throughout the country.[2] A modified giro system will be used, in which the payor will initiate the settlement process, but will do so by communicating, not with the payee, but with his bank—notifying it directly whom to pay, how much, and when.

Most of this information will be received at the bank in machine language; if not, it will be converted to that form, and the bank's computer will process the bookkeeping entries internally for amounts drawn on it. If one computer handles the accounts for several banks, the operation is still almost entirely an internal one. If payment is to an account in another bank, the information will be automatically routed into that bank's

[2] The number of computer centers given is conjectural but compromises an optimum operational size and a convenient geographical area. The very rapid growth of computer centers recently seems to presage the automation of all demand deposit accounting in the near future—using checks or any other settlement media. Banks will have a choice of their own equipment, a correspondent's facilities, a cooperative processing organization, or a commercial service bureau.

equipment. Bank positions will also be adjusted frequently throughout the day by debits and credits to member bank accounts with the Federal Reserve System. The computers will transmit printed-out confirmations to the payor and advices to the payee at appropriate intervals. The print-outs could be transmitted by mail or telephone wire, at the option of the customer. In the case of larger customers, the bank's computer will communicate directly with customer's equipment.

In this system there is no check sorting and re-sorting, no shipment of checks from bank to bank or bank to customer, no storage requirements for checks, no kited checks, no endorsement, no N.S.F. checks, no float, and a minimum of manual processing. Of course, different problems may later come to light. The machine must work; and the bank must make sure it is being instructed by the owner of the deposit. There is no reason, however, to fear that any such potential difficulties are beyond the technological capacities and, probably, the cost horizons now in view.

Furthermore, it seems logical and practical that at least some of the customer accounting antecedent and subsequent to settlement could be most economically done in a coordinated package with the settlement accounting. Every sales transaction, for example, by specifying a settlement date, might immediately be put into the bank's computer where it could accomplish immediate settlement or subsequent reminder and settlement. Similarly, a bank could handle payrolls and agree to bill and process many types of contractual payments for insurance, rent, and mortgage payments. In short, by virtue of its central position in the payments process, the bank is also able to perform ancillary and antecedent accounting and billing operations more economically than anyone else.

For willing business customers, the bank's service could include a large part of the accounting, analysis, and financing of receivables and even extend to provision of much current cash flow accounting—a basis of analysis that has become of increasing importance in both business and financial planning.

Tied into the possibility of, if not a prerequisite to, expanded service for most depositors is the introduction of a depositor combination cash-credit card. This device could be used for immediate payment, partially replacing the use of coin and currency, or it could be used for the processing of convenience credit or the scheduling and liquidation of installment or revolving credit.[3]

[3] The cash card involves some exposure to theft or counterfeiting but various identification devices such as voice "fingerprinting," or other technological developments now under study appear adequate to control losses. Security may be more importantly achieved, however, by the positive identification of all payees inherent in the system. To be a payee one must have an account with a bank and have met whatever identification and responsibility standards are found to be necessary for the protection of payors. There are no intermediate signatories in the system. Once the payor has directed his bank to make a given payment and the bank is satisfied with its identification of the payor, then there is no opportunity of intercepting and misappropriating the "document" used for this purpose.

All of these ancillary operations enhance profitable business prospects of a computerized settlement system outlined above. Obviously they and similar extensions of service have an important bearing upon the alacrity and enthusiasm with which banks will convert to or adopt EDP systems.

If the foregoing projections are realistic, they seem to promise, in the aggregate, a substantially more efficient settlement mechanism. And they imply additional profit opportunities for banks that can combine settlement with receivables accounting, payroll accounting, credit card operation, and a consumer credit system for depositors.

Today, no one really knows how much cost reduction, private and social, a fully computerized system might achieve. Some of those with the earliest and most extensive experience in partial EDP applications are taking a hard, if not skeptical, look at "hardware" costs of a full-scale operation. One of the difficulties of bringing the relevant evidence together is the problem of totaling up actual private costs in our present settlement system which could be eliminated or reduced in the "checkless-cashless" society. Another is the allocation of the new system's public and private costs among various public and private beneficiaries. If public costs presently involved in the distribution of currency and processing of checks, for example, are substantially reduced, how can the entrepreneur banker who brings this about collect a *quid pro quo?*

The question, then, of whether commercial banks will regard EDP as an opportunity for profitable service is not easily answered. The banking system is not distinguished for its innovative achievements—despite evidence of improvement in recent years. Its adaptability to change is hampered by regulatory constraints on structure and function. Entry, branching, and merger are closely regulated, as are prices paid for deposits and many of the conditions under which credit can be extended. Thus, there is a tradition of conservatism in management reinforced by competitive sheltering and regulatory constraints that act as inhibitions to innovative steps with any evident structural or functional consequences.

This opens the way for nonbank enterprises to become well established in the EDP record-keeping applications antecedent or related to settlement before banks even enter the field. If they do, their customers are likely to be relatively indifferent to tardily offered adjuncts to a banking settlement system.

The deferred entry of banks into the consumer credit business is a case in point. Today, credit for consumers is relatively independent of the banking system though it is also available there, and generally for less. However, even today, seldom does a bank's consumer credit system exploit the natural advantages of a continuing depositor relationship in the way that vendors, for example, have exploited the continuing patronage of their customers. Moreover, consumer credit is a natural extension of other banking operations. A bank's individual depositors use credit extended by its retail firm depositors with the proceeds of trade-credit bank lines. Vendors have established practical standards of credit worthiness for their customers and profitably priced the credit extended. At the most, very few banks have offered an aggressively competitive alternative to vendor credit by carrying the credit financing from producer or wholesaler through to the ultimate consumer.

As an industry, banks have moved into consumer credit far more slowly than vendors; they have not been innovative and, by and large, have made almost no use of their key position in settlement accounting to provide services more broadly and economically than anyone else.

Past experience suggests, therefore, that the banking system may well be reluctant or inhibited from exploiting the opportunities inherent in automation, particularly if more aggressively-minded EDP machine sellers or users can carve out large sectors of potential service in which, through lower costs and innovative flexibility, they can establish customer loyalties.

But if skepticism borne of experience leads me to expect opportunities to be missed in this area, logic compels me to insist that such a fate is not inevitable. A clear enough vision of future possibilities exists in some banks today. Hammered home hard enough by both intra-industry communication and private advice, it might serve to erode much of the inertia and inhibition now forestalling a full-fledged revolution in the settlements mechanism.

If this should happen—and assuming public policies are accommodative—not only banking services but also banking structure could be literally transformed. Profound structural changes seem almost a certainty. Automation can and will burst the locational constraints that are implicit in federal conformity to the provisions of fifty state banking laws pertaining to branching. Not only will metropolitan area-wide banking operations become commonplace everywhere at the option of bank managements, but remote control banking state-wide, and even across state lines, will also be feasible, limited by little more than the telephone toll costs of servicing more distant customers.

To be sure, banks have detoured branching restrictions for some time, as large banks in various parts of the country have solicited and made loans all over the United States—or over the world, for that matter—and have accepted deposits by mail or wire from customers wherever located. But this sort of substitute for branching is a reality only for large accounts. The dynamic change that will come into being is that computerizing the demand depositor-bank relationship will make it practicable and in all probability economically profitable for banks spectacularly to extend their present service areas for small and medium-sized accounts. This they can do, by using the U.S. mails or by hooking their computer onto a local telephone in any community they wish to serve.

The same features of automation that will enable banks to achieve many of the advantages of a far-flung branching system will also introduce a large element of obsolescence into many existing branch facilities. Branches that have been established to achieve proximity to depositors and are essential from the bank's standpoint only because they facilitate the sweeping up of loanable funds or minimize deposit fluctuations by more nearly encompassing the local payments cycle will become superfluous.

Depositors will have no need to visit their banking office any more often than they now visit their telephone or electric utility company office. They will not be making deposits of checks; rather their bank will notify them of credits to their accounts. They will rarely find it necessary to go to their bank to obtain cash, even for transactions that are now typically made with cash. Their credit line will be activated automatically. Their cash-credit card will be the equivalent of cash at a supermarket, the cleaners, or a department store. The coin and currency required for transactions that will continue to be most conveniently handled in that fashion will be supplied from commercial establishments that are regularly serviced by money truck pickup and delivery.

Perhaps there will be a place for "baby branches"—small field offices which might serve as headquarters for account salesmen and loan officers, and for performing custodial, certification, and routine financial advisory services, but it is hard to visualize the typical branch office in existence today as fitting into a computerized banking institution of the future.

Automation in banking will likely have lesser effects on such traditional types of bank credit extension as farm lending, mortgage lending, and loans to large businesses and to financial enterprises. But it should have a major impact upon consumer credit and trade credit between firms, particularly of small and medium size. These types of credit involve substantial investigative and bookkeeping costs relative to interest earned on a typical loan or line of credit. They also involve more surveillance and more losses, though of a readily insurable type, thus adding further to overhead costs.

With automation, banks can offer a credit system which ties settlement accounting into quasi-automatic credit extension; this combination has great operating advantages over other arrangements available to vendors or independent consumer finance companies. A bank depositor credit card is of superlative convenience for the purchaser when he can use it anywhere and in doing so express his preference for cash payment, convenience credit, installment credit or any combination of the three.

The bank, in offering this service, can extend credit to seller or buyer, or both, on the basis of prearranged lines—lines that have been fixed with access to unparalleled sources of information on the customer's financial activity and responsibility. Moreover, the computer continuously updates this information and can alert the bank's credit department on a timely basis to the emergence of credit abuses by whatever standard the bank may choose to employ. Imagine the convenience of a continuing scrutiny of the customer's cash inflow and outflow in relation to use of bank credit, and all monitored by a sentry who reports instantaneously!

Such a system would not be without losses, to be sure, but they could be controlled by fixing maximum credit lines for various types of accounts. And loan limits could serve another purpose: that of fostering larger demand deposit balances. If a line of credit, for example, were some multiple of average daily balance, it is quite likely that most depositors would gladly pay the "commitment fee" for the convenience and prestige of bank credit. And still another advantage so far as banks are concerned is the conventional preference of many bankers for self-liquidating short-term credit, met in this instance by the rapid turnover of consumer and sales credit of the type envisioned.

Particular beneficiaries of this more flexible and better disciplined credit use should be the many self-employed in the economy, ranging from part-time salesmen to proprietors. While their aggregate credit use is a small factor in bank lending, a significant public interest is served by uncovering any method of economically and conveniently making more bank resources available to them. Under current operating procedures, the overhead costs associated with such credit, when added to a regular interest charge, entail effective interest rates that are prohibitive or appear highly discriminatory. Automation offers a method of minimizing overhead costs and probably reducing risk, thereby making bank credit more accessible to a sector of the economy that has found all sources of credit "high priced."

In their continuous search for loanable resources, banks will find automation a far keener tool than they are accustomed to using. On the one hand, it will enable them to attract demand deposit customers with assurance of a simpler, safer, and more convenient means of payment than has ever been offered. Not only will the computer reduce the risk in paying bills, it will also take over the chores in banking—such as a trip to the bank and the standing in line to make a deposit, the writing of checks and mailing them to creditors, and similar routine tasks. Moreover, it will give the depositor "instant bookkeeping," as he will be able to find out as often as he likes the exact status of his account, and with that knowledge give the bank instruction as to whom to pay, and when. Thus he is enabled to manage his money position as closely as he likes.

From the standpoint of profitable operations, banks that offer a service making possible the close management of customers' bank accounts are almost certain to find their demand deposit totals wasting away as a manifestation of the automation program. Moreover, given the capabilities of a computerized economy, more frequent settlement periods are likely, if not certain, to come into widespread use and this development will diminish still further the size of a comfortable operating balance for the typical depositor. Just as weekly wage and salary payments go with a lower operating bank balance than is needed when payments are monthly, the shorter interval made possible by automation will call for even smaller cash balances.

Given declining need for demand deposit balance for these "technological" reasons, banks have the alternative of establishing fees to cover at least a portion of the costs incurred for processing flows through demand deposit accounts or of establishing minimum balances commensurate to the scope and cost of services rendered. If they rely heavily on fees, then in order to maintain their aggregate of loans and investments banks will need to attract time deposits (or to borrow) in one form or another in competition with other banks, other financial intermediaries, and the capital markets. The compensating balance alternative, on the other hand, if enhanced in appeal by linking it to a packaged credit line, would enable banks to minimize losses in demand deposit balances.

Other changes consequent to the automation of money flows—such as operating space and labor requirements of banking institutions—involve formidable housekeeping and management adjustments, but they are of a different order of concern.

Nor has any mention been made of the possibility of the settlement system being nationalized, along the lines of European experience, in the Post Office or the Federal Reserve System. While such a step is technically feasible, if not advantageously suited to a monopolistic operation, our preferences run strongly against extending government operations into service areas that can be satisfactorily performed privately.

If the views and speculations advanced here are at all persuasive, it will probably be with the assenter's proviso that "it won't happen in my time." To this skepticism I can only reply that most of the innovations I have alluded to are now in being, or about to be placed in operation. Individual banks in all sections of the country are adopting, piecemeal, elements of a system such as has been described. Before very long these experimental operations will provide a solid foundation for the new banking system of the future.

Cashing in on the Checkless Society

Robert L. Kramer and Putnam Livingston

FOREWORD

Technically speaking, the checkless society is virtually feasible now; the computer hardware is capable of handling it. But enormous problems remain, particularly in planning how the system will be instituted and financed, persuading the seg-

Harvard Business Review, September–October 1967.

ments of the economic community to accept it, and showing them how to take advantage of it. In this article the authors describe how each segment will be affected and venture some predictions as to how and when the checkless society will be launched.

Conversation today about the checkless society among those who have not considered it seriously resembles the popping of corn over a hot fire rather than serious dialogue.

Why this is so is a mystery, since the checkless society holds very significant promise in the computer age. It will be one of the most important so-called information utilities; in this case, a financial utility large enough eventually to be dedicated solely to the movement of money, the extension of credit, and the generation of data for the grist mills of our economists.

There are several basically synonymous terms that have been used by various authors in discussing what we shall call the "checkless society." Some refer to it as "cashless," and others use the term "paperless." All of them, though, forecast one thing: a major technological change in the payments mechanism.

The impact of the checkless society on the consumer and on banking has been discussed exhaustively.[1] Less attention, however, has been directed toward its effect on the business community at large. Since virtually all businesses, as well as the vast majority of individuals, deal with checks frequently and with money even more frequently, any change in the payments mechanism will have tremendous effects on industry. It is mainly with these effects of the forthcoming system that this article deals.

WHY DO WE NEED IT?

The primary impetus today for improving the payments mechanism stems from realization of the enormous cost of the rising tide of paper work and recognition that there are other ways of moving money besides the physical effort of preparing and exchanging documents.

Americans write 17 billion checks per year, and the number is increasing by 7% annually. The total value of checks written yearly is between $4 trillion and $5 trillion. It has been estimated that handling these billions of checks costs the banking system alone about $3.3 billion each year.[2] A recent survey for the Federal Reserve System by the Stanford Research Institute points out that commercial enterprises also spend billions annually in the payment process:

[1] See, for example, William D. Smith, "The Checkless Society: Human Beings Causing the Chief Delays," *The New York Times,* May 21, 1967; and W. Putnam Livingston, "Banking's Role in the Development of the Financial Information Utility," *American Banker,* December 1, 1966.

[2] George W. Mitchell, "The Impact of Automation on Bank Structure and Function," *American Banker,* December 30, 1965.

"The present system for transferring funds and extending credit to society . . . shows that the costs for granting, billing, and collecting credit are approximately of the same order of magnitude as those for the present checking system—i.e., $3 to $4 billion per year." [3]

On the checkless society's potential savings to check users and processors, John J. Clarke, vice president and special legal counsel for the Federal Reserve Bank of New York, has written:

"Preliminary indications are that if a DFT [Direct Funds Transfer] system is in widespread operation by 1975—which is fully predicted as a likely date—the average cost per transaction will be 7½ cents, with a spread of from 3 cents to 12 cents in individual transactions. Present costs of the demand deposit or checking account system appear to run to about 13 cents per transaction, to which must be added another 12 cents per transaction if the transaction involves an extension of credit. If these figures are even nearly right, and I believe they are, use of the DFT system in 1975 could at best save 17½ cents per transaction on average and at worst save 5½ cents per transaction on average." [4]

Applying these figures to their own businesses, readers can draw their own conclusions as to how much they will save in dispensing with check handling, not to mention credit losses. And they can visualize the impact that near-instant money transfer will have on cash flow, reserves, accounts payable and receivable, and other aspects of their businesses where cash plays a part—right down to postage costs.

It is likely that action on the part of commercial banks, the Federal Reserve System, and businesses will be forthcoming in the near future as their comprehension of the possible savings grows. What will the action be, and how will the checkless society be implemented?

WHAT WILL IT BE LIKE?

Important concepts evolve rather than spring into life as mature, complete systems; it is possible for several quite different practical designs to exist at the same time. So it may be with the checkless society. In different geographical areas or industries the system may evolve in various ways, depending on needs.

At this point such variations are unimportant. Whether a transfer of money is accomplished through a telephone or a computer terminal, and whether it is activated by an electronically sensitized "money card" or a personal identification card, the underlying purpose is the same. The idea is to harness the lightning-fast calculating speed and massive infor-

[3] *A Techno-Economic Study of Methods of Improving the Payments Mechanism* (Stanford, California, 1966), p. 19.

[4] "Hard Figures and Considered Judgments on Progress Towards Checkless Society," *American Banker,* February 17, 1967.

mation storage capabilities of modern electronic computers in a new and important way.

It was perhaps inevitable that people would begin thinking about completely eliminating the check. The first such proposal was made over a decade ago by a group at the Massachusetts Institute of Technology.[5] Its members delved deeply into the shortcomings of the present payments mechanism and described briefly a proposed system and its advantages. Though limited by then current technology, in basic concept their proposal was quite similar to those currently under discussion.

Case of Joe Smith

Perhaps the clearest way to provide an idea of what is to come is to put this brave new world in fictional form. Enter Joe Smith.

Joe Smith is traveling and needs some ready cash. He goes into a bank and presents an identification card (the only card he has to carry) to a teller, who puts the card into a terminal box. A green light appears. The teller punches a few buttons and hands Joe his money. Joe signs a receipt.

Joe is not worried about the size of the balance in his bank account back home because the day before was payday, and his employer passed the funds through the wire transfer system to his bank. Joe also knows his money is "good" money. Even if his wife has been drawing on their joint account, the bank (through a loan agreement) guarantees to place the necessary funds at his disposal.

Let us examine Joe's card and find out why it possesses a genie's magic touch. There are several forms of identification on it. It carries the name of his bank and his identification number (each in both readable print and machine language); it also carries his signature and photograph and has an invisible (magnetically encoded) two-digit number. The two-digit number—generated, recorded, and stored by the computer at the time of the last transaction—serves as a password to allow access to Joe's account. After each transaction, a new number is generated and stored; a counterfeit card would not have the correct number encoded on it. (When Joe Smith's card produced a green light in the terminal box, the teller immediately knew that the money was available and the card was authentic. He looked at the tamper-proof photograph and signature and established Joe as the card owner.)

Every few days Joe takes his machine-readable bills to a pay station on the corner. He calls the central computer exchange and inserts his identification card into a slot. A verification voice acknowledges him. One by one he drops in his bills, and the voice repeats instructions until the last bill has been processed. Joe is a shrewd man; he pays every bill promptly and obtains a discount, which shows up as a credit on his next bill. Joe

[5] See Robert H. Gregory and Herbert Jacobs, Jr., "A Study of the Transfer of Credit in Relation to the Banking System," M.I.T. Dynamic Analysis and Control Laboratory Report No. 87 (Cambridge, 1954).

knows the value of money and keeps ahead of the game, realizing that if an emergency arises, he may need to use his credit privileges to the fullest extent.

Readers can grasp the implications for business in this story. In the first place, the computer at Joe's company has "talked" to the computer at the bank, causing funds to be withdrawn from the company's account and distributed to hundreds of employees, not by checks mailed to their homes, but by instant transfer to each employee's bank account.

The company handles not only its payroll in this manner but also its other payables, so that money is constantly being withdrawn from its account and moved to vendors' accounts within the banking system. Accounts receivable are settled by customers the same way.

Retailers obtain immediate payment at the point of sale, but without the nuisance and risk of handling cash or the costs associated with credit cards. The banking system absorbs the burdens of transferring funds and of "carrying" credit payments.

The dominant factor in this instant money counterplay is the time value of money. The company pays promptly to gain a discount; its customers pay promptly for the same reason. Discounts and interest charges are computed on a daily basis.

Obstacles along the way

There is no question about the technological feasibility of a nationwide computer information network. Several regional, national, and even international computer networks are already in operation. "Touchtone" telephones with attachments capable of reading information from plastic credit or identification cards are in use. The problems of implementation lie mainly in the areas of financing, education, and marketing. If technology were the only hurdle, the checkless society would not be far away. As Clarke has estimated the situation:

"The hardware to create such a new system is practically here; the technical ability to make the hardware work in aid of the system is here; the general legal environment is hospitable to the system, though no doubt subject to some evolutionary development and refinement." [6]

Some major technical problems remain, however. These include:

Choosing and applying a numbering system to identify system users.
Perfecting security protection systems and devices for preventing accidental or fraudulent transactions.
Satisfying legal requirements and government agencies.
Designing and programming the system.
Standardizing subscribers' computer files so they are compatible with the system.
Reducing transmission costs.

[6] John J. Clarke, "Check-Out Time for Checks," *The Business Lawyer*, July 1966, p. 93.

The retailer cannot be relied on for verification of the cardholders' identity; he cares little who pays as long as he is assured of payment before releasing the goods. In contrast, the banker will be very concerned. Committees of the American Bankers Association and the American Standards Association are studying the user identification and verification problems.

So far, the Social Security numbering system, with possible modifications, seems most practical to the bankers. Almost every adult in the country (more than 130 million) has a Social Security number. This coverage makes it a strong contender for use in the checkless society. Further, financial institutions are already using Social Security numbers for reporting interest and dividend payments to customers, stockholders, and the Internal Revenue Service.

A number of methods have been suggested for identifying system users and for guaranteeing security (a combination of two or more would undoubtedly be safest). Among them are:

A picture and/or fingerprints on the card.
Transmission of the account holder's physical description.
Transmission of extra characters, numerical or alphabetical, known only to the account holder.
Feedback of a test word or number from the computer to the card, identifying it for the next transaction.
Facsimile transmission of the cardholder's signature.
A voice-print, kept in a central file, to be compared with words transmitted through the terminal.

The automated network will simplify or eliminate the following aspects of the present checking system:

Returning cancelled checks to the payer.
The extra handling required for certified and cashier's checks.
Stop-payment responsibilities.
The requirement that payment cannot be made unless an instrument (e.g., check) is presented.
Kiting (i.e., taking advantage of the false liquidity created by delay in processing checks).
Forgeries and alterations.
Errors in encoding.

Many questions still need to be answered: Will a nationwide network of remote computer terminals violate any branching regulations? How long will payment data have to be retained? What should be the counterpart to a stop payment? How can illicit access by electronic bugging be prevented?

Endless possibilities

Once these problems have been solved, we envision expanded use of the system in which it not only would handle the transfer of funds on instruction from the customer but would actually serve as a financial tool. The computer could be programmed, for instance, to:

Determine the advisability of a customer taking a discount for prompt payment rather than paying later.

Make periodic transfers from consumers' checking accounts to their savings accounts.

Invest excess corporate funds in appropriate instruments.

Transfer fixed payments automatically on the proper dates.

Keep track of businesses' inventories and reorder when necessary.

Another potential use is transferring stocks and bonds. The Swedish Bank Association is promoting a plan to tie the Stockholm Stock Exchange and that nation's banks into a central computer system that is expected to eliminate the enormous amount of paper work involved in this activity. The central computer would print the shares and stockholder lists, register changes in investors' holdings, and issue dividend checks, as well as transfer payments among the appropriate bank accounts.

Similar but smaller systems are already in use in Norway and Finland. While the task would be immeasurably more difficult in the United States, it certainly is not impossible; and the opportunities for the computer network here are almost endless. One observer has even proposed that it be used in elections to record voting! [7]

WHO WILL BE INVOLVED?

Eventually, a nationwide integrated payment system will embrace virtually every financial element of society: government, banks, credit bureaus, industrial firms, retailers, consumers.

Federal government

Of the many federal agencies to be affected by the checkless society, the most deeply involved, of course, will be the Treasury and the Federal Reserve System. Automation of the payments mechanism will reduce the Fed's huge volume of paper processing and eliminate its perennial problem of "float." The Fed provides for a maximum delay in credit availability of two days for check clearance. But the float period is longer; even with today's advanced check-handling methods, it is "difficult, if not

[7] Lawrence A. Welsch, "A Proposal to Automate Money," *Computer Digest,* March 1967, p. 3.

impossible, to route certain checks through the transit system in less than three or four days." [8]

This transit time in excess of the credit availability period, combined with unanticipated delays due to equipment breakdown, bad weather, transportation snarls, and the like, produces additional bank reserves of between $1 billion and $2 billion. These phantom funds will be eliminated when funds can be transferred instantaneously. James S. Duesenberry, a member of the Council of Economic Advisers, said this about the consequences:

"The size of the money supply relative to the economy will actually get smaller. The Fed will have to control the rate of increase of bank reserves to handle this smaller money supply.

"For government economists trying to tune and control the economy, it should make life easier. The quicker we can get consumer spending and other economic information in from the banks, the easier will be the task to make correct decisions." [9]

Individual and corporate taxes could be paid to federal, state, and local governments through the system. Transfer payments, such as Social Security, subsidies, and Medicare, could be similarly accomplished.

Financial community

There is some apprehension among bankers that the checkless society will radically change banking as we know it today. Of that there is no doubt; banks are service organizations, and they must respond to the needs and demands of their customers in order to survive. The development is also certain to alter the competitive positions of segments of the financial community.

For instance, since the system will allow a customer to transfer funds from his checking account to his savings account with comparative ease, it may increase these transactions in commercial banks and at the same time have a negative impact on deposits in savings banks and savings and loan associations. It is likely that this condition will be viewed with trepidation by the savings groups, whose managements will seek redress. One economist has predicted a possible result:

"Banks will be forced to act as common carriers do in the transportation industry—having to accept business from any and all comers. One can conclude then that either banks will offer the checkless society to their competitors willingly, or they will be forced to do so by governmental intervention." [10]

We are already witnessing moves by local and regional credit bureaus

[8] Stanford Research Institute, *A Techno-Economic Study of Methods of Improving the Payments Mechanism,* p. 1.

[9] Quoted in "Electronic Money," *Forbes,* April 1, 1967, p. 46.

[10] Paul S. Nadler in a speech before the annual convention of the American Bankers Association, San Francisco, October 1966.

to form computerized networks. It is obvious that these bureaus will be at least related to the checkless society system, if not a part of it, for credit cannot be separated from cash. Banks can play a great part in the credit data system, not by compiling extensive dossiers on consumers as they have traditionally done for corporate enterprises, but by preauthorizing the credit standing of individuals and businesses alike.

Business firms

As noted, both retailers and industrial corporations will be closely involved with the system. Not only will consumer purchases and salary payments be automated, but dealings of businesses with each other will also be done through the system. To a large extent banks will be handling both payables and receivables for business organizations without the need of paper documents.

Some industries may believe they have reason to fear a computerized payments mechanism. Retailers, especially, worry about elimination of their own credit-granting operations. They claim that the exclusivity of their credit card is important to them and their customers, that their credit standards are more liberal than those of banks, and that loss of this business would reduce their profits seriously.

But the rising tide of "universal" credit cards is rapidly making inroads on the exclusivity previously enjoyed by retailers. The fact that distribution of retail credit cards is becoming more liberal—perhaps alarmingly so—counters the second claim. Finally, the release of capital now tied up in retailers' own credit systems, added to the more rapid availability of receivables, should more than offset the loss of earnings from interest on consumer credit. A study undertaken for the National Retail Merchants Association concluded:

"It seems apparent that the average department store would enhance its profits by eliminating the credit function—if it could maintain the same sales volume. Not only would it make a greater profit, but it would be doing so on a much smaller investment since discontinuing credit services would also eliminate the need for investing capital in customers' accounts receivable.

"In a practical sense, eliminating the credit function would not necessarily enhance store profits as sales would undoubtedly be adversely affected. It is clear, therefore, that credit must be justified economically by the department store as a selling tool—not as a separate business venture. From the store's point of view, extending credit should increase sales by such an amount that profits resulting from these increased sales will be large enough to absorb any excess of credit costs over service charge revenue." [11]

[11] National Retail Merchants Association, Credit Management Division, *Study of Customer Credit Costs in Department Stores* (New York, 1963), p. 14.

The Joe Smiths

Enlisting the consumer's participation in the checkless society will be a major stumbling block. The public is frequently obstinate in refusing to accept innovations, especially if they are viewed as restricting personal freedom of action or choice.

Today many options exist within the payments mechanism. A consumer may:

1. Pay cash (part with money immediately).
2. Write out a check (delay actual transfer a few days).
3. Draw against a "piggyback," or automatic overdraft, account (for perhaps a 25-day grace period).
4. Use a credit card (with settlement due in 30 to 45 days).
5. Use a personal charge account (often carried 60 to 120 days).
6. "Take down" a line of credit (with monthly repayments over 12 to 24 months).
7. Obtain an installment loan (with payments spread over 36 months or more).

The checkless society must permit all these options to continue. Moreover, it has been argued that a major benefit of the proposed system would be the inclusion of additional options in an attempt to tailor the system to all consumer needs. Whatever the additional services and increased convenience the consumer will enjoy, a massive educational campaign is likely to be required.

Critics of the machine age and of the greater role that government plays in our lives fear that increased use of automation will result in an invasion of individual privacy. A Congressional subcommittee held hearings on this subject in 1966 and concluded that these fears may well be justified.[12] Certainly the concept of the checkless society poses dangers in this respect, and advent of the system must be accompanied by safeguards to protect privacy.

HOW DO WE ACCOMPLISH IT?

As we have suggested, the checkless society is certain to evolve over a period of years rather than spring, full blown, into its final form. Accomplished even in gradual stages, the transformation will require enormous effort and coordination among the various groups involved.

A major obstacle to overcome is supporting the system in the interim between its origin and the time when its impact on money and credit movement is great enough to offset the costs. While the checkless society is gaining acceptance, it will have to compete with all the present and comfortably familiar processes of moving money.

[12] *Twenty-second Report of the House Subcommittee on Government Operations*, 1966, p. 3.

The first step will undoubtedly be establishing a pilot system, in a test area that is large enough to be significant, by those who stand to gain by its successful outcome. A working pilot model is now being tested by the Bank of Delaware in Wilmington. It is enabling retailers to receive instant payment for merchandise at the bank via their customers' machine-readable identification cards.

Although the Federal Reserve System may be able to justify launching such a system, a "financial utility" financed and operated cooperatively in a Comsat-type arrangement seems more likely. Among the interested parties, in addition to the banking industry, would be communications companies, computer manufacturers, credit bureaus, other deposit-seeking and credit-granting institutions, and representatives of the retail and industrial sectors.

The utility could provide the hardware, programming and other "software," and the data transmission facilities. It is essential that the utility enlist the participants' cooperation at each stage of development, both technically and geographically. If only *some* of the business establishments and banks in a market area convert to an electronic system, for instance, maintenance of duplicate check processing would rob the direct funds transfer facilities of their effectiveness and place a severe strain on financing the undertaking.

The self-interest of the various groups whose cooperation is essential should prevent abuses or domination by a particular group. Furthermore, information in the system that would be proprietary (such as cash balances and credit history) would have safeguards making it unavailable to unauthorized subscribers.

Banks of all sizes would be free to subscribe to the system, much as they now can elect to join the Federal Reserve System. They in turn would be able to offer improved service to their customers (for which they would somehow be compensated). Since those banks that did not subscribe would be at a competitive disadvantage, it is reasonable to anticipate that the system will eventually achieve its necessary wide adoption. (The current trend toward universal acceptance of bank credit cards may well set the pattern for this.)

WHEN WILL IT BE HERE?

There are those who foresee a great many difficulties and drawbacks, some perhaps insurmountable, along the way to the checkless society. Some of these doubters question its economic justification. They point to recent improvements in the present system, such as speeding up credit reports through computerized credit bureaus, automatic bill payment, overdraft banking, direct payroll deposits, the growing use of credit cards, optical character recognition devices, and improved paper handling equipment.

But others—and we number ourselves in this group—see the checkless society as financially feasible and of great benefit to our economic welfare —see it, indeed, as a logical evolutionary outgrowth of current trends in automation, banking, and consumer financial behavior. The payments mechanism has evolved over the centuries and will continue to do so. The checkless society is part of this change.

Its challenge will require an unprecedented degree of coordinated planning and effort among banks, businesses of all types, and the Federal Reserve System. The greatest service performed by the current discussions is that they focus attention on our rapidly changing world, the importance of a social comprehension of the time value of money, and the potential of the computer age to supply a choice of payment settlements to meet the needs of all, including the consumer.

Obviously, since it is an evolutionary development, there will be no exact time when the new era will dawn. It is reasonable to forecast progress toward the checkless society along a continuum of steps, as we have done in Figure 1. Our time estimates do not represent an extreme position; some persons have predicted an integrated, nationwide system in operation by 1971, while others do not expect to see a checkless society before the year 2000.

As a group, bankers themselves are somewhat pessimistic about the development of the checkless society. A recent survey of them indicated that 53% regard the elimination of check writing as "not likely to happen"; another 32% feel it is "at least 10 years away." To a question on the paying of bills via telephone, the answers were only a little more encouraging: 25% believe it is not likely to happen, and 39% feel it is at least 10 years away. Even on the simple development of a national uniform identification number, 40% of the bankers think it is at least 10 years away, and 19% regard it as not likely to happen.[13] Bankers, however, have a reputation—probably well deserved—for being conservative.

Last year the British Government decided to put a "giro" bill-paying system into effect. The giro system operates through the general post office of a country allowing an individual who wishes to pay a bill to fill out a form and deposit the money at the post office. An identifying account number is used which simplifies the paper operation. There is no "float" involved because the funds are in the general post office and are merely transferred from one account to another with advices. If this system were computerized and operated through the banks, it would behave very much like the checkless society system. The British banks viewed this as direct competition and last December reacted with a proposal to spend £80 million to link some 11,500 of their branches to a centralized computer communications system by 1971. The Dutch banks are planning a similar program even sooner.

[13] Dale Reistad, "Credit Cards—Stepping Stones to the Checkless Society?" *Computers and Automation,* January 1967, p. 26.

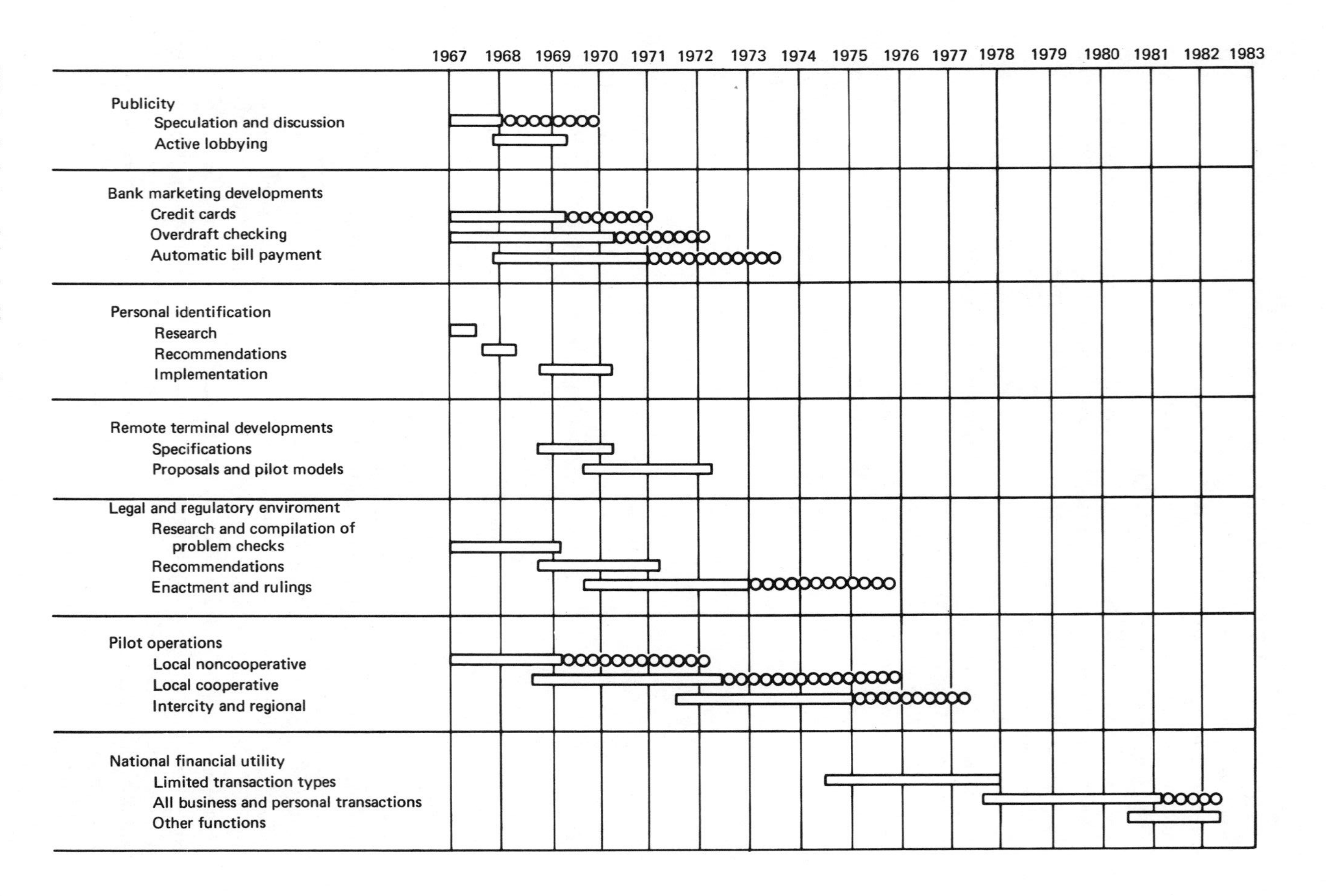

FIG. 1 Evolution of the checkless society.

We can anticipate somewhat slower progress in the United States for several reasons:

We do not face a government-sponsored giro system.

The task of coordination is far more difficult here. There are more than 14,000 banks in the United States, compared with about 24 in England. American banks range in asset size from under $100,000 to more than $15 billion.

There appears to be less room for improvement in the U.S. system; for example, the typical credit transfer takes two days here as against four days in England.

In sum, the approach to the checkless society in the United States is being undertaken by responsible groups. The wheels are in motion. The technological capabilities are virtually all available. Solutions must be found for the legal and marketing questions, but it appears reasonable to assume that within five years selected areas will have pilot systems operating, and in ten years the checkless society will be upon us.

INDEX

Index